The Development of
THE UNITED STATES
since 1865

NELSON P. MEAD

PROFESSOR OF HISTORY, COLLEGE OF THE CITY OF NEW YORK

HARCOURT, BRACE AND COMPANY
NEW YORK

PRINTED IN THE U. S. A. BY
QUINN & BODEN COMPANY, INC.
RAHWAY, N. J.

PREFACE

The territorial extent of the United States, the varied interests of the people, the heterogeneous character of the population, and the local peculiarities of the different sections of the country, make any generalizations concerning national development open to criticism. There have been, however, certain broad movements and tendencies in the history of the United States since the Civil War which provide a degree of unity to this period. In the following pages the record of recent American development has been grouped into two periods, one before, and the other since, 1900. The topical treatment has been adopted despite the fact that such a treatment presents certain obvious difficulties. On the whole it has seemed to the author the best method of presenting the story for college students who, for the most part, have had a high school course in American history in which the chronological account has been given.

NELSON P. MEAD

New York
January, 1930.

CONTENTS

v

THE DEVELOPMENT OF
THE UNITED STATES
SINCE 1865

CHAPTER 1

THE AFTERMATH OF THE CIVIL WAR

The final defeat of the Confederate armies in 1865 had preserved the union of states, but it was only nominally the union that had existed in 1860. In the first place the success of the national government in defeating the claims of state sovereignty added greatly to the prestige of the central government. And this prestige was enhanced by the outburst of national patriotism which the war had evoked. Then, too, the fundamental law of the land was shortly to be modified by three important amendments, all of which tended to fortify the power of the national government as against that of the states. Not for many years after the Civil War did the theory of States' Rights again arise to challenge seriously the steadily expanding power of the national government. In short there emerged from the war a new Federal union in which the relative authority of the states and the nation was quite different from that which had prevailed before 1860.

The Civil War, too, brought a significant change in the relative importance, politically and economically, of the sections of the country and of different economic groups. For thirty years before the war the Democratic party, under the leadership of the aristocratic planters of the South, and supported generally by the small farmers and artisans of the North, had controlled the politics and determined the economic policies of the nation. But the war ruined a large part of the planting aristocracy, and the leadership which they lost was seized by the captains of industry in the North, who, with the support of the farmers of the West, directed

3

the political and economic life of the nation during the last quarter of the nineteenth century.

PROBLEMS OF RECONSTRUCTION

For ten years following the close of the Civil War the thoughts of the people and the energies of public officials were devoted in large measure to attempts at solving the many perplexing questions raised by the war and its outcome.

First there was the problem of demobilization. Large numbers of men must be returned to civil life, and the industrial activities of the country changed from a war to a peace basis. Then came the question of the restoration of the former Confederate states to their normal position in the union, and the determination of the political, social, and economic status of the former slaves. Again, problems of financial readjustment were raised by the huge war expenditures, and serious foreign complications which had arisen while the war was in progress had to be adjusted. And all of these problems had to be solved in an atmosphere superheated by passions aroused through four years of bitter civil strife.

In the victorious North the problem of material reconstruction was not serious. With the exception of the battles of Gettysburg and Antietam, all of the important military engagements of the Civil War had been fought on Southern soil. Marching armies had not left a trail of destruction in the North as they had in the South. Nor had the economic life of the North been disrupted by the war. After the first shock to the business and financial interests caused by the outbreak of hostilities had subsided, these interests quickly adjusted themselves to war conditions, and during the greater part of the conflict the people of the North enjoyed a considerable measure of material prosperity.

Perhaps the most immediately pressing problem in the

North at the close of hostilities was the restoration of about a million men from military to civil life. That this was accomplished without serious difficulty was not due to intelligent planning or foresight on the part of the political authorities. Two fortunate circumstances contributed materially to the solution of the problem. First there was the disposal of the vast public domain. In 1862 Congress passed the Homestead Act, which provided that any citizen, or person who had declared his intention of becoming a citizen, could obtain title to 160 acres of public land by paying a nominal registration fee of $10.00 and cultivating the land for a period of five years. By taking advantage of this Act, returned soldiers who were so inclined could obtain a farm with little or no capital. In the second place the industrial expansion of the country in the decades following the war offered opportunities to those who were not attracted to rural life.

The collapse of the Confederacy left the defeated states in a demoralized condition. Marching armies had destroyed plantations, railroads, and public buildings. Millions of dollars invested in Confederate bonds and currency had disappeared. Capital amounting to two billion dollars invested in slaves had been wiped out. Organized government in the greater part of the South had ceased to function. The economic organization of these states, already seriously disrupted by military operations, was almost wholly destroyed as a result of the abolition of slavery.

Reconstruction in the South, therefore, involved three major problems. The first was the adjustment of the recently emancipated slaves to the new economic and social conditions of their free status. The second was the political and constitutional reorganization of the state governments, and the restoration of their former relations to the Federal union. The last was the rebuilding of the economic and industrial life of the South upon a basis of free labor. Under the most favorable conditions the solution of these questions would have been troublesome enough, but the difficulties were vastly increased by the spirit of vindictiveness displayed by the victors and that of sullen resentment shown by the vanquished.

The great majority of the emancipated negroes probably had only the vaguest idea as to what freedom meant. Under the conditions of slavery the negroes had not developed self-reliance, and they had had only the most meager opportunities for education. To many, emancipation meant freedom from work. Great numbers of them left the plantations and gave themselves up to tasting the pleasures of a life of idleness. The vicious, freed from the restraint of former masters, became a menace to society. To meet this danger the Southern state governments, set up under the Presidential plan of reconstruction, passed the so-called "Black Codes," among the provisions of which were the requirement of separate schools for the two races and separate accommodations on trains. Some states required negroes to obtain a license to carry weapons, to preach, or to engage in trade. Others allowed negroes to own property only in restricted areas. Apprenticeship laws were enacted providing that negro orphans could be bound out, and vagrancy laws empowered state authorities to hire out negroes found without employment.

In the North the need of extending aid to the negroes was early recognized. During the war this was at first undertaken by private individuals and organizations; but, as the number of refugees escaping into the Union lines, or freed as the Federal forces extended their conquest of the South, greatly increased, it became necessary for the government to take over this work. Just before the close of the war Congress passed the Freedmen's Bureau Act of March 3, 1865. This created in the War Department a Bureau of Refugees, Freedmen, and Abandoned Lands, which was to continue for one year, and was empowered to provide food, shelter, and clothing for the needy and to lease abandoned and confiscated property to the freedmen. The Bureau also took control of educational work among the negroes. Major General O. O. Howard was appointed head of the Bureau, and it is generally conceded that he was a capable and fair-minded official. Not so much can be said for many of the local agents of the Bureau in the South. Some of these men were merely misguided zealots; others were undoubtedly unscrupulous rogues. Simple-minded and credulous as children, the negroes who gathered about the depots of the Bureau were easily led to believe that the government would feed and clothe them for the rest of their lives. Moreover, a widespread rumor was current among the negroes that the government intended to confiscate a large amount of the land of former slave-owners and distribute it among the freedmen. "Forty acres and a mule" was the slogan. Swindlers went about among the negroes selling them fraudulent land certificates, while others sold painted red, white, and blue pegs which, it was stated, had been issued by the government for marking out land grants.

Despite the many handicaps that faced the freedmen, substantial progress was made by the negroes in the South within a comparatively short time after the close of the war. Many who had abandoned the plantations in the first outburst of enthusiasm over their freedom from slavery soon found their way back to their former homes and settled down to a normal life. A remarkable zeal for education rapidly spread among the negroes. After their restoration to the Union, all of the Southern states appropriated funds for the establishment of colored schools, and money for the same purpose was furnished by the Freedmen's Bureau and by private individuals and organizations in the North. The most important of these schools were Howard University; Fisk University at Nashville; Shaw University at Raleigh;

and the Hampton Normal and Agricultural Institute, at Hampton, Virginia.

POLITICAL RECONSTRUCTION

The collapse of the Confederacy brought to the fore the all-important question of the status of the Confederate states. Had the attempted secession taken these states out of the Union, or was secession a nullity from the beginning? If the states were out of the Union, was it the duty of the executive or of Congress to restore them to their former status? To these important questions the Constitution gave no clear answer. While the war was still in progress President Lincoln turned his attention to the restoration of the Southern states. By temperament he was not inclined to advocate any policy of vindictive punishment. Furthermore he was of the opinion that the task of political readjustment of the South belonged to the executive. Accordingly he issued a proclamation on December 8, 1863, in which he proposed to pardon all persons who took a prescribed oath of allegiance to the Union, with the exception of certain specified leaders of the Confederacy. Whenever as many as 10 per cent. of the voting population in 1860 of any of the seceded states had taken such oath and had established a state government, the President agreed to recognize such government as legal. At the same time Lincoln stated that it was the right of Congress to decide whether Representatives and Senators from such states should be allowed to take their seats.

Acting upon the President's proposal during the year 1864, state governments were organized in the states of Arkansas and Louisiana, followed by similar action in Tennessee the following year. Congress, however, was not disposed to concede the claim of the President that he had the power to devise a plan of reconstruction. It declined to allow the Representatives and Senators from the states organized under the Presidential proclamation to take their seats [1] and proceeded to enact the Wade-Davis Bill. This bill asserted the right of Congress to control reconstruction and laid down more rigid requirements for the Southern states to meet than those prescribed by Lincoln. In particular, Congress demanded that a majority, not merely 10 per cent., of the voters should take the oath of allegiance. The President disposed of this bill by means of a "pocket veto," stating that he was unwilling "to be inflexibly committed to any single plan of restoration." He indicated that he did not wish to discourage the loyal citizens of the Southern states which had established governments in accordance with his proclamation. At the same time he stated that he was prepared to recognize any other states which might adopt the Congressional plan.

Unfortunately for the country, and particularly for the South, Lincoln was removed from the scene by an assassin's bullet within less than a week after the surrender of General Lee's army at Appomattox. He was the one man who might have guided the country successfully through the troublous days of reconstruction. That he would have had to reckon with Congress there is no doubt, as the passage of the Wade-Davis Bill had clearly indicated. But his extraordinary understanding of human nature, and his wide popularity, would probably have enabled him to hold the extreme radical leaders of Congress in check. In any event he would have avoided the bitter controversy that his successor precipitated with Congress, and the South might have escaped the orgy of misgovernment that the radical Congressional program of reconstruction inaugurated.

Andrew Johnson's rise from poverty and obscurity had been quite as remarkable as that of Lincoln. His parents came from the class of "poor whites." Born in North Carolina, he

---

[1] The Representatives from Louisiana were at first allowed to take their seats but were later excluded.

was apprenticed at the age of ten to a tailor, and at the age of eighteen removed to eastern Tennessee, where he followed his trade. Such education as he received came largely from his wife. He entered politics early in life and was successively mayor of the village in which he lived, member of the state legislature, Congressman, Governor, and United States Senator. Throughout his political career he proclaimed the rights of the common man. His biographer says, "He cordially hated aristocracy and had decided objections to a gentleman." He realized that the miserable condition of the class from which he came was in large measure due to the slave system, and he became a bitter hater of the slavocracy of the South. He attracted attention in the North by his opposition to the secession of his state, and when the Union forces overran this region he was appointed by Lincoln military governor of Tennessee. In 1864 the Republican party, eager to refute the charge of being a sectional party, and in order to win the support of the war Democrats, nominated Johnson for the vice presidency as Lincoln's running-mate.

An unfortunate incident occurred at the time that Johnson was inaugurated as Vice-President. When he came before the Senate to take the oath of office, it was clear to many of those present that he was under the influence of liquor. Although little was said about the matter at the time, the incident was later recalled during his bitter controversy with the radicals in Congress. Whenever Johnson broke loose in one of his frequent tirades against his opponents, the charge was made that the President was drunk again. If the testimony of Secretary Welles, who was perhaps as close to Johnson as any one, is to be credited, these charges were unfounded.

In any event Johnson was manifestly not fitted, either by temperament or by training, for the delicate task confronting him. He possessed a rugged honesty and crude intellectual force, but he was violent of temper and intolerant of the opinions of those who did not agree with him. But Johnson's later difficulties are not to be explained wholly by the shortcomings of his character. It is to be remembered that he came to the presidency just as the war closed. During the war the normal relations between the legislative and executive departments of the government were thrown out of balance. The powers of government were concentrated largely in the hands of the President, and Congress was forced into the background. The members of Congress naturally became restive under this enforced subordination, and as soon as the crisis had passed they were determined to reassert their authority. President Johnson had to face, at the beginning of his administration, this aroused Congressional consciousness. His position resembled in many aspects that of President Wilson years afterward, at the close of the World War.

Upon his accession to the presidency Johnson was hailed by the radical Republicans as a firm ally. Senator Wade, one of the radical leaders, said at the time, "Johnson, we have faith in you. By the gods, there will be no trouble now in running the Government." In view of Johnson's record this confidence of the radicals seemed justified. Moreover, the President was deeply affected by the feeling of bitter resentment which swept the North as a result of the assassination of Lincoln. For a time it seemed that bloody reprisals would be inflicted upon the South. Numbers of the leaders of the Confederacy including President Davis, Vice-President Stephens, and former governors of the Confederate states were arrested and imprisoned. Only the vigorous opposition of General Grant prevented the arrest of General Lee. After the excitement in the North had abated somewhat, calmer counsels prevailed, and only four persons, three men and one woman, who were directly implicated in the plot to assassinate Lincoln, were executed, together with the commander of Andersonville prison, who was convicted of excessive cruelty to Federal prisoners of war.

To the deep chagrin of the radical leaders, when Johnson

came to formulate a program for dealing with the South, it was seen that he had greatly modified his earlier views. This change was due in part to the restraining influence of the members of Lincoln's cabinet whom Johnson had retained in office and in part to the sobering effect of the responsibilities of the presidency. The President began by recognizing the governments that had been organized in Louisiana, Tennessee, and Arkansas under the Lincoln plan, and also the somewhat shadowy loyal government of Governor Peirpoint in Virginia. For the remaining seven states of the Confederacy, Johnson, in a proclamation issued on May 29, 1865, set forth a plan which in all essential respects agreed with that of his predecessor.[2] It is true that Johnson refused amnesty to a larger number of persons than Lincoln had excepted. In particular, he excluded all persons worth twenty thousand dollars or more, obviously a reflection of his antipathy to the wealthy planter class.

Johnson had seven months in which to carry out his plan of reconstruction before Congress met, in December, 1865. The President appointed provisional governors in the seven states and issued instructions for the summoning of a constitutional convention in each state. He made it clear that these conventions must repudiate the ordinances of secession and also the Confederate war debt, and that the first state legislatures should ratify the Thirteenth Amendment abolishing slavery. During the summer and fall of 1865 all of the seven states except Texas had complied with the conditions required by the President. State governments were organized, state officials elected, and members of Congress chosen.

With growing concern and anger the radical Republican leaders watched the progress of presidential reconstruction. "If something is not done," said Thaddeus Stevens of Pennsylvania, "the President will be crowned King before

---

[2] Johnson's proclamation did not specify the percentage of voters required to declare loyalty before the state should be restored.

Congress meets." "What right," exclaimed Senator Sumner of Massachusetts, "has the President to reorganize states?" The ire of the radicals was greatly increased as they beheld the election of prominent Confederate officials to various state offices and to Congress. A former Confederate senator was elected Governor of South Carolina; the Governor of Mississippi had been a brigadier general in the Confederate army. The state legislature of Georgia chose as United States Senator Alexander H. Stephens, former Vice-President of the Confederacy.

Congress assembled in December, 1865, and immediately took up the problem of the Southern states. Both houses declined to allow the members elected from the Confederate states to take their seats. Charles Sumner in the Senate and Thaddeus Stevens in the House assumed the leadership of the radical Republican element. Sumner in the days before the war had been one of the most vigorous opponents of slavery, and his clashes with the slavery leaders in Congress engendered in him a bitter hatred of the South. He was a sincere but impractical doctrinaire, conceited in his opinions, and extremely irritating in his self-righteous pose. "He lived," says Professor Dunning, "in the empyrean, and descended thence upon his colleagues with dogmas which he discovered in that exalted region." In expounding his views concerning the South he developed what became known as the "State Suicide" theory of reconstruction. He contended that the Southern states by their attempted secession had committed suicide and had reverted to the condition of territories, and that their readmission as states depended upon the will of Congress. He further advocated granting full civil and political rights to the negroes. Thaddeus Stevens, the recognized leader of the radicals in the lower house, was a coarse, vindictive, narrow-minded old man who believed that the defeated South had no rights that the North was bound to respect. In dealing with the status of the Confederate states he formulated the so-called "Conquered Province" theory, which held that the South was a conquered province, wholly at the mercy of Congress. He would not concede to them even the status of territories, but insisted that the attempted rebellion had wiped out state lines and that it was within the power of Congress to combine or subdivide the former states as it saw fit.

The radicals were not, however, at first, in a majority in either house, and discretion on the part of President Johnson would probably have saved a large part of his program. His first message to Congress augured well for the future. The conciliatory tone of the document and the clear and forceful style in which it was written gave rise to laudatory comments on all sides. It was not disclosed until many years later that the literary quality, if not the substance of the message, was the work of the historian George Bancroft.

There were other reasons why Congress, apart from the desire to maintain its own prestige, should hesitate to endorse the policy of the President. In the first place, there were many sincere idealists in the North and in Congress who believed that the civil rights of the negroes in the South would be insecure unless they were given the suffrage. The "Black Codes" enacted by several of the Southern state legislatures were cited to prove that the white people of the South had no intention of conceding equal civil rights to the negroes. Of more practical importance to the Republican politicians was the realization of the fact that, if the Southern states were restored, with the negroes emancipated but not enfranchised, the effect would be to increase the representation of the South both in Congress and in the Electoral College, for the negroes would thereafter be counted the same as the whites in determining the population of a state, the three-fifths constitutional provision being no longer operative. Such a situation threatened the continued predominance of the Republican party in the nation, for it was very likely that the South would send solid Democratic delegations to Congress. The radical Republican leaders therefore determined to delay the restoration of the Southern states until Republican organizations, based upon negro suffrage, could be established in these states.[3]

The first act of Congress in dealing with the Southern question was the appointment of the "Joint Committee of Fifteen on Reconstruction," to which was referred all matters relating to the seceded states, and which was authorized to formulate a program for the consideration of Congress. Pending the report of this committee, Congress proceeded to enact legislation placing the negroes of the South under the protection of national law. The first of these measures was an act to extend the life and increase the powers of the Freedmen's Bureau. President Johnson promptly vetoed this bill on the ground that there was no further need for the activities of the Bureau and that some of the provisions of the act were an unwarrantable interference with the rights of the states. The attempt to pass the bill over the presidential veto failed. Johnson had scored his first and what proved to be his last victory in his contest with Congress. The thing that appears to have irritated many Congressmen was the President's implication that Congress as constituted had no right to legislate for the eleven unrepresented states.

Had the President acted with caution, he might have been able to consolidate the moderate sentiment in Congress and check the course of the radicals. Unfortunately his penchant for violent and coarse speech betrayed him. On Washington's birthday in 1866 a crowd of his supporters marched to the White House to serenade him. Against the advice of his closest friends the President appeared before the crowd and proceeded to harangue them after the manner of a back-

[3] The conservative Republicans would have been satisfied to solve this political problem by cutting down the representation of the Southern states as proposed in the Fourteenth Amendment without insisting upon negro suffrage.

woods politician. He denounced Stevens and Sumner for
their opposition to his policies, engaged in coarse repartee
with the crowd, declared that the radicals were seeking his
assassination, referred to his record as a friend of the people, and to other quite irrelevant subjects. The speech made
a most unhappy impression upon persons of moderate views
and was hailed with glee by the radicals as further evidence
of Johnson's unfitness for leadership.

The next move by Congress was the passage of the Civil
Rights Bill. This act declared the negroes citizens of the
United States and conferred upon them equal civil rights
with the whites. Federal officials were empowered to enforce
the law and the President was authorized to employ military
force, if necessary, to carry out its provisions. With a well-
reasoned and logical argument the President returned the
bill with his veto, but Congress was in no mood to listen to
even the most convincing statement from Johnson, and the
House promptly passed the bill over his veto. In the Senate
the required two-thirds majority was barely obtained after
the questionable action of that body in unseating a Democratic Senator from New Jersey. Then followed another
Freedmen's Bureau Bill, which the President vetoed and
which Congress immediately repassed over his veto.

In the meantime the Joint Committee had been formulating a program. Convinced that the white people of the South
were still disloyal and that they had no intention of respecting the rights of the freedmen, the majority of the committee was determined to deny the privileges of statehood to
the Southern communities until there were incorporated in
the Constitution guarantees of the rights of the negroes and
limitations upon the states to prevent any invasion of these
rights. With this end in view the committee recommended
the submission of a constitutional amendment incorporating
most of the provisions of the Civil Rights Bill. After some
modifications had been made by Congress, the amendment

was passed in both houses by the necessary two-thirds vote and was submitted to the states for ratification as the Fourteenth Amendment to the Constitution.

This amendment provided that all persons born or naturalized in the United States, and subject to the jurisdiction thereof, are citizens of the United States and of the state wherein they reside. It further prohibited any state from making any law which should abridge the privileges and immunities of citizens of the United States, or deny to any person the equal protection of the laws. Nor should any state deprive any person of life, liberty, or property without due process of law. The second clause was calculated to satisfy the practical politicians of the Republican party. It provided that any state which refused the vote to any adult male citizens should have its representation in Congress reduced in the proportion which the number of these disenfranchised citizens bore to the total number of adult males in the state. The third clause barred from Federal and state offices any person who had violated an oath previously taken to support the Constitution of the United States by engaging in rebellion against it, until pardoned by vote of Congress. Finally, it affirmed the validity of the public debt of the United States and prohibited the United States or any state from paying any part of the Confederate debt or any compensation to slave-owners for the loss of their slaves.

The amendment was submitted to all of the states, including those in the former Confederacy. It is difficult to see how these latter states were qualified to vote on constitutional amendments and yet were not entitled to assume their normal status in the Union. But nice questions of constitutional procedure did not deter the leaders in Congress from accomplishing the end that they had in view. The state of Tennessee promptly ratified the amendment and Congress thereupon restored this state to its full privileges in the Union. Unfortunately the other Southern states refused to follow the example of Tennessee and proceeded to reject the amendment, thus strengthening the hands of the radicals in Congress, who could point to this action as further evidence of the intransigent attitude of the people of the South.

The Congressional elections in the fall of 1866 brought the question of Southern reconstruction before the electorate of the Northern states. A large convention of delegates from all of the states, both North and South, met at Philadelphia to endorse the policy of President Johnson. The presence at this convention of numbers of prominent Confederate leaders, and also leading Copperheads [4] from the North, aroused bitter resentment among Republicans. An "address" was adopted by the convention, calling upon the people "to secure the election of members who, whatever other differences may characterize their political action, will unite in recognizing the right of every state of the Union to representation in Congress."

President Johnson, against the advice of his closest friends, threw himself into the campaign in defense of his policies. On a tour which took him through a number of the important cities of the East and Middle West he delivered speeches, in several of which he allowed himself to be drawn into undignified disputes with some of his auditors. Insults and epithets were bandied back and forth; cries of "traitor," "renegade," and "Judas Iscariot" were hurled at the President. The whole sorry spectacle saddened Johnson's friends and disgusted many in the North who had not sympathized with the radical Congressional policies.

Another incident occurred in the course of the campaign which was used to good advantage by the radicals. On July 30 there was a serious riot in New Orleans, which resulted in the death of about fifty persons, chiefly negroes. The Northern press made much of the affair and insisted that it

---

[4] The Copperheads were Northerners who sympathized with the South during the war.

foreshadowed what would happen in the South if the power of the Federal government was removed and the freedmen were entrusted to the tender mercies of their former masters.

The results of the election were a humiliating defeat for the President. Not only were all of the radicals reëlected, but their numbers were increased so that they would command a two-thirds majority in the new Congress and be able to ride roughshod over the President.

When Congress reassembled for its session in December, 1866, it reflected the influence of the election of the previous month. Thaddeus Stevens, with the ironic comment, "I was a conservative in the last session of Congress, but I mean to be a radical henceforth," began his vindictive and relentless drive for the punishment of the South. The first measure enacted was one conferring negro suffrage in the District of Columbia, although both Washington and Georgetown had a few weeks previously voted overwhelmingly against such a proposal. The Joint Committee then brought forward the first Reconstruction Act.

This act declared that "no legal state governments or adequate protection of life or property" existed in the South, and provided that the ten states should be grouped into five military districts, each under the command of a general officer of the army. These officers were empowered to preserve order and, if necessary, to suspend civil government and proclaim martial law. They were further required to summon state conventions, chosen by male citizens without regard to color, but excluding those disenfranchised under the proposed Fourteenth Amendment. These conventions were required to adopt state constitutions guaranteeing negro suffrage. Such constitutions must be ratified by the new electorate of the states and by Congress, and the first legislatures of these states must ratify the Fourteenth Amendment. When this amendment should have become ratified as a part of the Constitution of the United States, the states that had complied with all of the above cited provisions of the law should be entitled to resume their former status in the Union.

As was to be expected, Johnson vetoed the bill, and in a vigorous message accompanying the veto he contended that the bill was unconstitutional in that it established military rule after a state of war had ended. He also criticized the policy of forcing negro suffrage upon the South when only six states in the North allowed the negro to vote. But Congress contemptuously brushed aside the presidential objections and immediately repassed the bill.

On the same day that the Reconstruction Act was passed Congress enacted the Tenure-of-Office Act, which prohibited the President from removing officials without the consent of the Senate, thus denying to Johnson a privilege that every President since Washington had enjoyed. Congress further humiliated the President in depriving him of his constitutional privileges as commander-in-chief of the army by requiring that all military orders should come through the ranking officer of the army, General Grant.

The Reconstruction Act was passed only two days before the end of the term of the 39th Congress. The radical leaders feared that in the absence of Congress Johnson would obstruct enforcement of the Congressional policy. To meet this supposed danger it was provided that the new Congress should assemble immediately upon the expiration of the term of its predecessor. As we have seen, the 40th Congress had an increased number of radical Republicans in its membership and it vigorously pressed forward the program of military reconstruction. Two supplementary reconstruction acts were passed, which assured the carrying out of the Congressional policy and which gave to the military commanders in the South complete control of the civil authorities.

Apparently there were no lengths to which the radicals hesitated to go to enforce their will. When the Supreme Court in the case of *ex parte* Milligan declared that the writ of habeas corpus could not be suspended when the regular civil courts were freely functioning, and, in the cases of Cummings vs. State of Missouri and *ex parte* Garland, declared provisions of the Test Oaths, which excluded Confederate supporters from various professions, unconstitutional, the ire of the radicals in Congress was aroused. One member of the House declared that it was an outrage that five judges should be able to override the will of Congress. Another asserted that if the Court should "defy a free people's will," a constitutional amendment should be enacted "annihilating the usurpers in the abolition of the tribunal itself." A bill was actually passed by the House requiring a two-thirds majority of the Court to declare an act of Congress unconstitutional, but the bill failed to pass in the Senate. However, a law limiting the appellate jurisdiction of the Court was enacted by Congress. Warned by this belligerent attitude of Congress, the Supreme Court attempted to avoid becoming involved in the bitter controversy between the President and Congress. In two cases which were brought before the Court to test the constitutionality of the Military Reconstruction Acts the Court declined to render an opinion on the ground that it lacked jurisdiction, as the acts involved purely political questions with which the Court could not deal.[5]

Not content with the humiliation of the President, his enemies in Congress determined to remove him from office. Vigorous efforts were made by the radical leaders in the House during 1867 to force through impeachment proceedings, but they were unable to formulate charges that could command the support of even the none-too-scrupulous membership of the House. Although conservative Republican and Democratic victories in the state elections in the fall of 1867 indicated popular disapproval of the radical procedure

[5] Mississippi vs. Johnson (4 Wallace, 475); Georgia vs. Stanton (6 Wallace, 50).

in Congress, Johnson's enemies were not deterred by any such manifestations of popular feeling.

The opportunity to proceed against the President was offered by the action of Johnson in removing Edwin M. Stanton as Secretary of War. Johnson had retained Stanton along with the rest of Lincoln's cabinet when he assumed office. As the quarrel between the President and Congress developed, it became increasingly evident that Stanton was out of sympathy with the President. Obviously the normal action for Stanton to take was to resign from the cabinet. But from a curious notion of duty he determined to remain in office and hamper the President in every possible way. Confronted by this intolerable situation, Johnson finally, in August, 1867, suspended Stanton and appointed General Grant Secretary *ad interim*. When Congress reassembled, Johnson notified the Senate of his action in suspending Stanton, but the Senate declined to sustain the President, and under* the terms of the Tenure-of-Office Act Stanton was restored to office. General Grant promptly turned the office over to Stanton. This led to a dispute between Johnson and Grant. The President maintained that Grant had promised to retain the office and force Stanton to go to the courts to regain possession of the office. By this procedure the constitutionality of the Tenure-of-Office Act could be determined. Grant denied that there had been any such understanding, and the net result was to drive Grant into the camp of Johnson's enemies.

The President then precipitated matters by peremptorily removing Stanton and appointing General Lorenzo Thomas as Secretary *ad interim*. Immediately the House moved to impeach Johnson for high crimes and misdemeanors in office. The charges were incorporated in eleven articles which accused the President of obstructing enforcement of the Reconstruction Acts, of vilifying members of Congress, and of violating the law in the removal of Stanton. In speeches ac-

companying the passage of the resolutions members of the
House abandoned all restraint, not to say decency. "Traitor,"
"tyrant," "usurper," were some of the milder epithets applied
to the President. In Washington the wildest rumors were
circulated; among others that the President was contemplating a military *coup d'état* and that offers of troops had come
from sympathizers in both the North and the South.

The trial before the Senate was a travesty upon justice.
Instead of sitting as judges many of the Senators acted as
though they were prosecuting attorneys. Any evidence, however trivial or improbable, that tended to discredit the President was admitted, whereas counsel for the defense were
hampered in every way possible in presenting evidence in his
favor. Only the charge involving the removal of Stanton
presented a reasonable ground for impeachment proceedings.
Even if the very doubtful constitutionality of the Tenure-of-
Office Act was granted, there remained the question of its
applicability to Stanton. The act limited the tenure of cabinet
officers "during the term of the President by whom they
may have been appointed, and for one month thereafter."
Stanton had not been appointed by Johnson but had been retained by him along with the rest of Lincoln's cabinet. But
the trial had ceased to be, if it ever had been, a judicial procedure, and became a determined effort to remove the President for partisan reasons. On the final vote seven Republican
Senators defied the most extreme party pressure and joined
the twelve Democrats in voting for acquittal. The resulting
vote was 35 to 19, one less than the constitutional two-thirds
required for conviction. It is clear today that removal of the
President would have been outrageous injustice, for, whatever his shortcomings for the important office that he held,
Andrew Johnson had committed no "high crimes or misdemeanors."

This dramatic episode had diverted the attention of the
North for the moment from events in the South, where the

Congressional plan of military reconstruction was being worked out. The military commanders in due course had summoned constitutional conventions in the states under their control. A motley array of adventurous "Carpetbaggers " [6] from the North, unprincipled "Scalawags," [7] from the South, and illiterate negroes made up the bulk of these constituent bodies. Constitutions were drafted incorporating negro suffrage and, by the summer of 1868, the process of military reconstruction had been completed in all but three of the Southern states. Congress in an omnibus bill then hastened to restore the states of North and South Carolina, Georgia, Alabama, Florida, and Louisiana to representation in Congress. This hurried action was not due to any desire to speed the restoration of civil government in the South. The election of 1868 was approaching and the radicals wished to have these states, with their negro electorate, restored in time to participate in the election and assure the success of the Republican ticket.

RECONSTRUCTION COMPLETED

The radical Republicans approached the election of 1868 with some misgivings. The state elections of the previous year had shown a distinct reaction in the North against their reconstruction policies. Obviously their best strategy was to capitalize the patriotic services of the party in the war. Quite as clearly their candidate was indicated. General Grant, the "Hero of Appomattox," was best fitted to crystallize the patriotic sentiment in the North. He was nominated unanimously and had as his running mate Schuyler Colfax, the Speaker of the House. The platform of the party en-

---

[6] Carpetbaggers were Northern whites who went to the South at the close of the war carrying their belongings in carpetbags—hence the name.

[7] Scalawags were Southern whites who supported the radical reconstruction policy.

dorsed the Congressional policy of Reconstruction. On the question of negro suffrage the platform was equivocal, to say the least. While it defended the action of Congress in forcing negro suffrage in the South, it insisted that in the loyal states the question should be left to the people of those states to decide. On the financial question, which was soon to occupy a position of great political importance, the Republicans demanded the payment of the public debt "in the utmost good faith to all creditors."

The close of the Civil War found the Democratic party disorganized. Most of its ablest leaders had gone with the South in secession. As the Republicans were fond of saying, "While all Democrats were not rebels, all rebels were Democrats." It was clearly the strategy of the Democrats to divert the attention of the country from their war record. Quite naturally the Democrats denounced the Republican policy of Reconstruction as "unconstitutional, revolutionary, and void," but the party platform placed chief emphasis on the financial issue. Appealing to the farmers of the West, whose economic prosperity had been seriously disturbed by the fall in prices of agricultural commodities at the close of the war, the Democrats incorporated in their platform the so-called "Ohio Idea." This called for the payment of all government obligations in "lawful money," i.e., in greenbacks, unless otherwise specifically provided. As the platform stated, there should be "one currency for the government and the people, the laborer and the office holder, the pensioner and the soldier, the producer and the bond holder." The inflationists, however, were unable to nominate their favorite candidate, George H. Pendleton, of Ohio, and after a prolonged deadlock, the convention was stampeded to the presiding officer, Horatio Seymour, of New York.

The results of the election gave Grant 214 electoral votes to 80 for Seymour, but the popular vote showed no decisive endorsement of the Republican party in the country. In a total popular vote of 5,700,000, Grant received a majority of 300,000. But the negro vote in the South totaled more than 600,000, and without this vote Grant would have had a minority of the popular, and probably of the electoral, vote.

The Republicans promptly turned to the problem of completing reconstruction in the South. The election of 1868 had shown the value of the negro vote as a political asset to the Republicans and they determined to perpetuate it as part of the fundamental law of the nation. Accordingly the Fifteenth Amendment to the Constitution, prohibiting either the United States or any state from denying the right to vote to any citizen on account of "race, color, or previous condition of servitude," was passed by Congress and ratified by the states. The three states of Virginia, Mississippi and Texas, and also Georgia, which had again been placed under military control because of the action of its legislature in excluding negro members, were required to ratify the Fifteenth Amendment as a condition of their restoration. Finally, in July, 1870, these four states were declared entitled to representation in Congress and the process of political reconstruction was completed.

BIBLIOGRAPHICAL NOTE

There have been published a number of single-volume histories covering the period since the Civil War; C. A. Beard, *Contemporary American History* (1914); F. L. Paxson, *The New Nation* (1915); by the same author, *Recent History of the United States* (revised edition, 1928); P. L. Haworth, *The United States in Our Own Times* (1920); C. R. Lingley, *Since the Civil War* (revised edition, 1926); L. B. Shippee, *Recent American History* (1924); D. S. Muzzey, *The United States of America*, Vol. II (1924); R. G. Caldwell, *A Short History of the American People*, Vol. II (1927); A. M. Schlesinger, *A Political and Social History of the United States, 1829-1925* (1925). E. P. Oberholtzer has planned a comprehensive history of the period entitled *A History of the United States since the*

Civil War (1917-1926), of which the first three volumes, covering the years from 1865-1878, have thus far appeared. The last five volumes of *The American Nation; A History* (1907-1918) contain an excellent treatment of the period from 1865 to 1917. The later volumes of the *Chronicles of America* (1919-1921) contain good accounts of special phases of this period. C. A. Beard, *Rise of American Civilization,* Vol. II (1927), presents a stimulating synthesis of the period since the Civil War.

General accounts of the Reconstruction period are to be found in W. A. Dunning, *Reconstruction; Political and Economic* (1907); J. F. Rhodes, *History of the United States Since the Compromise of 1850,* Vols. VI and VII (1906); W. L. Fleming, *The Sequel to Appomattox* (1919); the same author's *Documentary History of Reconstruction* (1906) contains valuable illustrative material; P. J. Hamilton, *The Reconstruction Period* (1905); J. W. Burgess, *Reconstruction and the Constitution* (1902) is valuable for the discussion of the constitutional questions; C. G. Bowers, *The Tragic Era* (1929) is strongly critical of the whole reconstruction policy and aims to rehabilitate President Johnson; other recent favorable accounts of Johnson are R. W. Winston, *Andrew Johnson; Plebeian and Patriot* (1928), and L. P. Stryker, *Andrew Johnson, A Study in Courage* (1929). See also D. M. DeWitt, *The Impeachment of President Johnson* (1905), and C. F. Chadsey, *The Struggle between President Johnson and Congress over Reconstruction* (1896); H. K. Beale, *The Critical Year: A Study of Andrew Johnson and Reconstruction* (1930).

A series of monographs published in the Columbia University and Johns Hopkins University studies treat of the conditions in the various Southern states during the Reconstruction period; J. W. Garner, *Reconstruction in Mississippi* (1901); J. S. Reynolds, *Reconstruction in South Carolina* (1905); J. W. Fertig, *The Secession and Reconstruction of Tennessee* (1898); H. J. Eckenrode, *The Political History of Virginia during the Reconstruction* (1904); C. W. Ramsdell, *Reconstruction in Texas* (1910); W. W. Davis, *The Civil War and Reconstruction in Florida* (1913); T. S. Staples, *Reconstruction in Arkansas* (1923); J. R. Ficklen, *History of Reconstruction in Louisiana through 1868* (1910); C. Mildred Thompson, *Reconstruction in Georgia* (1915); E. Lenn, *Reconstruction in*

Louisiana after 1868 (1918) ; J. G. deR. Hamilton, *Reconstruction in North Carolina* (1914).

Vivid but prejudiced accounts of conditions in the South during Reconstruction are found in J. S. Pike, *The Prostrate State* (1874) ; Charles Nordhoff, *The Cotton States* (1876), and H. A. Herbert, *Why the Solid South* (1890). For the work of the Freedmen's Bureau see P. S. Peirce, *The Freedmen's Bureau* (1904).

CHAPTER 2

OUTCOME OF RECONSTRUCTION

CARPETBAG AND NEGRO RULE IN THE SOUTH

For periods of varying length, extending in the case of Louisiana, Florida, and South Carolina to eight years, the states of the South were subjected to an orgy of corruption and misrule probably never equaled in the history of civilized government. Northern Carpetbaggers in league with Southern Scalawags, supported by the misled enfranchised negroes, and aided and abetted by the radical Republican leaders in Congress, possessed themselves of the machinery of government in the South. The negroes were organized into so-called "Union Leagues" and encouraged by unscrupulous white leaders to commit acts of violence against their former masters. In all of the state legislatures there was a considerable number of negroes, and in South Carolina they were in a substantial majority. Many of these negroes were illiterate and others could scarcely write their own names. Possessed of little or no property upon which taxes were levied, the members of these legislatures proceeded to squander public money without let or hindrance.

The extent of fraud and corruption varied in the different states and reached its most revolting form in South Carolina and Louisiana. The state debt of the former was increased threefold in three years. Hundreds of thousands of dollars were wasted by inefficient public officials and larger sums dispensed in the form of bribes or stolen outright from the treasury. Over $100,000 was paid to corrupt members of the South Carolina legislature to assure the passage of one bill. Mirrors at $750 apiece, clocks at $480, cuspidors at $8, were a few of the items charged to the state. On one occasion the legislature voted to appropriate $1,000 to repay the Speaker for what he had lost in betting on a horse race. Government officials furnished their homes and dressed their families at the expense of the state. An impecunious Carpetbag governor in Louisiana retired after four years in office worth over a half million dollars. In South Carolina a "refreshment room" was maintained in connection with the legislature, at the expense of the state, in which the legislators were supplied with the most expensive liquors and cigars. In North Carolina the looters induced the legislature to issue bonds amounting to $25,000,000 for the construction of a system of railways and not a mile of track was built by the conspirators.

Not all of the large increase of the indebtedness in the Southern states at this time can be charged to official waste and corruption. Substantial sums for entirely legitimate purposes, such as the rebuilding of roads, bridges and public buildings destroyed during the war, and especially the construction of schools for both negroes and whites, were appropriated by the Carpetbag legislatures.[1]

To the decent whites of the South these conditions not only meant economic ruin, but they indicated a dissolution of organized society. Some persons simply resigned themselves to their fate, others sold their property for what it would bring and left the country, but the majority, with grim determination, set themselves to the task of salvaging all that was possible from the wreckage and restoring white supremacy. Appeals to the North and to the government at Washington met with little consideration. To wrest power from the negroes and their white leaders by legal means was in many of the states almost impossible because the negro voters outnumbered the whites. Recourse to extra-legal methods

[1] E. W. Knight, in *The Influence of Reconstruction on Education in the South* (1913), maintains that the money appropriated for schools by the Carpetbag régimes seldom reached the destination for which it was intended.

appeared, under the circumstances, both natural and justifiable.

Almost spontaneously there sprang up all over the South secret organizations of whites under various names such as the Knights of the White Camelia in Louisiana, the White Brotherhood in North Carolina, and the Knights of the Rising Sun in Texas. But the organization that attracted the widest attention and quickly spread to all parts of the South was the Ku Klux Klan. This society started in the little town of Pulaski, Tennessee, as a social group among former officers in the Confederate army. Similar groups were formed in other Tennessee towns and in those of neighboring states. In their social gatherings, these organizations quite naturally turned to a discussion of the political and social conditions in which they lived, and to consideration of ways and means of escaping from the intolerable situation.

With the spread of the order an imposing organization was erected. The whole South was designated the "Invisible Empire," presided over by a "Grand Wizard"; each state was a "Realm" under a "Grand Dragon"; each Congressional district a "Dominion" under a "Grand Titan"; each county a "Province," under a "Grand Giant"; each locality a "Den" under a "Grand Cyclops." The ideals of the order were stated to be the protection of the weak and innocent, the relief of the injured and oppressed, the defense of the Constitution of the United States, and the protection of people from unlawful arrest and prosecution. But in practice the Klan departed widely from these idealistic purposes. Intimidation of the negroes and their white associates became the chief if not the sole activity of the organization.

Garbed in awe-inspiring costumes, usually a white sheet with the face masked and the head covered with a high conical hat, groups of the Klansmen, mounted on horses similarly disguised, would appear at night before the cabins of negroes and threaten them with dire punishment if they did not cease their political activities. If this warning did not prove effective, more strenuous methods were employed, resulting in whippings, burning of cabins, and not infrequently killing of negroes. The better element among the members of the order tried to restrain these lawless actions, but the central organization was unable to control the local "Dens." In 1869 the "Grand Wizard" ordered the dissolution of the society and many of the conservative members withdrew. However, the local "Dens" continued their activities under reckless and lawless leaders.

The radical governors and legislatures tried to repress the disorders of the Klan by legislation imposing heavy fines and imprisonment upon those convicted of participating in its activities. Such legislation was generally ineffective, for it was almost impossible to procure convictions in the state courts. Failure of the state authorities to cope with the situation led to action by Congress. By two laws passed in May, 1870, and February, 1871, elections in the Southern states were placed under the control of Federal officials. The so-called "Ku Klux Law" of April, 1871, declared the activities of "unlawful combinations" to be "rebellion against the United States," and authorized the President to suspend the writ of habeas corpus and to use the military force of the United States to suppress disorder. Acting under these laws Federal forces were sent to various parts of the South, martial law was proclaimed in several counties of South Carolina, and several hundred persons were arrested and prosecuted in Federal courts. But the efforts of the Federal authorities to bolster up the disgraceful Carpetbag régimes were ineffective. The Ku Klux movement had paved the way for the restoration of white rule in the South. It not only solidified the whites of the South but it focused the attention of the North on the outrages of the Carpetbag governments. Northern sentiment was steadily turning against the radicals, new economic issues had arisen to divert the interest of people from the issues of the war, and in general there appeared a more tolerant attitude toward the South and its problems. As Tennessee was the first of the Confederate states to be restored to the Union, so also was it the first to escape from the rule of the radicals. In 1869 the conservatives succeeded in defeating the notorious "Parson Brownlow" for governor. In 1870 the Carpetbag régime in Georgia was overthrown, and in the same year the conservatives obtained control of the legislature in North Carolina. Success of the Democrats in the Congressional elections of 1874 further weakened the radicals in the South, and in that year Alabama, Arkansas, and Texas were reclaimed by the whites, followed by Mississippi the next year. In South Carolina, Florida, and Louisiana the Carpetbag governments retained a precarious hold for another year. The dubious victory of the Republicans in the presidential election of 1876 made it clear to the leaders of that party that the country was thoroughly tired of the Southern issue. Acting on this conviction, President Hayes, shortly after assuming office, withdrew the Federal troops from the South and the three remaining states passed quickly and peacefully under white control.[2]

White supremacy having been restored in the Southern states, various measures were resorted to to assure the permanence of this supremacy. Although intimidation of the negroes did not entirely disappear with the decline of the Ku Klux, other methods, such as stuffing the ballot boxes and shifting the boxes about so as to confuse the ignorant negro voters, were often found effective in keeping the negro vote at a minimum. Beginning in 1890, however, these extralegal devices were replaced by more formal constitutional and legislative provisions. It was in the decade of the nineties, as we shall see, that the Populist agitation divided the white voters of the South. In such a situation the negroes might be

[2] Virginia escaped the misfortunes of Carpetbag government by remaining under military rule until 1870.

used by one or both of the white factions, thereby threatening white supremacy. To avoid this danger the two factions of the whites joined forces to place the negro permanently beyond the political pale. Mississippi, in 1890, placed in her constitution a provision requiring of voters two years' residence in the state, one year in the election district, the payment of a two-dollar poll tax, and the ability to read any section of the state constitution or "to understand the same when read to him." Other Southern states soon followed the example of Mississippi. These residence, tax, and literacy tests effectively barred a large percentage of the negroes from voting, but they also had the effect of disfranchising a large number of shiftless and illiterate whites. An ingenious plan was then adopted in Louisiana to bar the negroes from voting without disfranchising the ignorant whites. By the so-called "grandfather clause" of the state constitution it was provided that any person who was entitled to vote prior to January 1, 1867, and the sons and grandsons of such persons, should not be deprived of the right to vote because of the inability to satisfy the property or educational qualifications, provided such persons registered before January, 1898. As the ancestors of most of the white inhabitants had voted before 1867, while few, if any, of the negroes' ancestors had done so, the effect of this provision was to exempt from the educational and property qualifications the illiterate whites while still holding the negroes to them. Other Southern states soon followed the example of Louisiana. Although many persons believed that these constitutional provisions violated the Fifteenth Amendment of the Federal constitution the courts did not at first so hold. It was not until 1915 that the Supreme Court declared unconstitutional the clause of the Oklahoma constitution which exempted whites from the literacy test.[3]

[3] The Court distinguished between the clause in the Louisiana constitution and that in the Oklahoma constitution. The former was applicable

Viewed in retrospect and judged by its fruits, the policy of political reconstruction was a stupendous blunder. In the first place, the ten years of political and social chaos that accompanied the reconstruction process delayed the economic recovery of the South for at least a generation. Further, the effort on the part of the radicals to force negro rule on the South seriously complicated the problem of race relations in this section. Agitators and unscrupulous politicians in the South for fifty years after the war were able to delay, if not to defeat, efforts of the intelligent leaders of both races to adjust the relations between the whites and negroes by raising the specter of negro rule and reviving the nightmare of reconstruction days.

Again, the reconstruction era bequeathed an unfortunate political heritage to the South. In the years before the Civil War the South was divided politically between Whigs and Democrats, much as was the North. But the bitterness aroused against the Republican party because of its creation and support of the Carpetbag governments, drove the vast majority of Southern whites into the Democratic party. Nor did this situation change with the passing of the Carpetbag régimes. Allegiance to the Democratic party became a tradition in the South and the former Confederate states voted solidly Democratic, irrespective of candidates or issues, while the Republican party, in many of these states, after the disfranchisement of the negroes, became a shadowy organization of Federal office holders.[4]

ECONOMIC CHANGES IN THE SOUTH

The war and its aftermath brought far-reaching changes in the economic life of the South. The old planter class, for

to the sons and grandsons of persons who voted in January, 1867, and was not intended to extend further. The Oklahoma provision contemplated an indefinite extension of the exemption (238 U. S. 347, 364).

[4] This was especially true in the southern tier of the former Con-

the most part, returned to their plantations impoverished by their losses sustained from investments in Confederate securities and from the confiscation of their slave property. With little or no capital, and with the necessity of adapting themselves to a system of paid labor, only the most capable and energetic among them were able to cope successfully with the changed conditions and hold their plantations together. Many, especially among the younger generation, left the plantations and entered trade or the professions. Others tried to retain control of their estates by dividing their land into plots, usually from twenty to fifty acres, and leasing these plots to white farmers or former slaves.

As the poor whites and freedmen had virtually no money with which to pay rent, a system of share tenancy became common in the South. Under this arrangement the landowner took an agreed-upon share of the crop each year as rent. Frequently the landowner also provided the tenant with tools, seed, and working animals. Credit for food, clothes, and other necessary supplies was usually furnished by the local merchant, who was secured by a lien upon the growing crop. When the crops were gathered, the landowner received his share and the merchant took a sufficient portion to reimburse himself for the advances that he had made. Improvidence and ignorance on the part of the farmers, coupled not infrequently by dishonesty of the merchants, kept many of the renters in a state of perpetual indebtedness. The practice of mortgaging the growing crop tended to discourage diversified farming and limited the economic opportunities of the farmer. He was obliged by the merchant-banker to confine himself to the production of cotton and tobacco because these crops were less likely to be total failures and commanded a more ready market than other crops.

federate states. In Virginia, North Carolina, and Tennessee the Republicans had a substantial minority.

The industrious middle-class farmers who constituted about two-thirds of the white population before the war saw their economic and social position improved as a result of the ruin of the planter class. The former social cleavage between the great landed aristocracy and the yeomen farmers was measurably lessened. If for no other reason, the planters and the white farmers had to make common cause in order to prevent the political domination of the negroes. Further, with the break-up of many plantations, white farmers were enabled to improve their land holdings by purchasing part of these plantations. During the ten years following the war the average size of farms in the South was reduced from three hundred and thirty-five acres to a little more than one hundred and fifty acres.

Social conditions in the post-bellum South indicated an increasing departure from old traditions. In ante-bellum days, although there were numbers of instances of men of standing who entered the field of trade as cotton factors or merchants, still the typical Southern gentleman of this time was either a planter, a lawyer, or an office holder. After the war a man could enter business or the professions without losing caste, and many did so. The old Southern aristocracy, with its exaggerated sense of personal "honor," slowly succumbed under the pressure of the new social order. Perhaps most striking was the change in the position of women. In the old days most women of the upper class had lived in an atmosphere of romance, wholly removed from contact with the business and political world about them. But the results of the war forced thousands of the gentlewomen to earn their own livelihood by entering the business world as shop-keepers, dressmakers, or, in some instances, directing the plantations that had been left by their husbands or fathers who had died on the battlefield. In short the "New South," although it lacked some of the geniality and hospitality of the old days, gave evidence of a greater alertness and vigor, which corresponded to the needs of the new age that was before it.

Moreover the South felt, in a measure, the effects of the industrial development that transformed the economic life of the nation in the decades following the Civil War. Railways were built into regions containing mineral and lumber resources. The site of the city of Birmingham was a cotton field in 1870; eight years later it was an important iron center. The census of 1880 showed that there were in the Southern states one hundred and sixty-four textile mills. In Tennessee and Georgia the annual value of the lumber output was nearly five million dollars. North Carolina had over one hundred tobacco factories, with a product valued at more than two million dollars annually.

POST-WAR FOREIGN RELATIONS

The Civil War closed with two serious controversies with foreign countries to be settled. One with France involved the French intervention in Mexico, and the other, with Great Britain, concerned the so-called "Alabama Claims."

The occasion for foreign intervention in Mexico was the failure of the Mexican government to pay certain of its financial obligations to foreign creditors. Early in 1862 a combined French, Spanish, and British military force landed at Vera Cruz. When Napoleon III disclosed his intention to assume political control of the country, the British and Spanish contingents were withdrawn and the French then proceeded to install the Austrian Archduke Maximilian as Emperor of Mexico.

Against this action of the French the United States protested, but no further steps could be taken at the time because of the exigencies of the war. With the close of hostilities in the spring of 1865, however, the State Department notified the French authorities in no uncertain terms that the United States would not tolerate the maintenance of a government in Mexico by French arms, and General Sheridan, with a veteran army, was sent to the Mexican border to lend emphasis to our protest. Coincident with this determined attitude of the government of the United States war clouds were gathering in Europe. Bismarck had despatched an ultimatum to Austria, and a major European war seemed imminent. In the face of these threatening European complications the French Emperor felt constrained to abandon the Mexican adventure. The French troops were withdrawn from Mexico and the Empire of Maximilian was promptly overthrown by the Republican army under Juárez.

More serious and complicated were the questions in controversy with Great Britain. Most prominent of these were the claims based upon the activities of Confederate cruisers built in Great Britain. In addition there was a boundary dispute between the United States and Canada, together with the long standing fisheries controversy. To add to the bitter feeling between the two countries, Irish-Americans in sympathy with the Fenian movement for Irish independence were attempting to stir up trouble for Great Britain in Canada.

Great Britain was not inclined at first to admit any responsibility for the depredations of the Confederate cruisers that had been built in British shipyards during the Civil War. But the strained international situation on the continent of Europe after 1868, especially between France and Prussia, raised the possibility of a European war in which Great Britain might become involved. In such an event it would be embarrassing to Great Britain if the United States and other neutral countries, using the precedent of the Confederate cruisers, should open their ports to commerce destroyers of Britain's enemies. This situation brought the British authorities to a different frame of mind, and when the American minister, Reverdy Johnson, proposed negotiations looking to a settlement of our claims he found the British ministry well disposed. As a result of the negotiations the Johnson-Clarendon Convention was drafted in January, 1869. This document made no direct reference to the Alabama Claims, but merely proposed that there should be submitted to arbitration all claims of the subjects of either country against those of the other which had arisen since the convention of 1853. The Senate by an overwhelming vote declined to ratify this blanket arrangement. This action of the Senate was due partly to the unwillingness of the Republicans to approve a measure which might reflect credit upon the administration of President Johnson and partly because the proposed settlement did not cover claims for national damage against Great Britain because of her encouragement of the Confederacy.

President Grant did not allow the issue to be dropped. Through his Secretary of State, Hamilton Fish, the British authorities were again approached and indicated their willingness to resume negotiations, influenced, no doubt, by the outbreak of the Franco-Prussian war. The situation was complicated as a result of a speech made by Senator Sumner, chairman of the foreign relations committee, in which he insisted that Great Britain should pay not only for the direct damages caused by the activities of the Confederate cruisers but also indirect damages, which he estimated at more than $2,000,000,000, on account of the prolongation of the war due to the unfriendly attitude of the British authorities.

The British government declined to discuss arbitration on any such basis. However, President Grant and Secretary Fish did not support the extreme claims made by Sumner, and a further personal controversy between the Senator and the President [5] led to the removal of Sumner from the chairmanship of the foreign relations committee. An agreement

[5] Sumner refused to support Grant in his effort to acquire the island of Santo Domingo.

was then reached for the appointment of a Joint High Commission to which was submitted all questions in dispute between the two countries. This commission drafted the Treaty
of Washington, which was signed on May 8, 1871, and
promptly ratified by the Senate. The treaty provided for a
mixed commission to deal with the fisheries question, and
for the reference of the Northwest boundary dispute to the
German Emperor for adjudication. Concerning the Confederate cruisers Great Britain expressed regret for the
escape of these vessels "under whatever circumstances" and
agreed to submit to the arbitration of an international
tribunal the question of damages to be paid to the United
States.

When the court of arbitration met at Geneva the American representatives made a belated attempt to revive the
claims for indirect damages, but the court ruled these out and
finally awarded to the United States $15,500,000 for direct
damages. The award of the German Emperor relative to the
Northwest boundary sustained the American claims, and
the mixed commission arranged a twelve-year agreement in
regard to the fisheries. Finally, an award of $2,000,000 was
allowed to British subjects, to be paid by the United States,
for British property confiscated and British subjects unlaw-
fully detained by the United States during the war.

In the higher ranges of international politics during the
decade following the Civil War, the American people seem
to have been wholly uninterested. The stirring events in
Europe which culminated in the creation of the German
Empire and the Italian kingdom affected but little the internal politics of this country. Nor is there any evidence
that America felt the urge for imperialist expansion which
at the time had gripped several of the large European
powers. It is true that Secretary Seward, an enthusiastic
expansionist, contracted a treaty for the purchase of Alaska
from Russia, but the response of the country to the action

of the energetic Secretary was anything but enthusiastic. The New York *Tribune* referred to the territory as "a frozen wilderness" and as "Seward's desert." There were loud complaints against spending seven million dollars for a worthless possession when the country was groaning under a huge war debt. The Senate finally ratified the treaty on April 9, 1867, influenced partly by a desire to show our gratitude to Russia because of the sympathy that she had shown for the North during the war, and partly by a desire to spite Great Britain. As one member of Congress put it: by the acquisition of Alaska, "We cage the British lion on the Pacific coast; we cripple that great and grasping monopoly, the Hudson's Bay Company." Even greater difficulty was experienced by Seward in persuading the House to appropriate the $7,200,000 [6] to pay for the territory, and it was not until July 14, 1868, that the measure passed the House, amidst charges that bribery had been used to facilitate its adoption.[7]

Seward's further efforts at expansion met with no success. He negotiated a treaty with Santo Domingo providing an American naval base on that island, and a second treaty for the purchase of the Virgin Islands, but the Senate refused to ratify either of these agreements. When President Grant entered office he tried to carry forward Seward's expansionist policy. A treaty was drafted providing for the annexation of Santo Domingo only to meet with rejection by the Senate, despite the strongest kind of presidential pressure

[6] It has recently been disclosed that only $1,400,000 of the amount paid to Russia was for the acquisition of Alaska. The remaining $5,800,000 was to reimburse Russia for the expense to which she was put in sending a fleet to New York during the Civil War as a demonstration of friendship for the North. See Muzzey, Vol. II, p. 47, note.

[7] A Congressional investigation later disclosed the fact that Robert J. Walker, former Secretary of the Treasury, had received $26,000 from the Russian embassy to aid in the adoption of the treaty, and that $5,000 of this sum had been paid to a brother of a Washington newspaper editor whose paper "had rendered valuable service" in supporting the treaty.

brought to bear on that body. Nor was Grant any more successful in persuading the Senate to approve his action in obtaining an American foothold in far-off Samoa. Clearly American imperialism was still in its infancy, and it was evident that the American people needed considerable education in the philosophy of "Manifest Destiny."

FINANCIAL RECONSTRUCTION

The effect of the Civil War upon the financial structure of the country was far reaching. In common with all wars this conflict brought a tremendous increase in government expenditures. In the four years of war the government had expended a greater amount than during the whole preceding period of national history. To meet this enormous financial burden the national government adopted measures that had political as well as financial implications. Of these the three most important were the imposition of high protective tariffs, the creation of a national banking system, and the injection of millions of dollars of fiat money into the currency of the country.

Beginning with the Morrill tariff of 1861, customs duties before the close of the war had been raised from an average of 19 per cent. to an average of 47 per cent. Excise taxes upon a great variety of manufactured commodities as well as upon business transactions were likewise imposed. Finally a Federal income tax, for the first time in our history, was levied on all incomes above $800. In addition to taxation the government resorted to borrowing on a large scale. By the issuance of long-term bonds and short-term notes the government borrowed $2,142,000,000 during the war.

But neither borrowing nor taxation sufficed to meet the mounting cost of war and resort was then made to non-interest-bearing Treasury Notes, which were made legal tender. In all, some $400,000,000 of these so-called greenbacks were issued during the war, and became a part of the currency system. Backed by nothing but the credit of the government, these notes soon depreciated in value in relation to gold and silver. They reached their lowest point in August, 1864, when a dollar greenback was worth thirty-nine cents. As the military fortunes of the North improved the greenbacks slowly appreciated in value. By the close of the war a paper dollar was worth about fifty-seven cents. With the depreciation of the greenbacks gold and silver disappeared from circulation. Even the fractional silver currency was hoarded, and to supply the need for such currency, small paper bills familiarly known as "shin plasters," were issued.

Another important result of war financing was the creation of a national banking system. The National Bank Act of 1863 provided for the granting of charters to groups of individuals who would invest at least one-third of their capital in government bonds. On the security of bonds thus purchased and deposited in the treasury as a reserve, each bank was authorized to issue circulating notes amounting to 90 per cent. of the value of the bonds deposited. This plan not only facilitated the disposal of government bonds but it furnished a standardized paper currency, badly needed in view of the unstable character of much of the paper money issued by state banks at the time. Incidentally this measure brought powerful financial interests to the support of the national government. Supplementing the National Bank Act, Congress in 1885 placed a prohibitive tax of 10 per cent. upon notes issued by state banks, which resulted in the retirement from circulation of some 7,000 different kinds of notes hitherto issued by state banking institutions.

In getting from a war to a peace basis of finance, significant political questions were involved. The demand for the removal of many of the war excise taxes aroused no opposition, and within two years after the close of the war most of these war levies were repealed. Similarly, incomes under two thousand dollars were freed from tax in 1867, and in 1872 Federal income taxes were abolished.

It was a different matter when it came to a reduction of the war tariffs. Representatives of tariff-protected interests flocked to Washington and demanded not only the retention of the tariff duties levied during the war but in many cases a substantial increase. In 1870, and again in 1872, some slight reductions in the war duties were made, but on the whole the powerful protected interests, strongly intrenched in the dominant Republican party, were able to retain the privileges that the exigencies of the war had conferred upon them.

Political and economic considerations, rather than those purely financial, determined the policy of Congress in dealing with the greenbacks. In conservative banking circles the opinion was generally held that these notes had been issued as a war measure and that as soon as the crisis had passed they should be retired and specie payments resumed as speedily as possible. Secretary of the Treasury McCulloch concurred in this opinion and Congress at first also appeared to hold to this view. In December, 1865, the House of Representatives passed a resolution stating its belief in the necessity of a contraction of the currency with a view to an early resumption of specie payments, and the next year Congress empowered the Secretary of the Treasury to retire $10,000,000 of greenbacks within six months, and not more than $4,000,000 in any one month thereafter. Acting under this authority Secretary McCulloch retired $44,000,000 of the notes during the following two years.

However, opposition to the withdrawal of the greenbacks soon developed, chiefly among the farmers of the West and South. The farmers, generally, were debtors, having borrowed large sums on mortgage loans. Many of these loans had been made in greenbacks when they were substantially depreciated in value. If the greenbacks were retired the farmer would be required to repay his debts in dollars worth one hundred cents whereas he had received paper dollars worth fifty cents or less when the loan was contracted. On the other hand the greater the amount of money in circulation the less would be its value in terms of wheat and other commodities. Plentiful money meant, therefore, high prices for grain. In response to this outcry from the agricultural regions Congress in 1868 enacted a measure which prohibited the Secretary of the Treasury from retiring any more of the greenbacks. In the presidential election of that year, as we have seen, the inflationists obtained control of the Democratic party and wrote into the platform the "Ohio Idea," which advocated the retention of the greenbacks and the payment of the public debt in the depreciated paper currency. Despite their defeat in this election, the advocates of inflation did not stop their agitation, and they were encouraged when Secretary Boutwell in 1871 issued $6,000,000 more of the notes and Secretary Richardson, during the panic of 1873, added another $26,000,000, making the total in circulation $382,000,000. Going still further, Congress in 1874 passed a bill providing for an increase of the greenbacks to $400,000,000, but this measure was vetoed by President Grant, who denounced the policy of inflation.

The success of the Democrats in the congressional elections of 1874 frightened the advocates of sound money and they hurried through the expiring Congress, January 14, 1875, the Resumption Act. This measure provided for the resumption of specie payments on January 1, 1879. For this purpose the treasury was authorized to accumulate a fund of gold, and, if necessary, to sell bonds in order to obtain a sufficient amount of specie. Concerning the greenbacks the Resumption Act adopted a compromise position. It provided for their retirement until the amount in circulation was reduced to $300,000,000,[8] after which no further reduction was to be made. To take the place of the retired notes, new national banknotes were authorized. The paper fractional currency was withdrawn and replaced by silver coin. In accordance with the provisions of this Act, during the four years before the date of the resumption of specie payment, the treasury accumulated a fund of $133,000,000 in gold and in the same interval the greenbacks steadily increased in value until a fortnight before the resumption date they were accepted at par with gold. As a result, when January 1, 1879, arrived, only a small fraction of the notes were presented for redemption.

The advocates of fiat money having failed to persuade either of the two major parties to accept their views completely, they determined to organize a new party to accomplish their purposes. In 1876 the Greenback or National party was formed. Its platform called for: (1) the repeal of the act for the resumption of specie payment; (2) the issue of legal-tender notes convertible into obligations bearing interest not exceeding one cent a day on each $100; (3) the suppression of bank notes; and (4) no gold bonds for sale in foreign markets. It was the contention of those who advocated these measures that the value of money is not dependent upon the intrinsic value of the metal from which it is made but rests solely upon the authority of the government that issues it. It was asserted that it is the purchasing power of money rather than its convertibility which determines its value. It was maintained that the dollar should have a fixed and stable value and should be issued only by the government. Its value would be sustained by the wealth and prosperity of the country.

[8] In 1878 Congress again stopped the retirement of the greenbacks, at which time they had been reduced to $346,681,616. These notes remain a part of the circulating medium at the present time.

The enthusiastic supporters of the greenbacks bitterly denounced their opponents as enemies of the common people. The effort to retire the greenbacks they asserted was a conspiracy of the money interests.

In the presidential election of 1876 the Greenback party polled about 80,000 votes. Two years later in the congressional elections they received more than a million votes, although part of this large increase was due to fusion with

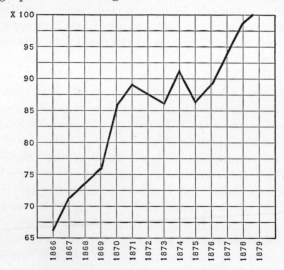

FLUCTUATION IN VALUE OF GREENBACKS

one of the major parties. In the election of 1880 the Greenback vote fell to about 300,000 and in 1884 to 175,000. By that time the advocates of an expanding currency had been won over to the movement for free silver.

The retention of the greenbacks as a permanent part of the national currency raised the question of the constitutional power of Congress to make paper money legal tender. The issue came before the Supreme Court in three important cases. In the case of Hepburn vs. Griswold, decided in 1869, the Court held by a vote of four to three that the legal tender provision, insofar as it applied to contracts made before the passage of the legal tender act, was unconstitutional. The decision aroused much popular criticism, and two years later a second case, Knox vs. Lee, came before the Court. In the meantime the composition of the Court had been changed by the addition of two judges, and the enlarged Court, by a vote of five to four, reversed the decision of Hepburn vs. Griswold. This action gave rise to the charge that the Court had been "packed," but there is no evidence to substantiate this accusation. A later decision upheld the right of Congress to issue legal tender notes in time of peace as well as in war.[9]

POST-WAR POLITICAL AND MORAL DEGRADATION

The decade following the Civil War presents an uninspiring picture of political corruption and loose financial methods, if not downright dishonesty, in business. The whole country was seized by a mania for accumulating wealth, and there were few who condemned the shady methods often employed in its acquisition. On all sides there was a vulgar display of wealth. Unscrupulous heads of large corporations corrupted legislators and prostituted the bench and the bar. At least two justices of the Supreme Court in New York, Barnard and Cardozo, dragged the ermine in the mire by submitting to the dictates of the notorious Jay Gould and Commodore Vanderbilt. Newspapers were, with few exceptions, open to corruption. Reporters from several New York papers were kept on the city payroll by Boss Tweed in order to assure favorable comment in their several journals.

Charles Francis Adams, in his entertaining essays called *Chapters of Erie,* thus depicts conditions: "The stock

[9] Juilliard vs. Greenman (1884).

exchange revealed itself as a haunt of gamblers and a den of thieves; the offices of our great corporations appeared as the secret chambers in which trustees plotted the spoliation of their wards; the law became a ready engine for the furtherance of wrong, and the ermine of the judge did not conceal the eagerness of the partisan; the halls of legislation were transformed into a mart in which the price of votes was haggled over, and laws, made to order, were bought and sold; while under all, and through all, the voice of public opinion was silent or was disregarded."

One or two illustrations will suffice to show the sordid conditions that prevailed in the business and political life of the time.

A trio of financial buccaneers, Daniel Drew, Jay Gould, and James Fisk, Jr., had obtained control of a majority of the stock of the Erie Railroad. "Commodore" Vanderbilt, who controlled the New York Central, determined to get possession of the Erie in order to control competition between New York and Buffalo. There ensued a bitter struggle in which Drew and his associates finally defeated Vanderbilt by the simple process of issuing new stock of the railroad to meet Vanderbilt's purchases. The courts and the state legislature became involved. Pliant judges issued injunctions and counter-injunctions at the behest of the rival conspirators. At Albany, around the legislature, which the New York *Independent* called "the worst assemblage of official thieves that ever disgraced the capitol of the Empire State," the Vanderbilt and Gould forces gathered to battle over a bill to legalize the stock issued by Gould and his associates. With liberal use of money Vanderbilt at first succeeded in defeating the measure, but when Gould appeared on the scene with large funds abstracted from the Erie treasury, the bill was passed amidst charges of wholesale corruption. The net result was the financial wrecking of a valuable railroad property.

A second exploit of Gould and Fisk attracted nation-wide attention and involved the national administration at Washington. Gould conceived a plan to corner the gold supply of the country then in circulation, amounting to about $15,-000,000. Gold was still at a premium in relation to greenbacks, and the metal was sold in Wall Street the same as stocks and bonds. At the time that Gould began his operations gold was selling at 132.

To insure the success of his scheme it was necessary to guard against the selling of gold by the national treasury. For this purpose Gould enlisted the support of President Grant's brother-in-law, Abel R. Corbin, by agreeing to purchase gold for his account. Through this intermediary Gould was able to meet Grant and apparently persuaded him that by raising the price of gold the Western farmers would be better able to market their crops. Grant further compromised himself by appearing in public at a theatrical performance in the company of Gould and Fisk, and by accepting the hospitality of Fisk on a trip from New York to Boston on one of Fisk's Fall River steamboats.

Feeling assured that the national administration would not interfere to break the corner the conspirators gave orders for the purchase of gold. Amidst the wildest excitement in the financial district gold was forced up to 140. Legitimate business interests were demoralized. But Gould apparently lost courage when he learned that Grant had been informed of Corbin's speculation and had told him to quit. In any event Gould displayed his financial morals by secretly giving orders to sell gold while his associate Fisk was still feverishly buying it. On Friday, September 24, 1869, the famous "Black Friday," came the crash. Fisk had forced gold to 163, and frantic appeals had been made to Grant to have the Secretary of the Treasury come to the relief of the market. Finally the order was issued to sell $4,000,000 of gold, and the corner was broken. Gould had managed to dispose of most of his gold before the crash and Fisk escaped by simply repudiating his contracts and allowing his brokers to fail.

Although a Congressional investigating committee exonerated the President from any guilt in connection with the gold conspiracy, the whole disgraceful affair created a most disquieting impression in the public mind.

Other incidents in President Grant's first administration caused serious misgivings in the minds of many leaders of the Republican party. The announcement of the selection of members of his cabinet at the beginning of his administration caused amazement. The list contained few if any prominent party leaders. A personal friend, Elihu B. Washburne, who possessed no known qualifications for the office, was named Secretary of State, and when he shortly afterward retired and was appointed to the less exacting position of ambassador to France, Grant selected as his successor the head of a socially prominent family in New York, Hamilton Fish, who proved to be an excellent choice. For Secretary of the Treasury Grant chose A. T. Stewart, a wealthy merchant prince of New York, and when it was discovered that a law dating from 1789 debarred any person who was actively engaged in trade from holding the office of Secretary of the Treasury, Grant tried to have Congress exempt Stewart from the provisions of this law. Failing in this move, the President then appointed as Secretary of the Treasury George S. Boutwell, who had been actively identified with the impeachment of President Johnson. Another man of great wealth, but otherwise inconspicuous, A. E. Borie, was named Secretary of the Navy. The two men of outstanding ability who entered the cabinet were J. D. Cox, Secretary of the Interior, and Judge E. R. Hoar, Attorney General. Cox later resigned because of his unwillingness to submit to the dictates of the professional politicians who surrounded Grant, and Hoar was removed by Grant to make way for an appointment by which he hoped to secure Congressional support for his move to annex Santo Domingo.

THE LIBERAL REPUBLICAN MOVEMENT AND THE ELECTION OF 1872

Leading Republicans, such as Carl Schurz, Charles Francis Adams, William Cullen Bryant, and Horace Greeley, had viewed with growing concern Grant's actions and policies and they determined, if possible, to prevent his renomination. Support for this movement came from such Republican papers as the New York *Nation,* the New York *Evening Post,* and the Springfield *Republican.*

The first evidence of revolt against the Grant régime appeared in Missouri, where, under the leadership of B. Gratz Brown, a former Democrat, and Carl Schurz, an organization was formed under the name of Liberal Republicans. The success of this movement in the state elections of that year encouraged the reformers to call a national convention at Cincinnati in May, 1872. At this gathering, which was more in the nature of a mass meeting than a political convention, there appeared men of widely differing views. Some were tariff reformers, others were interested chiefly in civil service reform, still others regarded a change in the Republican policy toward the South as the most important issue before the country. In their platform the Liberals arraigned Grant's administration and declared him unfit for the presidency; demanded complete amnesty for the South; and strongly endorsed the movement for civil service reform. Unable to agree upon a tariff policy the Convention referred this controversial question to the people in selecting their Congressmen.

In choosing their candidate for president the Liberals had an opportunity to name any one of a number of eminently qualified men, among whom were Charles Francis Adams, B. Gratz Brown, Justice David Davis of the Supreme Court, and Senator Trumbull of Illinois. But the convention, unfortunately, passed over all of these men and made the worst possible choice, namely, Horace Greeley, the nationally known editor of the New York *Tribune*. Not only because of his defects of temperament was Greeley's selection politically unwise, but because as editor of the most widely circulated newspaper in the country during the stirring days of the Civil War he had made a host of enemies. Then, too, Greeley had in the past opposed both of the issues most strongly advocated by the Liberals, namely, civil service and tariff reform. To cap the climax of absurdity, the Democrats in their convention proceeded to endorse Greeley as their candidate. This was too much for the sense of humor of the American people. Horace Greeley as the standard bearer of the party that he had denounced in season and out of season in the columns of his newspaper, seemed too ridiculous to be taken seriously. Only a few months before his nomination Greeley had said of the Democratic party, "May it be written on my grave that I never was its follower and lived and died in nothing its debtor."

The regular Republicans renominated Grant without a contest, and adopted a platform that strongly endorsed the Republican measures of reconstruction in the South. In the campaign that followed there was more than the usual amount of personal vilification and mudslinging. The result was never in doubt. Greeley received only lukewarm support from the liberal press and even less than that from Democratic newspapers. In the election Grant obtained a popular majority of 750,000 and received 286 electoral votes to 66 for Greeley. But even a more suitable candidate and a better managed campaign on the part of the reformers would probably have been unable to overcome Grant's personal popularity and the sectional feeling that survived. Patriotism was still a serviceable cloak to cover a multitude of sins, both of omission and of commission.

Grant's second administration has been well characterized as "the nadir of national disgrace." One revelation after another disclosed corruption in high places, besmirching the names of some leading members of Congress, of members of the President's cabinet, and reaching even to the vice presidency. First in point of time, if not of importance, were disclosures concerning the manipulation of the stock of a financial organization known as the Crédit Mobilier. This concern had been formed in connection with the building of the Union Pacific railroad. Oakes Ames, a member of Congress from Massachusetts, who was financially interested in the corporation, proceeded to distribute its shares to certain members of Congress where, as he stated, he thought they "would do most good." It is true that congressmen paid for the stock either directly or out of later accumulated dividends, but the whole procedure gave pointed evidence of the low tone of political morality of the time. Congress contented itself with censuring Ames, but several reputations were badly damaged, including that of the outgoing Vice-President Colfax.

To add to the distress of the Republicans, a very severe financial panic broke upon the country in 1873, shortly after the beginning of Grant's second term. The combined effect of financial depression and political corruption was clearly shown in the Congressional elections of the following year when, for the first time since the Civil War, the Democrats elected a majority of the House of Representatives. They also carried the state elections in twenty-three of the thirty-five states.

The events of the succeeding two years of Grant's administration did not improve the prospects of the Republicans in the approaching presidential election. Disclosures involving certain whisky distillers in the West, which indicated that they had been evading the internal revenue tax, brought to light the fact that Grant's private secretary, O. E. Babcock, had been closely associated with the conspirators. Largely through Grant's intervention, the prosecution of Babcock failed. Scarcely had the trial of Babcock ended when the country was further humiliated by evidence presented before a committee of the House of Representatives which showed conclusively that the Secretary of War, W. W. Belknap, had received sums of money paid by a subordinate official for the privilege of retaining his position as post-trader in the Indian Territory. The House unanimously voted to impeach Belknap. The Senate voted 37 to 29 to sustain the charges, and it was only Belknap's resignation before the vote was taken that prevented his conviction by the requisite two-thirds majority.

As a fitting culmination to the whole miserable record of wrongdoing came disclosures involving the brilliant Republican leader, James G. Blaine. While Speaker of the House in 1871 Blaine had become associated with a Boston business man named Fisher who was interested in promoting the Little Rock and Fort Smith Railroad. An agreement was reached between the two men by which Blaine was to receive a handsome commission for the sale of securities of the road to his friends. In a letter written by Blaine to Fisher he said: "I do not feel that I shall prove a dead-head in the enterprise if I once embark in it. I see various channels in which I know that I can be useful." When this letter became public Blaine's enemies charged that it showed that Blaine proposed to use his political influence to further the interests of the road and incidentally his own private fortune. Unfortunately for Blaine the railroad was soon in financial difficulties and he felt obliged to relieve his friends of the unprofitable investment that he had persuaded them to make. Blaine was then accused of inducing the Union Pacific and the Atlantic and Pacific Railroad Companies to purchase the securities at a figure much above their market value.[10] The failure of this financial venture led to a dispute between Blaine and Fisher, and the latter, in an effort to embarrass Blaine, turned over the correspondence that had passed between them to a clerk in his employ named Mulligan.

The presidential election of 1876 was impending, and Blaine had been prominently mentioned as the Republican candidate. Rumors had spread of Blaine's connection with the Little Rock enterprise and the Democratic House of Representatives, hoping to make political capital from the affair, just before the election of 1876 ordered an investigation by the Judiciary Committee. Fearing the disclosure of the letters in Mulligan's possession, Blaine persuaded Mulligan to "loan" him the correspondence, and then, on the advice of counsel, declined to return it. Blaine read extracts from the letters in the course of a dramatic speech which he made before the House in defense of his actions, but he refused to turn the correspondence over to the investigating committee. Although Blaine succeeded in convincing his ardent admirers of his innocence, nevertheless the "Mulligan Letters" remained to plague him to the end of his political career.

Political corruption was not confined to Washington or to the ranks of the Republicans. Municipal government at this time was a stench in the nostrils. In nearly every large city of the country political rings, Democratic or Republican according to local circumstances, took advantage of the low public morals of the time to fill their pockets at the expense of the local taxpayers. Most notorious of these corrupt machines was that headed by William M. Tweed, in New York. As leader of Tammany Hall, in 1868, he and a group of rascally associates obtained control of the city administra-

[10] In the subsequent investigation Blaine denied this charge and he was supported in his denial by the president of the Union Pacific. Stanwood, *Life of Blaine,* p. 146.

tion and for four years looted the city treasury of an amount estimated as high as $200,000,000. In connection with the building of the county court house the city was defrauded of over $8,000,000. A bill for repairing fixtures in the building before it was completed amounted to over a million dollars. One carpenter was paid $360,000 and a plumber $2,-800,000, most of which found its way into the pockets of the political grafters.

The overthrow of the ring was due largely to dissension within its ranks. A disgruntled Tammany politician who felt that he had not been duly rewarded for his services to the leaders turned over to the New York *Times* evidence of corruption which he had obtained from the comptroller's office. Efforts made by members of the ring to buy off the editor of the *Times* failed, and the incriminating material was published. The work of the *Times* was ably seconded by the telling cartoons of Tweed and his associates drawn by Thomas Nast and published in *Harper's Weekly*. As a result of the disclosures the ring was broken up. Tweed was arrested and convicted, escaped from prison, and was returned to spend his last days in jail. Samuel J. Tilden, a prominent New York attorney, played a leading part in bringing about the conviction of Tweed and for his services in this connection became the reform governor of the state in 1874, and two years later the candidate of the Democratic party for the presidency.

It was in no spirit of pride that the nation could celebrate its centenary in 1876. Senator Hoar, of Massachusetts, in that year lamented the fact that in his brief political career he had seen five Federal judges driven from office by threats of impeachment; the largest city of the country disgraced by a political administration that became a byword for corruption throughout the world; the building of the greatest railroad in the world accompanied by colossal fraud; and the astonishing doctrine proclaimed that political power should

be used to promote selfish ambition and gratify personal re-
venge. This was a discouraging but faithful portrayal of
the conditions in America on the hundredth anniversary of
her independence.

THE DISPUTED ELECTION OF 1876

It was with much trepidation that the Republicans looked
forward to the political reckoning that appeared to be in
store for them in the presidential election of 1876. The
Democrats, on the contrary, approached this election with
high hopes. Their success in the Congressional elections two
years before had encouraged them, and continued revelations
of political corruption in the closing years of Grant's administration materially strengthened the chances of Democratic success in the presidential campaign.

It was obviously necessary for the Republicans to divert
the attention of the country, if possible, from the distressing
incidents of the past eight years, and to rally once more the
patriotic sentiment of the country to the support of the party
that had saved the Union. The shrewd Republican leader,
Blaine, pointed the way. In the debate on a bill for the removal of the remaining disabilities upon Southerners under
the Fourteenth Amendment, Blaine moved to except Jefferson Davis, charging him with responsibility for cruelty inflicted upon Union prisoners of war. Some Southern Democratic members foolishly accepted the challenge and not only
defended Davis but made heated charges against the conduct
of the war by the Northern Republicans. This maneuver
gave the Republicans a much needed aggressive, if shopworn,
keynote; the identification of the Democracy with disloyalty
to the Union.

At the Republican convention, which met in Cincinnati,
Blaine was the leading candidate, but the reform element of
the party feared the effects of his connection with the shady

financial dealings of the past administration and there were doubts, furthermore, of Blaine's sincere desire for a political housecleaning. Moreover, Blaine had aroused the bitter personal animosity of certain leading Republican politicians, notably Senator Conkling of New York. There had been some talk among the old party war horses of nominating Grant for a third term, and there were indications that Grant himself would not discourage such a suggestion. But this move was checked before the convention met as a result of a resolution passed by the House of Representatives, with the support of a large majority of both Republicans and Democrats, declaring that a third term would be "unwise, unpatriotic, and fraught with peril to our free institutions." The convention finally nominated Governor Rutherford B. Hayes of Ohio. Hayes had the first essential qualification of a Republican candidate, namely, a satisfactory war record, and his career as Governor of Ohio appealed to the reformers in the party. Of necessity the Republicans could not follow the accepted practice of political parties of adopting a platform that "pointed with pride" to their record in office. Taking the cue from Blaine's speech, the platform makers prepared a document which extolled the services of the party in the war, touched gingerly upon the events of Grant's administration, advocated a protective tariff, and supported the movement for civil service reform.

The policy of the Democrats was clearly indicated. Repubelican corruption and misrule must be the rallying cry. The old rascals should be turned out, even if the result was to put some new rascals in. Quite as clearly was the standard bearer of the party indicated before the convention met. Samuel J. Tilden, the reform Governor of New York, had attracted national attention by his courageous action in smashing a corrupt canal ring in the state, and by the part that he had played in supporting the movement to rid the City of New York of the notorious Tweed Ring. Obviously the man who had done such a good job in cleaning house in New York was the man to clean house in Washington. When the Democratic convention met at St. Louis, Tilden was nominated without serious opposition and a platform was adopted which stressed the need for reform, in the tariff and financial policies of the nation, as well as in the civil service and administrative departments of the government.

There ensued a campaign in which the Republicans made every possible effort to fan into flame once more the dying embers of Civil War hatred. Tilden's war record was contrasted unfavorably with that of Hayes. It was asserted that if the Democrats attained control of the government, they would pay the Confederate debt and reimburse the former slave-owners for the loss of their slave property. The presence of ex-Confederates in Congress was cited as evidence of the danger of "rebel rule." Democratic orators quite naturally concentrated their attack upon the Republican record of corruption.

Election day in November passed with no more than the usual disorder. As the returns came in, it was clear that the Democrats had made remarkable gains in the North. They had carried the important states of New York, Connecticut, New Jersey and Indiana. On the morning following the election virtually all of the newspapers conceded the election of Tilden, but the Republican leaders were not willing to admit defeat. With the tabulation of the returns they saw an opportunity to win if they could hold the votes of three southern states, Florida, South Carolina, and Louisiana, which were still under the control of the Republican Carpetbag régimes.

When the returns from all of the states were in it was seen that Tilden had 184 electoral votes undisputed, while Hayes had 165 undisputed. The remaining 20 electoral votes from the states of Florida, South Carolina, Louisiana, and Oregon were in dispute. Of these votes Tilden needed but one to give him a majority of the electoral college, while Hayes needed all 20 votes.

Intense excitement prevailed throughout the country. President Grant sent orders to the military officers in the South urging them to preserve order. Prominent politicians from both parties, known as "visiting statesmen," went to the three southern states to watch the counting of the votes and to guard the interests of their respective parties. The case of Oregon was peculiar. There was no question that the Republicans had carried the state, but one of the Republican electors was a postmaster and hence disqualified under the Constitution to serve as an elector. The Governor of the state, a Democrat, therefore certified to the election of the other two Republican electors and of the Democratic elector receiving the highest vote. The Governor's action violated the law of Oregon, which declared that in such a case the remaining electors were to choose a substitute for the disqualified one.

In South Carolina the Republicans appeared to have a small popular majority but the Democrats maintained that this was due to fraud and the Democratic electors met, with the result that double returns were sent to Washington. In Florida the Democrats claimed a small popular majority, but the Carpetbag returning board certified to the election of the Hayes electors. In Louisiana the hopes of the Democrats seemed brightest. On the face of the returns the Tilden electors had majorities ranging from 6,000 to 9,000. But the returning board of the state was made up exclusively of Republicans, a circumstance contrary to the law of the state. The president of the board had been characterized by General Sheridan as a "political trickster and dishonest man," a second member had been involved in dubious financial dealings, while a third had been indicted for larceny. This body would obviously not be deterred in its actions by any conscientious scruples. After an unsuccessful attempt to sell out to the Democrats, the board proceeded to throw out the votes of enough precincts to assure majorities for all of the Hayes electors.

Neither the Constitution nor Congressional law offered a solution for the situation that had arisen. The Constitution provides that the electoral votes from the states shall be sent to Washington and that "the president of the Senate shall, in the presence of the Senate and House of Representatives, open all the certificates, and the votes shall then be counted." But counted by whom? If by the president of the Senate, a Republican, the returns of the Hayes electors would be sustained; if by Congress, the Senate, which was Republican would accept the Republican returns and the Democratic House would accept the Democratic returns. Thus a deadlock appeared inevitable and, as Grant's term was nearing its end, there loomed the possibility of an interregnum in the presidency which might lead, in view of the inflamed state of the public mind, to a renewal of civil strife.

Confronted by this alarming situation, Congress met in regular session in December, 1876. A joint committee of the two houses was appointed to work out a solution. A bill was drafted which was passed by both houses and signed by the President. It provided for the creation of an Electoral Commission, consisting of five members of the House, five members of the Senate, and five justices of the Supreme Court. Four of the justices were designated in the bill; two were Republicans and two were Democrats. The House selected three Democrats and two Republicans, while the Senate chose three Republicans and two Democrats. The fifteenth member, the fifth justice, was to be selected by the other four justices, and there was a tacit understanding that Justice David Davis would be chosen. He was credited with being an independent in politics and as free from partisan bias as was possible in the superheated partisanship of the time. But just at this juncture the Democratic legislature of Illinois elected Davis

United States Senator from that state. This action eliminated him from consideration as a member of the commission and the choice fell to Justice Bradley, a Republican. As thus constituted the commission comprised eight Republicans and seven Democrats. The act provided that all disputed returns should be referred to this commission and its decision on every point would be accepted unless both houses rejected it.

When the commission met the first important question that it had to decide was the extent of its authority. Should it go behind the returns and examine the charges of fraud at the polls, or must it confine itself to deciding which set of electors had the proper certificates from the legal state authorities? In arguing this question before the commission, the eminent legal counsel were quite ready to repudiate cherished party doctrines in order to sustain their contentions. The Democratic counsel discarded the traditional Democratic dogma of States' Rights and argued that the commission was empowered to go behind the returns and examine the election on its merits. Counsel for the Republicans suddenly became solicitous for the rights of the states and insisted that the commission must confine itself to deciding which of the disputed returns had official state authorization. By a strictly partisan vote of eight to seven the commission upheld the Republican contention. This virtually decided the contest, for in the three Southern states the Republican electors had the certification of the proper state authority. The commission therefore assigned all of the disputed votes to Hayes and Congress, in accordance with the terms of the act, ratified the decision and declared Hayes elected by a vote of 185 to 184.

Upon the justice of the decision there will probably never be agreement. Dr. Haworth,[11] in his exhaustive study of the election, reaches the conclusion that had there been an absolutely free and fair election, with no fraud or intimidation,

[11] Haworth, *The Disputed Presidential Election of 1876.*

Hayes would have carried all three of the disputed Southern states. In this conclusion Professor Burgess [12] concurs. On the other hand, Rhodes [13] is of the opinion that the Democrats were entitled to the votes of Florida and Louisiana.

The Democrats were naturally keenly disappointed and some of the more hotheaded among them advocated raising an armed force and marching upon Washington to seat Tilden in the presidency. But calmer counsels prevailed, and Tilden gave no countenance to his belligerently inclined supporters. It is a matter for sincere congratulation that the sense of order in the American democracy was so strongly rooted that it was able to weather a crisis that in many another country might have resulted in armed conflict and bloodshed.[14]

BIBLIOGRAPHICAL NOTE

Discussions of Carpetbag and negro rule in the Southern states will be found in the monographs cited in the bibliography at the end of Chapter 1. A good exposition of the activities of the Ku Klux Klan is given by W. G. Brown, *The Lower South in American History* (1902). See also J. C. Lester and D. L. Wilson, *Ku Klux Klan, Its Origin, Growth, and Disbandment* (1905), and E. P. Oberholtzer, *A History of the United States Since the Civil War,* Vol. II (1922).

For a discussion of the economic changes in the South after the war see Holland Thompson, *The New South* (1919) ; P. A. Bruce, *Rise of the New South* (1905), J. C. Ballagh (ed.), *South in the Building of the Nation* (1909).

On post-war foreign relations consult L. M. Sears, *A History of American Foreign Relations* (1927) ; T. W. Balch, *The Alabama Arbitration* (1900) ; F. W. Hackett, *Reminiscences of the Geneva Tribunal* (1911) ; J. B. Moore, *History and Digest of International Arbitration* (1898) ; C. F. Adams, Jr., *Lee at Appomattox and Other Papers* (1902).

[12] Burgess, *Reconstruction and the Constitution.*
[13] Rhodes, *History of the United States,* Vol. VII.
[14] It was later charged that the Hayes supporters obtained the acceptance of the commission's report by the Democratic House through a promise that Hayes would withdraw the Federal troops from the Southern states as soon as he became President.

Financial reconstruction is treated in D. R. Dewey, *Financial History of the United States* (1922) ; A. D. Noyes, *Forty Years of American Finance* (1907) ; W. C. Mitchell, *A History of Greenbacks* (1903) ; *History of the Coinage,* Senate Miscellaneous Documents No. 132, 41st Congress.

For a discussion of the political corruption of the time consult D. C. Seitz, *The Dreadful Decade, 1869-1879* (1926) ; D. T. Lynch, *"Boss Tweed": The Story of a Grim Generation* (1928) ; M. R. Werner, *Tammany Hall* (1928) ; J. B. Crawford, *Crédit Mobilier* (1880) ; R. H. Fuller, *Jubilee Jim: The Life of Colonel James Fisk, Jr.* (1928) ; C. F. Adams, Jr., *Chapters of Erie* (1886) ; T. S. Barclay, *The Liberal Republican Movement in Missouri, 1865-1871* (1926) ; D. C. Seitz, *Horace Greeley: Founder of the New York Tribune* (1926) ; Edward Stanwood, *James G. Blaine* (1905).

On the disputed election of 1876 see P. L. Haworth, *The Hayes-Tilden Disputed Election of 1876* (1906) ; J. W. Burgess, *Reconstruction and the Constitution* (1902) ; J. F. Rhodes, *History of the United States,* Vol. VII (1906) ; C. R. Williams, *Life of Rutherford B. Hayes* (1914) ; John Bigelow, *Life of Samuel J. Tilden* (1895).

CHAPTER 3

WESTWARD EXPANSION, 1875-1900

Although the activities of Congress and the thoughts of the people during the ten years following the Civil War had been concerned with the solution of problems that came from the war, it must not be overlooked that during these years there was being laid the foundation of a remarkable national development. While Congress was quarreling over the questions of reconstruction and Carpetbaggers were inflicting the orgy of misgovernment on the South, economic forces were emerging that were destined soon to usher in a new era in American history.

By the year 1876, as we have seen, the most insistent problems raised by the Civil War had been settled. With these troublesome questions out of the way the people turned with enthusiasm to the exploitation of the immense resources of the country. In the vast stretches of Western prairie land an imperial domain was brought under cultivation or devoted to cattle raising, adding millions of dollars to the national wealth and providing homes for hundreds of thousands of persons; from the mountains beyond the plains were obtained great quantities of gold, silver, and other metals, while primeval forests contributed their wealth of timber.

By the middle of the nineteenth century the westward drive of the pioneers, which had begun with the settlement of the first colonies, had reached beyond the Mississippi River. The discovery of gold in California in 1848 brought a large migration of white settlers to the Pacific Coast, thus establishing a second frontier. Between these two frontiers was a region of plain, prairie, and mountain, greater in extent than the whole settled area of the country at that time. The eastern portion of this great territory was a fertile prairie, but on the western border of the Mississippi valley the land rose into arid plains and desert land. Beyond were miles of lofty mountains and high plateaus.

At the opening of the Civil War this wide expanse from the Missouri River to the Rocky Mountains contained but few white men, with the exception of the Mormon settlements in Utah. The native Indians and the buffalo roamed at will over the prairies. To the Americans of the time it appeared that many generations would pass before this region would be occupied by white settlers. And yet within thirty years all of the best agricultural land west of the Mississippi had passed into private hands; towns and cities dotted the plains where the Indian and the buffalo had roamed; "boom" towns and mining camps were scattered over the mountain regions; a transcontinental railroad bound the Pacific to the East, and nine new states, carved from this Western domain, were admitted to the Federal Union. This remarkable Western development was destined to have far-reaching effects upon the social, economic, and political institutions of the whole country.

The settlement of the West was stimulated by the liberal land policy of the Federal Government. Prior to the Civil War the public domain had been subject to private entry upon payment of $1.25 an acre. But even this moderate payment was abandoned by the terms of the Homestead Act, passed by Congress in 1862, which allowed any adult citizen, or person who had declared his intention of becoming a citizen, to obtain a farm of 160 acres, by paying a small registration fee and living upon the land five years.[1] While the

[1] In the three years from 1865-1867 more than 4,500,000 acres were entered under the Homestead Act. In addition to these grants large estates were acquired by wealthy foreigners. Lord Dunmore owned 100,-000 acres in the West; the Duke of Sutherland, 500,000 acres; while two English syndicates held 7,000,000 acres in Texas.

Civil War was still in progress thousands of immigrants took advantage of this law and settled in the West. Still other thousands at the same time flocked to Nevada, Colorado, and Montana to seek their fortunes in the newly discovered silver mines.

Congress had taken a second important step in the development of the West with the granting of a charter in 1862 for the construction of a railroad from Omaha, Nebraska, to the Pacific coast. The Act of 1862, as amended in 1864, granted to each of two companies, the Union Pacific and the Central Pacific, a right of way across the public domain, twenty sections [2] of public land for each mile of road built, and a government loan ranging from $16,000 a mile for the portion crossing the plains to $48,000 a mile for the mountain region, to be secured by a second mortgage on the finished road. The exigencies of the war delayed the undertaking, but after 1866 the work was energetically pushed. The eastern section of the road, built by the Union Pacific, was advanced with remarkable speed while the western section, constructed by the Central Pacific, proceeded more slowly, owing to the difficult terrain over which it passed. Finally the two ends of the road met at Promontory Point, near Ogden, Utah, where the last spike was driven, amidst national rejoicing, on May 10, 1869.

In the meantime several other projects for the building of railroads in the Great West had been launched. In 1864 Congress granted a charter to the Northern Pacific Company for the construction of a line from some point on Lake Superior to Portland, Oregon. Two years later Congress gave a charter to the Atlantic and Pacific Company for a road from St. Louis through Kansas and New Mexico to the Pacific. This charter was later taken over by the Atchison, Topeka, and Santa Fé Company, which constructed a road following the course of the old Santa Fé trail. The Southern Pacific

[2] A section is 640 acres, or a square mile.

Company, a California corporation, built lines in that state and then pushed eastward through Arizona and Texas, where a connection was formed with a road under construction from New Orleans. In the north the Great Northern Railway, under the astute management of James J. Hill, was built, crossing the same territory as that penetrated by the Northern Pacific. By the close of the nineteenth century six transcontinental lines connected the Mississippi valley with the Pacific. Most of these roads received munificent grants of public land from the government.[3]

The managers of these enterprises soon discovered, however, that thousands of miles of railroad trackage running through unsettled prairies and desert land brought in meager revenue. They therefore addressed themselves to the task of stimulating settlement in the territory through which their roads ran. A campaign of advertising, both in this country and in Europe, was inaugurated. Alluring pictures were drawn of the opportunities that life in the West offered. Some of the more energetic boomers went further and offered aid to prospective settlers. James J. Hill, the head of the Great Northern Railroad, was an outstanding figure in his movement to stimulate settlement in the West. He not only provided free transportation for new settlers, but followed with interest their fortunes in their new homes by furnishing expert advice on farming methods, searching out markets for their products, and striving in every way possible to develop prosperous communities.

PASSING OF THE REDMAN

The winning of the West by the whites marked the last stand of the native Indian. For two hundred and fifty years, since the coming of the first white settlers to America, the

---

[3] In all some 242,000 square miles of public land, a region larger than the whole of France, were given to the different railroads.

Indians had been driven step by step from the Atlantic seaboard across the mountains into the Mississippi valley and beyond to the great plains. In this vast Western territory the government had set aside tracts of land for the use of the natives. The resistless pressure of the white settlers against the Indians entered a new phase after 1850, with the settlement of California. There were now two frontiers, one pushing eastward and the other westward. In these advancing frontiers even the untutored savage could not fail to realize that the last stage in the long struggle for the possession of a continent had been reached.

In the territory west of the Mississippi River there were, at the middle of the nineteenth century, approximately 300,000 Indians scattered over a wide area and organized into various tribes. The most important of these tribes were the two groups of Sioux, one in Minnesota and the other in the Dakota territory, the Cheyenne and the Arapaho in the Yellowstone valley, and the Apache and Comanche in Nevada and Arizona. In addition to these were the so-called civilized tribes, which had been induced to move from the region east of the Mississippi and had been concentrated in the Indian Territory, now a part of the state of Oklahoma.

Prior to the Civil War the Indian tribes on the great plains had been comparatively peaceful, but during the war increasing restlessness developed. Responsibility for this has been laid to the activities of Confederate agents, but there is no clear evidence to substantiate this charge. Causes in plenty existed to explain native unrest apart from any supposed Confederate intrigues. As has been noted, during the war thousands of prospectors, adventurers, and doubtless many war slackers, pushed out across the plains. In the year 1859 it is estimated that more than 100,000 miners and adventurers entered the Pike's Peak region. The discovery of gold in Idaho, in 1863, added more thousands. These fortune seekers were not likely to have a nice regard for the treaty rights of the Indians. To them the Indians were but one of the many obstacles that had to be overcome in their search for the precious metals. They entered the Indian reserves, staked out claims, built towns, and called upon the government at Washington to legalize their actions. In most cases this call did not go unheeded. Congress, in disregard of solemn treaty obligations, restricted the Indian tribes to increasingly narrower limits or moved them to less desirable lands. Further irritation was caused by the activities of the surveying parties during the later years of the war in laying out the line of the Union Pacific Railroad.

In government circles there was a sharp divergence of opinion as to the wise policy to pursue in dealing with the Indians. Among the officials of the Department of the Interior, who had immediate control of Indian affairs, there was in general a feeling that the Indians were the victims of unscrupulous white settlers, while many officials and active military leaders were generally inclined to the view expressed by General Sheridan that "there are no good Indians but dead Indians." Public sentiment in the country was similarly divided. In the East, where the people were far removed from the dangers of Indian attacks, there was a strong humanitarian feeling, which expressed itself in a demand that the government should protect its helpless wards against the greed of the whites, while in the West where the settlers had had abundant experience with the barbarous cruelties of Indian warfare there was strong approval of the stern methods advocated by the army officials.

The first period of Indian wars extended from the year 1862 to 1867. There was no concerted action by the different tribes in these struggles, but rather a series of local wars caused by particular grievances. The Sioux tribes in Minnesota were the first to go on the warpath. There appears to have been no connection between this outbreak and the war then in progress between the North and the South. After a year's fighting the uprising was suppressed and the Sioux were removed to poorer lands further west. The next important outbreak was that of the Cheyenne Indians in Colorado in 1864. By a treaty signed in 1851 these Indians had been assigned the region including the Pike's Peak country. Then came the gold rush in 1859 and the Indians were driven from the mountains down into the plains. No effort was made by the government to restrain the whites and a new treaty was signed in 1861 which removed the Indians to eastern Colorado. Dissatisfied with their new homes the Cheyenne, joined by portions of the neighboring Arapaho, Comanche, and Kiowa tribes, left the reservations and went on the warpath. There followed the usual cruel incidents of Indian warfare. The whites did not hesitate to adopt the worst methods of the Indians. A certain Colonel Chivington with a force of Colorado troops surrounded an Indian village and massacred the 500 inhabitants, mostly women and children. This action was later characterized by the Indian Commissioner as "butchery in cold blood by troops in the service of the United States." The war ended with the usual dispossession of the Indians. In 1866 the Sioux tribes of the plains region north of the Platte River were aroused by the activities of the army authorities in building fortifications and in opening an immigrant road through their finest hunting grounds along the Powder River. For two years, the Indians fought this invasion savagely and the struggle ended with the abandonment of the forts by the government in 1868.

With the Civil War ended, the national government was able to devote more attention to the Indian problem. In 1867 Congress authorized a commission consisting of four civilians and three generals to make a comprehensive study of the Indian question and suggest means of protecting the Indians, at the same time assuring a safe transit across the plains and the development of white civilization in the West. The commission succeeded in persuading most of the Indians to remove from the regions penetrated by the continental railroads. The report of the commission criticized severely many of the actions of the white settlers in the West and recommended that the Indians be placed under civilian governors "of unquestioned integrity and purity of character." In 1869 Congress appropriated $2,000,000 to be expended by a Board of Indian Commissioners "to promote civilization among the Indians, bring them, where practicable, upon reservations, and encourage their efforts to self-support." In 1871 Congress ordered that no more treaties should be made with the Indians, thus abandoning the policy of dealing with the Indian tribes as independent nations.

Despite these efforts to solve the Indian problem, further strife ensued. Following the building of the Pacific railroads increasing numbers of settlers found their way into the West and encroached steadily upon the hunting grounds of the natives. Still more serious was the action of many wealthy persons from the Eastern states and from Europe in organizing great hunting expeditions in which large numbers of buffalo were killed in the name of sport. It is estimated that in the three years from 1872 to 1874 more than 4,000,000 buffalo were slaughtered. To the simple-minded Indian the destruction of the buffalo appeared as further evidence of white hostility, for upon this animal the Indian depended for his meat supply and clothing.

In the year 1876 the Sioux of the plains, who had been removed after their defeat in 1863 from Minnesota to the Dakota territory, were once more aroused. To the grievances above noted were added others. Gross mismanagement on the part of some of the Indian agents in allowing spoiled and inferior rations to be issued to their charges led to complaints directed to Washington which brought little satisfaction. Then came the discovery of gold in the Black Hills region of southern Dakota, followed by the usual rush of prospectors to the spot. Foreseeing another forced removal from their lands, the Sioux, under their famous leader Sitting Bull, went on the warpath. In the conflict which followed, General Custer, already famous for his campaign against the Cheyenne, led a force of five companies. At the battle of Little Big Horn he was surrounded by a much larger force of savages and his whole force, with the exception of one man, was wiped out. Before the end of the year, however, Sitting Bull was badly defeated and fled to Canada with the remnant of his braves. With their leader gone and their lands confiscated, the Sioux quieted down.

Outbreaks among the Nez Percé Indians in the Snake River valley in 1877, the Modoc in northern California in 1873, the Apache in Arizona and New Mexico from 1871 to 1875, and again from 1882 to 1886, were incidents in the closing chapter of the long struggle between a virile and aggressive white civilization and an unprogressive and passive native civilization for the possession of a continent.

With serious resistance ended, the friends of the Indians turned to Congress once more and urged the enactment of legislation to protect the remaining Indians from further depredations by the whites. One obstacle to the growth of economic independence among the natives was the general practice of holding land in tribal rather than individual ownership. To meet this situation Congress passed the Dawes Act in 1887, which provided that the President might divide the reserves among the members of a tribe, assigning to each head of a family 160 acres and smaller amounts to unmarried adults and children. To protect the Indian against the wiles of land speculators the law prohibited the mortgaging or sale of land thus assigned for a period of twenty-five years. In addition the law granted United States citizenship to Indians who abandoned tribal organization. While many

Indians took advantage of this law a larger number preferred to retain their tribal status and remain the wards of the nation.[4]

LIFE IN THE GREAT WEST

In this western domain, there developed a civilization rich in color, romantic in appeal, especially to the youth of all countries, and unhampered by the conventions of the settled East and of Europe. Of those who followed the western trails many were drawn from the adventurous, the dispossessed, or the dissatisfied. Nearly all were alike in their desire and ability to break away from old habits and associations.

The discovery of gold in California brought the first influx of prospectors and adventurers into this territory. Ten years later, on the eve of the Civil War, gold was discovered in the Pike's Peak region in Colorado and about the same time silver was found in Nevada, followed at short intervals during the next decade by further discoveries in Idaho and Montana. Each new discovery led to a rush of prospectors to the neighborhood. Towns appeared as if by magic. Into these towns crowded a strange and motley aggregation of human beings. "A single street meandering along a valley, with one-story huts flanking it in irregular rows, was the typical mining camp. The saloon and the general store, sometimes combined, were its representative institutions. Deep ruts in the street bore witness to the heavy wheels of the freighters, while horses loosely tied to all available posts at once revealed the regular means of locomotion, and by the careless way they were left about showed that this sort of property was not likely to be stolen. The mining population centering here

[4] The Burke Act (1906) gave the Secretary of the Interior power to release any Indian from the twenty-five-year trust arrangement if satisfied that he was competent to manage his own affairs. By act of Congress passed in 1924 all Indians were made citizens.

lived a life of contrasts. The desolation and loneliness of prospecting and working claims alternated with the excitement of coming to town. Few decent beings habitually lived in the towns. The resident population expected to live off the miners, either in the way of trade, or worse. The bar, the gambling house, the dance hall have been made too common in description to need further account. In the reaction against loneliness, the extremes of drunkenness, debauchery, and murder were only too frequent in these places of amusement." [5]

Not unlike the mining towns were the railway towns which followed the progress of the transcontinental railroads across the prairies. Of the inhabitants of these towns Samuel Bowles of the Springfield *Republican* remarked that "hell would appear to have been raked to furnish them."

While restless and adventurous prospectors were penetrating the remote recesses of the mountains from Canada to the Mexican frontier, another equally colorful element in the variegated life of the West appeared on the rolling plains to the east of the mountains. For many years before the Civil War, in Mexico and Texas, great herds of cattle roamed at will over the wide plains. They were held in a somewhat loose ownership and had little value because of the inaccessibility to the eastern market. With the building of the transcontinental railroads in the years after the war, facilities were provided for the shipment of the cattle to the East. But the first of the railroads ran far to the north of the Texas range and to reach these roads it was necessary to drive the cattle in large herds across the open plains. Moreover, it was found that the Texas cattle improved in weight and quality when allowed to graze on the buffalo grass of the plains to the north. This led to the establishment of the "Long Drive" as a regular feature of the cattle industry. Twice each year, in

[5] Paxson, *The Last American Frontier,* p. 171.

the spring and fall, great numbers of Texas cattle, guided by cowboys, were driven northward over the vast unfenced public domain, feeding as they went—"processions of enormous wealth, owned by kings who paid no tribute, and guarded by men who never knew a master." When the herds reached the railroads in Wyoming or Nebraska they were shipped to the eastern market. For two decades, from the late sixties to the late eighties, the cattlemen, undisturbed by a benevolent government, reaped a rich harvest from the public domain. Brief as this period was it served to introduce into the life of the West one of its most characteristic features, the cowboy, with his picturesque garb, and his love for life in the open.

The open range as an institution of the cattle industry lasted for about two decades from 1865 to 1885. A number of factors contributed to its disappearance. The cowboys at the end of the long drive were forced to sell their cattle when they reached the railhead and if the market was overstocked they had to accept whatever price the meat packers were willing to pay. To remedy this condition enterprising cattlemen established ranches in favorable locations on the open plains and fenced in large areas with barbed wire where the cattle could be held until a satisfactory market price could be obtained. Then, too, the cattlemen had to meet the challenge of the sheep-raisers and the advancing farmer. The former needed to fence his land to protect his sheep from the depredations of wild animals, while the latter, in similar manner, needed to protect his growing crops. These fences broke up the continuity of the open range and seriously interfered with the "Long Drive." The cattle industry was therefore forced to adapt itself to these new conditions. With the extension of the railroads into the Southwest the cattle were placed on cattle trains and shipped to the ranches in the North or directly to the slaughterhouses.

THE AGRARIAN REVOLUTION

Through the combined effects of the Homestead Act and lavish grants to railroad companies, the Federal Government disposed of its rich heritage of western lands. Before the nineteenth century closed, the open frontier, with an abundance of free land, had passed as a factor in American life. And this disappearance of the frontier was destined to have important effects upon the economic and social life of the country. As long as there was good agricultural land to be had for the asking there were offered to the young and adventurous from the settled communities of the East and to the peasants and laborers from across the seas opportunities to obtain economic freedom. The West had rendered a very valuable economic service to the country in drawing from the congested urban centers of the East in times of industrial unrest the unemployed and the discontented. A submerged lower class was not likely to develop in a community where any ambitious and energetic person, with little or no capital, could become an independent farmer. But with the passing of the frontier such opportunities were greatly lessened and the mobility that had characterized American life since colonial days was measurably changed. Although for many years thereafter the static social and economic order that prevailed in Europe was not reproduced in America, there were indications that the trend in this country was toward the conditions obtaining in the Old World.

In the last quarter of the nineteenth century agricultural technique in the West underwent a significant change. In the early days of western settlement the pioneer had come in a covered wagon with his family, his live stock, and his primitive tools. On the open prairie he had staked out a farm and had there raised virtually all he needed for the support of his family. But the physical conformation of the West, with its vast stretches of prairie, lent itself naturally to large-scale farming. The one drawback to the development of such farming was the lack of an adequate labor supply; and this deficiency was largely supplied by the introduction of agricultural machinery. Even before the Civil War an improved reaper and thresher had been developed, but it was not until the decade between 1870 and 1880 that a remarkable number of inventions introduced labor-saving devices into every branch of agriculture. Mechanical corn planters and huskers, hay loaders, binders, and threshers, culminating in huge machines which cut, threshed, cleaned, sacked, and weighed grain without the touch of human hands, brought a revolution in agriculture.

Expensive agricultural machinery and the rising price of land due to the closing of the frontier made increasingly difficult the lot of the small farmers with little capital. Without the improved machinery they could not compete with the better equipped farms and to obtain the machines they found it necessary to mortgage their farms. Periodic depression in agricultural prices and crop failures added to their woes and many gave up the struggle and fell back into the condition of farm laborers or tenant farmers. By 1880, 25 per cent. of all the farms in the country were cultivated by tenant farmers, and by the close of the century the percentage had risen to 35. Those farmers who persisted in the unequal struggle found themselves saddled with a mounting burden of debt. Before the close of the century farm mortgages amounted to more than a billion dollars. Clearly Jefferson's alluring vision of a country filled with independent farmers owning their homes had not been realized.

In another respect the agricultural revolution worked an important change in rural economy. In place of the homesteader's self-sufficient farm, with its diversified crops, there appeared, throughout the West, farms thousands of acres in extent, devoted to the cultivation of specialized crops, chiefly wheat and corn. In the organization and management of these enterprises, and in the amount of capital needed for their successful operation, there developed many of the features characteristic of the great industrial organizations of the East.

AGRARIAN DISCONTENT

A revolution in agricultural economy so far-reaching was certain to arouse discontent in rural sections. Moreover, in the increase in national wealth which came in the last quarter of the nineteenth century the farmers felt that they had received too small a share. Although rural wealth had increased during this period from $4,000,000,000 to $16,000,-000,000, urban wealth had increased from $3,000,000,000 to $49,000,000,000.

Effective expression of rural discontent was not easily attained. The American farmer was a pronounced individualist. In the hard struggle with nature he had carried on life with little aid or direction from the government or coöperation with his fellow man. The isolation of the frontier compelled a large measure of self-reliance. And this isolation had not as yet been relieved by any of the modern conveniences, such as the telephone, the rural free delivery, the automobile, the Chautauqua, and the radio. The monotonous routine of work from sunrise to sunset in the summer was followed by an even more monotonous routine of leisure during the long winter. Only to a very limited degree did these self-sufficient families of pioneer farmers have the opportunity or inclination to develop social and cultural relationships with those about them. Efforts to organize the farmers have nearly always been greatly hampered by these conditions of isolation and of ingrained individualism.

In fact, the first important movement for the organization of the farmers in the period following the Civil War did not come from the farmers themselves, but was started by a government official in Washington. Oliver H. Kelley, a clerk in the Department of Agriculture, organized a society known as "the Patrons of Husbandry," patterned after the Masonic order, with a ritual, secret passwords, and symbols. The unit of organization was the local "Grange," from which the whole order later became known as the "Grangers." The purpose that Kelley had in mind in creating the society appears to have been purely social and cultural—to bring to the isolated rural parts of the country some of the educational and social advantages enjoyed by those living in settled communities. Beginning in 1867, the Grange made slow progress during the first three or four years, but after 1871 it grew rapidly, especially in the Western states, where it attained a membership of over 750,000 in 1874. This growth of the Grange was not due primarily to the social advantages that it offered but to its usefulness as a means for expressing agricultural discontent and for remedying the abuses of which the farmers complained.

And the grievances of the agricultural classes were real, however visionary some of the remedies that they advocated. With the close of the Civil War the prices of agricultural commodities declined rapidly, all out of proportion to the decline in the prices of manufactured articles. Moreover, the farmer saw a wide discrepancy between the price which he received for his grain and the price for which it sold in the New York market. Wheat, which sold for 90 cents a bushel on the farm brought $1.50 in New York. For these conditions the farmers blamed the railroads and the middlemen. The farmer was absolutely dependent upon the railroads for the marketing of his crops and, as he beheld the manipulation of these roads by financial buccaneers of the type of Jay Gould and Jim Fisk, he quite naturally concluded that he was being burdened by exorbitant freight rates which went to fill the coffers of Eastern financiers. For relief the farmer turned to his state legislature and demanded the enactment of legislation regulating railway rates and charges made by the privately owned grain elevators. In most of the Western states such laws, known as Granger laws, were passed.

The attempt on the part of the railroads and elevator interests to combat this legislation on the ground that it was an unwarranted interference with private property and that it violated the provisions of the Federal constitution was at first unsuccessful. In 1876 the Supreme Court, in the case of Munn vs. Illinois, upheld the right of a state legislature to fix maximum rates for the storage of grain in elevators. The Chief Justice in rendering the opinion in this case held that when "one devotes his property to a use in which the public has an interest, he, in effect, grants to the public an interest in that use, and must submit to be controlled by the public for the common good."

Coupled with the efforts of the farmers to obtain cheap transportation was their support of the movement to obtain cheap money. It is easy to see how the farmers were won by the advocates of an inflated currency. As has been noted, they had borrowed large sums on mortgage security and it was clearly to their advantage to pay the interest and principal of these loans in paper dollars exchangeable for a half bushel of wheat rather than in gold dollars exchangeable for a whole bushel of wheat. Moreover, cheap money meant high prices for agricultural commodities. True, it meant also high prices for all goods that the farmers bought, but the immediate advantage of a depreciated currency was sufficient to blind them to its ultimate effects. As we have seen, their efforts in this direction were successful to the extent of persuading Congress in 1868 to stop the further retirement of the greenbacks. It was from the Western farmers also that there came the chief support of the free silver movement, as will be noted later.

From the railroads and currency the leaders of the Grange

turned to more constructive measures. Coöperative societies of farmers were formed to control the prices of agricultural products and to purchase, or to engage in the production of, farm implements. Coöperative grain elevators were built and central agencies established to aid in the marketing of farm products. Bad management on the part of some of those in control of these enterprises, coupled with the inexperience of the farmers in coöperative undertakings, and the opposition of the middlemen, led to the failure of a number of these experiments.

After 1876 the political activities of the Grange rapidly declined and for a decade agricultural unrest was less in evidence, but in the nineties it appeared again in an intensified degree.

THE POPULIST MOVEMENT

If the Granger laws offered some relief to the farmers, they did not get to the root of the real problem in agricultural economy. Moreover, these laws soon lost much of their effectiveness as a result of judicial interpretation. As has been noted, the Supreme Court held in the Munn case that the state legislatures had the right to regulate railroad rates. But in 1886 the Court took a much narrower view of the powers of the state legislatures. Not only did the Court uphold the exclusive right of Congress to regulate interstate commerce but it maintained that the power to determine the reasonableness of railway rates rested with the Court and not with the legislatures. Checkmated in their efforts to control the railroads through state action, the farmers turned to Congress and succeeded in forcing through that body in 1887 the Interstate Commerce Act. In a later chapter we shall see that this act fell far short of correcting the abuses that it was intended to remedy.

But the fundamental difficulty in the agricultural situation was overproduction. The rapid extension of railroad building had greatly stimulated migration to the West. In the one state of Kansas the population increased in the twenty years from 1870 to 1890 from 364,000 to 1,427,000. As settlement pushed steadily westward it began to encroach upon the semi-arid plains. In the early eighties there were several years of excessive rainfall in the plains area and many settlers, unacquainted with normal conditions in this region, planted a large acreage to grain only to meet with disaster when the dry years came after 1887. Mounting crops brought decreased prices for all agricultural products. Wheat sold on the farm at less than 50 cents a bushel; cattle brought from 2 to 3 cents a pound on the hoof; corn was so cheap that farmers found it more profitable to burn it for fuel than to send it to market. The Southern farmer shared the distress of the West. Cotton, which had brought more than 11 cents a pound before 1890, sold at less than 8 cents in 1892.

Such conditions stirred up once more the slumbering agricultural discontent. Carrying forward the work started by the Grange, there were organized in the eighties a number of farmers' associations. Most important of these were the Southern Farmers' Alliance and the Agricultural Wheel, both of which orders drew their membership largely from the farmers of the South and Southwest, and the Northwestern Farmers' Alliance, which brought together the farmers of Northern and Western states. At the same time there appeared numerous other organizations of protest, advocating one panacea or another for the economic ills of the time. Some of these organizations voiced the discontent of the industrial workers of the East.

In 1889 a convention was held at St. Louis to bring about a union between the forces of agricultural and industrial unrest. But the resolutions adopted by the convention indicated that agrarian interests were uppermost in the minds of the delegates. They called for the abolition of national banks, free coinage of silver and an increased paper currency, government ownership of railroads, recovery by the government of unused lands granted to the railroads, and the prohibition of dealing in "futures" in the grain market.

As yet imperfectly organized, the protest groups entered the Congressional elections of 1890. In the South these bodies worked through the dominant Democratic party and succeeded in capturing the party organizations in several states. In the West the radicals generally broke away from the old line parties and formed new political organizations under varying names. As a result of the elections of that year eight Congressmen and two United States Senators supported by these protest groups appeared in Washington and in several Western and Southern states they returned large delegations to the state legislatures.

Encouraged by this initial success and stimulated by a further decline in the prices of agricultural commodities, the leaders of the various radical groups determined to present a united front in the approaching presidential election of 1892. With this end in view there gathered at Cincinnati, in May, 1891, some fifteen hundred delegates representing various agricultural and labor organizations. At this meeting it was determined to form a new political party to be known as the People's Party, and a call was sent for the meeting of the first national convention at Omaha, Nebraska, July 2, 1892.

The platform of the new party drew a severe indictment of social, economic and political conditions in the country. It flatly asserted: "Corruption dominates the ballot-box, the legislature, the Congress, and touches even the ermine of the bench. The people are demoralized . . . the newspapers are largely subsidized or muzzled; public opinion silenced; business prostrated; our homes covered with mortgages; labor impoverished; and the lands concentrating in the hands of capitalists. The urban workmen are denied the right of organization for self-protection; imported pauperized labor beats down their wages; a hireling standing army, unrecognized by our laws, is established to shoot them down, and they are rapidly degenerating into European conditions. The fruits of the toil of millions are boldly stolen to build up colossal fortunes for a few, unprecedented in the history of mankind; and the possessors of these, in turn, despise the republic and endanger liberty. From the same prolific womb of governmental injustice we breed the two great classes of tramps and millionaires."

Turning from indictment to remedies, the Populists demanded the free and unlimited coinage of silver, a more plenteous supply of paper money, a graduated income tax, postal savings bank, government ownership of railroads, telegraph and telephone, the suppression of alien ownership of land, the introduction of the Australian ballot, the initiative and referendum, the eight-hour day, a single term for the President, and the direct election of United States Senators. Although these proposals were greeted by the conservative press of the East as preposterous and as the work of unprincipled demagogues bent upon the destruction of the Republic, it is interesting to note, in passing, that most of the political changes and some of the economic reforms advocated by the Populists have been adopted during the past twenty-five years.

The results of the election clearly showed that the Populists spoke for a substantial body of discontent throughout the country. More than a million votes were cast for their presidential candidate, James B. Weaver, of Iowa, and they succeeded in winning twenty-two votes in the electoral college.[6] Moreover, as will be noted later, before another presidential election took place Populist ideas had gained control of one of the major political parties.

[6] The large Populist vote is accounted for, in part, by the fact that in five western states the Democrats fused with the Populists and did not nominate any ticket of their own.

POLITICAL AND ECONOMIC INFLUENCE OF THE WEST

The remarkable development of the West during the last quarter of the nineteenth century had a profound influence upon the political and economic life of the whole country. Following rapidly upon the westward drive of settlers came the political organization of the frontier. Before the close of the sixties territorial governments had been erected in Colorado, Wyoming, Nevada, Arizona, Montana, Idaho and Utah. But the western pioneer was not satisfied with the limited measure of self-government conferred by the territorial status. It irked him to have to resort to a distant government at Washington, in which he had no vote and in which the powerful railroad and other interests with a stake in the West were likely to have substantial support.

The road to statehood, however, was beset with difficulties. Eastern financial interests with large investments in the West were not inclined to entrust those interests to the radical proclivities of frontier politics. Then, again, nice considerations of partisan politics entered into the matter. Both Republican and Democratic politicians were likely to consider carefully the political complexion of the nascent commonwealths before admitting them, in order to avoid adding to the voting strength of their rivals in Congress.

The first of the western communities to obtain statehood was Nevada, admitted in 1864, largely because of exigencies of Civil War politics. Nebraska followed in 1867, and Colorado in 1876. It was not until 1889-1890 that the other western territories were able to muster sufficient support in Congress to obtain the coveted prize, at which time they were admitted as a group—the two Dakotas, Washington, Montana, Idaho, and Wyoming. Utah was forced to wait another six years until Congress was satisfied that polygamy, a Mormon practice which had aroused strong resentment in the

East, had been abandoned. Only New Mexico and Arizona, and the recently created territory of Oklahoma, remained in the territorial stage at the end of the century.

The addition of these western states to the Union brought important changes in political thought and action in the national administration. With the ruin of the planting interests of the South as a result of the Civil War, the victorious North, controlled largely by the industrial interests, had shaped the economic and political policies of the nation for twenty-five years. But the entrance of these new western commonwealths, together with the older western states of Kansas, Iowa, Oregon and California, into the arena of national politics, brought a significant challenge to the dominant position of the industrial classes. While the economic interests of these western states varied, none of them had large industries and all had a considerable, if not a predominant, agricultural economy. In a sense, then, the West had come to redress that balance between agriculture and industry which the Civil War had upset. This increased political influence of the agricultural sections of the country was reflected in national legislation. With the turn of the century the attention of Congress was directed in increasing measure to the solution of problems affecting rural life.

Western development played an important part in changing the economic status of the United States in relation to the rest of the world. In the building of the railroads of the country, foreign capital, chiefly British, had played a considerable part. Interest on these foreign loans, together with imports of foreign manufactures, turned the balance of trade generally against the United States. It was the precious metals and grain of the West, together with the cotton of the South, which enabled the country not only to pay these foreign obligations but also to accumulate surplus capital for the further development of the resources of the country.

From the West, too, came a number of novel contributions

to political science and governmental practice. Unrestrained by the conventions of the settled East, these new western communities felt free to experiment with political innovations. Virtually all of the schemes which aimed at a greater measure of popular control of governmental machinery, such as the initiative and referendum, the direct primary, the recall, direct election of United States Senators, and women's suffrage, had their origin in one or another of the western states.

BIBLIOGRAPHICAL NOTE

Good accounts of the westward migration are to be found in F. L. Paxson, *The Last American Frontier* (1910); by the same author, *History of the American Frontier* (1924); E. Hough, *The Passing of the Frontier* (1918); R. P. Porter, *The West from the Census of 1880* (1882); E. P. Oberholtzer, *A History of the United States,* Vol. II; K. Coman, *Economic Beginnings of the Far West* (1912).

For descriptions of the building of the western railroads consult John Moody, *The Railroad Builders* (1919); J. W. Starr, *One Hundred Years of American Railroading* (1928); R. E. Riegel, *Story of the Western Railroads* (1926); S. Daggett, *Chapters in the History of the Northern Pacific* (1883); J. P. Davis, *The Union Pacific Railway* (1894); E. L. Sabin, *The Building of the Pacific Railway* (1919); E. V. Smalley, *The Northern Pacific* (1883); J. G. Pyle, *James J. Hill* (1917); G. D. Bradley, *The Story of the Santa Fé* (1920).

The public land policy is discussed in B. Hibbard, *A History of Public Land Policies* (1925); G. M. Stephenson, *The Political History of Public Lands from 1842 to 1862* (1917); J. T. Du Bois and G. S. Matthews, *Galusha A. Grow, the Father of the Homestead Law* (1917); J. W. Taylor, *History of the Leasing of Public Lands* (1928).

For the Indian Wars consult Paxson and Hough cited above; see also W. A. Miles, *Serving the Republic* (1911); P. E. Byrne, *Soldiers of the Plains* (1926); G. A. Custer, *My Life on the Plains.* For a discussion of later phases of the Indian question see Jackson, *A Century of Dishonor* (1885); F. E. Leupp, *The Indian and His Problem* (1910).

Both Hough and Paxson give vivid descriptions of the colorful life of the West. Consult also P. A. Rollins, *The Cowboy* (1922); C. H. Shinn, *The Story of the Mine* (1901); E. S. Osgood, *The Day of the Cattleman* (1929); J. H. Cook, *Fifty Years on the Old Frontier* (1923); E. E. Dale, *The Ranchman's Last Frontier,* Mississippi Valley Historical Review, Vol. X (1924).

Western economic conditions are discussed by K. Coman, cited above; N. S. B. Gras, *History of Agriculture in Europe and America* (1925); H. N. Casson, *The Romance of the Reaper* (1908); H. W. Quitance, *The Influence of Farm Machinery on Production and Labor* (1904).

For discussions of agricultural discontent in the West consult S. J. Buck, *The Granger Movement* (1913); by the same author, *The Agrarian Crusade* (1921); F. L. McVey, *The Populist Movement* (1896); F. E. Haynes, *Social Politics in the United States* (1924).

CHAPTER 4

INDUSTRIAL DEVELOPMENT, 1865-1900

Side by side with the development of the agricultural and mining resources of the West there occurred an equally remarkable development of manufacturing and transportation. In coal, iron, steel, oil, and a great variety of industrial enterprises large corporations were organized; the quantity and value of manufactured goods increased enormously; fortunes, unprecedented in size, were accumulated; a great network of railroads was built reaching from the Atlantic to the Pacific. With the growth of industrial corporations went the growth of labor organizations, and between these two forces in the industrial machine there developed a bitter struggle. Finally, the population of the country in these two decades increased at a remarkable rate, owing largely to the influx of foreigners flocking to the Land of Promise. To a consideration of this striking material development and to a study of the many acute problems that it raised we shall now turn our attention.

Nature had been kind to the United States in placing within its boundaries an abundance of natural resources. Most of the essential commodities needed for large-scale industrial development could be found within its geographical limits. And a benevolent government stood ready to grant the land on which these valuable resources were to be found to enterprising individuals and corporations for a nominal financial consideration. No thought was given at this time by those in authority to conserving this immense national heritage for future generations. Nor did the national government restrict its bounty to private industry in placing at its disposal the wealth of natural resources. By means of a protective tariff it assured to the American manufacturer a large domestic market, freed from European competition. Finally, across the seas in Europe was an abundant labor supply which was drawn upon by the promoters of industrial enterprises.

With all of these advantages American industry advanced with confidence during the last quarter of the nineteenth century. Figures give a very inadequate impression of this remarkable growth in business enterprise. In 1860 there were a little more than one billion dollars invested in manufacturing, employing about 1,500,000 wage workers; at the close of the nineteenth century nearly nine billion dollars were invested, employing nearly 5,000,000 workers. In 1860 the production of steel in the United States was insignificant; in 1900 this country produced one-third of the total world's supply of steel. Similar figures might be given for substantially all forms of manufacturing enterprise.

But it is not only the striking growth of industry in this period that is significant. With this growth there went a fundamental change in the form of industrial organizations. It is true that even before the Civil War a beginning had been made in substituting the corporate form of industry for the older individual business and co-partnership. But in this earlier period industrial organizations were conducted on a comparatively small scale, in a restricted area, and with limited capital. It was not until the eighties that the integration of industry on a distinctly national scale became a characteristic feature of the business life of the country. The corporate form of industry lent itself to large-scale production. By the sale of stock a much larger amount of capital could be obtained than it was possible for an individual owner to raise. Increased capital brought larger factories, better machinery, more efficient management, less risk, and greater opportunity to use by-products. These advantages in turn brought a reduction in the cost of manufacturing and, assuming a willingness to pass on this saving to the consumer, a reduction in prices. Frequently, however, a large part of the saving due to large-scale production was absorbed in the form of increased dividends. When such dividends became so large as to arouse popular resentment they could easily be disguised by the simple process of stock "watering." This practice involved the issuance of corporate stock without a corresponding increase in the property or equipment owned by the corporation. In effect it was a capitalization of antici- pated future earning power of the company.

ORGANIZATION OF TRUSTS

The corporation was only the first step in the evolution of "Big Business." The upswing of business enterprise in the two decades following the Civil War was accompanied by cut-throat competition among corporations engaged in the same industry. The mad rush for wealth which characterized this era brought in its train wild speculation, over-extension of credit, and unsound business methods. The inevitable crash came in 1873, in one of the worst financial panics in our history. It was precipitated by the failure of Jay Cooke and Company, one of the largest and most respected bank- ing organizations in America. Thousands of business con- cerns were forced into bankruptcy and the country did not completely recover from the shock for more than five years.

Out of the economic chaos brought on by the panic there was evolved, under the guidance of a remarkable group of business leaders and financiers, a new and more highly integrated form of business structure. In the coal, iron, steel, oil, copper, sugar, and virtually every other important industry, as well as in transportation, the competitive corpo- ration was superseded by large organizations that were able to dominate, if not monopolize, their respective fields of business. Between 1880 and 1890 the number of woolen mills was reduced by one-third; factories manufacturing farm implements declined more than one-half, although the output in both cases increased materially; three-fourths of the companies in the leather industry disappeared in ten years, although the output was increased at the same time fivefold.

Among the outstanding personalities who provided the driving force to carry through these large undertakings were John D. Rockefeller in the oil industry; William H. Vanderbilt, Jay Gould, Collis P. Huntington, and Edward H. Harriman in railroad organization; Andrew Carnegie and H. C. Frick in steel; J. P. Morgan and Jay Cooke in the financial field. These men had certain characteristics in common. With few exceptions they were self-made men, starting life with meager financial resources and little more than an elementary education. They were all men of broad vision, of tremendous energy, of bold initiative, and of genius for organization. In general their methods were none too nice, judged even by the rather lax standards of the time. They did not hesitate on occasion to use ruthless and brutal expedients in crushing opponents or in removing obstacles from their path. "The end justified the means" sums up their business ethics.

Perhaps the best illustration of the new type of industrial organization is that furnished by the oil industry. In the process of integrating this industry there were displayed some of the most admirable as well as some of the most despicable traits of human nature. In forceful words Dr. Beard says, "All through this drama, from the start, dishonesty, chicane, lying, vulgarity, and a fierce passion for lucre are united with an intelligence capable of constructing immense agencies for economic service to the public and a philanthropic spirit that pours out money for charitable, religious, educational, and artistic plans and purposes."

Before the Civil War oil had been found in western Pennsylvania and neighboring states. Farmers had used the fluid found floating on the surface of streams to grease the axles of their wagons. An ingenious individual named Samuel M. Kier, who was engaged in the manufacture of salt obtained from artesian wells, conceived the idea of using the oil which frequently contaminated the salt water pumped from the wells. With a shrewd appreciation of the gullibility of the average American he bottled the oil and under the name of "Kier's Rock Oil," sold it as a cure for every imaginable human ill.

Experiments performed by a professor of chemistry at Yale College in the late fifties showed that the crude oil could easily be refined to produce an excellent illuminant, as well as valuable by-products such as paraffin and naphtha. A company was organized, and a man named Drake was sent to western Pennsylvania to drill a well. Despite the ridicule of the many persons living in the neighborhood who dubbed the enterprise "Drake's folly," the work was pushed, and in August, 1859, oil was pumped from the well at the rate of twenty-five barrels a day.

There immediately started a rush to the oil fields reminiscent of the gold rush to California ten years before. Towns sprang up overnight; impoverished farmers sold or leased their farms for fabulous sums; speculators and promoters launched companies by the hundreds. In short, all the features characteristic of the mining ventures in the Far West were reproduced on the hills of western Pennsylvania. Thus on the eve of the struggle for the preservation of the Union a new industry was started which was destined within twenty-five years to produce wealth far greater in extent than that represented by all of the slaves in the South.

The nature of the oil industry encouraged competition. One well sunk with comparatively inexpensive equipment might bring tremendous returns. The refining process likewise called for no large outlay of capital for expensive machinery. The uncertainty and the large rewards which characterized the industry encouraged speculation. As a result of these conditions competition was keen and the price of oil fluctuated violently, selling as high as twenty dollars a barrel in 1859 and as low as fifty-two cents a barrel in 1861.

Into this industry, highly volatile in a double sense, there entered the figure of John D. Rockefeller. As a young man Rockefeller had accumulated some capital in the produce commission business during the Civil War. In Cleveland, where his business was established, were a number of oil refineries, and in 1862 Rockefeller began to acquire an interest in one of these refineries. Three years later he organized a refining company under the name of Rockefeller, Andrews & Flagler.

Rockefeller apparently early conceived the ambition to organize the oil industry on a stable basis, eliminating the speculative and competitive features which brought periodic depressions in the industry. In 1870 he and a group of capitalists in Cleveland and New York incorporated the Standard Oil Company of Ohio. Within two years this company absorbed twenty of the twenty-five refineries in Cleveland. This combination of independent refiners was apparently facilitated by the activities of another organization called the "South Improvement Company," chartered by the Pennsylvania legislature. This company had arranged with the various railroads over which oil was shipped to receive from the latter a rebate of $1.06 on every barrel of oil shipped by companies affiliated with the South Improvement Company and, what was more remarkable, a rebate of the same amount to be paid to the company on all oil shipped by its competitors. Although the South Improvement Company was dissolved shortly after its practices were disclosed, the Standard Oil Company went ahead steadily in the process of combining independent refineries. Following the Cleveland combination the Standard absorbed the large refineries in Philadelphia and New York, in 1874, and in the next few years added most of those in western Pennsylvania. Thus within ten years Rockefeller and his associates had obtained control of 90 per cent. of the oil refining business of the country.

From refining, the Standard Oil Company turned its attention to shipping, and by building a pipe line from the refineries to tidewater it was enabled to force the railroads to grant favorable rates under the threat of shipping all of their oil through the pipe lines. In marketing its product the Standard Oil Company built up a most remarkable organization extending to every state of the Union and then reaching out to every part of the world. There is no question that through this organization the company furnished a better quality of goods to the consumer than he had previously been able to obtain.

In the process of this expansion of the Rockefeller interests, separate Standard Oil Companies had been formed in different states, while the Standard had also acquired control of a considerable number of other companies. To bring about closer articulation among these different organizations there was devised in 1882 a holding company called the Standard Oil Trust. The stock of all of the affiliated companies was placed in the hands of a group of nine trustees, the original owners of the stock receiving in exchange "trust certificates." This placed the management of the entire oil industry in the hands of a small group of men. Other lines of industry soon patterned their organizations after that of the Standard Oil Trust.

Many factors, good and bad, contributed to this development of "Big Business" in the closing decades of the nineteenth century. In the first place the captains of industry were men of remarkable ability. The magnitude of the organizations that they created, and the energy that they displayed in their work, compel admiration. But their success was undoubtedly furthered by other factors less admirable. Says

Beard of the practices of the Standard Oil Company: "It did receive rebates from time to time on its own and on its competitors' shipments of oil; it did crush out by methods none too delicate its rivals and its adversaries; its agents did resort to espionage and intimidation in destroying opposing concerns; its high spokesmen either lied deliberately or suffered from deficient memories on various stands; it had prominent politicians on its pay roll as counselors; and it contributed heavily to party campaign funds. On the other hand it was constantly assailed and blackmailed by men whose motives were no better and whose principles were no higher than its own." And the indictment here drawn could be made with equal force against other organizations of Big Business besides the Standard Oil Company.

RAILROAD CONSOLIDATION

Coincident with the integration of industry went a similar consolidation of the transportation facilities of the country. In the early days of railroad building there was little or no thought given to planning a comprehensive system of transportation serving the needs of the whole country. Usually a group of financiers would organize a company and obtain a charter from the state legislature for the construction of a road, generally between two important cities such as Baltimore and Washington or New York and Philadelphia. Not infrequently another group of financiers would organize another company and build a competing road paralleling one already built. The gauge on these early roads was not uniform, and thus it was impossible to interchange equipment. Hastily built, often through territory sparsely settled, many of these roads proved unprofitable, and when the panic of 1873 came a large part of the railroad mileage of the country was thrown into the hands of receivers.

In the years just before the Civil War a movement had

been started to tie together these isolated and competing lines. A leader in this movement was Cornelius Vanderbilt, who succeeded in bringing the several roads extending from New York to Buffalo into a single system called the New York Central and Hudson River Railroad. In the ten years from 1865 to 1875 this process of consolidation went on apace, and by the latter year five great trunk lines connected Chicago with the Atlantic seaboard.

Along with consolidation had gone a steady and rapid building of additional roads. By 1890 there were 163,000 miles of railroads in the country, nearly equal to half the railroad mileage of the entire world. In many cases this building had gone faster than the amount of freight and passenger traffic of the country warranted. Particularly was this true between such important centers as New York and Chicago. The five trunk lines serving these cities found it impossible to get enough business. There resulted an era of cut-throat competition, in which passenger and freight rates were slashed at times to a point below the cost of operating the trains. For example, the average freight rate on grain from Chicago to New York was reduced from 42 cents a bushel in 1868 to 14 cents a bushel in 1890. In the scramble to obtain freight the railroad managers adopted the practice of granting secret rebates from the published schedule of rates to large shippers such as the Standard Oil Company.

Various expedients were resorted to by the railroads to mitigate the losses due to competition. Sometimes the roads in a competitive field would agree to divide the limited business pro rata. Another plan provided for the pooling of earnings and their division on an agreed ratio. But rate agreements and pooling arrangements were difficult to maintain, for they depended upon the good faith of railroad operators, a virtue none too common at the time.

Another plan that was more successful until the government intervened to stop the practice was to charge a higher rate between certain places than between others. Forced to reduce rates between such competitive points as Chicago and New York, the roads attempted to make up the loss on this through traffic by charging excessive rates between points on their roads where they did not have to meet competition. As a result it was cheaper to ship goods from New York to Chicago than to a point several hundred miles east of Chicago. This discrimination between the "long and short haul" was felt particularly in rural areas served only by one railroad, and quite naturally aroused strong resentment among the farmers.

Another indictment brought against the railroads was that of reckless financing. In the early days of railroad building, the relatively modest financial needs were supplied by local banks or individuals; but with the tremendous expansion of railroads in the period after the Civil War, local and individual financial resources proved inadequate and recourse was had to the great banking interests, especially in New York. The manipulation of railroad securities soon became a leading feature of the activities of financiers and speculators in Wall Street and other financial centers. The exploits of Jay Gould and Jim Fisk in looting the Erie railroad were only the most spectacular of many similar incidents. As a result of these adventures in high finance the railroads of the country were loaded with indebtedness and capitalized far beyond their real value. It was estimated in 1883 that more than one-quarter of the railroad capitalization was "water." Railroading appeared to have lost its primary function of providing means of transportation and to have become an adjunct of high finance.

GOVERNMENT REGULATION OF TRUSTS AND RAILROADS

Such practices of large corporations, railroad managers, and financial magnates caused widespread popular protest.

Moreover, the social and political dangers involved in the accumulation of great fortunes by a few individuals gave rise to serious misgivings. Writers like Henry D. Lloyd and Edward Bellamy warned of dangers that inhered to the Republic in such concentration of wealth. But it was one thing to point out the abuses and shortcomings of existing conditions and another thing to find the remedy, for there were many obstacles to be overcome by those who urged that the government should intervene to protect the public from the unjust practices of industrial and railroad corporations. In the first place, the drafters of the Federal constitution in their efforts to protect private property had placed important restrictions upon the state and national governments in dealing with such property. The economic theory of *laissez faire* promulgated by Adam Smith had colored economic and political thought and action in America from the time the Republic was founded. Those who accepted this theory regarded any legislative interference with private business as unwarranted meddling. It is quite true that the adherents of the *laissez faire* doctrine were not consistent in applying it. Although they strongly protested against government regulation of private enterprise, they were equally insistent that the government should interfere with the free play of economic forces by enacting protective tariffs and granting subsidies. However, consistency is not a virtue when one's financial interests are at stake.

In the years following the Civil War the doctrine of *laissez faire* received added strength through judicial interpretation of the Fourteenth Amendment. The significant clause of this amendment stated that "no state shall make or enforce any law which shall abridge the privileges and immunities of citizens of the United States; nor shall any state deprive any person of life, liberty, or property, without due process of law; nor deny to any person within its jurisdiction equal protection of the laws." It is true that the Supreme Court at first took a narrow view of the meaning of the language of this clause. The opinion of the majority of the Court given in the Slaughter House cases in 1873 stated: "We doubt very much whether any action of a state not directed by way of discrimination against the negroes as a class, or on account of their race, will ever be held to come within the purview of this provision." This view still prevailed in 1876 as shown in the Granger decisions, when the Court upheld the power of state legislatures to regulate corporations and maintained that "for protection against the abuses by legislatures, the people must resort to the polls, not the courts." But the lapse of another ten years brought a decided change in the attitude of the Court. In arguing a case before the Court in 1882, Roscoe Conkling, who had been a member of the Congressional committee that drafted the Fourteenth Amendment, maintained that the amendment was designed not merely to protect the newly enfranchised slaves but also to protect corporations from unjust state legislation. He insisted that the word "person" as used in the amendment meant corporations as well as individuals. The Court soon came to take this view. In the case of Santa Clara County vs. The Southern Pacific Railroad, decided in 1886, the Court held that a corporation was a "person" in the meaning of the Fourteenth Amendment and was therefore entitled to the protection provided in the Amendment. Further, in the case of the Chicago, Milwaukee and St. Paul Railway Company vs. Minnesota, decided in 1889, the Court held not only that the Amendment applied to corporations but also that it was within the power of the Court to review the act of a state legislature which fixed railway rates and to set such rates aside if, in the opinion of the Court, they were unreasonable. In short, this decision had the effect of placing in the hands of the Federal judiciary the ultimate authority of determining how far a legislative body might go in regulating the earning power of business enterprises.

Added to these difficulties, inherent in the constitutional fabric, which confronted those who would lay a restraining hand on private business were others of a more insidious character. The directors of great business enterprises entered the political arena and, through the power of the wealth they controlled, were enabled to place in the halls of Congress and in state legislatures persons ready to do their bidding. Nor did they hesitate, on occasion, to resort to direct bribery to thwart legislative measures that they regarded as inimical to their interests.

In the face of all these obstacles it is not astonishing that the movement for the regulation of corporations was slow and halting, and that such legislation as found its way to the statute books was on the whole ineffective. The earliest efforts at regulation came from the states. In several of the eastern states railway commissions were appointed with power to investigate abuses such as the practice of granting rebates. The Massachusetts commission, under the able chairmanship of Charles Francis Adams, Jr., proposed a number of reforms. The Hepburn committee in New York disclosed the facts concerning rebates granted to the Standard Oil Company. In a number of the western states, where the complaints of the farmers were much more vigorous than in the East, the legislatures went much further and in the so-called Granger laws fixed maximum freight and passenger rates, prohibited the granting of free passes to public officials, and attempted to stop the abuse of the "long and short haul" by restraining any road from charging a higher rate for a short distance than for a long one.

But at best these efforts at state regulation could be only partially successful. Transportation was obviously a national problem, and any comprehensive plan of regulation must come from the national government. In 1874 the House of Representatives passed a bill for national regulation of railways, but the bill failed of adoption in the Senate. During the following ten years several other attempts were made by Congress to pass regulatory legislation, but without success. But in 1886 two incidents hastened Congressional action. The first was a decision of the Supreme Court holding that a state legislature could not fix rates on goods passing beyond the borders of the state, as the regulation of interstate commerce was an exclusive power of Congress. The second was the report of a Senate committee of which Senator Cullom of Illinois was chairman, which clearly showed the need of some form of effective regulation. As a result Congress passed the Interstate Commerce Act, which became a law by the signature of President Cleveland on February 4, 1887. This act declared illegal all rebates, pools, higher rates for short than long hauls, and all unreasonable charges. It required the railroads to publish copies of all rates, which could not be altered except after ten days' notice, and authorized the appointment of an Interstate Commerce Commission with authority to carry out the provisions of the law.

As a remedy for the abuses which had brought about its enactment, the Interstate Commerce Act proved a great disappointment. In the first place, the Commission was not given the power to fix rates, nor was a decision of the Commission that a rate was unreasonable final. If the carrier declined to comply with the ruling of the Commission in regard to rates or other matters, it was necessary for the Commission to take the question to the Federal court, where the decision was subject to review and was frequently modified or annulled. Further, the Commission could not deal with traffic conditions wholly within a single state, as its authority was confined to interstate commerce. In general the work of the Commission, in its early years, was restricted to making investigations and submitting recommendations.

While the results of the work of the Interstate Commerce Commission were disappointing at first, it is, perhaps, an exaggeration to say, as did a justice of the United States Supreme Court, that it was "a useless body for all practical purposes." The act of 1887 was the first effort at national regulation of large corporate enterprises and it at least served a useful purpose in challenging the dictum of "Commodore" Vanderbilt that the railroads were private property to be operated solely in the interest of their owners. Moreover, the Commission gathered considerable valuable information of which Congress made use in subsequent legislation.

The regulation of great industrial corporations met even greater difficulties than was the case with the railroads. The latter were semi-public institutions. They received charters from state legislatures, and they exercised the right to eminent domain in acquiring property. Endowed with these public attributes it was at least plausible to maintain that the railroads should be subject to public control. But the industrial corporations were private enterprises and it was a real challenge to the sacred doctrine of *laissez faire* to hold that they were subject to governmental regulation. Furthermore, there was no enlightened public opinion concerning the fundamental economic questions involved in the situation. Was monopoly an evil in itself? Did the mere size of a corporation constitute a menace to the public? How could the unjust practices of corporations be controlled without destroying the undoubted advantages of large-scale production? These and many other questions of equal significance gave rise to hopelessly divergent views among public officials. And those who controlled the great industrial organizations were determined, as well from conviction as for selfish reasons, to resist, with all the tremendous power that great wealth gave, any attempt at interference of their activities.

But the brutal methods employed by the Standard Oil and other corporations in crushing competition, corrupting legislatures, and in general showing a cynical disregard for the rights of others, gave rise to a widespread popular demand for government action. Public opinion had reached the point where it was prepared to discard economic theories long cherished in the face of what appeared to be a real public menace. In 1880 the Greenback party, and four years later the Anti-Monopoly party, placed planks in their platforms denouncing trusts and calling for governmental action to destroy them. In 1888 the platforms of both the major parties gave heed to the growing popular clamor and called for regulation of trusts and monopolies.

As with the railroads, so also with the industrial corporations, the first definite steps in government control came from the states. Before 1890 more than a dozen states had enacted legislation prohibiting combinations in restraint of trade. But here again the weakness of local regulation was apparent. Since some states failed to adopt restrictive legislation it was a simple matter for corporations to obtain charters in such states and then proceed to do business in every state. Obviously the remedy, if such there was, could be supplied only by Congressional action.

After much hesitation Congress, acting under its constitutional authority to regulate interstate and foreign commerce, passed the Sherman Anti-Trust Act, which became law by the signature of President Harrison on July 2, 1890. Its most important provision stated that "every contract, combination in the form of trust or otherwise, or conspiracy, in restraint of trade or commerce among the several states, or with foreign nations, is illegal." It further provided that any person injured in his business or property by reason of a violation of the provisions of the Act should be entitled to threefold damages. Hardly had the law reached the statute book, when there arose differences of opinion as to the meaning of its terms. What constituted "restraint of trade"? Did the law intend to forbid such "restraint" as would be involved in the combination of two small competing retail businesses? Or was it to be understood to prohibit only "unreasonable" restraint? Further the exact meaning of "trade or commerce" was not defined in the Act. Again did the law apply to combinations of labor as well as of capital? These and many other questions involving the meaning of the language of the law gave an opportunity to clever lawyers to advise their clients how to evade its provisions. Moreover, it opened the door wide to litigation and, in consequence, to judicial construction of the meaning of the law. In general the judicial interpretations of the law tended to restrict its effectiveness. For example the Supreme Court held, in the case of the United States vs. E. C. Knight, that the action of the American Sugar Refining Company in purchasing a number of refineries in Philadelphia, which enabled it to control virtually the entire refining business of the country, was not a violation of the Sherman Act on the ground that "purchase" did not involve interstate commerce, and that no direct evidence had been presented to show that the acquisition of the refineries would result in a restraint of trade.

In point of fact the Sherman Act was quite as ineffective in controlling industrial corporations as the Interstate Commerce Act had been in regulating railroad corporations. Nor does it appear that the governmental authorities made very vigorous efforts to enforce the law. During the two years of President Harrison's administration which remained after the passage of the Act only five prosecutions were started and of these four failed. During the administration of his successor, President Cleveland, eighteen cases involving the Sherman Act were prosecuted, and of these seven were cases involving combinations of labor. In six of the seven cases the Court held that the law applied to labor combinations. Of the remaining eleven cases involving corporations only one was successfully prosecuted.

Thus by one device or another the directors of Big Business were able to evade the provisions of the law. In the decade following the passage of the Sherman Act more than a hundred industrial combinations were formed, involving capital amounting to more than three billion dollars. In fact, in the closing years of the century the process of industrial combination reached the high-water mark, culminating in the formation of the United States Steel Corporation in 1901, the first billion dollar corporation in America.

However, it would not be strictly correct to call the Sherman Act a piece of futile legislation. Like the Interstate Commerce Act, it broke new ground, and that it failed at first to produce satisfactory results is not astonishing. Despite its failure to solve an extremely complicated economic problem, it was distinctly worth while as one more challenge to the doctrine of *laissez faire,* and it is probable that the Act did curb some of the more flagrant abuses of "Big Business." Nevertheless, the century closed with organized capital apparently triumphant. In its forward sweep it had reached virtually every field of commercial activity. And the large scale financial operations accompanying the process of consolidation gave rise to an intricate system of interlocking relations which placed in the hands of a small banking group an effective control of the business and commercial life of the nation. Neither state nor Federal Government appeared able to meet what seemed to an increasing number of thoughtful persons a serious challenge to democratic institutions.

BIBLIOGRAPHICAL NOTE

Surveys of the industrial development of the United States in the last quarter of the nineteenth century are given by H. U. Faulkner, *American Economic History* (1924) ; E. L. Bogart, *Economic History of the United States* (1907) ; Isaac Lippincott, *Economic Development of the United States* (1921) ; T. W. Van Metre, *Economic History of the United States* (1921).

For accounts of inventions see W. Kaempffert (ed.), *A Popular History of American Inventions* (1924) ; H. Thompson, *The Age of Invention* (1919) ; E. W. Byrn, *Progress of Invention in the Nineteenth Century* (1900).

For the growth of trusts and the question of their regulation consult J. W. Jenks and W. E. Clarke, *The Trust Problem* (4th ed., 1917) ; W. Z. Ripley, *Trusts, Pools and Corporations* (revised ed., 1917) ; H. D. Lloyd, *Wealth Against Commonwealth* (1894) ; Ida M. Tarbell, *History of the Standard Oil Company* (1914) ; B. J. Hendrick, *The Age of Big Business* (1919) ; L. H. Haney, *Business Organization and Combination* (1913) ; John Moody, *The Masters of Capital* (1914) ; M. W. Watkins, *Industrial Combination and Public Policy* (1927) ; W. H. Taft, *The Anti-Trust Act and the Supreme Court* (1914).

Railroad consolidation and regulation are treated by W. Z. Ripley, *Railroads: Rates and Regulation* (1912) ; by the same author, *Railroad Problems* (1912) ; John Moody, *The Railroad Builders* (1919). Consult also chapters in E. E. Sparks, *National Development* (1907) and D. R. Dewey, *National Problems* (1907).

CHAPTER 5

THE LABOR MOVEMENT, 1865-1900

The forward march of industry described in the preceding chapter led to the growth of the most powerful, wealthy and aggressive property class that had as yet appeared in American history. As we have seen, the leaders of this class were men who did things in a large way, who were predisposed to dictatorial methods, who were thoroughly committed to the doctrine of *laissez faire,* and who were not inclined to brook any interference with what they considered their property rights.

On the other hand, the wide expansion of business enterprise brought a formidable increase in the army of wage earners concentrated in industrial centers. This increase and concentration of labor forces gave rise to new and complicated problems concerning the relations of labor and the directors of industrial organizations. Given the point of view of the captains of industry at this time, there was little likelihood of their understanding or considering the interests and aspirations of the laboring class. At the same time the labor groups became increasingly aware of the divergence of interest of labor and of those who controlled the industrial machine.

In short, the closing decades of the nineteenth century showed unmistakable evidence of a widening breach between the forces of organized capital and those of organized labor. Each group was suspicious of the motives of the other, and each was determined to maintain its position with little or no consideration of the interests of the opposing group or of the general public. Clearly the stage was being set for a bitter struggle between the rival forces in American industrial life.

Prior to the Civil War labor organizations had been formed in various occupations, chiefly confined to the cities in the New England and Middle Atlantic states. These bodies were local in character, and loosely organized, and had meager financial resources. They were ill equipped to meet times of business depression and with each recurring financial panic the weak labor unions were disrupted if not completely dissolved. Such a period of industrial depression occurred in 1857, and before the labor organizations recovered from its effects the war came to complete the demoralization in the ranks of labor. During the war prices of all commodities rose much more rapidly than wages. In 1863 retail prices were 43 per cent. above the level of 1860, whereas wages were only 12 per cent. higher. To meet these conditions labor interests began rebuilding their shattered organizations. Former local unions were revived and new ones were established and, in addition, before the close of the war thirteen new national unions had been formed.

With these new foundations laid, the labor movement during the last quarter of the nineteenth century passed through a period of remarkable development and expansion. The causes of this striking growth are not difficult to discover. In the first place the rapid industrial expansion in the country in the decades following the Civil War greatly increased the number of wage earners. From slightly more than a million in 1860 the army of workers had increased to more than four millions in 1890. Moreover, the conditions under which the wage earners worked changed markedly during this period. In the pre-Civil War period, when industry was organized on a small scale, it was possible to maintain a fairly close personal relationship between employers and employees, but with the growth of large industrial corporations, employing thousands of workers, such personal relationship was impossible. Workers in these large organizations became part of a great industrial machine, wholly impersonal, owned by a large number of stockholders who were far removed from the business that they owned. This changed relationship of employer and employee increased greatly the chances of friction. Labor leaders realized that in order to deal with powerful organizations of capital with any reasonable chance of success it was necessary to present a united front through labor organizations.

The task that confronted the leaders of labor was not easy. In the first place, the raw material with which they had to deal was heterogeneous in character. American laborers, particularly the unskilled, were drawn from many nationalities with various cultural backgrounds. Their limited education would incline them to take a narrow and selfish view of the interests of labor. Moreover, the laboring class was more fluid and class consciousness less in evidence in America than in Europe. It was easier in the New World with its varied opportunities for the more ambitious and capable laborers to pass into the employing class. Then again, labor leaders could command no such financial resources as were at the disposal of the organizers of great corporations.

Another factor that greatly increased the difficulties confronting the leaders of labor organizations was the continual stream of immigrants from all parts of the world in the decades following the Civil War. This constant addition to the labor supply tended to keep wages down and to reduce the living standard of the working classes. Nor did the employers of labor hesitate, when confronted by a demand for increased wages or better working conditions, to import large numbers of immigrant laborers. It is interesting to note in passing that many of these employers who were beneficiaries of the protective tariff constantly urged the need for tariffs in order to protect American labor from the "pauper" labor of Europe. Confronted by all of these obstacles, it is surprising that organized labor made the substantial progress that it did make in the last quarter of the nineteenth century.

As has been noted, a large number of local unions, as well as several national unions, were started during the Civil War. In 1866 an attempt was made to form a loosely built federation of these local and national unions, together with various reform organizations, under the name of the National Labor Union. The leaders of this organization supported a variety of movements in the interest of labor. At first they concentrated their efforts on obtaining the eight-hour day, and were encouraged when Congress in 1868 passed a law fixing the eight-hour day for government employees. Several of the states in 1867 passed laws establishing the principle of the eight-hour day unless longer hours were specified by contract. The National Union also gave its support to the Greenback movement, and in 1872 entered the political arena with no very gratifying results. At another time the activities of the Union were directed to the formation of coöperative enterprises. Nearly all of the leading trades unions embarked on experiments in coöperation, most of which failed, sooner or later, because of mismanagement and the vigorous opposition of privately owned business. After six years of varied activity the National Union dissolved, to be succeeded by a more ambitious effort making for labor solidarity.

In 1869 there was organized in Philadelphia among the garment workers, under the leadership of Uriah S. Stephens, a secret society taking the name of the "Noble Order of the Knights of Labor." Disclaiming any antagonism to "legitimate enterprise" or "necessary capital," the principles of the order set forth its purpose "to create a healthy public opinion on the subject of labor (the only creator of values or capital) and the justice of its receiving a full, just share of the values or capital it has created." For nine years the order maintained its veil of secrecy and grew slowly. After 1878, however, it abandoned its secret practices and frankly announced its purpose to unite "all branches of honorable toil" without any distinction of race, color, nationality, or sex, into one comprehensive labor organization. Only liquor dealers, lawyers, bankers, stock brokers, and professional gamblers were barred from membership in the order, presumably because they did not live by "honorable toil."

The declaration of "First Principles" of the Knights indicated that their aims were as broad as their membership was inclusive. Idealistic purposes were stressed in their call for "the mutual development and moral elevation of mankind," and for the creation of a labor organization that "will develop more of charity, less of selfishness, more of generosity, less of stinginess and nearness, than the average society has yet disclosed to its members." In a more practical way they proposed to strive for the abrogation of all laws that did not bear equally upon capital and labor, and to advocate laws for the health and safety of laborers, the abolition of child labor, equal pay for both sexes, and the recognition of the eight-hour day. Following the example of the National Labor Union, the Knights of Labor urged the formation of producers' coöperative societies as a means of freeing the wage-earning class from the bondage of the wage system.

The growth of the order was remarkable. By the year 1886 it boasted a membership of more than 700,000, drawn chiefly from the ranks of unskilled labor. It had gained great prestige in labor circles by its successful contest with the Gould interests in the strike on the Missouri Pacific and Wabash railroads in 1885. But the decline of the order was almost as striking as its growth. Several factors contributed to this decline. Among the diverse elements that entered its membership during the period of rapid expansion were a considerable number of radicals bent upon committing the order to a program of socialism. The activities of these radicals brought discredit upon the organization, particularly after the Haymarket outrage in Chicago in 1886.[1] Again, the experiments of the Knights in various coöperative undertakings were not conspicuously successful and resulting financial losses caused friction in the order. But the chief element of weakness was the character of the organization itself. The ideal of the "one big union" based upon the conception of the solidarity of labor failed to make sufficient allowance for the particular and selfish interests of special groups of labor. Laborers, quite like other classes of society, were not willing to subordinate their peculiar interests for the sake of a "cause." Especially were the skilled laborers unwilling to have their identity lost in the mass of unskilled laborers. For these and other reasons the Knights of Labor declined rapidly after 1887, and their place in the labor field was taken by a body based upon a wholly different ideal of labor organization.

In 1881 some disaffected members of the Knights of Labor, together with representatives of various trades unions, launched a new labor organization called "The Federation of Organized Trades and Labor Unions of the United States of America and Canada." For five years this new order languished, and in 1886 it was reorganized under the name of the American Federation of Labor. From the first the Federation was controlled by the unions of skilled labor. The two outstanding figures in the organization of the Federation were Adolph Strasser and Samuel Gompers, both members of the cigarmakers' union. Gompers was chosen as its first president and held this office continuously, with the exception of one year, until his death in 1924.

In two important respects the Federation differed from the Knights of Labor. In the first place, it turned from idealistic schemes and radical programs for industrial reorganization and devoted its efforts to a realistic program of higher wages and shorter hours for labor. In the second

[1] See p. 121.

place, the promoters of the new organization discarded the idea of the "one big union" and determined to build upon the surer foundation of existing craft unions. The plan of organization adopted was a federation of autonomous trades unions. To the separate craft unions was left complete control of matters affecting the particular craft, including such questions as the arrangement of wage schedules, negotiations with employers, and the declaration of strikes. The central organization confined its activities to questions affecting labor as a whole, such as the encouragement of the organization of new labor unions, giving moral support to trade groups in their controversies with employers, and backing legislation favorable to labor.

The Federation quickly won the support of a large part of the skilled trades, and by the close of the century its membership had grown to more than 500,000. One important group of organized labor, the Railway Brotherhoods, declined to affiliate with the Federation. In the field of unskilled labor, which included the great majority of the laboring class, the American Federation, partly because of the peculiar character of its organization, made little effort to extend its activities.

With capital combined in the form of large corporations, and labor organized in unions, the stage was set for a trial of strength between these parts of the industrial machine. Although the controversies that ensued usually involved some concrete question such as wages or the length of the work day, the underlying cause of the industrial strife of this period was the fundamental difference in the points of view of the leaders of the contending forces. To the masters of business enterprise, imbued with the philosophy of *laissez faire,* the conduct of business was controlled by immutable economic laws. Labor was but one of many elements in a complicated industrial organism, and, like any necessary piece of machinery, should be bought in the cheapest market.

Wages should be regulated by the iron law of supply and demand. To the spokesmen for labor the situation appeared in quite a different light. They declined to view labor as a commodity to be bought and sold and finally to be scrapped. They insisted upon a consideration of the human factor in labor and contended that the laborer was entitled to a larger share of the wealth produced in order that he might enjoy greater material comforts and an opportunity to develop his cultural and spiritual life.

With two such opposing points of view, and with the leaders of both sides usually displaying an uncompromising attitude, bitter industrial warfare was inevitable. In the last quarter of the nineteenth century scarcely a year passed that did not record its full quota of strikes and lockouts, generally accompanied by disorder and the destruction of property, and occasionally taking on the aspect of civil war involving the use of state and Federal military forces. Statistics gathered by the United States Bureau of Labor show that in the twenty years from 1881 to 1900 there were some 24,000 strikes and lockouts, involving over 128,000 business establishments, and more than 6,600,000 employees. The direct monetary loss of these struggles has been estimated at more than $500,000,000 and the indirect losses cannot be computed.

Apart from questions of wages and hours of labor there was involved in nearly all of these industrial disputes the important principle of collective bargaining, that is, the right of workers to deal with employers in the adjustment of grievances through accredited representatives of labor organizations. In general employers were unwilling to admit that the development of large-scale industry necessitated any fundamental change in the direct personal relationship between employer and employee which had prevailed in earlier times. On the other hand, the leaders of organized labor insisted that it was manifestly impossible for the individual worker to bargain, with any hope of success, with the powerful organizations of capital. Only through the leaders of their craft unions, who were not subject to intimidation caused by threat of loss of employment, could the interests of the workers be adequately safeguarded. It was not until after the close of the nineteenth century that organized labor had any measure of success in establishing the principle of collective bargaining.

It is possible here to record only the high lights in this running warfare of twenty-five years between capital and labor. In the ten years following the close of the Civil War a condition of chronic disorder, approaching at times a reign of terror, prevailed in the anthracite coal region of Pennsylvania. A secret society, known as the Molly Maguires, had sprung up among the employees of the mines. The miners had legitimate grievances, but the methods pursued by the Molly Maguires aroused public indignation. Mine property was destroyed and mine owners and foremen were beaten and, in a number of cases, murdered. It was not until a Pinkerton detective named McParlan had succeeded in obtaining membership in the miners' society that the leaders of the movement were disclosed. Several of the conspirators were executed, others were imprisoned, and the society was broken up.

Hardly had the excitement caused by the activities of the Molly Maguires subsided, when the country was confronted by a widespread strike involving most of the railroads in the East. Following the panic of 1873, the railroads were in desperate financial straits. This condition was due to various causes: reduced traffic caused by the financial depression, cutthroat competition between rival roads, and reckless financing by those who controlled the railroads. In their efforts to escape bankruptcy the railroad managers determined to reduce wages. A reduction of 10 per cent. was made shortly after the panic, and this was followed in 1877 by a further horizontal cut of 10 per cent. This action precipitated strikes on nearly all of the railroads east of the Missouri River, apparently without any concerted action by labor leaders. The worst of the disorders occurred near Pittsburgh, where the strikers on the Pennsylvania Railroad inaugurated a veritable reign of terror. Long lines of freight and passenger cars were looted and set on fire. Two roundhouses with over a hundred locomotives and a grain elevator were destroyed. An appeal to the governor of the state led to the dispatch of state militia and finally of Federal troops. Clashes between the troops and the rioters resulted in the death of ten of the strikers and the wounding of a large number of others. At the same time a strike occurred in the anthracite coal fields of Pennsylvania accompanied by the usual disorder and necessitating the calling out of state militia and Federal forces under General Hancock. Two factors contributed to the lawlessness that accompanied these strikes. First was the lack of discipline in labor organizations, due to the primitive stage of development that trades unions had reached at the time. Second was the presence of a considerable number of radicals who were quite willing to use the prevailing industrial strife to hasten the social revolution they advocated.

The return of industrial prosperity in 1879 brought a temporary lull in the warfare between capital and labor, but in 1885-1886, following another business depression, there occurred a further outburst of industrial conflicts referred to as the "Great Upheaval." Only the most significant of these struggles can be noted here. In 1885 a cut of 10 per cent. in wages led to a strike on the Gould railway system. The sympathy of the public in general was with the strikers, because of Gould's unsavory reputation, and the railway management was forced to restore the former scale of wages. Encouraged by this success, the railway workers, except the members of the Brotherhoods, went on strike on the entire Gould system in protest against the discharge of a foreman who was a member of the Knights of Labor. In this struggle the strikers lost the sympathy of the public because of the tactics of the leader of the strikers, an ignorant ruffian named Martin Irons, and after two months of interrupted traffic the strike was abandoned.

Coincident with the strikes caused by specific grievances, the American Federation of Labor in 1886 inaugurated a nation-wide movement for the eight-hour day. Some of the better organized trades obtained their object, but the cause of the workingmen was set back by an outrage in Chicago, attributed to the activities of a small group of anarchists.

A strike was in progress at the McCormick Reaper Works, in the course of which a clash occurred between the police and the strikers resulting in the death of four of the strikers. The following day a protest meeting was held in Haymarket Square. Leaders of the radical International called upon the workers to "arm yourselves and appear in full force." Near the close of the meeting, while the police were attempting to disperse the crowd, a bomb was suddenly hurled into their midst by an unknown hand, resulting in the death of one policeman and the fatal injury of seven others. In the popular excitement that followed the outrage the strike and its causes were lost sight of, and the issue was declared to be the preservation of social order. Eight anarchists were arrested and tried for murder, although it was not shown that any of the eight had been directly connected with the bomb explosion, but in the opinion of the judge who presided at the trial it was sufficient to show that they "had generally by speech and print advised large classes to commit murder and had left the commission, the time, place, and when to the individual will, whim or caprice or whatever it may be of each individual man who listened to their advice." The jury convicted all eight men, of whom seven were condemned to death and one to the penitentiary. Of the seven sentenced to be hanged, four were executed, one committed suicide and two had their sentences commuted to life imprisonment by the governor of the state. Although the bomb outrage was attributed to a small group of anarchists the public indignation that it aroused was turned against all forms of labor agitation. Even the reasonable demands of labor obtained little popular support until the excitement over the Haymarket incident had died down.[2]

The next significant event in the labor warfare occurred in the steel industry. In 1892 a strike was declared in the plant of the Carnegie Steel Company at Homestead, Pennsylvania. There were involved in the dispute both the question of wages and that of the recognition of the union. Pinkerton detectives were brought in by the management to protect the property of the company and a clash occurred between the strikers and the detectives resulting in the death of ten persons. A call for the militia brought troops to the number of 8,000 men to the scene and after a lingering struggle the strike was broken and organized labor lost its grip upon the steel industry.

The year 1894 produced a further crop of labor disturbances, caused in part by the business depression that followed in the wake of the panic of 1893. The number of workers involved in the strikes of this year reached nearly 750,000, exceeding even the mark set in 1886. The strike of the United Mine Workers and the Pullman strike in Chicago were the most important of the various labor struggles of this year. The strike of the coal miners ended in the complete defeat of the workers. The Pullman strike, which began in May, 1894, grew out of a demand of some of the employees of the Pullman Palace Car Company for a restoration of the wages paid during the previous year. The Pullman employees were affiliated with the American Railway Union, an organization that aimed to bring into one large labor organization

---

[2] Governor Altgeld later pardoned the three surviving anarchists, to the dismay of conservatives throughout the land.

all railway workers. The moving spirit in this union was Eugene V. Debs, who had been formerly associated with the Brotherhood of Locomotive Firemen. In support of the Pullman employees the Railway Union voted to stop handling Pullman cars unless the Pullman company would agree to arbitrate its dispute with its employees. The struggle then developed into a contest between the railway managements, which were bound by contracts with the Pullman company, and the union, supported by many members of the Brotherhoods, although the Brotherhood organizations had opposed the strike.

Scenes of violence reminiscent of the great railway strike of 1877 accompanied the struggle. The center of disturbance was in and around Chicago, where lawless crowds of strikers and the criminal fringe, always present on such occasions, destroyed railway property and terrorized the community. Governor Altgeld of Illinois, who had aroused the ire of conservative elements in the country by his pardon of three of the men convicted in the Haymarket incident, gave further offense to these same interests by declining to call for Federal aid to preserve order.

Despite the expressed opposition of the Illinois governor to Federal interference, President Cleveland determined to use the strong arm of the national government to restore order. The leaders of the strikers were charged with maintaining a conspiracy in restraint of trade in violation of the Sherman Anti-Trust Act. Basing their action upon the constitutional duty of the Federal Government to maintain the unrestricted movement of the mail, the Federal officials obtained from the court a sweeping "blanket" injunction, which enjoined the strikers from interfering directly or indirectly with the delivery of the mail. Debs and the other officers of the Railway Union were promptly arrested and charged with contempt of court in disobeying the injunction. President Cleveland followed this action by sending 2,000 troops to Chicago. The effect of the vigorous action of the Federal authorities was seen in the complete collapse of the strike, which was already virtually beaten.

As the leaders of organized labor surveyed the incidents connected with the Pullman strike they realized that new and formidable obstacles had been raised to hamper labor in its contest with organized capital. First was the unexpected application of the Sherman Anti-Trust Law to combinations of labor as well as to combinations of capital. More important was the use of the injunction in industrial disputes. It is true that this was not the first time that this judicial weapon had been used in labor controversies, but the sweeping character of the injunction in the Debs case caused profound concern in labor circles. To the spokesmen for organized labor the intervention of the Federal courts in labor disputes seemed to be always to the advantage of the employers. More serious was the fact that punishment for a violation of an injunction could be inflicted without a jury trial, thus denying to the accused a fundamental constitutional privilege. Backed by the steadily growing power of the American Federation of Labor, a determined effort was inaugurated to relieve labor organizations from the penalties of the Anti-Trust Law and to restrict the issuance of injunctions in industrial disputes. Twenty years of agitation for these changes, as we shall see, met with only partial success.

LABOR LEGISLATION

For twenty-five years the forces of organized capital and organized labor had carried on an embittered warfare resulting in considerable loss of human life, besides property losses running into hundreds of millions of dollars. At first the political authorities, both state and national, were inclined to view these controversies as private affairs calling for governmental interference only when public order was threatened. The theory of *laissez faire* was still potent, and the time had not yet arrived when industrial conflicts were regarded as having a public interest. Moreover, the constitutional inhibitions, particularly upon the national government, placed many obstacles in the way of any comprehensive plan for legislative control of industrial relations. By the Federal constitution Congress is limited in dealing with industrial controversies, to such as affect interstate or foreign commerce. The state legislatures, on the other hand, enjoy a wider scope of power in regulating these matters, being limited only by the constitutional provisions for the protection of private property and individual liberty. Despite these constitutional difficulties some progress was made in this period in placing labor legislation upon the statute books. The first national law concerning labor was that enacted in 1868 establishing the eight-hour work day for all laborers and mechanics "employed by or on behalf of the United States government." In 1882, under pressure from the wage earners of the Pacific coast, Congress passed the Chinese Exclusion Act, and in 1885, under similar pressure from labor organizations, the Alien Contract Labor Law was passed. This Federal statute bars from the country aliens who arrive under contract to work for an American employer of labor. In 1884 Congress provided for a Bureau of Labor. The widespread labor disturbances in 1885-1886 led President Cleveland to call the attention of Congress to the desirability of providing governmental agencies to aid in the settlement of industrial disputes. In response to this suggestion Congress in 1888 enacted a law for the voluntary submission of disputes between railway corporations and their employees to arbitration but without any obligation upon either party to the dispute to accept the decision of the arbitrators.

In the states the record of labor legislation during this period is more extensive. Most of the states made provisions for labor bureaus for the collection of information relative to labor conditions. Eight-hour laws were enacted in a number of states, but the effect of these laws was limited, as they were applicable only when a longer work day was not provided by contract. Factory laws and laws regulating the employment of children were also placed upon the statute books in many states.

<h2 style="text-align:center">LABOR AND POLITICS</h2>

The growth of labor solidarity in the last quarter of the nineteenth century raised the question of the entrance of labor into the political field. In 1867 the National Labor Union resolved that the time had arrived when "the industrial classes should cut themselves aloof from party ties and predilections and organize themselves into a National Labor party." This suggestion bore fruit in the organization of the Labor Reform party in 1872, but the results of the election were not encouraging, as the candidate of the party polled only 29,000 votes. In the presidential election of 1876 the labor interests were divided. A small but aggressive element joined the socialist organization known as the Workingmen's party, while a larger group affiliated with the Greenback party. In the eighties several ephemeral labor reform parties made their appearance, such as the Union Labor party, the United Labor party, the Progressive Labor party, the American Reform party, the Homesteaders, and the Anti-Monopoly party.

With the growth of the American Federation of Labor as the dominant factor in organized labor in the country the efforts to form a distinct labor party were definitely checked. Samuel Gompers, the president and guiding spirit of the Federation, was consistently opposed to the organization of such a party. He held the view that the interests of labor would be better maintained by influencing existing political parties to support labor measures and by supporting candidates for office who would pledge themselves to vote in the interests of labor.

However, labor interests not affiliated with the American Federation of Labor continued the agitation for political organization. Most of these joined one or another of the Socialist organizations. In 1864 Karl Marx had started the International Workingmen's Association and within a short time branches of this Association appeared in America, drawing their membership chiefly from the foreign element in the industrial centers. In 1874 these groups entered the political arena by organizing the Social Democratic party, but the class-conscious appeal of Marxian socialism roused little response among native American laborers. Reorganized in 1877 under the name of the Socialist Labor party, the radical elements continued their political activities, with few tangible results except, perhaps, to furnish conservative orators with ammunition to be used, on occasion, to defeat even the most moderate reform measures.

LABOR AND IMMIGRATION

Not until the closing decades of the nineteenth century was there any considerable feeling in this country that the influx of alien immigrants was a problem worthy of serious consideration.[3] During the first hundred years of our national history such attention as Congress had given to the question was in the direction rather of encouraging immigration than of restricting it. A vast unoccupied continent seemed to offer abundant room for all who wished to come. Nor was there lacking artificial stimulation to the natural desire of the European peasant and worker to reach the land of promise. The steamship companies, the land speculators, and

[3] It is true that the Know Nothing movement during the fifteen years before the Civil War was an expression of opposition by the native American stock to immigrant groups.

the employers of cheap labor, all had a pecuniary interest in the steady flow of aliens to the New World.

Under these favorable conditions the immigrant tide rose steadily. From a little more than 2,000,000 in the decade between 1860 and 1870 it had risen to more than 5,000,000 in the decade between 1880 and 1890. The bulk of the immigration in these years had come from racial strains in Europe closely related to those from which the native Americans had come. Prior to 1880 more than five-sixths of the foreign-born population in the United States had come from the British Isles, Germany, and the Scandinavian countries.

After 1880 two significant factors forced the attention of the country for the first time to a serious consideration of the immigrant question. The first of these factors was the rapid exhaustion of cheap western lands. When it no longer was possible for incoming aliens to obtain free farms in the West they tended to congregate in increasing numbers in the industrial centers of the East. Owners of railways, mills, and mines, unmindful of the effect upon the nation of large numbers of unassimilated aliens, welcomed this abundant supply of cheap labor. The other new factor was the changed character of the immigrants. After 1882 the influx from southern and eastern Europe began to assume large proportions and by 1896 the arrivals from these countries exceeded in volume the immigrants of the earlier types.

The economic standards of a large proportion of the new class of immigrants were lower than those of the older type and of the native laborers, and their willingness to work for low wages threatened the standard of living of American wage earners. Moreover, the racial traits of these new arrivals contrasted sharply with those of the native American stock, and the latter generally raised a social barrier against these strange and so-called inferior races. Forced to live together in congested slums of the large cities and factory towns, retaining their own language and institutions, and possessing little or no incentive to acquire American ideals, this steadily growing mass of unassimilated aliens gave rise to new and perplexing problems.

It was from the ranks of organized labor that the first demand came for a curb upon the flood of immigration. The leaders of labor realized that it was an impossible task to raise or even to maintain the living standard of American labor as long as employers could import from Europe and the Orient armies of laborers accustomed to low standards of living. As we have seen, it was largely at the behest of labor organizations that Congress had passed the Chinese Exclusion Act in 1882 and the Contract Labor Law in 1885. But the efforts of labor leaders to obtain a more comprehensive restriction upon immigration met with little success at this time. It is true that both of the great political parties in 1892 adopted planks in their platforms favoring the restriction of immigration. The Republicans demanded "the enactment of more stringent laws and regulations for the restriction of criminal, pauper, and contract immigration," while the Democrats approved "all legislative efforts to prevent the United States from being used as a dumping ground for the known criminals and professional paupers of Europe." When, however, Congress in 1896 passed an act which provided that all immigrants between the ages of fourteen and sixty should be excluded "who cannot both read and write the English language or some other language" it met a veto at the hands of President Cleveland. He stated that he could not concur in so radical a departure from the traditional liberal policy of the United States, and he believed that it was better "to admit a hundred thousand immigrants who, though unable to read and write, seek among us a home and opportunity to work, than to admit one of those unruly agitators and enemies of governmental control who can not only read and write, but delights in arousing by inflammatory speech the illiterate and peacefully inclined to discontent and tumult." Two more decades passed, adding millions more to the immigrant horde, before an effective barrier was raised against the alien flood.

BIBLIOGRAPHICAL NOTE

A number of good accounts of the rise of labor organizations and of labor problems have appeared in recent years. Brief surveys are found in S. P. Orth, *The Armies of Labor* (1919) ; and Mary A. Beard, *A Short History of the American Labor Movement* (1920) ; a more comprehensive treatment is given in J. R. Commons and Associates, *History of Labor in the United States* (1918) ; consult also R. F. Hoxie, *Trade Unionism in the United States* (1917) ; S. Perlman, *A History of Trade Unionism in the United States* (1922) ; by the same author, *A Theory of the Labor Movement* (1928) ; S. Gompers, *Seventy Years of Life and Labor* (1925) ; John Mitchell, *Organized Labor* (1903) ; T. V. Powderly, *Thirty Years of Labor* (1890) ; R. T. Ely, *Labor Movement in America* (1890) ; T. S. Adams and H. L. Sumner, *Labor Problems* (1905).

The story of the Knights of Labor is told by D. D. Lescohier, *The Knights of St. Crispin* (in the *University of Wisconsin Economic and Political Science Series,* Vol. VII, No. 1, 1910) and by D. Wright, *An Historical Sketch of the Knights of Labor* (*Quarterly Journal of Economics* I, 137-168).

A discussion of the labor conflicts of this period can be found in the work of T. S. Adams and H. L. Sumner cited above and in F. T. Carlton, *The History and Problems of Organized Labor* (1920) ; consult also J. P. Altgeld, *Reasons for Pardoning Fielden, Neebe and Schwab* (1893), E. Berman, *Labor Disputes and the President of the United States* (1924).

The efforts of labor organizations in the political field are described by N. Fine, *Labor and Farmer Parties in the United States* (1928). Labor legislation is considered in most of the histories of the labor movement noted above. See especially on this subject J. B. Andrews and J. R. Commons, *Principles of Labor Legislation* (1927) ; and C. G. Groat, *Attitude of the American Courts to Labor Cases* (1911).

A brief discussion of the immigration question can be found in S. P. Orth, *Our Foreigners* (1919) ; more extended treatment of the subject is contained in J. W. Jenks and W. J. Lauck, *The Immigration Problem* (1926); E. Abbott, *Historical Aspects of the Immigration Problem* (1926); J. R. Commons, *Races and Immigration in America* (1920); G. M. Stephenson, *The History of American Immigration* (1926).

CHAPTER 6

POLITICAL PARTIES AND POLITICS, 1877-1896

The Republican party emerged from the Civil War with the prestige that came from having saved the Union. It is true that thousands of Democrats in the North had supported the Union cause but it is undeniable that a large majority of those who fought under the Confederate flag had been enrolled in the Democratic party. And the Republicans had not neglected to capitalize to the fullest extent, in the years following the close of the war, the patriotic asset that they had inherited. As we have seen, "waving the bloody shirt" was a potent, if not a decisive, factor in most of the political campaigns during the ten years after the close of the sectional struggle.

But the strength of the Republican party in the last quarter of the nineteenth century did not by any means rest wholly upon an appeal to national patriotism. Forces much more substantial, at least from the financial point of view, account for the success of the Republicans in this period. In general, the same economic interests that had constituted the backbone of the Whig party in the days before the Civil War were enrolled in the ranks of the Republican party after the war. These interests included the major part of the manufacturing and financial forces of the country. And these forces had grown tremendously in numbers and wealth due to the industrial development of the country in the closing decades of the nineteenth century. Then, too, the Republican party was able to retain the loyalty of a large part of the farmers of the Middle West, except on occasion when agricultural depression led to sporadic revolts. This loyalty was partly due to tradition. The Republican party was born in the Middle West and its first President came from this section. And this traditional loyalty was fortified by the generosity of the party in granting to millions of farmers free homesteads.

The close of the Civil War found the Democratic party broken and discouraged. For years thereafter it had to bear the onus of having been the mainstay of an unsuccessful rebellion. Moreover, the planter class of the South, which had furnished the leaders of the Democracy in the ante-bellum days, had been ruined by the collapse of the Confederacy, and for some years most of those who survived the loss of their property were barred from political activity by the provisions of Reconstruction legislation. When the Southern states were finally restored to the Union and the disabilities had been removed from Confederate leaders, the Democratic party began to renew its strength. With a nucleus of states constituting the former Confederacy and a substantial following among the working classes in the North, the Democratic party was able, after 1870, to challenge with some hope of success the entrenched forces of the Republicans.

The two major political parties in the United States did not represent distinct social and economic classes, as was the case in many European states. Economic conditions in this country had not as yet produced a static condition of social classes comparable to that which prevailed in Europe. The fluidity of social groups was reflected in the composition of political parties. Both the Republican and Democratic parties had within their ranks representatives of all economic classes from the highest to the lowest. As a consequence the principles set forth in the platforms of the two major parties in the last quarter of the nineteenth century, with the possible exception of the tariff question, indicate no clear-cut differences between the parties based on economic questions. The politicians who guided the destinies of both parties felt the necessity of treating gingerly any really controversial question, for fear of alienating some part of the heterogeneous elements which constituted the rank and file of the party membership. As a result the typical party platform was made up of a collection of platitudinous generalities couched in language sufficiently ambiguous to satisfy the varied party clientele.

PRESIDENT HAYES AND POLITICAL REFORM

President Hayes was in an extremely trying position when he assumed office as a result of the decision of the Electoral Commission. A substantial body of opinion in the country believed that he was not entitled to the office of President. Democratic orators and newspapers referred to him as the "Fraud President" and "Old Eight-to-Seven." Nor did Hayes have the enthusiastic support of the politicians of his own party. His nomination was a grudging concession to the reform element in the party, made necessary by the scandalous revelations of Grant's administration.

Hayes was not a man to arouse popular enthusiasm. He was conscientious and industrious but lacked the magnetic qualities essential to successful political leadership. He was quite overshadowed in the public mind by leaders in his own party like Blaine and Conkling. Moreover, at the time Hayes became President, the executive had not recovered from the loss of prestige and dignity that it had suffered during the time of President Johnson. The announcement of his cabinet selections by Hayes aroused the ire of the old line Republican politicians. The die-hards, who still cherished the resentments of the Civil War, were outraged by the selection of David M. Key, an ex-Confederate soldier, as Postmaster General, while the professional politicians did not relish the appointment of William M. Evarts, one of the counsel for the defense in the impeachment of President Johnson, as

Secretary of State or of Carl Schurz, a leader of the reformers, as Secretary of the Interior.

President Hayes promptly gave evidence that his promise to wipe out dishonesty and inefficiency in administrative circles was not made simply for campaign purposes, and in his determination to clean house he had the courage to throw down the gauntlet to some of the most powerful politicians of the Republican party. Against the determined opposition of Senator Conkling he reappointed Thomas L. James, a strong advocate of reform in the postal service, as postmaster in New York. Displaying even greater courage, he removed from office Chester A. Arthur, the Collector of the Port of New York, a henchman of Conkling, and the naval officer of the Port, Alonzo B. Cornell, chairman of the Republican National Committee, on account of gross frauds and inefficiency in the administration of the Custom House.

Hayes' earnest efforts to advance the movement for civil service reform met with little success. Although he issued an executive order that no officer of the government should be required or permitted to take part in the management of political organizations, and that no assessments for political purposes should be made upon such officers, there is evidence that the order was honored more in the breach than in the observance. The repeated recommendation of the President to Congress to renew the appropriation for the Civil Service Commission, which had been allowed to lapse during Grant's administration, was frustrated by the opposition of politicians in Congress. President Hayes gave further offense to the "Stalwarts" [1] in his party by the withdrawal of Federal troops from the South and his refusal to support any longer the Carpetbag régimes there. He was savagely attacked for his action in this matter by Republican politicians and news-

[1] There were two factions in the Republican party in New York at this time, the regular or machine element called Stalwarts, and the reform faction dubbed Half-Breeds.

papers and was charged with carrying out a bargain made with Southern Democratic leaders at the time he became President.

From the viewpoint of constructive legislation the four years of Hayes' administration are virtually barren.[2] This was due to the fact that the President never obtained effective leadership of his own party in Congress and to the further fact that during his term of office the Democrats controlled the House of Representatives and during the last two years, the Senate as well.

The Democratic House of Representatives, with an eye to the coming presidential election, authorized the Potter committee to investigate the validity of the decision of the Electoral Commission in the disputed election of 1876. As might be expected, a majority of this committee reached the conclusion that Tilden had been elected president. The effect of the report of this committee, however, was considerably weakened by disclosures made by the Republican Senate Committee of certain "Cipher Despatches" sent in the interest of Tilden in which offers were made to bribe the returning boards in Florida and South Carolina. The partisan character of this whole sorry business is revealed by the fact that despatches sent by Republicans were conveniently lost or destroyed.

During the last two years of Hayes' administration there took place a prolonged struggle between the President and Congress, controlled by the Democrats, over the efforts of the latter to do away with the remnants of Reconstruction legislation. Most important of these measures were the so-called "Force Bills," which provided for the supervision of elections by officials appointed by Federal courts, and authorized Federal marshals to preserve order at the polls with the use of United States troops if necessary. Lacking the necessary

---

[2] The most important legislative enactment of the Hayes administration was the Bland-Allison Silver Purchase Act noted in a later chapter.

two-thirds majority in Congress which would enable them to pass measures over the veto of the President, the Democrats attempted to accomplish the repeal of the Force Bills by attaching "riders" to appropriation bills which prohibited the use of the army in elections and struck out the funds provided for the payment of deputy marshals and supervisors of elections. President Hayes disapproved all of these measures not so much because he wished to maintain Federal control of elections as because he regarded the action of Congress in placing riders on essential appropriation bills as an unwarranted attempt to deprive the executive of his constitutional prerogative to exercise a qualified veto of Congressional acts.

CONTINUED EFFORTS FOR REFORM, 1881-1885

When President Hayes assumed office he declared himself opposed to a second term for the presidency. Apart from his own unwillingness to serve, however, it is doubtful whether he could have been renominated by his party. The old war horses of the Republican party were determined to have no more "goody-goody" Presidents who refused to play the game of practical politics as they understood it. With a determination to regain their lost prestige the Stalwart leaders—Conkling, Cameron, and Logan—undertook to nominate General Grant, who had just returned from a triumphal tour around the world, for a third term. They argued plausibly that as four years had elapsed since Grant's second term his nomination would not violate the third term tradition. Grant at first hesitated to give his consent to the movement to nominate him, but he finally agreed to accept "if the party unanimously, or nearly unanimously, demand it." But unanimity in the party was far from evident. Conkling and his associates did succeed in lining up a block of 300 delegates for Grant before the convention met. But both

Blaine and Sherman had substantial support, and the reform element in the party was unalterably opposed to four years more of Grant.

When the Republican Convention met at Chicago on June 2, 1880, 304 delegates cast their votes for Grant on the first ballot, but he was not able to secure the required majority on subsequent ballots. After a prolonged deadlock the Convention turned to the proverbial "dark horse," and nominated James A. Garfield, of Ohio. As a sop to the Stalwart faction the vice-presidential nomination was given to a protégé of Conkling, Chester A. Arthur, of New York. Garfield was an "available" candidate, although hardly an outstanding personality. He had the essential military record for a Republican aspirant for office, having risen to the rank of Brigadier General in the Union army. He had not been involved in the factional quarrels of the party during Hayes' administration, and he could capitalize his humble beginnings as a "canal-boat boy."

The Democrats failed to improve the promising situation that recent elections had disclosed. The attempt to nominate Tilden again, on the theory that he was entitled to "vindication," failed because of his poor health and also because of the vigorous opposition of the party organization in New York, led by "Boss Kelly." The convention finally selected as the nominee General Winfield Scott Hancock, who had a creditable war record, but who was wholly inexperienced in governmental affairs. By nominating a Union general as their candidate the Democrats hoped to refute the claim of the Republicans to a monopoly of patriotism.

In the ensuing campaign the Democrats stressed the issue of the "steal" that the Republicans had perpetrated in 1876, and called upon the voters to right the wrong that had then been done. But the passage of time had robbed this appeal of its former effectiveness. Nor were the Republicans much more successful in their efforts again to "wave the bloody shirt." The results of the election showed that the voters were about equally divided between the two parties. Although Garfield won by 214 electoral votes to 155 for Hancock, his plurality in the popular vote was less than 10,000 in a total vote of more than 9,000,000.[3]

It is impossible to say whether Garfield would have fared better than Hayes in reconciling the discordant elements within his party, for he had served but four months of his term when he was shot by a disgruntled office-seeker named Guiteau. During his brief tenure of office Garfield precipitated a quarrel with the Stalwarts by refusing to follow the wishes of the senators from New York in making important appointments in that state. Senator Conkling tried to prevent the ratification of the presidential nominees by the Senate, but in vain, whereupon he and his colleague, Thomas C. Platt, resigned from the Senate and called upon the state legislature to reëlect them as a rebuke to the President. Much to their chagrin the legislature refused to do this, and Conkling retired permanently, and Platt temporarily, to private life.

That the disclosures of corruption during the Grant régime had not resulted in any great reformation of the political morals of the professional politicians was evidenced by the exposure of the "Star Route Frauds" in the post office department during Garfield's administration. The Star Routes were chiefly in the West, in regions not reached by railroads. Contracts for the delivery of mail in these areas were let to private individuals or companies, but the Post Office Department was authorized to increase the compensation without calling for bids where growth of population warranted it. The secretary of the Republican National Committee, Senator S. W. Dorsey, was interested in one of the

[3] The Greenback Party nominated J. B. Weaver, of Iowa, on a platform demanding that legal-tender currency (greenbacks) should be issued by the government in place of the national bank notes and that gold and silver be coined in unlimited amounts. It also denounced child labor and called for the exclusion of Chinese coolie labor.

companies which held a number of these contracts. By collusion with Second Assistant Postmaster General Brady this company received more than $400,000 above the amount of its contract in one year. Estimates of the total amount of the frauds were as high as five million dollars and it was disclosed that a considerable part of the misappropriated funds was paid into the treasury of the Republican National Committee.

The accession of Vice-President Arthur to the presidency caused consternation among the reformers. His whole political career had been that of the machine politician. He had been removed from the office of Collector of Customs by President Hayes because of gross mismanagement, and there would seem to have been abundant justification for the apprehension entertained when he assumed the presidential office. But the grave responsibilities suddenly thrust upon him appear to have had a sobering effect upon the new President. He indicated his determination to carry out the policies of his predecessor and gave evidence of his courage by vetoing an extravagant Rivers and Harbors bill that Congress had passed. Moreover, to the delight and surprise of the reformers, he gave earnest support to the movement for civil service reform.

The assassination of President Garfield by a disappointed applicant for office awakened the public conscience to the evils of the spoils system, and the advocates of reform took advantage of the favorable situation to press upon Congress the need for action. The result was the passage, in January, 1883, of the Pendleton Bill, which authorized the President to appoint three commissioners who should classify employees of the government into grades. Appointment to, and promotion within, these grades were to be made from a list of eligibles prepared after competitive examination. It further prohibited political assessments upon office holders. The act itself applied to only some 14,000 positions, amounting to about one-tenth of the total number of Federal employees, but the President was empowered to extend the scope of the classified service at his discretion. Succeeding Presidents made use of this discretionary power, not always from purely disinterested motives,[4] and the merit system was steadily extended until at present more than half of the vast army of Federal officials are in the classified service.

ADMINISTRATION BY THE DEMOCRATS, 1885-1889

President Arthur felt that he was entitled to nomination by his party in 1884, but he lacked the qualities of aggressive leadership. Although he had alienated the support of his old associates among the Stalwarts by his advocacy of reform measures, he had failed to convince the reformers of the sincerity of his conversion. In the Republican convention Blaine, who had failed to obtain the nomination in the two preceding elections, had an enthusiastic following and despite the opposition of the reformers who favored Senator Edmunds of Vermont, Blaine was nominated on the fourth ballot. "It is now Blaine's turn," was the characteristic comment of ex-Senator Platt, of New York. Some disappointed reformers deserted the Republican party and openly advocated support of the Democrats. Others, like young Theodore Roosevelt and Henry Cabot Lodge, remained regular but displayed no enthusiasm for the party candidate.

The Democrats on this occasion took full advantage of their opportunities. They selected as their standard bearer Grover Cleveland, then Governor of New York, and adopted a platform that made sweeping promises of reform. Cleveland had been elected Mayor of Buffalo in 1881 on a reform ticket and had attracted the attention of those who had

---

[4] Retiring presidents, especially if their successors were of the opposite party, took advantage of the discretion allowed them by the law to cover into the protected service officials who might have been removed by the incoming administration.

become disgusted with the time-serving and corrupt politicians. In 1882 he was nominated for Governor by the Democrats, not because they wanted him but because they wanted
to win, and was elected by the unprecedented majority of
190,000.[5] During his term as Governor he continued his attitude of fearless and aggressive independence, to the delight
of the reformers and the distress of the politicians. Cleveland lacked those qualities of brilliancy which Blaine possessed but he was credited with just the sort of homely
honesty demanded by the situation at that time. He was slow
and deliberate in formulating his opinions on public questions but once having reached a conclusion he maintained his
position with great stubbornness, and apparently with little
consideration for his own political fortunes. His statement
that "public office was a public trust" was calculated to win
him favor among men of all parties who were aroused by
the constant revelations of wrong-doing in public life. Although Cleveland was opposed by some of the influential
politicians of his own party, he won the support of a group
of leading Republicans and independents, such as Carl
Schurz, George William Curtis, and Henry Ward Beecher,
and such influential newspapers as the New York *Times,* the
Springfield *Republican,* the New York *Evening Post,* and
the *Nation.*[6]

The campaign was a contest of personalities rather than
of principles. Never before had the country witnessed such
an exhibition of scurrility as that which characterized the
"oratory" of this campaign. Speakers on both sides exceeded

[5] Cleveland's success was undoubtedly furthered by factional quarrels
in the Republican party.

[6] The Anti-Monopoly party nominated Benjamin F. Butler, of Massachusetts, for President and adopted a platform calling for the regulation
of corporations by the government, a graduated income tax, direct election of U. S. senators and the prohibition of grants of public lands to
corporations. The National (Greenback) party also nominated Butler on
a similar platform but with the additional demand for the issuance of
greenbacks in place of national bank notes. The combined popular vote
of the two parties was 175,370.

the bounds of decency in their efforts to blacken the character of the opposing candidate. Cleveland was charged with being a libertine and habitual drunkard. It was shown that he was the father of an illegitimate child, a fact which Cleveland frankly admitted. On the other hand the opponents of Blaine once more brought forth evidence of his connection with the scandals of Grant's administration. The Mulligan letters were republished and sent all over the country. Vicious cartoons of both candidates appeared in the press. In this welter of vilification, political issues were quite forgotten. In point of fact the platforms of the two parties presented no real differences. Both dealt somewhat vaguely with the tariff and both were eloquent in the endorsement of civil service reform, while neither gave any evidence of a desire to grapple with the significant economic questions that the industrial development of the country had raised in abundance.

As the campaign neared an end Blaine attended a reception given by a delegation of clergymen in New York, in the course of which the Reverend Dr. Burchard referred to the Democrats as a party of "Rum, Romanism and Rebellion." Blaine's opponents immediately raised the cry that the Republicans had insulted the Irish Catholics who constituted a substantial number of voters in the city. There were many who afterward claimed that the indiscreet remark cost Blaine the electoral vote of New York and the presidency.

The election returns disclosed the extremely close division of the electorate between the two major parties. Each party polled slightly more than 48 per cent. of the popular vote, and the Democrats had a plurality of only 62,000 in a total vote of more than 10,000,000. A change of fewer than a thousand votes in New York would have given the election to Blaine.

For the first time since the Civil War a Democrat occupied the presidential office and, despite the dire forebodings of Republicans, the country survived and the people continued to pursue the even tenor of their ways. Even had Cleveland been inclined to try any novel experiments he would have been blocked by a Senate controlled by the Republicans, but Cleveland was naturally conservative, and he advocated no radical political or economic changes. The new President was beset with difficulties from the outset. On the one hand thousands of hungry and deserving Democrats who had long been denied the spoils of office clamored for jobs. On the other hand the reformers who had supported Cleveland in the election urged him to uphold the merit system. As might have been expected, the President failed to satisfy either group. He removed a sufficient number of Republicans from office to disappoint the advocates of civil service reform and not enough to satisfy the Democratic politicians. But on the whole the merit system did not suffer at his hands and by the close of his administration the number included in the classified service had been more than doubled. The Republican Senate tried to protect Republican office holders from removal by reviving the Tenure of Office Act. The President accepted the challenge and firmly disputed the right of the Senate to control the executive power of removal. In the end Cleveland prevailed and Congress repealed what remained of the Tenure of Office Act.[7]

Cleveland's administration was characterized by negative rather than positive accomplishment. In particular he made a vigorous use of the presidential veto, directed particularly against special pension legislation. Pensions had been granted to persons who had no reasonable claims to them. Men who had been dishonorably discharged from the army were on the pension rolls. One claimant had asked a pension because he had hurt his ankle while intending to enlist; another had fallen from a ladder and fractured his skull; still another asked for government largess because he had broken his leg

[7] The clause of the Tenure of Office Act that required reasons for suspensions was repealed in 1869.

many years after the war. In rejecting these absurd claims the President caustically remarked: "We are dealing with pensions, not with gratuities." In all, Cleveland vetoed over 200 bills of this character on the ground that they constituted unjustifiable raids on the public treasury. He also vetoed a general pension bill passed by Congress in 1887 which applied to all dependent veterans who had served three months or more in the Union forces. In his message returning the measure to Congress he criticized the loose language of the bill and pointed out that its effect would be to place thousands of men still in the prime of life on the pension rolls. Although the President's action in these matters was applauded by those who were interested in efficient business methods in governmental affairs it aroused the ire of the members of the Grand Army of the Republic who accused Cleveland of being in sympathy with the cause of the Rebellion.

Cleveland aroused further resentment among the super-patriots of the North by his approval of a suggestion made by the Adjutant General that certain Confederate flags in the possession of the war department should be restored to the states from which the regiments which bore them had come. The commander of the Grand Army denounced the suggestion as an outrage and an insult to those who had fought under the Stars and Stripes. So great was the clamor which ensued that Cleveland rescinded the order on the ground that it was the function of Congress to determine the disposition of the matter. In the interest of economy Cleveland also defeated an extravagant Rivers and Harbors bill by means of a pocket veto and returned to Congress without his approval a bill to refund to the Northern states direct taxes paid during the Civil War.

In the field of constructive legislation the outstanding measure of Cleveland's first administration was the Interstate Commerce Act, already discussed. Of significance, too, was the vigor displayed by Cleveland in recovering more than

80,000,000 acres of public lands illegally obtained by individuals and corporations. Two other important measures passed in this administration were the Presidential Succession Act (January, 1886) and the Electoral Count Act (February, 1887). The former provided that the succession to the presidency in case of death, resignation or incapacity should pass, after the Vice-President, to the members of the cabinet in the order of the creation of their offices. The latter act aimed to prevent a recurrence of a disputed election such as had happened in 1876. By its provisions Congress was required to accept a single electoral return from a state unless both houses rejected it. In case there should be more than one set of returns from a state and the two Houses could not agree as to which should be counted, Congress was required to accept the electoral vote certified by the executive of the state from which it came.

Finally, Cleveland gave offense to the strongly intrenched protected interests of the country by challenging the sacredness of the protective tariff. As the question of the tariff is treated in a later chapter it is sufficient at this point simply to note that Cleveland by his vigorous attacks succeeded in committing his party to the principle of tariff revision. The Republican leaders were quite willing to accept the challenge and boldly defended the protective principle, thus providing a clear-cut issue for the approaching presidential election.

REPUBLICANS AGAIN IN COMMAND, 1889-1893

The Democrats renominated Cleveland in 1888, albeit with somewhat wry faces on the part of the old-line politicians of the party. The platform endorsed the President's stand on the tariff question, and commended his efforts at reform. A bid for the Irish vote was made by expressing sympathy for the efforts of Ireland to obtain home rule, and the western farmer was enticed by the demand for admission of five western territories as states.

The Republicans adopted a platform that strongly upheld the principle of protection and advocated a reduction in internal revenue taxation if it should be deemed necessary to reduce the surplus in the treasury. It approved the aspiration of the western territories for statehood and, oddly enough, in view of later developments, it denounced the Democratic party for its efforts to demonetize silver. The selection of a candidate caused some difficulty. Blaine, who was traveling in Europe, declined to allow his name to go before the convention. The nomination finally went to Benjamin Harrison, of Indiana, grandson of a former president, himself a distinguished officer in the Civil War, and an ardent advocate of protection.[8]

The ensuing campaign was made up of about equal parts of the usual political buncombe and serious discussion of the outstanding tariff question. The Republicans accused the Democrats of advocating free trade, despite the fact that President Cleveland had distinctly repudiated any desire to make a wholesale reduction of tariff schedules. The Republican campaign chest was filled through a frank appeal to the protected interests. President Cleveland was charged by the Republicans with being a "British candidate." They stated, in all seriousness, that he had received British gold in appreciation of his efforts to reduce the tariff. An incident that occurred at the height of the campaign was hailed by the Republicans as evidence of the truth of their charge. A man who signed himself C. F. Murchison, and who pretended to be a naturalized Englishman, wrote to the British Minister at Washington, Sir Lionel Sackville-West, asking the Minister's advice as to how he should vote at the coming election. Not

[8] Minor parties participating in this election were the Prohibition party, the Union Labor and the United Labor parties, and the American party. The last-named group made a feeble attempt to revive Know-nothingism.

suspecting a trap, the British diplomat replied that he be, lieved that President Cleveland would be fair and reasonable in dealing with questions which might arise between the United States and Great Britain. The publication of this correspondence just before the election caused the Democrats much embarrassment because of the importance of the Irish vote. The indiscretion of the Minister led President Cleveland to demand his recall, and when the British authorities declined to regard the incident as of sufficient importance to warrant such action the President informed the British government that Sackville-West was *persona non grata* and he was given his passports.

The election returns indicated that the campaign of education had not resulted in any material change in the opinions of the electorate. Although Harrison carried enough states by small pluralities to give him 233 electoral votes to 168 for Cleveland, the Democrats had a popular vote of nearly 100,000 more than that cast for the Republican ticket.

Harrison lacked those qualities which make for popularity. He was a cultured gentleman, whose personal integrity was unquestioned, but his manner was so reserved that it gave rise to the remark that "Harrison sweats ice water." He conceived the duties of the President to be confined literally to those enumerated in the Constitution. It was his view that the President should enforce legislation enacted by Congress rather than attempt to impose upon that body his own ideas. Party policies during Harrison's administration were determined by such forceful Congressional leaders as Speaker Reed in the House and Senators Sherman and Quay in the Senate.

In the matter of the civil service Harrison's record was uneven. In the unclassified service patronage was dispensed by the professional politicians without let or hindrance. On the other hand he gratified the supporters of civil service reform by appointing Theodore Roosevelt to the civil service commission, and, toward the end of his administration, he extended the application of the merit system, perhaps not unmindful of the fact that the political signs were none too favorable for Republican success in the approaching election.

In the Congressional elections of 1888 the Republicans returned 166 members, and the Democrats 159. This narrow majority of Republicans made it possible for the Democrats, under the existing rules of the House, to obstruct the work of the House. By the simple expedient of refusing to answer to their names when the roll was called they could claim the lack of a quorum, whenever a few Republicans failed to attend. Speaker Reed, against the vehement protests of the Democrats, checked this practice by noting such Democrats as were present in the House and ordering the clerk to record them as present. The Speaker took the position that it was the business of the majority to legislate and that a minority should not be enabled to defeat the will of the majority. In furtherance of the views of the Speaker the rules committee presented two important modifications of the rules of the House. The first empowered the Speaker to refuse to entertain dilatory motions, made simply for the purpose of obstructing action. The second allowed the Speaker to count members actually present for the purpose of determining a quorum. Reed's somewhat arbitrary methods of dealing with the members of the House earned for him the sobriquet of "Czar."

Of the important legislation of the Harrison administration the McKinley Tariff Act, the Sherman Silver Purchase Act and the Sherman Anti-Trust Law are considered in other chapters. Other measures of importance were a dependent pension bill, similar to the one Cleveland had vetoed, and a bill for refunding the direct taxes paid by the states during the Civil War, another measure which Cleveland had vetoed. The Congressional elections of 1890, which resulted in a landslide for the Democrats, ended all constructive legislation by the Republicans during the last two years of Harrison's administration.

THE RETURN OF THE DEMOCRATS, 1893-1897

The game of party see-saw brought the Democrats once more into control of the national administration as a result of the election of 1892.

Although Harrison had aroused no enthusiasm among the rank and file of his party he had done nothing which would seem to justify the leaders in denying him a renomination. A belated effort of Blaine's friends to arouse interest in his candidacy failed and Harrison was renominated on the first ballot. As a matter of course the platform endorsed in emphatic terms the principle of the protective tariff.

During Harrison's administration ex-President Cleveland had been quietly practicing law in New York, but he managed to keep in the public eye by means of frequent addresses made before public gatherings. At one such meeting called by the Reform Club in New York he took occasion in a letter sent to the chairman, due to his inability to attend, to express his views on the question of free coinage of silver. Politicians of both parties had been extremely cautious about committing themselves on this controversial question for fear of alienating the strong free-silver sentiment in the West and South. But Cleveland with his usual courage stated his belief that the attempt to establish free coinage was "dangerous and reckless." Although the politicians freely predicted that this statement would cost him the nomination, apparently many persons welcomed the blunt honesty of Cleveland as a refreshing contrast to the "pussyfooting" of the average politician. In any event Cleveland was nominated on the first ballot despite the determined opposition of the Democratic organization of his own state, then dominated by David B. Hill.

After some hesitation the Democrats incorporated in their platform a ringing denunciation of the protective tariff as "a fraud" and "a robbery of the great majority of the American people for the benefit of the few," and declared it "a fundamental principle of the Democratic party that the Federal Government has no constitutional power to impose and collect tariff duties except for the purpose of revenue only." Cleveland in his letter of acceptance, however, somewhat modified this unequivocal declaration by the statement that "we contemplate a fair and careful distribution of necessary tariff burdens rather than a precipitation of free trade." On the question of the currency the platforms of the two parties were virtually indistinguishable. Both favored the maintenance of the parity of gold and silver by "appropriate legislation." Both platforms, too, made the customary gesture of sympathy for Ireland and for the oppressed Jews of Russia.

The campaign lacked dramatic interest. Both candidates were well known and neither was calculated to arouse much popular enthusiasm. The outbreak of the strike in the Carnegie steel works at Homestead in the midst of the campaign was used effectively by Democratic orators. They pointed out that the reduction of wages in this highly protected industry made but a hollow mockery of the Republican pretension that the tariff was a benefit to American labor.

The result of the election was a sweeping victory for the Democrats. They carried such important Northern states as New York, New Jersey, Connecticut and Indiana, in addition to California, Illinois and Wisconsin, which with the "solid South," gave Cleveland 277 electoral votes to 145 for Harrison and 22 for Weaver, the Populist candidate. In the popular vote the Democrats had a plurality of 380,000.

Undoubtedly the most significant aspect of the election of 1892 was the showing made by the Populist party. Here was a party that made its appeal to the electorate on the basis of a realistic dealing with some of the significant social and economic questions of the day. In no uncertain terms the platform declared that "we have witnessed for more than a quarter of a century the struggles of the two great political parties for power and plunder, while grievous wrongs have been inflicted upon the suffering people. We charge that the controlling influences dominating both these parties have permitted the existing dreadful conditions to develop without serious effort to prevent or restrain them. Neither do they now promise us any substantial reform. They have agreed together to ignore in the campaign every issue but one. They propose to drown the outcries of a plundered people with the uproar of a sham battle over the tariff, so that capitalists, corporations, national banks, rings, trusts, watered stocks, the demonetization of silver, and the oppression of the usurers may all be lost sight of. They propose to sacrifice our homes, lives, and children on the altar of mammon; to destroy the multitude in order to secure corruption funds from the millionaires." With such a challenge the Populists were able to rally to their standard more than a million votes and win 22 votes in the electoral college.[9] Here was clearly a warning to both of the old parties that there was an ominous spirit of protest spreading over the country which could not be satisfied by ambiguous and insincere pronouncements of party platforms, and that the time was fast approaching when both parties would have to face real issues which the events of the past two decades had been steadily pushing to the front.

In 1893 the Democrats, for the first time since the administration of President Buchanan, controlled the executive and both branches of the legislature, but on the two major questions confronting the administration President Cleveland led a divided party. On the question of the currency

[9] In addition to the Populist party the radical element in this election was represented by the Socialist Labor party, which polled an insignificant vote.

a considerable number of Democratic Senators and Representatives from the South and West bitterly opposed the President's attitude on the silver question, while on the tariff issue there were enough Democratic Congressmen favorable to protection to defeat, in large measure, the efforts of the President to redeem the pledge given in the party platform to revise the tariff downward.

To add to Cleveland's difficulties the Republicans had turned over to him a national treasury virtually empty, a condition in part due to the extravagant expenditures of Harrison's administration. Then, too, at the outset of his administration, there came a financial panic which brought in its train business depression, unemployment, and widespread labor disorders. To all these difficulties were added serious international problems which threatened to disturb the peaceful relations between this country and Great Britain.

Such a formidable list of trying problems was calculated to test the qualities of leadership of even the ablest statesman. And Cleveland, with all his rugged honesty, lacked certain characteristics necessary for successful political leadership. Reaching his conclusions on important questions as a result of patient study, he was prepared to maintain his position, reckless of consequences. A man of stubborn temperament, he seemed unable to understand or appreciate the point of view of those who differed with him. Throughout his political career he had refused to submit to the dictation of leaders of his party, and the evidence of popular confidence in him whenever he was a candidate for office tended to strengthen his belief in the correctness of his own judgments. Although Cleveland probably recognized the reality of the grievances of which Western farmers and Eastern workmen were complaining, he was such a firm believer in the theory of strict construction that he was unwilling to sanction novel constitutional experiments, even to remedy admitted social wrongs.

For the first two years of his second administration Cleveland struggled doggedly to guide the ship of state through extremely troubled waters. The Congressional elections of 1894 brought disaster to the Democrats, resulting in the control of both houses of Congress passing to the Republicans. During the remaining two years of his term the President pursued his way, unmoved by the clamor raised by his opponents, apparently content to leave to the judgment of posterity the justification of his course. When he retired from office his party had repudiated his leadership to follow a new prophet from the West.

For twenty years the political pendulum had swung first to the Republican and then to the Democratic side. And throughout this period of oscillating control of the machinery of government, professional politics and politicians dominated the scene. In both parties there appeared an unwillingness to face frankly significant issues. Party platforms were models of evasion and the characterization once made of the two major parties as two bottles, of the same size and shape, with different labels—and both empty, seems more than a little apt. But beneath the surface there were stirring forces that would no longer tolerate this political make-believe and before the century closed the politicians of both parties, as well as the powerful economic groups that had guided their destinies, realized the necessity of coming to grips with the vital economic and social problems of the day. The opening of the new century marked the dawn of a new era.

BIBLIOGRAPHICAL NOTE

For a good general treatment of political parties and issues consult, D. R. Dewey, *National Problems* (1907), and E. E. Sparks, *National Development* (1907). For the period after 1885 H. T. Peck, *Twenty Years of the Republic* (1906) is excellent. Party platforms and the statistics of elections can be found in E. Stanwood, *History of the Presidency* (1898). Consult also H. R. Bruce, *American Parties and Politics* (1917) ; E. M. Sait, *American Parties and Elections* (1927).

Civil service reform is discussed by C. R. Fish, *The Civil Service and the Patronage* (1905) ; and H. C. Thomas, *The Return of the Democratic Party to Power in 1884* (1919). See also S. P. Orth, *The Boss and the Machine* (1919) ; H. J. Ford, *The Cleveland Era* (1919). A discussion of Speaker Reed's domination of the House is found in M. P. Follett, *The Speaker of the House of Representatives* (1896), and D. S. Alexander, *History of the Procedure of the House of Representatives* (1916).

For biographical accounts of the leading statesmen of the period consult T. C. Smith, *The Life and Letters of James A. Garfield* (1925) ; E. Stanwood, *James G. Blaine* (1905) ; L. A. Coolidge, *Old Fashioned Senator, O. H. Platt, of Connecticut* (1910) ; T. E. Burton, *John Sherman* (1906) ; A. R. Conkling, *Life and Letters of Roscoe Conkling* (1889) ; J. L. Whittle, *Grover Cleveland* (1896) ; R. McElroy, *Grover Cleveland, the Man and Statesman* (1923) ; S. W. McCall, *The Life of Thomas B. Reed* (1914) ; G. F. Hoar, *Autobiography of Seventy Years* (1903).

CHAPTER 7

FINANCE AND CURRENCY PROBLEMS, 1876-1896

Out of the far-reaching economic changes described in the preceding chapters came a number of perplexing financial and monetary problems. In the handling of these problems political expediency and sectional interests were more in evidence than sound financial and economic considerations.

As has been noted before, the high tariff rates imposed during the Civil War were not repealed in the process of post-war financial adjustment. Neither of the major political parties seemed inclined at first to take any definite stand on the question of the maintenance of a protective tariff as a permanent fiscal and economic policy. In the absence of any aggressive action by either party the protected interests were able to retain, for nearly twenty years, with only slight reductions, the advantageous rates that the war tariffs imposed.

In fact, when the first earnest attempt at the revision of the war tariffs was undertaken, in 1883, it was not owing simply to a consideration of the justice or injustice of the existing duties but rather because the operation of the tariff had resulted in piling up an embarrassing surplus in the Federal treasury. With the return of business prosperity following the depression caused by the panic of 1873, foreign imports increased greatly and custom receipts grew proportionately. The treasury surplus, which had stood at $10,-000,000 in 1870, reached $68,000,000 in 1880, and $145,-000,000 in 1882. During the fiscal years from 1882 to 1885

156

the excess of receipts over expenditures amounted to $446,-000,000.

A large surplus, if retained in the treasury, would seriously interfere with legitimate business enterprises by the withdrawal of this money from circulation. Furthermore, the presence of these large unused funds in the treasury was a constant temptation to extravagance on the part of Congress. Some portion of the surplus could be and was used to redeem the national debt. However, many of the outstanding bonds did not fall due for some years and in applying the surplus to the retirement of these bonds the government was obliged to buy them in the open market at a premium above their par value. Moreover a further redemption of the bonds would have necessitated a modification of the national banking act for it was upon these bonds that the national bank notes rested as security. The two main expedients resorted to by Congress in disposing of the surplus were appropriations for pensions and for internal improvements. By various measures the amount appropriated for pensions increased from $27,-000,000 in 1878 to $56,000,000 in 1880. In the case of internal improvements the chief expenditures were for the improvement of rivers and harbors. In 1870 such appropriations totaled $4,000,000; in 1880 nearly $9,000,000; and in 1882 Congress, in a particularly generous mood, passed a rivers and harbors bill carrying a total of more than $18,-000,000. Among the items included in this measure were funds for improving such waterways as the Popinowut, the Choptank, the Scuppernong, the Waccamaw, the Yallabusha, and the Cheesequake. As one member of Congress facetiously remarked, the only way to make these rivers navigable was to pave them.

Even with such generous appropriations the surplus still stood at $140,000,000. Further retirement of government bonds or the legal tender greenbacks would result in a reduction of the circulating medium. There remained therefore only one other method of preventing the accumulation of unnecessary funds in the treasury, namely, by reducing tariff duties, which were the chief source of such revenue. But by this time the powerful protected interests had made their influence felt in both of the major parties. In 1884 the Republicans came out boldly in favor of the protective principle, while the Democrats rather cautiously recommended such reduction as "would not injure any domestic industry but rather promote their healthy growth."

In 1882 Congress had provided for a tariff commission, which recommended a reduction of tariff duties ranging from 20 to 50 per cent. But the protected interests immediately descended upon Congress and the result was a tariff measure passed in 1883 which made some slight reductions but which also raised others so that the general level remained virtually unchanged. A bill calling for a "horizontal" reduction of 20 per cent. in tariff rates, was introduced into the House, only to meet defeat when a group of protectionist Democrats, under the leadership of Samuel J. Randall of Pennsylvania, voted with the Republicans against the measure.

In his messages to Congress in 1885 and 1886 President Cleveland pointed to the necessity for a reduction of government revenue, and in urging a revision of the tariff schedules he questioned whether the farmers and laborers of the country were benefited by the protective system. His recommendations brought no response from Congress and in 1887 he determined to bring the issue squarely before the country by devoting his entire message to Congress to a discussion of revenue reform.

In this famous document Cleveland insisted that it was indefensible for the government to collect in taxes much greater sums than were needed for government expenditures. He directed attention again to the danger of a large unused treasury surplus in encouraging extravagance and in curtailing the amount of money in circulation. Turning to remedies,

he indicated the difficulty of using the surplus in making a
further reduction of the public debt and insisted that the only
logical thing to do was to reduce the revenue by revising
the tariff. He then discussed the effects of tariffs in raising
the price of commodities and denounced the existing tariff as
"vicious, illegal, and inequitable." At the same time he insisted that he was not advocating free trade, and that the
question was practical and not academic. As he put it, in his
memorable phrase, "It is a *condition* which confronts us,
not a *theory.*"

Despite his attempt to forestall the charge that he was
advocating an assault upon the principle of the protective
tariff, the Republican press immediately hailed the message
as a free trade document. Said the New York *Sun,* "The
most striking and interesting part of the message was devoted
to that sort of argument which a free-trade text-book of
political economy would follow"; and the Philadelphia *Press*
stated, "A thousand thanks are due to him for his bold,
manly, and unequivocal avowal of his extreme free-trade
purposes."

Urged on by the vigorous leadership of the President, the
Democrats in Congress, somewhat reluctantly, took up the
question of tariff revision. A bill was introduced into the
House by Roger Q. Mills, the chairman of the Ways and
Means Committee, providing for a thoroughgoing revision
of substantially all the tariff schedules. The bill was forced
through the House by party pressure but the Republican
Senate substituted a bill of its own and tariff legislation in
this Congress was defeated.

The issue was then placed before the country in the election of 1888. The Democrats renominated Cleveland on a
platform that endorsed his stand on the tariff, while the Republicans put forward Benjamin Harrison with a ringing
reaffirmation of the principle of protection. The ensuing campaign centered largely on the tariff issue, but the resulting

election gave no evidence that popular sentiment was strongly committed one way or the other for, while the Republicans succeeded in electing their candidate the Democrats had the larger popular vote.

Accepting the somewhat dubious verdict of the election as a mandate to maintain the protective principle, the Republicans as soon as they were in possession of all branches of the government proceeded to the framing of a new tariff measure. In preparing the schedules the protected interests were given a free hand, while a sop was thrown to the western farmers by raising the duties on certain agricultural products. By removing the duty on raw sugar [1] and by raising some schedules so high as to make foreign imports virtually impossible, it was hoped that the troublesome surplus in the treasury would be materially reduced. Owing largely to the insistence of Blaine, then Secretary of State, there was incorporated in the bill a provision for "reciprocity." But it was reciprocity of a novel sort. Instead of providing for the usual reciprocal reduction of rates the President was empowered to raise the rates on commodities coming from countries that placed "unreasonable or unjust" tariff duties on American commodities. In general the completed measure, bearing the name of its sponsor, Representative William McKinley, raised the tariff to the highest point yet reached in the course of tariff legislation.

Scarcely had the McKinley Act been placed upon the statute books when the retail prices of a large number of commodities were sharply raised. Opponents of the tariff were quick to charge that this increase in the cost of living was due to the extortionate rates of the new tariff bill. Apparently the people took this view, for in the congressional elections in the fall in 1890 the Republicans suffered a stinging defeat.

---

[1] A bounty of two cents a pound, the amount of the former duty, was given to producers of beet and cane sugar in the United States.

When the new House met in December, 1891, with its overwhelming Democratic majority, several measures were passed providing for a material reduction of the rates of the McKinley Act but, as the Republicans retained control of the Senate, it was impossible to enact these measures into law. It was the obvious intention of the Democrats to keep the tariff issue before the country in anticipation of the presidential election of 1892.

When President Cleveland returned to office as a result of the election of 1892 the financial condition of the country was in striking contrast to that which had prevailed in his first term. By the close of the Harrison administration the treasury surplus had been reduced to the vanishing point, as a result of greatly increased appropriations for pensions, of decreased imports due to business depression, and of the loss of revenue due to the repeal of the sugar duty and the bounty paid to domestic sugar producers. Clearly the argument of a plethoric treasury which President Cleveland had formerly urged as a reason for reducing the tariff could not now be presented. Nevertheless, when in 1893 the Democrats obtained control of both houses of Congress, President Cleveland called upon his party to redeem the pledge made in the election of 1892 to reduce the tariff. As a result the so-called Wilson Bill was introduced in the House. It was in no sense a radical measure. It extended somewhat the free list and made reductions in the prohibitive rates of the McKinley Act, but made no general onslaught upon the protective duties. Nevertheless the beneficiaries of the tariff were up in arms and they concentrated their efforts upon the Senate when the measure reached that body. These efforts were highly successful, for when the bill finally passed the Senate it bore slight resemblance to the measure that came from the House. Under the expert guidance of Senator Gorman, of Maryland, the bill was amended so as to restore many of the rates that the House had reduced and, despite the efforts of the President to preserve the principles of the original bill, the Senate stood firm with the result that the measure which was finally agreed upon by both houses was only slightly less protectionist than the McKinley Act. Cleveland bitterly denounced the action of Democratic Senators as "party perfidy and party dishonor" and further expressed his disapproval by declining to sign the bill when it came before him, allowing it to become a law without his signature.

The turn of the political wheel brought the Republicans once more into power as a result of the election of 1896. While the tariff question had played little or no part in this election the Republicans once more assumed that the country had endorsed their tariff policy. Impatient to repair what little damage had been done by the Wilson-Gorman Act to the protected interests, President McKinley within two weeks after he had assumed office called Congress in special session to frame a new tariff measure. With assurance the forces of protection, now in undisputed control of the Republican party, wrote the new Dingley Law, which raised the average rates even higher than those of the McKinley Act. Protectionism was now triumphant, and with the Democratic party demoralized no serious challenge to the dominance of the protective principle was made for more than a decade.

Twenty years of tariff agitation thus ended with the Republican party definitely committed to high protection, principally to the advantage of the large industrial interests, while the Democratic party, at least in theory, took its stand in support of a tariff for revenue only.

THE INCOME TAX LAW OF 1894

In connection with the Democratic tariff of 1894 there was passed a measure providing for an income tax of 2 per cent. on incomes of $4,000 or over. Two factors contributed to the enactment of this law. First, the desire to provide for the estimated loss of revenue caused by the reduction of the tariff and second, to satisfy the Populist members of Congress whose votes were needed and who insisted that a part of the burden of taxes should be shifted from commodities consumed by the poor to the incomes of the wealthy. While the measure was before Congress the defenders of property interests inveighed against the proposal as class legislation. Senator Hill denounced it as "paternalistic, discriminating, inquisitorial, and populistic" and Senator Sherman declared, "In a republic like ours, where all men are equal, this attempt to array the rich against the poor, or the poor against the rich, is socialism, communism, devilism."

Defeated in the halls of Congress the opponents of the income tax turned to the courts. Some of the most eminent legal talent in the country, headed by Joseph H. Choate, were engaged to persuade the Supreme Court that the law was unconstitutional. This was a difficult task, for the Court had held as recently as 1870 that an income tax was not a direct tax and therefore did not violate the constitutional provision that direct taxes must be apportioned among the states according to population. Nevertheless Choate undertook to convince the Court that the law menaced our whole constitutional structure. He warned the judges that this measure was but the beginning of a "communistic march," which threatened the sanctity of private property, and urged the judges not to be influenced by popular clamor in favor of the law. This impassioned appeal evidently affected some of the judges, for Justice Field observed: "The present assault upon capital is but the beginning. It will be but the stepping stone to others larger and more sweeping till our political conditions will become a war of the poor against the rich; a war growing in intensity and bitterness." However the Court divided four to four, one justice being ill, on the main issue of the constitutionality of the law. Such a result aroused bitter disappointment in the conservative circles. Said the

New York *Sun,* "Twice in great national crises the Supreme Court of the United States has failed to meet the expectations of the people or to justify its existence as the ultimate tribunal of right and law. In both instances the potent consideration has been neither right nor law, but the supposed demands of political expediency. . . . Yesterday the failure of the Supreme Court to decide the main question of constitutionality submitted to it was brought about by political considerations. It was not Democracy against Republicanism as before, but Populism and Clevelandism against Democracy, and the vote was four to four."

But those who were bent upon overturning the law did not despair. The Supreme Court consented to a rehearsing of the case and, while Justice Jackson who had not participated in the previous decision gave his vote in favor of the constitutionality of the law, one of the other judges changed his opinion and by a vote of five to four the essential parts of the income tax law were declared null and void.

The joy of the conservatives was now quite as striking as had been their gloom after the first decision. Now the *Sun,* which had so recently held doubts whether the Court could "justify its existence as the ultimate tribunal of right and law" apparently had these doubts dispelled for it declared: "There is a safe future for the national system under which we were all born and have lived and prospered according to individual capacity. The wave of socialistic revolution has gone far, but it breaks at the foot of the ultimate bulwark set up for protection of our liberties. Five to four the Court stands like a rock."

But among liberals and radicals the decision appeared in quite a different light. By them the Court was denounced for having surrendered to the power of wealth and it is difficult to avoid the conclusion today that, whatever the merits of the decision may be, it was not based wholly on abstract constitutional interpretation but was influenced by the economic views of the judges. One of the justices who dissented from the majority stated that the decision "gives certain kinds of property a position of favoritism and advantage inconsistent with the fundamental principles of our social organism," while another justice even more vigorously declared that "it is the first step toward the submergence of the liberties of the people in a sordid despotism of wealth."

CURRENCY PROBLEM

Of the problems thrown up in profusion by the industrial revolution none was more perplexing and none stirred so deeply class and sectional feeling as those which involved the determination of the monetary system of the country. There is nothing strange about this. From the early colonial days onward there were periodic struggles between the debtor and property-less classes on the one hand and on the other, those whose incomes were derived from fixed investments, over the question of the amount and character of money in circulation. The former groups constantly urged a plenteous supply of money, for this meant increased prices and low interest rates; while the latter favored a currency restricted in volume and on a sound basis which would assure the payment of interest and principal in money equal in value to that which had been loaned or possibly, in case the amount of money in circulation did not keep pace with the expansion of business, in money having an enhanced purchasing power.

In a previous chapter we have discussed one of these struggles over the monetary system in connection with the process of financial readjustment at the close of the Civil War. The advocates of cheap money on this occasion took their stand in favor of retaining and expanding the system of fiat currency which had been resorted to in the exigencies of the war. But in this effort they were only partially successful, for while the greenbacks were retained as a part of the circulating medium, Congress declined to expand the amount of fiat money. This victory of the so-called "Wall Street" interests aroused resentment among the agrarian classes, particularly in the South and West. However, at the very moment that the advocates of an expanding currency lost their battle for the greenbacks, circumstances seemed to offer an opportunity of accomplishing their desire for an expanded currency in another direction, namely by a resumption of the free coinage of silver.

Shortly after the formation of the national government, Congress had provided for the coinage of both gold and silver into dollars at a fixed ratio. The fixing of such a ratio, however, involved great, if not insurmountable, difficulties. Gold and silver are commodities used in industry as well as for currency and, like other commodities, such as wheat and corn, their market value is fixed by the law of supply and demand. If the supply of one of the precious metals increases faster than that of the other, or if the demand for one metal grows out of proportion to that for the other, the scarcer metal or the one in greater demand will command a higher relative market value. Hence any fixed ratio of value between the two metals is certain to differ, in a comparatively short time, from the market value. In consequence the legal ratio sooner or later undervalued one of the metals.

Thus in 1792 the Federal Government fixed the ratio for coinage purposes between gold and silver at 15 to 1, that is 15 ounces of silver were to be regarded as equivalent to one ounce of gold. But within a short time it was found that this ratio undervalued gold, and therefore the owners of gold would not present it for coinage at that ratio. Then Congress in 1834 changed the ratio to 16 to 1. Now the situation was reversed. Silver was undervalued and was not presented for coinage. This condition continued for nearly forty years and Congress in 1873, in connection with a revision of the coinage laws, omitted the silver dollar from the list of coins, apparently because it had not been coined for so many years.

AVERAGE MARKET RATIO OF SILVER TO GOLD

Year	Ratio	Year	Ratio	Year	Ratio	Year	Ratio
1793	15.00	1819	15.33	1845	15.92	1871	15.57
1794	15.37	1820	15.62	1846	15.90	1872	15.63
1795	15.55	1821	15.95	1847	15.80	1873	15.92
1796	15.65	1822	15.80	1848	15.85	1874	16.17
1797	15.41	1823	15.84	1849	15.78	1875	16.59
1798	15.59	1824	15.82	1850	15.70	1876	17.88
1799	15.74	1825	15.70	1851	15.46	1877	17.22
1800	15.68	1826	15.76	1852	15.59	1878	17.94
1801	15.46	1827	15.74	1853	15.33	1879	18.40
1802	15.26	1828	15.78	1854	15.33	1880	18.05
1803	15.41	1829	15.78	1855	15.38	1881	18.16
1804	15.41	1830	15.82	1856	15.38	1882	18.19
1805	15.79	1831	15.72	1857	15.27	1883	18.64
1806	15.52	1832	15.73	1858	15.38	1884	18.57
1807	15.43	1833	15.93	1859	15.19	1885	19.41
1808	16.08	1834	15.73	1860	15.29	1886	20.78
1809	15.96	1835	15.80	1861	15.50	1887	21.13
1810	15.77	1836	15.72	1862	15.35	1888	21.99
1811	15.53	1837	15.83	1863	15.37	1889	22.09
1812	16.11	1838	15.85	1864	15.37	1890	19.76
1813	16.25	1839	15.62	1865	15.44	1891	20.92
1814	15.04	1840	15.62	1866	15.43	1892	23.72
1815	15.26	1841	15.70	1867	15.57	1893	26.49
1816	15.28	1842	15.87	1868	15.59	1894	32.56
1817	15.11	1843	15.93	1869	15.60	1895*	30.73
1818	15.35	1844	15.85	1870	15.57		

* July 1. From White, Money and Banking.

Just at this juncture a combination of circumstances radically changed the relative value of gold and silver. In the first place the opening of several new silver mines in Nevada greatly increased the amount of silver on the market. At about the same time several European countries either stopped entirely the coinage of silver or limited the amount coined. Thus a large increase in supply, coupled with a decrease in demand, brought an inevitable decline in the market price of silver. By 1876 silver sold in the market at the ratio of 17 to 1.

The same economic and social classes that had supported the greenback movement now started the agitation for the resumption of free coinage of silver. Their ranks were reënforced by a small but wealthy group of silver mine owners. It was freely charged that the demonetization of silver, the "Crime of 1873," was a sinister move on the part of the wealthy classes of the East to limit the amount of money in circulation in order to depress prices of commodities, lower wages, and increase interest rates. To add to the forces of discontent the business depression that followed the panic of 1873 brought widespread unemployment among the laboring classes in the industrial centers and great suffering to the debt-ridden farmers of the West. In their search for relief from distress these discontented groups quite generally grasped at the elusive remedy of cheap money. If the government would enlarge the volume of circulating medium by resuming the coinage of silver they reasoned that the prices of farm products would be increased, better wages would be paid to labor, and it would be easier to obtain money to pay their debts.

It was inevitable that this discontent should affect the politicians in Congress. In 1875 a Congressional committee was appointed to study the currency situation and make such recommendations as it should deem wise to meet the existing conditions. The report that was submitted contained an elaborate review of the history of bi-metallism but the members of the committee were unable to agree upon any remedy for the existing situation. The leaders of both the major political parties approached the problem with great caution, for there were free-silver advocates in both parties and the issue threatened to split the parties much as slavery had done before the Civil War.

In 1877 the champions of free silver assumed the aggressive, and under the leadership of Richard P. Bland, a Democratic representative from Missouri, a bill was passed in the

House providing for the resumption of the unlimited coinage of silver dollars at the ratio of approximately 16 to 1. When the measure reached the Senate, however, an amendment was introduced by Senator Allison, of Iowa, which struck out the provision for unlimited coinage, and substituted a clause which required the Secretary of the Treasury to purchase not less than two million and not more than four million dollars' worth of silver each month to be coined into silver dollars which were to be made legal tender. The silver advocates in the House reluctantly accepted this compromise. The vote on the bill indicated that it was in no sense a party measure for the affirmative votes were almost equally divided between Republicans and Democrats. President Hayes vetoed the Bland-Allison Act, contending that it would be a breach of faith for the government to pay its obligations in depreciated currency. The silver interests, however, were able to muster sufficient strength in Congress to repass the bill over the presidential veto.

The next move on the part of the inflationists was to stop the retirement of the greenbacks which had been provided for in the Resumption Act of 1875. They succeeded, as we have seen, in getting through Congress a bill which prohibited the treasury department from retiring any more of the paper notes. A further effort to postpone the resumption of specie payments beyond the date agreed upon January 1, 1879, failed. As the date for resumption approached, the depreciated greenbacks moved steadily nearer and nearer to par, thus adding a further grievance to the debtor classes. Debts that had been contracted in paper money worth sixty or seventy cents in gold now had to be repaid in paper dollars worth nearly one hundred cents. Debtors pointed out, with considerable force, that the creditor class, which had so loudly denounced the proposal to have debts paid in money worth less than that in which the debts had been contracted, saw no objection to having those same debts repaid in money worth more than that which the debtors had borrowed.

Neither the silver interests nor the debtor classes obtained from the Bland-Allison Act the relief that they had expected. It is true the effect of the law was to add about $31,000,000 annually to the circulating medium but this increase was partially offset by the retirement of national bank notes, through the reduction of the bonded indebtedness upon which these notes were based. In the decade between 1880 and 1890 the amount of national bank notes in circulation declined more than $173,000,000. Nor did the purchase of silver by the government stop the decline of the market price of the metal. The market value of the silver in a dollar, which was ninety-three cents in 1878, had fallen to about seventy cents in 1889. To add to the woes of the western farmer the prices of agricultural commodities during the eighties suffered a calamitous decline. Corn, which sold for 63 cents a bushel in 1881, was selling in 1890 for 28 cents.

Once again the distressed farmers turned to Congress for relief. Their influence in this body had been materially strengthened by the admission of six new Western states to the Union in 1889-1890. Still clinging to the belief that the remedy for their ills was to be found in the further expansion of the currency, they carried through Congress in July, 1890, the Sherman Silver Purchase Act.[2] By the terms of this measure the treasury department was required to purchase each month 4,500,000 ounces of silver, which was about twice the amount which had been purchased under the Bland-Allison Act. In payment for the silver the treasury was authorized to issue treasury notes which were made a full legal tender and which were redeemable in gold or silver at the option of the government. Curiously enough, in view of the later position of the two parties on the silver issue, the Sherman Act passed both houses by a strictly party vote, all

[2] The Senate had passed a free-coinage bill, in 1890, which was defeated in the House. The Sherman Act was adopted as a compromise.

of the Republicans supported it while all of the Democrats opposed it. This does not mean that the Democratic party was opposed to cheap money. On the contrary many Democrats voted against the measure because they felt that it did not go far enough in expanding the currency. On the other hand, many conservative Republicans supported the bill because they feared that, if it failed, a more radical measure might be passed. They also felt that, unless something was done for silver the Western members of their party in Congress would retaliate by defeating the McKinley Tariff Bill then before Congress.

Despite the fact that the amount of silver to be purchased under the terms of the Sherman Law was equivalent to nearly the total silver production of the country at the time, the market value of silver continued to decline. In 1890 the ratio of silver to gold was approximately 20 to 1, in 1891 it fell to 21 to 1, and in 1893 to 26 to 1. This meant that the actual bullion value of the silver in a silver dollar in 1893 was about sixty cents. According to a principle known as Gresham's law, if there are two kinds of money of the same face value but of different intrinsic value in circulation at the same time the money having the lesser intrinsic value will drive the money having the greater intrinsic value from circulation. Thus, with the silver dollar in 1893 being worth only sixty cents, while the gold dollar was worth one hundred cents, people hoarded gold and it was evident that within a very short time gold would disappear from circulation entirely.

The monetary situation of the country had reached an acute stage when President Cleveland entered upon his second term in the spring of 1893. As we have seen, only a small fraction of the greenbacks had been presented for redemption when specie payment was resumed in 1879. For the future redemption of the $346,000,000 in these notes which remained in circulation the treasury had maintained a fund known as the gold reserve. By custom this fund had been kept at $100,000,000. In addition to the greenbacks there were about $150,000,000 in treasury notes which had been issued for the purchase of the silver under the provisions of the Sherman Act. Thus there were nearly $500,000,-000 of fiat paper money in circulation which the government was pledged to redeem in coin. Fearing that the government might redeem these paper notes in depreciated silver instead of gold many persons presented the notes and demanded payment in gold.

During his first term President Cleveland had stated his position on the silver question with characteristic boldness. He had urged Congress to repeal the Bland-Allison Act and had pronounced the free silver agitation as "dangerous and reckless." With his return to office in 1893 he promptly summoned Congress in special session and urged upon them the necessity for the immediate repeal of the Sherman Silver Purchase Act. In the House the repeal was voted without delay, but in the Senate the silver forces rallied and by filibustering were able to delay the final vote until the end of October. Finally the repeal was passed, but unlike the vote that had passed the measure it was not along party lines. Half the Democratic Senators refused to accept the advice of the President and voted against the repeal and they were joined by twelve Republicans and three Populists. Cleveland's insistence upon the repeal of the Sherman Law so embittered many Democratic members of Congress that they retaliated by refusing to follow the advice of the President in regard to the revision of the tariff.[3]

While the repeal of the Sherman Law stopped the flow of silver into the treasury, it did not serve immediately to restore confidence in the financial stability of the government. Moreover, the disastrous industrial crisis which came at this time greatly enhanced the feeling of uneasiness in the country. As a consequence there began a rush to hoard gold.

[3] See p. 161.

Thousands of persons presented the greenbacks and treasury notes for redemption at the treasury. This of course caused a rapid depletion of the $100,000,000 gold reserve. By the close of 1893 the reserve had been reduced to less than $70,000,000.

President Cleveland was convinced that the financial credit of the government could be maintained only by continuing gold payments, and in order to replenish the depleted fund of gold in the treasury he decided to sell government bonds, and $50,000,000 of such bonds were issued. The relief to the treasury, however, was only temporary, for many persons presented the greenbacks and treasury notes to the treasury to obtain the gold for the purchase of the bonds. A further issue of $50,000,000 in bonds in November, 1894, brought similar results. Obviously here was a vicious circle; gold drawn into the treasury from the sale of bonds was almost immediately withdrawn by bankers in exchange for government notes.

In desperation President Cleveland summoned Mr. J. P. Morgan to Washington and arranged with him for the formation of a financial syndicate which agreed to purchase $65,000,000 of government bonds for gold, at least one-half of the metal to be obtained from abroad. At the same time the bankers agreed to use their influence to prevent further withdrawals of gold from the treasury. By this expedient the gold reserve was restored, but it brought down upon the head of Cleveland bitter denunciation from those who believed that he was a tool of Wall Street bankers. It was pointed out that the Morgan syndicate had sold the bonds to the public at a large profit and the criticism of the transaction became so insistent that when it was necessary to issue an additional $100,000,000 of bonds in January, 1896, they were sold directly to the public, to the decided advantage of the government. By this time the worst phase of the financial panic had passed, and with the gradual restoration of normal business conditions confidence was restored and the hoarded gold was returned to circulation.

But in the agrarian centers of the South and West economic recovery was less rapid than in the industrial East, and the discontent which still prevailed among large numbers of farmers was reflected in a striking manner in the approaching presidential election of 1896.

BIBLIOGRAPHICAL NOTE

For a discussion of the tariff consult P. Ashley, *Modern Tariff History* (1920); T. W. Page, *Making the Tariff in the United States* (1924); F. W. Taussig, *Tariff History of the United States* (1924); I. M. Tarbell, *The Tariff in Our Times* (1911); D. R. Dewey, *Financial History of the United States* (1922); E. Stanwood, *American Tariff Controversies in the Nineteenth Century* (1903).

The question of the income tax is treated by E. R. A. Seligman, *The Income Tax* (1914); H. T. Peck, *Twenty Years of the Republic* (1906); D. R. Dewey, *National Problems* (1907).

The best general account of the financial controversy of this period is by A. D. Noyes, *Thirty Years of American Finance* (1898); a brief discussion of the silver issue can be found in F. W. Taussig, *The Silver Situation in the United States* (1892); see also A. B. Hepburn, *History of Coinage and Currency in the United States* (1903); J. T. Laughlin, *History of Bimetallism in the United States* (1897); John Sherman, *Recollections* (1895); D. R. Dewey, *Financial History of the United States* (1918).

CHAPTER 8

THE BATTLE OF THE STANDARDS

As the time for the presidential election of 1896 approached it was apparent to those accustomed to observe the trend of political events that a struggle was impending which in all likelihood would be more significant than any that had taken place since the first election of Lincoln in 1860. Events of the preceding four years gave abundant evidence that there was abroad in the country a widespread spirit of discontent. The remarkable growth of the Populist party in the rural areas and the bitter labor struggles in the industrial centers were ominous signs of the prevalent unrest. And the recent action of Congress in repealing the Silver Purchase Act and of the Supreme Court in nullifying the Income Tax Law added fuel to the discontent.

It is true that the campaign of this year revolved about the issue of the free coinage of silver, but to regard this election as a struggle over a technical financial question would be to miss its true significance. It was a conflict in which the cleavage between social and economic classes was more clearly in evidence than had been the case in any previous election. In fact gold and silver took on a symbolic meaning. Silver was regarded as the money of the poor, toiling masses, while gold, in the eyes of many persons in the lower classes, was a weapon in the hands of the predatory rich.

The political leaders of both major parties viewed the evidences of discontent with anxiety, for the spirit of unrest was not confined to one party. Clearly the situation called for something more than the insincere juggling with issues such as had been common in most of the past presidential campaigns. On the whole the Republicans were in a better position than the Democrats. They had been out of office during the preceding four hectic years and could therefore disclaim responsibility for the unsettled condition of the country. Furthermore the Republicans, through long tenure of office, had developed experienced and capable party leaders. On the other hand the Democrats, rightly or wrongly, had to shoulder responsibility for the unfavorable economic conditions that prevailed during Cleveland's second administration. Moreover, a large part of the rank and file of the party as well as many of the politicians had repudiated the guidance of President Cleveland, the one conspicuously successful leader whom the Democrats had produced since the Civil War.

Among the Republican leaders there appeared at this juncture a man who showed marked ability in guiding the party through the greatly troubled political waters. Marcus A. Hanna, or Mark Hanna, as he became popularly known, was a typical example of the successful business man of that time. He was the son of a prosperous wholesale grocer and he apparently inherited the business acumen of his father. He engaged in a variety of business activities, including coal, oil, shipping and banking, and like many other outstanding figures in the industrial life of the time, he used methods which the business ethics of a later day have condemned as unscrupulous. But he had at least the merit of frankness and never assumed a moral pose. He had fought his way to the top in business and he adopted the same methods in politics. No evidence has been disclosed that he entered politics for personal financial gain. He handled large sums of money in the course of his political activities and none of it appears to have stuck to his fingers. He was honest and courageous as well as patriotic according to his lights. He identified the welfare of the country with the success of the Republican party and the control of that party by the large business in-

terests. But he had no sympathy with those men of wealth
who regarded the working class as a lower order of human
beings. On one occasion he bluntly remarked to a millionaire
who had referred to the "lower classes": "Do you mean
workingmen or do you mean criminals and that sort of
thing? These latter are the lower classes."

With all his cynicism and outward roughness of character
he had many attractive human qualities, among which was
his ability to form warm personal friendships. Of these none
was more genuine than that which developed between Hanna
and William McKinley. When McKinley was defeated for
Congress in 1890 it was largely through Hanna's influence
and money that he was elected Governor of Ohio in 1891.
Shortly afterward, when McKinley became involved in heavy
financial losses, it was Hanna who raised $100,000 among
his wealthy associates to save McKinley from bankruptcy.

In 1895 Hanna withdrew entirely from business and devoted all his time and energy to obtaining for his friend Mc-
Kinley the Republican nomination for the presidency. In
this undertaking he displayed the same shrewdness, aggres-
siveness, and capacity for organization that had characterized his business activities.

It was not an easy task which Hanna had set for himself.
It is true that McKinley was a well-known figure in public
life, chiefly as a result of his connection with tariff legislation. He had, moreover, a pleasing personality and he could
point to a satisfactory, if not a brilliant, military record in
the Civil War. But McKinley's Congressional career covered
the period of the controversy over the currency and his record
in this connection had not been such as would commend him
to conservative Republicans in the East. He had voted for
a free silver bill in 1877 as well as for the Bland-Allison Act
the following year, and had supported the Sherman Silver
Purchase Act in 1890. However, in his campaign for governor of Ohio a year later he modified his earlier views and

declared his opposition to free silver unless it could be brought about by international agreement.

Hanna was a thorough believer in the gold standard but he realized the danger of committing himself or his protégé McKinley before the Republican convention should meet. He tried to divert public attention from the currency issue and to emphasize the tariff question. By extensive newspaper publicity McKinley was put forward as "the advance agent of prosperity." At the Ohio State Convention Hanna succeeded in having a financial plank incorporated in the platform which was a masterpiece of ambiguity. It stated: "We contend for honest money, for a currency of gold, silver, and paper . . . that shall be as sound as the Government and as untarnished as its honor." There was no difficulty in interpreting this statement to the satisfaction of the silver interests in the West and the gold interests in the East.

In the meantime Hanna was industriously gathering delegates, especially in the South and West, pledged to support the nomination of McKinley, and he succeeded in lining up more than half of the delegates before the convention met. Having accomplished his main object, Hanna was then prepared to deal with the financial question. When the convention met at St. Louis, on June 16th, some of the leading Republican politicians from the East conferred with Hanna and stated that they would insist upon writing into the platform a plank declaring unequivocally for the gold standard. McKinley was inclined at first to balk at this proposal, but Hanna, who all along had favored such a move, accepted, albeit with simulated reluctance, the demands of the conservatives. As finally framed the financial plank stated: "We are unalterably opposed to every measure calculated to debase our currency or impair the credit of the country. We are, therefore, opposed to the free coinage of silver, except by international agreement with the leading commercial nations of the world, which we pledge ourselves to promote, and until such agreement can be obtained the existing gold standard must be preserved." The remainder of the platform consisted of the usual stereotyped pronouncements. The Cleveland administration was denounced as "a record of un-paralleled incapacity, dishonor, and disaster." The protective tariff was defended as "the bulwark of American industrial independence and the foundation of American development and prosperity." The Monroe Doctrine was reaffirmed and "a firm, vigorous, and dignified foreign policy" was advocated which, among other things, should include the acquisition of the Hawaiian Islands as well as the Danish West Indies.

The adoption of the plank upholding the gold standard precipitated a revolt among the silver forces in the convention. Under the leadership of Senator Teller, of Colorado, thirty-four delegates, chiefly from western states, withdrew from the convention. The conservative forces, then in complete control of the situation, proceeded to nominate Mc-Kinley on the first ballot.

For some time before the meeting of the Democratic National Convention it was apparent that the silver interests would dominate the body. State conventions in thirty of the states had adopted resolutions supporting free silver, whereas in only ten states had the gold standard been approved. In fact many conservative Democrats were at first inclined not to attend the national convention, but they were dissuaded from this action by President Cleveland, who took the position that "a cause worth fighting for is worth fighting for to the end." As soon as the convention assembled at Chicago on July 7 the silver forces indicated their determination to seize the helm at once. When the national committee, which was still under control of the conservative element of the party, presented the name of Senator Hill, of New York, as temporary chairman of the convention, the silver advocates put forward in opposition Senator Daniel, of Virginia, who was elected by the decisive vote of 556 to 349. They followed up this victory by seating contesting silver delegations from Nebraska and Michigan.

While awaiting the report of the Committee on Resolutions the convention listened to a number of speeches from prominent Democrats, among whom were Governor Altgeld, of Illinois, and Senator Tillman, of South Carolina. In the course of his speech Altgeld said: "We have seen the streets of our cities filled with idle men, with hungry women, and with ragged children. The country today looks to the deliberations of this convention to promise some form of relief." Senator Tillman, amidst great excitement and considerable hissing from the delegates, declared that the issue before the convention was as much a sectional issue as slavery had been. Such pronouncements were ominous. They gave pointed evidence of the deep-seated class feeling that animated a large number of the delegates.

On the third day of the convention the Committee on Resolutions submitted a majority and a minority report. The former denounced "the interference by Federal authorities in local affairs" and particularly "government by injunction," which was declared to be "a new and highly dangerous form of oppression, by which Federal judges become at once legislators, judges, and executioners." It expressed the sympathy of the Democratic party for labor and demanded "the passage of such laws as may be necessary to protect it in all its rights." The action of the Supreme Court in nullifying the Income Tax Law was denounced and it vaguely suggested the possibility that Congress might bring about a reconstitution of the Court. The most important part of the majority report, however, was that which dealt with the money question. It declared its opposition to monometallism, "which has locked fast the prosperity of an industrial people in the paralysis of hard times," and demanded "the free and unlimited coinage of both gold and silver at the present

legal ratio of 16 to 1 without waiting for the aid or consent
of any other nation."

The minority report took exception to some of the proposals made by the majority as "extreme and revolutionary,"
and it declared that the attempt to inaugurate the free coinage
of silver "would place this country at once upon a silver basis,
impair contracts, disturb business, diminish the purchasing
power of the wages of labor, and inflict irreparable evil upon
our nation's commerce and industry." Finally the minority
proposed a resolution commending "the honesty, economy,
courage and fidelity of the present Democratic national administration."

The presentation of the two reports precipitated an acrimonious and disorderly debate. Senator Tillman led off with
a denunciation of the proposal to endorse the administration
of Cleveland. He referred to the President as "the tool of
Wall Street" and declared: "If this Democratic ship goes to
sea on storm-tossed waves without fumigating itself, without express repudiation of this man who has sought to destroy his party, then the Republican ship goes into port and
you go down in disgrace, defeated in November." Tillman
lost his temper so completely that at times he was incoherent
and his violence caused a revulsion of feeling in the convention.

Senator Hill then spoke for the minority. In a calm and
dispassionate voice he criticized the majority report for its
endorsement of the income tax and questioned the wisdom
of that report in its attack upon the Supreme Court. He appealed to the convention not to "drive old Democrats out of
the party who have grown gray in the service, to make room
for a lot of Republicans and Populists, and political nonde-
scripts." Senator Vilas, of Wisconsin, supported the views
of Senator Hill and declared that the free silver proposal was
"the beginning of the overthrow of all law, of all justice, of
all security and repose in the social order." He appealed to

the convention not to "pull down the pillars of the temple and crush us all beneath the ruins."

Neither the ranting of Tillman nor the cold reasoning of Hill and Vilas, in voices that did not carry, appealed to the mood of the delegates. At this juncture there appeared on the platform a man, unknown to a large part of the turbulent audience whom he faced, William Jennings Bryan, of Nebraska. There was something in the calm assurance and dignity of this young man which caught the fancy of the crowd, and before he had said a word the disorder that had prevailed in the convention subsided. In a remarkably pleasing voice which penetrated, apparently without effort, to all parts of the vast auditorium, Bryan began his historic address. He opened with a courteous reference to those who had preceded him on the platform, but he said that "this is not a contest between persons. The humblest citizen in the land, when clad in the armor of a righteous cause, is stronger than all the hosts of error." He declared that he came "to speak in defense of a cause as holy as the cause of liberty—the cause of humanity." Having won the attention of every person in the huge audience he proceeded with increasing fervor and power. "We stand here," he said, "representing people who are the equals before the law of the largest cities of Massachusetts. When you come before us and tell us that we are about to disturb your business interests, we reply that you have disturbed our business interests by your course.

"We say to you that you have made the definition of a business man too limited in its application. The man who is employed for wages is as much a business man as his employer. The attorney in a country town is as much a business man as the corporation counsel in a great metropolis. The merchant at the crossroads store is as much a business man as the merchant of New York. The farmer who goes forth in the morning and toils all day—who begins in the spring and toils all summer—and who, by the application of brain and muscle to the natural resources of the country, creates wealth, is as much a business man as the man who goes upon the Board of Trade and bets upon the price of grain. The miners who go down a thousand feet into the earth, or climb two thousand feet upon the cliffs, and bring forth from their hiding places the precious metals to be poured into the channels of trade, are as much business men as the few financial magnates who, in a back room, corner the money of the world.

"We come to speak for this broader class of business men. Ah, my friends, we say not one word against those who live on the Atlantic coast; but those hardy pioneers who brave all the dangers of the wilderness, who have made the desert to blossom as a rose—those pioneers away out there, rearing their children near to nature's heart, where they can mingle their voices with the voices of the birds—out there where they have erected schoolhouses for the education of their children and churches where they praise their Creator, and the cemeteries where sleep the ashes of their dead—are as deserving of the consideration of this party as any people in this country.

"It is for these that we speak. We do not come as aggressors. Our war is not a war of conquest. We are fighting in the defense of our homes, our families, and posterity. We have petitioned, and our petitions have been scorned. We have entreated, and our entreaties have been disregarded. We have begged, and they have mocked when our calamity came. We beg no longer; we entreat no more; we petition no more. We defy them."

As Bryan uttered these striking words pandemonium broke loose in the convention. With a shout which seemed to rock the great hall the Western Democracy hailed its new champion.

When a measure of quiet was restored Bryan resumed his speech. He answered the objection that the platform criticized the Supreme Court by pointing out the fact that the income tax had been declared unconstitutional only after one of the justices had changed his mind, and he said, "We cannot be expected to know when a judge will change his mind." The tariff question he regarded as less significant than the currency questions for while "protection had slain its thousands, the gold standard had slain its tens of thousands." He maintained that the contest was "a struggle between the idle holders of idle capital and the struggling masses who produce the wealth and pay the taxes of the country.

"There are two ideas of government. There are those who believe that if you just legislate to make the well-to-do prosperous their prosperity will leak through on those below. The Democratic idea has been that if you legislate to make the masses prosperous, their prosperity will find its way up and through every class that rests upon it.

"You come to us and tell us that the great cities are in favor of the gold standard. I tell you that the great cities rest upon these broad and fertile prairies. Burn down your cities and leave our farms, and your cities will spring up again as if by magic. But destroy our farms, and the grass will grow in the streets of every city of this country.

"If they dare to come out in the open and defend the gold standard as a good thing, we shall fight them to the uttermost, having behind us the producing masses of the nation and the world. Having behind us the commercial interests and the laboring interests and all the toiling masses, we shall answer their demands for a gold standard by saying to them, you shall not press down upon the brow of labor this crown of thorns. You shall not crucify mankind upon a cross of gold."

An indescribable scene of tumult and enthusiasm followed the conclusion of this speech. "Twenty thousand men and women went mad with irresistible enthusiasm. This orator had met their mood to the very full. He had found magic words for the feeling which they had been unable to express. And so he had played at will upon their very heart-strings until the full tide of their emotion was let loose in one tempestuous roar of passion, which seemed to have no end."

The conservatives were overwhelmed. All of their proposals were voted down and the platform as reported by the majority of the committee was adopted by a large majority. Even the proposal of the minority to commend the administration of President Cleveland was defeated by a vote of 357 to 564. Many of the conservatives abandoned the struggle in despair and turned to the Republican party. Others, such as Senator Hill, remained within the party fold but declined to participate in the campaign. Still others, among them President Cleveland, organized the National Democratic party, which adopted a platform affirming the traditional principles of the party and nominated John M. Palmer for the presidency.

It may be conceded that there is much in Bryan's speech that is trite. It was by no means a spontaneous production. Incorporated in it were a large number of platitudes that he had developed in earlier political addresses. Nevertheless there is no doubt that he expressed what was in the minds of many of his listeners and the effect of his words was heightened by the remarkable oratorical ability of the speaker. Bryan's speech had transformed him overnight from a comparatively unknown western politician into a national figure and had placed him among the leading contestants for the presidential nomination. His chief rival was Richard P. Bland, of Missouri, known as the "Father of Free Silver." While Bland received the largest vote on the first ballot, the enthusiasm for Bryan among the delegates did not subside, and on the fifth ballot he was nominated. For the vice presidency the convention chose Arthur Sewall, a wealthy Maine shipbuilder.

The Populists and "Silver Republicans," who met in convention in St. Louis, were in a quandary. The Democrats had stolen most of the Populist thunder and there was nothing to be gained by putting another radical candidate in the field. After some hesitation they decided to endorse Bryan as their candidate, although they substituted the name of Thomas E. Watson, of Georgia, for that of Sewall for the vice presidential nomination.

In the campaign that followed deep-seated class feeling appeared to a degree never approached in any former presidential election. Throughout the West and parts of the South popular leaders such as Mary Ellen Lease, "Sockless" Jerry Simpson, and "Pitchfork" Ben Tillman stirred the people to a veritable frenzy. Whole communities gave themselves over to political discussions which frequently resembled religious hysteria. William Allen White thus pictures the situation in the West. "It was a fanaticism like the Crusades. Indeed the delusion that was working on the people took the form of religious frenzy. Sacred hymns were torn from their pious tunes to give place to words which deified the cause and made gold—and all its symbols, capital, wealth, plutocracy—diabolical. At night from ten thousand little white schoolhouse windows, lights twinkled back vain hope to the stars. For the thousands who assembled under the schoolhouse lamps believed that when their legislature met and their Governor was elected, the millennium would come by proclamation. They sang their barbaric songs in unrhythmic jargon, with something of the same mad faith that inspired the martyrs going to the stake. . . . It was a season of shibboleths, fetishes, and slogans. Reason slept; and the passions—jealousy, covetousness, hatred—ran amuck, and whoever would check them was crucified in public contumely."

And the fanaticism of the West was matched by an unreasoning bitterness among the conservatives in the East. When Bryan came to New York to deliver his speech of acceptance he attempted to refute the charge that the Democrats contemplated an attack upon the rights of property or a revolutionary change in the social order. But his protest was of no avail. It is difficult to understand today the terror that Bryan inspired in the East. Conservative newspaper editors indulged in the most extravagant language in denouncing the Democratic party and its candidate. Thus the New York *Tribune* referred to Bryan as "the wretched, rattle-pated boy, posing in vapid vanity and mouthing resounding rottenness" who was "the puppet in the blood-imbued hands of Altgeld, the anarchist, and Debs, the revolutionist, and other desperadoes of that stripe." From the pulpit, too, came language better fitted to the street corner. One eminent clergyman in Brooklyn declared that the Democratic platform "was made in hell"; another stated that the free silver movement was "accursed and treasonable"; still another referred to Bryan as "a mouthing, slobbering demagogue whose patriotism is all in his jawbone."

Whether or not the Republican leaders believed that Bryan was as great a menace as their language indicated they made full use of the terror which his candidacy inspired among conservative business men to forward the interests of their party candidate. Hanna visited the financial centers of the East and obtained from men of wealth and large corporations great sums of money to be used in launching a nation-wide "campaign of education." Hundreds of thousands of pieces of campaign "literature" were distributed; thousands of speakers were sent throughout the country; hundreds of campaign "clubs" were organized. Contracts were made by business men contingent upon the election of McKinley, while others let it be known that the success of the Democratic party would be followed by widespread unemployment, through the shutting down of factories.

The campaign methods of the two candidates were in striking contrast. McKinley remained at his home in Canton, Ohio, where he received visiting delegations from various states and to whom he read carefully prepared addresses. At first he attempted to keep the currency question in the background, and to emphasize the tariff question, together with the claim that prosperity would return with the success of the Republican party. But Bryan's vigorous tactics forced the silver issue to the front, and before the campaign was far advanced this question had dwarfed all others.

Bryan made a whirlwind campaign, traveling thousands of miles into every part of the country, and addressing more than five million persons. His eloquence held thousands spellbound, even if his arguments did not convert them. It is doubtful if Bryan could have succeeded, under any circumstances, against the tremendous power of organized wealth that was arrayed against him, and his chance of success was lessened by his insistence upon the currency question as the paramount issue, which tended to alienate many who recognized the reality of the grievances of the farmers and industrial laborers, but who regarded free silver as a financial heresy.

In any event, the fact that Bryan, with a disorganized party and against tremendous handicaps, was able to poll 6,500,000 votes in a total of 13,600,000 gave striking evidence of the extent of political unrest in the country, for there can be little doubt that a considerable part of his vote represented a protest against existing economic and social conditions. While the conservative forces that had shaped the political and economic history of the country since 1865 had again triumphed in this election, in time these forces had to face the realities of the social and economic problems that had come to the surface in this significant campaign. In fact, it would seem to be a question today, in view of the events of the twenty years following the election of 1896, whether Bryan was a revolutionary radical or merely a prophet ahead of his time. Within these twenty years most of the reforms that Bryan advocated were written into the law of the land. A progressive income tax, far larger than any that was contemplated in 1896, was placed on the statute books; legislation limiting the use of injunctions in labor disputes was approved; a restraining hand was laid upon the power of corporate wealth; and political reforms even more radical than those put forward by Bryan were introduced. In fact only the issue of free silver passed into the limbo of lost causes, and even here it is a question whether the Federal Reserve Act was not a recognition of the same principle which prompted the demand for free silver, namely the need for a more adequate circulating medium.

The election of 1896 was in some respects similar to the election of 1860. As in the earlier struggle the electorate in 1896 divided along sectional lines. The East and the Middle West were aligned against the South and the Far West. Again, in 1896 as in 1860, the cleavage between the sections of the country was along economic lines. But the defeated party in 1896 did not resort to secession as had been done in the earlier crisis. This was not because the feeling between the sections was any less bitter in 1896 than it was in 1860, nor because the right of secession was any less legal in 1896 than in 1860. The constitution of the United States, so far as the right of secession was concerned, was precisely the same in 1896 as it was in 1860. The reason that secession was not resorted to in 1896 is to be found, largely, in the economic development of the country in the thirty-five years that had elapsed since the outbreak of the Civil War. In these years the business interests of the country had been organized on a national scale. Great corporations carried on their activities from Maine to California and from the Gulf to the Great Lakes. Artificial state boundaries were merely a nuisance to these national enterprises. Then, too, the continental railroads had bound the East to the West. It is the simple fact that economic forces had integrated the nation and had made the theoretical nationality which Webster had proclaimed so eloquently a reality. However strongly the West may have felt on the question of free silver, its economic interrelation with the East was sufficiently developed to prevent any suggestion of secession.

The outcome of the election of 1896 was a triumph for business enterprise. The large business and financial interests of the country were now so strongly intrenched in politics that it seemed unlikely that any successful challenge to their dominance could be made for many years to come. Little did these interests realize that within five short years a new champion of the forces of discontent would appear in the person of Theodore Roosevelt, who was to succeed where Bryan had failed. But for the moment everything seemed to be for the best in the best of possible worlds for those engaged in large business enterprises. In the words of Andrew Carnegie, it was "high noon," and not a cloud appeared in the sky to disturb the serenity of the great captains of industry. Moreover, at this juncture, there came a foreign war which, by arousing national patriotism, served to divert the attention of the people for the time being from economic complaints.

BIBLIOGRAPHICAL NOTE

Brief discussions of the campaign of 1896 can be found in Dewey, *National Problems* (1907), and in S. J. Buck, *The Agrarian Crusade* (1921). For more extended and vivid accounts see H. T. Peck, *Twenty Years of the Republic* (1905), and Mark Sullivan, *Our Times,* Vol. I (1926). For Bryan's personal account see W. J. Bryan, *The First Battle* (1897). A clever presentation of the arguments for free coinage of silver is given by W. H. Harvey, *Coin's Financial School* (1894). A criticism of these arguments is presented by Horace White, *Coin's Financial Fool: The Artful Dodger Exposed* (1896). Two good critical biographies of Hanna have been published, H. Croly, *Marcus A. Hanna* (1912), and Thomas Beer, *Hanna* (1929). The best study of Bryan is Paxton Hibben, *The Peerless Leader: William Jennings Bryan* (1929); see also J. C.

BIBLIOGRAPHICAL NOTE 191

Long, *Bryan, The Great Commoner* (1928), and M. R. Werner, *Bryan* (1929). A sympathetic study of McKinley is given by C. S. Olcott, *William McKinley* (1916). Interesting sidelights on the leading statesmen of this period may be found in H. L. Stoddard, *As I Knew Them* (1927), and L. J. Platt, ed., *Autobiography of Thomas C. Platt* (1910).

CHAPTER 9

SOCIAL AND CULTURAL CONDITIONS, 1865-1900

The material development of the United States in the period from the Civil War to the close of the nineteenth century brought about important changes in the social life of the people, accompanied by a rapid growth of urban centers of population, especially in the industrial regions of the North. In 1865 there was no city with a population of a million; in 1900 New York had reached nearly three and one-half million, Chicago over one and one-half million and Philadelphia over one and one-quarter million, while there were nine cities having a population of over three hundred thousand. Before the close of the century life presented striking contrasts in these rapidly growing cities. To them came thousands of persons who had accumulated fortunes from the mines and forests of the West or in the varied industrial enterprises of the East. For the most part lacking a cultural background or inherited traditions these *nouveaux riches* lavished huge sums of money upon the construction of palatial residences, which they stocked with furniture, canvases, statuary, tapestries, rugs and bric-a-brac gathered from every part of the world. Having meager intellectual interests and being unrestrained by the need of earning a living, many representatives of this new plutocracy conjured up costly and bizarre forms of entertainment to beguile their idle time. Sumptuous feasts in exotic surroundings were given in the great houses of the rich or at the large hotels. "At a dinner eaten on horseback," says Beard, "the favorite steed was fed flowers and champagne; to a small black and tan dog wearing a diamond collar worth $15,000

192

a lavish banquet was tendered; at one function, the cigarettes were wrapped in hundred dollar bills; at another, fine black pearls were given to the diners in their oysters; at a third, an elaborate feast was served to boon companions in a mine from which came the fortune of the host. Then weary of such limited diversions, the plutocracy contrived more freakish occasions—with monkeys seated between the guests, human goldfish swimming about in pools, or chorus girls hopping out of pies."

The reverse of this picture of life among the idle rich in the "Gilded Age" presents a sordid aspect. Into cities flocked hundreds of thousands of workers from rural parts of the country or directly from Europe. Municipal authorities did little or nothing in the way of planning housing accommodations for this rapidly increasing mass of laborers. In general they were crowded into tenements offering the meagerest provisions for health and comfort. Garbage and all manner of filth were left to accumulate in congested parts of cities, often making streets impassable. Many cities had inadequate, if any, sewerage provisions. The inevitable result of such conditions was frequent scourges of disease and high mortality figures. In Philadelphia in 1865 more than seven hundred persons were victims of typhoid and over three hundred of typhus. In the same city over a thousand died of scarlet fever in 1869 and 1870. A smallpox epidemic struck New York in 1871. Other cities presented equally shocking conditions.

Unable to afford the expensive pastimes of the wealthy, the working classes of the cities found relief from the squalor of their surroundings by patronizing cheap theaters, museums, and circuses, or by passing their leisure time in the ubiquitous saloon. Prominent among those who furnished amusement to the masses were P. T. Barnum, with his "Greatest Show on Earth," and "Buffalo Bill" Cody, with his "Wild West Show," depicting the life of the rapidly disappearing frontier.

Between these upper and lower crusts of urban society was a large and energetic middle class. This class comprised most of those engaged in trade, in the professions, and in clerical pursuits. Its majority was drawn from descendants of early American stock, although in the latter years of the century the more energetic and intelligent among the immigrant groups found their way in increasing numbers into trade and the professions. Most of the members of the middle class in the early decades of this period were housed in private dwellings, but French "flats," forerunners of modern apartment houses, had appeared in New York in the seventies, and before the century closed, large numbers of the middle-class families had abandoned private houses for the "conveniences" of apartments. Various inventions and new devices brought a greater degree of comfort to the urban household. Sewing machines became common, while refined kerosene and, later, gas and electricity, gave better illumination. With the development of the Pennsylvania coal fields anthracite coal was widely used for heating purposes. Pianos, steel engravings, reproductions of famous paintings, plush albums, marble-topped tables and "whatnots" graced the "parlors" in the homes of many middle class families.

Constituting as they did a large majority of the population of the country, the members of this middle class gave to the civilization of the United States its tone and quality. In general both the men and women of this group were industrious and serious-minded persons, who for the most part upheld rigid moral standards. The Puritan tradition was still strong among them. They attended and supported the churches, educated their children in school and college and showed an earnest effort to improve themselves culturally. The popularity of the Chautauqua and other lecture courses at this time attest the wide interest in popular education for adults.

Despite the growth of urban centers of population during the last quarter of the nineteenth century, a majority of the people of the United States still dwelt in rural regions at the close of the period. In 1900 the urban population numbered 30,380,433 and the rural population 45,614,142. Although at this time life on the farm and in the small towns retained some characteristics of the earlier frontier, nevertheless, with the extension of the railroad into rural areas, farmers and village folk were able to obtain some of the comforts and conveniences enjoyed by middle class families of the cities. In their cultural interests and general outlook upon life the farming population did not differ essentially from urban dwellers, although inhabitants of country districts were inclined to be more rigidly orthodox in their religious beliefs, less responsive to the disturbing scientific discoveries of the time, and more insistent upon the observance of the conventional moral code than were those in urban centers.

Southern plantation life, as we have seen, did not survive the shock of the Civil War and of the days of Reconstruction. While Southern orators arose on occasion to lament the passing of chivalric ante-bellum manners, members of the younger generation in the South in the last quarter of the nineteenth century, however much they might continue to revere the great leaders of the old South, frankly faced the realities of the world about them and entered trade and the professions. Before the century closed Southern life had lost most of the characteristic features of pre-Civil War days and, with the growth of towns and cities and the rise of industrial pursuits, life in the South became in large measure similar to that which prevailed in the North.

Life in the West during the closing decades of the nineteenth century also underwent important changes. With the building of transcontinental railways, the subjugation of hostile Indians and the passing of the frontier, many picturesque aspects of Western life disappeared. During these years the population of the Western states and territories grew at a remarkable rate. In the period from 1870 to 1900 Minnesota had increased in population from 439,706 to 1,751,394; North Dakota from 2,405 to 319,146; South Dakota from 11,776 to 401,570; Nebraska from 122,993 to 1,066,300; and Kansas from 364,399 to 1,470,495. Similar impressive figures might be given for all the Western communities. Towns and cities sprang up on the plains. Many settlers who found their way to the West had come from the states of the East and the South, and in their new homes quickly established the essential features of the civilization to which they had been accustomed. Schoolhouses and churches were built, and most Western towns could boast of one or more local newspapers. "The little sun-baked, blizzard-chilled hamlet that was talking of Indian raids one day might be talking of the *Atlantic Monthly,* the suffragist lecturer, and Paris fashions the next."

Among the social changes that marked the decades under review should be noted the challenge to the traditional position of women. Before the Civil War the "Woman's Rights" agitation had been launched under the leadership of Mrs. Elizabeth Cady Stanton and Miss Susan B. Anthony. After the war these veteran leaders revived their crusade and they were joined by a group of able and energetic women, among whom were Lucretia Mott, Mrs. Horace Greeley, and the notable sisters, Victoria Woodhull and Tennessee Claflin. For a decade these last two carried on picturesque and checkered careers before the American public. Their ventures in spiritualism, as Wall Street brokers under the patronage of Commodore Vanderbilt, as publishers of a weekly magazine and as ardent advocates of the "emancipation" of women, gave interesting "copy" to the newspapers and scandalized staid members of society. Although the suffragist leaders at this time failed to realize their program for the full political emancipation of women by means of an amendment to the Federal constitution, substantial progress was made through state action in extending the suffrage to women. By the close of the century there was abundant evidence that the position of women in the home and in society was fast changing. In all parts of the country women's clubs had been organized, and these soon departed from their original programs of a cultural type to discuss questions having social and political bearings. Women, in these years also, either through necessity or through choice, found their way in increasing numbers into the business world, where they obtained a measure of economic independence and a knowledge of the world of men which their mothers had not experienced.

The thirty-five years following the Civil War witnessed a remarkable growth of, and fundamental changes in, organized education in the United States. In the former Confederate states the war and its aftermath brought a serious check to the development of public education. Impoverished by the war and then mulcted by the Reconstruction governments, the people of the South had neither the means nor the incentive to go far in the rehabilitation of their educational facilities. It was not until near the close of the century that the public school system in some of the southern states was restored to the standards prevailing before 1860. In this process of slow recovery the southern communities were materially aided by substantial funds furnished by wealthy philanthropists in the North.

Throughout the country as a whole, however, a much more satisfactory condition prevailed. The large increase in national wealth during these years provided adequate means for the expansion of educational facilities. Between the years 1870 and 1900 public expenditures for elementary and secondary schools increased from $63,000,000 to more than $200,000,000. The pupils enrolled in public schools increased from 6,871,522 to 15,503,110. Illiteracy, despite the large influx of uneducated immigrants, was reduced from more than 11 per cent. to less than 8 per cent. The development of secondary education in this period was particularly striking. At the close of the Civil War there were fewer than two hundred public high schools in the country; by the close of the century there were more than six thousand, with an enrollment of more than 500,000 pupils.

With this growth of publicly supported elementary and secondary schools went a notable expansion of collegiate and university education. Through the munificence of Johns Hopkins, a Baltimore merchant, a university bearing his name was opened in that city in 1876. A decade later the struggling University of Chicago received the first of its princely gifts from John D. Rockefeller. Following these examples most of the other colleges in the East made successful appeals to men of wealth, thus adding large sums to their endowments. Supplementing these donations from private sources for higher education were grants made by national and state authorities. In 1862 Congress passed the Morrill Act for the encouragement of education in agriculture, in the mechanic arts and in the natural sciences. By its terms the states received 30,000 acres of public land, for the support of such education, for each senator and congressman to which they were entitled. With funds obtained from this source, in addition to grants made by the state legislatures, state universities were founded, especially in the newer states of the Middle and Far West. Differing from the older colleges in the East, which were exclusively for men, the western state universities were co-educational, in response to the growing demand for higher education for women. In the East, too, collegiate education for women made noteworthy progress in this period. To mention only a few of the more important, Vassar College was founded in 1861; Wellesley and Smith in 1875; Radcliffe, in connection with Harvard, in 1879; Bryn Mawr, in 1880; and

Barnard, associated with Columbia, in 1889. By the close of the nineteenth century there were in the United States more than six hundred colleges and universities having a total enrollment of nearly 120,000 students.

Quite as significant as the expansion of higher education in these decades was the change in the character of the training given in colleges and universities. The older colleges had been founded, in most instances, by religious organizations, and the rigidly prescribed curriculum placed emphasis upon the ancient classics, philosophy, and rhetoric. In many of these institutions no modern languages had been offered; history, when given, was a branch of belles-lettres or philosophy; and only the most elementary courses in science, with little or no laboratory practice, had been provided. Frequently one professor would be expected to teach half a dozen subjects, and the instruction given consisted, generally, of rote recitations from prescribed textbooks. Technical and professional schools for training in law, medicine and engineering, where they existed at all, fell far below the standards set for such institutions at the present time.

Obviously the colleges and universities had not kept pace with the rapidly moving world about them. To remedy this situation a group of able and energetic college administrators, including Andrew D. White, of Cornell; Charles W. Eliot, of Harvard; James McCosh, of Princeton; James B. Angell, of Michigan; and Daniel Coit Gilman, of Johns Hopkins, inaugurated a veritable revolution in the content and methods of college instruction. In the first place, with the increased endowments derived from wealthy business men rather than from ecclesiastical foundations, the larger colleges and universities of the East were freed, in great measure, from clerical domination, whereas the new state universities had never been subjected to such control. With the passing of clerical influence in these institutions there came sweeping changes in the rigid system of classical training which had formerly prevailed. The curriculum was enriched by the addition of courses in the natural and social sciences. Better trained instructors, fresh from study in European universities, were added to the faculties; library and laboratory facilities were greatly augmented; and better methods of instruction were introduced. At Harvard, President Eliot shocked the conservatives by sweeping away the rigid curriculum of prescribed studies and introducing a system of free electives. Although this arrangement allowed frivolous students to slip through college with a minimum of work by a judicious selection of easy courses, on the other hand it offered to serious-minded students splendid opportunities for an enriched education.

Coincident with these changes in the liberal arts college went greatly improved methods in professional and technical education. Among the reforms introduced by President Eliot at Harvard was the raising of standards in the medical school, requiring three full years of attendance to obtain the degree. He further revolutionized the teaching of law with the introduction of the case system. First-class technical institutions, such as the Massachusetts Institute of Technology, Worcester Polytechnic, Lehigh University, and the Case School of Applied Science, were established, bearing witness to the increased importance of training in applied science. Advanced research work in all branches of learning also marked the educational development of this period. Johns Hopkins University at the outset announced that scientific research would be the chief aim of the institution. At Columbia, Harvard, and other leading universities graduate schools of political and social science, philosophy, literature, and pure science were founded. In short, by the close of the nineteenth century the institutions of higher education in the United States had come to compare favorably with similar institutions in Europe.

The development of American literature in the last quarter

of the nineteenth century presents some interesting characteristics. At the close of the Civil War the great figures of the
New England school, Emerson, Lowell, Longfellow, Haw-
thorne, Holmes, still held the center of the literary stage.
But much of their best work had been done in the days before
the war, and the sway of the "Brahmin caste of New England" was approaching an end. In the years immediately following the war the literary output in America was not
especially notable. Some of the leading poets of the old
school, apparently having exhausted their creative powers,
turned to translation. In these years Longfellow published
his translations from Dante and Bryant his translation of
Homer.

But beginning in 1870 there came a new era in American
literature. With the single outstanding exception of Henry
James, whose development of the so-called international
novel led him increasingly to apply his talents to European
subjects, American writers devoted their efforts to descriptions of America, its component races, their manners and
their speech. The nation had begun to take an interest in
itself, and fiction was not slow to provide a varied and
profuse literature to satisfy this interest. Mark Twain, Bret
Harte, and Joaquin Miller revealed the wild regions and life
of the West; Edward Eggleston and Hamlin Garland por-
trayed the heroic struggles of the men and women who
settled in the Middle West; George W. Cable pictured the
colorful life of the Creoles of Louisiana; Joel Chandler
Harris and Thomas Nelson Page turned to the romantic
days of the old South; James Lane Allen found inspiration
in Kentucky scenes; Miss Mary N. Murfree ("Charles Eg-
bert 'Craddock") disclosed to the world the primitive people
of the Tennessee mountains; and William Dean Howells
came from the West to depict the life of New England.
Similarly the poets turned from romanticism to realism,
finding inspiration for their poetic works in the homely life

of the people among whom they lived. Typical of this trend in poetic writing are the productions of John Hay, James Whitcomb Riley, and Eugene Field. Perhaps the most distinctively American poet of these years, however, was Walt Whitman. His inspiration is neither sectional nor European. Whitman's free verse, sometimes lyrical, often formless, did not meet with approval among his contemporaries, and it was not until after the opening of the new century that his true worth was recognized. His message is "comradeship," the free and loyal devotion of strong individualities of whatever race or condition. He is an exultant prophet who beholds in America a race of strong men and women, building a new civilization based on "the love of comrades."

This period, too, saw the rise of a group of American humorists who seized upon the incongruities and follies of the life of the time to formulate grotesque and shrewd comments that appealed strongly to the primitive sense of humor of the American people. Most notable in this group were David Ross Locke ("Petroleum V. Nasby"), Charles Farrar Browne ("Artemus Ward"), Robert Henry Newell ("Orpheus C. Kerr"), and H. W. Shaw ("Josh Billings").

Symptomatic of the reading taste of a large number of Americans in these years was the vogue of the "dime novel." Themes for these productions were taken largely from the stirring life of the West. In their pages were depicted the wild adventures of "Diamond Dick," the blood-curdling exploits of "Idaho Tom," or the deep-dyed villainies of "Spitfire Saul." On every page of these works was a thrill, and they always concluded with virtue triumphant over vice. Literally millions of copies of such novels were circulated and read, often surreptitiously, by the men and boys of the time.

In the drama little of permanent value was produced in the last quarter of the nineteenth century. Many of the plays presented were adaptations from European writers. Perhaps

the most characteristic theatrical productions were melo-
dramas, frequently of the lurid type. Nevertheless there were
changes taking place similar to those mentioned in speaking
of the novel. Steele Mackaye set himself the task of reform-
ing the American stage and of introducing some of the
naturalism that was asserting itself in European theaters.
His *Hazel Kirke,* first acted in Providence in 1879, held the
stage for thirty years and was played in England, Australia,
Japan, Hawaii and elsewhere. More significant, perhaps, is
the work of Bronson Howard. His *Shenandoah* is an effective drama of the Civil War that remained popular for
years; but his *Aristocracy* is more important, since it is a
criticism of one of the most deplorable weaknesses of American society. It is in the capacity of critic of society that he is
of greatest interest to the historian, since in it he gives evidence of the growth of self-consciousness in the American
people and of attempts to appraise conditions.

In the theaters the last decade of the century saw the
passing of the old stock companies with their repertoire of
plays. In their place came the "star system," in which brilliant or popular actors and actresses were featured in plays
selected by theatrical managers. Moreover, the theatrical
field was affected by the general drift toward "big business"
which marked these years. Theatrical managers and producers became more interested in the profits to be derived
from the enterprise than in the artistic quality of the plays
produced. But the best traditions of the theater did not
wholly disappear, as is evidenced by the success of Edwin
Booth in the portrayal of Shakespearean drama, of Joseph
Jefferson in comedy, and of Augustin Daly with his famous
company consisting of Ada Rehan, John Drew, and others.

Notable progress in the development and encouragement
of the fine arts was made in America in the closing decades
of the nineteenth century. Men of wealth made liberal donations for the foundation of art museums. In 1869 the Cor-

coran Art Gallery was founded in Washington through the generosity of a wealthy banker. In 1876 the Boston Museum of Fine Arts was opened to the public and three years later in New York was established the Metropolitan Museum of Art supported by both public and private funds. The construction and decoration of public buildings and the call for memorial monuments to war heroes provided opportunities for rising young artists and sculptors.

Much of the work produced by American artists in these years was influenced strongly by the classical traditions of European art. Their themes were more frequently derived from the masterpieces of Renaissance artists than from the scenes of the America in which they lived. However, the technical quality of the work of these American artists was of a high order. The portraits by John Singer Sargent, the paintings of Edwin A. Abbey, and the etchings of James McNeill Whistler aroused admiration in both Europe and America.

Despite the influence of classical traditions upon American art there were those who revolted against the rigid standards of the old school. Among these were John La Farge, George Inness, and William Morris Hunt, who returned from their studies in Paris influenced by the Barbizon school of French painters. Under the leadership of La Farge there was established the Society of American Artists, as a protest against the conservatism of the older American Academy. Prominent among those who sounded the realistic note in art was Winslow Homer. He had little or no formal training, either in this country or Europe. Like Abbey, he had received the stimulus for his career in sketching for Harper's publications. His experience at the front in the Civil War furnished him with stirring subjects of war scenes. To these he added realistic portrayals of the simple seafaring people and farmers of his native New England.

In addition to these American contributions to the field

of art mention should be made of the work of cartoonists and illustrators. Thomas Nast won enduring fame by depicting, in the pages of *Harper's Weekly,* in telling cartoons, the chief figures in the scandals of Grant's administration and of the Tweed Ring. In the closing decade of the century the cartoons by Homer Davenport in the Hearst press of the "Money Trust" lent spice and vigor to the political campaigns of the period. Less controversial, though of greater artistic merit, were the illustrations drawn for the current magazines by Howard Chandler Christy, Frederick Remington, and Joseph Pennell. Of American engravers whose work placed them among the leaders of their craft mention should be made of Kruell, Closson, Frank French, Kingsley and Wolf. American sculptors, too, were producing work of undoubted merit in these decades. In the forefront of the workers in this field were Augustus Saint-Gaudens, Daniel Chester French, George Grey Barnard, and Gutzon Borglum.

America's contribution to the realm of music, in the years under review, was very limited, and such compositions as were produced gave no evidence of distinctly American characteristics. On the other hand, the American people, especially in the middle and upper social ranges, displayed commendable efforts to stimulate appreciation of good music. As in the field of art, so here men of wealth gave large sums for the support of orchestral and operatic performances. The Boston Symphony Orchestra, the New York Philharmonic Society, the Metropolitan Opera Company, and similar organizations throughout the country won the support of those who had wrested wealth from the bounteous resources of America. In many a middle-class family the fond mother saw in her growing daughter a potential musical genius and inflicted upon her wearisome hours at the piano. Concerts, recitals, and great music festivals were given in all parts of the country, showing further evidence of popular interest in things musical. Lured by American gold, European musical

teachers and directors came to this country to inspire bud-
ding genius or to direct musical organizations. Further
stimulus was given to the growth of musical taste in America
by the large influx of immigrants from Europe, especially
from Germany, who brought their native love of music.

In the last quarter of the nineteenth century American
journalism underwent a transformation. In earlier years the
large newspapers had reflected the personalities of their
editors. The New York *Tribune* was the personal organ of
Horace Greeley; Henry J. Raymond presided over the destinies of the New York *Times;* James Gordon Bennett, the
elder, dominated the New York *Herald;* and Samuel Bowles
made the Springfield *Republican* one of the outstanding
journals of the country. The editorial pages of all these
papers were widely read and the views there expressed influenced in no small measure national and local politics in
the stirring days of the Civil War and the Reconstruction
era. But the day of the one-man newspaper was fast coming
to an end. New inventions in printing and typesetting machinery called for large investments in mechanical equipment. Furthermore, the reading public had come to value
more highly the news than the editorial columns, and this
brought additional expense for reportorial work. These
mounting costs in newspaper production made it impossible
for aspiring young newspaper men to repeat the exploits of a
Greeley or a Raymond. Moreover, the rapid growth of commercial advertising in these years made newspaper editors
more cautious in expressing editorial opinions that might
offend those who contributed to the financial success of the
paper. In short, by the close of the century newspaper production had ceased to be a personally conducted enterprise
and had taken on many of the characteristics of large commercial business.

These years beheld also a new departure in American
journalism, the rise of the so-called "yellow press." In 1883

Joseph Pulitzer, the energetic editor of the St. Louis *Post-Despatch,* came to New York and purchased the *World.* He promptly announced his intention to launch a campaign against the possessors of swollen fortunes. He denounced "the aristocracy of Central Park" and called for the imposition of income, inheritance, and luxury taxes to deprive these persons of a part of their superfluous wealth. His appeal was frankly directed to the lower middle and working classes, and he shrewdly adapted the form and content of his paper to meet the mental equipment and intellectual interests of these classes. By the lavish use of heavily leaded headlines, comic supplements, special articles having an emotional appeal, and sensational accounts of crime, he won a large following, many of whom had never read a newspaper before. The success of Pulitzer soon attracted others into the same field. In 1896 William Randolph Hearst, son of a California millionaire, came to New York and bought the *Journal.* He adopted and greatly expanded the methods employed by Pulitzer in his efforts to reach the masses. Varicolored headlines, striking cartoons, crude "comics," and editorial articles with a class appeal, written by Arthur Brisbane, became features of the Hearst publication.

Although the sensational methods of Pulitzer and Hearst brought forth denunciation from the staid newspapers of the old school and shocked the sensibilities of many of the respectable middle class, there is no doubt that the "yellow" press performed a real public service in rousing the public conscience and in stirring up the complacent editors of "respectable" newspapers to a realization of existing social and political abuses. Moreover, it provided reading matter of a kind and aroused an interest in public affairs for a mass of the population that had never before been reached by the newspaper press.

Supplementing the daily paper in providing literary sustenance to an increasing number of readers were several new periodical magazines. In 1865 E. L. Godkin started the *Nation* and in its pages put forth vigorous denunciation of the political corruption of the times and biting criticism of the manners and morals of the vulgar rich. At about the same time four monthly magazines, *Scribner's, Lippincott's,* the *Galaxy* and the *Overland,* were founded, and *Putnam's* was revived. Profiting by the experience of the newspapers, *Scribner's* in 1870 began the practice of printing general advertising matter in connection with the magazine. To meet the needs of women readers the *Ladies' Home Journal* was started in 1883, and quickly won a large circulation. S. S. McClure struck a new note in periodical literature with the publication of a magazine bearing his name in 1893. In its make-up sprightly romance and stirring biography were interspersed with pictures of the leading figures in the political, theatrical, and sporting world of the day. The phenomenal success of this venture soon brought imitators, such as the *Cosmopolitan* and *Everybody's.*

In the field of science, especially of applied science, American contributions, in the period under review, were noteworthy. Scarcely a year passed in this era that did not record some important invention, destined to have far-reaching effects upon the life of the people. In 1872 Edison perfected the duplex telegraph; in 1876 Alexander Bell sent his first public telephone message; in 1879 the first patent for a gasoline-driven wagon was granted; and in the same year Edison produced the first practical incandescent electric light; in 1880 the first electric railway was run at Menlo Park by Edison; in 1893 Henry Ford operated his first motor car; in 1894 the first motion picture demonstration was given; in 1896 the Langley model airplane made a successful flight. To these should be added inventions which revolutionized the printing industry and others which provided greatly improved agricultural machinery. Many of these inventions were still in the experimental stage and their full effects upon the economic and social life of the country were not felt until the early decades of the new century.

In pure science, although Americans produced no work comparable to that of Helmholtz, Tyndall, or Pasteur in Europe, nevertheless, American workers made important scientific contributions. Among those whose reputations for sound scholarship was recognized both in this country and in Europe were Lewis H. Morgan, in ethnology; Simon Newcomb, in astronomy; Benjamin Peirce, in mathematics; Josiah Willard Gibbs, in physics; and Wolcott Gibbs, in chemistry. To these should be added Louis Agassiz and Asa Gray who, although they belonged to the previous generation, continued their work for a decade after the Civil War, the one in the broad field of natural history and the other in botany.

It was inevitable that scholars in the United States should be affected by the storm raised in England in scientific and religious circles as a result of the work of Charles Darwin, Alfred Russel Wallace, and Herbert Spencer. In 1859 was published Darwin's epoch-making *Origin of Species,* which formulated the theory of evolution. Thomas Huxley, himself an eminent scientist, devoted his remarkable gifts of exposition to the task of popularizing the new ideas of Darwin. Spencer, in his synthetic philosophy, undertook to apply the evolutionary theory to the whole range of human knowledge and experience. These disturbing ideas reached across the Atlantic and aroused here both earnest support and vigorous opposition. E. L. Youmans, editor of *Popular Science Monthly,* raised a fund to aid Spencer in the publication of his philosophic studies. At Harvard, John Fiske delivered a series of lectures expounding the theories of Darwin and Spencer. Andrew D. White, president of Cornell University, came forward with a lecture on "The Battlefields of Science," later expanded into a book called *The Warfare between Science and Theology,* in which he showed the age-old conflict between science and orthodox religion. To the work of these men was added that of the masters themselves. Both Huxley and Spencer visited the United States and delivered addresses to large audiences. But the upholders of the old order did not lack defenders. From pulpit and from press came violent protests against these "atheistical" ideas. At Yale President Noah Porter conducted a course for the purpose of combating the Spencerian philosophy. Thus was inaugurated a controversy the rumblings of which are still heard half a century later.

Upon organized religion in America the intellectual ferment and the social and industrial changes of the last quarter of the nineteenth century left their mark. The discussion of the theory of evolution, coupled with the work of a group of scholars known as "Higher Critics," who had made a fresh study of the books of the Bible as historical and literary documents, led to a sharp division among both clergy and laity in most of the Protestant denominations in the United States. The liberal group advocated a modification of traditional creeds and dogmas to make them conform to new scientific knowledge, whereas the conservatives clung to the old beliefs. In some instances means were found by which the rival factions were held within the same fold but in others the differences could not be composed. Dr. Charles Briggs of Union Theological Seminary and Professor Henry Preserved Smith, of Lane Theological Seminary, who expressed approval of the new views, were suspended from the ministry by the General Assembly of the Presbyterian Church. In the Episcopal Church repercussions were felt of the "Oxford Movement" in England, leading to the formation of "High Church" and "Low Church" groups, and to the secession of a faction which organized the Reformed Episcopal Church.

The Roman Catholic Church in the United States did not feel, to the same degree, the impact of these disturbing forces, resting as it did upon ancient dogma and tradition and accepting implicitly Papal authority on questions of faith and morals. The rapid growth of the Catholic Church in the closing decades of the nineteenth century, due largely to the great influx of immigrants, caused some apprehension in Protestant circles. There were those who maintained that the doctrines of the Catholic Church were inimical to American institutions, citing as evidence the "Syllabus of Errors" issued by Pope Pius IX in 1864, in which he condemned many convictions and institutions cherished in this country. On the other hand the undoubted loyalty of the great mass of Catholics in the United States and the robust Americanism of Catholic leaders like Cardinal Gibbons and Archbishop Ireland tended, in large measure, to allay such suspicions.

In addition to the old established religious orders there appeared in the closing quarter of the nineteenth century a number of new departures. Prominent among these was the Ethical Culture Society, a movement which drew its chief support from Jews who had departed from the traditions of orthodox Judaism. More successful was the movement started by Mrs. Mary Baker Eddy in 1866, known as Christian Science. The basic principle proclaimed by Mrs. Eddy is the supremacy of mind over matter. "Nothing possesses reality or existence except the Divine Mind and His ideas," she wrote. "The notion that both good and ill are real is a delusion of the material sense which Science annihilates." The supposed naturalness of sin, sickness and death were declared to be abnormalities of the "carnal mind." In place of the medicaments of physicians Christian Science offered spiritual healing, for all sorts of so-called human ailments, administered by specially trained "practitioners." The movement spread with great rapidity to all parts of the country. Fine churches were built and large numbers of adherents were attracted, especially from the prosperous middle class. By the end of the century Christian Scientists were numbered among the important religious organizations in America.

The swiftly changing social and economic conditions that accompanied the industrial development of the United States raised troublesome questions for religious leaders. How could the glaring contrasts between luxury and poverty and the bitter conflicts between capital and labor be made to square with the Sermon on the Mount and the simple teachings of Jesus? Some bolder spirits among the clergy bluntly asserted that the capitalist system was contrary to fundamental Christian ideals and frankly advocated the establishment of some form of collectivism or socialism. Other more cautious spiritual leaders proposed an expansion of the social activities of the churches in order to ameliorate conditions of life among the less fortunate classes. Out of these suggestions came the development of the so-called "institutional" church, with its program of boys' and girls' clubs, clinics for free medical treatment, and organizations for recreational work. Similar in character were the "settlements" established in the congested centers of large cities by socially minded leaders like Jane Addams and Florence Kelley in Chicago and Lillian D. Wald in New York. It was through such institutions as these that many members of the middle class got first-hand knowledge of the life of the working class and thus were prepared to deal sympathetically and intelligently with some of the pressing social problems of the time.

Viewed in the large, American civilization from the Civil War to the close of the nineteenth century presents a varied aspect. There was about it much that was cheap and flashy. There was lacking a refinement of taste and there appeared a tendency to glorify bigness and to confuse it with greatness. On the other hand it was a richer and fuller life that Americans lived in these days than their fathers before them had lived. As a contemporary observer remarked, the American people "are far less raw and provincial than their fathers; they have seen more, they have read more, they have mixed more with people of other nationalities, they have thought more and had to think more, they have spent more for ideas and given more away." In short America at the close of the nineteenth century was still in the adolescent stage. It exhibited both the strength and crudities of youth, and it experienced youth's growing pains. America was yet to come of age.

BIBLIOGRAPHICAL NOTE

An illuminating discussion of American social and cultural conditions in the last quarter of the nineteenth century is to be found in C. and M. Beard, *Rise of American Civilization,* Vol. II, Chap. XXV (1927) ; A. Nevins, *The Emergence of Modern America* (1928), discusses social conditions during the fifteen years following the Civil War. T. Beer, *The Mauve Decade* (1926), gives a witty account of society in the nineties. Numerous memoirs have appeared that picture the life of these years. Among these may be noted, G. C. Eggleston, *Recollections of a Varied Life* (1924) ; H. Garland, *A Son of the Middle Border* (1917) ; H. C. Lodge, *Early Memories* (1913) ; B. Matthews, *These Many Years* (1917) ; Mark Twain, *Life on the Mississippi* (1889).

For the educational development of this period consult E. P. Cubberly, *Public Education in the United States* (1919) ; E. G. Dexter, *History of Education in the United States* (1904) ; C. F. Thwing, *A History of Higher Education in the United States* (1906) ; E. C. Moore, *Fifty Years of American Education* (1917).

The development of American art is discussed by S. Hartman, *A History of American Art* (1901) ; S. Isham, *History of American Painting* (1905) ; C. F. Coffin, *Story of American Painting* (1905) ; for sculpture and architecture consult L. Taft, *History of American Sculpture* (1903) ; J. W. Dow, *The American Renascence: A Review of Domestic Architecture* (1918) ; F. Kimball and G. H. Edgell, *A History of Architecture* (1918).

For the development of American music see L. C. Elson, *History of American Music* (1925) ; R. Hughes and A. Elson, *American Composers* (1914) ; W. Damrosch, *My Musical Life* (1923) ; C. E. Russell, *The American Orchestra and Theodore Thomas* (1927).

For a discussion of American literature and drama consult *The Cambridge History of American Literature,* Vols. III and IV (1917-1921) ; F. L. Pattee, *A History of American Literature Since 1870* (1915) ; G. E. Woodberry, *America in Literature* (1903) ; G. H. Putnam, *Memories of a Publisher* (1915) ; B. Perry, *The American Spirit in Literature* (1921) ; E. Pearson, *Dime Novels; or, Following an Old Trail in Literature* (1929) ; A. H. Quinn, *A History of the American Drama from the Civil War to the Present Day* (1927) ; J. R. Towse, *Sixty Years of the Theatre* (1916) ; T. A. Brown, *History of the New York Stage* (1903).

For journalism see W. G. Bleyer, *Main Currents of American Journalism* (1927) ; J. M. Lee, *History of American Journalism* (1923) ; A. Nevins, *The Evening Post: A Century of Journalism* (1922) ; J. K. Winkler, *W. R. Hearst, An American Phenomenon* (1928) ; D. C. Seitz, *Joseph Pulitzer, His Life and Letters* (1924).

CHAPTER 10

FOREIGN RELATIONS, 1876-1896

By the year 1876 the foreign complications that were a heritage of the Civil War had been adjusted, and during the years that followed the energies of the American people were directed largely to domestic questions. The development of the West offered abundant opportunities for the investment of such surplus capital as the country possessed, and American manufacturers, protected by a benevolent tariff, had a large domestic market in which to dispose of their products. For the moment American public opinion was quite unconcerned with the significant questions in world politics then agitating European nations. In general our relations with European nations during these two decades were confined to questions that involved the interests of those countries on this continent. As Great Britain had larger territorial possessions in the New World than any other European power it was natural that the diplomatic relations between the United States and Great Britain should be more important than those with other European states.

Of the controversies with Great Britain none had been more persistent than that involving the fisheries on the coast of British North America. In 1818 a convention had been agreed upon by the two nations that defined the privileges of American fishermen on the coasts of Labrador and Newfoundland and in the ports of Canada. A reciprocity treaty, signed in 1854, restored most of the rights that American fishermen had enjoyed under the treaty of 1783. This treaty, however, as a result of the animosities aroused by the Civil War, was denounced by Congress in 1866, and there was

no regulation except the convention of 1818. The Treaty
of Washington in 1871 revived the rights of American
fishermen in Canadian ports and granted similar rights to
Canadian fishermen in American ports. As Great Britain
maintained that the privileges granted to American fishermen were more valuable than those allowed to Canadians it
was agreed that additional compensation to be paid by the
United States should be determined by arbitration. An arbitration commission in 1877 awarded Great Britain $5,500,000
for the twelve years during which the agreement was to run.
Regarding this amount as excessive, Congress in 1883 gave
the required two years' notice of the termination of the
agreement. This was followed in 1888 by a *modus vivendi,*
whereby the American fishermen were granted yearly licenses
to enter Canadian bays and harbors and the final settlement
of the whole controversy was postponed for another twenty
years.[1]

The acquisition of Alaska by the United States in 1867
gave rise to two diplomatic controversies with Great Britain.
The first of these involved the seal fisheries in Bering Sea.
On the Pribilof Islands was the breeding ground of thousands of seals. In the fall the herds went south into the
Pacific and returned in the spring to the islands to rear their
young. In 1870 Congress declared the Pribilof Islands a
government reserve and leased the privilege of hunting the
seals to the Alaska Commercial Company. The business
became so profitable that foreigners who were excluded from
the islands resorted to the killing of the seals in the open sea
on their way to and from the islands. The resulting slaughter
of the seals threatened the annihilation of the herds. To
meet this danger the United States authorities advanced the

[1] In 1909 the dispute was referred to the Hague Court, which rendered
an award defining the authority of Canadian officials for the protection
of the fisheries and the maintenance of public order, delimiting the territorial waters of Canada, and specifying the rights of American fishermen
in these waters.

claim that the Alaska peninsula and the Aleutian Islands enclosed the Bering Sea making it a closed sea (*mare clausum*) over which the United States had exclusive jurisdiction.

Because of this contention three British vessels were seized in 1886, while engaged in catching seals between sixty and seventy miles from shore. The British government protested the seizures as a violation of international law. An effort on the part of President Cleveland's Secretary of State, Bayard, to obtain an international agreement for the protection of the seals, met with no success. Further seizures of British vessels in 1889 brought renewed protests from Great Britain. Blaine, who was Secretary of State in the Harrison administration, advanced two arguments in defense of the action of the American authorities. He maintained, first, that extermination of the seals was *contra bonos mores,* and would involve "a serious and permanent injury to the rights of the government and people of the United States." In the second place, he claimed that the seal fisheries had been controlled exclusively by Russia without question and that this right had passed to the United States with the purchase of Alaska. To neither of these propositions would the British authorities agree, and after an extended diplomatic correspondence, the matter was referred to arbitration, in 1892. The decision of the arbitrators denied the claims of the United States to exclusive jurisdiction in the Bering Sea and further held that the United States had no right of protection of fur-seals found outside the three mile limit. Acting under the terms of the arbitration, the tribunal drew regulations for the protection of the seals that were incorporated in a convention signed by the United States, Great Britain, Japan, and Russia, in 1911.

The second diplomatic controversy with Great Britain related to the Alaskan boundary. The United States acquired Alaska in 1867, with the boundaries that had been agreed on by Russia and Great Britain in the treaty of 1825. By the terms of this treaty the boundary between Alaska and British Columbia was to be marked by a line ten marine leagues from the ocean. For many years this line was not determined by either government because of the inaccessibility of the territory. With the discovery of gold in this region, however, the boundary question became of considerable importance. The chief point in controversy was whether the ten marine leagues specified in the treaty should be measured from the prominent headlands of the coast or whether it should follow the sinuosities of the shore line. If the former interpretation was valid Canada would receive several ports giving access to the interior, while, if the latter contention was upheld, the United States would control the entire coast.

For several years the question threatened serious difficulties because of the conflict of authority between the American and Canadian officials. Finally, in 1903, the matter was referred to a mixed commission consisting of three Americans, two Canadians and the Lord Chief Justice of England.[2] In the decision the Lord Chief Justice voted with the three American representatives to uphold the contention of the United States. The Canadians were naturally disappointed, some going so far as to charge that Lord Alverstone had sacrificed the interests of Canada in order to further the friendly relations between Great Britain and the United States.

Far more acute was the controversy that arose over the question of the boundary line between Venezuela and British

[2] President Roosevelt refused to submit the dispute to an arbitral tribunal but agreed to refer the question to "six impartial jurists." The three "impartial" jurists appointed by the President had, according to Roosevelt's own statement, "already committed themselves on the general proposition." Moreover, Roosevelt stated in a letter to Justice Holmes of the Supreme Court that in case of a disagreement by the joint commission he intended to advise Congress to give him authority "to run the line as we claim it, by our own people, without any further regard to the attitude of England or Canada." Bishop, *Theodore Roosevelt and His Time*, I, p. 259.

Guiana. When England came into possession of part of Dutch Guiana, at the close of the Napoleonic wars, the boundary between this territory and the adjacent Spanish territory that later became the Republic of Venezuela had not been determined. In 1841 a surveyor named Schomburgk, under British direction, ran a line that Venezuela claimed invaded her territory. In 1850 the two governments made a "diplomatic agreement," by which each agreed not to occupy any of the territory in dispute. Great Britain, however, steadily increased her claims in the disputed area, and the question assumed added importance with the discovery of gold in the region. In 1876 Venezuela attempted to have the dispute submitted to arbitration, but Great Britain declined, and in protest Venezuela in 1887 severed diplomatic relations with England.

The development of the controversy had been watched with interest and concern by the American authorities. Repeated efforts were made at Washington to promote the re-establishment of diplomatic relations between the contending parties without success, and the proffer of its good offices by the United States to bring about an adjustment of the controversy was declined by Great Britain. Finally President Cleveland determined to bring the question of the vital interests of the United States in the dispute forcibly to the attention of the British authorities.

Secretary of State Olney, in a despatch to the British government, in July, 1895, after reviewing what he considered the important features of the controversy, proceeded to set forth its relation to the Monroe Doctrine. While disclaiming any desire on the part of the United States to establish a protectorate over other American states or to interfere in the internal affairs of such states, he asserted that when a dispute between an American and a European power involved the possible extension of European territorial possessions on this continent, the United States was vitally interested. In language fitted to an ultimatum rather than to an invitation to friendly discussion he asserted that "the United States is practically sovereign on this continent, and its fiat is law upon the subjects to which it confines its interposition. Why? It is not because of pure friendship or good will felt for it. It is not simply by reason of its high character as a civilized state, not because wisdom and equity are the invariable characteristics of the dealings of the United States. It is because, in addition to all other grounds, its infinite resources combined with its isolated position render it master of the situation and practically invulnerable against any or all other powers."

After waiting four months Lord Salisbury replied to this somewhat truculent pronouncement. He declined to accept what he declared was an unwarranted extension of the principle of the Monroe Doctrine and further denied that the Doctrine was a part of international law. On the question at issue between Great Britain and Venezuela he stated that the British government was willing to arbitrate the conflicting claims to a part but not all of the territory in dispute.

In the meantime President Cleveland had transferred the question from the diplomatic to the political sphere. In his message to Congress in December, 1895, he insisted that the Monroe Doctrine was applicable to the case in question and requested Congress to authorize him to appoint a commission to investigate the merits of the controversy. His closing words were clearly in the nature of a challenge to Great Britain. He declared: "When a report is made and accepted it will, in my opinion, be the duty of the United States to resist by every means in its power, as a willful aggression upon its rights and interests, the appropriation by Great Britain of any territory which, after investigation, we have determined of right belongs to Venezuela. In making these recommendations I am fully alive to the full responsibility incurred, and keenly realize all the consequences that may follow. I am nevertheless firm in my conviction, that, while it is a grievous thing to contemplate the two great English-speaking peoples of the world as being otherwise than as friendly competitors in the onward march of civilization and strenuous and worthy rivals in all the arts of peace, there is no calamity which a great nation can invite which equals that which follows supine submission to wrong and injustice, and the consequent loss of national self-respect and honor, beneath which is shielded and defended a people's safety and greatness."

The President's vigorous words met with hearty popular approval. Newspapers that had accused Cleveland of being a paid agent of the British government now hailed him as a patriot. Congress responded by an appropriation of $100,000 for the proposed investigation. For the moment feeling in England and America alike ran high. Irresponsible persons on both sides of the water indulged in belligerent talk. But saner counsels prevailed and vigorous efforts were put forth to prevent warlike moves. In England such prominent individuals as the Prince of Wales, Lord Rosebery, and Mr. Balfour, took a firm stand in favor of conciliation, while in America newspapers like the *Nation* criticized the President for endangering the peace of the country by the extreme position that he had taken.

The tension was distinctly relieved when the British foreign office indicated its willingness to coöperate in every possible way with the commission appointed by the President. This was followed by a statement from Lord Salisbury in which he agreed to waive his former contention and allow a consideration of all matters in dispute. With these conciliatory gestures the way was opened for a peaceful settlement of the whole controversy. A treaty was signed by Great Britain and Venezuela which provided for the submission of the questions in dispute to a commission consisting of two Americans, two Englishmen and a Russian.

The decision of this commission was on the whole favorable to the British claims.

The incident has a number of interesting aspects. It unquestionably gave new life and vigor to the Monroe Doctrine and further indicated that popular sentiment in America was rapidly developing to the point where it would approve even more pretentious excursions into world politics. The surprisingly conciliatory attitude of the British government was not due wholly to the desire to preserve peaceful relations between the English-speaking peoples, nor, despite the flamboyant statement of Mr. Olney, to a fear of the military power of the United States. British imperial interests and the ominous state of the European international situation at the time were factors that impelled the British authorities to avoid, if possible, complications on this side of the Atlantic. In South Africa relations between the Boers and the British had become strained almost to the breaking point, while in Europe the organization of the Triple and Dual Alliances gave British statesmen serious food for thought concerning Britain's international relations. Clearly the time was not propitious for raising further international difficulties. These considerations also doubtless influenced the British authorities at the time in proposing to the United States a general treaty of arbitration for the settlement of all disputes arising between the two countries. Political considerations in this country, however, prevented the consummation of this proposal.

RELATIONS WITH SPANISH AMERICA

Any consideration of the relations between the United States and the Spanish American republics naturally begins with the issuance of the Monroe Doctrine. During the fifty years following the publication of this famous pronouncement the activities of the United States in its relations with its southern neighbors had been confined largely to the settlement of disputes arising between these states and European powers or to controversies among the Spanish American states themselves. Thus in 1876 a territorial dispute between Argentina and Paraguay was referred to the President of the United States for arbitration. Similar controversies between Costa Rica and Nicaragua, Argentina and Brazil, Mexico and Guatemala, and Chile and Argentina were settled by the aid of the American government. American participation in the dispute between Great Britain and Venezuela has already been recounted.

Such incidents reveal the Monroe Doctrine chiefly as a factor in maintaining the political *status quo* on this continent. It was James G. Blaine, the brilliant Secretary of State, first under President Garfield and later under President Harrison, who recognized the wider possibilities of the Doctrine as a means for extending the commercial interests of the United States. In the decades following the Civil War, while American economic activity was devoted largely to the internal development of the country, American trade in South America languished. Great Britain, France and Germany took advantage of the situation to expand greatly their commercial interests in these countries.

In 1881 Blaine inaugurated his plan by sending an invitation to the Latin-American countries to join in a conference with the United States for the purpose of promoting the friendly relations among the states on this hemisphere. However, the assassination of Garfield and the subsequent retirement of Blaine from the State Department caused an abandonment of the conference at that time. Out of office, Blaine continued to advocate his idea, and his efforts bore fruit when Congress in 1888 authorized the President to extend an invitation to the countries of Latin-America to meet in a conference at Washington. When the conference met the following year Blaine was once more at the head of the State Department and he presided over its sessions. There was presented a somewhat ambitious program, including a plan for a customs union among the American states, suggestions for a uniform currency system, the establishment of uniform weights and measures, of international copyright, trademarks, and patents, and better means of communication among the states of this continent. The net results were disappointing; the one outstanding accomplishment was the establishment of a Bureau of American Republics, later to be known as the Pan-American Union, with headquarters at Washington, to serve as a clearing-house for information concerning all of the American Republics.

This propitious beginning in Pan-American accord was in a measure nullified by an incident that arose in 1891 in connection with the civil war in Chile. The American minister to Chile, Patrick Egan, overstepped the bounds of diplomatic practice in openly expressing his sympathy with President Balmaceda, who had been defeated by the insurgents. Further resentment against the United States was aroused by the attempt of the American authorities to seize a Chilean vessel that had been sent by the insurgents to San Diego, California, for military supplies. The vessel escaped, but it was later turned over to the naval authorities of the United States at Valparaiso in order to avoid diplomatic complications.

The bitter feeling aroused by these events culminated in a clash between Chilean and American sailors in the streets of Valparaiso in which two Americans were killed and several others wounded. Secretary Blaine called upon the Chilean government for an apology and the payment of an indemnity, to which demand the Chilean authorities at first declined to accede. Blaine was disposed to find a reasonable accommodation, if possible, in accordance with his policy to promote our friendly relations with Latin-American countries, but when the Chilean foreign minister accused Presi-

dent Harrison of deliberately misstating the facts of the
controversy in his message to Congress, the American authorities lost their patience and an ultimatum was sent to
Chile calling for an immediate compliance with our demands. This vigorous action, coupled with the preparation
of an American naval squadron, brought a complete submission from the Chilean government.

The project for building an inter-oceanic canal, which
was more or less persistently discussed in the last quarter
of the nineteenth century, involved our relations with both
Latin-American and European countries. In 1878 a French
company obtained a concession from the Republic of Colombia for the construction of a canal across the Isthmus of
Panama. Ferdinand de Lesseps, who had recently completed
the Suez Canal, became identified with the enterprise for
building the new canal and a large amount of stock in the
company was sold to French investors. De Lesseps paid a
visit to the United States in order to interest American
capital in the enterprise.

Public sentiment in America, however, was steadily growing in favor of a canal built under American auspices.
President Hayes in 1880 stated that "the policy of this country is a canal under American control." But there were difficulties in the way of accomplishing this purpose. In the
Clayton-Bulwer treaty signed with Great Britain in 1850
there was a provision that if either Great Britain or the
United States should build a canal across Nicaragua or "any
other practical communication between the two oceans" its
neutrality should be jointly guaranteed by the two powers
and, in case of war between the United States and Great
Britain, each party should have free use of the waterway.
In effect this meant British control of the canal in time of
war, so long as Great Britain maintained her naval supremacy. There were those in this country who proposed to overcome the restriction that the treaty imposed by the simple

expedient of denouncing the treaty. Secretary Blaine, unwilling to go to this extreme, approached the British government in 1881 with the suggestion that the treaty be modified. To this proposal the British foreign office replied that Great Britain was a New World power interested equally with the United States in the construction and neutrality of the canal and equally entitled to participate in its political control. Further efforts in the same direction made by Blaine's immediate successors met with no greater success.

In answer to the activities of the French company at Panama, in 1886 a syndicate was organized in New York which obtained from the government of Nicaragua a concession for building a canal across that country. The syndicate then organized the Maritime Canal Company and obtained a charter from Congress in 1889, with the proviso that the United States should not be committed to any financial obligations for the building of the proposed canal. Excavations were started at Greytown, but the disastrous failure of the French company in 1889, coupled with the business depression in 1893, led to the abandonment of the enterprise. Thus matters rested until the results of the Spanish-American War made the construction of a canal an enterprise of vital concern to the United States.

INTERESTS IN THE PACIFIC

The foreign relations thus far considered concerned matters relating to the American continents and involved no departure from the traditional American policy of isolation from world affairs. We now come to consider two incidents that may be regarded as marking the entrance of the United States into the arena of world politics.

In 1872 an American naval officer, while cruising in the Pacific, touched at the Samoan Islands and negotiated with one of the native chiefs a treaty granting to the United

States a naval station in the harbor of Pago-Pago on the island of Tutuila. The Senate was at first not inclined to ratify the action of an overzealous officer; but, six years later, after an uprising in the islands had been followed by the raising of the American flag over the native "capital," the Senate saw the matter in a different light and a treaty was concluded which ceded the naval base to the United States. In the meantime German and British commercial interests had gained a foothold in the islands. There followed ten years of intrigue, interspersed with native wars, in which rival "Kings" received the support of the several foreign interests. Finally conditions reached such a pass that in 1889 each of the three powers concerned sent a naval force to the islands to protect its national interests. An armed conflict seemed inevitable when suddenly a terrific storm struck the islands, resulting in the loss of all of the war vessels except one British ship. This common disaster relieved the tension for the moment and an agreement was reached by which a tripartite protectorate was extended over the Samoan group.

For another ten years affairs in the islands continued in their troubled course. President Cleveland, who seems to have had some misgivings concerning this new departure in American diplomacy, expressed the opinion that our participation in the formation of the protectorate "was in plain defiance of the conservative teachings and warnings of the wise and patriotic men who laid the foundations of our free institutions," and he invited Congress to express an opinion "on the propriety of steps being taken by this government looking to the withdrawal from its engagements with other powers." But Congress did not see fit to retrace the steps that had been taken, and thus matters rested until the events of the Spanish-American War dispelled, at least for the moment, whatever reluctance there had been in the country to endorse American imperial enterprises. In 1899 the triple protectorate was abandoned and the Senate ratified a treaty by which the United States received the island of Tutuila, while Germany took the remainder of the group. Great Britain received compensation elsewhere in the Pacific.

The second incident, and one that further discloses a growth of American imperial tendencies, was the series of events resulting in the acquisition of the Hawaiian Islands. Early in the nineteenth century Yankee traders had become acquainted with these islands while carrying on commerce with China. Then, too, American missionaries had found their way there as early as 1820. As the years passed the numbers of Americans who took up residence in the islands steadily increased, and they were joined by Chinese, Japanese, and settlers from various European countries. In competition with aggressive foreigners the primitive native population soon succumbed. Before the close of the century more than half of the land and virtually all the trade were in the hands of foreigners, chiefly Americans. In 1875, a treaty was made with the Hawaiian king that provided for reciprocity between Hawaii and the United States, thus allowing the importation of Hawaiian sugar duty free. It also included a provision that no Hawaiian territory should be alienated except to the United States, thus foreshadowing future annexation of the islands. This was followed in 1884 by the grant of Pearl Harbor to the United States as a naval station. Obviously "Manifest Destiny" had determined the fate of these lovely islands. As Secretary of State Bayard remarked, all that we needed to do was to "wait quietly and patiently and let the islands fill up with American planters and American industries until they should be wholly identified in business interests and political sympathies with the United States. It was simply a matter of waiting until the apple should fall."

The falling of the ripened fruit was hastened by two events. The first was the McKinley Tariff Bill of 1890, which provided for the removal of the duty on raw sugar and compensated American sugar producers with a bounty. The effect upon the sugar industry of Hawaii was disastrous. The advantage that Hawaiian sugar planters had enjoyed under the treaty of 1875 disappeared and they now had to meet the competition of Cuban sugar. American owners of Hawaiian plantations called loudly for annexation to the United States. To add to the economic distress the Hawaiian Queen, Liliuokalani, who came to the throne in 1891, took her position seriously, disregarding the realities of foreign domination in the islands. She proceeded to revoke the constitution of 1887, which conferred substantial privileges upon foreigners and indicated her determination to restore the autocratic power of the monarch. Quite naturally foreign residents resented this interference with their "rights," and under the guidance of the American minister, J. S. Stevens, they proceeded to foment a revolution. Supported by American marines, the revolt quickly succeeded. A provisional government was established, the American flag was raised, and a commission was promptly sent to Washington with a treaty calling for annexation to the United States. While the whole enterprise had been carried through with neatness and despatch it failed, chiefly through lack of time. President Harrison, who was about to retire from office, received the commission cordially and promptly sent the treaty to the Senate, with his endorsement. Before action could be taken by the Senate, however, President Cleveland had assumed office. Once again Cleveland showed his lack of sympathy with American expansionist enterprises. He at once withdrew the treaty from the Senate and sent a personal representative to Hawaii to make an investigation. The report he received stated that there was no doubt that the revolution had been instigated by foreign residents in the islands and that it could not have succeeded except for the support given by American marines.

Acting upon this report the President sent a message to Congress in which he denounced the attempt to annex the islands, declaring that "the control of both sides of a bargain acquired in such a manner is called by a familiar and unpleasant name when found in private transactions." He then sent a new minister to Honolulu to negotiate with the deposed Queen, but the envoy found Her Majesty in an ugly mood, determined not only to regain her throne but to execute those who had been responsible for the revolution. When the Queen was finally won over to a more reasonable point of view, the provisional government, which had had a year in which to consolidate its authority, determined to resist any attempt to restore the monarchy. The Hawaiian republic was proclaimed, and after some hesitation Cleveland abandoned the effort to restore the native monarchy and welcomed the new republic. At the same time the Senate passed a resolution declaring that the United States should not interfere in Hawaiian affairs and that it would regard interference by any other country as an unfriendly act.

But neither Senate resolutions nor Presidential scruples could stop the inevitable march of events. The dominant economic forces in Hawaii were bent upon bringing the islands under the American flag, and they bided their time until an administration in sympathy with their views was installed at Washington. With the return of the Republicans to office as a result of the election of 1896, and under expansionist enthusiasm in the country aroused by the events of the Spanish War, there came at last the picking of the ripened Hawaiian fruit. By joint resolution of Congress in 1898 the Hawaiian republic was annexed to the United States.

Viewed in retrospect, the diplomatic history of the United States in the last quarter of the nineteenth century discloses no consistent policy or any comprehensive program. In general the issues that arose dealt with isolated incidents concerning matters on the American continents. In the higher ranges of European diplomacy in this period the United States participated only in a halting and tentative manner. In 1884 and again in 1890 American representatives attended European conferences that dealt with African affairs. Although the agreements reached at these conferences were signed by the American delegates they were not submitted to the Senate for ratification because of the fear that such formal ratification might involve this country in European complications. Only in the Samoan and Hawaiian incidents do we get clear evidence of the dawning of a new era in American diplomacy.

BIBLIOGRAPHICAL NOTE

For general discussions of American foreign relations consult R. G. Adams, *History of the Foreign Policy of the United States* (1924) ; C. R. Fish, *American Diplomacy* (1924) ; by the same author, *The Path of Empire* (1919) ; J. B. Moore, *American Diplomacy* (1905) ; J. H. Latané, *History of American Foreign Policy* (1927) ; L. Sears, *History of American Foreign Relations* (1927) ; J. Q. Dealey, *Foreign Policies of the United States: Their Bases and Development* (1927) ; S. F. Bemis, ed., *American Secretaries of State and Their Diplomacy*, 10 Vols. (1927-1928), contains biographies and estimates of the achievements of all of the secretaries of state.

For special treatments of our relations with Great Britain see R. M. McElroy, *Pathway of Peace: An Interpretation of Some American and British Crises* (1927) ; R. B. Mowat, *The Diplomatic Relations of Great Britain and the United States* (1925) ; J. M. Callahan, *The Alaska Purchase and American-Canadian Relations* (1908).

For accounts of the relations of the United States with Latin-American countries consult D. Y. Thomas, *One Hundred Years of the Monroe Doctrine* (1923) ; W. S. Robertson, *Hispanic-American Relations with the United States* (1923) ; J. Agan, *The Diplomatic Relations of the United States and Brazil* (1926) ; H. C. Evans, Jr., *Chile and its Relations to the United States* (1927) ; W. R. Shepherd, *The Hispanic-Ameri-*

can Nations of the New World (1919); G. T. Stuart, *Latin-America and the United States* (1928); J. H. Latané, *The United States and Latin America* (1920).

American relations in the Pacific are considered by J. M. Callahan, *American Relations in the Pacific and the Far East* (1901); E. J. Carpenter, *America in Hawaii* (1899); C. A. Conant, *The United States in the Orient* (1900); J. W. Foster, *American Diplomacy in the Orient* (1903).

CHAPTER 11

OVERSEAS EXPANSION

It has been noted that in the last quarter of the nineteenth century the American people were little concerned with the affairs of the outside world. Their activities had been devoted largely to the exploitation of the abundant natural resources of the country. During these years, too, American manufacturers had at their door a domestic market that absorbed a large part of the goods produced. In these circumstances there was no need to search for foreign markets or to acquire outlying possessions to provide an added source of raw materials. But in the closing years of the century there were stirring beneath the surface forces that were destined to alter materially these conditions. The remarkable economic development of the country provided capital resources not only to satisfy most of the domestic demand but, in time, also a surplus beyond these needs. Moreover, shrewd industrial leaders could foresee the time when the domestic market would not be able to absorb the steadily growing output of American factories and mines. The accumulation of surplus capital seeking investment and of manufactured goods seeking a market was certain, sooner or later, to give rise to a challenge to the traditional American policy of isolation from world affairs. For the search for markets and investment opportunities in undeveloped parts of the world almost inevitably brings in its train friction with native people or with rival economic interests. This in turn is followed by appeals for intervention on behalf of the interests involved and frequently results in a greater or less degree of political control of backward countries.

233

In the major European countries, notably Great Britain, this process of economic penetration of undeveloped areas was well advanced before the close of the nineteenth century. In the United States the first manifestations of this tendency, in the Samoan and Hawaiian enterprises, did not arouse any widespread feeling among the American electorate. It is doubtful, in fact, whether any considerable number of persons in the country realized the implications of this new departure in the economic and political life of the nation. It was not until the Spanish War, which resulted in the acquisition of insular dependencies, that the American people appreciated the fact that the country was faced by a significant change in its traditional world policy. It required some finesse on the part of those who had a stake in this development to educate public opinion to the point where it was willing to accept the new policy. The materialistic appeal alone would probably have been insufficient. Only a small fraction of the people stood to gain economically by the acquisition of foreign markets or outlying possessions. Some broader appeal, preferably with an altruistic ring, seemed desirable. This was found first in the stirring of national patriotism. Westward the star of empire had taken its way from the Atlantic to the Pacific. There appeared to be no logical reason why this advance should stop at the shores of the Pacific. Territorial expansion had been characteristic of American history since colonial days and, with the occupation of the West and the disappearance of the frontier, this passion for territory could be counted upon to sanction further expansion. Then there was the appeal of the "white man's burden." Surely America should not refuse to play its part in carrying the blessings of Anglo-Saxon civilization to the backward peoples of the world. Last but not least was the religious appeal. Missionary zeal had long been a feature of American life and the call to carry the blessings of Christianity to the benighted heathen was calculated to touch a responsive chord in thousands of American breasts.

Complex forces, economic, patriotic, and religious thus appeared, in the closing years of the nineteenth century, to prepare the way for the entrance of the United States upon the stage as a world power. Hesitatingly, at first, and apparently without any definite program, we entered upon the path of empire, but experience brought confidence and by the turn of the century the leaders of the new movement were boldly proclaiming the "Manifest Destiny" of the United States.

The island of Cuba had long been an object of interest to the people of the United States. Its geographic position made it a matter of concern to this country. At one end it commands the entrance to the Gulf of Mexico while at the other it faces the Caribbean Sea and the approach to any isthmian canal that might be built. Even Thomas Jefferson, who certainly was not inclined to an aggressive foreign policy, declared he had always considered that "Cuba is the most interesting addition which can be made to our system of states." During the fifteen years prior to the Civil War the slave interests of the South made repeated attempts to acquire the island in order to provide additional slave territory. For ten years from 1868 to 1878 civil war raged in Cuba and Cuban sympathizers in the United States organized filibustering expeditions, which were sent to the island. The charge made by the Spanish authorities that the American government connived at the departure of these expeditions led to much recrimination between the two governments and when one of these filibustering vessels, the *Virginius,* was captured by the Spaniards and several Americans on board were shot, the incident nearly precipitated a war between the United States and Spain.

For seventeen years following the close of the Ten Years' War there was comparative quiet in the island, but in 1895 a new revolt started. By this time a new factor had entered the situation. Southern slaveholders were no longer pressing for the annexation of the island, but American capital in large amounts had been invested in Cuban business and the trade between the island and the United States had reached $100,000,000 annually. The economic conditions in Cuba were seriously disturbed as a result of the action of the United States, in 1894, in placing a duty on raw and refined sugar, one of the chief exports from the island. Many Cuban sugar producers were forced to curtail production and thousands of laborers were deprived of work, many of whom drifted into the ranks of the insurgents.

The struggle that followed between the insurgents and the Spanish forces was characterized by atrocities on both sides, accompanied by widespread destruction of property and trade. The Cuban leader, Gomez, adopted a policy of destroying plantations and mills, doubtless with the hope that such action would force American intervention. The Spanish general, Weyler, in an effort to crush the rebellion, ordered the concentration of the rural population near garrisoned towns. Thousands of miserable peasants were crowded into unsanitary barracks where they were insufficiently fed and clothed.

Here was a combination of circumstances calculated to arouse intense feeling in the United States. In the press, notably in those papers controlled by William Randolph Hearst, the barbarous conditions in Cuba were painted in lurid colors and a cry was raised for American intervention in the cause of humanity. This humanitarian appeal had the substantial support of important financial interests whose investments in the island were threatened by continuance of the war. The call for action reached the halls of Congress and a Congressional resolution was passed which declared that the United States should recognize the rebel government in Cuba and should intervene, if necessary, to put an end to

Spanish control of the island. But President Cleveland, then about to retire from office, was unwilling to enter upon such an important adventure, which, in the nature of things, he could not see through, and which might embarrass his successor. He therefore insisted upon maintaining an attitude of strict neutrality, although in his final message to Congress he called attention to the great damage done to American interests in Cuba as a result of the disturbed conditions there and intimated that the United States would not continue much longer to tolerate these conditions.

Thus matters stood when President McKinley assumed office in March, 1897. Lacking the aggressive independence of his predecessor, McKinley was disinclined to assume the responsibility for checking the growing sentiment in the country and in Congress for vigorous action in the Cuban situation. For a short time there was a prospect of improvement. A new liberal ministry had come into office in Spain and a change of military commanders in Cuba was accompanied by a promise of reform and the concession of autonomous government. But the Cuban leaders were unwilling to accept anything short of complete independence.

At this juncture two incidents greatly strengthened the position of those urging American intervention. Señor de Lome, the Spanish minister at Washington, in a private letter written to a friend in Havana, gave expression to some rather uncomplimentary remarks concerning President McKinley. The letter was stolen from the mail and published in the Hearst newspapers. As De Lome admitted the authenticity of the letter the State Department at Washington requested his withdrawal, and the affair tended to strengthen popular belief in Spanish duplicity throughout the United States.

The other incident was of a decidedly more tragic nature. In January, 1898, the American Consul General at Havana, in view of the popular demonstrations there against Americans, requested his government to send a war vessel to that harbor. In compliance with this request the battleship *Maine* was ordered to Havana. The Spanish authorities received the naval visitors with every evidence of good will, but three weeks later, on February 15, the American people were horrified by the news that the battleship had been destroyed by an explosion in which 260 of the officers and crew lost their lives. Despite the appeal of Captain Sigsbee of the *Maine* for suspension of judgment until the cause of the disaster should be established, popular indignation in the United States was roused to fever heat. The Spanish government offered to facilitate in every possible way the determination of the cause of the explosion. An American board of naval experts examined the hull of the sunken vessel and reported that the keel had been driven upward, thus showing that the explosion had come from outside the ship. This report was corroborated years afterward when the vessel was raised. A Spanish board, however, after a similar examination, gave its opinion that the battleship had been sunk as the result of an explosion in the forward magazine of the vessel. Quite naturally the American people accepted the views of the American experts and popular feeling in the country became daily more inflamed.

President McKinley was personally desirous of avoiding war, but he was unwilling or unable to withstand the popular clamor in the press and in the halls of Congress. On March 29 he sent an ultimatum to Spain which demanded the revocation of the *reconcentrado* order and the proclamation of an armistice for the purpose of ending the civil war in Cuba. To the first of these demands the Spanish government acceded, but it temporized in regard to the second demand, for fear of arousing patriotic resentment in Spain. In the meantime the Pope and the representatives of various European powers put forth earnest efforts to preserve peace. At Washington the representatives of Great Britain, Austria-Hungary, France, Germany, Italy, and Russia presented a collective note to the President requesting him to make every effort to preserve peace. Harassed by the advocates of both peace and war, McKinley determined to throw the responsibility upon Congress. Just before he sent his message to Congress, on April 11, the President received word that the Spanish government had agreed to the proclamation of an armistice and to grant to the Cubans "all the liberty they could expect." In his war message the President reviewed at length the Cuban situation and stated his opinion that intervention by the United States was the only solution that remained. He justified American intervention on four grounds. First, in the cause of humanity to stop the barbarities in Cuba; second, to afford protection to American lives and property in the island; third, to protect American trade and commerce; and last, to remove the constant menace to our peace which Cuban disorders entailed. He referred briefly to the latest concession promised by Spain but he did not lay before Congress a complete statement of the Spanish proposals. For this action the President has been severely criticized, but there is little reason to believe that any promise from Spain would have stayed the hand of Congress. In concluding his message the President wrote, "The issue is now with Congress. I await your action."

In both houses of Congress resolutions were passed by overwhelming majorities authorizing the President to employ the armed forces of the United States to compel Spain to withdraw from Cuba. In the Senate, largely because of the insistence of a small group of Populist members, there was added to the war resolution a pledge that the United States would claim "no sovereignty, jurisdiction, or control over the said island, except for the pacification thereof," and that at the close of the war we should "leave the government and control of the island to its people." On April 20, 1898, the Congressional resolutions were signed by the President and the Spanish War began.

Although all of the European powers promptly declared their neutrality, there was a sharp division of popular sentiment in the different countries. In Germany and France public opinion distinctly favored the cause of Spain, while in England the press, generally, and a number of prominent public men expressed warm sympathy for the United States.

From the point of view of preparedness there was a striking contrast between the American army and its navy when the war began. During the fifteen years before the Spanish War the United States had formed the nucleus of a modern navy and largely through the energetic activities of Theodore Roosevelt, Assistant Secretary of the Navy, the fleet had been brought to a high state of efficiency. On the other hand, conditions in the army aroused widespread criticism. There was evidence that politics influenced the selection of commanding officers, while incompetence, if nothing worse, appeared in the commissary department and in the sanitary arrangements at the army encampments that were formed. The regular army was increased to 62,000 men and a call for 200,000 volunteers was made by the President. Among the latter was a picturesque cavalry organization called the "Rough Riders," created chiefly through the energy of Theodore Roosevelt, who resigned his position as Assistant Secretary of the Navy in order to take an active part in the military campaign in Cuba. In recruiting his regiment of "Rough Riders" he gathered a striking group of cowboys, hunters, full-blooded Indians, and prominent athletes from leading universities of the country.

In the nature of things the navy was destined to play the more significant part in the armed conflict that followed. As soon as hostilities began Admiral Sampson, who was placed in command of the fleet in the Atlantic, was ordered to blockade Cuba and also to watch for the approach of

the Spanish fleet from Spain. At the same time Commodore
Dewey, who commanded the American fleet in the Pacific,
was directed to proceed from his base at Hong Kong to the
Philippines and attack the Spanish fleet at Manila. With
six cruisers and a revenue cutter Dewey started on his six-
hundred mile voyage to the Spanish islands.

At midnight on April 30, 1898, the American squadron
entered the bay of Manila and at daybreak the next morning the battle of Manila Bay began. The Spanish squadron
was distinctly inferior to that which Dewey commanded,
but the Spaniards made poor use of such equipment as
they had. For two hours Dewey cruised slowly back and
forth before the Spanish ships, sending broadsides from his
port and starboard batteries alternately. The Spanish fire
was wild and ineffective. The American commander then
drew off out of range to give his men a rest and to examine
the damage done. At eleven o'clock Dewey resumed the attack and completed the destruction of the Spanish fleet as
well as the reduction of the shore batteries. This astonishing
victory was accomplished without the loss of a single American life.

When the news of Dewey's achievement reached Washington on May 7, the country went wild with joy and many
Americans, doubtless, hurriedly consulted their atlases to discover where the Philippine Islands were. President Mc-
Kinley cabled the congratulations of the people to Dewey
and immediately advanced him to the rank of rear admiral.

The destruction of the Spanish fleet and fortresses at
Manila did not end Dewey's difficulties. He sent home word
that while he could take the city at any time he did not have
sufficient men or munitions to hold it. In answer to his call
the authorities sent ten thousand troops, under command of
General Merritt, from San Francisco. In the meantime British, French, Japanese, and German warships appeared at
Manila. Dewey had proclaimed a blockade of the harbor

and all of the foreign warships, except the German, observed the customary regulations of international courtesy by reporting to the American commander before entering the harbor. The German admiral, however, failed to do so until he was somewhat pointedly reminded by a shot fired across the bow of one of his ships. The arrival of additional German warships made the squadron under the command of Admiral von Diederichs equal to that of Dewey's. The German leader then proceeded to act in a most arrogant manner. He moved his ships about the harbor at will and even went to the extent of landing provisions at Manila for the Spaniards. He inquired of the British commander, Captain Chichester, what his instructions were in case of a clash between himself and Dewey, and the British captain replied that his instructions in such an event were known only to himself and Commodore Dewey. His patience exhausted, Dewey finally sent word to the German commander vigorously protesting against his "extraordinary disregard of the usual courtesies of naval intercourse" and bluntly stated that such actions would not be longer tolerated. This ultimatum brought an apology from the German admiral and the arrival of American reënforcements shortly afterward ended all interference with American authority in the harbor.

While these stirring events were taking place in the far-off Pacific other incidents scarcely less dramatic occurred in the West Indies. Shortly after the declaration of war a Spanish fleet under the command of Admiral Cervera left the Cape Verde Islands for a destination unknown. When news of its departure reached this country a panicky feeling spread throughout cities and towns on the Atlantic seaboard. Proprietors of summer resorts along the coast suffered financial loss because many persons avoided these places through fear of a possible attack by the Spanish fleet. But the navy department was convinced that the Spanish admiral would proceed to some one of the West Indies in order to refuel

after his long voyage across the Atlantic. Two fast American
scout vessels were sent to the eastward of the island of
Martinique to look out for the approach of the Spaniards.
Admiral Sampson with a part of the Atlantic fleet sailed for
Porto Rico in the hope of intercepting the Spanish fleet there.
Not finding any evidence of the Spaniards, he returned
toward Havana and the two patrol vessels off Martinique
abandoned their watch on May 10, according to instructions.
The following day the Spanish fleet slowly approached the
island of Martinique and then proceeded to the Dutch island
of Curaçoa to coal. When the whereabouts of the Spaniards
was learned by the American naval authorities Admiral
Sampson ordered Commodore Schley to proceed to the port
of Cienfuegos on the southern shore of Cuba, where it was
expected that Cervera would go. But while Schley was maintaining a blockade of Cienfuegos the Spanish admiral with
his fleet quietly slipped into the harbor of Santiago, about
three hundred miles to the eastward. When it was finally
determined that Cervera was at Santiago the entire American fleet under Admiral Sampson established a blockade of
the harbor. The American force included four first-class
battleships, one second-class battleship, two cruisers, and
several converted yachts. Among these was the battleship
Oregon, which had recently joined the fleet after a remarkable voyage from the Pacific coast around South America.

Now that the Spanish fleet was securely bottled up the
American authorities could turn their attention to the task
of conquering the Spanish forces in Cuba. Amidst scenes of
almost unbelievable confusion the American military forces,
regular and volunteer, were gathered at camps in the southern states. Trainloads of food and munitions stood for days
along the railroad sidings, no one apparently knowing where
they were to go. Heavy woolen clothing was issued to troops
about to campaign in a tropical climate. Unsanitary conditions in the training camps caused more deaths than all of

the military and naval battles of the war. The transport service was disorganized, and commanders of regiments placed their men on any ship that was available. When news of these deplorable circumstances became public, popular indignation was expressed throughout the country and it resulted in the removal of the Secretary of War, General Russell A. Alger. Although Alger was not a conspicuously able administrator, the real difficulty was that he was at the head of an antiquated military organization.

The expeditionary force, under command of General William R. Shafter, landed some fifteen miles to the eastward of Santiago. From this point General Lawton, in command of an infantry division, advanced westward and captured the village of Siboney. General Wheeler, in command of the cavalry, captured Las Guasimas after spirited fighting. Further progress was difficult because of the lack of roads through the jungle. Two important engagements marked the approach of the American forces toward the city, one on the right at El Caney, a fortified village, and the other on the left of San Juan Hill. In each of these battles the Spaniards offered stubborn resistance but the American forces succeeded in driving the Spaniards from both positions and took possession of the heights above the city.

The advance of the American forces toward Santiago made it necessary for the Spaniards to determine what should be done with the fleet in the harbor. If it remained and the Americans captured the city, the fleet would be doomed. Rather than meet this fate Governor General Blanco ordered Admiral Cervera to leave the harbor and make a dash for safety. On the morning of July 3 the American blockading squadron discovered the Spanish fleet, led by its flagship, the *Maria Teresa,* emerging from the harbor. As soon as the Spanish ships reached the open sea they turned westward under full speed, in the hope of escaping.

Just before the Spanish fleet left the harbor Admiral

Sampson, on the flagship *New York,* had gone to Siboney
for a conference with General Shafter. The *Massachusetts*
was also away, coaling at Guantánamo. The remainder of
the American fleet quickly started in pursuit of the fleeing
Spaniards and one after another the Spanish ships were
destroyed or driven ashore. Admiral Sampson, who had
heard the firing from a distance, hurried back in time to
see the last of the Spanish vessels destroyed. A second
great naval victory had been won by the Americans with
the loss of only one American life, while the Spaniards
lost over 500 in killed and wounded and 1,750 surrendered
as prisoners of war. The brilliance of this victory was somewhat dimmed by an unfortunate controversy between the
partisans of Commodore Schley, who was in command of
the fleet during the greater part of the battle, and those of
Admiral Sampson, as to the relative credit which should
be given to each. For three years the controversy was carried on in the newspapers and in Congress. A naval court
of inquiry criticized the actions of Schley both before and
during the battle at Santiago, although Admiral Dewey,
who was a member of the court, stated his opinion that
Schley was in actual command at the time of the battle
and was "entitled to the credit due to such commanding
officer for the glorious victory which resulted in the total
destruction of the Spanish ships." The Secretary of the
Navy approved the findings of the majority of the court
and disapproved the separate findings of Admiral Dewey
and this conclusion was upheld by President Roosevelt.

The destruction of the Spanish fleet was followed shortly
by the surrender of the Spanish forces at Santiago to General Shafter. General Miles was then sent with an army to
Porto Rico but before he could complete the subjugation
of that island the war had been brought to a close.

Realizing the futility of further resistance, the Spanish
government on July 18, 1898, requested the French ambas-

sador at Washington to arrange preliminary terms of peace
with the American authorities. Ambassador Cambon presented this request to President McKinley, and on July 30
a formal reply was given which stated the following terms
which the United States would be willing to accept: (1)
The immediate evacuation of Cuba and the relinquishment of
Spanish sovereignty over the island; (2) the cession to the
United States of the island of Porto Rico and one of the
islands in the Ladrones in lieu of an indemnity; (3) the
occupation by the United States of "the city, bay, and
harbor of Manila, pending the conclusion of a treaty of
peace which shall determine the control, disposition, and
government of the Philippines." On August 12 a protocol
was signed containing these provisions and the further
stipulation that a peace conference should meet at Paris
not later than October 1. On the day after the protocol was
signed the American forces in the Philippines, who had not
learned of the suspension of hostilities, captured the city of
Manila and raised the American flag.

The peace conference met at Paris on October 1. The
American delegates were William R. Day, who had resigned
as Secretary of State to head the commission, Senators
Cushman K. Davis, and William P. Frye, and George Gray,
and Whitelaw Reid, editor of the New York *Tribune,* with
John Bassett Moore as secretary. While agreeing to re-
linquish control of Cuba the Spanish representative attempted
to make the United States assume the Cuban debt. This proposal was firmly rejected by the American delegates. More
serious was the question of the disposition of the Philippines. When the Spanish War began it is doubtful whether
one American in a thousand knew where the Philippine
Islands were, and it is certain that even fewer Americans
conceived the possibility that these far-off islands would
come into the possession of the United States. Nor does it
appear that those in authority at Washington were them-

selves at all clear in their minds as to what disposition should
be made of this territory, which the fortunes of war had
placed in our hands. It is true that President McKinley in
the instructions given to the American commissioners when
they left for Paris stated that while the war had been undertaken without any thought of conquest, "The march of events
rules and overrules human action." He further observed that
the possession of the Philippines offered "commercial opportunity to which American statesmanship cannot be indifferent." He therefore concluded that the United States
must demand at least the cession of the island of Luzon.

Among the American delegates at Paris there was sharp
division of opinion concerning the disposition of the islands.
Davis, Frye, and Reid held that the United States should
demand the cession of the whole archipelago; Day favored
taking only Luzon, while Gray was opposed to taking any of
the islands because he regarded their acquisition by the
United States as a dangerous experiment in imperialism.

In the country at large public opinion, stimulated by the
press, was slowly but surely reaching the point where it
was prepared to approve the demand for the acquisition of
the islands. Powerful commercial interests were quick to
point out advantages which their possession offered. Moreover, McKinley was also much influenced, as he later declared, by the humanitarian appeal. He felt that it was our
duty to hold the islands and "to educate the Filipinos, and
uplift and civilize and Christianize them." In the end, therefore, Secretary Hay notified the American delegates at Paris
that "on political, commercial, or humanitarian grounds"
the United States must demand the cession of all of the
islands. The Spanish delegates at first protested that this
demand was a violation of the protocol but they were finally
persuaded to accept the proposal when the American commission agreed that Spain be paid $20,000,000 to relinquish
her claims to the islands.

When the treaty of peace was submitted to the United States Senate it met with determined opposition, chiefly from the Democrats and Populists. A few Republican senators, who had not been converted to the doctrine of "Manifest Destiny," added their protest against the new departure that the treaty contemplated. Senator Hoar, of Massachusetts, stated that colonial dominion over distant and alien peoples could not be made to square with the principles of the Declaration of Independence and that our expansion into the Pacific would make a mockery of the Monroe Doctrine. Senator Platt, of Connecticut, on the other hand, brushed aside these constitutional difficulties and advanced the view that "the United States is a nation; that as a nation it possesses every sovereign power not reserved in its constitution to the states or the people; that the right to acquire territory was not reserved, and is therefore an inherent sovereign right." But neither of these extreme views was accepted by a majority of the senate. Most of that body were inclined to follow the advice of Senator Lodge, which was to accept what the fortunes of war had brought and to leave to the future the determination of a definite policy in regard to the islands.

As the time for the final vote on the treaty approached it was evident that the necessary two-thirds majority could not be obtained without the aid of the Democrats. At this critical juncture Bryan came to Washington and persuaded ten Democratic senators to vote for the treaty and thus assured its ratification by the narrow majority of one vote. A further factor that aided ratification was the outbreak of an insurrection in the Philippines against the authority of the United States. Many felt that the national honor was now involved and that under the circumstances we could not withdraw from the islands. Bryan later explained that he had urged ratification of the treaty in order to bring the war to an end and that it was his purpose to demand the immediate independence of the Philippines under American protection.

For better or for worse the United States had entered upon a "Great Adventure." In Porto Rico we had acquired nearly a million new subjects of mixed negro and Spanish blood, and in the Philippines we had added seven and a half million persons, black, white, yellow, and brown, and ranging in civilization from head-hunting savages to highly cultured natives who had acquired at the least the appearance of Western civilization. Whither this "Adventure" would lead us only the future could tell.

BIBLIOGRAPHICAL NOTE

The most comprehensive and reliable treatment of the diplomatic and military aspects of the Spanish War will be found in F. E. Chadwick, *The Relations of the United States and Spain,* 3 Vols. (1909-1911) ; consult also H. E. Flack, *Spanish-American Diplomatic Relations preceding the War of 1898* (1906) ; E. J. Benton, *International Law and Diplomacy of the Spanish-American War* (1908) ; S. F. Bemis, ed., *American Secretaries of State* (1927-1928). Good surveys of the war are given by J. H. Latané, *America as a World Power* (1907) ; H. T. Peck, *Twenty Years of the Republic* (1907) ; and J. F. Rhodes, *The McKinley and Roosevelt Administrations* (1922). For the naval events of the war see J. D. Long, *New American Navy* (2 Vols., 1903) ; and A. T. Mahan, *Lessons of the War with Spain* (1899). T. Roosevelt, *Rough Riders* (1899) records the exploits of that famous regiment. For the war in the Philippines consult O. K. Davis, *Our Conquest in the Pacific* (1899). For the Dewey-Von Diederichs incident in Manila Bay see L. B. Shippee, "Germany and the Spanish-American War" in *American Historical Review,* Vol. XXX, July, 1925. Consult also in this connection, B. A. Reuter, *Anglo-American Relations during the Spanish-American War* (1924) ; and J. Keim, *Forty Years of German-American Political Relations* (1919). For a consideration of the drafting and ratification of the treaty of peace consult R. Cortissoz, *Life of Whitelaw Reid* (1921) ; and G. F. Hoar, *Autobiography of Seventy Years* (1906).

CHAPTER 12

THE FRUITS OF VICTORY

The outcome of the Spanish War forced upon the attention of the American people new and perplexing questions. What should be the attitude of the United States toward its new protégé, Cuba? Was it desirable to add millions of unassimilable aliens to the already heterogeneous population of the country? What was to be the status of the new colonial possessions in relation to the continental United States? Granted that it was desirable to acquire these new dominions, did our constitutional system warrant the acquisition of colonies that could never become states of the Union?

Of necessity these questions played an important part in the first presidential election following the war. In the nature of the case the Republican party defended the policy of expansion that it had inaugurated. Moreover, the leaders of the party were convinced that public opinion in the country was now prepared to endorse the new adventure. In a speech in the Senate in January, 1900, Senator Beveridge of Indiana, proclaimed the articles of the new faith in ringing terms. "We will not renounce," he declared, "our part in the mission of the race, trustee, under God, of the civilization of the world. . . . He has made us the master organizers of the world to establish system where chaos reigns. . . . He has made us adepts in government that we may administer government among savage and senile peoples. . . . And of all our race, he has marked the American people as His chosen Nation to finally lead in the regeneration of the world. This is the divine mission of America, and it holds for us all the profit, all the glory, all the happiness possible to man. We are trustees of the world's progress, guardians of its righteous peace. The judgment of the Master is upon us : 'Ye have been faithful over a few things; I will make you ruler over many things.' . . . Pray God the time may never come when mammon and the love of ease will so debase our blood that we will fear to shed it for the flag and its imperial destiny." Here we have the undiluted doctrine of "Manifest Destiny" and of the "white man's burden." Of course there was some dissent, even among Republicans, from these grandiose pronouncements. The Anti-Imperialist League, made up largely of "intellectuals" from New England, condemned the acquisition of dependencies as a violation of the finest traditions of America.

Doubtless many factors besides the issue of imperialism contributed to the success of the Republicans in the election of 1900. The injection of the free silver question into the campaign solidified the East against the Democrats, while it failed to arouse the enthusiasm in the West that it had excited four years before. The West was now prosperous and, moreover, the large increase in the world's gold supply which came from the opening of new mines in South Africa and the Klondike in recent years had increased the monetary supply of the country and thus deprived the free silver slogan of much of its effectiveness. Then, too, the Republicans could point to four years of unparalleled prosperity under Republican rule. But, making full allowance for all of these other factors, there would seem to be little question that a substantial majority of the American electorate had expressed its approval of our adventure as a world power.

THE UNITED STATES AND CUBA

One of the first problems that confronted the administration at the close of the Spanish War was the determination of the relations between the United States and Cuba. The first

task that the American authorities in the island had to face
was the relief of thousands of the Cuban people who were
on the verge of starvation. Major General Leonard Wood,
who served as Governor General of Cuba until 1902, did a
splendid piece of work in bringing order out of the chaos
that prevailed when Spain withdrew from the island. He
cleaned the indescribably dirty streets of Havana and other
cities, enforced sanitary regulations, built sewers, and
through scientific methods stamped out the yellow fever
scourge. In addition, he improved greatly the educational
facilities; firmly checked all attempts at factional strife; put
an end to the slipshod financial practices of the Spanish
authorities, and at the end of three years left a well-filled
national treasury.

Having set the Cuban house in order, it was important
next to fix its future economic relations with the United
States. The chief Cuban crops are sugar and tobacco, and a
large part of both crops was exported to the United States.
The Dingley tariff rates had seriously affected the importation of these commodities to the United States, and General
Wood, with the earnest support of Secretary of War Root
and President Roosevelt, urged the desirability of reducing
these rates in order to promote the economic rehabilitation of
the island. But when the President brought this matter to
the attention of Congress, the domestic beet sugar interests,
as well as the cane sugar planters of Louisiana, insisted that
a reduction of the tariff rates would ruin their business. It
was not until 1903 that Congress was finally persuaded,
largely by the insistence of President Roosevelt, to agree
to a reduction of 20 per cent. in the Dingley rates on Cuban
products, in return for which Cuba agreed to grant a reduction on American imports into Cuba ranging from 25 to 40
per cent.

Lastly, there was the question of the permanent political
relations that should obtain between the United States and

the Cuban republic. It will be recalled that the United States
on the eve of the war with Spain had declared that it had
no intention of exercising any sovereignty or jurisdiction
over Cuba except to establish peace, and that it was its purpose, as soon as this was accomplished, to leave the government of Cuba to its own people. Despite the cynical comments
in European newspapers at the time to the effect that this
pronouncement was merely a thin disguise to cover American
imperialist ambitions, there was no inclination on the part
of the Administration or of any considerable part of the
American people at the close of the war to repudiate the
promise to withdraw from the island. Nevertheless there was
a distinct feeling, particularly among those Americans who
had property interests in Cuba, that the United States should
maintain a restraining hand upon the new republic for the
purpose of protecting property and preserving order. With
this end in view Secretary Root communicated to General
Wood a number of suggestions which he proposed should
be incorporated in the Cuban constitution. The Cuban convention, which had met to draft the constitution, was not
inclined to adopt these suggestions and the question was then
brought up in Congress, where Senator Platt of Connecticut
introduced as an amendment to the army appropriation bill a
series of resolutions which provided that (1) the government of Cuba shall never enter into any treaty with any foreign power which will impair the independence of Cuba or
allow any foreign power to acquire any part of the island,
(2) the government shall not incur public debts which cannot
be defrayed by the ordinary revenues, (3) the United States
reserves the right to intervene in Cuba to preserve its independence and to maintain "a government adequate for the
protection of life, property, and individual liberty," (4) all
of the acts of the United States during its military occupancy
shall be validated, (5) the Cuban government shall adopt
adequate sanitary regulations, (6) the Isle of Pines shall

be omitted from the constitutional boundaries of Cuba, "the title thereto being left to future adjustment by treaty," [1] (7) Cuba shall lease to the United States land for coaling and naval stations. The Cuban authorities at first protested against these resolutions, particularly the one concerning the right of American intervention, on the ground that they violated Cuban independence, but upon receiving official assurance from President Roosevelt that the right of intervention would not be exercised for the purpose of "intermeddling with the affairs of the Cuban government," the provisions of the Platt Amendment were adopted as an appendix to the Cuban constitution.

On a number of occasions since the withdrawal of the American forces from Cuba in 1902 the United States has exercised the authority provided by the Platt Amendment. In 1906 Secretary Root somewhat sharply reminded the Cuban authorities that they had failed to make adequate sanitary regulations, which had been provided for in the treaty. In the same year factional strife between the Moderates and the Liberals threatened civil war and upon the urgent request of the Cuban President American forces were sent to the island and for three years a provisional government under Governor Charles E. Magoon conducted the affairs of the Republic until a new president was elected. Further internal strife in 1912 and again in 1917 necessitated American intervention, which was accompanied by a warning to the Cubans that these repeated disturbances were threatening the independence of the republic. It is a matter for sincere congratulation that the United States did not take advantage of the opportunity, on any of these occasions, to extend permanent political control over Cuba.

[1] A treaty recognizing the sovereignty of Cuba over the Isle of Pines was negotiated in 1908 and finally ratified by the U. S. Senate in 1925.

THE UNITED STATES AND PORTO RICO

The passing of sovereignty over the island of Porto Rico from Spain to the United States raised the problem of its future political relationship to the continental United States. This was not an easy matter to determine. Although a majority of the inhabitants of Porto Rico were white, more than 80 per cent. were illiterate and under Spanish rule they had had no experience in self-government. It was obvious, therefore, that they were not fitted for statehood in the Union or even for that degree of self-government which territories within the United States enjoyed. On the other hand, to have retained the island under military rule would have given rise to serious criticism in this country.

To meet the situation Congress in 1900 enacted the Foraker Act, which established in Porto Rico a modified form of territorial government. By its terms the inhabitants were made "citizens of Porto Rico and as such entitled to the protection of the United States." Such laws of the United States as were applicable were to be extended to the island. The government was placed in the hands of a governor, with a council consisting of six Americans and five Porto Ricans, all appointed by the President of the United States, and a representative legislative body chosen by a limited suffrage. The Governor's council acted both in an administrative capacity and as the upper house of the legislature. All laws passed by the insular legislature were subject to the veto both of the Governor and of Congress.

With the passing years this limited grant of self-government did not satisfy the Porto Ricans. The denial of United States citizenship hurt their pride and caused some legal confusion, for while they were not citizens of the United States they were not, on the other hand, aliens. Their status resembled that of the American Indians. Then, too, the preponderance of Americans in the upper branch of the legislature was resented. To satisfy these grievances President Wilson in 1914 issued a presidential order so reconstituting the executive council as to give the Porto Ricans a majority, and Congress in 1917 passed the Jones Act, which granted to the Porto Ricans American citizenship and deprived the council of its legislative functions, substituting in its place an elected Senate of nineteen members. Congress, however, still retained the power of veto over the acts of the legislature. While these concessions were welcomed by the people of the island, many intelligent Porto Ricans cherished the hope that some day Porto Rico would become one of the states of the Union or at least would enjoy the measure of self-government exercised by British dominions.[2]

In adjusting the economic relations of Porto Rico with the United States difficulties arose. The people of the island depend largely upon the production of certain staple agricultural products, mainly coffee, sugar, tobacco, and fruits. Shortly after the island passed under American control President McKinley stated that it was "our plain duty to abolish all customs tariffs between the United States and Porto Rico, and give her products free access to our markets." But, as in the case of Cuba, the protected sugar and tobacco interests in the United States objected, and Congress somewhat grudgingly agreed to a compromise by which Porto Rican goods were to be admitted to this country at 15 per cent. of the rates fixed in the Dingley tariff. In 1901, however, complete free trade between the island and the United States was established.

The economic and cultural development of Porto Rico

[2] The Republican party in the island for a number of years advocated statehood, while the Unionist party advocated an autonomous government along the lines of that in the British Dominions. Recently the two parties have combined in an attempt to obtain an elective governor. A petition to President Coolidge in 1928 for this change brought a somewhat sharp rebuke to the petitioners, in which the President defended the policy of this country in Porto Rico.

since its acquisition by the United States has been remarkable. The external trade of the island increased from $17,-500,000 in 1901 to $202,000,000 in 1927. Ninety per cent. of this trade is with the United States. Many miles of modern roads have been constructed; sanitary conditions have been greatly improved; public schools have been established in which more than 200,000 pupils are enrolled; and in general the standard of living of the people has been materially bettered. It does not appear, however, that this apparent prosperity of the island has been spread evenly over the native population. Wages of labor are still miserably low. Much of the property and most of the business of the island are in the hands of Americans.

THE UNITED STATES AND THE PHILIPPINES

The most troublesome problem that the Spanish War bequeathed to the United States was that of the Philippine Islands. As we have seen, it was not until after the peace conference was in session at Paris that the American authorities made up their minds to demand the cession of the islands to the United States. In the nature of the case, therefore, little or no thought had been given to the question of their political organization when they passed under American control. In fact, the first problem that confronted the American authorities in the islands was the pacification of the natives. For two years before the outbreak of the war between the United States and Spain the Filipinos, especially in Luzon, had been in a state of revolt against the Spanish administration. With the outbreak of hostilities between Spain and the United States a group of Filipino refugees, including their leader Aguinaldo, returned to the islands on Dewey's ships. For a time the insurgents and the American forces coöperated in the attack upon the Spaniards. Whether with justification or not the Filipinos cherished

the hope that the United States would pursue the same
policy toward them that had been followed in Cuba and

would grant the Filipinos independence as soon as Spanish
authority was overthrown. When, therefore, the Filipino
leaders were informed at the close of the Spanish War that
the United States had no intention of withdrawing immediately from the islands, they determined to resist American

control. For more than two years hostilities continued between the American military forces and the Filipinos, in the course of which the accepted canons of "civilized" warfare were disregarded by both sides. In the end the insurrection was suppressed, after the expenditure of more than $170,-000,000 and the loss of nearly a thousand American and more than five thousand Filipino lives.

With American authority secured, there next came the problem of formulating political institutions for the islands. Both President McKinley and Congress moved cautiously in this matter. It was no simple task to devise a political organization for more than 7,000,000 persons of alien blood, ranging all the way from extreme barbarism to advanced civilization, scattered over three thousand islands, seven thousand miles away from our shores. In order to obtain information which might aid him in determining a policy; President McKinley, in January, 1899, sent a commission headed by Jacob G. Schurman to the Philippines. On the basis of the report of this commission a second commission, with William H. Taft at its head, was sent to the islands to inaugurate civil government. In the instructions given to the commission it was directed to start with the local governments, and later proceed to the organization of the provincial and central governments. It was further advised to leave as large a measure of control in the hands of the local authorities as possible and to avoid centralization. The commission was authorized to make regulations for the collection of taxes, the expenditure of funds, the organization of an educational system, the establishment of courts, and the creation of an efficient civil service. In the appointments to civil offices competent natives were to be given preference over Americans.

Fortified by the popular mandate as expressed in the election of 1900, the Republicans proceeded with greater assurance to the elaboration of a definite colonial program. In

March, 1901, Congress, in.the so-called Spooner Amendment, vested complete power for the establishment of civil government in the Philippines in the hands of the President, until otherwise provided by·Congress. Acting under this sweeping grant of authority, President McKinley appointed Taft civil governor of the islands and directed him to take over the authority which had been exercised by the military governor. Shortly afterward, by presidential decree, three Filipinos were added as members of the commission. In accordance with the presidential instructions, the commission proceeded first to the organization of municipal and provincial governments. In the municipalities the suffrage was granted to male persons twenty-three years of age who had held any municipal office, or who owned property to the value of five hundred pesos or paid thirty pesos taxes, or who could speak, read, and write English or Spanish. The provincial officers, except the governor, were appointed by the commission.

On July 1, 1901, Congress passed the Philippine Government Act. This act confirmed the action of the President and of the commission in organizing the Philippine government and declared the inhabitants of the islands to be "citizens of the Philippine Islands, and as such entitled to the protection of the United States." It further provided that as soon as peace should be restored in the islands a census should be taken, and that two years after the completion of the census an election should be held for delegates to a Philippine assembly. The census was duly taken in 1905 and the first elections for the assembly were held in 1907. The Philippine government thereafter consisted of a governor and a civil commission, which also acted as the upper house of the legislature, appointed by the President with the consent of the Senate, and an assembly chosen by popular vote.

One of the earliest problems which the new Philippine government had to meet was that of the church lands. More than 400,000 acres of the best agricultural land in the islands were held by various religious orders. During the insurrection the friars had been driven out and, when the United States assumed control, they demanded the return of their property. The Philippine commission proposed to solve the problem by having the American government purchase the church lands and sell them to the tenants. Governor Taft visited Rome for this purpose and it was agreed that the United States should pay $7,239,000 to the religious orders for their holdings.

As we have seen, the question of the permanent retention of the Philippines was an important issue in the presidential election of 1900. In the Republican platform of that year it was stated that the Filipinos should have the "largest measure of self-government consistent with their welfare and our duties," but the Republicans declined to make any promise of ultimate independence for the islands. On the other hand the Democrats demanded an immediate declaration of the purpose of the United States to withdraw from the islands. The success of the Republicans in that election and their continuous control of the national administration during the succeeding twelve years removed the question of Philippine independence from practical politics during this period. When, however, the Democrats came into power as a result of the election of 1912 the issue was revived. The Democratic platform in that year called for "the immediate declaration of the Nation's purpose to recognize the independence of the Philippine Islands as soon as a stable government can be established." In furtherance of this promise the Democratic Congress in 1916 passed the Jones Act, which provided for an elected Filipino Senate to replace the appointed commission, extended the suffrage to all male adults who could speak or write a native dialect, and declared the intention of the United States to withdraw from the islands as soon as a stable government should be established. Mr.

Burton Harrison, who was appointed governor of the Philippines by President Wilson, further raised the hopes of the Filipinos by replacing many American office holders in the islands by natives. Thus matters stood when the United States entered the Great War and it was agreed on all sides that the question of Philippine independence should be postponed until peace was restored. But by the time that the war was over the Democrats had lost control of Congress and, as a result of the election of 1920, of the presidency as well. In his final message to Congress in December, 1920, President Wilson called attention to the fact that the people of the Philippines had maintained a stable government since the passage of the Jones Act and he therefore proposed that they be granted the independence, which had been promised them and which they desired. The Republican-controlled Congress, however, declined to carry out this suggestion. Shortly after entering office President Harding appointed a commission, headed by General Leonard Wood, to investigate conditions in the Philippines. In its report this commission conceded that a large part of the Christian population in the islands desired some form of independence but it nevertheless recommended that the present political status should continue "until the people have had time to absorb and thoroughly master the powers already in their hands." It further proposed that "under no circumstances should the American Government permit to be established in the Philippine Islands a situation which would leave the United States in a position of responsibility without authority." This report aroused great disappointment and resentment among the advocates of independence in the islands and when General Wood returned as Governor General he was met by a policy of passive resistance by the members of the Independence Party, which had gained control of both houses of the Philippine legislature.

With the view of adjusting the difficulties that had developed between the Governor General and the legislature and also of obtaining another general survey of conditions in the islands President Coolidge in May, 1926, sent Mr. Carmi A. Thompson as his special representative to the Philippines. As a result of his investigations Mr. Thompson submitted to the President a number of recommendations. In his opinion complete independence was impossible "for a long time to come," for a variety of reasons. In the first place the financial resources of the islands are not sufficient to maintain an independent government; then, the lack of a common language in the islands retards the development of a national spirit; further, the abandonment of the islands would hurt American commercial interests in the Orient and might complicate international relations in this region: finally, complete independence would deprive the Philippines of the advantage of free trade with the United States. While he opposed the granting of independence to the islands, Mr. Thompson made a number of constructive suggestions the most important of which were that the administration of our overseas territory should be taken from the War Department and assigned to a new colonial department; that civil instead of military advisers to the Governor General should be appointed; that the proposal to divide the Philippine group of islands should not be adopted; that the Jones Act should not be amended or repealed at this time; that the policy of granting further autonomy to the Filipinos should be continued; and that the Philippine government should withdraw from private business at the earliest possible date.[3]

Whatever differences of opinion there may be in this country concerning the political status of the Philippines, every American can feel proud of the record that has been

[3] In the session of Congress in 1930 the proposal to grant Philippine independence was strongly supported by representatives and senators from western states because of the competition of Philippine imports, especially sugar, with domestic products.

made in the economic and social development of the islands under American control. It is true that at first the protected interests in the United States were able to prevent the establishment of free trade between the islands and the United States. By the act of March 2, 1902, Congress allowed Philippine exports to the United States to enter at a 25 per cent. reduction from the rates of the Dingley tariff. In the Payne-Aldrich tariff of 1909, all Philippine exports, except sugar and tobacco, were admitted free of duty, and finally in the Underwood tariff of 1913 complete free trade between the islands and the United States was established. During the twenty years following the American occupation of the Philippines the agricultural and industrial products increased at a remarkable rate. In 1895, when the native revolt against Spain began, the total trade of the islands amounted to $32,000,000, in 1925 it had reached $267,000,000. A splendid piece of work had been accomplished by the Americans in roadbuilding and in sanitation. In 1913 there were 60,000 fewer deaths in the islands than in 1905. But it is in the educational development of the Filipinos that the American administration has made the most significant contribution. A complete system of education extending from the primary school to the University of the Philippines, including trade and agricultural schools, has been established. More than 7,000 school buildings have been built, housing over 1,000,-000 children, under the supervision of 25,000 teachers, nearly all of whom are natives. In the University there are nearly 5,000 students.

ANNEXATION OF HAWAII

It was in the midst of the Spanish War, and doubtless hastened by that event, that the movement for the annexation of the Hawaiian Islands was brought to a successful conclusion. President McKinley negotiated a treaty in 1897 with the Hawaiian Republic providing for annexation to the United States, but ratification in the Senate by the necessary two-thirds majority could not be obtained because of Democratic opposition. The advocates of annexation then accomplished their purpose by means of a joint resolution of the two Houses, which requires only a simple majority. The acquisition of Hawaii did not give rise to the problems that had appeared in the case of Porto Rico and the Philippines for those who controlled the island republic had long advocated its annexation to the United States. There was, however, the question of the large Asiatic population in the islands. The Chinese and Japanese constituted nearly 60 per cent. of the population, and the American and European settlers were determined to prevent the Orientals from gaining political control. This was accomplished by the organic law passed by Congress April 30, 1900. By its terms Hawaii was given the status of a United States territory, thus assuring to its people a fuller measure of constitutional rights than had been granted to the Filipinos or the Porto Ricans. All of the citizens of the former Hawaiian republic were granted United States citizenship. The act provided for a governor appointed by the president of the United States and a territorial legislature elected by the people. The voting privilege, however, was restricted to citizens who were able to speak, read or write the English or Hawaiian language—thereby excluding a large part of the Asiatic inhabitants from political privileges.

The close economic ties between the United States and Hawaii are indicated by the trade statistics of the islands. In 1927 imports into Hawaii amounted to $88,802,428 and of this sum $79,630,613 came from the United States, while of the $111,504,035 worth of exports, $109,236,321 went to the United States.

THE CONSTITUTIONAL STATUS OF DEPENDENCIES

The acquisition of outlying colonial possessions as a result of the Spanish-American War gave rise to a number of significant and perplexing constitutional questions. When Spain turned over the Philippines and Porto Rico to the United States, did these islands become immediately an integral part of this country? Did the Constitution of the United States extend automatically to these new possessions? Were Congress and the President, in dealing with these territories, bound by the same constitutional limitations which controlled their actions in dealing with the states of the Union? Were the inhabitants of these islands entitled to the privileges of citizens of the United States?

To these questions the Constitution itself gave no conclusive answers; for it contained no express provisions concerning the government of dependencies. Both President McKinley and Congress had proceeded on the assumption that the constitutional restrictions on their authority did not apply to the recently acquired island possessions. Ultimately, of course, the answers to these important questions had to be given by the Supreme Court. To persons given to strict constitutional interpretation there appeared to be no doubt that the Constitution extended to every place where the American flag floated, and a long line of judicial decisions upheld this point of view. But to apply all the provisions of the Constitution to primitive natives of tropical islands would be inconvenient if not wholly impracticable.

The Supreme ·Court resolved the difficulty by strained judicial interpretation of the Constitution in a series of decisions known as the Insular Cases. The first of these cases (DeLima vs. Bidwell, 182 U. S. 1) involved the question of the right of the Federal Government to collect duties on imports from Porto Rico under the provisions of the Dingley Tariff Act. The Dingley Act provided for duties on goods imported "from foreign countries." In its decision the Court held that Porto Rico had ceased to be foreign territory when it passed under the jurisdiction of the United States and that therefore the provisions of the Dingley law were no longer applicable to the island. This decision, however, did not answer the question whether Congress could pass a special tariff law for Porto Rico. Congress had assumed the right to do so and the Foraker Act levied duties on Porto Rican imports equal to 15 per cent. of those provided in the Dingley Act. Did this act violate the constitutional provision that all duties must be "uniform throughout the United States"? The Supreme Court attempted to answer this question in the case of Downes vs. Bidwell (182 U. S. 144). By a vote of five to four the Court upheld the constitutionality of the Foraker Act, but the five justices who constituted the majority reached a common decision along widely different lines of reasoning. Justice Brown, who delivered the majority opinion, held that Porto Rico was a "territory appurtenant and belonging to the United States, but not a part of the United States," and that therefore the Foraker Act did not violate the constitutional provision that tariff duties must be uniform throughout the United States. The four justices who dissented from the decision vigorously denied that Congress was freed from constitutional limitations in dealing with any territory over which the American flag floated. Justice Harlan said, "I confess that I cannot grasp the thought that Congress, which lives and moves and has its being in the Constitution, and is consequently the mere creature of that instrument, can, at its pleasure, legislate or exclude its creator from the territories which were acquired only by authority of the Constitution." In a later case the Court held that there are certain parts of the Constitution which are "fundamental" and that there are other parts which are merely "formal," and that while Congress is bound to observe the fundamental provisions it is free to disregard the formal ones in legislating for the territories.

In short, the Supreme Court, in these Insular Cases, by a process of forced judicial interpretation, attempted to apply the Constitution to conditions that the drafters of that instrument had never contemplated. Perhaps it would have been better to accomplish this by the more regular procedure of constitutional amendment but, in any event, public opinion in the country approved the view that the inhabitants of Porto Rico and the Philippines should not be incorporated into the body politic of the United States, and in the words of Mr. Dooley, "The Supreme Court followed the election returns."

BIBLIOGRAPHICAL NOTE

A brief survey of American colonial expansion is given by C. R. Fish, *The Path of Empire* (1921); consult also J. H. Latané, *America as a World Power* (1907); A. L. P. Dennis, *Adventures in American Diplomacy* (1928); J. W. Garner, *American Foreign Policies* (1928). For a criticism of American imperialism see G. F. Hoar, *Autobiography of Seventy Years* (1906); S. Nearing, *The American Empire* (1921).

For our relations with Cuba see L. H. Jenks, *Our Cuban Colony: A Study in Sugar* (1928); C. E. Chapman, *A History of the Cuban Republic: A Study in Hispanic-American Politics* (1927); A. G. Robinson, *Cuba and the Intervention* (1905); G. H. Stuart, *Cuba and Its International Relations* (1921); E. Root, *Military and Colonial Policy of the United States* (1916). On Porto Rico consult M. Knowlton, *Porto Rico, History and Conditions* (1926); W. F. Willoughby, *Territories and Dependencies of the United States* (1905); L. S. Rowe, *United States and Porto Rico* (1905). A good history of the Philippines is D. C. Worcester, *Philippines: Past and Present* (1914); for a vigorous defense of American policy in the islands see W. C. Forbes, *The Philippine Islands* (1921); for a criticism of American policy see M. Storey and M. P. Lichauco, *Conquest of the Philippines by the United States, 1898-1925* (1926); W. H. Taft, *Report on the Philippines,* Senate Documents, 60th Congress, 1st Series, No. 200, is an illuminating account by the first Governor General of the islands. On

Hawaii see W. F. Blackman, *The Making of Hawaii* (1899);
E. J. Carpenter, *America in Hawaii* (1899); W. R. Castle,
Hawaii, Past and Present (1917).

For a discussion of the constitutional status of dependencies
consult W. F. Willoughby, *Territories and Dependencies of the
United States* (1905); C. F. Randolph, *The Law and Policy
of Annexation* (1901); W. W. Willoughby, *The Constitutional
Law of the United States* (1910).

CHAPTER 13

THE POLITICAL TREND, 1901-1908, THE ROOSEVELT ERA

During the twenty years from 1877 to 1897 the Republican and Democratic parties had contended for control of the national government. Neither party had succeeded in holding both branches of Congress as well as the Presidency, for more than two years consecutively during these twenty years. This period of alternating party control closed with the election of 1896. For the next sixteen years the Republican party held the presidential office and, except for the last two years, both branches of Congress as well. Several factors contributed to this long lease of power by the Republicans. An effective organization under capable leaders was one. Again, these years were marked by widespread national prosperity which the Republican leaders capitalized to the advantage of their party. The directors of large business enterprises, for the most part, coupled the success of the Republican party with their own economic interests. And there can be no doubt that those who were high in the councils of the Republican party held economic views which harmonized closely with those of "Big Business." Moreover, the idea that prosperity was bound up with the success of the Republican party permeated the minds of a large number of Americans who were not closely identified with large business enterprises and led them to give their support to that party. Finally the Republicans profited by dissensions within the ranks of the Democrats. The election of 1896 left the Democratic party broken and disorganized. The western Democracy, under the leadership of Bryan, had obtained control of the party machinery but the conservative Democrats of the East refused, during the years which followed, to give to Bryan anything more than nominal support.

MC KINLEY AND THE FULL DINNER PAIL

In the election of 1896 the Republicans had presented McKinley as the "advance agent of prosperity," and the business revival which came during the following four years was naturally hailed by the Republican leaders as justifying their prediction. Then, too, the party leaders could "point with pride" to a successful war, which had carried the American flag to distant shores. Furthermore, the Republicans had redeemed the pledge made in 1896 to maintain the gold standard, and the return of prosperous times had restored government finances and brought a surplus to the treasury.

With this striking record of achievement the Republicans approached the election of 1900 with confidence. When their National Convention met in Philadelphia there was little opposition to the renomination of McKinley. He had made many friends both in Congress and throughout the country by his courtesy and his winning personality. He had, moreover, the support of Senator Hanna, who had been instrumental in securing his first nomination and who was now chairman of the National Committee. Therefore, despite some opposition from Republican leaders who were opposed to the colonial policy of the administration, McKinley was unanimously renominated for the presidency. The chief interest in the convention was aroused in connection with the selection of a candidate for the vice presidency. Senator Platt, of New York, urged the choice of Theodore Roosevelt, not because of any admiration for the man but because he hoped thereby to remove a disturbing influence in his political bailiwick. Platt had agreed to the nomination of

Roosevelt as Governor of New York in 1898, hoping to profit by the popularity which Roosevelt had gained in the Spanish War. In office, Roosevelt refused to submit to the dictation of the party Boss and Platt determined to get rid of him by forcing his nomination for Vice-President. Roosevelt understood Platt's motives and he declared that under no circumstances would he accept the nomination. Furthermore, neither McKinley nor Hanna welcomed the suggestion of Roosevelt's name. Hanna felt that Roosevelt's record and character would not fit into the "safe and sane" scheme of things which had characterized the McKinley era, while the President had had an opportunity to become acquainted with the restless and energetic Governor when he was Assistant Secretary of the Navy at the outbreak of the Spanish-American War. But the reluctance of Roosevelt and the opposition of McKinley and Hanna combined failed to overcome the enthusiastic support which Roosevelt received from western delegates and he was nominated on the first ballot, receiving every vote in the convention except his own.

The Republican platform strongly endorsed the administration of President McKinley and justified the acquisition of our colonial possessions. It gave full credit to the Republican party for the notable prosperity of the country during the preceding four years; advocated extension of American trade in the Orient; and favored government aid in building up the merchant marine. The trust plank, drafted by Hanna, was conveniently vague in its statement about "the necessity and propriety of the honest coöperation of capital to meet new business conditions, and especially to meet our rapidly increasing foreign trade."

The Democratic party entered the campaign of 1900 still handicapped by the factional division that had marked the election of 1896. At the Democratic convention at Kansas City the conservatives were unable to present any formidable opposition to Bryan, and he was nominated by acclamation.

For the sake of consistency Bryan insisted that the platform of the party should include a plank indorsing free silver. The chief emphasis of the platform, however, was placed upon the "trust question" and "the burning issue of imperialism." Private monopolies were declared to be indefensible and intolerable and the party was pledged "to an increasing warfare in nation, state, and city against private monopoly in every form." Imperialism was declared to be the paramount issue which "threatened the very existence of the Republic and the destruction of our free institutions." The subjection of the Philippines and the retention of the islands against the wishes of the natives was declared to be a repudiation of the principles enunciated in the Declaration of Independence. A bid for the labor vote was made by incorporating a plank denouncing "government by injunction." To conciliate the conservative wing of the party the vice presidential nomination was offered to David B. Hill, of New York, and, upon his refusal to accept, the convention named Adlai E. Stephenson, of Illinois, who had held this office during President Cleveland's second term.

In the campaign Bryan once more toured the country and appealed to the masses to rally to the support of the Democratic party in its war on "Plutocracy." But this appeal was far less effective than it had been four years before. Returning prosperity had relieved in a measure the distress of the farmers and laborers and the spirit of discontent was for the time being quiescent. The free silver slogan also had lost much of its potency. Recent discoveries of gold in the Klondike and South Africa had added materially to the world supply of the precious metal and had enabled the government to increase substantially the amount of money in circulation,[1] thereby satisfying to an extent the demands of those who had advocated the free coinage of silver. Although McKinley

[1] Between 1896 and 1902 nearly twice as much gold was coined by the government as in any five-year period since 1873.

conducted his campaign quietly from the front porch of his home in Canton, Ohio, Roosevelt injected a lively element into the political contest by following Bryan about the country and denouncing the Democratic candidate for his advocacy of a policy of "scuttle" in the Philippines. Hanna, in the meantime, was effectively appealing to the large business interests to save the country from the menace of Bryanism and he succeeded in raising a campaign fund of more than $2,500,000.

The results of the November election indicated that the electorate had not been greatly aroused by the "paramount" isue of imperialism. Bryan's vote was 142,000 less than in the previous election and he lost the states of Kansas, Nebraska, South Dakota, Utah, Wyoming, and Washington, which he had carried in 1896. These losses were partly offset by gains in eastern states due to the return of some conservative Democrats to the party and to support from disgruntled Republicans who were opposed to the colonial policy of their party. McKinley received a popular vote of 7,219,-525, and Bryan 6,358,737. The electoral vote was 292 to 155. On March 4, 1901, President McKinley entered upon his second term, fortified by a striking demonstration of popular support. The large business interests of the country looked forward with confidence to another four years of prosperity under the fostering care of a benevolent administration.

Fate decreed otherwise. On the sixth of September, 1901, while attending the Pan-American Exposition at Buffalo, President McKinley was shot by a young Polish fanatic. For a few days it looked as though the wound would not prove fatal. He withstood the operation for the removal of the bullet successfully and was apparently on the road to recovery when complications set in and on September 14th he died. Vice-President Roosevelt heard of the death of the President while in a camp in the Adirondacks, and he made a hurried trip to Buffalo where he took the oath of office as President.

The universal and evidently sincere expressions of popular grief which came when word of the President's death was received demonstrated the affection in which he was held by the American people. His career as President forms a striking contrast to that of his predecessor Cleveland or of his successor Roosevelt. Lacking the stubborn qualities of the former and the vigorous personality of the latter, McKinley accomplished his purposes by means of persuasion and compromise. His Congressional experience stood him in good stead. He understood how to work with Congress instead of attempting to drive that body. In temperament he was distinctly conservative and showed little understanding of or sympathy with the forces of discontent that came to the surface during his administration. His inclination to follow rather than to lead public opinion caused many persons to believe that McKinley was dominated by Hanna and other party leaders. But those who were nearest to him have insisted that he had a will of his own which he did not hesitate, on occasion, to assert. How McKinley would have met the formidable problems that confronted his successor it is not possible to say, but in the last speech he made before his assassination he seemed to sense a coming change and a willingness to modify his views accordingly. He warned his fellow tariff protectionists that "we must not repose in fancied security that we can forever sell everything and buy little or nothing," and boldly asserted that if "some of our tariffs are no longer needed for revenue or to encourage and foster our industries at home, why should they not be employed to extend and promote our markets abroad?" These were strange and disturbing ideas to come from the lips of the high priest of protection.

THE ROOSEVELT ERA

After Theodore Roosevelt had taken the oath of office as President he added solemnly: "I wish to state that it shall be my intention and endeavor to continue, absolutely unbroken, the policy of President McKinley, for the peace, prosperity and honor of our beloved country." Doubtless this was said in all sincerity, but the personality of the new President coupled with the rapidly moving tide of events made this resolution impossible of accomplishment.

At the time he assumed the presidential office Roosevelt was not quite forty-three years of age, but he had already had a wide experience in public life. Shortly after his graduation from Harvard College he began his public career as a member of the New York legislature. Then followed in rapid succession his appointment as a member of the United States Civil Service Commission, as President of the Board of Police Commissioners of the city of New York, as Assistant Secretary of the Navy in the first McKinley administration, as colonel of the "Rough Riders" in the Spanish War, and, finally, his election as Governor of New York. In all of these positions he had given evidence of the fearlessness and untiring activity which made the old-line politicians extremely apprehensive when fate brought him to the presidency.

Few, if any, of Roosevelt's predecessors in the presidency could compare with him in versatility, forcefulness, buoyant energy, and ability to sense public opinion and win popular support. He displayed a lively interest in a great variety of subjects. He had read to an astonishing extent in the fields of history, science, art, literature, politics, sport, in fact in nearly every realm of human endeavor—and he delighted to discuss with leading authorities the latest productions in these diverse subjects. In addition he found time to write innumerable letters to a host of friends and to publish upward

of thirty volumes on history, politics, war, and sport. To
an unusual degree Roosevelt possessed the ability to make
friends, and his friends were drawn from every social class.
He met with equal facility littérateurs and prize-fighters,
politicians and cowboys, clergymen and labor leaders. He
had a keen appreciation of the value of publicity, and
seemed to sense instinctively the drift of public opinion.
With vigorous and picturesque language he was able to focus
public attention upon even the most unappealing subjects.
A reformer and a propagandist, in the best sense of that
word, Roosevelt never permitted his idealism to get the better
of his practical common sense. He fought with vigor and
sincerity for those things he thought were right, but he understood, none the less, how to employ the devices of the
politician to accomplish his ends.

Concerning such a dynamic personality it was difficult to
maintain a neutral opinion. Persons were apt to be either devoted followers and vigorous supporters of Roosevelt or his
equally intense opponents. Convinced of the righteousness of
the cause that he espoused and of the soundness of his own
judgment Roosevelt was inclined to be impatient with those
who did not agree with him and even to impute to them base
motives. Given to the use of superlatives and impatient to
accomplish results, he laid himself open to the charge of
being superficial and hasty in reaching his decisions. Few
would claim that Roosevelt's views on public questions were
always sound or that the means that he used in accomplishing his purposes were never open to criticism, but on the
other hand few would deny his sincerity or his high sense of
public duty. He surrounded himself with an unusually able
group of advisers and associates and he succeeded in instilling
into them a large measure of his own enthusiasm.

Roosevelt's experience in public life had been largely in
executive and administrative positions. He was accustomed
rather to giving than to receiving orders. When he became

President it was natural that he should use to the full the large powers of that office and, in fact, extend the scope of those powers. As he afterward said, "I did and caused to be done many things not previously done by the President and the heads of executive departments. I did not usurp power, but I did greatly broaden the use of the executive power. In other words, I acted for the common well being of all of the people, whenever and in whatever manner was necessary, unless prevented by direct constitutional or legislative prohibition. I did not care a rap for the mere form and show of power; I cared immensely for the use which could be made of the substance." Roosevelt here indicates his conception of the President as the spokesman of all of the American people. In his dealings with Congress he was wont to refer to "my policies" and to regard that body as the instrument for giving effect to such policies. He did not scorn the politicians in or out of Congress but utilized them for his own purposes. To near the end of his political career he remained a party man, believing that more was to be accomplished by working within the party than by bolting.

When Roosevelt entered upon his duties as President, conditions in the country were ripe for just such a forceful leader who could crystallize sentiments which had formed in the minds of a large number of people. It will be recalled that the election of 1896 gave evidence of the existence of widespread discontent throughout the country. The results of that election, coupled with the return of prosperity and the outbreak of the Spanish War, quieted for the time being these disturbing influences. But the underlying causes of economic unrest still remained. In fact, during the four years of McKinley's administration they became more acute. As has been pointed out elsewhere, the directors of large business enterprises took advantage of the benevolent attitude of the Republican administration to indulge in questionable financial practices and to show a cynical disregard of the interests of the public. By the year 1901 the glamour of the Spanish War had passed and economic questions once more pressed to the front. In labor and agrarian circles doubts were expressed as to whether the boasted McKinley prosperity was being generally shared by all classes of society. Out in Wisconsin Robert M. La Follette, after a long and bitter fight against the political domination of the railroads and other corporations in that state, was finally elected governor in 1900 and proceeded to launch the "Wisconsin idea," which, among other things, advocated the control and equitable taxation of railroads and other corporations, direct primaries which might enable the voters to control the party machinery, and the conservation of the natural resources of the state. It was left for Roosevelt to apply these principles on a national scale.

Roosevelt's first message to Congress, in December, 1901, was a confession of faith and a declaration of policy. In this voluminous document he set forth his views on nearly every important public question. In the first place he hastened to reassure conservative business interests that he had no intention of making a rash assault upon industry. He expressed the view that the growth of large-scale industry was the result of natural economic causes and that it would be both unwise and futile to attempt to prevent such development. He praised the work of the captains of industry who had contributed so much to the material development of the nation and criticized those who made it their vocation to denounce all large fortunes. Yet he observed, "There is a widespread conviction in the minds of the American people that the great corporations are in certain of their features and tendencies hurtful to the general welfare." To remedy current abuses he stated that business combinations should not be prohibited but should be regulated by the Federal Government. It was essential, in order to act intelligently in dealing with industrial combinations, to obtain the facts; and he therefore urged that full and exact information as to the operation of corporations should be made public at regular intervals. In order to have adequate governmental machinery to handle these industrial problems he recommended that a Department of Commerce and Industries should be created with a Secretary having a seat in the Cabinet.

Stubborn resistance to such a program was sure to come from industrial leaders unwilling to concede that the era of *laissez faire* was ended. As Roosevelt later said, "The big reactionaries of the business world and their allies and instruments among politicians and newspaper editors . . . fought to keep matters absolutely unchanged." But Roosevelt was not to be turned from his course. He carried his appeal directly to the people in a speaking tour of the New England states and the West, and the popular response was generally favorable. Nor did he confine himself to words. In 1902, as we shall see, he interfered with vigor in the anthracite coal strike and also directed the Attorney General to bring suit against the Northern Securities Company for violation of the Sherman Anti-Trust Law. In 1903 Congress carried out the suggestion of the President for the establishment of a Department of Commerce and Labor. This included a Bureau of Corporations, authorized to investigate the organization and methods of business corporations. In the same year was passed the Elkins Act, by which it was hoped to stop the practice of granting rebates by railroads.[2]

Nor did Roosevelt restrict his efforts to the field of domestic affairs. His prompt intervention in the Venezuelan dispute [3] and his brusque handling of Colombia in the Panama controversy [4] gave rise to much public acclaim and not a little criticism. But whether one agreed or disagreed

[2] See p. 370.
[3] See p. 446.
[4] See p. 450.

with Roosevelt's multifarious activities none could deny that
in the three and a half years in which he was completing the
unexpired term of McKinley he succeeded in winning a large
and enthusiastic popular following and became the outstanding political figure of his time.

It was only natural that Roosevelt should desire an expression of approval from the American people by being chosen
President in his own right in the election of 1904. Apart
from the personal gratification that this would bring, Roosevelt believed that he needed another four years in the presidential office in order to carry out the policies close to his
heart. At first it appeared that there would be considerable
opposition to his nomination by the Republican party. The
professional politicians of the party resented the independent
attitude he had assumed. The large financial and business
interests were irritated at his interference with their "rights"
and were apprehensive of further action he might take to
curb their power. It was rumored that these forces in the
Republican ranks would back Senator Hanna against Roosevelt for the nomination. If such was the intention the plan
was frustrated by the death of Hanna, on February 15, 1904.
It was then too late to rally the anti-Roosevelt forces behind
any other candidate, and when the convention met at Chicago in June, Roosevelt was nominated by acclamation, with
Senator Fairbanks, of Indiana, as his running mate. The
platform perforce "pointed with pride" to the record of the
Republican party, upheld the protective tariff, defended
Roosevelt's action in Panama, advocated civil service reform,
and reaffirmed the maintenance of the gold standard. But
there is little indication in the platform that the party leaders
approved or even understood the new trend in economic and
political thought of the preceding three years. There was no
ringing denunciation of the evils of the trusts but only a
statement that combinations of both labor and capital should

not be permitted to infringe upon the rights of the people and that both are entitled to legal protection if formed for lawful purposes.

When the Democratic convention assembled at St. Louis a·bitter struggle ensued between the radical and conservative elements in the party. The latter were determined to wrest control of the party machinery from the Bryan forces, which had carried the party to defeat in the two preceding campaigns. The conservative insisted that the only hope of success in the coming election lay in the return of the party to the principles it had advocated before 1896. In fact there was considerable talk among the eastern Democrats of drafting Grover Cleveland once more to lead them to victory. But this suggestion met with a prompt refusal on the part of the ex-President to allow his name to come before the convention. The Bryan forces rallied behind William Randolph Hearst, who had attained national notoriety by means of his sensational newspapers. In the end the conservative forces in the convention triumphed and they nominated for President Alton B. Parker, Chief Judge of the New York Court of Appeals. A platform was adopted that denounced the Republican administration as "spasmodic, sensational, spectacular, and arbitrary," called for a revision of the tariff, upheld civil service reform, advocated the enforcement of the anti-trust laws and the popular election of United States Senators. Against the vehement protest of Bryan all mention of the currency question was omitted from the platform. In order that his position on this question should be clearly understood by the delegates Judge Parker sent a telegram to the convention in which he stated that he regarded the gold standard as "firmly and irrevocably established," and that if his views did not meet the approval of the convention he desired to have some one else nominated. Despite the strong opposition of the Bryan forces the convention notified Parker that the platform was silent on the question of the monetary standard because it was not regarded as an issue in the campaign and that his views would not preclude him from accepting the nomination.

In the campaign that followed the Democratic candidate utterly failed to arouse popular enthusiasm. He had made an excellent record as a judge but he was scarcely known outside of New York and his colorless personality stood out in striking contrast to that of his popular opponent. On the question of the trusts and other economic and social problems then to the front Parker offered no program to catch the popular imagination. Moreover he was unable to convince any large part of the business and financial interests that his brand of conservatism was preferable to Roosevelt's radicalism. The one incident that aroused some excitement in an otherwise listless campaign arose from a charge made by Parker that the chairman of the Republican National Committee, George B. Cortelyou, had used information concerning actions of certain corporations which he had obtained while he was Secretary of Commerce to force these corporations to make large contributions to the Republican campaign fund. Just before the election Roosevelt issued a statement denouncing these charges as "unqualifiedly and atrociously false" and Parker was unable to produce any evidence to substantiate his accusation, although later investigation disclosed that both the Republican and Democratic parties had received large contributions from corporations in this campaign.

The election resulted in an overwhelming victory for Roosevelt. The Democrats carried no state outside of the solid South. West of the Mississippi the Democratic vote was 500,000 less than it had been in 1900. In only seven states did Parker's vote exceed the votes cast for Bryan four years before. It is evident that a considerable number of Bryan supporters did not vote at all, or cast their ballots for Roosevelt with the conviction that a radical Republican was preferable to a conservative Democrat. The popular vote was 7,624,489 for Roosevelt and 5,084,422 for Parker, thus giving Roosevelt the largest vote as well as the largest majority which had ever been obtained by a presidential candidate. Immediately after the election Roosevelt issued a statement to the effect that he regarded the three and a half years which he had served as his first term and that under no circumstances would he be a candidate for or accept another nomination.

Strengthened by the impressive popular endorsement given him in the election Roosevelt determined to press with greater vigor the policies he had advocated. In his first message to Congress after the election he reaffirmed his earlier views concerning the necessity for governmental control of corporations and he lost no time in putting into practice his convictions. As a result of an investigation made by the Commissioner of Corporations a suit was instituted against the "beef trust" and the Supreme Court rendered a decision ordering its dissolution. Prosecutions were also started against the Standard Oil Company of New Jersey and the American Tobacco Company, although the final decrees in these cases were not entered until after President Roosevelt left office. Charges brought against the Standard Oil Company of Indiana for receiving rebates from the Chicago and Alton Railroad resulted in a verdict against the corporation in the Federal district court and the imposition of a fine of $29,240,000. On appeal to the circuit court, however, the company succeeded in having the decision reversed and the fine remitted, chiefly on a technical interpretation of the meaning of the law. Another corporation that ran afoul of the law was the American Sugar Refining Company. In November, 1907, a Federal official discovered that the company had defrauded the government out of a large amount due on tariff duties by manipulating the scales on which the imported sugar was weighed. Suit being brought for the recovery of the sums due resulted in a verdict for the government and the payment of more than $2,000,000 by the American Sugar Refining Company and $1,500,000 by other companies which had been guilty of the same practices.

In his efforts to secure additional legislation to strengthen the hands of the Federal Government in dealing with the trust and railroad problem the President met with determined opposition from the conservative members of his own party in Congress. Only by making an appeal directly to the people did he succeed in bringing sufficient pressure to bear upon Congress to obtain the legislation for which he asked. Most important of these measures was the Hepburn Act, which increased the size and added to the powers of the Interstate Commerce Commission. In response to the public interest that had been aroused by the publication of Upton Sinclair's *Jungle*, Roosevelt in 1906 appointed a commission to investigate the conditions in the Chicago stockyards. The report of the commission called attention to unsanitary conditions prevailing in the packing industry and urged the enactment of remedial legislation in the interest of public health. The result was the passage by Congress of the Meat Inspection Act, which authorized the Federal authorities to inspect meat shipped in interstate commerce and also to see that sanitary conditions were maintained in slaughtering houses. Another piece of legislation of a similar character was the Pure Food and Drugs Act, which prohibited the "manufacture, sale or transportation of adulterated, misbranded, poisonous, or deleterious foods, drugs, or liquors." The law required that all such articles should carry a label stating the character of the contents and that no "deleterious drug, chemical, or preservative" could be used.

Although Roosevelt energetically supported these and other measures which were aimed at undoubted abuses in the business world he was not in sympathy with the indiscriminate onslaught upon "big business" which was made in a number of "muckraking" magazines and by sensational writers. He realized that exaggerated or unfounded accusations would inevitably lead to a reaction in popular feeling and discredit the whole movement for reform. As he forcefully put it, "I want to let in light and air, but I do not want to let in sewer gas. If a room is fetid and the windows are bolted I am perfectly contented to knock out the windows, but I would not knock a hole in the drain pipe. In other words, I feel that the man who in a yellow newspaper or in a yellow magazine makes a ferocious attack on good men, or even attacks bad men with exaggeration or for things they have not done, is a potent enemy of those of us who are really striving in good faith to expose bad men and drive them from power. I disapprove of the whitewash brush quite as much as of mud slinging, and it seems to me that the disapproval of one in no shape or way implies the approval of the other."

It was in the nature of things that many of the large business and financial leaders should resent what they were pleased to consider Roosevelt's meddling with their affairs and they eagerly sought an opportunity to discredit him. They felt that this opportunity had come when the financial panic of 1907 struck the country. The President's opponents were quick to point out that the unstable condition was caused by the unwarranted governmental interference with private business. Not only the conservative press but many of the President's warmest supporters urged him to modify his policies but he declined to heed any of these suggestions. In a letter to President Scull of Bryn Mawr College he said: "That some trouble has been caused by the action which I have taken against great and powerful malefactors, I have no doubt; and in any such case there are always people of little faith who at once scream in favor of a continuance of corruption and dishonesty rather than see any unsettlement of values because of the enforcement of the principles of honesty. I shall pay no heed whatever to these people whose attitude I regard as profoundly foolish and profoundly immoral. In other words, their attitude is precisely like that of a man who, having a cancer which can be cured by the use of the knife, nevertheless screams and refuses to submit to an operation because he knows that there will be temporary pain and discomfort."

In fact the fundamental cause of the financial disturbance in 1907 was the speculative fever that had swept over the country during the preceding six years and the unsound, if not reckless, financial operations of some of the large industrial enterprises. When the crash came President Roosevelt did everything in his power to restore confidence. He kept in constant communication with the financial leaders in New York and tried in every legitimate way to prevent the spread of the panic to other parts of the country. One of his actions in this connection subjected him at a later time to severe criticism. Two of the leading figures in the United States Steel Corporation, Judge E. H. Gary and Mr. H. C. Frick, called on the President to ascertain the attitude that the government would take if the Steel Corporation should purchase a large block of stock of the Tennessee Coal and Iron Company. They assured the President that the contemplated purchase had been urged by a number of leading bankers in order to prevent the failure of an important financial institution that held the stock. They stated that under normal conditions the Steel Corporation would not regard the transaction as of advantage to that body but they were willing to go through with the project for the purpose of relieving the financial tension, provided that the government would not regard such action a violation of the anti-trust law. After consultation with the Attorney General the President told Gary and Frick that although he could not advise them to take the action proposed he felt that he had no public duty to interpose any objection.

His willingness to coöperate with those who were striving to ease the financial situation did not prevent him from striking out at those who attempted to load the responsibility for the business disturbance upon his shoulders. Early in 1908 the Louisville and Nashville Railroad served notice of a reduction in wages because of the "drastic laws inimical to the interests of the railroads that have in the past year been enacted by Congress and the State Legislature." President Roosevelt promptly accepted this challenge and directed the Interstate Commerce Commission to make a thorough investigation in order to ascertain the merits of the case. In his letter to the Commission he said: "If the reduction in wages is due to natural causes, the loss of business being such that the burden should be, and is, equitably distributed between the capitalist and the wage-earner, the public should know it. If it is caused by legislation, the public and Congress should know it; and if it is caused by misconduct in the past financial or other operations of any railroad, then everybody should know it, especially if the excuse of unfriendly legislation is advanced as a method of covering up past business misconduct by the railroad managers, or as a justification for failure to treat fairly the wage-earning employees of the company." The managers of the railroad saw a light and no reduction in wages was made.

From the point of view of the future welfare of the nation Roosevelt's efforts to control the great industrial combinations were not so significant as his activities in furthering the movement for the preservation of the natural resources of the country. During the nineteenth century, as has been noted, the Federal Government had dispensed with a lavish hand a large part of the immensely valuable national domain. Public opinion either approved of or was indifferent to the policy of transferring to private ownership the agricultural, timber, and mineral resources of the nation. Not content with the liberality of the government in disposing of

its valuable heritage, many unscrupulous individuals and corporations obtained large amounts of public land by methods
of dubious legality and frequently by downright fraud. In private hands these national resources were exploited in the most
ruthless fashion. Timber was cut recklessly, little or no effort
being made to select the ripe from the growing timber or to
reforest cut-over land. Disastrous forest fires, usually caused
by carelessness, annually destroyed millions of feet of valuable lumber. Crude and wasteful methods of coal mining resulted in leaving inaccessible in the ground large quantities
of coal. Natural gas and oil were allowed to escape, apparently on the assumption that the supply of these valuable
commodities was inexhaustible.

By such criminally wasteful processes was national wealth
of inestimable value threatened with rapid and permanent
exhaustion. Experts pointed out that unless new methods of
lumbering were adopted the standing timber of the country
would not last more than thirty years. Scientists demonstrated that destruction of forests caused vast losses due to
floods and the erosion of agricultural lands. But the public
conscience was slow in becoming aroused to the menace of
the situation, and those profiting from the process quite
naturally resisted every effort on the part of the government
to interfere with their accumulation of wealth. There was
need for a leader who could stir the dormant public interest
in the movement to conserve what remained of our natural
resources, and such a leader was found in President Roosevelt.

In 1891 Congress had enacted a law which conferred upon
the President the right to set aside and withhold from sale
public lands partly or wholly covered by timber or undergrowth. Presidents Harrison, Cleveland and McKinley made
moderate use of the authority given to them by this act, but
it was left for Roosevelt to exercise to the full the power
granted, and during his seven and a half years as President

he withdrew from sale one hundred and fifty million acres of forest land. To administer these forest reserves there was formed the United States Forest Service, under the able and energetic Gifford Pinchot as Director. A systematic plan of fire prevention and reforestation was inaugurated. Agricultural land in the forest reserves was thrown open to settlement under regulations that favored the settler rather than the large stockowner. Grazing privileges, which had formerly been enjoyed without any expense to the stockowners were thereafter to be paid for at a reasonable rate. From this source and from the sale of timber and the leasing of water-power rights a substantial sum was turned in yearly to the public treasury.

Out of the movement for the preservation of the forests there developed the general conservation movement. In March, 1907, President Roosevelt appointed an Internal Waterways Commission for the purpose of improving the system of water transportation and to "consider the relations of the streams to the use of all the great permanent natural resources and their conservation for the making and maintenance of permanent homes." Later in the year the President made a trip down the Mississippi for the purpose of arousing public interest in the development of the inland waterways, and at the same time he announced his intention of summoning a conference, to consider ways and means of conserving our natural resources.

In May, 1908, this notable gathering met in Washington. In addition to the President, Vice-President, members of the Cabinet and Justices of the Supreme Court, there were in attendance the Governors of thirty-four states and representatives of twelve others, the Governors of all the territories, representatives of sixty-eight national societies, and a number of distinguished invited guests. The conference adopted a declaration of principles which set forth "that the great natural resources supply the material basis upon which our civilization must continue to depend and upon which the perpetuity of the nation itself rests," and that it was of vital importance to conserve these resources. Concretely it recommended the extension of the forest policies already established; the improvement of inland waterways; the conservation of water resources for irrigation and water-power; and the elimination of waste in mining. It further recommended the appointment of National and State conservation commissions. Acting upon this suggestion President Roosevelt appointed a national conservation commission with Gifford Pinchot as chairman. This body accomplished an important piece of work in making an inventory of the natural resources of the country, despite the fact that Congress refused to make any appropriation and attempted to prevent government bureaus from doing any work for the commission.

Another phase of the conservation movement was the reclamation of arid and waste lands. Millions of acres of land in the western states suitable for agriculture were not cultivated because of an insufficient water supply. Upon the recommendation of President Roosevelt Congress, in 1902, passed the Newlands Act, which provided that 95 per cent. of the money received from the sale of public lands in sixteen of the western states should be used for the construction of irrigation works. Money obtained from the sale of water to settlers was to be placed in a revolving fund to be used for further construction. Within ten years after the passage of this law huge dams had been constructed in several western states which supplied water to over 3,000,000 acres of farm land.

Seven and a half years of almost uninterrupted effort on the part of President Roosevelt and his supporters to curb the power of organized wealth had brought important results. They had succeeded in establishing, at least for the time being, the principle that private property rights were subordinate to the broader interests of the public. Railroad and

industrial corporations had been forced to modify to a degree
their former arrogant attitude toward the public. Remnants
of the vast national domain had been saved from the grasping hands of selfish exploiters. Most important of all, the
national conscience had been aroused to the existence of glaring evils in the economic and political life of the nation.
Taking advantage of this awakened public conscience, the
reform leaders extended the scope of their activities. To a
consideration of this wider reform movement we shall now
direct our attention.

BIBLIOGRAPHICAL NOTE

General accounts of the Roosevelt era are to be found in
H. Howland, *Theodore Roosevelt and His Times* (1921) ; F. A.
Ogg, *National Progress* (1918) ; J. F. Rhodes, *McKinley and
Roosevelt Administrations* (1922) ; M. Sullivan, *Our Times,*
Vol. II (1927) ; J. H. Latané, *America as a World Power*
(1907).

Roosevelt's personality and policies have been set forth in a
number of volumes, most of which, however, are uncritical.
J. B. Bishop, *Theodore Roosevelt and His Times* (1920) was,
in part, prepared under Roosevelt's supervision and is necessarily sympathetic ; Roosevelt's own estimate of his times can
be found in his *Autobiography* (1913), and in *Selections from
the Correspondence of Theodore Roosevelt and Henry Cabot
Lodge* (1925). Other biographical sketches are W. D. Lewis,
The Life of Theodore Roosevelt (1919) ; W. R. Thayer, *Theodore Roosevelt: An Intimate Biography* (1919) ; L. F. Abbot,
Impressions of Theodore Roosevelt (1919) ; G. R. R. Charn-
wood, *Theodore Roosevelt* (1923), is by an English writer. See
also O. K. Davis, *Released for Publication: Some Inside Political History of Theodore Roosevelt and His Times* (1925).

On the policy of Roosevelt toward the corporations consult
Ogg cited above and B. P. De Witt, *The Progressive Movement*
(1915) ; B. H. Meyer, *A History of the Northern Securities
Case* (1906) ; J. Mitchell, *Organized Labor* (1903) ; G. Ken-
nan, *E. H. Harriman* (1922) ; J. R. Day, *The Raid on Prosperity* (1907), is a criticism of Roosevelt's policy.

The best study of the conservation movement is C. R. Van Hise, *The Conservation of National Resources in the United States* (1910) ; see also G. W. James, *Reclaiming the Arid West* (1917) ; G. Pinchot, *The Fight for Conservation* (1910) ; J. J. Hill, *Highways of Progress* (1910).

CHAPTER 14

THE POLITICAL TREND, 1908-1912

THE PROGRESSIVE MOVEMENT

In the course of the long struggle for governmental control of corporations described in the preceding chapter, abundant evidence had been disclosed of the powerful influence exercised by business organizations in state and national legislatures and in the organizations of both of the major political parties. Time and again legislation favored by large corporate enterprises had been enacted and measures to which they were opposed had been defeated by methods that would not stand the light of day. What Elihu Root described as the "invisible government" in New York state could be found in nearly every state of the Union, and at the national capital. In both political parties the leaders were often men like Thomas C. Platt in New York, who had close affiliations with large business organizations. Confronted by this situation, the reform leaders reached the conclusion that there was little chance of placing upon the statute books progressive legislation until the alliance between "big business" and the government was broken; and to accomplish this a number of fundamental changes were proposed in governmental procedure and party organization.

Turning first to the state legislatures, the advocates of reform brought forward two devices for curbing the power of these bodies. The first of these was the incorporation into the state constitutions of provisions for the regulation of a large number of subjects that had formerly been left to the legislatures. Prominent among these new constitutional limitations upon the powers of the legislatures were regulations concerning the control of corporations. As a result of this practice some of the state constitutions were transformed from brief documents containing general statements of fundamental constitutional principles into elaborate compilations of laws dealing with a large number of social and economic questions. In most cases these new constitutional provisions were a clear indication of the popular distrust of legislative bodies.

Proceeding further, the proponents of reform determined to limit the power of the legislatures by giving to the voters directly the right to propose and enact laws, by means of the initiative and the referendum. By these devices a certain percentage of the voters was empowered to submit a petition for the enactment of a measure to the legislature, and in case the latter refused to pass the proposed law, to have it submitted directly to the people at the polls. Similarly, the voters might petition to have any law enacted by the legislature referred to the people for approval or rejection. Starting in South Dakota in 1898, the movement for the adoption of the initiative and the referendum spread to a number of other western states and then, when the progressive movement got well under way, it reached the more conservative states of the East. By 1912 sixteen states had adopted this method of direct government and then, the enthusiasm for reform having spent itself, the movement was checked. Ultimately twenty states in all adopted the initiative and the referendum in one form or another. In practice these devices have neither justified the extravagant claims of their advocates nor produced the dire results predicted by those who opposed them. When they were first introduced the voters usually displayed an interest in the proposals submitted to them and showed intelligent discrimination in accepting or rejecting them, but it was not long before the people became weary of being called upon to express their views at each election upon a great variety of subjects and they manifested resentment either by refusing to vote at all on the measures submitted or by rejecting all of them without distinction. It was only the exceptional voter who was sufficiently interested and intelligent enough to inform himself concerning the merits and demerits of all of the proposals upon which he was asked to vote, even when, as in the case of Oregon, he was furnished with a printed summary of the arguments for and against the proposed measure.

Reaching beyond the legislature, the leaders in the forward march of reform proposed to strengthen popular control of all governmental officials by means of the recall. By this device a public official might be removed from office before the expiration of his term. By means of a petition, signed by a specified number of voters, a special election is held in which the voters determine whether to retain the incumbent in office or to replace him by some one else. Eleven states in all have adopted the recall, and seven of these provide for its use against judicial as well as executive and administrative officers. The application of the recall to judges gave rise to bitter denunciation in conservative circles. Much eloquence was expended in the effort to prove that it would bring about the degradation of the courts and the establishment of mob rule. With fearsome alliteration one congressman referred to the proposal as the work of "agrarian agitators, the culpable confederates of convicted criminals, and daring demagogues," who would "drag the upright and stainless judge from the bench." In fact, no such terrible calamity has occurred. In practice the recall has generally been used for the removal of municipal officials. On only one occasion has it been successfully applied against higher state officials, and then, interestingly enough, it was used by the conservatives to get rid of a radical state régime.[1]

[1] In 1921 the Governor, Attorney General, and the commissioners of agriculture and labor in North Dakota, who had the support of the Non-Partisan League, were removed in a recall election.

Shifting their attack, the prophets of the new democratic era turned to the reform of party organizations and practices. From the days of Andrew Jackson it had been the custom for political parties to select their candidates for office by means of conventions composed of delegates. In theory the delegates to these conventions were chosen by the enrolled voters of the party but in practice the political leaders controlled the so-called primary elections in which the delegates were selected. At a typical party convention a few leaders arranged the slate of candidates for the various offices to be filled and the delegates went through the motions of ratifying the selections made by the party bosses. Such a procedure made the working of the "invisible government" easy and effective.

To meet this situation and to break the power of the political machine the so-called direct primary was instituted. It was in Wisconsin, where Robert M. La Follette had been carrying on a bitter struggle with the reactionary forces, that the first state-wide direct primary law was enacted,[2] in 1903, and from there the reform spread rapidly to other western states and more slowly to the East. Ultimately all but five of the states adopted the new system, either by legislative enactment or by party regulation. The essential feature of the direct primary is that it gives the enrolled party voter an opportunity to express his choice of candidates for various elective offices. The usual procedure requires prospective candidates to circulate petitions among the enrolled voters of the party and, if they are able to obtain the required number of signatures, their names are placed on the primary ballot. At the ensuing primary election the party voters indicate their choice from among the names submitted, and the person receiving the largest vote obtains the nomination. Although the direct primary has not brought the political

---

[2] In the southern states direct primaries had been used before 1903, but they were held under party regulations and were not prescribed by state law.

millennium there is little doubt that it has eliminated some of the glaring abuses of the old convention system. It is true that under the direct primary the person having the backing of the party organization obtains the nomination in nine cases out of ten, but at least the voters have an opportunity, if they care to use it, of forcing the party leaders to name satisfactory candidates for office.

About a dozen states have extended the principle of the direct primary to the selection of presidential candidates. By the laws of these states the voters are allowed to express their preference for a particular candidate and to instruct the delegates to the national convention to support their choice. It is significant that in the two presidential elections since the adoption of the preferential primaries, in which there was a sharp contest for the nomination, the candidates who received the largest popular preference vote did not obtain the nomination.[3]

Pressing forward in their assault upon the old order of things the leaders of the new dispensation turned their attention to the method of electing United States Senators. Those who drafted the Federal constitution provided for the election of Senators by the state legislatures, with the idea of providing a conservative body which would serve as a check upon the popularly elected House. In the course of time this fear of democracy was dissipated and the demand arose for the direct election of the upper house. Strength was given to this movement by the repeated disclosures of political manipulation, if not downright bribery, which accompanied the election of Senators by state legislatures. Not infrequently men of wealth bought their way into the Senate and it was not alone the Populists who came to regard that body as a millionaires' club. Then, too, the feeling became widespread that the Senators, removed from

[3] In 1912 Roosevelt carried the preferential primaries in most of the states having large Republican votes. In 1920 Gen. Leonard Wood obtained a similar endorsement.

the fear of popular control, were inclined to become the spokesmen of special interests and the difficulty experienced in getting through the Senate legislation designed to control corporations intensified this feeling.

Beginning in 1893 the House of Representatives on several occasions passed resolutions calling for a constitutional amendment providing for the direct election of Senators, only to have the resolution defeated in the Senate. Undeterred, the proponents of the change turned to the states, where by means of the direct primary they substantially accomplished their aim. The names of senatorial candidates were placed on the primary ballots and the voters were allowed to express their preferences. The names of the candidates so designated were then· placed on the ballot at the following· election and the members of the state legislature were pledged to vote for the candidate receiving the largest popular vote, irrespective of party affiliation. In this rather cumbersome fashion more than three-fourths of the states accomplished what was essentially popular election of Senators until finally, in 1911, the Senate submitted to the inevitable and passed by the necessary two-thirds vote the resolution providing for a constitutional amendment, establishing thd change, which was promptly ratified by three-fourths of the states and became the Seventeenth Amendment in May, 1913.

In this onward sweep of political reform it was natural that interest should be stimulated in a movement that had made slow but steady progress in the last half of the nineteenth century; namely, the enfranchisement of women. In 1869, under the leadership of Elizabeth Cady Stanton and Susan B. Anthony, a constitutional amendment was introduced into the House of Representatives which provided for the granting of the suffrage to women; but there the matter rested for nearly half a century, except for an occasional debate started by some member favoring the change. In the meantime the suffrage leaders turned their attention to the individual states and, as with most of the other reform movements, the first success was obtained in the West. The territory of Wyoming led the way by granting women the right to vote in 1869, and when it was admitted as a state in 1890 the right was confirmed. Three years later Colorado followed the example of Wyoming, and in 1896 Utah and Idaho were added to the list of women-suffrage states. Then the movement was checked, and for the next fourteen years no other states adopted the reform. The general progressive swing was not the only factor that caused a revival of the suffrage movement. The opening years of the twentieth century found women entering in increasing numbers into the economic life of the country. As they began to work side by side with men in factories, offices, and in the professions, the old conception of the domestic position of women and of their economic dependence upon men underwent a decided change. And with this change came a more insistent demand for political enfranchisement. In 1910 the movement got under way again, with the addition of Washington to the suffrage states. Then in quick succession California, Oregon, Kansas, Arizona, Nevada, and Montana fell into line. Nor did defeat in several of the eastern states discourage the suffrage leaders, for with women voting in one-fourth of the states they could make their influence felt in presidential elections and in the halls of Congress. However, it required another decade of agitation to bring about the full political enfranchisement of women.[4]

Accompanying these changes in the field of politics and government in the early years of the twentieth century, there went a notable expansion of the activities of state and national authorities. More and more the people turned to the government, and especially to the Federal Government, for a solution of social and economic problems. This brought

[4] See p. 337.

not only a large increase in legislation but also a multiplication in the number of government officials. In the state and local governments most of these new officials were added to the already imposing list of officers that the voters were called upon to elect. As a result the ballot in many states became unwieldy and intelligent voting almost impossible. Thus in New York the voters were called upon at each state election to vote for governor, lieutenant-governor, secretary of state, state treasurer, state engineer and surveyor, attorney-general, and state comptroller, not to mention members of the legislature and a large number of municipal and county officers. It is doubtful if one voter in ten could name, the day after election, the person for whom he had voted for state engineer and surveyor, and it is certain that an even smaller number had any knowledge of the technical qualifications of the candidate. More serious was the fact that the election of the heads of the various state departments made it difficult to fix the responsibility or obtain unity in the state administration. The governor could not control officials who, equally with himself, had received their mandate from the people.

It was to remedy this condition that the so-called short ballot movement was started. In 1910 the National Short Ballot Association was formed to press the reform. In general, it was proposed to reduce materially the number of elective officers, thereby enabling the voters to cast their ballots with greater intelligence. At the same time, by allowing the chief executive to appoint the heads of departments, responsibility for efficient administration could be fixed. Advocates of the reform met many obstacles. Political bosses regarded it as an encroachment upon their prerogatives, for it would deprive them of the privilege of selecting a large number of officials. Upholders of things as they were denounced, with much eloquence, the proposal as an invasion of the sacred right of the people to elect their own officials.

Nevertheless, substantial progress was made. In New York, for instance, under the energetic leadership of Governor Smith, a constitutional amendment was adopted which reduced the number of elected state officers to four, the governor, lieutenant-governor, attorney-general, and comptroller, and gave to the governor the right to appoint the other heads of departments.

Similar in character was a change made in municipal government. The tremendous growth in the size of cities in the last quarter of the nineteenth century, chiefly as a result of the industrial development of the country, increased greatly the difficulties of efficient municipal government. Even the most conscientious city officials floundered in their efforts to administer these unwieldy urban centers. And, unfortunately, all too frequently those into whose hands the control of the cities fell were not actuated by the best of intentions. It was in the cities that American politics was seen at its worst. It was there that the arch type of political boss flourished. That sympathetic and well-informed foreign commentator on American government, James Bryce, referred to the government of our cities as "the one conspicuous failure" of American democracy.

This failure was partly due to the archaic system of city government which prevailed in American cities until the end of the nineteenth century. Virtually all municipalities were governed by an executive, called a mayor; a city legislature, frequently of two houses; and a system of municipal courts. In city elections the voters divided along political lines much as they did in state and national elections. Frequently the political leaders would inject into a municipal election national political issues, which had not the remotest relation to the problems of city administration. In short, the cities were regarded as appendages to the state and national political organizations, whereas the modern city has taken on many of the aspects of a large business corporation which demands, primarily, expert administration.

It was as a result of a calamity that a new type of city government was inaugurated which was based on the conception of the city as a business rather than a political organization. In September, 1900, the city of Galveston, Texas, was struck by a great tidal wave which destroyed it in large part. The existing city government was unable to cope with the disaster and the citizens petitioned the legislature to place the affairs of the city in the hands of a group of prominent citizens for a period of one year. So successfully did the emergency government function that it has been continued ever since, and has been copied in about four hundred other cities throughout the country. The essential features of the commission form of city government are first, that it discards the traditional partisan political alignment, and second, that it concentrates power and responsibility in the hands of a small group of officials. Under this system the voters choose, without reference to the party affiliations of the candidates, a group of commissioners, usually five in number. Each commissioner acts as the head of one of the municipal departments, with authority to appoint his subordinates, and the commission as a whole takes over the functions formerly exercised by the mayor and the city legislature. A modification of the commission system, which carries the principle of business organization of municipalities a step further, is the city-manager system, which has been adopted in about two hundred cities. Under this plan the commissioners employ a city-manager in much the same way in which a board of directors selects a president or general manager for a corporation. Not infrequently the commissioners go outside of their own city to obtain a manager—perhaps a man who has made a success in administering some other city. The manager has the authority and responsibility for administering the affairs of the city, but is accountable to the commission.

THE ELECTION OF 1908, AND THE TAFT INTERLUDE

The progressive movement was in full swing when President Roosevelt came to the end of his eventful seven-and-a-half years in the presidential office. As the time for the election of 1908 approached many of Roosevelt's ardent admirers urged him to run again, pointing out that a large part of the progressive program was still unrealized and that only by his vigorous leadership could it be successfully accomplished. They argued that his acceptance of the nomination would not violate the third-term tradition, inasmuch as during his first three-and-a-half years in office he was merely serving out the unexpired term of McKinley. But Roosevelt declined to listen to these suggestions and served notice that he adhered to the declaration he had made in 1904 not to accept another nomination.

Although Roosevelt eliminated himself, he was determined to have a decisive voice in the selection of his successor. Among his intimate associates in the Cabinet he considered Secretary Root as the man who would make the ablest President but he realized that, as a candidate, Root would be handicapped by his record as a corporation lawyer. Of the other members of his official family none was more highly regarded by Roosevelt than his Secretary of War, William Howard Taft. Taft had had a long and honorable career in public life, both in judicial and in administrative offices. Despite obvious differences in temperament, there developed a warm personal friendship between Roosevelt and Taft. In their official relations the energetic President frequently called upon his genial and capable Secretary to represent him on important foreign missions, and when the question of his successor arose he fixed upon Taft as best qualified "to carry on the work upon which we have entered during the past four years." Backed by the influence of Roosevelt and by the power of the Federal organization, Taft had no difficulty in securing the Republican nomination on the first ballot by an overwhelming majority, although some of Roosevelt's most enthusiastic supporters tried to stampede the convention into renominating their idol.

Not only did Roosevelt select the Republican nominee but he also took an active part in writing the platform adopted by the convention. This document quite naturally praised the work of the outgoing Administration and pledged the party to a continuance of the "Roosevelt policies." The protectionist principle was upheld, although promise was made of an immediate revision of the existing tariff schedules. Increased government control of corporations was advocated through amendments to the Sherman Law and the Interstate Commerce Act. A vague promise was made to labor to restrict the use of injunctions in labor disputes.

Having made a dismal failure to rally the country to the support of the Democratic party under conservative auspices in 1904, the leaders of that party in 1908 turned once more to Bryan. Despite his two former defeats Bryan still held a large following among the rank and file of the party. Moreover, Bryan's radicalism in 1908 did not arouse the fear that it had aroused in 1896. Progressive ideas were now in vogue. Seven years of Roosevelt had brought the country to accept readily many proposals for the advocacy of which Bryan had been bitterly denounced a decade before. Under these changed conditions the conservative wing of the Democratic party showed no repugnance to enlisting under the banner of the "peerless leader." When, therefore, the party met in convention at Denver, in July, 1908, there was no serious opposition to Bryan's leadership and he was nominated with great enthusiasm on the first ballot.

The Democratic platform tried to outbid the Republicans for the support of the progressive forces. The Republican tariff was denounced as a breeder of trusts. The currency question was handled with caution, in view of the two former defeats of the party on this issue. Private monopoly was declared to be "indefensible and intolerable," and the party was pledged to enact laws that would make it impossible for such monopolies to exist in the United States. Concretely, it advocated a law prohibiting interlocking directorates, a Federal license system for corporations controlling as much as 25 per cent. of any commodity, and a law compelling such corporations to dispose of their commodities to all purchasers without discrimination. To meet the demands of labor a plank was inserted which stated that "injunctions should not be issued in any cases in which the injunctions would not issue if no industrial dispute were involved." Other planks advocated a Federal income tax, a physical valuation of the railroads to aid in regulation, and publicity for campaign expenditures.

The campaign that followed was without special interest and the election resulted in a victory for the Republicans. Taft polled a slightly larger popular vote than Roosevelt had received four years before, whereas Bryan's vote exceeded Parker's in 1904 by 1,324,615. Although Taft received 321 electoral votes to 162 for Bryan the results of the election did not indicate an unqualified indorsement of the Republican party throughout the country. The Democratic vote for state and local officers in many states ran far ahead of the vote for the national ticket. In five states carried by Taft, Democratic governors were elected, while in several others the Republican vote for state officials was far below the Taft vote. The results showed that the political situation was in a state of flux and that the forces of unrest that had come to the surface during the Roosevelt era still had to be reckoned with. It remained to be seen how successful the new President would be in guiding the ship of state through the troubled political waters.

Mr. Taft brought to the presidential office a long and varied experience in public life. As judge, first in the state and then in the Federal courts, then as a member of the Philippine Commission and the first Governor General of the Islands, and finally as Secretary of War, he had had an opportunity to become acquainted with many problems that he was called upon to deal with as President. In these various activities he had displayed a finely trained legal mind, coupled with a marked degree of administrative ability. But these qualities alone were not sufficient to assure success to the new President. In the first place he came into office at a time when the country was expecting the political millennium. During the preceding half-dozen years, from press, pulpit, and public platform had come a steady stream of agitation for political and social reform. Various panaceas for our political and social ills had been urged and, when these schemes failed to realize the extravagant claims made for them by their advocates, the people in their disappointment held the President responsible. Moreover, Taft had to face the handicap of succeeding one of the most virile and picturesque personalities who had ever occupied the presidential office. Scarcely a week had passed during the seven-and-a-half years of the Roosevelt régime that did not bring from the presidential office some striking pronouncement on a live public question or a vigorous challenge to "malefactors" and "mollycoddles." By temperament Taft was not fitted to carry on the Roosevelt tradition. As Beard says, Taft "simply could not spring into the limelight booted and spurred, grinning from ear to ear. Matter-of-fact in outlook and procedure, he thought it was his duty to take stock rather than to drum up trade and keep the people excited every moment." Roosevelt had aroused enthusiasm; Taft could merely inspire respect. His judicial training influenced his conduct as President. He was inclined to weigh evidence rather than to make snap judgments, and he displayed greater regard for the constitutional limitations of the presidential office than his predecessor had shown.

The charge brought against Taft by his critics that he was a reactionary is not justified by the record of his administration. During his four years as President there was placed upon the statute books a substantial amount of progressive legislation. Among these measures were laws for the establishment of a postal savings system, a parcel post, taxation of corporation profits, and two constitutional amendments, providing for the Federal income tax and the direct election of Senators. It is true that some of these laws were merely the fruition of the work inaugurated by Roosevelt, but Taft nevertheless gave them his earnest support. Then, too, Taft pushed forward the program of his predecessor concerning trusts and railroads. He brought to a successful conclusion the prosecution of two of the largest trusts, the American Tobacco Company and the Standard Oil Company. But this creditable record was offset by two incidents that occurred early in the new administration and that were seized upon by the President's critics to discredit him with the progressive forces in the country. These were the Payne-Aldrich Tariff and the Ballinger-Pinchot controversy.

Elsewhere we have noted that the tariff issue had come more and more to the front in the closing years of Roosevelt's administration.[5] Taking note of this public interest the Republican platform in 1908 had declared "unequivocally for a revision of the tariff by a special session of Congress immediately following the inauguration of the next President." The upshot was the Payne-Aldrich Tariff, which left the level of protective duties little, if any, below the Dingley rates.[6] This was interpreted not only by the Democrats but also by a large number of progressive Republicans as a direct

[5] See p. 433.
[6] See p. 434.

repudiation of the platform pledge. President Taft might have escaped a measure of responsibility for this action had he not seen fit to come out in a speech at Winona, Minnesota, and defend the law as the "best tariff bill ever passed by the Republican party." To the Western insurgents this statement of the President served to identify him with the protected industrial interests of the East and with the reactionary element of his party led by Senator Aldrich and Speaker Cannon.

The second incident aroused even greater resentment in the ranks of the progressives. Taft had selected, as Secretary of the Interior, Richard A. Ballinger, who had been closely associated as attorney with some of the large corporations. Shortly after assuming office Ballinger revoked an order that had been issued by President Roosevelt providing for the withdrawal from sale of certain public lands containing valuable water-power sites. The Secretary took the position that the order had been issued without sufficient legal authority. The conservationists were immediately up in arms. Gifford Pinchot, the Chief Forester and an ardent defender of the conservation movement, openly criticized the action of Ballinger as favoring the water-power trust. Fuel was added to the flames by a charge brought by L. R. Glavis, an official in the Forestry Service, that the Morgan-Guggenheim Syndicate, for some of the members of which Ballinger had formerly acted as attorney, were interested in certain fraudulent claims to valuable mineral lands in Alaska. The issue was taken up by the newspapers and resulted in much personal recrimination. President Taft stood by his Secretary and dismissed Glavis from the government service. Pinchot then jumped into the breach and wrote a letter to Senator Dollinger criticizing Ballinger. For this action the President removed Pinchot from office.

This unfortunate controversy served to confirm the views of many progressives that Taft had deserted their cause, and it deprived him of the credit for furthering the conservation movement by two important recommendations that he made to Congress. The first of these proposed that Congress should authorize the President to withdraw lands containing water-power sites from sale, and the second provided for the separation of the title to surface lands on the public domain from the title to the sub-surface mineral rights, and for the lease instead of the sale of the latter. Congress enacted into law both of these recommendations. Further evidence of President Taft's interest in the conservation movement was given by his action in signing the bill for the creation of the Appalachian Forest Reserve.

In the meantime a political storm was brewing in Congress. For many years the Speaker of the House of Representatives had exercised dictatorial power over that body by means of his authority to appoint all committees of the House and to designate their chairmen, coupled with his influence as chairman of the Committee on Rules, which body determined the legislative procedure of the House. In the Speaker's chair at this time was Joseph G. Cannon, a typical representative of the stand-pat school of Republicans, and reformers both within and without Congress had become convinced that Cannon was making free use of his power as Speaker to defeat progressive legislation. In March, 1910, the storm broke. A group of insurgent Republicans, under the leadership of George W. Norris of Nebraska, presented an amendment to the rules of the House which provided that the Committee on Rules, increased in size to ten members, should be elected by the House, and that the Speaker should not be a member of the committee. Cannon and his followers tried to defeat the proposal by parliamentary tactics, but the progressives, with the aid of the Democrats, forced a vote and the amendment was adopted. Having accomplished their purpose the insurgents refused to support a further resolution declaring the Speaker's chair vacant, as they did not want the issue to be shifted into a personal attack upon Cannon. The following year, when the Democrats obtained control of the House, the prerogatives of the Speaker were further curtailed by transferring to the Ways and Means Committee the power to appoint the remaining standing committees of the House.

One year of the Taft administration had made clear the deep rift in the ranks of the Republican party. The "Old Guard" element had hoped, with the retirement of Roosevelt, to resume their control of the party but they found their efforts vigorously resisted by a group of insurgents, coming chiefly from the Middle West. Confronted by this cleavage in the ranks of his party President Taft showed neither the ability to close the breach nor a willingness to assume effective leadership of either faction. During this year ex-President Roosevelt had been out of the country on a hunting expedition in Africa and the progressives were anxiously awaiting the return of their former chief in the hope that he would once more assume the leadership of their cause. In fact, Gifford Pinchot had made the trip to Europe to lay before Roosevelt the grievances of the progressive forces against the Taft administration.

When Roosevelt reached home, in June, 1910, he promptly became involved in the political controversy. He went to the New York State Republican Convention, where he succeeded in preventing the nomination of the regular organization candidate for governor and forcing the nomination of Henry L. Stimson. The fact that Stimson was defeated in the ensuing election apparently did not affect adversely Roosevelt's prestige. In the course of a trip through the West he took occasion in a speech at Ossawatamie, Kansas, to define anew his political creed. Designating his program as the "New Nationalism," he reiterated his belief in the effective governmental control of corporations, and endorsed the other items in the platform of the progressives, including a graduated income tax, protective labor legislation, direct primaries, conservation, and the recall of elective officers. He contended that the former conception of the distribution of powers between the Federal Government and the states did not meet the needs of the new economic conditions. He insisted that there should be no "neutral ground" between the jurisdiction of the Federal Government and that of the states "to serve as a refuge for lawbreakers, and especially for lawbreakers of great wealth, who can hire vulpine legal cunning which will teach them how to avoid both jurisdictions." He declared that the New Nationalism "puts the national need before sectional or personal advantages. It is impatient of the utter confusion that results from local legislatures attempting to treat national issues as local issues. It is still more impatient of the impotence which springs from the over-division of governmental powers, an impotence which makes it possible for local selfishness and for legal cunning hired by wealthy special interests to bring national activities to a deadlock." Such pronouncements could leave no one in doubt as to where Roosevelt would stand in the impending struggle between the progressive and reactionary forces in the Republican party.

The fall elections in 1910 showed clearly that the Taft administration had lost the confidence of the people. Normally Republican states such as Maine, Massachusetts, Connecticut, New York, New Jersey, Ohio, Indiana, and Oregon chose Democratic governors. In the Congressional elections the Democrats succeeded in turning a Republican majority of 47 in the House into a Democratic majority of 63, while in the Senate the Republican majority was reduced from 28 to 10. In a number of Western states where the Republicans retained their hold the progressive element replaced the stand-pat group in control of the party organization. This political overturn made the enactment of any considerable amount of constructive legislation in the last two years of the Taft administration out of the question. The Democrats, in control of the House, did everything that they could to embarrass the Republicans, with an eye to the election of 1912. In particular they kept the tariff issue to the front by passing bills providing for the reduction of the duties on a considerable number of commodities, all of which measures met the presidential veto.

President Taft caused further dissatisfaction among western Republicans by his advocacy of a reciprocity agreement with Canada. This arrangement provided for free trade between the two countries in a number of food products and for the mutual reduction of duties on manufactured products. Western farmers objected to this proposal because they feared that the free admission of Canadian wheat and other food products would depress agricultural prices. On the other hand the protected manufacturers of the East would get the advantage of reduced Canadian tariffs on their exports to Canada without having to meet any great competition from Canadian manufacturers. When the President submitted the proposed agreement to Congress, in January, 1911, he succeeded in getting it through the House with the aid of Democratic votes, but the insurgent Republicans in the Senate were able to prevent a vote on the measure before Congress expired in March. Determined to force a vote on the question, the President summoned a special session of the new Congress in April. After a delay of three months both houses approved the measure, largely as a result of Democratic support. Taft had carried his point, but only after embittering still further the insurgent faction of his party, and then he suffered the humiliation of having the whole reciprocity agreement rejected by the Canadian parliament. Canadian sentiment had been turned against the proposal partly through the activities of the Canadian industrialists and partly because of the condescending attitude and ill-advised remarks of persons on this side of the border. The Speaker of the House of Representatives, Champ Clark, stated in the House that he favored the reciprocity agreement because he hoped "to see the day when the American flag would float over every square foot of the British North American possessions clear to the north pole," a remark that was not calculated to win favor with patriotic Canadians.

The closing year of the Taft administration was given over largely to a preparation for the struggle all political observers foresaw coming in the presidential election the following year. Taft's record, as we have seen, was far from being reactionary, but he had signally failed to win the confidence of the Progressives and they were determined to prevent his renomination, if possible. All signs pointed to one of the most interesting political battles in American history. And so it proved to be.

ELECTION OF 1912

The Progressive leaders took the first step in organizing their forces in January, 1911, with the formation of the National Progressive League and the adoption of a set of principles that reaffirmed all of the well-known progressive ideas. This was followed by the summoning of a national Progressive conference, which met in Chicago in October. At this meeting resolutions were adopted indorsing the program of the League and putting forward Senator La Follette as the logical candidate for President because "his experience, his character, his courage, his record in constructive legislation, his administrative ability, meet the requirements of leadership such as a presidential candidacy demands."

While doing these things many leading Progressives were casting longing eyes toward Theodore Roosevelt. He had declined to join the Progressive League, but in various speeches he had left no doubt as to where his heart was. In fact, Roosevelt was in a most trying position. Openly to join Taft's enemies would mean the repudiation of the man he had placed in the presidency and he was perfectly aware of the fact that if he allowed his name to be used it would certainly split the Republican party and assure the success of the Democrats in the coming election. On the other hand, Roosevelt was convinced that Taft had failed to carry forward the principles in which he was deeply interested. In a letter dated December 29, 1911, he wrote, "Taft is utterly hopeless. I think he would be beaten if nominated, but in any event it would be a misfortune to have him in the presidential chair for another term." Both the Taft and La Follette supporters were eager to have Roosevelt definitely decline to allow his name to be considered for another nomination, but this he refused to do. As he wrote in a letter to Frank A. Munsey, in January, 1912, "I shall not seek the nomination, nor would I accept it if it came to me as the result of an intrigue. But I will not tie my hands by a statement which would make it difficult or impossible for me to serve the public by undertaking a great task if the people as a whole seemed definitely to come to the conclusion that I ought to do that task." This statement gave encouragement to the ardent Roosevelt followers and led them to press forward in the movement to make him the standard bearer of the Progressive cause. On the other hand La Follette resented Roosevelt's attitude and he later accused Roosevelt of using him as a stalking horse until he was ready to assume control of the Progressive forces.

Early in February, 1912, the Progressive leaders determined that the time had come for a definite decision concerning the presidential nomination. A group of seven Republican governors addressed a joint letter to Roosevelt in which they stated their belief that a large majority of the Republican voters desired his nomination, and that a large majority of the people desired his election. They urged him not to consider his personal interests, but the interests of the people as a whole, and that if he declined he would show himself unresponsive to a plain public duty. Two days after this letter was sent, while Roosevelt was still considering what answer he should make to this call, President Taft took occasion in the course of an address before the Republican Club in New York to denounce persons who "are seeking to pull down those things which have been regarded as the pillars of the temple of freedom and representative government and to reconstruct our whole society on some new principle," and to characterize them as "political emotionalists or neurotics." This was a direct challenge to Roosevelt and there is little question that it influenced materially his determination to accept the invitation of the Republican governors. On February 21st he delivered an address before the Ohio Constitutional Convention in which he reaffirmed his adherence to the Progressive program, and three days later he notified his supporters that he would accept the nomination if it should be tendered to him.

Having made his decision Roosevelt threw himself into the contest with his accustomed vigor. During the following seven months the country beheld the distressing spectacle of a campaign of bitter personal recrimination between the President of the United States and his predecessor in that high office. In the campaign for delegates to the national convention Taft had the great advantage of controlling the national party organization. Through this, and by a judicious use of patronage, he was assured in advance of the support of the delegates from a considerable number of states, especially those of the South. On the other hand in thirteen states provision had been made for a system of preferential presidential primaries and in these states an opportunity was given to register the opinions of the rank and file of the Republican voters. The results of these primaries were an impressive victory for Roosevelt. Of the 382 delegates chosen from these states, 278 were instructed to vote for him, whereas Taft obtained only 68 delegates, 28 of whom were from

Georgia, which was certain to go Democratic in the presidential election. La Follette received the 36 votes from Wisconsin and North Dakota. In Taft's own state of Ohio, Roosevelt delegates were chosen by a majority of 47,000. There was therefore no doubt that where the Republican voters had been given chance to state their preference Roosevelt was their overwhelming choice, and the Roosevelt support came from the states that were normally Republican and that any Republican candidate would have to carry to be elected.

When the Republican convention met at Chicago, in June, more than 200 of the seats for delegates were contested, and upon the decision of these contests the nomination depended, for no candidate would have a majority without these contested seats. The Taft forces had the advantage of controlling the national committee, which made up the temporary roll of the convention, and they used this advantage to the full. In deciding the contested delegations the committee seated 235 Taft delegates and only 19 for Roosevelt. The Roosevelt forces were up in arms and Roosevelt himself came to Chicago to look after his interests. But the conservatives were evidently determined upon a policy of rule-or-ruin, and the "steam roller" was run over the Progressives without compunction. The Taft supporters chose Elihu Root as temporary chairman of the convention and they firmly resisted all efforts of the Roosevelt followers to "purge" the convention roll of delegates seated by the national committee. Thereafter the Progressives sat sullenly in their seats and most of them declined to participate further in the work of the convention.

In complete control of the situation, the conservatives proceeded to adopt a platform which, in accordance with tradition, "pointed with pride" to the achievements of the Republican party during the preceding sixteen years, with special emphasis upon the record of the Taft administration. It solemnly declared the "unflinching faith of the party in government of the people, by the people, and for the people," and promised the enactment of further progressive social and economic legislation. On the other hand it declared the proposal for the recall of judges "unnecessary and unwise." For the rest there was the usual defense of the protective tariff, a pledge to enforce the Sherman Law, and recommendations for currency reform, immigration restriction, and the regulation of campaign contributions. Only Taft and La Follette were formally placed in nomination and on the first ballot Taft received 561, Roosevelt 107, La Follette 41, Cummins 17, and Hughes 2, with 344 Roosevelt supporters not voting. The convention completed its work with the renomination of Vice-President Sherman.

Immediately after the adjournment of the Republican convention the Roosevelt delegates, accompanied by a large number of loyal followers, met in another hall in the city and adopted resolutions calling for the organization of a Progressive party and the nomination of Roosevelt as its candidate for the presidency. When Roosevelt appeared in the hall there followed a scene of the wildest enthusiasm. He addressed the gathering in a fiery speech stating that the time had come when "all men who believe in those elementary maxims of public and private morality, which must underlie every form of successful free government, should join in our movement." Before accepting the proffered nomination he advised the delegates to go home and sound out the sentiment of the people and then assemble again in a mass convention "to nominate for the presidency a Progressive on a Progressive platform that will enable us to appeal to the Northerner and Southerner, Easterner and Westerner, Republican and Democrat alike, in the name of our common citizenship." He declared his willingness to make the fight even if only one state supported him. "I am in this fight," he declared, "for certain principles, and the first and most important of these goes back to Sinai, and is embodied in the commandment

'Thou shalt not steal.' Thou shalt not steal a nomination. Thou shalt neither steal in politics nor in business. Thou shalt not steal from the people the birthright of the people to rule themselves."

After the dramatic scenes at the Republican convention it seemed that the gathering of the Democrats would be in the nature of an anti-climax. But such proved to be not the case. In the Democratic ranks there was the same cleavage between the conservative and radical forces that had appeared among the Republicans. Bryan was the acknowledged leader of the liberal wing of the party and although he had no intention of attempting to secure his own nomination for a fourth time, he was bent upon playing a decisive rôle in determining who should be the candidate and in writing the party platform. The bright hopes for Democratic success in the coming election because of the threatened split in the Republican ranks brought out an unusual number of candidates for the Democratic nomination. Among these were Governors Harmon of Ohio, Wilson of New Jersey, and Folk of Missouri, Speaker Champ Clark, and Representative Oscar Underwood of Alabama.

As soon as the convention met at Baltimore, on June 25th, the clash between the liberals and conservatives began. Bryan opposed the choice of the conservative Alton B. Parker as temporary chairman. In this he failed, but he succeeded in having one of his staunch supporters, Senator Ollie James, chosen as permanent chairman. Bryan followed this up by obtaining the passage of two resolutions which reaffirmed the party's position as "the champion of popular government and equality before the law" and declared against the nomination of any candidate representing "the privilege-hunting and favor-seeking class."

In the pre-convention contest for delegates Champ Clark had obtained a larger number of delegates pledged to his support than had any other candidate, and among those so pledged was the Nebraska delegation, headed by Bryan. On the early ballots Clark led Wilson by about 100 votes and when, on the tenth ballot, the New York delegation shifted its vote to Clark his nomination seemed assured; but Bryan once more stepped into the breach with the declaration that the Nebraska delegation would withhold its support from Clark, despite its instructions, as long as he had the support of the New York delegates who, Bryan declared, were allied with the reactionary forces in the party. Amidst much recrimination Bryan threw his strength to Wilson, and this proved to be the turning of the tide. Steadily Wilson's vote increased until, on the forty-sixth ballot, he received 990 votes and the nomination. In the following words a journalist in attendance described the scene that accompanied the balloting: "It was halloing, yelling, screaming, roaring, raised to the nth power. When a telling speech was successfully shouted or a significant vote was cast, they carried banners up and down and around the aisles; they sent up toy balloons; and tossed pigeons into the air; horns, whistles and infernal contrivances without name contributed to the diabolical din. . . . Uproar that shattered the voice of a new chairman every five minutes, and wore out fresh platoons of police every hour; the efforts of bands drowned under the vocal din, and the chromatic color of banners assailed the delegates and left them stubborn at their posts."

The platform of the Democratic party placed chief emphasis upon the tariff, which was declared to be a burden upon the farmer and the laborer, and the party was pledged to "immediate downward revision." More rigid trust legislation was demanded in order to end private monopoly. Banking and currency reform were urged; publicity of campaign contributions, rural credits, conservation, and the physical valuation of railways were indorsed. A constitutional amendment was advocated making the President ineligible for reëlection, and the nominee of the party was pledged to this principle. Finally it favored "an immediate declaration of the nation's purpose to recognize the independence of the Philippine Islands as soon as a stable government can be established."

Despite the colorful and stirring scenes at the Democratic convention, the climax in the political drama of this eventful year remained still to be staged at Chicago. It was there, in August, that in accordance with the suggestion of Roosevelt, the Progressive hosts assembled. Nothing quite like this gathering had ever met in the political history of this country. Of typical professional politicians there was a minimum. In their place were some two thousand earnest men and women, many of whom had never been to a political convention before. An enthusiasm, bordering on religious fervor, swept the meeting. Instead of engaging in the common form of convention din and horse-play, the delegates joined in singing the "Battle Hymn of the Republic" and "Onward Christian Soldiers." The convention oratory was also on a high plane, free from the cant and hypocrisy usually found on such occasions.

In the minds of the delegates there was but one thought as to the man who should lead their crusade. That man was Theodore Roosevelt, and on the second day of the convention he was nominated for President by acclamation, with Hiram W. Johnson of California, as his running mate. When Roosevelt appeared before the convention he was greeted with tremendous enthusiasm. In a speech accepting the nomination, which he called his "confession of faith," he reaffirmed his adherence to the Progressive principles which he had so frequently enunciated; appealed to those ready to join "in the endless crusade against wrong," and who were prepared to "strive in a spirit of brotherhood for the betterment of our nation"; and closed with a slogan befitting the religious atmosphere of his surroundings: "We stand at Armageddon and we battle for the Lord."

The platform of the new party was as novel as the convention that framed it. Of the usual platitudinous pronouncements and political straddling this document was refreshingly free. It was designated "A Contract with the People" and came to grips in no uncertain terms with most of the insistent political and social problems then stirring the country. It indorsed all of the newer experiments in political democracy, including direct primaries, nation-wide preferential primaries for the selection of candidates for the presidency, direct popular election of United States Senators, the short ballot, the initiative, referendum and recall, "a more easy and expeditious way of amending the Federal Constitution," woman suffrage, and the recall of judicial decisions. Concerning the trusts it advocated rigid governmental control rather than indiscriminate dissolution. Most significant was its advocacy of a wide program of social legislation, including minimum wage laws; the abolition of child labor; laws furthering industrial health, education, and social insurance; the eight-hour day; the promotion of agricultural credit and coöperation; the creation of a department of labor; and publicity in regard to wages and working conditions.

In the ensuing campaign the Democratic and Progressive candidates strove for the support of the liberal voters. Wilson set forth his economic and political philosophy under the caption of "The New Freedom," which appeared to be a combination of economic individualism and States' Rights. He criticized the Republicans for allowing big business to dominate the government, but at the same time he rejected Roosevelt's remedy of strict governmental regulation of industry. He visioned the return of the small business man and farmer to their former condition of economic independence but, when called upon to indicate exactly how this was to be accomplished, he stated that he was not presenting "specific measures and programs," but "the new spirit of our politics." Roosevelt threw himself into the campaign with his usual energy. He characterized one of his opponents as reactionary and the other as visionary. One dramatic incident of the campaign came near being a tragedy. On the 14th of October Roosevelt, while on his way to deliver a speech in Milwaukee, was shot by a fanatic. Despite the warning of his friends he insisted on proceeding to the hall and delivering the scheduled address, with the bullet in his chest.

In the November elections Taft carried only two states, Vermont and Utah; Roosevelt received the electoral votes of Pennsylvania, Michigan, Minnesota, South Dakota, and Washington, and 11 of the 13 votes of California—88 in all; Wilson carried all of the remaining states, receiving the unprecedented electoral vote of 435. However, the popular vote indicated no landslide to the Democratic party. Wilson received 6,286,214 votes; Roosevelt 4,126,020; Taft 3,483,-922; and Debs, the perpetual Socialist candidate, 897,011. These figures show that Wilson was chosen President by a minority of the popular vote, and they show also that the temper of the country was distinctly liberal, for the two liberal candidates, Wilson and Roosevelt, polled more than three-quarters of the popular vote. In short, the Progressive cause had triumphed although the Progressive party was defeated. Finally, for Roosevelt to be able, with only an improvised organization, to poll more than four million votes, was a striking demonstration of the hold that he still had upon the affections of a large number of his fellow citizens.

In the congressional elections the Democrats also triumphed. They obtained an overwhelming majority of 147 in the House and a narrow majority of 6 in the Senate. Thus for the first time in eighteen years the Democratic party was in control of all branches of the Federal Government, and the country waited, with apprehension in some quarters and lively anticipation in others, to see what use the party would make of its opportunities.

BIBLIOGRAPHICAL NOTE

General surveys of the Taft administration are to be found in F. A. Ogg, *National Progress* (1918), and H. Howland, *Theodore Roosevelt and His Times* (1921). Especially good on the relations between Roosevelt and Taft is H. H. Kohlsaat, *From McKinley to Harding* (1923).

For a sympathetic treatment of the philosophy underlying the progressive movement consult H. Croly, *Promise of American Life* (1914); by the same author, *Progressive Democracy* (1915); F. C. Howe, *Privilege and Democracy in America* (1916); W. Lippman, *A Preface to Politics* (1913); by the same author, *Drift and Mastery* (1914); W. E. Weyl, *The New Democracy* (1912). For a conservative criticism of the new movement see N. M. Butler, *Why Should We Change Our Form of Government?* (1912); W. H. Taft, *Political Issues and Outlook* (1909).

For a discussion of the new democratic experiments see J. D. Barnett, *Operation of the Initiative, Referendum and Recall in Oregon* (1915); C. A. Beard, *American Government and Politics* (1925); F. C. Howe, *Wisconsin, An Experiment in Democracy* (1912); E. Kimball, *State and Municipal Government in the United States* (1922); W. B. Munro, *The Initiative, Referendum and Recall* (1912). On Woman Suffrage see W. H. Allen, *Women's Part in Government* (1911); C. C. Catt and N. R. Shuler, *Woman Suffrage and Politics* (1926); R. C. L. Dorr, *Susan B. Anthony* (1928); K. R. Porter, *A History of Suffrage in the United States* (1918); I. H. Harper, ed., *History of Woman Suffrage*, Vols. V and VI (1922).

For the formation of the Progressive party consult B. P. De Witt, *The Progressive Movement* (1915); S. J. Duncan-Clark, *The Progressive Movement, Its Principles and Progress* (1913); F. E. Haynes, *Third Party Movements Since the Civil War* (1916); R. M. La Follette, *Autobiography* (1913). See also *Selections from the Correspondence of Theodore Roosevelt and Henry Cabot Lodge*, Vol. II (1925).

For the election of 1912 see Ogg and Haynes cited above. Consult also W. J. Bryan, *A Tale of Two Conventions* (1912); C. Clark, *My Quarter Century of American Politics* (1920); W. F. McComb, *Making Woodrow Wilson President* (1921).

CHAPTER 15

THE POLITICAL TREND, 1913-1929

WOODROW WILSON AND PROGRESSIVE DEMOCRACY

The man who entered the White House in March, 1913, was born in Virginia, of Scotch-Irish parentage. His early academic training was received at Princeton, followed by a short law course at the University of Virginia. His experience in the practice of law did not prove to be particularly attractive, and Wilson soon returned to academic circles. He pursued graduate courses in political science at Johns Hopkins University, from which place he passed in succession to the faculties of Bryn Mawr College, Wesleyan University, and Princeton. In 1902 he was chosen president of his alma mater. In this position he attracted wide attention and won much praise by his vigorous, though unsuccessful, effort to curb the influence of the aristocratic clubs at the university.

Wilson's writings on political and historical subjects seemed to stamp him as a Democrat of the Jefferson and Cleveland school and as such he was singled out by George Harvey, editor of the *North American Review* and *Harper's Weekly,* as the man to save the Democratic party from the blighting influence of Bryan. Wearied by the long struggle with his academic foes at Princeton, Wilson listened with sympathy to the suggestion that he enter the political arena.

His opportunity came in 1910, when the Democratic organization in New Jersey, feeling that the political situation called for a man differing from the professional politician, nominated Wilson as its candidate for governor. Carried into office on the wave of popular revolt against the Taft administration, Wilson promptly assumed a position of independence in relation to the machine politicians of his party. He successfully opposed the effort of the Democratic boss, James Smith, to have himself elected to the United States Senate and then won the plaudits of the liberals by forcing through the legislature a notable program of reform legislation, including a direct primary law, a law regulating public utilities, an employers' liability act, and a corrupt-practices act. Both conservatives and liberals could, therefore, point with satisfaction to the past record of the new President, for, as Beard says, "If the conservatives felt they could trust a man who had steered a safe course in his youth and through his middle period, backers tinged with radicalism could now point to the cautious scholar made progressive by experience."

In the personal characteristics and experiences of President Wilson there were elements both of strength and of weakness. Few of his predecessors had come to the presidency with as thorough knowledge of the theory of the American government as Wilson possessed, and yet few had had so little experience with its practical operation. He had a definite conception of the duties and functions of the presidency. Like Roosevelt, he regarded the President both as a party leader and as the spokesman for the entire American people, and he was just as insistent as Roosevelt had been in pressing upon Congress the administration policies. He lacked that ability, which Roosevelt possessed to such an eminent degree, to mobilize public opinion and win popular support. A certain austereness of manner coupled with the habit of reserving his judgment until he had satisfied himself of the justice of his decisions, led many of his enemies to charge him with being cold, stubborn, opinionated, and unwilling to take advice. Yet those who came in closest contact with him have testified to the warmth of his affection for his friends and his receptiveness to the ideas of others. He was shy and reserved, although always courteous, and was extremely sensitive to hostile criticism. He had neither capacity nor taste for those social contacts that might have smoothed his path on many occasions, nor did he have the ability to arouse warm personal devotion in his followers, or to inspire them, as did Roosevelt, with his own enthusiasm. His public papers are characterized by a literary style of a high order and throughout them there appears an idealism which at times seemed to put him out of touch with the realities of the everyday world. Above all, Wilson had a real passion for democracy. He seemed to have unbounded faith in the common man and a deep-seated conviction that, in the long run, the people could be trusted to make right decisions.

Just before he entered upon his duties as President he published a collection of his campaign speeches under the title of *The New Freedom,* wherein are set forth his program of reform and his vision of a new era for the people of this country. He would give to every citizen equal opportunity to enjoy the benefits that Providence had showered upon America. Our country, he asserted, "stands for a free field and no favors, America stands for a government responsive to the interests of all." He summoned "all honest men, all patriotic, all forward-looking men," to join him in hastening the dawn of the new era, with a view to "fitting a new social organization to the happiness and prosperity of the great body of citizens."

It was no easy task which confronted the new President in his effort to realize his ambitious program. In the first place his election had been due to a split in the ranks of the Republicans and he could therefore lay no claim to an overwhelming popular mandate in support of his policies. Then, too, the Democratic party had been out of power for so many years that it had not had the opportunity to develop a group of experienced administrators such as the Republicans had developed. Moreover it was not at all certain that many of the practical politicians in the Democratic party understood or sympathized with the idealism of the President.

In selecting the members of his cabinet President Wilson faced the necessity of satisfying Bryan, partly because the latter had played such a prominent part in bringing about his nomination, and partly because the "Great Commoner" still had a large following among the rank and file of the party. The President therefore offered Bryan the position of Secretary of State, despite the fact there was little in Bryan's career to indicate that he possessed any marked qualifications for the position. In point of fact, however, when circumstances made the foreign relations of the country the most significant problem confronting the administration, the President assumed personal control of the conduct of our foreign policies and, when Bryan resigned, in 1915, because of his unwillingness to support the presidential diplomacy, Wilson became, to all intents and purposes, his own Secretary of State during the remainder of his administration. In the nature of things the other members of the President's official family came largely from the South, the stronghold of the Democracy. Neither New England nor the Middle West, except Nebraska, obtained recognition in the cabinet appointments.[1]

In his inaugural address Wilson specified three major reforms that would have to be accomplished before the era of the "New Freedom" could be inaugurated. The first of these was the reform of the tariff "which cuts us off from our proper part in the commerce of the world, violates the just principles of taxation, and makes the Government a facile

[1] The other members of the cabinet were William G. McAdoo, of New York, a Southerner by birth, Secretary of the Treasury; L. M. Garrison, of New Jersey, Secretary of War; A. S. Burleson of Texas, Postmaster General; Josephus Daniels, of North Carolina, Secretary of the Navy; James C. McReynolds, of Tennessee, Attorney General; David F. Houston, of Missouri, Secretary of Agriculture; William C. Redfield, of New York, Secretary of Commerce; William B. Wilson, of Pennsylvania, Secretary of Labor; Franklin K. Lane, of California, Secretary of the Interior.

instrument in the hands of private interests." The second was the modification of "a banking and currency system based on the necessity of the Government to sell its bonds fifty years ago, and perfectly adapted to concentrating cash and restricting credits." Lastly was a readjustment of "an industrial system which, take it on all sides, financial as well as administrative, holds capital in leading strings, restricts the liberties and limits the opportunities of labor, and exploits, without renewing or conserving, the natural resources of the country."

Determined to lose no time in launching his program of reform, President Wilson summoned Congress in special session on April 7, 1913, and, reverting to the practice of our first two Presidents, Washington and John Adams, he appeared before Congress in person to read his message. He also departed from precedent by confining his recommendations to one subject, namely, the revision of the tariff. Acting upon the President's recommendation, Congress enacted the Underwood tariff.[2] Having carried his first point, the President again appeared before Congress and once more he devoted his attention to a single subject, this time the question of currency reform. Again Congress responded to the presidential recommendation by enacting the Federal Reserve Law.[3] The third item in the presidential program of reform was legislation providing for a more effective control of trusts and corporations. On January 20, 1914, the President once more addressed Congress in person and recommended legislation that would remedy the defects in the Sherman Anti-Trust Law. In response to the President's suggestions Congress passed the Federal Trade Commission Act on September 26, 1914, and the Clayton Anti-Trust Act on October 15th.[4]

[2] See p. 436.
[3] See p. 367.
[4] See p. 367.

In a little more than a year-and-a-half after he had assumed office President Wilson had succeeded by aggressive leadership in having placed upon the statute books four pieces of legislation of major importance. How much further he might have gone in elaborating a program of social and economic reform it is impossible to say for, in August, 1914, the Great European War broke out, which raised international problems, involving the United States, of the first importance. As a result during the remaining six years that President Wilson was in office he was forced to devote his attention mainly to pressing problems of foreign policy, to the exclusion of questions of domestic reform. A consideration of the relation of the United States to the European cataclysm is left to a later chapter. At this point it is necessary to consider only the influence of these events upon the internal political situation.

The mid-term Congressional elections in November, 1914, resulted in something more than the normal reaction against the party in power. The Democratic majority in the House was reduced from 147 to 29. Various causes contributed to this overturn. The protected interests resented the lowering of the tariff and "Big Business" in general objected to the trust legislation, while the administration was denounced for surrendering to the demands of organized labor in the Clayton Law. Moreover, there had been a business depression during 1913 which was considerably aggravated by the economic confusion brought about by the outbreak of hostilities in Europe.

With the approach of the presidential election of 1916 the Republicans were confronted with the problem of healing the breach that had been made in the party in the previous election. If the Progressives and the regular Republicans again nominated opposing candidates it would assure success to the Democrats once more. To meet one of the criticisms made by the Progressives in 1912, that the nominee of the Republican party was frequently determined by hand-picked delegates from Southern states in which the party had no chance of obtaining any electoral votes, the National Republican Committee voted to submit to the various state conventions a proposal to apportion the delegates in the national convention so as to give to each state four delegates at large, with one additional delegate for each congressman at large, one delegate from each congressional district, and an additional delegate from each district in which the Republican vote in the presidential election of 1908 or the congressional election of 1914 had been not less than 7,500. The proposal was adopted and the convention of 1916 was made up on this basis. The effect was to give to the states having a large Republican vote a greater weight in determining the party candidate, although the distribution of delegates under the new arrangement was still not representative of the voting strength of the party in the various states.

Both the Republican and the Progressive National Conventions met in Chicago on June 7, 1916. This had been arranged by the leaders of the two groups in the hope that a fusion of the two factions might be accomplished. But when the two conventions did meet common action seemed unlikely. The Progressives were determined to nominate Roosevelt once more, whereas the regular Republicans would not accept him under any conditions. On the other hand conservative Republicans favored the nomination of Elihu Root, who was anathema to the Progressives because of his attitude toward them in the convention of 1912. Committees from the two conventions conferred together but were unable to reach a basis of agreement, and each body proceeded to work independently.

The regular Republican convention after some hesitation passed over Root and a number of "favorite sons" and finally selected as their candidate Associate Justice Charles E. Hughes of the United States Supreme Court, who resigned from the bench to accept the nomination. A brief platform was adopted, in which the Democratic Administration was accused of failure to protect the rights of American citizens. It denounced Wilson's interference in Mexico and pledged the Republicans to an adequate protection of American interests abroad. Military preparedness was stressed and the principles of the protective tariff reaffirmed.

The Progressives went forward with their program, naming Roosevelt for President with John M. Parker, of Louisiana, for Vice-President. A platform was adopted which declared anew the faith of the party in the program of social justice set forth in 1912. In line with the views of their leader the platform called for adequate military and naval preparedness. Action of the convention was telegraphed to Roosevelt who responded that he could not consent to accept the nomination at the time as he wished to wait until Mr. Hughes had had an opportunity to define his views on the vital issues of the day. He suggested that his conditional refusal be placed in the hands of the Progressive National Committee, and this was done. On June 26th he informed the committee that he was satisfied with Mr. Hughes as a candidate and proposed to support him, albeit with no great enthusiasm. As he put it in a letter to James Bryce, "At his worst he (Hughes) will be better than Wilson, and there is always a chance that he will do very well indeed." Many of the Progressives followed Mr. Roosevelt back into the Republican fold but others, embittered at what they considered his desertion of the Progressive cause, threw their support to the Democrats.

The Democratic convention met in St. Louis, June 14th. The gathering failed to develop any of the dramatic incidents that had characterized the meeting four years before. President Wilson had established himself in undisputed leadership of his party, and despite the declaration of the party platform of 1912 in favor of a single term for the President,

Wilson indicated his willingness to accept a renomination if public opinion demanded it. No opposition to such action developed in the convention and he was renominated by acclamation. With pardonable pride the platform recounted the truly remarkable legislative achievements of the past three years and called upon the electorate to give a vote of confidence to the party that had so signally redeemed its platform pledges. It denied the charge that the administration had failed to protect American interests abroad and pointed to the success of the President in forcing Germany apparently to abandon its ruthless submarine activities.[5]

In the campaign that followed Mr. Hughes devoted much of his time to a denunciation of the foreign policy of the Wilson administration and insisted that if elected he would "stand for the firm and unflinching maintenance of all rights of American citizens on land and sea." When challenged to state exactly how he would accomplish this without involving the country in war, the Republican candidate failed to make any convincing reply. The Democrats responded that Wilson had maintained peace with national honor. The slogan "He kept us out of war" was used with telling effect, for the people of this country, especially in the Middle West, had no desire to become involved in the terrible European catastrophe. In the closing weeks of the campaign the Democrats lost ground in the eastern states as a result of the action of the President in signing the Adamson railroad law.[6] The Republicans charged that he had surrendered to the unjust demands of the labor leaders in order to avoid a threatened railroad strike. On the other hand Hughes did not succeed in reconciling the Progressives; in fact his tactless dealing with the Progressive forces in California, led by Governor Hiram Johnson, probably cost him the electoral vote of that state and with it the presidency.

[5] See p. 505 ff.
[6] See p. 395.

The election in November resulted in the closest contest since 1876. Early returns from the eastern states indicated the success of Hughes; in fact on the day after the election most of the press, including Democratic papers, conceded his election. But as the returns from the western states began to come in Democratic hopes were revived. In two states, Minnesota and California, the vote was so close that it required an official count to determine the result. In the end Wilson won by the narrow majority of 11 electoral votes. With 266 electoral votes required to elect, Wilson received 277 and Hughes 254. The popular vote was 9,128,837 for Wilson, and 8,536,380 for Hughes. Wilson had carried the agricultural South and West while Hughes held the industrial East. That Hughes failed to win fully the confidence of the Progressives who had left the party in 1912 was strikingly shown in California where the Progressive leader Hiram Johnson was elected to the United States Senate by a majority of 300,000 while Wilson carried the state by 3,700.

One month after President Wilson was inaugurated for his second term the United States entered the World War. For the next two years the energies of the Administration and the thoughts of the American people were devoted in large measure to the many perplexing problems that this stupendous event entailed. A consideration of the very remarkable response of the country to the call to arms is left for treatment in a later chapter. At this point we shall note merely the effect of the war upon certain domestic institutions. Under the supposed exigencies of the war the time-honored American principles of freedom of speech and of the press were either wholly discarded or greatly curtailed. It is, of course, difficult to say just how far the individual should be allowed to go in criticizing his government at the time of a great national crisis. The distinction between legitimate criticism and disloyalty is not easily drawn. Nevertheless, there can be little doubt that government officials, so-called patriotic societies, and over-enthusiastic private individuals exceeded reasonable bounds during the war in their efforts to make individuals conform, and to suppress dissent.

Upon the recommendation of President Wilson, Congress, in June, 1917, passed the Espionage Act, which laid heavy penalties upon persons who disclosed information concerning the national defenses, advocated forcible resistance to the laws of the United States, or interfered in any way with the mobilization of the military and naval forces. Still more drastic was the Sedition Act of May 16, 1918, which made persons liable to a fine of $10,000 or twenty years' imprisonment, or both, who were found guilty of uttering abusive language concerning the American form of government, the Constitution, the flag, or the military forces of the country. A further law of October, 1918, authorized the Secretary of Labor to deport aliens who advocated the overthrow of the government or the unlawful destruction of property, or who belonged to any organization that advocated such doctrines. Supplementing these Federal laws, state and local authorities hastened to adopt restrictive measures, in some instances even more drastic.

Acting under the vague provisions of these laws, a host of government officials, augmented by an even larger number of private individuals, inaugurated a nation-wide campaign of spying upon their fellow citizens, and reported to Washington anything said or done by any one which was regarded by the amateur detectives as "disloyal." In similar manner educational officials kept close watch upon the teaching profession. Teachers in schools and colleges, suspected of unorthodox opinions, were dismissed from their positions. Nearly 2,000 persons were prosecuted under the Espionage and Sedition Acts. Hundreds of so-called undesirable aliens were arrested and 249 of these were deported in December, 1919, more than a year after the war was over.

Although these widespread inquisitorial activities contributed little towards apprehending active enemy spies in this country, they were used by enterprising individuals, who would otherwise have been inconspicuous, to obtain for themselves a fleeting sense of importance and they were seized upon by conservatives as a means of discrediting persons whom they disliked and whose opinions they feared.

Another significant effect of the war upon the life of the American people is seen in the culmination of the movement for national prohibition of intoxicating liquors. Moral and religious reformers had long urged this reform. As early as 1869 had been formed the National Prohibition Party, which thereafter regularly nominated candidates for the presidency and state offices. In 1883 the Women's Christian Temperance Union was organized and in 1893 the Anti-Saloon League. Through the activities of these organizations slow but steady progress was made in advancing the prohibition movement until at the time that the United States entered the World War more than two-thirds of the states had adopted state-wide prohibition by constitutional amendment or had provided for local option. The exigencies of the war were seized upon by the advocates of prohibition to further their campaign. It was urged that the use of intoxicating liquors by the man in uniform would lessen the efficiency of the army and navy. Further, it was pointed out that at the time that the government was calling upon the people to conserve the food supply of the country, large quantities of cereals were being used in the manufacture of intoxicating beverages. Then, too, many business men lent support to the movement, convinced that the use of liquor by their workmen lessened their efficiency.

Influenced by these various factors Congress, on August 1, 1917, passed the Eighteenth Amendment by the requisite two-thirds vote and by January 16, 1919, three-fourths of the states had ratified the Amendment. Under its terms, one year after the ratification was secured, the manufacture, sale, or transportation of intoxicating liquors throughout the United States was prohibited. Both Congress and the states were given concurrent power to enforce the amendment by appropriate legislation. It will be noted that the amendment does not define the alcoholic content that would constitute an intoxicating beverage. This was left for legislative action. Accordingly Congress, on October 28, 1919, passed the famous Volstead Act, which fixed the alcoholic content of beverages at not more than one-half of 1 per cent.

The effort to enforce prohibition on a national scale gave rise to serious problems. Sentiment among the people was sharply divided. In general the rural areas favored the experiment, while the industrial centers were violently opposed. There were those who insisted that the prohibition amendment violated the fundamental principles upon which our government was founded, and that in any event it would be impossible to enforce a law to which large numbers of persons were opposed. In practice there is no question that the law has been flagrantly violated. "Bootlegging" has become something of a vested interest, and in many sections of the country huge sums of money have been paid to government officials by those engaged in the illicit traffic. In time agitation for the repeal of the amendment, or at least a modification of the prohibition law, became an acute political issue and played an important part, as we shall see, in the presidential campaign of 1928.

The war period brougnt a second change in the fundamental law of the land. As we have seen, the movement for the political enfranchisement of women had made substantial progress in the first decade of the twentieth century. Having received the vote in more than one-fourth of the states, the militant suffragist leaders determined to renew the struggle for complete enfranchisement by means of a national constitutional amendment. Their efforts were aided by the extensive activities of women in war work, which called at-

tention to the increasing participation of women in publii.
affairs and emphasized the anomaly of their political subordination. In the presidential election of 1916 both of the leading candidates, Mr. Hughes and Mr. Wilson, endorsed the
principle of women's suffrage, although the latter still clung
to the conviction that it should come by state action rather
than by an amendment to the Federal Constitution. Great
encouragement was given to the suffragist cause in 1917 by
the addition of the important state of New York to the
growing list of suffrage states. The following year President
Wilson was won over. Perhaps not unmindful of the approaching congressional election, the President appeared before Congress in September, 1918, and urged the passage of
the national suffrage amendment. It took another ten months
to muster the necessary two-thirds vote in Congress to pass
the amendment, and then there ensued a year of intensive
work by the suffrage leaders to obtain ratification of three-
fourths of the states. Finally in August, 1920, after nearly
a hundred years of agitation, women were placed on a basis
of political equality with men by the addition of the Nineteenth Amendment to the Federal Constitution.

The Congressional elections in November, 1918, occurred
just before the signing of the armistice that brought to a
close the great struggle in Europe. In the course of the campaign President Wilson issued an appeal to the people to
return a Democratic Congress in order that his hands might
be upheld in bringing the war to a successful conclusion and
in the negotiations with the European powers that would
necessarily follow. What effect the appeal had upon the
voters it is impossible to say, but the election resulted in a
decisive victory for the Republicans. The President's party
lost control of both branches of Congress, and Wilson went
to Paris to undertake the arduous work at the peace conference handicapped by this political reverse at home.

The dramatic incidents, in connection with President Wilson's activities at Paris and his struggle with the Senate over the ratification of the peace treaty are reserved for later consideration. Humiliated by the failure to secure the ratification of his labors at Paris and broken in health, the President served through the last year-and-a-half of his administration. By the irony of fate a President who had entered office bent upon a crusade for domestic reform had been forced to assume the rôle of military dictator in a great foreign war and was fated to see his hopes for economic and social regeneration at home blasted and many of his cherished ideals trampled under foot.

The Democrats approached the presidential election of 1920 with much misgiving. Their great leader, who had piloted the party during the past eight eventful years, presented a pathetic figure on his sick bed in Washington, and there was no one else who appeared able to wield the scepter that he was about to lay down. It was inevitable, too, that a party that had been in control of the government during the momentous years of the war should have aroused bitter resentments that would embarrass the party in a national election. On the other hand, the Republicans looked forward to the coming election with confidence. The breach between the Progressives and the conservatives had been healed, or perhaps it would be more accurate to say that the Progressive movement was a thing of the past. Roosevelt had died in January, 1919, and there was no other Progressive leader even remotely approaching him in popularity to whom the Progressive forces could turn. With a united and confident party the conservative Republican leaders were prepared to take full advantage of the misfortunes and mistakes of their political opponents.

The Republican National Convention met at Chicago on June 8, 1920. The leading contenders for the presidential nomination were General Leonard Wood, a close friend of Roosevelt; Senator Hiram Johnson, Roosevelt's running mate in 1912; and Governor Frank O. Lowden, of Illinois. The conservative Republican Senators who dominated the convention did not look with favor upon any of the leading aspirants and, when the early balloting indicated that no one of the three would be able to obtain the necessary majority, a group of Senators gathered in a hotel room and agreed to give their support to their colleague, Senator Warren G. Harding, of Ohio. The following day Harding was nominated on the tenth ballot. For the vice presidency the convention chose Governor Calvin Coolidge, of Massachusetts. The platform adopted by the convention denounced President Wilson for his "dictatorial course" in dealing with Congress; declared that the policies of the administration had been "humiliating to America and irritating to other nations" and had resulted in impairing our moral influence, leaving us "discredited and friendless among the nations of the world." It pledged the Republican party to "fulfill our world obligations without sacrifice of our national independence," without indicating, however, just how this was to be accomplished.

The Democrats met at San Francisco on June 28th. President Wilson from his sick bed declined to support any candidate for the presidential nomination but indicated his desire that the convention would choose a man who had supported his policies. The names most prominently mentioned for the Democratic nomination were William G. McAdoo, Secretary of the Treasury and a son-in-law of President Wilson; Attorney General A. Mitchell Palmer; Governor James M. Cox, of Ohio; and Governor Alfred E. Smith, of New York. McAdoo led on the first ballot but his vote fell far short of the two-thirds requirement. It took forty-four ballots before Governor Cox received sufficient votes to obtain the nomination. The platform strongly endorsed the administration of President Wilson and called for the ratification of the Treaty of Versailles "without reservations which would imperil its essential integrity."

In the campaign Cox attempted to make the question of American entrance into the League of Nations the dominant issue. In this he had the hearty approval of President Wilson, who expressed the wish that the election might be a "solemn referendum" on the question of the treaty and the League. Harding had some difficulty in meeting this issue. There was a sharp division of opinion among prominent Republicans concerning the policy that this country should take toward the League and during the campaign the Republican nominee obviously attempted to avoid the troublesome issue. As events proved, it was unnecessary for him to commit himself, for the voters were determined to rebuke the Wilson administration irrespective of what the Republicans stood for. The outgoing President and his party associates had piled up an accumulation of grievances. Citizens of German descent or sympathies resented the fact that Wilson had espoused the cause of the Allies and further accused him of betraying Germany at the peace conference; Irish-Americans were grieved because he had refused to take up the cause of the Irish republic; liberals accused him of having deserted his "Fourteen Points" at Paris, and of giving aid and comfort to the activities of Attorney General Palmer in enforcing the Espionage and Sedition laws; large business interests resented his trust legislation and his alleged surrender to labor in the Adamson Law and the Clayton Act; and, finally, the mass of the people were restless under the high prices for commodities, which reached their peak in the summer of 1920. The unprecedented Republican majority of more than 7,000,000 was therefore not so much an indorsement of the Republican party as a condemnation of the Wilson Democracy. The Republican landslide gave that party an overwhelming majority in the House and an ample majority in the Senate.

HARDING AND COOLIDGE—CONSERVATISM TRIUMPHANT

The character of President Harding stood in sharp contrast to those of the two dynamic personalities, Roosevelt and Wilson, who had occupied the center of the political stage during the preceding two decades. He laid no claim to exceptional intellectual ability and his political record gave no indication that he would assume a dominant position as a party leader. His record in Congress had been that of a faithful supporter of the party organization. He lacked the moral fervor to become the spokesman of a "cause." In fact, he prided himself upon being just an average American citizen or, in the words of Mrs. Harding, they were "just folks." And the temper of the country at the time welcomed such a man in the White House. Sixteen years of Roosevelt and Wilson had tended to weary the people of the brilliant leader who was constantly advocating reform and they yearned for a return to the "normalcy" that Harding proclaimed and typified.

But the advent of Harding meant more than the change of personalities in the presidency: it marked the end of the era of progressive reform that Roosevelt had inaugurated and which Wilson had carried forward, and it ushered in a period of conservative reaction. There were two reasons for this change. First was the inevitable reaction which follows every reform wave. The average citizen is unable or unwilling to maintain through a stretch of years that "moral overstrain" which gives the driving force to reform movements. After the initial rush of enthusiasm has passed there invariably follows a feeling of lethargy. Such appeared to be the mood of a large part of the American people in 1920, after the long crusading era of Roosevelt and Wilson. More potent, however, in furthering the retreat to conservatism, was the reaction to the Russian Bolshevist revolution in the

United States. Expressions of sympathy with the Russian experiment among the left wing labor and liberal groups in this country were eagerly seized upon by conservative and reactionary forces to frighten timid people with the specter of a similar upheaval in America. Even the most moderate suggestions of reform were denounced as "Bolshevistic" and "un-American." Leaders of liberal thought could make no headway in the prevailing atmosphere of suspicion that swept the country; in fact, they were exposed to the attacks of the professional witch-hunters who had constituted themselves the guardians of undiluted Americanism. Ideas that a few years before had been acclaimed by the people were now rejected as sinister proposals of foreign agitators bent upon undermining American institutions. Conservative leaders took full advantage of this trend in public opinion to bring about not merely a halt in the Roosevelt-Wilson program of reform but to effect a substantial return along many lines to the ideals of the McKinley era.

President Harding was in full accord with the swing to conservatism. In the selection of his Cabinet no consideration was given to the former Progressive leaders who had returned to the ranks of the Republican party. As Secretary of State he chose Charles E. Hughes; for the Treasury he selected Andrew Mellon, a wealthy Pennsylvania banker; Herbert C. Hoover, who had established a world-wide reputation through his relief work in Europe, was made Secretary of Commerce. Two cabinet appointments which later brought discredit upon the Administration were those of Senator Fall as Secretary of the Interior and Harry M. Daugherty as Attorney General.

To hasten the "return to normalcy" President Harding summoned Congress in special session on April 11, 1921, for the enactment of the requisite legislation. As was to be expected, attention was promptly given to the tariff. An emergency tariff law, designed to satisfy the demands of the farmers, which had been vetoed by President Wilson on the last day of his term, was repassed and signed by President Harding. This was followed by the enactment of a general tariff act, the Fordney-McCumber Law, which effectively closed the breach in the wall of protection that had been made by the Underwood Tariff.[7]

Having restored normalcy in the tariff the conservative leaders turned to the revision of the war taxes. The war brought a veritable revolution in the system of Federal taxation. Prior to 1913 the national government had been sustained wholly by indirect taxes on customs and excises. By the close of the war nearly one-half of the Federal revenues were obtained from inheritance and income taxes. The rates on the largest incomes reached 65 per cent. In addition, heavy levies were made upon the excess profits of corporations. As soon as the war ended there arose an insistent demand, particularly among the large taxpayers, for relief from the burdensome war taxes. They were successful in bringing about a prompt repeal of the excess profits tax. Secretary Mellon followed this by a suggestion that the surtax on incomes should be reduced from a maximum of 65 per cent. to 25 per cent. In Congress, however, the remnant of the insurgent element from the West joined with the Democrats in refusing to make this concession to the wealthy taxpayers and the surtax maximum was fixed at 50 per cent. in the revenue law of 1921.

The prophets of the new era met a further check in their efforts to solve the shipping problem. During the war, the government had purchased and built a large fleet of merchant ships to facilitate the transport of troops and goods to Europe. With the close of the war the Shipping Board attempted to keep these ships in operation, but the decline in the demand for shipping facilities made their maintenance unprofitable.

[7] See p. 438.

The Merchant Marine Act of 1920 provided for the sale of government-owned ships to American citizens but, in the depressed condition of the shipping business, purchasers could not be found who would take the vessels on any reasonable terms. President Harding then urged upon Congress the enactment of legislation providing for a subsidy to be paid from the national treasury to American-owned merchant vessels, but the proposal was rejected by the Senate, largely because of the opposition of Senators from the agricultural states.

There were other indications that serious obstacles would be met on the road back to normalcy. In 1922 two great strikes, one in the bituminous coal fields and the other among the railway shopmen, showed that all was not well in the ranks of labor. Moreover, the numbers of unemployed had increased to an alarming extent. Finally, in the halls of Congress the agricultural bloc was calling loudly for legislation to relieve the distress of the farmers. To suggest ways and means of remedying these evidences of discontent President Harding appointed a Coal Commission to make a thorough survey of the whole coal industry, summoned a Conference on Unemployment to suggest means of relieving unemployment and an Agricultural Conference to study the ills of the farmers. The Coal Commission accomplished little of practical importance. The Unemployment Conference made a number of recommendations to provide temporary relief and also suggested a program for permanent recovery from the existing depression. The Agricultural Conference consisted of representatives of farmers, packers, bankers, and government officials. On the basis of the recommendations of this conference Congress enacted three measures in the interests of the farmers: a Futures Trading Act, designed to prevent speculation of the grain exchanges; a Filled Milk Act, prohibiting the sale of adulterated milk; and an Agricultural Credits Act, which provided for government credit to farmers through Intermediate Credit Banks, which were authorized to discount farmers' notes.

The mid-term Congressional elections in November, 1922, resulted in the customary reaction against the party in power. The Republican majority in the House was reduced from 168 to 14, and in the Senate from 24 to 10. Moreover, a number of Senators and Representatives in the new Congress, though nominally classed as Republicans, could not be depended upon to support the party program. In fact, the balance of power was held by a group of Progressive Representatives and Senators, chiefly from the West.

A cloud was cast upon the Harding Administration through disclosures of maladministration, if nothing worse, by the heads of three of the Government departments. Certain sources of oil supply on public lands in Wyoming and California had been reserved for future use by the navy. Shortly after his inauguration President Harding transferred the control of these lands from Secretary of the Navy Denby to Secretary of the Interior Fall. Fall then proceeded to lease the "Tea Pot Dome" fields in Wyoming to Harry F. Sinclair and oil lands in California to E. M. Doheny. Both Sinclair and Doheny were prominent figures in the oil industry. Investigation by a Congressional committee disclosed the fact that Fall had received from Doheny a "loan" of $100,000, apparently without any security. Popular indignation aroused by these disclosures resulted in the retirement of Secretaries Fall and Denby from the Cabinet. Suits brought by the Government in the Federal courts led to the cancellation of the leases made by Fall on the ground of fraud and conspiracy. Criminal prosecutions against Denby and Sinclair [8] failed despite the fact that the Supreme Court had declared that the

---

[8] Sinclair was later convicted and imprisoned for contempt of the Senate in refusing to answer questions and also for shadowing the jury in his trial for conspiracy.

whole affair was tainted by fraud and corruption. In the meantime another Congressional committee had unearthed evidence of flagrant corruption in the Department of Justice, which brought about the forced resignation of Attorney General Daugherty, in March, 1924.[9]

In June, 1923, President and Mrs. Harding, with a party of friends, started on a tour of the West, including a visit to Alaska. The President's health was none too good when he began the trip and it is probable that worry over the disclosures of corruption among his trusted associates aggravated his condition. When he reached San Francisco upon his return from Alaska it became apparent that his condition was serious and on August 2d the country learned with genuine grief that the President was dead. Political animosities were forgotten for the time being, and from all sections of the country there came expressions of admiration for the unaffected simplicity and the lovable character of the late President.

The succession of Vice-President Coolidge to the presidency brought no material change in the policies of the administration. The political and economic philosophy of the new President were in general agreement with those of his predecessor. His early political career had not been conspicuous and he had always shown a willingness to work in harmony with the leaders of the Republican organization. National attention was first directed to him in 1919 while he was Governor of Massachusetts. In that year the policemen in Boston went on strike for increased pay and for several days the city was left without police protection. Appealed to by the local authorities, Governor Coolidge called out the militia to restore order, for which action he was loudly praised by the press of the country, although there

[9] In 1929 ex-Secretary Fall was convicted of accepting a bribe from Doheny and was sentenced to pay a fine of $100,000 and to serve a year in prison. The prison term was suspended.

were those who later insisted that the Governor did not intervene until the strike had virtually collapsed. Coolidge himself never claimed credit for settling the difficulty.

Although President Coolidge obtained a national reputation as a shrewd man of few words, he, in fact, both wrote and spoke with facility. In his writings and speeches there is no profound political or economic philosophy. The homely virtues of thrift and economy were the attributes that appealed to him most and that he never failed to emphasize in his public addresses. Despite the remarkable support which Coolidge received from the press of the country while in the presidency he never succeeded in making himself the dominant leader of his party as did Roosevelt and Wilson. Time and again he failed to obtain from Congress support for the policies that he advocated.

President Coolidge met his first Congress in December, 1923, and delivered to it his message in person. The keynote of the President's address was economy and tax reduction. But Coolidge had even greater difficulty than Harding in persuading Congress to accept his point of view. As we have seen, the balance of power in both houses of Congress was held by a small group of Progressives who were not at all inclined to see eye to eye with the President. The administration met its first rebuff in its recommendation for the revision of the tax laws. Secretary Mellon submitted a proposal to reduce the normal income tax to 3 per cent. and the maximum surtax to 25 per cent. But the insurgents in Congress regarded this as being too tender to the large taxpayers and passed a bill that reduced the rate on small incomes to 2 per cent. and kept the maximum surtax at 40 per cent. Congress further declined to accept the suggestion of the President that the great water power plant built by the government at Muscle Shoals should be sold to private individuals.

Despite his failure to control Congress the approach of the presidential election of 1924 found Coolidge in a strong strategic position to secure the Republican nomination. During the year-and-a-half that he was serving out the term of President Harding he had had an opportunity to build up a substantial personal following through the judicious use of presidential patronage. Moreover, he could disclaim responsibility for the corruption that had been disclosed in the administration of his predecessor. The conservatives, who controlled the party organization, regarded with satisfaction the continuance of Coolidge in the presidency. Under the circumstances no serious opposition to the nomination of the President developed at the Republican Convention and he was chosen on the first ballot. For the vice presidency Governor Lowden, of Illinois, was at first selected but upon his refusal to accept the nomination the convention chose Charles G. Dawes of the same state. The Republican platform, as was to be expected, advanced no novel proposals. It opened with a tribute to the late President Harding and eulogized President Coolidge and the Republican party for the correction of "the ills we received from the last Democratic administration." For the rest there was the usual praise of the protective tariff; a demand for further tax reduction; a declaration in favor of the United States joining the International Court of Justice; a proposal for a further conference on the limitation of armaments; a pledge to bring about "a balanced condition between agriculture, industry and labor"; and, without referring to the scandals of the Harding administration, a demand for the impartial prosecution of all wrongdoers. On the much mooted question of prohibition the Republicans contented themselves with a pledge to use "the full strength of the government for the enforcement of the Constitution and of all laws."

Democratic hopes of profiting by the disclosures of Republican corruption were blasted as a result of a bitter factional fight within the party. At the Democratic Convention which met in the city of New York the leading aspirants for the presidential nomination were Governor Smith, of New York, and William G. McAdoo, of California.[10] The requirement of a two-thirds vote to nominate made it difficult in Democratic conventions to agree upon a candidate whenever more than one proposed nominee had substantial support. When the balloting for the nomination began it appeared that neither of the leading candidates would obtain the required vote. Day after day the sweltering delegates continued at their task amidst scenes that gave evidence of bitter sectional and religious animosity. It was not until the 103rd ballot that the convention, worn out by the long struggle, abandoned the effort to nominate either of the leading contestants and selected John W. Davis, a conservative Democrat from West Virginia. The Democratic platform presented no striking contrast to that of the Republicans. Quite naturally the Democrats made much of the corruption in Republican ranks, but they were just as evasive as the Republicans on the prohibition issue, using almost identical language in their pledge "to respect and enforce the Constitution and all laws." The protective tariff was condemned; tax reduction promised, although the proposals of Secretary Mellon were denounced; the League of Nations and the World Court were praised as "constituting the supreme effort of statesmanship to organize the world for peace," and a popular referendum was proposed to determine the question of American membership in the League. The effort to arouse religious or racial dissension was deplored. Both platforms advocated the ratification of the child labor amendment to the Constitution.[11]

There was little in the platforms of the two parties or in the records of the candidates that would appeal to persons of a liberal or progressive point of view. Increasing evidence of discontent in both agricultural and industrial regions in the

[10] McAdoo had changed his residence from New York to California.
[11] See p. 404.

years after 1920 encouraged those who saw no hope in either
the Democratic or the Republican party to attempt to organize the progressive forces once more and present a candidate for the presidency in 1924. In 1923 a convention of
the Farmer-Labor party was held, but, as the Communist
element played a leading rôle in its deliberations, many conservative labor leaders withdrew their support and participated in the formation of a new organization called the Conference for Progressive Political Action. At a meeting held
in St. Louis in February, 1924, this body adopted resolutions
endorsing most of the well-known progressive principles and
called a nominating convention to meet in July. In the meantime Senator La Follette, the veteran leader of the Progressives, had announced his intention of running for President
independently, and when the convention of the Conference
for Progressive Political Action met it endorsed his candidacy. Similar action was taken by the American Federation
of Labor and by the Socialist party, which had been seriously weakened by the Communist defections since 1920.

The Democrats entertained hopes that La Follette might
split the Republican vote as Roosevelt had done in 1912, but
their hopes were not realized. In the first place, the Democratic candidate, despite his acknowledged ability, aroused no
great popular enthusiasm and, moreover, the bitterness engendered at the Democratic convention was not wholly dissipated during the campaign. The Republicans made much of
the menace that the candidacy of La Follette offered and
urged all who believed in the sanctity of American institutions to support the "safe and sane" policies of President
Coolidge. Despite the fact that La Follette advocated no
more radical a program than Roosevelt had supported twelve
years before, the Republican appeal was effective. Times had
changed. The Bolshevist bugaboo was used to advantage to
frighten timid voters, and the fact that the Socialists had
endorsed La Follette probably convinced many persons that

he was the dangerous radical pictured in the Republican press.

The election resulted in a substantial victory for the Republicans. Coolidge polled more than 54 per cent. of the popular vote, receiving 15,718,789 votes to 8,378,962 for Davis and 4,822,319 for La Follette. The electoral vote was Coolidge 382, Davis 136, and La Follette 13. Outside of the "Solid South" the Democrats carried only one state, Oklahoma, while La Follette won only in his own state of Wisconsin. It is significant, however, that in twelve western states the popular vote for La Follette exceeded that for Davis. The Republicans undoubtedly profited by the fact that the country was generally in a prosperous condition and the voters saw no advantage in a change in party control. Agricultural discontent was temporarily quieted as a result of a large wheat crop in 1924, which was sold in the world markets at satisfactory prices. In the Congressional elections the Republicans increased their majorities in both Houses.

As President in his own right Mr. Coolidge did not propose any strikingly new program. He held to the view that American social and economic conditions were fundamentally sound, that the country was enjoying prosperity, and that the less done by the government in interfering with the conduct of private business the better. In his message to Congress in December, 1924, he emphasized again the need for economy and tax reduction and this time he had little difficulty in persuading Congress to adopt at least the second of these proposals. The Southern Democrats in Congress, who for the most part represented the same economic interests as the conservative Republicans, were quite sympathetic with the demand for the reduction of taxes on large incomes. Nor did the Democratic leaders sense any party advantage to be obtained from opposing the proposals of Secretary Mellon, who was widely proclaimed in the press of the country as "the greatest Secretary of the Treasury since Alexander Hamilton." This left only the handful of western Progressives to resist the administration program. With remarkable speed Congress passed the new tax law, which reduced the maximum surtax on incomes from 40 to 20 per cent., repealed the provision of the former law providing for publicity of income tax returns, and made less drastic reductions in the rates on smaller incomes. Although Congress declined to adopt the suggestion of Secretary Mellon for the repeal of the Federal inheritance tax, it did reduce the maximum rate of this tax from 40 to 20 per cent., and further allowed a credit of as much as 80 per cent. on the Federal tax in the case of estates that paid a state inheritance tax.

More than a year before the time for the presidential election of 1928 the ardent supporters of President Coolidge started a movement for his renomination. To those who raised the issue of a third term it was replied that the year-and-a-half in which Coolidge was serving out the term of President Harding should not be counted as a full term, and that the President was entitled to a second "elective" term. For some time Coolidge made no move either to encourage or to stop the movement to nominate him, and the friends of other possible candidates hesitated to launch their booms until the President had definitely declared his intentions. Finally, on August 2, 1927, the anniversary of his taking the oath of office four years before, he gave to the press a statement which read, "I do not choose to run for President in 1928." Although the majority of persons took this to mean that Coolidge had definitely eliminated himself from the presidential race, some of his most enthusiastic supporters insisted that it meant that although the President did not "choose" to run he might be persuaded to accept a nomination if the popular demand was sufficiently emphatic. Despite the fact that Coolidge declined to elaborate upon his original statement, in his quiet way he made it evident that he would oppose any move to "draft" him.

With the President definitely removed from consideration the supporters of Herbert C. Hoover, Secretary of Commerce in the Coolidge Cabinet, inaugurated a vigorous campaign to obtain his nomination by the Republicans. It was generally believed that Hoover's selection was favored by Coolidge, but no public statement to that effect came from the White House. The primary elections indicated a strong Hoover sentiment among the Republican voters and by the time that the national convention met he had far outdistanced the other suggested candidates. The chief opposition to Hoover came from the representatives of the Western farmers because of his action during the war when as Food Administrator he had fixed the price of wheat. Despite this opposition Hoover was nominated on the first ballot. For Vice President the convention chose Senator Charles Curtis, of Kansas.

Even more impressive than Hoover's strength among the Republicans was that of Governor Alfred E. Smith, of New York, among the Democrats. Ever since the memorable struggle in the Democratic convention of 1924, Governor Smith had grown steadily in popularity, not only in his own state but in the nation at large. He had been elected Governor for a third time in 1924 by more than 100,000 plurality, although President Coolidge carried the state by nearly 900,000. In 1926 he was elected Governor for the fourth time by nearly 250,000 plurality, and from that time on he was the foremost candidate for the Democratic presidential nomination. Opposition to his selection came from various parts of the country, first, because he was known to be opposed to prohibition, second, because he was a Roman Catholic, and lastly, because of his Tammany affiliations. However, no other candidate appeared who could compare with Smith in popularity among the rank and file of the Democratic voters and at the convention he was nominated on the first ballot. For Vice President the Democrats chose Senator Joseph T. Robinson of Arkansas.

The platforms of the two parties were even less distinguishable than they had been four years before. Concerning foreign relations both parties pledged their support to the outlawry of war and to plans for the limitation of armaments. The Republicans reaffirmed their opposition to the United States joining the League of Nations, while the Democrats omitted any reference to that body. The Democrats advocated non-interference in the internal affairs of Latin America and the Republicans disclaimed any idea of conquest or exploitation in these countries. Even on the question of the tariff the Democrats departed from their traditional policy in failing to incorporate in their platform a ringing denunciation of the principle of protection. They contented themselves with a demand for a tariff which would maintain legitimate business and the high standard of wages for American labor, and for the equitable distribution of the benefits and burdens of the tariff. On the two controversial questions of farm relief and prohibition the party platforms presented no sharp contrast. The Republicans promised to promote the establishment of a farm marketing system with financial assistance from the Government. The Democrats, with an eye to the vote in the Middle West, were somewhat more specific in their promises of aid to the farmers. On the thorny question of prohibition the Republicans pledged their party to "the observance and vigorous enforcement" of the Eighteenth Amendment, while the Democrats promised to make "an honest effort to enforce the Eighteenth Amendment and all other provisions of the Federal Constitution and all laws enacted pursuant thereto."

However, it was of little consequence what was contained in the party platforms. The people were interested in the personalities and views of the candidates rather than in the ambiguous or meaningless pronouncements of party programs.

The personalities of the two leading candidates disclosed some points of similarity and others of striking contrast. Both had risen in life from humble beginnings, one starting on an Iowa farm and the other on the sidewalks of New York. Both were distinctly self-made men and, again, both had established national reputations for possessing administrative capacity to an unusual degree. On the other hand Hoover was an unknown quantity in politics. He had never held an elective office and had no experience in the practical game of politics. Smith, on the contrary, had the most remarkable vote-getting record of any man in the country, and had held numerous elective offices in city and state to which he had been chosen by overwhelming majorities. Further, Hoover lacked Smith's ability to arouse deep personal affection among the mass of the people. Hoover won admiration for his ability as a great engineer and administrator; Smith stirred popular feeling because of his human qualities.

In the campaign the Democratic candidate, despite the equivocal statement of the party platform on the question of prohibition, came out boldly in favor of a modification of the Volstead Act and further advocated the ultimate repeal of the Eighteenth Amendment, leaving to the people of each of the states the problem of regulating the liquor traffic. At the same time he stated that he was firmly opposed to the revival of the saloon and suggested the possibility of having the state governments handle the sale of liquor in somewhat the same manner as was done in some of the Canadian provinces. The Democratic campaign orators made a somewhat weak attempt to capitalize the disclosures of corruption during the Harding administration, but there was little evidence of moral indignation on this score among the voters. Finally the Democrats labored to prove that the success of their party would not be disturbing to business and in this connection they pointed to the fact that a number of men, prominent in the business world, had declared their intention to support the Democratic ticket.

Mr. Hoover restricted his campaign efforts to a comparatively few speeches in the important cities of the East and South. On the subject of prohibition he said little but indicated that he was opposed to any change in what he called "a noble experiment." In general the Republicans stressed the issue of prosperity and claimed full credit for the generally prosperous condition of the country. Despite Mr. Hoover's denunciation of those who tried to raise the religious issue, there was carried on a widespread "whispering" campaign against Governor Smith on account of his Catholic faith.

The results of the election presented some remarkable aspects. The popular vote was the greatest ever cast, both in the total number of ballots and in the percentage of eligible voters who went to the polls. In all 36,879,414 votes were cast, of which Mr. Hoover received 21,392,190 and Governor Smith 15,016,443. Of the electoral votes the Republicans received 444 and the Democrats 87. Despite the apparent overwhelming victory of the Republicans, Governor Smith polled the largest popular vote ever cast for a Democratic candidate for the presidency and he received a larger percentage of the total popular vote than the Democratic candidates in the two preceding elections had obtained.

The most striking feature of the election was the victory of the Republican candidate in the states of Virginia, North Carolina, Florida, and Texas, which for the first time in more than fifty years gave their electoral votes to a Republican. On the other hand, Governor Smith carried the normally strong Republican state of Massachusetts, as well as its little neighbor Rhode Island. A further surprising result was the failure of Governor Smith to carry his own state of New York, despite the fact that the Democratic candidates for United States Senator and Governor in that state were successful.

Doubtless many factors contributed to the success of the Republicans in this election, but the comment of one shrewd political observer would not seem to be far amiss, viz., that it was "the three P's"—Prohibition, Prejudice, and Prosperity—that were mainly responsible for the result.

During the first year of the administration of President Hoover there were indications that the "normalcy" of the Harding-Coolidge era had passed. In the fall of 1929 a severe decline in the prices of securities on the stock market resulted in the wiping out of many "paper" fortunes. More serious was the evidence of a distinct slowing up in industrial activities, bringing in its train an alarming increase in unemployment. In agricultural circles, too, unrest appeared because of the low prices of agricultural commodities. It was inevitable that these unsatisfactory conditions should be reflected in Congress. In the Senate "insurgency" once more was strongly in evidence. A group of progressive Republican Senators from the West joined with the Democrats to wrest control of the Senate from the regular Republicans, at least temporarily, during the discussion of a proposed new tariff bill. Personal animosities, reminiscent of the days of 1912, were displayed in the halls of Congress. A leading Republican Senator referred to his insurgent party colleagues from the West as "sons of wild jackasses." Further evidence of the undercurrent of revolt was given in the debate that took place in the Senate in connection with the confirmation of the appointment of Mr. Charles E. Hughes as Chief Justice of the Supreme Court to succeed Justice Taft. Several Senators openly opposed his confirmation, not because of any doubt concerning his judicial qualifications but because they were opposed to adding another justice of conservative temperament to a Court already strongly inclined toward conservatism. One Senator went so far as to predict that, if the

Court persisted in its policy of nullifying progressive legislation, the time was not far distant when action would be taken to curtail the powers of the Court.

At this time (1930) it is not possible to state whether these manifestations of protest against the era of "normalcy" are only a temporary flare-up or whether they foreshadow a real revival of progressivism.

BIBLIOGRAPHICAL NOTE

General accounts of the important political events since 1913 are to be found in H. H. Kohlsaat, *From McKinley to Harding* (1923); O. S. Straus, *Under Four Administrations* (1922); E. Stanwood, *History of the Presidency* (rev. ed., 1928); Ogg, *National Progress* (1917), covers the period to 1917. Consult also *The American Year Book* (1910- ——); *The New International Year Book* (1907- ——).

President Wilson's economic and political philosophy is set forth in his *The New Freedom* (1913). See also R. S. Baker and W. E. Dodd, *Public Papers of Woodrow Wilson* (1927). Numerous biographical sketches of Wilson and estimates of his work have been published. The authorized biography is by Ray Stannard Baker, of which two volumes were published in 1927. Consult also R. E. Annin, *Woodrow Wilson: A Character Study* (1924); W. E. Dodd, *Woodrow Wilson and His Work* (1921); W. A. White, *Woodrow Wilson: The Man, His Times and His Task* (1924); H. J. Ford, *Woodrow Wilson: The Man and His Work* (1916); B. J. Hendrick, *Life and Letters of W. H. Page* (3 Vols., 1922-1925); Charles Seymour, *Intimate Papers of Colonel E. M. House* (4 Vols., 1926-1928); D. F. Houston, *Eight Years with Wilson's Cabinet* (1926); J. P. Tumulty, *Woodrow Wilson as I Knew Him* (1925). For a discussion of the war restrictions on freedom of discussion see Z. Chaffee, *Freedom of Speech* (1920). On prohibition consult E. H. Charrington, *The Evolution of Prohibition in the United States* (1920); J. A. Krout, *The Origins of Prohibition* (1925).

For the Harding-Coolidge period consult W. G. Harding, *Our Common Country* (1921); J. M. Chapple, *Warren G. Harding: The Man* (1920); C. W. Gilbert, *Behind the Mirrors: Psychology of Disintegration at Washington* (1922); C.

Coolidge, *The Price of Freedom* (1924) ; H. Green, *The Life of Calvin Coolidge* (1924) ; W. A. White, *Calvin Coolidge: The Man Who Is President* (1925).
   On Hoover and Smith see H. C. Hoover, *American Individualism* (1922) ; W. H. Irwin, *Herbert Hoover, A Reminiscent Biography* (1928) ; V. L. Kellog, *Herbert Hoover: The Man and His Work* (1920) ; A. E. Smith, *Progressive Democracy* (1928) ; by the same author, *Up to Now: An Autobiography* (1929) ; H. F. Pringle, *A. E. Smith: A Critical Study* (1927).

CHAPTER 16

INDUSTRY AND TRANSPORTATION, 1900-1929

It is difficult to avoid the use of superlatives in describing the industrial development of the United States in the period after 1900. The figures measuring the output of American mines and factories in these years are so huge that it is almost impossible to comprehend their meaning. The total value of manufactured goods in 1900 was 13 billions of dollars, in 1925 it exceeded 62 billions. Iron and steel manufactures in this period grew from $1,800,000,000 to over $6,000,000,-000. In 1925 the United States produced 38 per cent. of the world's coal, 70 per cent. of the petroleum, 38 per cent. of the electrical power, 33 per cent. of the iron ore, and 54 per cent. of the copper.

It is not merely the remarkable increase in the industrial output of these years that is significant. This expansion was accompanied by fundamental changes in industrial methods of such far-reaching importance as to warrant the statement that they constituted a new industrial revolution, quite as striking as that which occurred at the end of the eighteenth century. The distinguishing features of this new industrial revolution are the widespread use of electricity and of the internal combustion engine in place of steam power, and, secondly, the mass production of standardized goods. To a consideration of these new industrial methods and of the problems that have arisen from the industrial growth of the United States in recent years we shall now turn our attention.

We have noted the growth of great industrial combinations in the closing decades of the nineteenth century and the ineffectual attempt to control these large aggregations of capital by the Sherman Anti-Trust Law.[1] A temporary check was given to the development of business concentration by the panic of 1893, but before the close of the century the country had recovered from the financial depression and there followed a number of years of remarkable business prosperity, accompanied by a renewal of the development of large-scale business enterprises. Industrial and financial leaders like Morgan, Vanderbilt, and Rockefeller, who had gained their business experience and laid the foundations of their fortunes in the eighties and nineties, were the outstanding figures in the new era of business and financial development and their operations were conducted on a scale that dwarfed their earlier activities.

A few typical examples of industrial concentration and capital inflation may be noted. In 1899 the Standard Oil Company of New Jersey was organized, as the successor to the Standard Oil Trust, with a capitalization of $102,233,-000. In the same year there was formed, under the favorable corporation laws of New Jersey, the Amalgamated Copper Company, capitalized at $175,000,000, although the par value of the stocks of the constituent companies was only $47,-748,500. The most striking example of corporate financing at this time was that involved in the organization of the United States Steel Corporation in 1901. There was issued a total of approximately $1,400,000,000 in stocks and bonds of the new corporation which were exchanged for the securities of the companies brought into the combination or were given as commissions to the underwriting syndicate. It is not possible to estimate accurately the physical value of the properties that were consolidated, but there is no question that in many instances these values had been greatly inflated. In the purchase of the Carnegie concern a total of $303,450,000 in bonds and nearly $200,000,000 in stock was given for property that could have been obtained a year or two before for

[1] See p. 105.

$157,000,000. To the syndicate which undertook the forma-
tion of the corporation there was given more than $150,-
000,000 in stock as compensation for promotion and underwriting services. The Bureau of Corporations valued the
tangible property of the combination in 1901 at $682,000,000,
against which there had been issued $1,400,000,000 in securi-
ties. However, whatever water there was in the capitalization
of the United States Steel Corporation was largely squeezed
out later. Each year the directors of the corporation voted
large sums out of earnings for building new plants or extending old ones. Within fifteen years more than $500,000,000
was expended in this manner, thus placing physical value behind virtually the full capitalization of the company.

From oil, copper, and steel the mania for consolidation
spread to substantially every field of industrial activity. In
the six years from 1898 to 1904, 236 industrial trusts were
organized with an aggregate capitalization of $6,049,618,223.
In public utilities the same tendency is found. Eight telegraph
and telephone combinations, all but two organized after 1898,
brought together 136 smaller companies with a combined
capitalization of $629,700,500. Gas, electric light, and street
railway consolidations numbered 103, representing over 1,200
original companies, and having a total capitalization of
$3,105,755,571. In the years before 1900 railway consolida-
tion had brought a great part of the railroad mileage of the
country into a number of large systems, through the activities of such men as Vanderbilt and Gould. In the early years
of the new century the process was continued on a still larger
scale. In 1897 E. H. Harriman obtained control of the Union
Pacific Railway and, after reorganizing the company, made
it the nucleus of a vast network of railroads extending from
Chicago to the Pacific and southward to the Gulf of Mexico.
James J. Hill and J. P. Morgan, after a spectacular struggle
with Harriman, effected a combination of the Great Northern, the Northern Pacific, and the Chicago, Burlington, and

Quincy Railroads. Having obtained control of these three great railroad properties the Hill-Morgan group organized the Northern Securities Company for the purpose of effecting a unity of control and operation of their extensive transportation interests. This new corporation, which was simply a holding company, was organized under the laws of New Jersey, in 1901, with a capital of $400,000,000. The stock of the company was to be exchanged for the stock of the Northern Pacific and the Great Northern Railroads, thus securing a virtual consolidation of these two great parallel railroad systems.

The trust fever had largely spent itself by the year 1903, and four years later when a financial panic struck the country the combination movement met a definite check. Although most of the larger combinations weathered the financial storm, a more conservative spirit characterized the activities of financial and industrial leaders after 1907.

The mere enumeration of business combinations given above presents but an inadequate idea of the extent to which the industrial activities of the country were concentrated in the hands of a small group of men. The enormous amounts of capital that the development of large-scale industry called for led to the transfer of authority in many business enterprises from individual men of practical business experience to the large banking organizations. In the formation of substantially all the large trusts their promoters found it necessary to resort to great banking concerns, especially in New York, to obtain the requisite capital. This process is shown strikingly in the financial operations of the firm of J. P. Morgan & Co. In addition to underwriting the financing of the United States Steel Corporation this company was the dominant factor in the organization of the steamship trust, the harvester trust, and the reorganization of several important railway consolidations, not to mention a large number of less important combinations.

Naturally financial control brought in its train control of the management of these business enterprises, for on the boards of directors of great corporations were placed representatives of banking interests. An eminent authority on the trust problem, John Moody, described the intimate relation between the banking and business interests of the country in 1904 as follows: "Around these two groups (the Rockefeller and the Morgan groups), or what must ultimately become one greater group, all the smaller groups of capitalists congregate. They are all allied and intertwined by their various mutual interests. . . . Viewed as a whole we find the dominating influence in the Trusts to be made up of an intricate network of large and small groups of capitalists, many allied to one another by ties of more or less importance, but all being appendages to or parts of the greater groups, which are themselves dependent on and allied to the two mammoth or Rockefeller and Morgan groups. These two mammoth groups jointly (for, as pointed out, they really may be regarded as one) constitute the heart of business and commercial life of the nation, the others all being the arteries which permeate in a thousand ways our whole national life, making their influence felt in every home and hamlet, yet all connected with and dependent on this great central force, the influence and policy of which dominates them all."

Such a remarkable concentration of economic power was sure to arouse strong opposition. Even though the captains of industry and their banker allies avoided in most cases the cruder forms of political corruption and financial debauchery that had marked the earlier exploits of Gould and Fisk, there were not a few persons who professed to see in this growth of giant business organizations a serious menace to many cherished American ideals. To these critics the disappearance of the small independent business men threatened to destroy that spirit of self-reliance and self-direction which they regarded as a striking and valuable characteristic of the social and economic life of America. There were others who were not particularly alarmed by the size of the business organizations but who believed that adequate government supervision of these enterprises should be maintained so that they might not use their tremendous power to the detriment of the public. Of those who held this latter view Theodore Roosevelt was a conspicuous leader.

In his first message to Congress, in December, 1901, President Roosevelt expressed the opinion that great business organizations were the result of natural causes in the business world and that legislative attempts to break up such organizations would be futile. In later statements on the same subject he maintained that the remedy for the abuses of the trusts was to be found in publicity and government regulation. In his message to Congress in December, 1907, he said: "The anti-trust law should not be repealed; but it should be made more efficient and more in harmony with actual conditions. It should be amended so as to forbid only the kind of combination which does harm to the general public, such amendment to be accompanied by, or to be an incident of, a grant of supervisory power to the Government over these big concerns engaged in interstate business. . . . Provision should also be made for complete publicity in all matters affecting the public, and complete protection to the investing public in the matter of issuing corporate securities."

The Trust policy advocated by Mr. Roosevelt was not, however, adopted by the state legislatures or by Congress. In general, state legislation showed a determination to destroy all trusts, without distinction, and by the year 1914 every one of the forty-eight states had placed upon its statute books or had written into its constitution more or less stringent anti-trust provisions. Nor did Congress show any inclination to distinguish between good and bad trusts in accordance with the President's suggestion. However, Congress did adopt the proposal of Mr. Roosevelt for strengthening the governmental machinery for trust supervision and for greater publicity of trust affairs. In 1903 Congress established the Department of Commerce and Labor and provided for a Bureau of Corporations in this Department. During the decade following its organization the Bureau of Corporations published elaborate reports concerning most of the larger trusts and upon information derived from these reports Congress in 1914 made the first important changes in Federal anti-trust laws since 1890.

The first of these measures was the Federal Trade Commission Act. By this law a commission was created to "prevent persons, partnerships, or corporations, excepting banks and common carriers subject to acts to regulate commerce, from using unfair methods of competition in commerce." The Commission took over the work which had formerly been done by the Bureau of Corporations and in addition it was given wider powers of investigation, publicity, and recommendation. It was authorized to require corporations to make reports in such form as the Commission might prescribe; to investigate and report concerning alleged violations of the anti-trust laws; to investigate trade conditions in other countries with reference to combinations; and to make public such portions of the information obtained in its investigations as it should deem expedient. The activities of the Commission have not been, however, wholly of a restrictive character. It has aimed to be of service to industry by recommending uniform and simplified systems of accounting, and it has given special assistance in the expansion of American foreign trade.

The second measure dealing with the trust question was the Clayton Anti-Trust Act, which was approved October 15, 1914. This act prohibits the following: Discrimination in prices charged to different purchasers; interlocking directorates; the acquisition by any corporation of the stock in another corporation where the effect may be "to substantially lessen competition"; and dealing in supplies and securities by common carriers. To meet the demands of labor and farmers' organizations there was incorporated in the Clayton Act a proviso that labor, agricultural, and horticultural organizations, not conducted for profit, should not be construed as combinations in restraint of trade, under the anti-trust laws. The Act further attempted to limit the use of injunctions in industrial disputes.

The effectiveness of anti-trust legislation depended upon the vigor displayed by the executive branch of the government in prosecuting alleged violations of the laws and upon the way in which the Federal courts interpreted the laws. As has been previously noted, for a decade after its enactment the Sherman Law had failed to accomplish the purposes for which it had been enacted. During the administration of Presidents Harrison, Cleveland, and McKinley only eighteen prosecutions were instituted under the Sherman Law and the decisions of the courts in these cases, in general, tended to restrict narrowly the provisions of the law. With the advent of President Roosevelt, however, there was inaugurated a vigorous enforcement of the anti-trust legislation. During President Roosevelt's seven and a half years as President forty-four prosecutions were started and this activity was continued under his two immediate successors, Presidents Taft and Wilson. In the former's four years no fewer than eighty cases were brought into the courts and during Mr. Wilson's first term thirty-two.

Accompanying this increased activity on the part of the executive department of the government there appeared a tendency on the part of the Federal courts to interpret the Sherman Law so as to give it greater effectiveness. In the Trans-Missouri Freight Association case, decided in 1897, the Supreme Court held that the anti-trust law applied to all contracts in restraint of interstate or foreign commerce and was not confined to cases where the restraint was unreasonable. In the Joint Traffic Association case, decided the following year, the Court held that an agreement among thirty-one railroads to determine what rates should be charged and what proportion of the business each company should do was in violation of the Sherman Law. Again, in 1899, the Court declared illegal an agreement among six corporations manufacturing cast-iron pipe not to compete with one another.[2] Still more significant was the view expressed by the Court in the Northern Securities case, decided in 1904. This case involved the legality of the Northern Securities Company which, as we have seen, was a holding company formed to unite the railway interests of the Great Northern and the Northern Pacific Railways. In its decision holding that the combination was illegal the Court reaffirmed the opinion expressed in the Trans-Missouri case that the Anti-Trust Act is not limited to restraints of trade or commerce that are unreasonable in their nature, but embrace all direct restraints imposed by any combination. It further held that "it need not be shown that the combination, in fact, results or will result in a total suppression of trade or in a complete monopoly, but it is only essential to show that by its necessary operation it tends to restrain interstate or international trade or commerce or tends to create a monopoly in such trade or commerce and to deprive the public of the advantages that flow from free competition."

This sweeping condemnation of all combinations in restraint of trade was not followed in later decisions of the Court. In the cases involving the Standard Oil Company of New Jersey and the American Tobacco Company, while the Court held in both instances that these combinations violated the Sherman Law, the majority opinion departed from the view expressed in the Northern Securities case and earlier cases and laid down the dictum that the Sherman Law did not intend to prohibit combinations "which did not unduly

[2] Addyston Pipe and Steel Co. vs. U. S. (175 U. S. 211).

restrain interstate or foreign commerce," and that the Court would apply the "standard of reason" in determining in a given case whether a particular act violated the anti-trust law. From this interpretation of the law Mr. Justice Harlan strongly dissented, holding that the Court was indulging "in judicial legislation by inserting in the act the word 'unreasonable' or any other word of like import."

Fifteen years of anti-trust agitation had brought no clearcut solution of the trust problem. The effort to enforce competition by legislative enactment or judicial fiat had at best been only partially successful. Industrial integration was as striking a feature of the economic life of America in 1915 as it had been in 1900. It is probable, however, that the earnest efforts to enforce the anti-trust laws during these years had the effect of slowing up the process of industrial combination, and there is no doubt that popular agitation had made the captains of industry more circumspect in the methods they employed.

In dealing with the railroad problem in the years after 1900 the Federal authorities followed much the same policy they had taken toward the trusts. Through legislative enactment and administrative activity efforts were put forth to give to the Interstate Commerce Commission the vitality it had formerly lacked. Thus in 1903 Congress passed the Elkins Law, which defined more clearly what constituted unfair discrimination between shippers and provided more effective methods for suppressing such discrimination by making railroad officials personally liable for violations of the law. In the Hepburn Act, passed in 1906, the Interstate Commerce Commission was increased to seven members and its jurisdiction extended to cover pipe lines, express companies, bridges, ferries, and railway terminals. The Act further empowered the Commission to fix just and reasonable freight and passenger rates, subject to review by the Federal courts. Finally, the Law attempted to divorce transportation and commercial enterprises by forbidding any railroad to carry any commodities, except timber, which were owned by the railroads themselves. Again, in 1910, Congress enacted the Mann-Elkins Law, which extended the jurisdiction of the Interstate Commerce Commission over telegraph and telephone companies and authorized the Commission to proceed against any common carrier on its own initiative. It provided also for the creation of a Commerce Court to expedite appeals from the decisions of the Commission, but this feature of the Act was repealed in 1913. Finally, in 1913, Congress passed an act providing for a physical valuation of all the railroads of the country with the view of furnishing the Interstate Commerce Commission data upon which it might determine reasonable rates. All of this legislation, it will be noted, was restrictive in character, with the idea either of enforcing competition among the railroads or of preventing discrimination among shippers. In none of these laws does there appear any conception of the railroads as a part of a unified system of transportation. It required the crisis of a great war to bring about a fundamental change in the attitude of the Federal authorities toward the railroad problem.

The entrance of the United States into the World War in 1917 brought about a profound and, what appeared to many persons, a revolutionary change in American industrial organization and practices. Not only were the various anti-trust laws scrapped for the time being, but the whole fabric of private business was subjected to a degree of governmental direction and control for which there was no precedent in American history. In fact, before the war ended, the economic life of the country presented many aspects of state socialism. In the effort to mobilize the material resources of the country for war purposes Congress in a series of laws placed in the hands of the President dictatorial power over the economic system of the country. The powers thus conferred were freely used by Wilson. Numerous new governmental agencies were organized for the purpose of supervising or directing virtually every economic activity in the country. Thus was created the United States Food Administration, which by means of a licensing system, controlled the distribution and consumption of the most important food products. It fixed the price of wheat, both to avoid speculation and to assure the farmer against loss in case of a sudden termination of the war. Similarly the United States Fuel Administration fixed the price of fuel and apportioned its distribution throughout the country. The railway, telegraph, telephone, and cable lines and the express companies were taken over and operated as government enterprises. The Capital Issues Committee, with the support of the large banking organizations, substantially controlled the issuance of new securities by firms and corporations. The United States Shipping Board, with its Emergency Fleet Corporation, was authorized to commandeer ships and shipbuilding plants, to inaugurate an extensive program of shipbuilding, to charter and operate vessels, to prescribe freight rates, and to determine the order of priority in which goods could be shipped.

With the close of the war the country was confronted with the problem of determining how much, if any, of the elaborate governmental economic organization should be retained as a permanent feature of the economic structure of the country. To those inclined to liberal or radical economic thought it appeared that the war experience would mark the beginning of a new era in the industrial life of the country and that the days of economic individualism were definitely ended. On the other hand, those of a more conservative turn of mind saw in the business activities of the government during the war a dangerous departure from traditional American policies that should be abandoned as soon as the war ended. In general the press of the country supported the conservative view, and vigorous attempts were made to discredit governmental activities in business. Then, too, a large number of persons had been irritated by the manifold governmental restrictions upon their individual activities during the war and they were quite ready to support the demand for a return to "the good old days."

President Wilson, engrossed in his contest with the Senate over the Treaty of Versailles, was unable to devote attention to the problem of economic reconstruction. With the return of the Republicans to power as a result of the election of 1920, the conservative forces dominated the situation. Harding, during the campaign of that year, asserted that the country needed "not nostrums but normalcy; not revolution but restoration," and he acted upon this theory consistently. His successor, President Coolidge, held essentially the same view. In his annual message to Congress in December, 1926, he said, "What the country requires is not so much new policies as a steady continuation of those which are already being crowned with such abundant success. . . . I am in favor of reducing, rather than expanding, government bureaus which seek to regulate and control the business activities of the people." And popular opinion in the country seemed, in general, to accept this philosophy. The enthusiasm for "trust busting," which had characterized the early years of the century, was no longer in evidence.

Congressional legislation in the years following the war reflected the changed attitude of the government toward business combinations. In the Export Trade Act, commonly known as the Webb-Pomerene Act, which was approved April 10, 1918, Congress removed the restrictions of the Sherman Act so far as they applied to industrial combinations engaged in the export trade. In dealing with the railroads, which had been taken over by the government during the war, Congress in 1920 enacted the Esch-Cummins Law, which provided for return of the railroads to private operation on March 1, 1920. The law extended financial aid to the railroads, by means of loans, to meet their needs during the period of readjustment. The Interstate Commerce Commission was authorized to establish such rates as would insure a "fair return" to the roads and it was provided that the net income of any railroad in excess of 6 per cent. should not be distributed to the stockholders but should be retained, one-half to be turned over to the government to be placed in a revolving fund from which loans might be made to roads needing assistance, and one-half to be held by the road itself as a reserve fund. Abandoning completely the earlier attitude of the government toward consolidation of competing roads, the law provided for the voluntary combination of the railroads of the country into regional systems under the supervision of the Commission. With a view to preventing the reckless financing that had characterized earlier railroad operations, it was provided that thereafter no new securities could be issued by any road without the consent of the Interstate Commerce Commission, nor could any new roads be built or old roads abandoned without similar consent. The law further set up elaborate machinery for the settlement of labor disputes on the railroads; but both railway operators and employees were dissatisfied with the way in which the machinery worked, and in 1926 Congress repealed that part of the law which provided for the establishment of the Railroad Labor Board. The effort to carry out the provisions of the Esch-Cummins Law for the consolidation of the railroads into a number of systems met with many difficulties. The powerful financial interests that controlled the various railroads were unable to agree upon a satisfactory plan of unification. After waiting nine years for the railroads to adopt a voluntary plan for consolidation the Interstate Commerce Commission took the initiative and in December, 1929, proposed a comprehensive plan for the grouping of the railroads of the country into nineteen systems. It remains to be seen whether this plan will meet with approval of Congress and of the private financial interests involved.

The decisions of the Supreme Court in the post-war period likewise reflected a changed attitude on the part of the Court toward large business combinations. In 1911 the Government brought suit against the United States Steel Corporation and asked the Federal court to order its dissolution on the ground that it was a combination in restraint of trade. The case did not reach the Supreme Court until 1920, when a decision was rendered denying the government's plea on the ground that the Corporation did not possess a monopoly of the steel business of the country and had not used its vast power to fix prices or to control its competitors. Further, the Court stated that it did not believe that the public interest would be subserved by a dissolution of the corporation. The view expressed by the Court in this case is in striking contrast to that held in the Northern Securities decision. It was apparently the opinion of a majority of the judges in the Steel case that the mere size of a corporation, short of actual monopoly, did not involve a violation of the Sherman Law, nor was the possession of potential power to restrain trade illegal provided that this power was not actually used. This view of the majority of the Court did not pass without vigorous dissent from one of the judges. In his dissenting opinion Justice Day said: "I know of no public policy which sanctions a violation of law, nor of any inconvenience to trade, domestic or foreign, which should have the effect of placing combinations, which have been able to thus organize one of the greatest industries of the country in defiance of law, in an impregnable position above the control of the law forbidding such combinations. Such a conclusion does violence to the policy which the law was intended to enforce, runs counter to the decisions of the Court, and necessarily results in a practical nullification of the Act itself." Again in 1925 the Supreme

Court modified its view in regard to the legality of trade associations. A former decision of the Court [3] held that these associations were combinations in restraint of trade, but in the case brought by the government to dissolve the Maple Floor Manufacturers Association,[4] the Court held that trade associations which merely gathered and disseminated information and met to discuss such information without making any attempt to control prices or to restrain competition were not combinations in unlawful restraint of commerce.

With the various departments of the Federal government thus favorably disposed, and with public opinion quiescent, the directors of large business enterprises felt free to resume the activities that had been temporarily checked by the policies of the Roosevelt and Wilson eras. The combination and integration of industry were resumed at a quickened pace, and on a scale that dwarfed the earlier activities along these lines. The Standard Oil Company in 1873, with a capitalization of only $3,500,000, was regarded as a menace to the economic life of the country. Contrast this with the American Telegraph and Telephone Company, which in 1927 boasted total assets of $3,250,000,000, and net earnings of $204,870,000. In 1901 there was only one billion-dollar corporation in the country; in 1925 there were twelve corporations with assets of over a billion dollars each; five were capitalized at over a billion dollars; and five had annual sales of over one billion. In many instances the huge capitalization of corporations had no relationship to the physical value of the property used in the business. Instead of upon physical value capitalization was based upon anticipated earning power of the business. It became the practice of large corporations to issue common stock of no nominal or par value, and in case the enterprise proved prosperous to add to the capitalization by issuing stock dividends or by exchanging

[3] 257 U. S. 377; also 262 U. S. 371.
[4] 268 U. S. 697.

the outstanding stock for new stock at the ratio of two, three, or, in some instances, as high as twenty, to one.

It is not only in the size of their capitalization and in the magnitude of their undertakings that the gigantic business organizations of the present time differ from their predecessors at the close of the nineteenth century. The business leaders of the McKinley era were aptly called "Captains of Industry." There was in their activities much of the ruthlessness that characterizes warfare and also some of the same spirit of adventure that is found in military exploits. These leaders were pioneers, and they had to blaze new trails. They had few precedents to guide them and there was a considerable element of luck which determined the success or failure of their ventures.

The situation at the present time is quite different. Business processes have become highly technical. Those who control large business organizations have come to depend more and more upon trained experts and scientists in the conduct of their business. The element of chance has been largely eliminated and plans are frequently made for future developments many years in advance, based upon careful scientific study. Nor are the large business organizations at present dominated by single individuals to the same extent as they were in the days of Commodore Vanderbilt, Jay Gould, and John D. Rockefeller, Sr. It is beyond the ability of any individual to dominate the gigantic business enterprises in America today.

The tremendous increase in capital investment in recent years raises the question as to where the vast amount of money for these purposes was found. In the years before 1914 large business enterprises were financed by a comparatively few men of great wealth. But the huge demands of the financial operations of corporate enterprises in the last ten or fifteen years could not be met by a few wealthy investors or even by the resources of the large banking institutions. The additional capital resources were found by the diffusion of stock ownership among a large number of small investors. Thus the Vanderbilt family at one time owned 87 per cent. of the stock of the New York Central Railroad, whereas at present the company has about 64,000 stockholders. A majority of the stock of the old Standard Oil Company was owned by six men, but its successor, the Standard Oil Company of New Jersey, has 80,000 stockholders. More than 150,000 persons hold shares in the United States Steel Corporation, 140,000 in the Pennsylvania Railroad Company, and 399,000 in the American Telegraph and Telephone Company.[5] This wide distribution of stock ownership did not, in many cases, carry with it a corresponding diffusion of corporate control. A considerable number of companies adopted the expedient of issuing two kinds of common stock, usually designated as Class A and Class B stock. The former, which was sold to the investing public, carried no voting rights, whereas the latter, which was reserved for a small group of insiders, carried full voting rights. This device enabled the promoters of corporate enterprises to obtain large amounts of capital and at the same time to retain control of the management in their own hands.

It is not only the huge capital investments in the present-day industrial organizations that is worthy of note. In many of these enterprises there has taken place in recent years a veritable revolution in methods of production. The so-called "mass production" has become the characteristic feature of the remarkable industrial development in the United States. This process involves the extensive use of labor-saving machinery, the utilization of vast quantities of material, and the manipulation of the material in a continuous series of operations. The Ford automobile works offer a striking illustration of the operation of this new process. The standardized

[5] It has been estimated by the actuary of the United States treasury that in 1928 there were about 3,000,000 persons who owned corporate stock and about 1,000,000 persons who held corporate bonds.

and interchangeable parts of the automobile are brought together in an assembling plant. An endless conveyor belt moves between two lines of workers and each man in turn performs his allotted task in the construction of the machine as it moves slowly by him on the conveyor. By this method labor is reduced to a minimum and all lost motion is eliminated. Although "mass production" has its advantages in turning out commodities at less cost and greater speed than was formerly possible, it has on the other hand distinct disadvantages. There is a tremendous nervous strain upon the worker who is compelled to perform many times a day a definite piece of work in a strictly limited period of time. As has been well said, "The men are not running the machines, but the machines are running the men, setting for them an inexorable pace with which they must hurry and struggle to keep up." Again, any important change in the style or form of the finished product entails huge expenditures for new machinery. When Henry Ford changed the model of his automobile it necessitated the scrapping of millions of dollars worth of machinery, the practical cessation of the operation of the plant for more than a year, and the temporary unemployment of thousands of workers.

Another significant development in the industrial organization of the country during the last ten or fifteen years has been the remarkable growth of the chain store and mail order business. In the earlier years "Big Business" had confined its activities largely to manufacturing and the extractive enterprises, and had left the retail trade in the hands of the small merchant. But in recent years companies such as Sears, Roebuck, F. W. Woolworth Company, The Atlantic and Pacific Tea Company,[6] to mention only a few of the largest, have applied to the retail field the characteristic features of large-

[6] The Great Atlantic and Pacific Tea Company has 17,500 stores scattered throughout the country with annual sales of $750,000,000. The F. W. Woolworth Company has 1,581 stores with annual sales of $272,000,000.

scale industry. As a result, the small retail merchant today finds himself in much the same position as was the small manufacturer when trusts began to develop. This whole process of business integration raises some significant social as well as economic questions.

Coincident with the growth of American industry in the first quarter of the twentieth century and especially in the period since the Great War there has appeared a constant tendency toward a wider geographical distribution of industrial activities. In earlier years large industrial enterprises were concentrated chiefly in the New England and Middle Atlantic group of states but in recent years the Middle West has made giant strides in industrial development, notably in the manufacture of automobiles, while the South bids fair to deprive New England of its primacy in the textile industry.[7] Another recent industrial tendency has been the migration of industrial enterprises from large urban centers to suburban or rural areas. Better means of transportation, easy access to power through the wide distribution of electrical power, and cheaper land and labor in rural regions have' facilitated this movement.

In the period since 1900 there has taken place a revolution in methods of transportation, due to the appearance of the automobile and the aëroplane, in many ways more remarkable than that which came with the development of the railroads in the nineteenth century. The growth of the automobile industry in America has been nothing less than amazing. Since 1900 the number of automobiles built yearly has increased from 5,000 to 5,000,000. In 1929 there were some 24,000,000 cars in operation in the continental United States, approximately four times the number in all other countries of the world combined.

In its early years the automobile industry was highly com-

[7] In the first quarter of the twentieth century the capital invested in manufactures in the South increased from $1,200,000,000 to $6,880,000,000.

petitive, but in the years since 1920 there has appeared the same trend toward combination in this field that we have noted in other industrial lines. The General Motors Corporation has brought together several formerly independent companies and other combinations of a similar nature have taken place in recent years.

The development of the motor truck and the automobile bus has affected materially both passenger and freight transportation on the railroads, and especially on the electric railways connecting rural and urban regions. In fact, the motor bus has displaced the electric trolley lines in many sections of the country.

Coincident with the growth of motor transportation has appeared a widespread program of highway building by the Federal, state, and local governments. A network of concrete or other hard-surfaced roads now stretches from the Atlantic to the Pacific and from the Gulf to the Great Lakes, displacing the dusty, rough, and frequently impassable roads that were formerly found in all rural communities. In the building of these improved highways more than a billion dollars was expended in 1929.

Although the aëroplane is still in its early stage of development it has already become a factor in freight and passenger transportation. The mail is now carried to all parts of the country through the air and regular passenger service by aëroplane is daily becoming more common. Several of the larger railroads have attempted to meet this threatened competition by establishing combined rail and air transportation.

There resulted from this industrial development a large increase in national wealth, but not all classes or sections of the country appeared to be satisfied with the distribution of this added national wealth. Among the farmers of the West and South and the laboring classes in the industrial centers there were doubts expressed as to whether they were receiving an adequate share of the boasted prosperity. And these classes, particularly the farmers, possessed greater political power than they had in the days of the Granger and Populist movements. Their leaders in Congress boldly asserted that agriculture was as deserving of the fostering care of a benevolent government as organized industry. The directors of "Big Business" therefore found that the return to the "normalcy" of the McKinley era could, at best, be only partially realized, and that in the process substantial concessions would have to be made to satisfy agrarian demands.

REVIVAL OF AGRICULTURAL DISCONTENT

In addition to the general complaint of the farmers that they had not received a due proportion of the national wealth there were specific grievances that stirred agricultural discontent in the decades after 1900 as it had been roused in the earlier Granger and Populist movements. It was charged by the farmers that they received unfair treatment from the privately owned grain elevators in the grading of wheat. They maintained that the grain and cattle markets of the Northwest were controlled by the Chambers of Commerce of Minneapolis, Chicago and Duluth. Finally they insisted that the wide difference between the price that the farmer received for his grain and that which it brought in the eastern markets was due to the speculative dealings in the grain markets and to the extortionate charges of the middlemen.

It was to remedy these conditions that the so-called Non Partisan League was organized in North Dakota in 1915. The program of this organization called for state-owned grain elevators, warehouses, flour mills, packing houses, cold storage plants, creameries, stockyards, a state-owned bank, wide extension of rural credits and the exemption of farm improvements from taxation.

Instead of following the example of the Populists in forming a new political party the leaders of the League felt that they could more readily accomplish their purposes by obtaining control of one of the existing party organizations. In 1916 the League succeeded in capturing the Republican primaries in North Dakota and nominating a state ticket pledged to the support of the League's program. The following year the organization spread its activities to the neighboring states of Minnesota, South Dakota, and Montana. For a time it seemed that the movement would sweep through the West as had the Populist movement in the nineties. A number of factors, however, contributed to check the advance of the League and finally to bring about its practical dissolution. In the first place the chief organizer of the League, Arthur C. Townley, as well as some of his associates, was strongly tinged with Socialist ideas, and it was charged that they were not concerned simply with remedying the ills of the farmers but were aiming at a fundamental change in the existing economic order. Then Townley and some of the other League leaders opposed the entrance of the United States into the World War and their unguarded language was seized upon by their opponents to convict them of the charge of disloyalty. Moreover, the conservative reaction that came at the close of the World War added to the difficulties of those who advocated novel social and economic ideas.

In 1919 the legislature of North Dakota, under control of the League, adopted an ambitious program, which incorporated many of the measures advocated by the League but before this program could be fully carried out, internal dissensions, coupled with the vigorous opposition of the conservatives, brought about the defeat of the League. In a recall election in 1921 the state administration in North Dakota, which was supported by the Non Partisan League, was removed from office.

But the decline of the Non Partisan League did not mean that agricultural discontent had disappeared. On the contrary, the agrarian leaders in Congress insisted that the government must do something to relieve agricultural depression. In response to this demand as we have seen Congress passed the emergency tariff act in 1921, increasing the duties on agricultural products and in the following year President Harding summoned an Agricultural Conference which made a number of recommendations that were enacted into law by Congress.[8]

Apparently these measures did not fully meet the demands of the farmers, for although agricultural discontent was temporarily quieted by the high prices of grain in 1924 it was once more in evidence in 1926. In Congress in this year much of the time of both houses was spent in a discussion of plans for farm relief, and a measure known as the McNary-Haugen bill was finally passed in February, 1927. This act provided for the creation of a Federal Farm Board, empowered to purchase the surplus of agricultural products and sell it abroad. Any loss was to be made up by an equalization fee levied on the farmers in proportion to the size of their crops. It further provided for a "revolving fund" of $375,000,000, drawn from the Treasury, to be used for the purpose of financing the carrying and sale of the surplus products. President Coolidge returned this measure with his disapproval and in a long veto message criticized its provisions in language of unaccustomed vigor. He objected to the equalization fee as "a tax for the special benefit of particular groups" and he characterized the proposal for government price-fixing as "an economic fallacy from which this country has every right to be spared." An attempt to pass the bill over the President's veto failed, and the question of farm relief remained unsolved, to become one of the leading issues in the presidential campaign of 1928.

The platforms of both of the major parties in this election, as we have seen, promised legislation in the interest of agriculture. Shortly after President Hoover assumed office he

[8] See p. 345.

summoned a special session of Congress to deal with the agricultural problem and on June 15, 1929, he signed a measure passed by Congress to provide better means for marketing agricultural products. By the terms of this act a Federal Farm Board was created and endowed with broad authority to promote the effective merchandising of agricultural commodities by minimizing speculation, preventing inefficient and wasteful methods of distribution, encouraging the formation of farmer-owned and farmer-controlled coöperative associations and warehousing agencies, and eliminating crop surpluses. The Board was also authorized to determine methods of reducing the acreage of unprofitable land; to study means for developing by-products from agricultural commodities; to expand markets both at home and abroad; and to adopt measures to prevent overproduction. To aid in the inauguration of this large program the act authorized the appropriation of $500,000,000 to be placed at the disposal of the Board.

In general this measure aims to apply to agriculture many of the principles that have transformed manufacturing industry and commerce in the United States during the first quarter of the twentieth century. It remains to be seen how the distinctive characteristics of agricultural economy and the individualism of the farmer will respond to these efforts to apply to agriculture the technique of "big business."

BIBLIOGRAPHICAL NOTE

General descriptions of the recent industrial development of the United States are to be found in V. S. Clark, *History of Manufactures in the United States,* Vol. III (1929); R. G. Tugwell, *Industry's Coming of Age* (1927); F. W. Wile, ed., *A Century of Industrial Progress* (1928); E. E. Hunt, *An Audit of America* (1930); Report of the Committee on Recent Economic Changes of the President's Conference on Unemployment. On the growth of industrial combinations and the efforts at governmental control consult, Annual Reports of the Federal Trade Commission; J. B. and J. M. Clark, *The Control of Trusts* (1912); J. M. Clark, *The Social Control of Business* (1926); A. S. Dewing, *The Financial Policy of Corporations* (1920); G. C. Henderson, *The Federal Trade Commission* (1924); A. J. Eddy, *The New Competition* (1916); J. W. Jenks and W. E. Clarke, *The Trust Problem* (rev. ed., 1919); C. R. Van Hise, *Concentration and Control* (rev. ed., 1921). A keen criticism of corporation financing can be found in W. Z. Ripley, *Main Street and Wall Street* (1927). On railroad regulation see W. J. Cunningham, *American Railroads: Government Control and Reconstruction Policies* (1922); F. H. Dixon, *Railroads and The Government: Their Relations* (1922).

On the subject of agricultural discontent consult A. A. Bruce, *Nonpartisan League* (1921), which is critical and H. E. Gaston, *The Nonpartisan League* (1920), which is favorable. On farm relief see E. R. A. Seligman, *Economics of Farm Relief* (1929); R. W. Kelsey, *Farm Relief and Its Antecedents* (1929); F. E. Haynes, *Social Politics in the United States* (1924).

CHAPTER 17

LABOR PROBLEMS, 1900-1929

As we have seen, the labor movement in the last quarter of the nineteenth century was marked by bitter struggles between organized labor and organized capital, frequently accompanied by loss of life and destruction of property. Only rarely did either side in this warfare appreciate the point of view of the other, or attempt to find any common basis for understanding. Furthermore, as has been noted, the political authorities in both state and nation during these years failed to adopt any comprehensive constructive policy looking to a solution of the problem of industrial warfare. In general they pursued a policy of *laissez faire,* except, on occasion, when the executive or the courts intervened to preserve order or to protect property. But in the opening years of the new century there appeared a striking change in the attitude of all three of these forces, capital, labor, and the government. The leaders both of capital and of labor showed a distinctly less uncompromising spirit in dealing with each other. Trade agreements were entered into and the principle of collective bargaining was widely accepted. Equally significant was the change in the attitude of the political authorities. No longer was industrial strife to be regarded as a species of private warfare with the government a more or less disinterested observer. Abandoning the policy of *laissez faire,* the political leaders in both state and nation displayed an active interest in the solution of labor troubles and in the promotion of plans for improving relations between capital and labor.

With the return of industrial prosperity in 1898 there came a rapid expansion of labor organizations. From a membership of about 320,000 in this year the American Federation of Labor increased its numbers to 1,676,000 by 1904. This remarkable growth was checked during the succeeding six years, but in 1910 the forward movement was resumed, bringing the membership in the organization to nearly two million in 1913. If there be added to these numbers the organizations not affiliated with the Federation, the total union membership in 1913 was nearly 2,700,000. Most of this striking growth of the American Federation of Labor was confined to the ranks of the skilled and semi-skilled labor. The Federation made little effort to extend its activities to the mass of unskilled and migratory labor. In this neglected field of labor there appeared in 1905 an organization known as the Industrial Workers of the World. The promoters of this movement obtained most of their followers from among the workers in the mines and lumbering camps of the western states and in some of the unorganized textile industries in the East. In both aim and method the I.W.W. differed from the American Federation of Labor. Strongly tinged with Socialist doctrines, the leaders of the I.W.W. rejected the moderate demand of "a fair day's wage for a fair day's work" and called for the complete abolition of the wage system. In method of organization the I.W.W. abandoned the autonomous craft union and advocated the formation of industrial unions, including all grades of skilled and unskilled labor. In this manner they hoped to be able to present a united front against the employing class and to bring about an overthrow of the capitalist system by means of revolutionary political or "direct" action. The I.W.W. did not develop sufficient strength to challenge the position of the American Federation of Labor, but it did serve to arouse the leaders of the latter organization to consider the interests of the unorganized and unskilled laborers.

The growth of labor organizations brought an intensified activity on the part of trade unions to obtain higher wages

and shorter hours, and their efforts in these directions met
with substantial success. Public opinion, aroused at this time
by the unscrupulous practices of some of the large organizations of capital, was, in general, sympathetic to the demands
of labor. Moreover, there was abroad in the country a humanitarian spirit which demanded a remedy for the distress
and abuses, among the laboring classes, which had formerly
been disregarded.

Further evidence of the advance in the influence of labor
is seen in the spread of trade agreements, involving recognition of the union and collective bargaining. The earlier
efforts to form such agreements had met with slight success,
but after 1900 noteworthy progress along this line was made,
chiefly in the bituminous coal fields, among the railway
Brotherhoods, and in the clothing industry. In 1901 the National Civic Federation, representing leaders of both labor
and capital, was formed for the purpose of promoting trade
agreements and, in general, of furthering the movement for
the peaceable solution of labor problems.

Although organized labor made substantial progress in the
ten years following 1900, there were many employers who
declined to accept the principle of union recognition or of
collective bargaining for which organized labor contended.
Organizations such as the National Association of Manufacturers carried on a vigorous campaign against labor unions
and urged the maintenance of the principle of the "open
shop." In that part of the industrial field which was still competitive, the unions were generally able to enforce their demands, but they were less successful in their efforts to union-
ize the more highly integrated industries. A notable instance
was the steel industry. After the disastrous Homestead strike,
in 1892, union activity virtually ceased in the Pittsburgh steel
plants. With the organization of the United States Steel Corporation, in 1901, the directors of this large corporation inaugurated the policy of the "open shop" and they successfully

resisted every attempt of the labor leaders to organize their workers.

In the anthracite coal industry the United Mine Workers had begun organizing the miners in 1897, and in 1900 they had made sufficient headway to call a strike for the purpose of enforcing the demand for a 10 per cent. increase in wages and the abandonment of certain practices, enforced by the operators, of which the miners complained. The presidential election was impending, and Senator Mark Hanna, who was promoting the interests of his friend McKinley, had no desire to have a serious labor controversy threaten the success of the Republican candidate. Hanna, therefore, used his influence with the coal operators and persuaded them to accept the most important demands of the miners. Although these concessions brought an end to the strike, and thus served a useful political purpose, they did not bring permanent peace in the industry. The miners still insisted that wages were inadequate; they complained of abuses in the company stores from which the miners were obliged to purchase their supplies; they objected to the practice of the operators in reckoning 3,000 pounds of ˙coal as a ton; and, finally, they demanded the right to have union officials negotiate with the operators for the adjustment of grievances. Early in 1902 the representatives of the miners presented a series of demands involving all of the foregoing complaints and asked for a conference with the representatives of the operators.

The presidents of the coal companies, still resentful at what they considered interference with their private business in the previous strike, declined to have any dealings with the union, and as a result a strike was called that lasted from May until October and that kept nearly 150,000 miners idle. Senator Hanna again tried to adjust the dispute, but he was rebuffed by the operators. Mr. George F. Baer, President of the Philadelphia and Reading Company, was reported to have referred to the owners of the coal mines as "Christian men to whom God in His infinite wisdom has given the control of the property interests of the country," a remark that won for him the sobriquet "Divine Right" Baer.

As the strike dragged on and winter approached, popular feeling in the North was deeply stirred, for in these sections most people depended entirely upon anthracite coal for heating purposes. Public sentiment generally favored the miners. They had conducted the strike without violence and had repeatedly expressed a willingness to arbitrate their grievances, whereas the operators persisted in their unyielding attitude. Quite apart from the merits of the dispute, there was a widespread feeling that the mine owners were taking advantage of their control of one of the necessities of life and were showing a callous disregard for the health and comfort of hundreds of thousands of their fellow citizens.

Faced by a situation that daily became more critical, the newspapers in northern states, together with state and local officials, appealed to President Roosevelt to use his influence to avoid a national calamity. Mr. Roosevelt fully realized that in his official capacity he had no authority to act, but he determined to use both his personal prestige and the dignity of his office in an effort to end the strike. He summoned the representatives of the miners and the operators to meet him in Washington. At the conference the President made it clear that he disclaimed any right to interfere in the controversy on legal grounds but that he felt impelled to appeal to the patriotism of all concerned to "make individual sacrifices for the common good." In answer to this appeal Mr. Mitchell, representing the miners, offered to submit the controversy to any tribunal that the President might select, and to accept the award even if it should be against the claims of the miners. On the other hand Mr. Baer, speaking for the operators, declined to accept the arbitration proposal, and at a subsequent meeting prepared statements were read by the operators in which resentment was shown toward Roosevelt.

They intimated that he had failed in his duty by refusing to break the strike by the use of troops.

Realizing that further parley with the operators was futile, the President sent Elihu Root to visit J. P. Morgan, whose financial power in railroad circles was greater than that of any other man in the country. Root informed Morgan that the President proposed to appoint a commission of investigation, headed by former President Cleveland, and if the operators declined to accept his proposal he was prepared to send Federal troops into the anthracite fields and mine coal regardless of the wishes of the owners. Apparently Morgan applied the necessary pressure upon the operators for on October 13th they notified the President that they were prepared to submit all matters in dispute to the consideration of a commission. The commission that was finally appointed was headed by Judge Gray of Delaware. After taking a large amount of testimony and investigating the conditions in the mines, the commission rendered a decision that conceded some of the demands of the miners. A 10 per cent. increase in wages was granted and provision was made for the submission of future disputes to a Board of Conciliation, consisting of representatives of the miners and operators. Although recognition was not accorded to the union the creation of the joint arbitration board was a recognition of the principle of collective bargaining for which the union had contended.

The intervention of President Roosevelt in the coal strike has a significance beyond the settlement of an important industrial controversy. It involved a bold challenge to the doctrine of *laissez faire* and inaugurated a new theory, viz., that when industrial strife threatened the comfort and well being of the public at large, it was the duty of the government to protect the public interest. It required no little courage to take the stand that Roosevelt took in this matter, for the political power of organized capital at this time, especially in the Re-

publican party, was very great, and the President frankly
stated his belief that this action probably would end his political career. But events soon proved that public sentiment
throughout the country supported the stand taken by the
President in this significant industrial controversy.

Indicative of the changed attitude of the government toward labor controversies are the measures passed by Congress for the adjustment of industrial disputes. The Erdman
Act, passed in 1898, provided for the mediation and arbitration of labor disputes on railroads by the chairman of the
Interstate Commerce Commission and the Commissioner of
Labor, and during the following fifteen years more than
forty disputes were settled in this manner. In 1913 the Newlands Act was passed which created a Board of Mediation
and Conciliation by means of which sixty-one labor controversies were adjusted during the succeeding three years. In
the same year the Department of Labor was formed, with a
Secretary in the President's cabinet. Through conciliation
commissions appointed by the Secretary of Labor more than
two hundred labor disputes were settled in the years between
1913 and 1916. In 1912 Congress passed an act creating an
Industrial Relations Commission which was directed to "in-
quire into the general condition of labor in the principal
industries of the United States." The Commission was to
consist of nine members, three representing the public, three
representing employers, and three representing labor. The
selections for membership on the Commission made by President Taft did not meet with the approval of the Senate, and
the Commission was not finally appointed until President
Wilson assumed office. No practical results came from the
deliberations of this body. The labor members in their report
stressed the need of strengthening labor unions; the employers group emphasized compulsory arbitration; and one
of the public group advocated the establishment of a permanent governmental industrial commission.

Striking as was the growth of organized labor in the decade following 1900, there was an even more significant development in the succeeding decade. Two circumstances contributed to this growth. First the success of the Democratic party in the Presidential election of 1912 brought in an administration at Washington which was distinctly sympathetic to the interests of labor. In the Department of Labor, which was given cabinet rank in 1913, the American Federation of Labor obtained a decisive influence. The second factor that increased the economic and political power of organized labor at this time was the outbreak of the European War in 1914. The war brought a check to the flow of immigrant labor, thereby reducing the labor supply of the country. At the same time the large purchases of war supplies in this country by the European belligerents stimulated industrial activity in many lines and in consequence increased the demand for labor. With the entrance of the United States into the war, in 1917, the labor situation in the country became acute. Every industrial enterprise engaged in the production of war materials was urged to increase its output and in doing so it was necessary to expand greatly the number of laborers employed. At the same time the government withdrew more than a million men from productive enterprises as a result of the operation of the draft law.

It was in the nature of things that organized labor should take advantage of these favorable circumstances to strengthen its position. Not only was union membership increased by nearly a million during the war period, but the labor leaders succeeded in extending materially two of the major planks in the labor program, i.e., the eight-hour day and the principle of collective bargaining. Early in 1916 the four railway brotherhoods made a joint demand for the eight-hour day. The railway officials claimed that the demand for the reduction of the working day was not made in good faith as it would be impossible to operate the roads on the eight-hour basis, and that in reality the men were demanding ten hours' pay for eight hours' work. The unions stood firm in their position and threatened to tie up the whole transportation system of the country if their demands were not granted.

To obviate the calamity of a general railway strike at a time when the foreign relations of the country were at a critical stage President Wilson summoned representatives of the railway executives and of the brotherhoods to Washington, but he was unable to induce them to settle the dispute. He then turned to Congress and recommended the passage of an eight-hour law for all train operatives without any reduction in wages. He also suggested that a special commission should be appointed to report on the operation of such a law for a period of six months, after which the subject might be reconsidered. Finally he proposed that the Newlands Act should be so amended as to make it illegal to call a strike or a lockout pending the investigation of a controversy by a government commission. Congress promptly enacted the so-called Adamson Law, which incorporated the first two suggestions of the President but omitted the proposal to place restrictions upon strikes and lockouts.

When in March, 1917, it seemed inevitable that the United States would be drawn into the Great War the national officers of all of the important unions met in Washington and adopted resolutions pledging the support of organized labor to the government. At the same time they insisted that national necessity should not be given as an excuse to deprive labor of "the advantages, the protections, and guarantees of justice that had been achieved after ages of a struggle." They demanded that the government should recognize the organized labor movement as the agency through which it dealt with the wage earners and that labor should be represented on all bodies for determining and administering policies of national defense. Finally they insisted that whatever sacrifices were demanded of labor should be accompanied by similar burdens on property and profits. In the realization of this program the leaders of organized labor met with substantial success.

When in 1916 President Wilson established the National Council of Defense he appointed Samuel Gompers as one of the seven members composing the Advisory Commission in charge of all policies dealing with labor. The Council promptly put itself on record in favor of maintaining existing standards for the protection of labor during the war. The Federation of Labor was also given representation on the Emergency Fleet Construction Board, The Fuel Administration Board, The Woman's Board, The Food Administration Board, and the War Industries Board. In addition to granting representation to labor on boards and commissions the government entered into agreements with the Federation concerning conditions of employment on government contracts which provided for the maintenance of existing trade union standards. When the government took over the railways on January 1, 1918, it extended to all railway workers the eight-hour day and the principle of union recognition, which formerly had been enjoyed only by the four brotherhoods.

On March 29, 1918, the National War Labor Conference Board, composed of five representatives of the Federation of Labor, five representatives of employers' associations, and two joint chairmen, William H. Taft for the employers and Frank P. Walsh for the unions, reported to the Secretary of Labor certain "Principles and Policies to govern Relations between Workers and Employers in War Industries for the Duration of the War." These "principles and policies" were to be enforced by a War Labor Board organized on the same lines as the Labor Conference. The report recommended that employers and employees should agree to the voluntary relinquishment of the right of the strike and of the lockout upon certain conditions. These included recognition of the right of both employers and employees to organize and of trade unions to employ collective bargaining; observance of pre-war conditions concerning union or open shop organization in any given establishment; maintenance of the basic eight-hour day in all cases in which existing law required it; abandonment of restriction of output by trade unions; and recognition of the right of all workers to a "living wage."

The war had given organized labor its great opportunity; the return of peace tested its real strength. Would it be able to retain permanently the advantages that the exigencies of war had brought? That it would not be able to do so without a struggle seemed inevitable. Many employers had submitted to the demands of labor during the war unwillingly and it was certain that they would make an effort to restore pre-war conditions as soon as the crisis had passed. At the close of the war public opinion appeared to be none too favorably disposed toward the claims of labor. Many persons felt that labor had taken an unfair advantage of its opportunities during the war to exact unreasonable demands. Furthermore, the return of hundreds of thousands of men to civil life, with the demobilization of the armies, coupled with slackening of war-time activity in many industries, brought an end to the labor shortage in the country. Finally there was within the labor ranks a radical minority which had expressed sympathy with the Russian Communist movement and, in the inflamed condition of the public mind at this time, there was a tendency to denounce all labor agitation as Bolshevistic. All of these circumstances were calculated to place labor on the defensive and to test the qualities of leadership of those who controlled organized labor.

Two great strikes in the fall of 1919 demonstrated clearly the changed situation that had come with the close of the war. One of these was the strike in the steel industry and the other the strike of the soft coal miners. During the war period organized labor had not succeeded in unionizing the steel industry and the strike in 1919 was a belated attempt to accomplish this together with the establishment of the eight-hour day. In this struggle organized labor had to face the most powerful aggregation of capital in the country, and it received no aid or comfort from the government, now that the war crisis had passed. Furthermore, the leader of the strike, William Z. Foster, was identified with the left wing of the labor movement and the conservative press denounced the strike as an attempt to spread Bolshevism in this country. Under the circumstances it is not astonishing that the strike resulted in a complete defeat for the workers.

In the bituminous coal industry the miners had entered, in 1917, into a wage agreement for the duration of the war. The rise in the cost of living during the war caused much discontent among the mine workers and as soon as the Armistice was signed they demanded an abrogation of the wage agreement and asked for a 60 per cent. increase in wages. The operators insisted that the agreement was still in force as the war was not legally over until a treaty of peace was signed by this country. The Fuel Administration, which had not as yet been disbanded, attempted to adjust the dispute, but was unsuccessful. The strike was called and the Attorney General tried to break it by obtaining an injunction against the union under the wartime Lever Act.[1] It is obvious that times had changed when the same administration, which had shown so much consideration for organized labor during the war, should make use of a wartime measure, designed for a quite different purpose, to hamper a union in an important labor controversy. The strike was finally settled by a commission appointed by the President which granted the miners a wage increase of 27 per cent.

Further evidence of the passing of the wartime spirit of

[1] The Lever Act gave the President dictatorial power over the food and fuel supply of the country and made it a penal offense to conspire or take action leading to the interference with the production of food or fuel.

give and take on the part of capital and labor was given by the failure of the Industrial Conference summoned by President Wilson in October, 1919. The Conference was composed of three groups, one representing organized labor, one capital, and one the general public. On the all-important question of collective bargaining through union representatives which was proposed by the labor group no agreement could be reached, the employers group taking a determined stand against this proposal, and the Conference disbanded without accomplishing any concrete results. A second Conference was called by the President the following year. This time the body was not divided into groups, but all the members presumably represented the general public. This Conference made a number of definite proposals, including a recommendation to extend employee representation in industry and a suggestion for the creation of somewhat elaborate machinery for the settlement of industrial controversies. As President Wilson was about to retire from office, he made no move to carry out the recommendations of the Conference, and his successor in the presidential office showed no inclination to go forward with the proposals.

Labor met with further disappointment in connection with the adjustment of the railway problem at the end of the war. As we have seen, the government had taken over all of the railways of the country as a war measure, and at the end of the war an agitation was started for permanent government ownership and management of the roads. The railway labor organizations supported this move and presented to Congress the so-called Plumb Plan, prepared by Glenn E. Plumb, the legal representative of the brotherhoods. This plan proposed that the government should purchase the railways from their present owners and entrust their operation to a board composed of government officials, representatives of the unions, and representatives of the technical staffs. This proposal was doomed, if for no other reason, because it savored too much of socialism to obtain any considerable popular support in the existing conservative temper of the country.

Taking advantage of the post-war reaction, conservative employers started a concerted drive against labor unions. A widespread propaganda was launched calling for the establishment in industry of the so-called "American System," which among other things, insisted upon the maintenance of the principle of the "open shop." In many sections of the country, notably in San Francisco, where the grip of the unions upon industry had been strongest, and where their arbitrary methods had aroused considerable popular feeling, the movement met with striking success. In Chicago the unions lost their wartime control of the packing industry, and in many other industrial centers union influence was weakened. Between 1920 and 1926 membership in the American Federation of Labor declined over 1,000,000.[2]

Although organized labor failed to retain all of its wartime gains in the post-war period, important progress was

[2] TRADE UNION MEMBERSHIP

Year	All Unions	A. F. of L. Unions
1900	868,500	548,321
1910	2,184,000	1,562,112
1915	2,607,000	1,946,347
1918	3,508,000	2,726,478
1919	4,169,000	3,260,068
1920	5,110,800	4,078,740
1921	4,815,000	3,906,528
1922	4,059,400	3,195,635
1923	3,747,200	2,926,468
1924	3,746,600	2,865,799
1925	3,817,900	2,877,297
1926	3,900,500	2,803,966
1927	3,903,800	2,812,526
1928	....	2,896,063
1929	....	2,933,545

The figures for all unions were compiled by Dr. Leo Wolman for the National Bureau of Economic Research; the A. F. of L. figures represent average paid-up membership in the Federation as reported for fiscal years ended August 31. Reports of the Federation for recent years state that in addition to the paid-up members there have been at least 500,000 others not paying dues on account of unemployment, strikes, or lockouts, and therefore not reported. Both sets of figures include some Canadian made during these years by labor forces in advancing their program for shorter hours and higher wages. Despite the failure of the steel strike in 1919, the workers in this industry obtained, within three years thereafter, one of their major demands, namely, the abolition of the twelve-hour day. Public opinion clearly condemned a practice which called for not only a twelve-hour day but also a twenty-four-hour turn, usually every fortnight, when changing from night to day work or vice versa. At the earnest solicitation of President Harding the officials of the United States Steel Corporation in 1922 agreed to introduce three eight-hour shifts in place of the two twelve-hour shifts that had formerly prevailed.[3]

Of greater significance was the new principle put forth by a number of large employers of labor that it would be to the advantage of industry for employers to pay the highest possible wages to labor in order to increase the purchasing power of the laboring classes and thus expand the market for manufactured goods. Henry Ford was a leader in this movement. He established a minimum wage of five dollars a day in his great automobile manufacturing plant, and followed this by an even more remarkable announcement, in 1926, that all of his plants would immediately adopt the five-day week schedule. The principal reason assigned for his action was that the shorter work week would give the workers more time for consumption.

"The country is ready for the 5-day week," he said. "It is bound to come through all industry . . . because without

membership, which has been about 200,000 during the last few years. The Wolman figures on total membership appear to be conservative. According to a Bureau of Labor Statistics study the aggregate membership of American trade unions in 1926 was 4,443,523 (including 201,951 in Canada)—3,383,997 in the A. F. of L. and 1,059,526 in independent unions and the I.W.W.

[3] An investigation made by Mr. E. M. Hartl and E. G. Ernst in 1929 covering 300,000 workers in the steel industry disclosed the fact that more than 150,000 were working ten hours or more a day and more than 77,000 were working seven days a week. (See *The New Republic,* March 7 and 12, 1930.)

it the country will not be able to absorb its production and
stay prosperous. . . . The industry of this country could
not long exist if factories generally went back to the 10-hour
day, because the people would not have time to consume the
goods produced. For instance, a workman would have little
use for an automobile if he had to be in the shops from dawn
until dusk. And that would react in countless directions, for
the automobile, by enabling people to get about quickly and
easily, gives them a chance to find out what is going on in
the world—which leads them to a larger life that requires
more food, more and better goods, more books, more music,
more of everything. . . . Just as the 8-hour day opened our
way to prosperity, so the 5-day week will open our way to
still greater prosperity." [4]

The American Federation of Labor enthusiastically endorsed Ford's announcement and proclaimed its purpose to
launch a campaign for the general adoption of the five-day
week. During the three years from 1926 to 1929 slow but
steady progress was made in furthering this program. In
May, 1929, the Building Trades Employers Association and
the Building Trades Council of New York City reached an
agreement whereby approximately 150,000 building trades
workers in that city would be placed on a five-day work
schedule beginning in August, 1929. It has been estimated
that by the end of 1929 there were at least 500,000 wage
earners in the United States on a year-round five-day work
schedule. Although this number represents only about 1 per
cent. of the persons gainfully occupied in this country it is,
nevertheless, of sufficient size to mark the movement for the
five-day week as one major importance.

If a balance is struck between the gains and losses of

[4] When in October, 1929, a severe decline in stock market securities
appeared to foreshadow an industrial depression, Henry Ford met the
situation by announcing a further increase in wages. President Hoover
called a number of industrial leaders to Washington and got them to
agree not to reduce wages because of the stock market crash.

American labor in the first quarter of the twentieth century there can be no doubt not only that the workman is far better paid in America than anywhere else in the world, but also that the real wages and the standard of living of the American laborer have increased materially in this period, especially in the years since 1920. This is clearly shown from the following chart.

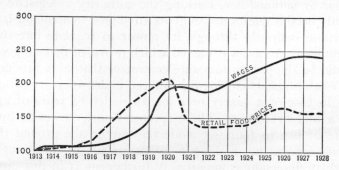

It will be seen that from 1913 to 1920 both retail prices and wages rose steadily, but that since 1920, while prices have declined, wages have continued to rise. It is obvious therefore that the working-man is receiving a real wage considerably above the 1913 standards.

SOCIAL LEGISLATION

It has been noted that in the early years of the twentieth century there came a distinct challenge to the *laissez faire* tradition. Further evidence of this tendency is seen in the passage of a substantial body of social legislation by the state and national legislatures.

Congressional action along this line was limited by the nature of our Federal system of government. Under the Constitution Congress can deal with the labor problem only indirectly, through its power to regulate interstate commerce.

In 1906 Congress passed an Employers' Liability Act, which provided for the compensation for injuries sustained by employees of railroads engaged in interstate commerce. This act was set aside by the Supreme Court on the ground that Congress had exceeded its constitutional authority, and in 1908 a second act was passed to meet the objections of the Court. In 1916 Congress made an effort to regulate child labor by national law. Lacking the authority to legislate directly on this question, Congress attempted to accomplish its purpose indirectly through its power to regulate interstate commerce. An act was passed which provided that no goods could be shipped in interstate commerce that were produced in establishments employing children under 16 years of age, in the case of a quarry or mine, or under 14 years of age, in a mill or factory. The Supreme Court, however, by a vote of five to four, set aside the law on the ground that Congress was not making a legitimate use of its power to regulate interstate commerce. A further effort in this direction was made by Congress in 1919 by means of a law which placed a prohibitive tax on the profits of factories employing children under fourteen years of age; but again the Supreme Court nullified the law on the ground that Congress had no right to do indirectly what it did not have the authority to do directly. To meet these constitutional objections which the Court had raised, Congress in 1924 passed a constitutional amendment which provided that Congress should have the "power to limit, regulate and prohibit the labor of persons under eighteen years of age." By this time, however, the enthusiasm for social legislation had spent itself and there was, moreover, a determined agitation throughout the country against the tendency to increase the power of the Federal Government at the expense of the states. As a result, the proposed amendment failed of ratification in the state legislatures. In 1916, as has been noted, Congress passed the Adamson Law, which established the eight-hour

day for employees on interstate railways, and the Supreme
Court upheld the law as a valid exercise of the power of
Congress to regulate interstate commerce. In 1918 Congress
enacted a law providing for the fixing of minimum wages
for women and children in the District of Columbia by a
board of three members representing the employers, the employees, and the public; but five years later the Supreme
Court set this law aside on the ground that it violated the
constitutional right of liberty of contract.

In the field of social legislation the activities of the states
were less restricted by constitutional limitations than those
of the Federal government. As we have seen in an earlier
chapter, some of the states, in the years before 1900, when
the doctrine of *laissez faire* still held sway, had passed legislation dealing with labor questions; but it was not until the
opening decade of the twentieth century, when public opinion
concerning the relations of the government to social and industrial problems underwent a marked change, that the state
legislatures placed upon the statute books a substantial
amount of social legislation.

The appalling number of accidents to workmen in industrial enterprises gave rise to a demand for legislation providing compensation to injured workers. Until 1900 it had
been the practice in this country to follow the old English
common law concerning compensation for industrial accidents, by which an employer was responsible for accidents
only in case negligence on his part could be shown. If a
worker was injured through his own negligence or that of a
fellow worker no liability rested upon the employer. Between
1900 and 1920, however, the legislatures in forty-two states
modified the common law principle and passed workmen's
compensation laws, which provided for payment to injured
workers irrespective of the responsibility for the accidents.

In this same period most of the states enacted legislation
for the protection of women and children in industry. In

all but four of the states the working day for women was
fixed, varying from eight to eleven hours. Night work for
women was prohibited in certain occupations in thirteen
states. Nearly all of the states prohibited or restricted the
employment of children in gainful occupations. The age limit
varied from twelve years in some states to sixteen in others.
Minimum wage laws for women in certain occupations were
passed in twelve states. Forty of the states have passed laws
providing for widows' pensions. State legislation regulating
the working conditions of men has been much less extensive
than that for women and children. However, most of the
states have passed laws that provide an eight-hour day on all
public work, and several states have limited the hours of
labor in certain occupations, notably in mining.

THE COURTS AND LABOR LEGISLATION

It is probable that the amount of social legislation, both
state and national, would have been considerably more extensive had it not been for constitutional limitations upon the
legislative power. Congress and the state legislatures derived
their right to pass legislation of this type, not from any specific constitutional grant, but from the very indefinite "police
power," which had been defined by the Supreme Court as the
power "to prescribe regulations to promote the health, peace,
morals, education, and good order of the people, and to legislate so as to increase the industries of the state, develop its
resources, and add to its wealth and prosperity." On the other
hand the Constitution of the United States in the Fifth and
Fourteenth Amendments prohibits Congress and the state
legislatures from enacting any legislation which deprives a
person of "life, liberty, or property, without due process of
law." The question arose, therefore, how far the police power
might be extended without encroaching upon the property
rights guaranteed by the Constitution. In any specific in-

stance the answer to this question had to be given by the
courts, and ultimately by the Supreme Court. The indefinite
nature of the police power of necessity gave to courts wide
discretion in fixing its metes and bounds, and the opinions
of different courts or of the same court at different times
varied greatly, in the efforts to define it.

A few typical cases which show the shifting attitude of
the courts in this matter may be noted. In 1898 the Supreme
Court of the United States upheld the constitutionality of a
law of the state of Utah which limited the hours of labor for
coal miners to eight, on the ground that the hazardous character of the work warranted the states under the police power
in fixing a limitation to the length of the work day.[5] On the
other hand the same court in 1905 declared that a state law
of New York which limited the hours of labor of employees
in bakeshops to ten a day was unconstitutional because, in the
opinion of the court, the business of baking bread was not
essentially dangerous and therefore could not be regulated
under the police power.[6] But three years later the Supreme
Court upheld the constitutionality of an Oregon law which
limited the employment of women to ten hours a day,[7] and
even more significant was the opinion of the Court in 1917
which sustained a law of the same state fixing a ten-hour day
for all persons employed in manufacturing establishments,[8]
In the same year the Court upheld the constitutionality of
the Adamson Law which fixed the basic eight-hour day on
interstate railways.[9] *Per contra,* in 1923, a majority of the
Supreme Court held that a law of Congress fixing a minimum wage for women and children in the District of Columbia was unconstitutional in that it violated the constitutional freedom of contract.[10]

[5] Holden vs. Hardy (169 U. S. 366; 1898).
[6] Lochner vs. New York (198 U. S. 45; 1905).
[7] Muller vs. Oregon (208 U. S. 412; 1908).
[8] Bunting vs. Oregon (243 U. S. 426; 1917).
[9] Wilson vs. New (243 U. S. 332; 1917).
[10] Adkins vs. Children's Hospital (261 U. S. 525; 1923).

The history of this last case demonstrates clearly how eminent judges, interpreting the same constitutional provision, can differ widely in their views. Congress in 1918 had enacted a law setting up a board to fix minimum wages for women and children in the District of Columbia. A case to test the constitutionality of the law was brought before the Court of Appeals of the District of Columbia. One of the judges of the court was unable to sit because of illness and the other two judges designated a Justice of the Supreme Court of the District to sit in his place. The decision of the court was two to one in favor of the statute. When Justice Robb, who had been ill, returned to the bench a rehearing was granted and this time the vote was two to one against the statute. The case was appealed to the Supreme Court of the United States, which held, by a vote of five to three (Justice Brandeis not participating), that the law was unconstitutional. Justice Sutherland, speaking for the majority of the Court, held that the statute in question involved an unwarranted interference with the freedom of contract. He further maintained that since the passage of the Nineteenth Amendment had given women an equal political status with men they could no longer be treated as a special class to be protected by regulatory legislation. Chief Justice Taft and Justice Holmes in vigorous dissenting opinions bluntly indicated that the majority opinion was based upon the social and economic views of the individual judges rather than upon abstract constitutional considerations. Said the Chief Justice, "I agree that it is a disputable question in the field of political economy how far a statutory requirement of maximum hours or minimum wages may be a useful remedy for the evils of a sweating system; but it is not the function of this Court to hold Congressional acts invalid simply because they are passed to carry out views that the Court believes to be unwise or unsound." And to the same point Justice Holmes asserted that "the criterion of unconstitutionality is not whether we believe a law to be for the public good." These observations of two eminent justices of the highest tribunal of the land give point to the argument of those who maintain that the fate of any piece of social legislation in this country depends not upon specific constitutional provisions but upon the economic views of the justices who happen to constitute a majority of the Supreme Court at a particular time.

The action of the courts in nullifying social legislation is not, however, the chief cause of resentment on the part of organized labor. The principal ground for dissatisfaction is to be found in the decisions of the courts in defining and limiting the rights of organizations of labor, particularly in connection with strikes. In a previous chapter we have noted the intervention of the courts on labor disputes through the issuance of injunctions and the objection of organized labor to this practice on the ground that it deprived the defendant of his ordinary constitutional safeguards when his case came up in court. In the years following 1900 there came a wide extension of the use of the injunction in labor disputes. For relief the leaders of organized labor turned to the state legislatures and to Congress. Several states passed laws forbidding or limiting the issuance of injunctions in labor disputes, but in most cases these laws have been set aside by the courts as unconstitutional. Congress responded to the appeal of labor by incorporating in the Clayton Anti-Trust Law of 1914 provisions designed to restrict materially the use of injunctions in labor controversies. It declared that, "No injunction shall be issued by a Federal court in any labor dispute, unless necessary to prevent irreparable injury to property; and no injunction shall prohibit any person from quitting work, or from peacefully advising or persuading others to quit. No injunction shall forbid any person to cease to patronize or to employ any party to a labor dispute, or by peaceful and lawful means to recommend, advise, or persuade others so to do. No injunction shall forbid persons to assemble peaceably in a lawful manner, for lawful purposes, or for doing anything which might be lawfully done in the absence of the dispute, by any party to the dispute." While these provisions of the law were hailed by labor leaders as a Magna Charta for organized labor, the frequent use of such qualifying words as "peaceful," "peaceably," "lawfully," "lawful manner," and "lawful purposes" left to the courts wide discretion in the use of the injunctive process. And the courts did not fail to make use of this discretion in such a manner as to make the advantages that labor hoped to gain from the law more seeming than real.

Thus the courts have narrowly restricted the use of picketing in strikes [11] ; they have set aside laws designed to prevent an employer from discharging a man on account of membership in a union [12] and also laws that forbid an employer to compel a worker to sign a non-union contract.[13] Unions have been enjoined from inducing workers who have signed a non-union contract to join a union.[14] The use of the boycott by labor organizations has been virtually destroyed as a result of two decisions of the Supreme Court holding labor unions financially liable for damages under the anti-trust law where resort has been made to the boycott.[15]

DEMOCRATIZATION OF INDUSTRY

Many thoughtful persons both in the ranks of labor and among employers have viewed with concern the ebb and flow of industrial strife in this country in recent years, and earnest efforts have been made to discover ways and means for bridging the gap between capital and labor. In this connec-

[11] Truax vs. Corrigan (257 U. S. 312).
[12] Adair vs. U. S. (208 U. S. 161).
[13] Coppage vs. Kansas (236 U. S. 1).
[14] Hichman Coal & Coke Co. vs. Mitchell (245 U. S. 229).
[15] Lowe vs. Lawler (208 U. S. 274); Gompers vs. Bucks Stove & Range Co. (221 U. S. 418).

tion a number of interesting experiments have been tried which, for want of a better name, have been called "Industrial Democracy." The plans tried vary greatly in details but they have certain characteristics in common. All start with the assumption that labor is not a commodity to be bought and sold, but hold that there is in labor a human factor to be considered. They all aim to restore in a measure the contact between employer and employee, which has been destroyed by the growth of large-scale industry. The practical means adopted to accomplish these aims have usually taken the form of some plan of employee representation, not merely for the purpose of providing machinery for settling labor disputes but also, in many cases, to give to employees an actual share in the management of industry. It has been estimated that between the year 1915 and 1923 nearly a thousand distinct plans of employee representation were put into effect in American industrial establishments. Leaders of organized labor have been inclined to look with suspicion upon some of these experiments. They regard them as veiled attempts to undermine the influence of labor unions. The fact that many of the most conspicuous examples of employee representation have been in industries that, in the past, have been opposed to organized labor has been enough to make labor leaders skeptical of the motives of those advocating the new idea. Then, again, there has been the fear that if the plan of employee representation should be largely successful it would make the old form of labor unions unnecessary.

Another development that may have a far-reaching effect upon the relations of capital and labor is the remarkable growth of investments by employees in recent years in the stocks and bonds of the corporations by which they are employed. The directors of some of the largest corporations in the country have encouraged this movement by offering to their employees securities of their companies upon very favorable terms. Nearly one hundred thousand of the em-

ployees of the American Telephone and Telegraph Company
have purchased stock in the company. Seventy per cent. of
the workers of the International Harvester Company hold
common stock in the company to an aggregate value exceeding $5,000,000. Virtually every workman employed by the
Procter and Gamble Company is a shareholder in the enterprise and 90 per cent. of the employees of the Firestone Tire
and Rubber Company are stockholders.

Still another recent development that shows the tendency
of labor to encroach upon the traditional field of capital is
the establishment of banks controlled by labor organizations.
The Brotherhood of Locomotive Engineers and the Amalgamated Clothing Workers have been leaders in this movement. Since 1920 thirty-six labor banks have been opened in
different parts of the country having resources in excess of
$127,000,000. Some of these enterprises have been finan-
cially successful, others, notably those conducted by the
Brotherhood of Locomotive engineers, have failed, owing
partly to the inexperience of those in control, and partly to
unfortunate investments and bad management. By 1929 the
number of labor banks had been reduced to twenty-four and
their resources had shrunk to $110,500,000. Whether this
indicates the passing of an interesting experiment or merely
a temporary set-back remains to be seen.

LABOR AND INDUSTRIAL PRODUCTION

In recent years there has been a remarkable increase in the
amount of goods produced in the United States without a
corresponding increase in the number of laborers employed.
This has been brought about partly by the introduction on a
large scale of labor-saving machinery and partly by more
efficient organization of industry. The increase in the output
per worker in manufacturing during the last 30 years is
shown by index numbers in the following table:

Year	Output per Worker	Year	Output per Worker
	(1899 = 100)		
1899	100.0	1920	107.9
		1921	107.3
1904	104.0	1922	128.5
		1923	132.5
1909	109.6	1924	133.0
		1925	145.4
1914	108.5	1926	148.7
		1927	149.5
1919	104.5	1928	....

The trend here indicated has had two important results. In the first place it is apparent that if an increased amount of goods can be produced with a smaller amount of labor there will arise the problem of unemployment. Herein is to be found at least a partial explanation of the apparent paradox that national prosperity and increasing unemployment went hand in hand in the years following 1920. In the second place if goods can be produced with a smaller labor cost the margin of profit is increased. Doubtless in some cases, but not in all, a part of the increase has been passed on in the form of higher wages and lower prices. But there was a distinct feeling, especially in labor circles, that the employers have benefited chiefly from the increased productivity of industry.

INCREASE IN PRODUCTION AND DECREASE IN EMPLOYMENT

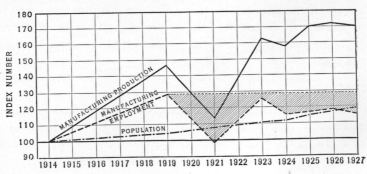

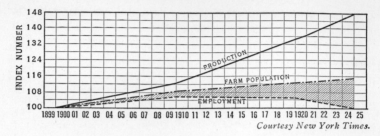

Courtesy New York Times.

At the convention of the American Federation of Labor held in 1925 the whole problem of the relation of labor to industrial production was thoroughly discussed and a set of resolutions was adopted setting forth a significant change in the attitude of organized labor. Frankly abandoning the policy that had been pursued by some labor unions of restricting the output of labor the resolutions stated that "the best interests of wage earners, as well as the whole social group, are served by increasing production in quality as well as in quantity." At the same time it was maintained that labor should receive a just share of the financial benefits that come from increased production, whether these are the result of greater efficiency of the individual worker or of improved industrial technique. Labor leaders insisted that it is not enough for wage earners to be able to buy more of the necessities and comforts of life if others who share in the distribution of the national income find their position improved to an even greater extent. Higher productivity without corresponding increase in real wages means that the social position of wage earners in relation to other consumers becomes worse, because their standard of living does not advance proportionately with those of other groups.

To what extent these new trends in the industrial organization and practices in this country indicate the dawn of a new era in the relations of capital and labor it is as yet impossible to say. In any event, it is evident that the more intel-

ligent and wider-visioned leaders of capital and labor at the
present time are inclined to regard the relations of the two
forces in the industrial world from a new and more hopeful
point of view. Rejecting the idea that labor and capital are
of necessity opposed to each other's interests, these men are
making an earnest effort to find a solution to the age-old
problem of industrial conflict.

LABOR AND IMMIGRATION

Closely related to the problem of labor is that of immigration. In a previous chapter we noted not only the steady rise
in the immigrant tide in the last half of the nineteenth century but also the marked change in the character of the immigrant groups entering the country after 1890. The following table indicates the percentage of immigrants from the
countries of northwestern Europe and from those of southeastern Europe—by decades from 1860 to 1914.

Period	Total Immigrants Admitted	Immigrants from			
		Northern and Western Europe	Southern and Eastern Europe	Northern and Western Europe %	Southern and Eastern Europe %
1861-1870	2,314,824	2,031,642	33,628	87.8	1.4
1871-1880	2,812,191	2,070,373	201,889	73.6	7.2
1881-1890	5,246,613	3,778,633	958,413	71.0	18.3
1891-1900	3,687,564	1,643,492	1,915,486	44.6	51.9
1901-1910	8,795,386	1,910,035	6,225,981	21.7	70.8
1911	878,587	202,391	562,366	23.0	64.0
1912	838,172	161,290	557,585	19.2	66.5
1913	1,197,892	182,886	872,969	15.3	72.9
1914	1,218,480	164,133	894,258	13.4	73.4

Despite the efforts of the leaders of organized labor to
place a curb upon the rising immigrant tide, slow progress
was made in the first decade of the twentieth century in
arousing public opinion to the seriousness of the problem.
We have noted the failure to enact a law providing a literacy

test in 1897, due to the veto of President Cleveland. A similar measure was vetoed by President Taft in 1913. It was the outbreak of the Great War in 1914 that brought the first important check to the flow of immigration into this country. Most of the European states that became involved in the gigantic struggle placed an effective embargo upon emigration, as a means of conserving their man power for military service.[16] Even more significant was the effect the war had in stirring up a country-wide discussion of our whole immigration policy. Sooner or later most of the countries from which we obtained the larger part of our immigration became involved in the war. Immigrants who had come from these countries quickly expressed their sympathies for the country of their birth. In fact, in many instances, it seemed doubtful whether their loyalty to their adopted country was greater than that to their native land. Apparently the "melting pot" had not functioned as effectively as many Americans had fondly believed.

Aroused by these demonstrations of divided loyalty, public opinion was prepared to support the demand made by the labor leaders for an effective curb upon immigration, at least until we were able to digest the unassimilated mass of aliens within our borders. Circumstances, too, brought a change in attitude of large employers of immigrant labor. The Bolshevist upheaval in Eastern Europe, with its radical program of social and economic reconstruction, stirred the imagination of the masses of immigrants from these regions in the mines

Fiscal Year	Total Immigrants	[16] Per Cent. of Total Immigrants from			
		Northern and Western Europe	Southern and Eastern Europe	Canada	Mexico
1914	1,218,480	13.4	73.4	7.1	1.2
1915	326,700	24.2	36.3	25.2	3.8
1916	298,826	17.1	31.7	33.9	6.2
1917	295,403	13.0	32.0	35.7	6.0
1918	110,618	11.7	16.4	29.3	16.8

and factories of America. Many among them accepted with enthusiasm the picture of the Communist millennium that was presented by radical agitators. Some of the more thoughtful of the captains of industry began to realize that the hordes of immigrants, whose admission to this country they had encouraged as a means of curbing the demands of organized labor, might prove to be a far greater menace to the existing economic order here than even the most extravagant claims of the labor unions. Thus for various reasons, some patriotic and others selfish, powerful interests and sentiments joined in the movement for restrictive legislation upon immigration.

In response to this demand Congress in 1917 passed a bill over the veto of President Wilson which provided for the exclusion of all aliens over sixteen years of age "who cannot read the English language or some other language or dialect" unless they were physically incapable of reading. The literacy test did not act as a serious check upon the flow of immigration to this country. As soon as the war was over immigration took a sharp turn upward, and by 1921 was back to almost three-quarters of its pre-war volume. At this time it was reported from American consular officers in Europe that millions were awaiting transportation facilities to carry them to the United States. These reports created deep concern in this country, coming as they did at a time when industrial depression, accompanied by widespread unemployment, was prevalent. As a result there arose an insistent demand that Congress should take steps to put a drastic limitation upon immigration. In response to this demand Congress, in May, 1921, passed an act providing for a definite numerical restriction of immigrants coming to the United States. By this law the number of aliens admitted to this country in any one year from any European, Asiatic, or African country was limited to not more than 3 per cent. of the number of people of that country residing in the United States according to the census of 1910. Not satisfied with this substantial curb, Congress in 1924 reduced the yearly quota from 3 to 2 per cent., based upon the census of 1890. The figures for 1890 were taken as the standard in order to reduce the quotas from the nations of Eastern and Southern Europe. This law was to continue in effect for three years, after which the number of immigrants to be admitted in any one year from all non-American countries was limited to 150,000 and each nationality was entitled to a percentage of this number equal to its percentage of the total population of the country according to the census of 1920. By the same law all aliens ineligible to citizenship were excluded, thus completely shutting out all Asiatic immigration.

The quota acts of 1921 and 1924 did not apply, nor does the present act apply, to any immigrant born in the Dominion of Canada, Newfoundland, the Republic of Mexico, Cuba, Haiti, the Dominican Republic, the Canal Zone, or any independent country of Central or South America. All of these were designated as non-quota immigrants. This class at present includes also (1) any immigrant who is the unmarried child under eighteen years of age, or the wife, of a citizen of the United States; (2) any immigrant previously lawfully admitted, who is returning from a temporary visit abroad; (3) any minister of a religious denomination, or professor of a college, academy, seminary or university, provided that for two years immediately preceding his application for admission he has been such and seeks to enter for the purpose of carrying on his vocation; (4) any immigrant who is a bona fide student at least fifteen years of age and who seeks to enter the United States solely for the purpose of study at an accredited school or college.

The numbers admitted as quota immigrants, and the numbers of immigrants admitted without reference to quotas, during the years the quota plan has been in effect, are shown in the following table:

Fiscal Year	Total Im- migrants	Quota Im- migrants	Non-quota Immigrants	Per Cent. of Total: Quota	Non-quota
1922.........	309,556	243,953	63,603	78.8	21.2
1923.........	522,919	335,480	187,439	64.1	35.9
1924.........	706,896	357,642	349,254	50.6	49.4
1925.........	294,314	145,971	148,343	49.6	50.4
1926.........	304,488	157,432	147,056	51.7	48.3
1927.........	335,175	158,070	177,105	47.2	52.8
1928.........	307,255	153,231	154,024	49.9	50.1

During the last five years only about one-half the immigration to the United States has been subject to quota limitations. This has been due principally to the large volume of immigration from the neighboring countries of Canada and Mexico. The numbers of immigrants received from those countries during the years the present immigration act has been in effect are shown below:

Fiscal Year	Total Non-quota Immigrants	Immigrants from Canada	Immigrants from Mexico	Per Cent. of Total from: Canada	Per Cent. of Total from: Mexico
1925.........	148,343	102,753	32,964	69.2	22.2
1926.........	147,056	93,368	43,316	63.5	29.4
1927.........	177,105	84,580	67,721	47.4	32.2
1928.........	154,024	75,281	59,016	48.8	38.3

The following table shows the general effect of the post-war immigration legislation. It compares the original quotas, the present quotas, and the national-origin quotas of the two grand divisions of Europe with the numbers of immigrants received from those divisions in the last year before the war, and the last year before numerical restriction went into effect.

	Total	Numbers from Northern and Western Europe	Numbers from Southern and Eastern Europe	Per Cent. from Northern and Western Europe	Per Cent. from Southern and Eastern Europe
Immigration:					
Fiscal year 1914....	1,218,480	164,133	894,253	13.4	73.4
Fiscal year 1921....	805,228	138,551	513,813	17.2	63.8

	Total	Numbers from Northern and Western Europe	Numbers from Southern and Eastern Europe	Per Cent. from Northern and Western Europe	Per Cent. from Southern and Eastern Europe
Immigration quotas:					
Original quotas, Act of 1921, 3 per cent. of foreign born in 1910	356,995	198,082	157,630	55.5	44.1
Existing quotas, Act of 1924, 2 per cent. of foreign born, 1890	164,667	140,999	20,423	85.6	12.4
Quotas under national-origin plan ...	153,714	125,853	24,638	81.9	16.0

It is not possible to estimate yet the effect that the policy of restricted immigration, if it is maintained, will have upon the labor situation of the country, and especially upon the fortunes of organized labor. That it is likely to have far-reaching results admits of little doubt.

BIBLIOGRAPHICAL NOTE

On the subject of social legislation consult J. R. Commons and J. B. Andrews, *Principles of Labor Legislation* (1920); F. T. Carlton, *The History and Problems of Organized Labor* (1920); J. E. Rhodes, *Workmen's Compensation* (1917); E. H. Downey, *Workmen's Compensation* (1924); A. Epstein, *The Challenge of the Aged* (1928); on the relation of the government to the settlement of industrial disputes see H. Feis, *Settlement of Wage Disputes* (1921); A. R. Ellingwood and W. Coombs, *The Government and Labor* (1926); E. Berman, *Labor Disputes and the President of the United States* (1924); for the radical labor movement consult M. D. Savage, *Industrial Unionism in the United States* (1922); D. J. Saposs, *Left Wing Unionism* (1928); P. F. Brissenden, *The I.W.W.* (1919); J. G. Brooks, *American Syndicalism* (1913). For the use of the injunction in labor disputes see J. P. Frey, *The Labor Injunction* (1922); G. G. Groat, *Attitude of the American Courts in Labor Cases* (1911). For experiments in industrial democracy consult G. James and others, *Profit Sharing and Stock Ownership for Employees* (1926); J. Myers, *Repre-*

sentative Government in Industry (1924) ; National Industrial Conference Board, *Employee Stock Ownership Plans in the United States* (1928). For the effects of the new industrial revolution on labor see S. Chase, *Men and Machines* (1929) ; W. J. Lauck, *The New Industrial Revolution and Wages* (1929).

CHAPTER 18

PROBLEMS OF FINANCE AND CURRENCY, 1900-1928

The defeat of the Democratic party in the elections of 1896 and 1900 brought to an end the agitation for the expansion of the currency by means of the unlimited coinage of silver. On March 14, 1900, a Gold Standard Act was passed by Congress, which provided that the dollar should consist of twenty-five and eight-tenths grains of gold nine-tenths fine, and that all forms of money issued by the United States should be maintained at a parity value with this standard. It was further provided that a fund of $150,000,-000 should be set aside in the Treasury, to be used solely for the redemption of the greenbacks still in circulation.

Although these measures satisfied the demands of the advocates of "sound money," they did not provide an adequate currency system for the country. The chief defect of the currency was its lack of elasticity. In the ordinary course of business the demand for currency in different parts of the country fluctuates from year to year and from season to season. In the West during the crop-moving season there is need for a large supply of currency, while at other times the need is not so great. Similarly in industrial centers periods of great business activity give rise to a demand for large quantities of currency, while in slack times the demand is much less.

The currency of the United States, prior to 1914, could not be expanded and contracted to meet these varying demands of business. The paper currency consisted of gold and silver certificates, greenbacks, and national bank notes. The first might be increased in amount by additional coinage of gold by the Treasury. The greenbacks were fixed in amount and the national bank notes were limited to the amount of government bonds outstanding which had the "circulation privilege." The currency system was therefore not adjusted to meet the strain of a financial crisis, or even the ebb and flow of normal business conditions.

The defects of the inelastic currency were shown in a forcible manner in 1907, when a severe financial crisis befell the country. For several years prior to the crash a wave of speculation had swept the country and large quantities of securities had been sold at inflated values. When the day of reckoning came the banking and currency system was unable to meet the strain. Country banks attempted to withdraw their funds from New York banks. Depositors started a run on several financial institutions and one of these, the Knickerbocker Trust Company, was forced to close its doors. From New York the panic spread to other parts of the country. Currency went to a premium and to tide over the situation "clearing-house certificates" were issued. By this device a bank could deposit bills receivable or securities and receive in exchange "certificates," which were accepted in place of cash at the clearing house in the settlement of balances. These clearing-house certificates were in the nature of an emergency currency, and provided the elasticity that the currency system lacked.

The incidents of the panic of 1907 led Congress and the banking interests of the country to search for a remedy. The immediate result was the passage by Congress of the Aldrich-Vreeland Act in 1908. This authorized national banks in time of emergency to obtain circulating notes by the deposit of commercial paper and other securities with a "national currency association." The law was avowedly a temporary measure designed to meet such a critical situation as had arisen the previous year, but it made no provision to meet the needs of business in normal times. It did, however, authorize the appointment of a National Monetary Commission, composed of members of the two houses of Congress, to make a thorough study of the currency problem and to recommend to Congress such changes in the currency and banking system of the country as were thought desirable. After more than three years, during which the Commission made an exhaustive study of the monetary systems of the leading European countries, a voluminous report was submitted to Congress. Its recommendations were incorporated in the so-called Aldrich plan, which provided for the creation of a central reserve bank to be owned and controlled by private banking interests and for an elastic currency secured by commercial paper. As the presidential election of 1912 was pending when the report reached Congress that body took no action and the whole matter of currency reform was left to be dealt with by the incoming Democratic administration.

Upon assuming office President Wilson promptly turned his attention to the problem of the currency. He appeared before a special session of Congress and recommended the enactment of legislation that would provide a currency "elastically responsive to sound credit, the expanding and contracting credits of everyday transactions, the normal ebb and flow of personal and corporate dealings." He further stated that the banking laws must provide for the mobilization of reserves and must not permit the concentration of the monetary resources of the country in a few banks, or their use for speculative purposes to such an extent as to hamper the conduct of legitimate business. Finally he insisted that the new system of banking should be under public and not private control. It will be noted that in two important respects the recommendations of the President differed from those of the Monetary Commission; first, in the rejection of the idea of a central bank, and, second, in the demand for public rather than private control of the system. For these and possibly other reasons some of the most important banking interests in the country opposed the bill introduced in Congress incorporating the President's recommendations. In the end, however, the measure known as the Federal Reserve Act, which embodied all of the principles outlined by Wilson, was passed and received the Presidential approval on December 23, 1913.

The law provided for the appointment of a commission, which body divided the country into twelve districts, in each of which there was to be a Federal Reserve Bank. All of the national banks in each district were required to become members of the Reserve system and state banks and trust companies might also become members under certain conditions. Each member bank had to subscribe to the capital stock of the Reserve Bank of its district an amount in proportion to its own capital, and keep a part of its reserves in the regional bank. The Reserve Banks were to act as central banks for their members and not deal directly with the public except in the purchase and sale of gold, Government bonds, and bills of exchange. The control of the system was placed in the hands of a Federal Reserve Board, composed of the Secretary of the Treasury, the Comptroller of the Currency, and five (later six) persons appointed by the President for terms of ten years. Each regional bank has nine directors, six elected by the member banks and three named by the Federal Reserve Board. One of the last group is Federal Reserve agent, and acts as chairman of the local board.

To meet the need for a mobilization of the banking resources of the country the law provided that each regional bank might rediscount the notes of its member banks, and, if directed to do so by the Federal Reserve Board, render a similar service for other regional banks. In this way funds not needed in one section might be used to finance the business operations in another section.

The most noteworthy feature of the new system, however,

is the device for giving elasticity to the currency. This is accomplished through the issuance of Federal Reserve Notes. If the supply of currency in any district is inadequate to meet the demands of legitimate business the Reserve Bank of the district may apply to the Federal Reserve Board for a sufficient amount of Federal Reserve Notes to meet the business demands and deposit as security approved commercial paper such as notes of reputable business concerns. If business becomes less active and there is less demand for currency the Reserve Notes may be returned to the Federal Reserve Agent and be withdrawn from circulation. In order to avoid excessive expansion of the currency the regional banks are required to keep a gold reserve equal to 40 per cent. of the amount of Federal Reserve Notes that they have received, and if at any time the gold reserve falls below this per cent., a tax is placed on the bank, which the bank adds to the rediscount rate. The Reserve Notes are obligations of the United States and are redeemable in gold at the Treasury.

In operation the Federal Reserve system not only has justified the hopes of those who were instrumental in its establishment but has brought praise from the same banking interests that vigorously opposed its adoption by Congress. Coming into operation on the eve of the outbreak of the Great War in Europe, there is little doubt that the new system contributed materially to relieving the financial strain which that event precipitated, and it is equally certain that it served admirably in meeting the unprecedented financial problems that arose when the United States entered the Great War.

In recent years there has been considerable discussion of the possibility of using the Federal Reserve system for the purpose of stabilizing prices. Those who advocate such a policy point to the evils of constantly changing price levels. The so-called business cycles of the past have each been characterized by a period of rising prices accompanied by speculation and over-extension of credit, followed by a period of falling prices, slack business, and unemployment. If the curve of the business cycle could be flattened out and prices kept reasonably stable, some of the universally admitted evils of existing conditions would be remedied. A number of leading economists have urged the feasibility of using the Federal Reserve system to prevent wide oscillations of prices, first by raising or lowering the rediscount rate in order to control credit and prevent undue speculation, second by increasing or decreasing the Federal Reserve Bank's investments in securities, third by moral suasion over member banks, and finally by publicity, designed to stimulate or check optimism on the part of the business community. Other economists and banking authorities, however, maintain that such action by the Federal Reserve authorities would be both ineffective and unwise, inasmuch as there are many factors that affect price changes that are wholly outside the control of the Federal Reserve system.

Although the reform of the banking and currency system met most of the needs of the commercial and industrial interests of the country, it did not satisfy the demands of the agricultural interests. Commercial loans are usually limited to ninety days, whereas the farmer needs credit for at least six months for planting and marketing his crops, as well as long-term loans for permanent improvements secured by farm mortgages. The spokesmen for the agricultural groups turned to Congress for relief and succeeded in bringing about the enactment, in 1916, of the Federal Farm Land Bank Act. This measure was patterned after the Federal Reserve Act. The country is divided into twelve districts in each of which there is a Federal Farm Land Bank. Farm Loan Associations, made up of farmers who desire to borrow money, are organized in each district. A farmer desiring to make a loan gives a mortgage to the Association, which in turn deposits the mortgage with the Farm Land Bank, from which the loan is received. To obtain additional funds for loans the Land Bank is authorized to sell bonds to the public, secured by the pledged mortgages. By this method the farmers are able to get loans at a lower rate of interest than had formerly been possible. In addition to this measure, Congress in 1923 passed the Agricultural Credits Act. This act provided for government credit to farmers and for the making of private loans by private organizations on livestock and farm products. Intermediate Credit Banks were authorized, one for each of the existing Federal Land Banks. The capital stock of these banks ($5,000,000 each) was to be subscribed by the United States Government. The Intermediate Credit Banks were authorized to sell debenture notes, secured by farmers' notes discounted by banks, to investors. The farmers' notes could be carried for terms varying from six months to three years. The bill also provided for the establishment of private farm credit corporations supervised in the same manner as national banks.

Paralleling the huge combinations of industrial organizations in the period since 1920, went similar combinations in the banking field. In 1929 there were fewer banks in the United States than there were in 1914, despite the enormous increase in the country's wealth during these years.[1] In the first quarter of 1929 there were over one hundred bank mergers involving assets of more than 13 billion dollars. That

[1] Year	Number of Banks	Capital and Surplus	Total Resources	Resources of Average·Bank
			(thousands of dollars)	
1914	26,765	3,846,600	26,971,400	1,007.7
1919	29,123	4,619,359	47,615,447	1,644.0
1920	30,139	5,132,985	53,079,108	1,761.1
1921	30,812	5,445,993	46,671,390	1,612.1
1922	30,389	5,641,359	50,425,367	1,659.3
1923	30,178	5,851,861	54,034,911	1,790.5
1924	29,348	6,081,562	57,144,690	1,947.1
1925	28,841	6,343,045	62,057,037	2,151.7
1926	28,146	6,745,271	64,893,362	2,305.6
1927	27,061	7,141,025	68,132,558	2,517.7
1928	26,213	7,671,051	71,574,328	2,730.5

this concentration of the banking resources of the country may have far-reaching effects upon American business appears obvious. Heretofore, business enterprises have been able to avail themselves of various credit resources as competition for banking business has been keen, but if the present trend toward banking consolidation continues unabated it can have but one result; the concentration of credit control and the placing of an immense power over business in the hands of a relatively few men in control of the great banking institutions.

The entrance of the United States into the World War, in 1917, gave rise to financial problems of the first magnitude. The equipment and maintenance of an army of more than two million men, not to mention the enormous loans made to our allies, called for government expenditures on an unprecedented scale. Between April 6, 1917, and October 31, 1919, the expenditures of the Federal government amounted to $35,413,111,000. How was this huge sum obtained? In previous wars the government had depended largely upon the sale of bonds at high rates of interest to raise needed money, but now from many quarters there came the demand that this practice should not be repeated. It was urged that if the young men were called upon to sacrifice their lives for their country, persons of wealth should be required to contribute their money for the same purpose. In fact, many persons demanded that the whole cost of the war should be defrayed from taxes upon large fortunes and upon profits gained from business incident to the war.

Although Congress did not adopt these extreme proposals, it did resort to taxation upon an unprecedented scale. Fortunately the scope of the Federal taxing power had been greatly widened by the adoption of a constitutional amendment in 1913, giving Congress the right to levy Federal income taxes without having to meet the former constitutional limitation that such taxes had to be distributed among the states according to population. Acting under this authority Congress laid steeply graded taxes upon incomes, reaching in the case of the largest incomes as high as 65 per cent. In addition, heavy taxes were placed upon excess profits of corporations. More than one-half of the revenues collected by the treasury during the war came from income and excess profits taxes. Of the actual expenditures made by the Government for war purposes nearly 40 per cent. was raised by taxation.

The remaining 60 per cent. of the cost of the war was met by the issuance of government bonds. Between April, 1917, and April, 1919, five huge loans were floated, amounting in all to $21,448,120,300. Differing from former practice, these bonds were not sold to banking syndicates, but were disposed of directly to the public. All of the devices of modern high-powered salesmanship were employed to induce persons to invest in these bonds. Organizations were formed in every city and village of the country to stimulate popular enthusiasm. Appeals to patriotism were made by means of huge posters depicting the sacrifices made by our soldiers in France. Refusal to respond to the call to buy "Liberty Bonds" exposed a person to the charge of disloyalty. As a result of this nation-wide appeal more than 21,000,000 individuals bought bonds in the fourth war loan.

Although the war period saw a huge increase in the national debt, on the other hand it brought a striking change in the financial position of this country with relation to the rest of the world. For many years before the war the United States had been a debtor nation. The excess in the value of our exports over imports in these years had been offset by the interest charges on foreign investments in this country, together with payments for freight and passenger service on foreign-owned ships and expenditures of American tourists abroad. With the outbreak of the war in Europe the belligerent nations, especially Great Britain and France, turned to the United States for huge quantities of war materials and food products. To pay for these purchases the European countries sent large amounts of gold to this country and also most of the American securities held by foreign investors. When these means proved inadequate to balance the account they placed immense loans in the United States. Until we entered the war these loans were taken by private banking interests in this country, but with our entrance into the war Allied purchases in this country were covered by loans made directly by the United States government. The amount and subsequent funding of these loans will be considered in a later chapter. Nor did the raising of capital funds in the United States by foreign governments and corporations cease with the close of the war. In the decade following the close of the World War American investors continued to supply capital to Europe on a large scale, as is indicated in the following table:

EUROPEAN CAPITAL ISSUES FLOATED IN UNITED STATES
(excluding refunding operations)

Year	Government Issues *	Corporate Issues	European Securities
1914	$ 11,000,000	....	$ 11,000,000
1915	600,000,000	....	600,000,000
1916	796,900,000	....	796,900,000
1917	395,000,000	....	395,000,000
1918	....	....	....
1919	323,587,000	$ 19,871,500	343,458,500
1920	174,951,250	42,910,000	217,861,250
1921	180,324,300	1,000,000	181,324,300
1922	136,278,200	77,570,000	213,848,200
1923	78,000,000	30,057,000	108,057,000
1924	508,090,555	22,000,000	530,090,555
1925	408,652,000	242,917,400	651,569,400
1926	188,337,500	306,691,550	495,029,050
1927	289,343,000	281,950,625	571,293,625
1928	367,035,000	230,871,500	597,906,500
	$4,457,498,805	$1,255,839,575	$5,713,338,380

* Governmental, provincial, and municipal issues, including corporate issues officially guaranteed.

These figures cover only securities that have been publicly offered, and do not include securities privately taken in large blocks by American corporations and other investors. Nor do they include direct investments in physical properties which have not involved the transfer of securities or investments in countries outside of Europe. The total of American capital invested abroad at the end of 1928 has been estimated to reach the huge sum of $15,601,000,000.

This "dollar invasion" of Europe has caused considerable apprehension in foreign banking and industrial circles, and has led to the adoption of measures to curtail American financial domination in these countries. The General Motors Corporation in 1929 obtained a "substantial interest" in the Adam Opel Company, the largest manufacturer of automobiles in Germany. The General Motors Corporation, the Ford Motor Company, and other large American automobile companies have established branch organizations in several foreign countries. American investments in public utilities and mining corporations, particularly in England, France, and Italy, in recent years have also been on a large scale.

Aroused by this threat of American control of some of the most important industrial enterprises in Europe, both political and financial interests in these countries have urged the adoption of defensive measures. Among the devices used for this purpose are, the restriction of the sale of securities of domestic corporations to citizens, the requirement that the boards of directors and officers of such corporations must be citizens and the limitation of the voting power of stock held by foreigners.

To what extent this significant change in the financial position of the United States will affect its domestic policies and its international relations presents an interesting speculation. To a consideration of the influence that this new situation may have upon one important economic policy we shall now turn our attention.

THE TARIFF, 1900-1928

In the discussion of the tariff before 1900 we saw that the Republican party by the close of the nineteenth century had become definitely committed to the principle of high protection. Although the election of 1896 had been fought largely on the issue of free silver, the Republicans interpreted their success in that contest as evidence of popular approval of the protective tariff principle. As a result, in 1897, they promptly enacted a new tariff law, the Dingley Act, which raised the duties on many commodities higher than in any previous tariff. For twelve years following the passage of this law the tariff remained unchanged. This comparative stability was due in part to the fact that the Republicans were in continuous control of the government during that period. Moreover, these were years of widespread prosperity, and there was no insistent demand for a change in tariff policy so long as good times lasted. Finally other issues—the trusts imperialism, political reform—diverted the attention of the public for the time being from the tariff.

In 1907 came a change. The financial panic of that year brought to an end the decade of almost uninterrupted industrial prosperity. Besides, the remarkable growth of trusts and monopolies in the preceding ten years was attributed in some quarters to the advantages that these enterprises received from high protective duties. In consequence, the trusts and the tariff became associated in the public mind, and the hostility toward the former stimulated opposition to the latter. The Republican party could not afford to ignore the popular clamor for an overhauling of the ten-year-old tariff schedules, and its party platform in the presidential campaign of 1908 pledged a "revision" of the tariff—this term being generally understood to mean a reduction. At the same time it was stated, "In all protective legislation the true principle of protection is best maintained by the imposition of such duties as will equal the difference between the cost of production at home and abroad, together with a reasonable profit to American industries."

Just how this "principle" would work in practice remained to be seen. Thoroughly applied, it meant that duties should be high enough to allow anything and everything to be made in this country. As one of the leading authorities on the tariff puts it, "Pineapples can be grown in Maine, if only a duty be imposed sufficient to equalize the cost of production between the growers in Maine and those in more favored climes. Tea, coffee, cocoa, raw silk, and hemp—any quantity of things that are now imported can be grown in the United States provided only that a duty high enough is imposed." Moreover, it would be extremely difficult, if not impossible, to determine the difference in cost of production at home and abroad, not to mention the question of what was to be considered "a reasonable profit."

In point of fact the drafting of the tariff bill of 1909 was attended by the same scenes that had marked earlier tariff legislation. The representatives of protected industries flocked to Washington to look after their respective interests, and on the whole they were eminently successful. The bill as reported by the House Ways and Means Committee and passed by the House gave evidence of a disposition to bring about a real reduction in the Dingley tariff rates, notably on such commodities as iron, steel, coal, lumber, and hides. When the bill reached the Senate, however, it underwent a complete transformation. Under the guidance of Senator Aldrich, the high-priest of protection, more than 800 changes were made in the House bill, nearly all in the direction of raising rates. Protests from the Democrats and from a small group of "insurgent" Republican Senators from the West were of no avail, and the measure as finally passed by the two Houses and signed by President Taft left the average of tariff rates, at least on the most important commodities, scarcely, if at all, lower than that of the Dingley law.

A new principle was incorporated in this tariff law in the provisions made for the imposition of maximum and minimum rates. The rates fixed in the law were declared to be minimum rates and to these rates 25 per cent. was to be added on goods coming from countries that "unduly discriminated" against the United States by way of tariff rates, export bounties, or duties, trade regulations or "in any other manner." These maximum rates were to be applied unless the President by proclamation declared that there was "no undue discrimination" against the United States. President Taft, in April, 1910, stated that he was satisfied that there was no undue discrimination against the United States by any nation and hence the minimum rates were declared in force.

Despite President Taft's vigorous defense of the Payne-Aldrich tariff there was a widespread feeling in the country that the Republican party had repudiated the pledge made in its platform in 1908, and there is no question that this feeling contributed to the defeat of the Republicans in the Congressional elections of 1910. Other factors doubtless played a part in this political overturn. The business depression that followed the panic of 1907 was one. For ten years the nation had ridden on the wave of prosperity, and the Republicans had claimed full credit for it. Now that the tide had turned they had to shoulder the responsibility for hard times. Moreover, there were ominous rumblings from the progressive wing of the party, giving evidence of discontent with the forces that had guided the destinies of the Republican party for so many years.

The success of the Democrats in the election of 1910 gave them a majority in the House alone. The Senate was still controlled by the Republicans. With the Senate and the presidency in the hands of the opposition party the Democrats were unable to pass any general tariff legislation, but they were determined to keep the tariff question before the public in anticipation of the presidential election of 1912. With this end in view the House passed bills lowering the duties on a number of commodities, notably on wool, steel and iron, and also a "farmers' free list" bill, which removed the duties on certain goods purchased in agricultural regions. Some of these measures got through the Senate with the aid of Progressive Republicans, but they were all vetoed by President Taft on the ground that he was opposed to a piecemeal modification of the tariff. He urged that Congress should wait until the Tariff Board, which had been created by the provisions of the Payne-Aldrich Act, had had an opportunity to make a comprehensive study of the entire tariff question on the basis of which a "scientific" revision could be accomplished.

As a result of the election of 1912 the Democrats, for the first time since 1894, obtained control of all branches of the Federal government and President Wilson immediately after his inauguration called a special session of Congress to consider a general revision of the tariff. Under his effective leadership the Democrats in both House and Senate displayed remarkable unity of action and succeeded in passing the Underwood Tariff Act, October 3, 1913, unaccompanied by the selfish manipulation that had so often characterized tariff legislation.

In this Democratic tariff measure there is no evidence of an attempt to inaugurate a program of free trade, or even any onslaught upon the principle of protection. It is true that the Democrats stated that this tariff was based upon a new principle, namely, that of a "competitive tariff." In general, this meant that the tariff rates should not be made so high as to eliminate the possibility of foreign competition. In applying this principle in the Underwood Act some of the existing duties were sharply cut, while others were only moderately reduced. Wool was placed on the free list and the duties on woolen manufactures were reduced from 100 per cent., or more, to 35 per cent., or less. The duty on sugar was to be gradually reduced until, in 1916, all sugar was to be admitted free. In fact, however, the final reduction was not made, and a rate of 1¼ cents a pound was retained under an amendment passed in 1916. All agricultural implements were placed on the free list, as well as leather, boots, shoes, wheat, flour, cattle, meats, coal, lumber, iron ore and steel rails. Less drastic reductions were made in many other duties. The provisions of the act of 1909 to guard against "dumping" were retained. The Secretary of the Treasury was authorized to impose additional duties equal to the amount of bounty on exportation granted by a foreign country.[2]

Whether the disaster to American industry predicted by the advocates of protection as a result of the passage of the Underwood bill would ever have materialized it is impossible to say, for within less than a year after it went into effect the Great War in Europe broke out. This event brought about such an abnormal economic situation in this country that no conclusions can be drawn concerning the effect of the reduced tariff rates upon American industry.

The election of 1920 brought the Republican party into power once more. Although the tariff question played an insignificant part in this election the Republicans, as in 1896, maintained that the electorate had again endorsed the protective tariff principle, and they acted promptly upon this theory. The decline in war prices that came in 1920-1921 was particularly marked in agricultural commodities. The prices of wheat, corn, meats, and cotton were cut to one-half, or even less than one-half of the war figures. The out-

[2] The Tariff Board, which had been provided by the Payne-Aldrich law was not retained in the Underwood Act. However, in 1916, the Democrats revived the principle of an expert tariff board by providing for a bi-partisan Tariff Commission of six members appointed by the President for terms of twelve years.

cry of the farmers was heard in Congress and that body turned to the tariff for a remedy for the farmers' distress. In 1921 The Emergency Tariff Act was passed which placed high duties on various agricultural products. As a relief to the farmer this measure was almost entirely ineffectual, for the prices of agricultural products continued to decline despite the high tariff; but it did serve to bring support from the agricultural states to the movement for a general boosting of the tariff. Having received from Congress all that they demanded in the way of protection for agricultural products, the farmers' representatives could not readily oppose similar demands from manufacturing interests. The result was a tariff that imposed rates higher than any in the long history of tariff legislation. The so-called Fordney-McCumber Tariff Law was pushed through Congress in 1922, the protected interests encountering little difficulty in having their desires satisfied. Certain industries that had sprung up during the war demanded and received protection in the new tariff. Chief among these was the dye industry, which had been controlled largely by Germany before the war. From American manufacturers of dyestuffs came "patriotic" appeals in which they pointed out that the encouragement of this industry would be of value in preparing this country for future wars. The same plant that was used for making coal tar products could be used for the production of explosives and poison gas. Their pleas were effectual and the new rates of duties on coal tar derivatives were placed extremely high.

A novel feature of the tariff law of 1922 was the provision that authorized the President to increase or decrease the rates fixed in the law, not to exceed 50 per cent., when it was shown that the duties did not equalize the cost of production in the United States and in competing foreign countries. Before using this power, however, the President was required to base his action upon investigations made by the Tariff Commission. In practice this resulted in a number of increases but in very few decreases in the tariff schedules.[3]

The platform of the Democratic party in the election of 1928 indicated an important change in the traditional policy of that party concerning the tariff. The tariff plank stated that, "The Democratic tariff legislation will be based on the following policies: (a) The maintenance of legitimate business and a high standard of wages for American labor. . . . (b) Duties that will permit effective competition, insure against monopoly, and at the same time produce a fair revenue for the support of the government. Actual difference between the cost of production at home and abroad, with adequate protection for the wage of the American laborer, must be the extreme measure of every tariff rate. . . . (c) Equitable distribution of the benefits and burdens of the tariff among all." Contrast this with the pronouncement of the same party in the platform of 1912: "We declare it to be a fundamental principle of the Democratic party that the Federal government has no right or power to impose or collect tariff duties except for the purpose of revenue."

What is the explanation of this remarkable change? It is to be found chiefly in the new economic conditions in the "Solid South," the stronghold of the Democratic party. As has been noted elsewhere, the South since 1900, and especially since 1920, has experienced an extraordinary industrial development. Southern manufacturers, no less than those of the North, are desirous of having a benevolent government stand between them and their foreign competitors. Thus did economic forces once more display their ability to play havoc with cherished traditions.

It was suggested above that the changed financial position of the United States since the Great War may bring a new alignment of powerful economic forces in this country on the tariff question. Prior to the war banking and commercial

---

[3] President Coolidge increased rates on eighteen commodities and decreased rates on five.

interests were, in general, united in support of the principle of protection. Large financial concerns had their investments chiefly in American industrial enterprises and were therefore interested in stimulating the growth of such industries. But in the period since the war there has come a significant change. Billions of dollars have been invested by American bankers in foreign securities upon which millions of dollars in interest will have to be paid. Such payments can only be made, in the long run, by the acceptance of foreign manufactured goods or raw materials, and the purpose of a high protective tariff is to discourage the importation of foreign goods. In this situation there appear the elements of a conflict between the interests of American bankers having large foreign investments and American manufacturers determined to preserve the home market. Rumblings of such a clash have already been heard. Thus we find the Wall Street *Journal,* mouthpiece of the large banking interests, referring to the Fordney-McCumber tariff as "one of the most selfish, short-sighted and extravagant laws of the kind ever enacted." Furthermore, it may be noted that there are important manufacturing interests in this country, notably the automobile industry, and manufacturers of typewriters and agricultural machinery, who have nothing to fear from foreign competition, but who on the other hand are very much interested in finding foreign markets for their products. Such manufacturers stand to benefit by a lowering rather than a raising of the tariff rates, thereby making possible a greater foreign consumption of their products. In short, the power of organized wealth no longer stands united behind the advocates of a protective tariff. This cleavage in the ranks of the banking and manufacturing interests may have important political as well as economic effects.

An important constructive measure dealing with government finance was passed by Congress in 1921. This was the so-called Budget Act. Prior to the passage of this law the

financial operations of the Federal government were conducted in the most unscientific manner. No attempt was made
by Congress to adjust expenditures to income. Various committees in House and Senate brought forward at each session
appropriation bills without making any effort to formulate a
comprehensive budget plan. Any country less favorably endowed than the United States could not have survived under
such slipshod financial practices. The huge increase in government expenditures that came with the entrance of the
United States into the World War finally brought home to
Congress the necessity of adopting a more scientific method
of handling government finances. Under the provisions of
the Budget Law the President is required to submit to Congress at the opening of each regular session a budget containing the estimate of the government expenses for the
ensuing year. This estimate is prepared by the Director of
the Budget after consultation with the heads of the various
government departments. Congress thus has each year a complete picture of the financial needs of the government, although it is not obligated to accept the estimate prepared by
the budget director and is free to make such alterations as it
may deem fit.

BIBLIOGRAPHICAL NOTE

For recent tariff history consult I. Tarbell, *The Tariff in Our
Times* (1911); F. W. Taussig, *The Tariff History of the
United States* (7th ed., 1923); D. R. Dewey, *Financial History
of the United States* (8th ed., 1922); R. W. Kelsey, *The Tariff*
(1929). On the Federal Reserve system see A. B. Hepburn,
A History of Currency in the United States (rev. ed., 1924);
R. L. Owen, *The Federal Reserve Act* (1919); C. Glass, *An
Adventure in Constructive Finance* (1927); W. P. G. Harding,
The Formative Period of the Federal Reserve System (1925);
E. A. Goldenwasser, *The Federal Reserve System in Operation*
(1925); E. W. Kemmerer, *The A.B.C. of the Federal Reserve
System* (1918); H. L. Reed, *The Development of Federal Re-
serve Policy* (1922). On the relation of the Federal Reserve

system to the stabilization of prices consult J. L. Lawrence, *Stabilization of Prices* (1928). For the treatment of farm loans see I. Wright, *Bank Credit and Agriculture Under the National and Federal Reserve Banking Systems* (1922); H. Myrick, *The Federal Farm Loan System* (1916). On war taxation consult A. D. Noyes, *The War Period of American Finance* (1926); A. W. Mellon, *Taxation: The People's Business* (1924). On the changed financial situation of the United States after the World War see *Proceedings of the Academy of Political Science*, Vol. XII, No. 4 (1928); report of the National Industrial Conference Board, *The International Financial Position of the United States* (1929).

CHAPTER 19

THE UNITED STATES AS A WORLD POWER

The emergence of the United States as a world power at the opening of the twentieth century gave rise to significant and perplexing questions concerning the relations of this country with the Spanish-American republics. Most Americans apparently assume that these relations are sufficiently regulated by the Monroe Doctrine, which has become to the average American almost as sacred as the Declaration of Independence and the Constitution. And yet if called upon to give an exact definition of the Monroe Doctrine this same average American would probably take refuge in some such general remark as: "Europe must keep her hands off of America." But such a statement fails utterly to define the relations of the United States with its independent neighbors. Did President Monroe when he stated that this continent was no longer to be regarded as a field for European colonization, intend to bind the United States not to acquire territory at the expense of our sister republics? The results of the Mexican War in the middle of the nineteenth century, by which we acquired a large part of the Mexican Republic, appeared to answer this question conclusively. Clearly the Monroe Doctrine was not a self-denying ordinance. Intelligent Spanish-Americans began to query whether the Doctrine was an unmixed blessing from their point of view, but as the United States during the fifty years that followed the Mexican War acquired no further territory [1] at the expense of its neighbors, in the course of time such fears were quieted.

[1] Except the Gadsden Purchase from Mexico.

In the first decade of the twentieth century, however, a series of events occurred that once more aroused in Spanish-American countries the latent suspicion and fear of the United States, and led a prominent Argentine statesman to declare: "The Monroe Doctrine is not a doctrine of America for Americans, but of America for North Americans. It has served as an admirable instrument for the United States to separate Europe from America and to establish its hegemony over the latter. The United States has been at all times preoccupied in obtaining concessions of every kind at the cost of the sovereignty of the rest of the American states. The doctrine is dangerous because it is North American imperialism hidden under a principle of international law." To a consideration of the events that called forth such a statement we must now turn our attention.

At the opening of the twentieth century there was in full swing the movement that has been called "Economic Imperialism." In undeveloped parts of the world, chiefly in Africa and Asia, the leading industrial countries of Europe were adding colonial possessions or staking out "spheres of influence." While the Monroe Doctrine prohibited the further acquisition of European colonies in the New World, it did not prevent the investment of large amounts of European capital in the republics of Central and South America. Moreover, American capital, in the closing decades of the nineteenth century, began to seek investment in these areas.

In many Spanish-American countries there occurred frequent revolutionary disturbances. These political upheavals were a source of irritation to the business interests, and not infrequently they threatened the security of foreign investments. Foreign capitalists, quite naturally, turned to their respective governments for the protection of their property rights, and in most cases these appeals received the desired support.

The government of the United States was especially con-

cerned in these controversies. Not only was it besieged by
American bankers and business men to protect their threatened property but, when European governments threatened
to take vigorous action against some defaulting Spanish-
American state, there was involved the question of a possible
violation of the Monroe Doctrine. Several incidents will serve
to illustrate the expansion of American political and economic control in Spanish-American countries.

THE VENEZUELAN CONTROVERSY

Venezuela presents a typical example of the revolution-
ridden Spanish-American republic. In the closing decades of
the nineteenth century there prevailed in that country a condition of chronic disorder. One revolutionary leader after
another seized control of the government, and each in turn
looted the treasury and left the country with a mounting
burden of debt. Grants, concessions, and privileges were
made to foreigners by these ephemeral rulers, sometimes for
legitimate purposes but often without any material benefit to
the country. The numerous insurrections resulted in injury
to foreign property interests and led to large claims for indemnity.

In 1899 Cipriano Castro established himself as a virtual
dictator of this disturbed country. He soon found himself in
difficulty because of his unwillingness or his inability to meet
the claims for damages made by foreign investors. Failing
to obtain satisfaction from the Venezuelan government, these
interests called upon their respective governments for protection. In response to these appeals Great Britain, Germany,
and Italy joined in an ultimatum to Venezuela demanding
satisfaction of the claims of their nationals. In the meantime
the American government had been sounded by the foreign
powers concerning its attitude in case they found it necessary
to take coercive measures against Venezuela. Secretary Hay

assured them that the United States would raise no objection
to any measures that might be adopted provided they did not
result in the permanent acquisition of Venezuelan territory
by a European power. Having received this assurance, the
three powers proceeded to declare a blockade of Venezuelan
ports. Confronted by this determined action President Castro
proposed that the question of the foreign claims should be
submitted to arbitration, and this suggestion was strongly
supported by the United States authorities. In an account of
the controversy written many years later President Roosevelt
stated that the German government refused to agree to arbitration until he threatened to send an American fleet under
Admiral Dewey to Venezuela.[2]

At all events the controversy was satisfactorily adjusted
by having the foreign claims submitted to mixed commissions. The equity of these claims may be judged from the
fact that the awards made by the commission totaled about
one-fifth of the sums demanded. The three powers that had
participated in the blockade insisted that their claims should
take priority over those of other nations. This phase of the
controversy was submitted to the Hague Tribunal, which
rendered a decision favorable to the contention of these
powers.

Out of this controversy there developed an animated discussion of the use of force in the collection of public debts.
The question came up at the Second Hague Conference, and
a resolution was adopted by this body which provided that
"the contracting powers agree not to have recourse to armed

[2] This version has been seriously questioned by Professor Howard C.
Hill, who, after an exhaustive examination of all of the documentary
evidence, reached the conclusion that Germany showed no greater un-
willingness to arbitrate than did Great Britain, and he is unable to find
any evidence that Germany changed her attitude as a result of the
American threat.—Bishop, *Life and Times of Theodore Roosevelt*, I, 222.
Thayer, *John Hay*, II, 412. H. C. Hill, *Roosevelt and the Caribbean*,
Ch. V.

force for the recovery of contract debts claimed from the government of one country by the government of another country as being due to its nationals," unless the debtor state should refuse to submit the claims to arbitration or should decline to accept the award of arbitrators.

ISTHMIAN CANAL DIPLOMACY

The growing interests of the United States in the Caribbean after the Spanish war led to a revival of the project for building an interoceanic canal. Preliminary to such an undertaking it was necessary to make certain diplomatic adjustments. We have seen that the efforts of Secretaries Blaine and Frelinghuysen to persuade Great Britain to agree to a modification of the terms of the Clayton-Bulwer treaty were unsuccessful. At the close of the nineteenth century, however, conditions seemed to be decidedly more favorable for a satisfactory adjustment of this question. During the Spanish-American War British public opinion supported the American cause, and this friendly attitude tended to soften the ancient animosities in this country toward Great Britain. British statesmen at this time were desirous of strengthening cordial relations with the United States. The international European situation at the opening of the new century was threatening. The major continental Powers had formed two rival military alliances and Great Britain began seriously to consider whether she could longer follow with safety her traditional policy of "splendid isolation," particularly in view of the threat of German naval rivalry. To add to Britain's difficulties war clouds were gathering in South Africa. Obviously it was to the interest of Great Britain to remove any cause of friction with the United States, in view of these disturbed European and African conditions.

Under these favoring circumstances Secretary Hay in

1899 revived the question of the Clayton-Bulwer treaty. The British authorities met these advances cordially and in February, 1900, was drafted the Hay-Pauncefote treaty, which authorized the United States to construct and assume the management of an interoceanic canal, but which retained the provision of the earlier treaty providing for neutralization. The United States Senate amended the treaty in three important respects: (1) by declaring that the Clayton-Bulwer treaty was superseded; (2) by providing that the restrictions in the regulations governing the use of the canal should not apply to measures which the United States might adopt for its own defense or for the maintenance of public order along the canal; (3) by eliminating the article providing for the adherence of other powers. The British government declined to accept these changes, and a year passed before a compromise agreement was reached. The treaty as finally agreed upon provided for the abrogation of the Clayton-Bulwer convention, thus allowing for the construction of a canal under the exclusive jurisdiction of the United States. While the principle of neutralization was retained, it was to be under the sole guarantee of the United States, and the clause of the original draft forbidding fortifications was omitted.

Diplomatic obstacles to the construction of the canal having been cleared away, the next important question to be determined was the route. The opinions of expert engineers in this country had generally favored the Nicaraguan route, and two commissions, one in 1895, and the other in 1897, had recommended it. However, considerations other than purely engineering ones influenced the determination of this matter. The French Panama Canal Company, which had undertaken the construction of a canal across the Isthmus of Panama, was bankrupt, and its concession would expire in 1904. Unable to raise the necessary funds to continue the work on the canal the stockholders of the French Company were threatened with the loss of their concession and property.[3] Their only recourse seemed to be to dispose of their interests to the American government, and for this purpose an active lobby was maintained in Washington.

In 1901 the Walker Commission, which had been appointed to make a thorough investigation of the Panama and Nicaragua routes, reported that in its opinion "the most practicable and feasible route for the isthmian canal, to be under the control, management, and ownership of the United States, is that known as the Nicaragua route." A bill was promptly introduced in Congress providing for the construction of a canal through Nicaragua, but the Panama Canal interests, realizing that if this measure were passed their investment at Panama would be virtually worthless, made a definite offer to sell all their rights to the United States for $40,000,000.[4] The bill before Congress was then so amended as to authorize the President to acquire the rights and property of the Panama Company at a cost not to exceed $40,000,000; to acquire from the Republic of Colombia perpetual control of a strip of land six miles wide extending across the Isthmus; and, as soon as these rights were acquired, to proceed to the construction of a canal. In case satisfactory arrangements could not be made with both the French Company and the Republic of Colombia "within a reasonable time and upon reasonable terms," the President was authorized to turn to the Nicaragua route.

No difficulty was found in reaching an agreement with the canal company to purchase its rights, but it was different when it came to negotiating with Colombia. A treaty was signed by Secretary Hay and Mr. Herran, the Colombian representative at Washington, which provided that the United States should pay to Colombia $10,000,000 in cash and an annuity of $250,000 for the perpetual lease of a strip of land across the isthmus. The treaty was ratified by the

[3] A considerable amount of the stock of the company had been bought by American speculators.
[4] The company had originally demanded $100,000,000.

United States Senate, but the Senate of Colombia held up the measure, probably because it was felt that better terms could be obtained from the United States. At this juncture things began to happen behind the scenes. President Roosevelt, who strongly favored the Panama route, did not avail himself of the congressional authorization to turn to Nicaragua. In the meantime the French stockholders, thoroughly aroused over the threatened loss of the $40,000,000 which they were to receive from the United States, sent to this country Mr. Philippe Bunau-Varilla, former chief engineer of the company, to look after their interests. The inhabitants of the Isthmus, who were keenly disappointed at the failure of the treaty, considered the advisability of organizing a revolution against Colombia, and sent Dr. Amador to Washington to sound the American authorities concerning the attitude of this country in the event that Panama should revolt. While President Roosevelt and Secretary Hay declined to commit this country to the support of such a movement, it was clear to the conspirators that the President did not frown upon their undertaking. In a letter written on October 10, 1903, to Mr. Albert Shaw, editor of the *Review of Reviews,* the President said: "Privately, I freely say to you that I should be delighted if Panama were an independent state, or if it made itself so at this moment; but for me to say so publicly would amount to an instigation of a revolt, and therefore I cannot say it." The revolutionists were further encouraged by an order issued by the President to the commander of the cruiser *Nashville* to proceed to the Isthmus and "to prevent the landing of any armed forces with hostile intent, either government or insurgent, at any point within fifty miles of Panama."

On November 3rd the anticipated revolt on the Isthmus occurred, and events followed one another with startling rapidity. American marines prevented the landing of Colombian troops sent to suppress the revolt, and three days later the United States recognized the independence of Panama. Such precipitate action was unprecedented in American history, and it gave rise to considerable criticism in the press of the United States. Efforts were made to justify the action of the administration by citing our obligations under an old treaty signed in 1846 with the republic of New Granada which guaranteed that transit across the Isthmus "shall be open and free to the government and citizens of the United States"; but Roosevelt probably expressed the truth in a speech delivered after he had retired from the presidency when he said: "If I had followed traditional conservative methods I should have submitted a dignified state paper of probably two hundred pages to the Congress and the debate would be going on yet, but I took the Canal Zone and let Congress debate, and while the debate goes on the canal does also."

Following the recognition of the Panama Republic a treaty was promptly ratified between that country and the United States which provided that the United States should guarantee the independence of Panama and should pay to the Panama Republic a sum of $10,000,000 and an annuity of $250,000 beginning nine years after the ratification of the treaty. In return, Panama agreed to grant to the United States full authority over a strip of territory ten miles wide extending across the Isthmus, for the construction of a canal. After some delay because of change in plans, the construction of the canal began. A marvelous piece of work was accomplished by army engineers in overcoming the many difficult engineering problems, and an almost equally striking success is to be credited to American medical authorities in conquering the malarial and other epidemic conditions on the Isthmus. In August, 1914, the canal was opened to traffic.

The incidents surrounding the acquisition of the Canal Zone aroused resentment not only in Colombia but throughout Latin America. To appease this feeling efforts were made by President Taft, after Mr. Roosevelt retired from office, to compensate Colombia for the loss of the Panama territory. The proposal that Panama should assign to Colombia the first ten annual installments of the rental for the canal zone and that the United States should pay an additional sum of $10,000,000 to Colombia was rejected by Colombia. When the Wilson administration assumed office negotiations with Colombia were renewed, and a treaty was drafted by the terms of which the United States expressed "sincere regret that anything should have occurred to interrupt or to mar the relations of cordial friendship that had so long subsisted between the two nations"; and $25,000,000 was to be paid to Colombia. Roosevelt denounced this treaty as a reflection upon his actions in acquiring the Canal Zone, and his supporters in the Senate were able to prevent its ratification. Shortly after the Harding administration came into office a new treaty was drafted which stated that both countries desired "to remove all misunderstandings growing out of the political events in Panama in November, 1903," and which again provided for the payment of $25,000,000 to Colombia. This treaty was accepted by Colombia and was ratified by the United States Senate, friends of the then deceased Roosevelt voting for it. It is probable that the fact that American oil interests had found difficulty in doing business in Colombia because of the strained relations between the two countries facilitated the ratification of the treaty in the Senate.

Two years before the completion of the Panama Canal, Congress had enacted legislation regulating the rates to be charged on traffic passing through the canal, and providing that American vessels engaged in the coast-wise trade should be exempt from the payment of tolls. Great Britain protested that this was a clear violation of the Hay-Pauncefote treaty, which required that the canal should be opened to all nations "on terms of entire equality." In reply to this protest the United States stated that as only American vessels could engage in the coast-wise trade there was no discrimination against the vessels of other nations. Great Britain, however, renewed her protest and, with the advent of the Democratic administration in 1913, President Wilson urged upon Congress the repeal of the tolls law on the ground that it was a violation of a treaty pledge.[5] Despite vigorous opposition from members of his own party in Congress, the President succeeded in forcing through the repeal measure.[6] During the Harding administration an attempt was made to reënact the exemption law but, as the Washington Conference on the Limitation of Armaments was just about to meet, it seemed unwise to revive a diplomatic controversy that might put in jeopardy the success of the Conference, and the matter was allowed to drop.

THE UNITED STATES IN THE CARIBBEAN

In the nature of things the construction of the Panama Canal stimulated the interest of the United States in the whole area adjacent to the canal. A glance at the map will show the strategic importance for the defense of the canal of the group of islands that bound the Caribbean Sea on the north and the east. The results of the Spanish-American War had given the United States a predominant position in two of these islands, Cuba and Porto Rico. Between these was a large island divided politically into the two republics of Haiti

[5] In making the plea for the repeal of the tolls law Wilson said, "I ask this of you in support of the foreign policy of the administration. I shall not know how to deal with other matters of even greater delicacy and nearer consequence if you do not grant it to me in ungrudging measure." Perhaps some light is thrown upon this cryptic statement by the account given in the *Life and Letters of Walter H. Page* of the visit of Colonel House to Great Britain, France, and Germany at this time for the purpose of trying to find some peaceful solution of the delicate European situation. Wilson probably felt that the tolls dispute would prevent the success of the House mission.

[6] It has been charged that the transcontinental railroads were behind the movement for the repeal of the tolls exemption for American vessels, because of the competition of traffic by way of the canal.

and Santo Domingo. During the nineteenth century political conditions in both of these republics had been most unstable. In this period two presidents of Haiti were assassinated, one committed suicide, six were exiled, and several others were overthrown by revolutionary movements. And the record in Santo Domingo was scarcely less tumultuous. Such unsettled political conditions caused acute disturbance to the island's business interests, which were largely in the hands of foreigners. Moreover, the various ephemeral governments had contracted large foreign loans, which could not be met by the meager revenues of the island. At the close of the nineteenth century foreign claims against the government of the Dominican Republic were estimated at between thirty and forty million dollars. Creditors in various European countries were constantly urging their governments to take measures to protect their investments.

President Roosevelt realized the danger of intervention by one or more European states and he was determined to prevent, if possible, a repetition of the crisis that had arisen in the Venezuelan controversy. In his message to Congress of December 6, 1904, he said, "Any country whose people conduct themselves well can count upon our hearty friendship. If a nation shows that it knows how to act with reasonable efficiency and decency in social and political matters, if it keeps order and pays its obligations, it need fear no interference from the United States. Chronic wrongdoing, or an impotence that results in a general loosening of the ties of civilized society, may in America, as elsewhere, ultimately require intervention by some civilized nation, and in the Western Hemisphere the adherence of the United States to the Monroe Doctrine may force the United States, however reluctantly, in flagrant cases of such wrongdoing or impotence, to the exercise of an international police power."

Convinced that conditions of "wrongdoing and impotence" obtained in the Dominican Republic, he directed the Ameri-

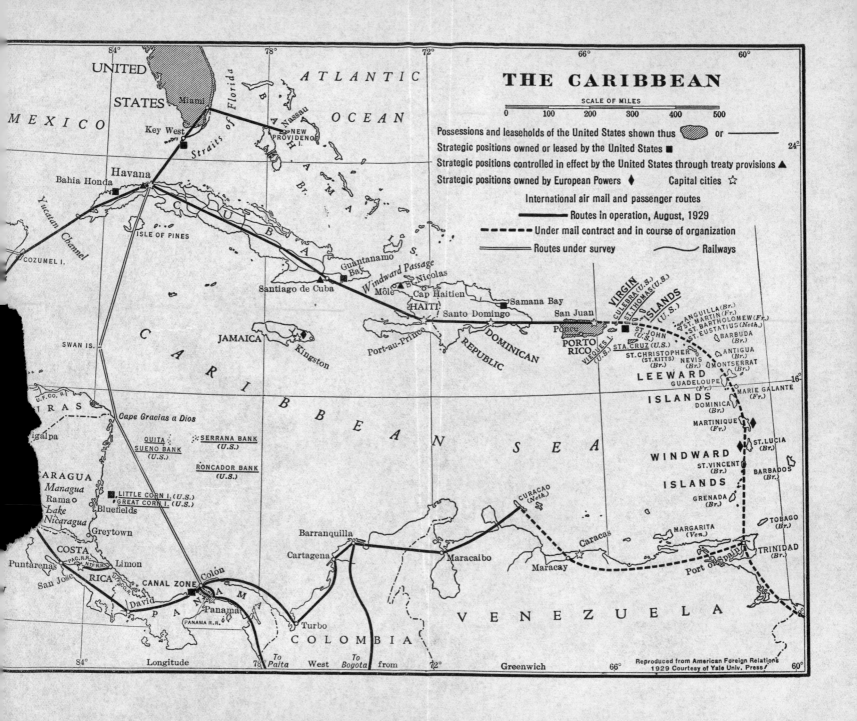

THE CARIBBEAN

SCALE OF MILES

0 100 200 300 400 500

Possessions and leaseholds of the United States shown thus [hatched] or ——

Strategic positions owned or leased by the United States ■

Strategic positions controlled in effect by the United States through treaty provisions ▲

Strategic positions owned by European Powers ◆   Capital cities ☆

International air mail and passenger routes

—— Routes in operation, August, 1929

– – – Under mail contract and in course of organization

═══ Routes under survey   ⌒ Railways

UNITED STATES

MEXICO

ATLANTIC OCEAN

Miami

Key West

Straits of Florida

Nassau
NEW PROVIDENCE

BAHAMAS Br.

Havana

Bahia Honda

Yucatan Channel

COZUMEL I.

CUBA

ISLE OF PINES

Guantanamo Bay

Santiago de Cuba

Windward Passage

Môle St. Nicolas

Cap Haitien

HAITI

Port-au-Prince

Santo Domingo

Samana Bay

DOMINICAN REPUBLIC

San Juan

Ponce

PORTO RICO

VIRGIN ISLANDS
CULEBRA (U.S.)
ST.THOMAS (U.S.)
ST. JOHN (U.S.)
STA. CRUZ (U.S.)
VIEQUES I. (U.S.)

ANGUILLA (Br.)
ST. MARTIN (Fr.)
ST. BARTHOLOMEW (Fr.)
ST. EUSTATIUS (Neth.)
BARBUDA (Br.)
ST. CHRISTOPHER (ST. KITTS) (Br.)
NEVIS (Br.)
ANTIGUA (Br.)
MONTSERRAT (Br.)

LEEWARD ISLANDS

GUADELOUPE (Fr.)

MARIE GALANTE (Fr.)

DOMINICA (Br.)

MARTINIQUE (Fr.)

ST. LUCIA (Br.)

WINDWARD ISLANDS

ST. VINCENT (Br.)

BARBADOS (Br.)

GRENADA (Br.)

JAMAICA

Kingston

SWAN IS.

CARIBBEAN SEA

QUITA SUENO BANK (U.S.)

SERRANA BANK (U.S.)

RONCADOR BANK (U.S.)

HONDURAS

U.F.CO. R.R.

Tegucigalpa

Cape Gracias a Dios

NICARAGUA

Managua
Rama
Lake Nicaragua
Bluefields
Greytown

LITTLE CORN I. (U.S.)
GREAT CORN I. (U.S.)

COSTA RICA

Puntarenas

San Jose

Limon

David

PAC.R.R.
N.I.F.R.R.

CANAL ZONE

Colón

PANAMA

Panama

PANAMA R.R.

Turbo

COLOMBIA

To Paita   To Bogota

Barranquilla

Cartagena

Maracaibo

Maracay

Caracas

VENEZUELA

CURACAO (Neth.)

MARGARITA (Ven.)

TOBAGO (Br.)

Port of Spain

TRINIDAD (Br.)

Longitude   West   from   Greenwich

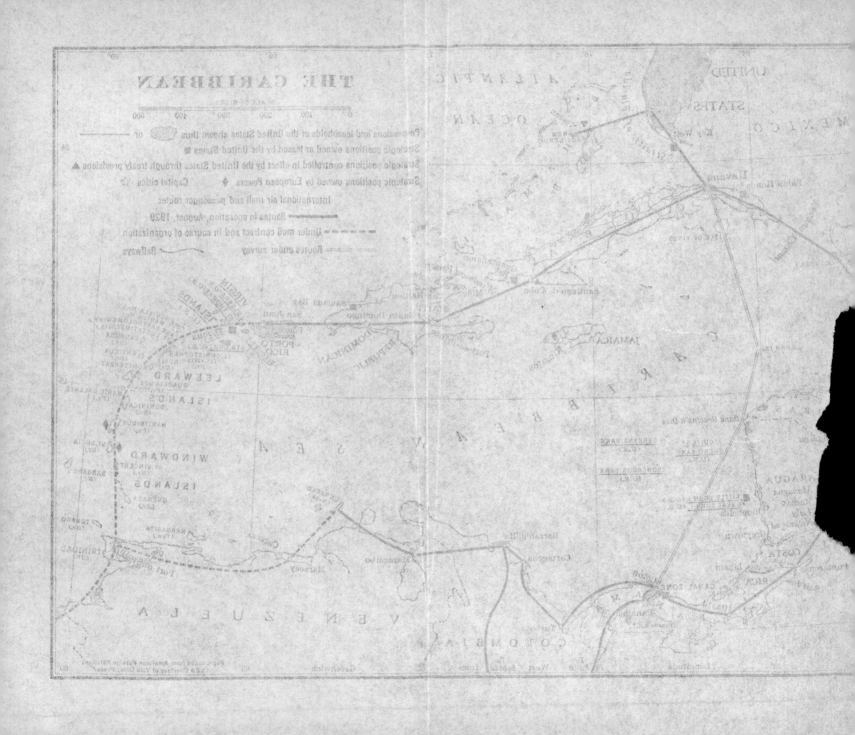

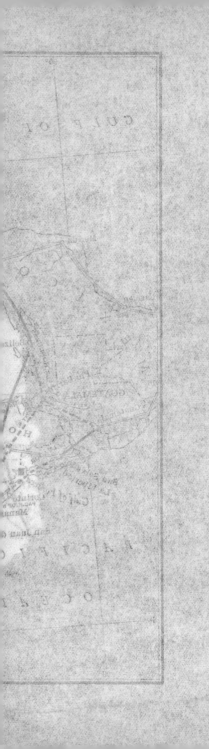

can minister to propose to the Dominican government that the United States should take charge of its customs. Acting upon this suggestion a "protocol" was signed by the representatives of the two governments which provided that the United States should guarantee the territorial integrity of the Dominican Republic, take charge of the custom houses, administer its finances, and settle its foreign and domestic obligations.

When the protocol came before the Senate, President Roosevelt urged its ratification on the ground that "those who profit by the Monroe Doctrine must accept certain responsibilities along with the rights which it confers." But the Senate was unable or unwilling to see the matter in this light, and it adjourned without acting upon the protocol. Undeterred by senatorial disapproval, President Roosevelt arranged a *modus vivendi* with the Dominican government by which the Dominican President appointed a receiver of customs selected by President Roosevelt and this officer entered upon his duties under the protection of American war vessels. Despite determined opposition in Congress this arrangement was continued until in February, 1907, the Senate finally ratified a treaty giving legal sanction to the tentative arrangement made by President Roosevelt. In the meantime an agreement had been made whereby the claims against the Dominican Republic were scaled down from $40,000,000 to $17,000,000, based upon a cash payment. Although the financial and commercial conditions in the island republic improved remarkably under American supervision, political conditions continued unsettled, and in 1916 American marines were landed at the capital to suppress a revolt. For the next nine years the republic was virtually ruled by American military forces and the Dominicans resented the loss of their political and civil rights. Finally, in 1925, civil government was restored, and the American marines were withdrawn after a new treaty had been agreed to, which provided for the continuance of American control of the finances of the republic until the outstanding foreign bonds were paid.

The republic of Haiti, which occupies the western end of the island of Santo Domingo, had been in a condition of almost continual political unrest during the nineteenth century. In 1914 the situation in this negro republic had reached a critical stage. Foreign intervention by Great Britain, France, and Germany, to enforce the payment of obligations due to their nationals, was averted only by the outbreak of the Great War in Europe. In the summer of 1915 the American government ordered Admiral Caperton to proceed to the island. He arrived just in time to learn that President Sam had ordered the execution of a large number of his political opponents and had in turn been assassinated by the enraged populace. Faced by a condition of political chaos, Admiral Caperton landed American marines at Port au Prince and took control of the custom houses. A presidential election was then held under American protection, and M. Dartiguenave was elected. This was followed by the negotiation of a treaty which virtually established an American protectorate. By its terms a Haitian receivership of customs was to be placed under American control; an American financial adviser was to assist in straightening out the finances of the republic; the Haitian constabulary was placed under the command of American officers; all revolutionary forces were to be disarmed; and Haiti was to guarantee not to cede any territory to any foreign country except the United States.

The Haitian Congress was not inclined at first to ratify this treaty, but Admiral Caperton notified President Dartiguenave that no funds collected at the custom houses would be turned over for the payment of salaries of officials until the treaty had been accepted. Submitting to this pressure, the Haitian Congress reluctantly ratified the convention. The treaty was to remain in force for ten years and to continue for another ten years unless its purpose had been fully accomplished.[7] In 1917 a new constitution, drafted by Franklin D. Roosevelt, Assistant Secretary of the Navy, was presented to the Haitian assembly for approval. Largely because it contained a clause giving foreigners the right to own land, despite the former constitutional prohibition of such ownership, the Assembly refused to ratify the constitution. The American authorities in the island promptly dissolved the Assembly and secured ratification of the constitution by means of a farcical plebiscite. Later amendments were adopted, presumably with the approval of the American authorities, which authorized the President to remove judges of the courts, and conferred upon the government authority to suppress the freedom of the press and to dispense with the jury system.

The results obtained from American control of Haitian affairs have been both good and evil. There can be no question that the living conditions in the island have materially improved during the period of American occupation, and the finances of the republic have been put upon a sound basis. On the other hand, many serious charges have been made against American officials in the island, and at least some of these charges have been upheld by impartial investigators. Among other things it was maintained that American marines had killed many natives without just cause and had visited upon others cruel and inhuman treatment. In their work of road-building the Americans revived the hated corvée, or system of forced labor. No doubt the difficulties that the Americans met in Haiti were aggravated by the fact that they had to deal with the negro race, and the experience with the race problem in the United States gave abundant

[7] In 1917 the treaty was extended to 1936, although this extension was not ratified by either the United States Senate or the Haitian National Assembly.

evidence of the unwillingness of the whites to treat the negroes on a basis of equality.[8]

Upon the overthrow of Spanish authority in Central
America in the early part of the nineteenth century five new
republics were organized in this area. In 1825 these five
states were joined in a federal union patterned after that of
the United States, but the union lasted only fifteen years,
after which the states resumed their independent status. During the latter half of the nineteenth century the relations of
the United States with these Central American republics
were concerned chiefly with various unsuccessful efforts to
restore the former federal union of these states. With the
completion of the Panama Canal, however, the interest of the
United States in the whole Caribbean area assumed greater
importance.

Political conditions in all five of the Central American republics during the greater part of the nineteenth century had
been extremely unstable. The frequent revolutionary outbreaks were of course disturbing to the security of foreign
investments, which had flowed into these countries in increasing volume in the closing decades of the nineteenth century.
It was inevitable that sooner or later one or more of the
foreign powers would be called upon to protect the threatened
interests of their nationals.

Confronted by such conditions President Roosevelt, in
1906, determined to make an effort to end the political chaos
that had prevailed in these states. Taking advantage of the
war then in progress between Guatemala, Salvador, and
Honduras, he invited President Diaz to Mexico to join with
him in an offer of mediation. This offer was accepted and
hostilities were suspended. President Roosevelt followed this
success by an invitation to the representatives of all Central

[8] In December, 1929, an outbreak occurred in Haiti which was suppressed by American marines. Following the suppression of the revolt
President Hoover sent a commission to Haiti to prepare plans for the
termination of American control of the Republic.

American states to meet in Washington to discuss plans for stabilizing political conditions in these countries. At this conference a general treaty of peace and arbitration was agreed upon, by the terms of which all disputes arising in the future among these states should be adjudicated by a Central American court of justice, composed of five judges, one to be elected by the legislature of each state. The hope that this new venture would inaugurate an era of peace and order in Central America was, unfortunately, not realized.

President Zelaya, of Nicaragua, a stormy petrel in Central American politics, continued to stir up revolutionary movements in the neighboring republics and when, in 1909, a revolution broke out in Nicaragua against the Zelaya régime the revolt was regarded with considerable favor in the other Central American states and at Washington. Aroused by the attitude of the American authorities President Zelaya, in November, 1909, ordered the execution of two Americans, apparently without any legal justification. Following this action President Taft immediately broke off diplomatic relations with Zelaya. This caused his speedy downfall, and a new régime, first under President Estrada, and later under Adolfo Diaz, was recognized by the United States.

Diaz, however, was unable to pacify his disturbed country, and in July, 1912, he requested the United States to send American forces to Nicaragua to protect the rights of American citizens. In answer to this appeal President Taft sent a detachment of marines to Managua and later, as the revolutionary disturbances continued, to other points in the republic. With order restored the American authorities proceeded to negotiate a treaty with the Diaz government which provided for the payment by the United States to Nicaragua of $3,000,000 in return for the exclusive privilege of building a canal through Nicaragua, the grant of a naval base on the Gulf of Fonseca, and a lease for ninety-nine years of the Great Corn and Little Corn Islands in the Caribbean. This treaty was before the United States Senate when the Taft administration went out of office, but the Democratic administration of President Wilson was apparently quite willing to continue the policy inaugurated by its predecessor. At all events, the treaty, with some modifications, was ratified by the Senate in February, 1916. In reference to this treaty Senator Borah said: "I have never regarded the Nicaraguan treaty as binding upon the Nicaraguan people. We were making a treaty with ourselves. We were making a treaty with a government which was our puppet. We were making a treaty with a government which represented us at the other end of the treaty-making negotiations. It is one of the most indefensible transactions of which I have knowledge in international affairs."

The governments of Costa Rica and Salvador protested that the treaty between the United States and Nicaragua violated their rights and they submitted their protests to the Central American Court of Justice. The Court rendered an opinion upholding the contentions of Costa Rica and Salvador but both the United States and Nicaragua declined to accept the decision of the Court. As a result the Court, which it will be recalled had been organized largely through the efforts of the United States, went out of existence.

As long as the American military forces remained in Nicaragua a condition of comparative order and peace prevailed. When, however, in August, 1925, the marines were withdrawn from the capital, revolutionary outbreaks almost immediately followed. General Chamorro, who had been defeated in the recent presidential election, executed a *coup d'état,* forced the constitutionally elected president to resign, and had himself chosen president by a subservient Congress. The United States authorities notified Chamorro that it would not recognize a President chosen in this unconstitutional manner. Encouraged by this statement, the liberals stirred up a revolution against Chamorro. Appeals from

American business interests in the country resulted in the landing of American marines once more. While it was officially declared that they had been sent simply to protect American property and lives, the American forces speedily took control of the country. Chamorro was induced to resign, and the Congress chose Adolfo Diaz as President over the protests of the liberals, who supported General Sacasa. The United States recognized the Diaz régime and the liberals under Sacasa once more took up arms. American marines were again sent to the distracted country, and President Coolidge, with the hope of finding a solution of the long-drawn-out controversy, sent Henry L. Stimson to Nicaragua in April, 1927, as his personal representative. After prolonged negotiations Stimson succeeded in persuading the liberal and conservative factions to agree to a cessation of hostilities on condition that the United States would agree to supervise the presidential election in 1928, in order to assure a fair election. A portion of the liberals, under the command of General Sandino, declined to accept this arrangement and continued a guerrilla warfare against the American forces during the following year. In accordance with the above agreement American military and civil officials organized and supervised the election machinery in the ensuing national election, at which time the liberal candidate was successful. With the installation of the new president it was announced by the Washington authorities that the American marines would be withdrawn from Nicaragua at an early date.

In recent years the United States has had occasion to intervene to a greater or less extent in the affairs of other Central American states. In 1911 Secretary Knox proposed a plan for adjusting the tangled finances of Honduras, but the United States Senate declined to ratify the convention. In the same year President Taft accepted a proposal to mediate between two rival factions in Honduras, and a satisfactory adjustment was made. A boundary dispute between Costa Rica and Panama was submitted to Chief Justice White of the United States Supreme Court as arbitrator. Panama at first declined to accept the decision of Justice White, but in the end grudgingly consented. At the suggestion of the United States in 1922-1923, a conference of the Central American republics was held in Washington and there was drafted a series of treaties, the most important provisions being (1) a strict limitation of armaments, (2) the appointment of international commissions of inquiry to settle disputes arising among these states, (3) the non-recognition of governments established by revolution, (4) the organization of a new Central American Court of Justice, less political in character than the one established in 1908.[9]

BIBLIOGRAPHICAL NOTE

The works of Fish, Latané, and Garner cited in the bibliographical note at the end of Chapter 12 contain useful material concerning the relations of the United States and Latin-America. These should be supplemented by W. S. Robertson, *Hispanic-American Relations with the United States* (1923); A. C. Coolidge, *The United States as a World Power* (1908); C. L. Jones, *Caribbean Interests of the United States* (1916); G. H. Stuart, *Latin-America and the United States* (rev. ed., 1928); S. G. Inman, *Problems in Pan-Americanism* (1922); G. H. Blakeslee, *Recent Foreign Policy of the United States* (1926). For the evolution of the Monroe Doctrine consult D. Y. Thomas, *One Hundred Years of the Monroe Doctrine* (1923); and A. B. Hart, *The Monroe Doctrine: An Interpretation* (1916).

For a discussion of the Venezuelan policy of Roosevelt see J. F. Rhodes, *The McKinley and Roosevelt Administrations* (1922); J. B. Bishop, *Theodore Roosevelt and His Times* (1920); H. C. Hill, *Roosevelt and the Caribbean* (1927).

On Panama and the isthmian canal see Bishop and Rhodes

---

[9] In 1916 the United States added to her interests in the Caribbean by the purchase of the Virgin Islands from Denmark for $25,000,000.

mentioned above and J. H. Latané, *America as a World Power* (1907).

On American intervention in Haiti, Santo Domingo, and Nicaragua consult Blakeslee, cited above, and C. P. Howland, *Survey of American Foreign Relations, 1929* (1929).

CHAPTER 20

THE UNITED STATES AS A WORLD POWER (*Cont.*)

In 1876 Porfirio Diaz, a pure-blooded Indian, gained control of the government of Mexico. During the following thirty-four years, with the exception of a single term of four years, he occupied the presidential office and enjoyed substantially dictatorial powers. Under the Diaz régime law and order prevailed throughout Mexico; banditry was virtually abolished; the railroad mileage was increased from 400 to 15,000; the foreign credit of the country was greatly improved; mines were opened, and factories were built. While these conditions were highly pleasing to the small ruling class, and to foreign investors, the mass of the Indian peons, who constituted about three-quarters of the population, enjoyed little of the seeming prosperity of the country. Most of the land in Mexico was held in large estates, and the peons who cultivated the soil were in a condition bordering on slavery. The development of mines, oil wells, and railroads gave rise to an industrial proletariat whose condition was little better than that of the agricultural peasant.

So long as Diaz retained his health and vigor his dictatorial system worked, but with advancing age his grip upon the governmental machine relaxed, and various politicians appeared upon the scene as expectant successors. Finally, in 1911, the break came. Under the leadership of Francisco Madero, a sincere but unpractical theorist, there was started a revolutionary movement which spread rapidly to various parts of the republic. Unable to stem the rising tide of revolution, Diaz resigned and retired to Europe. Madero entered

Mexico City and in the election that followed he was chosen President by a large majority.

It is doubtful whether, even under the most favorable conditions, Madero could have realized the program of political and social reform that he had promulgated. And conditions were far from favorable. Madero lacked the ability to control the revolutionary forces that he had aroused. Then, too, the economic groups that had flourished under the Diaz régime quite naturally resisted his efforts at reform, especially the proposal to divide the large landed estates. For two years Madero retained a somewhat precarious hold upon the presidential office until General Huerta, who was in command of the military forces of the Republic, staged a *coup d'état*. Madero and Vice President Suarez were seized and later murdered in cold blood, and a provisional government was established with Huerta in control. These events occurred just before President Wilson assumed office in March, 1913.

Many foreign financial interests in Mexico looked with favor upon Huerta, apparently with the hope that he might prove to be a second Diaz. Most of the European governments promptly extended recognition to the Huerta régime, and similar action by the United States was urged by the American ambassador in Mexico City. But President Wilson would not be hurried. In a statement issued one week after his inauguration he said, "We hold, as I am sure all thoughtful leaders of republican governments hold, that just government rests always upon the consent of the governed, and that there can be no freedom without order based upon law and upon the public conscience and approval. We shall look to make these principles the basis of mutual intercourse, respect, and helpfulness between our sister republics and ourselves. We shall lend our influence of every kind to the realization of these principles in fact and practice, knowing that disorder, personal intrigue, and defiance of constitutional rights weaken and discredit government. . . . We can have no sympathy with those who seek to seize the power of government to advance their own personal interests and ambition." Here was a clear warning to the Spanish-American states that Wilson proposed to discourage military *coups d'état* by declining to recognize governments not established by constitutional methods.

Acting upon this determination, President Wilson declined to recognize the Huerta régime, and suggested that a free election should be held in which Huerta should not be a candidate for President. Quite naturally this proposal was rejected by Huerta and then President Wilson inaugurated his policy of "watchful waiting," convinced that the failure to obtain American recognition would be fatal to Huerta. Encouraged by the attitude of the United States, revolutionary leaders such as Carranza and Villa instigated revolts in various parts of Mexico. On April 9, 1914, an incident occurred at the port of Tampico that added greatly to the difficulties of the Mexican president. Some of the crew of the U.S.S. *Dolphin,* who had landed to purchase supplies, were arrested by a Mexican officer. When General Huerta learned of this action he ordered the release of the prisoners and expressed his regret, but declined to meet the demand of Admiral Mayo for a salute to the United States flag. President Wilson upheld Admiral Mayo, and when Huerta persisted in his refusal the President ordered the American fleet to establish a pacific blockade of the eastern Mexican coast. This was followed by the seizure of the port of Vera Cruz to prevent the landing of a consignment of arms for the Huerta forces. At this juncture, when war between the United States and Mexico seemed imminent, the representatives of Argentine, Brazil, and Chile tendered their good offices to effect a settlement of the difficulty. This offer was accepted by the United States, and Huerta, harassed by enemies both from within and from without, could not refuse. The revolutionary leaders were also requested to suspend hostilities and send representatives to a conference at Niagara Falls, but Carranza, anticipating the speedy fall of Huerta and his own accession to power, declined to accept the proposal. After deliberating six weeks the conference adjourned without any practical accomplishment save to convince the leading South American states that the United States had no desire to ride roughshod over its unfortunate southern neighbor. Shortly after the conference ended Huerta gave up the struggle and Carranza took over the hazardous job of ruling Mexico.

Hardly had Carranza been seated in the presidential chair when his erstwhile fellow revolutionist Villa started a revolt in the northern provinces. Other leaders followed his example, and in a short time chaotic conditions prevailed throughout the country. President Wilson once more turned to the leading states of Spanish-America and a joint note was signed by the representatives of the United States, Argentine, Brazil, Chile, Bolivia, Uruguay, and Guatemala, calling upon the various Mexican factions to join in the establishment of a constitutional government in Mexico. Villa accepted the proposal, but Carranza, who was rapidly regaining control of a large part of the country, declined to sanction what he was pleased to consider outside interference in the internal affairs of Mexico. Carranza's continued success, however, led the representatives of the Spanish-American states to recommend his recognition, and this suggestion President Wilson finally accepted.

Angered by the success of his rival, Villa determined to force the intervention of the United States in Mexico. In January, 1916, a band of Mexican outlaws seized a train and shot in cold blood eighteen Americans who were on board. This outrage was followed on March 9th by a raid made by Villa on the town of Columbus, New Mexico, resulting in the death of seventeen Americans. President Wilson immediately ordered General Pershing to pursue the bandits into Mexico and capture or destroy them. President Carranza gave unwilling consent to this expedition, but showed no desire to coöperate with the Americans. As Pershing's forces penetrated farther and farther into Mexican territory the attitude of the Mexican government became increasingly hostile. The situation reached a critical stage on June 21, when a pitched battle was fought between the Americans and the Carranza forces in which twenty-one American soldiers were killed and a number were taken prisoners. President Wilson immediately ordered 150,000 troops to the Mexican border, and war between the countries seemed imminent. At this juncture Carranza agreed to release the American prisoners and to submit the matters in dispute to a joint conference. At this conference a protocol was signed which provided for the withdrawal of the American forces from Mexico within forty days, provided no new raids should occur in the meantime, the United States reserving the right to cross the border in pursuit of bandits. Claims for damages were left for future negotiations. Despite the fact that the Carranza government did not ratify this agreement, the American forces were withdrawn from Mexico in February, 1917. The resumption of unrestricted submarine warfare by Germany at this time followed by the severance of diplomatic relations between the United States and that country, diverted the attention of the Washington administration for the time being from Mexican affairs.

Freed for the moment from the menace of foreign intervention, the Mexican government turned its attention to internal problems. In February, 1917, a convention was called to draft a new constitution. The instrument that was accepted by this body contained a number of drastic provisions concerning land ownership, the control of natural resources, religious organizations, and the regulation of industry. There was written into the fundamental law of the land a complete code of social legislation, providing for the eight-hour day; regulation of the employment of women and children; minimum wage scales; old age, sickness, life, and unemployment insurance; and measures for the settlement of industrial disputes. All church property was declared to belong to the nation and all schools and charitable institutions were brought under the control of the civil authorities.

The provisions of the new constitution which attracted most concern in foreign countries and especially in the United States were those dealing with the ownership of land and natural resources. Article XXVII provided that measures should be taken to divide large landed estates. The ownership of all sub-surface mineral deposits was declared to be in the nation and to be inalienable. Only Mexicans by birth or naturalization, and Mexican companies, could acquire ownership in lands, waters, and their appurtenances, or obtain concessions to develop mines or fuel deposits in the Republic. The nation might grant these rights to foreigners, provided they would agree to be considered Mexicans in respect to such rights and not to invoke the protection of their governments concerning such rights. Further, within a zone of 100 kilometers of the frontiers and 50 kilometers of the coasts, no foreigner could under any condition acquire direct ownership of lands or waters.

Despite the fact that the constitution stated that "no law shall be given retroactive effect to the injury of any person whatsoever," American financial interests with large investments in Mexico felt that their property rights were seriously menaced. The state department at Washington, in spite of its preoccupation with the European war, sent a vigorous protest to the Mexican government against the enforcement of any regulations that would confiscate the property rights of American citizens. An organization called the Association for the Protection of American Rights in Mexico was formed, with strong financial backing, which carried on a widespread newspaper agitation in favor of the oil interests. Anti-Mexican sentiment in this country was also stimulated by many persons who felt that the provisions of the Mexican constitution relating to church property threatened the historic rights of the Catholic Church and in effect would result in religious persecution.

Carranza had aroused strong foreign opposition, and he had not succeeded in stabilizing conditions at home. Only a feeble effort was made to inaugurate the ambitious program of social reform, and the economic conditions in the country remained unsatisfactory, while the President devoted his attention to perpetuating his control of the government. Although the constitution forbade his reëlection, Carranza determined to choose his successor and assure his election through governmental control of the elections. His plans were frustrated, however, by a combination of Mexican leaders who raised the standard of revolt and forced Carranza to flee from the capital. In his effort to leave the country Carranza was assassinated by a treacherous guard. At the ensuing election General Obregon was chosen president and President Wilson was again confronted with the problem of recognizing a régime that had seized power by revolution, accompanied by assassination. However, as he was approaching the end of his term as President, Wilson decided to pass the question on to his successor.

The Republican administration that came into office as a result of the election of 1920 was apparently not greatly concerned about the methods by which Obregon had obtained control in Mexico, but it was determined not to extend recognition to the Obregon government until a satisfactory agreement had been reached in regard to American property rights in Mexico. For two years the two governments debated the issue. In May, 1923, a settlement was reached on the questions of the foreign debt, indemnity for confiscated lands, and the oil concessions. Following this agreement the

Obregon government was formally recognized by the United States. In 1924, for the first time in a dozen years, a presidential election was held in Mexico, unaccompanied by revolution, and the presidential office passed peacefully from General Obregon to Señor Calles.

Despite the apparent settlement of the oil controversy in 1923, the issue flared up again in 1926 with the issuance of presidential regulations by the Mexican executive concerning the operation of the petroleum law. Among other things these regulations required that all owners of land who had acquired their titles before May 1, 1917 (the date of the promulgation of the new Mexican constitution), should exchange these titles for Government "concessions" running for fifty years. The United States authorities insisted that this requirement would result in the confiscation of American property rights. A number of the oil companies declined to comply with the regulation and when the Mexican authorities withdrew their drilling permits they appealed to the Mexican Supreme Court. In November, 1927, the Court rendered an opinion upholding the claims of the oil companies and declared two of the important articles of the petroleum law unconstitutional. This decision greatly eased the tension between the two countries and apparently pointed the way to a final adjustment of the long-standing controversy.

PAN-AMERICANISM AND THE PAN-AMERICAN CONFERENCES

As has been noted, chiefly through the activity of James G. Blaine there met in Washington in 1889 the first Pan-American Conference.[1] While few of the measures discussed at this conference were immediately realized, there is no doubt that a gathering of all of the American republics on a basis of equality produced a favorable reaction among the states of Central and South America. The most important

[1] See p. 223.

concrete accomplishment of this first conference was the establishment at Washington of a Bureau of American Republics, later known as the Pan-American Union. This organization is maintained by the twenty-one American republics and its governing body is composed of the Secretary of State of the United States and the diplomatic representatives in Washington of the twenty other American nations.[2] It gathers and distributes information of all kinds concerning the material and cultural development of the American republics.

The second Pan-American Conference was held at Mexico City in 1901, the third at Rio de Janeiro in 1906, and the fourth at Buenos Aires in 1910. At each of these gatherings chief consideration was given to proposals for developing the commercial relations among the nations on this continent. A fifth conference was to have been held in 1914, but the outbreak of the war in Europe caused its postponement and it did not finally meet until 1923, at Santiago, Chile. In the interval between the meeting of the fourth and fifth conferences much water had flowed under the bridges. It was during these years that the Caribbean policy of the United States was fully disclosed. The "Dollar Diplomacy" of Secretary Knox, the intervention in and financial control of Haiti, Santo Domingo, and Nicaragua; and the long-drawn-out controversy between the United States and Mexico, gave rise to serious misgivings among the statesmen in Spanish American countries concerning the ultimate aims of this country. Moreover, the various statements made by leading American statesmen did little to clarify the situation or to reassure our neighbors to the south. When former President Roosevelt visited South America in 1913 he expressed the view that the Monroe Doctrine should no longer be maintained exclusively by the United States but should be upheld as a joint obligation of all of the nations on this continent.

[2] Later changed by the sixth conference.

"All nations," he said, "which are sufficiently advanced, such as Brazil and the United States, should participate on an absolute equality in the responsibilities and development of this doctrine so far as the interests of the western hemisphere as a whole are concerned. It must be made a continental and not a unilateral doctrine." Ex-President Taft afterward stated in a public address that he agreed with the view of Roosevelt. Similarly President Wilson in an address to a group of Mexican editors said, "Let us have a common guarantee, that all of us will sign, of political independence and territorial integrity. Let us agree that if any one of us, the United States included, violates the political independence or territorial integrity of any of the others, all the others will jump on her." On the other hand Mr. Wilson said in January, 1916, "The Monroe Doctrine was proclaimed by the United States on her own authority. It has always been maintained, and always will be maintained, upon her own responsibility." Likewise Mr. Elihu Root expressed the view that the Monroe Doctrine could not be "transmuted into a joint or common declaration by American states or any number of them." In face of these divergent views of men who at one time or another had controlled the foreign policy of the United States it is not astonishing that statesmen and publicists in Latin American countries were bewildered and concerned about the precise meaning of this much discussed but vaguely defined Doctrine. To many it appeared that Monroe's famous pronouncement had been adjusted to meet the exigencies of various incidents to which it had been applied.

Then, too, it must not be forgotten that the Great War and its aftermath brought an important change in the relation of the Spanish American states to world affairs. Most of these states had followed the United States into the war against Germany and were represented at the peace conference, however little influence they may have had upon the decisions of that body. Moreover, eighteen of the twenty

Latin American republics became members of the League of Nations and representatives from these countries have met at Geneva on a basis of equality with the representatives of the great European nations. The Presidents of three recent League Assemblies were Latin Americans, and three of the fourteen members of the League Council at present (1929) come from Latin America. Of the eleven judges of the Permanent Court of International Justices, two are from Latin America. It is in the nature of things that this participation in world affairs would give rise to an increased national consciousness and dignity among the Latin American states and to a feeling of resentment against any effort on the part of the United States to control their destinies.

It was under these changed conditions that the fifth Pan-American Conference met at Santiago in 1923. It was apparent before the Conference assembled that it would not confine its attention to the more or less innocuous questions that had been presented to previous Conferences. On its program were a number of important and complicated political problems, such as disarmament, proposals for an American League of Nations, a possible modification of the Monroe Doctrine, and a reorganization of the Pan-American Union. The conference accomplished little in solving these thorny questions. When the President of Uruguay presented a plan for an American League of Nations it was received coldly by the delegates from the United States, and the proposal was not pressed. A suggestion made by the Uruguayan delegation for a consideration of the Monroe Doctrine brought a blunt statement from the chairman of the United States delegation that the Monroe Doctrine was a unilateral policy of the United States, to be interpreted and enforced by it alone. The Costa Rican delegation submitted a proposal to have representatives to the Pan-American Union appointed directly instead of having the various diplomatic representatives at Washington act as such representatives. It was urged that a state that had failed to receive the recognition of the United States was thereby deprived of representation in the Union. It was further argued that diplomatic representatives at Washington were not free, as representatives in the Union, to criticize the policy of the government to which they were accredited. After a prolonged discussion it was agreed to have the diplomatic representatives continue as members of the governing board of the Union and to allow any country not having a diplomatic representative at Washington to appoint a special representative to the Union. It was further provided that the governing board should thereafter select its president instead of having the Secretary of State of the United States hold this position *ex officio*.

Shortly after the Santiago Conference, Secretary of State Hughes, with the evident desire to clarify if possible the confusion that appeared in the minds of many Latin Americans as to our present interpretation of the Monroe Doctrine, made two notable addresses on the occasion of the celebration of the hundredth anniversary of the issuance of the Doctrine. He frankly admitted that the Spanish American Republics no longer feared encroachments and control from European powers, but that they looked with apprehension at the formidable strength of the United States. He then stated that the Monroe Doctrine had not been changed in any essential respect since its first declaration. In only two particulars had modifications been made: (1) "What was said with Europe exclusively in view must be deemed equally applicable to all non-American powers," and (2) the opposition to the extension of European colonization has been extended to embrace opposition to acquisition of additional territory through voluntary transfer of dominion or sovereignty. Hughes proceeded to define the Doctrine to mean opposition "(1) to any non-American nation encroaching upon the political independence of American states under any guise, and (2) to the acquisition in any manner of the

control of additional territory in this hemisphere by any
non-American power." It will be noted that this definition
does not preclude the possibility of the United States adding
to its territorial possessions at the expense of its neighbors or
of encroaching upon their political independence. And this is
precisely what the countries of Latin America fear. It is
true that Hughes went on to state that "the Monroe Doctrine is not a policy of aggression; it is a policy of self-
defense," and that it does not aim to infringe upon the independence and sovereignty of other American states or attempt
to establish a protectorate over them. Nevertheless he insisted
that as the Doctrine "is distinctively the policy of the United
States, the government of the United States reserves to itself
its definition, interpretation, and application." Hughes made
the further significant statement that "the Monroe Doctrine
as a particular declaration in no way exhausts American right
or policy; the United States has rights and obligations that
that doctrine does not define. And in the unsettled condition of certain countries in the region of the Caribbean it
has been necessary to assert these rights and obligations as
well as the limited principles of the Monroe Doctrine." In
other words the United States affirms the right to exercise in
the Caribbean area a control beyond that contemplated in
other parts of Spanish America.

The sixth Pan-American Conference assembled at Havana
in January, 1928. The American delegation included more
men of distinction than had appeared at any previous conference. Heading the delegation was former Secretary of
State Charles E. Hughes, and other members were Henry
P. Fletcher, American Ambassador to Italy, Dwight W.
Morrow, American Ambassador to Mexico, Judge Morgan
J. O'Brien, and James Brown Scott. To add luster to the
gathering, President Coolidge and Secretary of State Kellogg attended the opening session of the Conference. Delegates from all of the twenty-one states that are members of

the Union were in attendance. At the time the Conference met American marines were 'actively engaged in the effort to suppress the revolution in Nicaragua, and it seemed inevitable that the whole question of the relations of the United States to its southern neighbors would be injected into the debates. The most important questions discussed were the organization and powers of the Pan-American Union, the policy of intervention, tariffs, immigration, and arbitration.[3] A proposal to allow member states to appoint representatives on the governing board of the Union, other than their diplomatic representatives at Washington, was adopted, but the suggestion to enlarge the functions of the Union by conferring upon it political powers was rejected, opposition to this proposal coming not only from the United States but also from Mexico and other states who apparently feared that a strengthened Union might give the United States greater influence in Latin America. The head of the Argentine delegation made an earnest effort to have the Conference adopt resolutions calling for the reduction of tariff barriers between the nations on this continent but the vigorous opposition of the American delegation on the ground that the tariff was purely a domestic question, brought about the rejection of the proposal. Perhaps the most significant discussion at the Conference involved the question of the right of intervention. A delegate from Salvador introduced a resolution proposing that "no state has the right to intervene in the internal affairs of another." This precipitated an animated discussion in which the representatives of several

[3] At a special Pan-American Congress held in Panama City in 1926 to commemorate the hundredth anniversary of the Congress summoned by Simon Bolivar in 1826, a resolution was adopted favoring the formation of an American League of Nations "on the basis of the juridical equality of all States." The United States delegates to the Congress, on instructions from the State Department, declined to discuss or vote on this resolution, on the ground that it was the understanding of this country that the Congress had been called as a ceremonial and commemorative body and "it had not been expected that the Congress would seek to adopt conclusions or make recommendations of a political character."

of the Latin American states earnestly supported the resolution. Hughes, realizing that the proposal was aimed at the
policy of the United States, made a long and vigorous defense of our activities in Latin American countries. He
refuted the charge that this country desired to infringe upon
the independence of any of its neighbors, but insisted that
international law justified interposition by a government for
the purpose of protecting the lives and property of its
nationals. The resolution was finally withdrawn, but the debate had indicated the significance of the issue. The only
action of the Conference which might operate to restrict the
freedom of action of the United States in the future was the
adoption of a resolution which stated that "all aggression
is considered illicit and as such is declared prohibited."

The Havana conference took a further step toward the
peaceful adjustment of disputes between nations on the
American continent in providing for a subsequent conference
of American states for the purpose of drafting treaties of
arbitration and conciliation. Pursuant to this action representatives of twenty of the twenty-one republics assembled at
Washington on December 10, 1928. After three weeks of
discussion the Conference adopted two treaties, one providing for the compulsory arbitration of all disputes of a
juridical nature and the other for the submission to conciliation commissions of all disputes not deemed suitable for
arbitration. Questions submitted to arbitration are to be
referred to the World Court, the Hague Tribunal, or to a
special tribunal selected by the parties to the dispute. Questions referred to conciliation are to be submitted to one of
the two permanent committees of diplomats, one at Monte-
video and the other at Washington, which were provided by
the fifth Pan-American Conference. The only matters excepted from the arbitration convention are domestic questions "not controlled by international law" and questions
affecting states not parties to the convention. On the assump-

tion that these treaties are ratified [4] and loyally carried out it is not too much to hope that they will go a long way toward preventing a recurrence of such unfortunate incidents as our recent exploits in Haiti, Santo Domingo and Nicaragua.

It is doubtful whether the earnest efforts of Hughes either before or at the Conference contributed much toward dispelling the fear and suspicion of the purposes of the United States held by Latin Americans; nor have they served to advance the sentiment of Pan-Americanism which American statesmen have so earnestly advocated. It must not be forgotten that the cultural inheritance of Latin America comes from Europe, not from the United States. These countries have many spiritual and sentimental ties with European nations, notably France and Spain, and every effort has been made by statesmen and publicists of these nations to strengthen such ties. Then, too, as we have seen, the membership of the Central and South American states in the League of Nations has created a political bond with Europe. Already a number of disputes between Latin American states have come before the League and although the Council of the League in each instance has sought to avoid assuming jurisdiction, out of deference to the United States, it is by no means certain that this policy will be continued indefinitely. It is quite possible, moreover, that some of the Latin American countries may demand that the League fulfill the obligations to its members defined in the Covenant.

Herein lies a real challenge to Pan-Americanism and the continuance of this ideal as a vital force would seem to depend largely upon the attitude of the United States. The situation calls for a sympathetic understanding on our part of the ideals and problems of Latin American countries and

[4] The first of these treaties was ratified by the United States Senate early in 1929.

the avoidance of a spirit of condescension in our dealings with them.[5]

AMERICAN INTERESTS IN THE PACIFIC

In the two decades before the Civil War the United States had coöperated with the European Powers in forcing Japan and China to open their ports to the commerce of the West. These two countries met the impact of Western civilization in quite different ways. While China clung to her ancient civilization and resisted every effort of the Western powers to enter her domain, Japan, on the other hand, determined that the best way to meet the challenge of the West was to adopt Western methods. As a result Japan, in the last quarter of the nineteenth century, passed through a remarkable transformation. The economic life of the nation was reorganized, following European experience, and an army and navy were created patterned after the latest European models. By the close of the nineteenth century, therefore, Japan was in a po-

---

[5] During his tour of Latin American countries just before he assumed office, President Hoover said in one of his addresses, "There are no older and younger brothers on the American continent. They are all friendly and equal states of a great continent. . . . The fear of some persons concerning supposed intervention ideas of the United States are unfounded." Literally interpreted this statement would seem to indicate a new and more hopeful interpretation of the Monroe Doctrine. In March, 1930, the State Department issued a memorandum in which the effort was once more made to clarify the meaning of the Monroe Doctrine. It was stated that the activities of the United States in recent years in Cuba, the Dominican Republic, Haiti and Nicaragua do not fall within the Monroe Doctrine as originally proclaimed but "may be accounted for as an expression of a national policy, which, like the Doctrine itself, originates in the necessities of security and self-preservation." It was further asserted that the Doctrine "states a case of the United States vs. Europe, and not of the United States vs. Latin America." At the same time the memorandum set forth that the Doctrine was purely unilateral and that the United States alone should determine when and if the principles of the Doctrine are violated and what measures should be taken to vindicate it. It is difficult to see how this statement can allay the fears of Latin-American states. After all it makes little practical difference whether we intervene in their affairs under the terms of the Monroe Doctrine or by virtue of "an expression of a national policy."

sition not only to resist the imperialistic encroachments of European powers but also to dispute with them the economic domination of the Asiatic continent.

China's effort to maintain her oriental exclusiveness proved futile. On one pretext or another the European powers seized parts of her vast dominions or staked out "spheres of influences" in the great sprawling Empire. France appropriated a large slice in Indo-China; Great Britain from her vantage point at Hong Kong obtained control of the trade of Canton; the great Russian "bear" pushed on irresistibly from Siberia into Manchuria and Mongolia; Japan, in 1895, now well advanced in her process of "Westernization," joined the scramble in China and after a successful war appropriated Formosa and was only prevented from taking much more by the intervention of Russia, France, and Germany, which countries suddenly became solicitous about the "integrity" of China; Germany took advantage of the murder of two German missionaries to extort from China the port of Kiao-chau and, ultimately, the control of the whole province of Shantung.

These imperialist enterprises in China were in full swing when the United States went to war with Spain. As we have seen, the outcome of this war was to transform the United States into a world power. The acquisition of the Philippines, in particular, stimulated the interest of the American people in the affairs of the Far East. Moreover, it was at this juncture that American business enterprise, which had advanced with giant strides in the preceding decades, began to look for new opportunities in distant places. When American merchants and capitalists began to extend their activities to China they found themselves handicapped by the monopolistic rights which the European governments had staked out for their own nationals. Confronted by this situation, the American government, solicitous for the advancement of American interests in China, had to pursue one of two courses. It could decide to join in the movement for the partitioning of China and obtain for American business interests a part of the spoils. But there was no certainty that public opinion in this country was as yet prepared to approve so bold an imperialist adventure. On the other hand, it might attempt to check the further extension of special economic privileges in China and keep what was left of the Chinese market and Chinese resources open to American business enterprise. The latter alternative the American authorities determined to follow. In September, 1899, John Hay, President McKinley's Secretary of State, sent to the principal European powers and to Japan a communication in which he requested each of them to declare (1) that it would not interfere with any treaty port or vested interest in its so-called sphere of influence; (2) that it would permit the Chinese tariff to continue in force and to be collected by Chinese officials; and (3) that it would not discriminate against other foreigners within its special sphere of influence in the matter of port dues or railway rates. While the replies made by the several countries to this note were somewhat evasive, Mr. Hay stated that he considered their acceptance of the proposals as "final and definitive."

Meanwhile the Chinese took matters into their own hands and struck out blindly against the "foreign devils." Patriotic societies, known as Boxers, sprang up throughout the country. These societies were connived at, if not supported, by the Chinese authorities. An energetic propaganda was carried on against all aliens and in a short time the lives and property of foreigners in many parts of China were endangered. The situation reached a critical stage in June, 1900, when the German minister was killed in a street of Peking. The members of the diplomatic corps, with their families and other foreigners, took refuge in the enclosure of the British legation, where they were besieged by the Chinese forces. When news of the plight of the foreigners reached the outside world a relief expedition consisting of Japanese, British, French, German, and American troops was dispatched to China and after a ten days' march reached the capital and rescued their beleaguered nationals. The foreign troops, with the possible exception of the Americans and the British, then indulged in an orgy of looting and murder, which equaled, if it did not surpass, the outrages of the Boxers.

When it came to exacting an indemnity from China some of the European powers desired to take advantage of this opportunity to dismember the empire still more; but Secretary Hay insisted that a solution should be sought which, while it assured the protection of foreigners in China, would secure the integrity of the empire and "safeguard for the world the principle of equal and impartial trade with all parts of the Chinese empire." In the end the American view prevailed and the foreign powers contented themselves with levying a huge indemnity of $334,000,000 upon China. The amount assigned to the United States was $24,000,000, but, when it was found later that this was just about double the amount of the damage sustained by American citizens, Congress authorized the return of the excess to China to be set aside as a fund to be used for the education of Chinese students in American universities.

Despite the efforts of Secretary Hay to check foreign aggression in China the great powers showed no intention of surrendering the privileges that they had extorted from this unhappy country nor, indeed, of abandoning their attempts to extend their control. Russia retained her troops in Manchuria after the Boxer uprising with the intention of making this Chinese province a Russian sphere of influence. Great Britain and Japan, aroused by the Russian advance, joined hands in a defensive treaty of alliance in 1902, by the terms of which each nation recognized the special rights of the other in China and agreed to support the other in case of an attack by two or more other powers.

With this assurance that in case of war she would not again be subjected to the humiliation that she had suffered in 1895, Japan assumed a more determined attitude in face of the Russian threat. In 1904 she submitted a number of proposals to Russia by which the respective interests of the two countries in northern China were to be delimited and recognized. When Russia declined to agree to these proposals Japan promptly declared war. Not only did Japan have the assurance of British support in case any other power joined Russia in the war, but President Roosevelt privately warned the French and German authorities that, if either of those countries intervened on the side of Russia, America would come in on the side of Japan. This was, to say the least, a startling proposal from an American President, in view of the fact that under the Constitution Congress alone has power to declare war.

Fortunately the contingency which would have tested the reality of President Roosevelt's threat did not arise for neither France nor Germany came to the aid of Russia. While Japan won a number of striking victories on land and sea, the war placed a heavy strain upon the financial resources of the nation and when foreign bankers indicated an unwillingness to extend further aid, the Japanese Emperor turned to President Roosevelt with the request that he approach the Russian government and learn whether it was willing to discuss peace terms. Having obtained a satisfactory reply from Russia, Roosevelt invited the representatives of the two powers to meet at Portsmouth, New Hampshire, in the summer of 1905. In the peace negotiations that followed the President played an important part. He persuaded the government of Japan to abandon its demand for a large indemnity, an action which aroused bitter resentment among the Japanese people. On the other hand Japan received the Russian concession at Port Arthur and Dairen, as well as the control of the South Manchurian railroad in addition to the southern half of the island of Sakhalin.

President Roosevelt did not restrict his diplomatic activities in the Far East to the restoration of peace between Japan and Russia. He entered into secret negotiations with Japan and agreed to recognize Japanese control of Korea in return for Japanese recognition of American dominion in the Philippines. Then with a breezy disregard for constitutional formalities he assured the Japanese authorities that the American people were "so fully in accord with the people of Japan and Great Britain in the maintenance of peace in the Far East that, whatever occasion arose, appropriate action of the government of the United States, in conjunction with Japan and Great Britain, for such a purpose, could be counted upon by them quite as confidently as if the United States were under treaty obligations."

Whatever unanimity of opinion there may have been among the peoples of these countries in regard to the preservation of peace in the Far East, it is clear that those who shaped national policies in these three nations did not have the same outlook in regard to the Chinese situation. Japan had not fought the war with Russia because of any altruistic desire to maintain the integrity of the Chinese empire or to assure economic equality for the commercial interests of all nations. On the contrary, the Japanese were determined to secure to the full the economic advantage in Manchuria which the fortune of war had brought them. When, therefore, enterprising American interests began to enter this region at the close of the Russo-Japanese war the Japanese quickly forgot their animosity toward their recent enemies and entered into a secret agreement with Russia by which Manchuria was divided into a Russian and a Japanese sphere of influence, and each power agreed to support the other in case of a threat from a third power to their interests in north China.

From official circles in the United States there came distinct encouragement to the policy of promoting American concessions and loans in foreign countries. President Taft and his Secretary of State, Philander C. Knox, earnestly supported the movement which became known as "Dollar Diplomacy." In 1912, a group of international bankers, including prominent American banking interests, were contemplating making a large loan to the recently formed Chinese republic, on condition that the Chinese government would agree to place certain sources of revenue under the control of the banking group as a guarantee for the security of the loan. President Taft favored American participation in this undertaking but before the negotiations could be completed Taft's term as President had ended. With the advent of the Wilson administration in 1913 there came a temporary check to the program of "Dollar Diplomacy" which his immediate predecessors had supported. When President Wilson was asked to give official sanction to the participation of American bankers in a projected international loan to China he declined to do so. On the other hand when Japan in 1915 sought to take advantage of the preoccupation of the European powers in the Great War to strengthen her grip upon China Mr. Wilson vigorously protested. Japan submitted to China a series of demands, the most important of which were that China should transfer to Japan Germany's former rights in the Shantung peninsula; recognize Japan's special rights in Southern Manchuria; grant monopolistic rights to a Japanese-Chinese coal and iron company; refuse to cede to any third power any harbor, or island; allow Japan to have control of Chinese police; employ Japanese political advisers and purchase yearly from Japan a fixed amount of munitions. The United States government promptly notified Japan that it would not recognize any of these demands, which violated our treaty rights, the territorial integrity of China, or the principle of the "open door." Nevertheless Wilson, two years later, authorized the signing of the Lansing-Ishii agreement, which provided that "the governments of the United States and Japan recognize that territorial propinquity creates special relations between countries, and consequently the government of the United States recognizes that Japan has special interests in China, particularly in the part to which her possessions are contiguous." The agreement went on to state that both nations wished to preserve the independence and territorial integrity of China and that "they are opposed to the acquisition by any government of any special rights that would deny to the subjects or citizen of any country full enjoyment of equal opportunity for commerce and industry in China." The language of this agreement was decidedly ambiguous and offered serious possibilities of friction between the two governments concerning its meaning.

At the Peace Conference at the close of the Great War Japan determined to reap her rewards in the Far East. She insisted that the Conference should ratify the agreement which she had forced upon China in 1915 by which Germany's rights in Shantung were to be transferred to Japan. Wilson reluctantly agreed to this proposal after the Japanese representatives assured him verbally that Japan would restore the political sovereignty of China in Shantung and would retain only the economic privileges that Germany had enjoyed there.

When the political seers both in this country and abroad surveyed the world situation at the close of the Great War the prediction was freely made that the next great struggle would take place in the Pacific, with the United States and Japan as protagonists. To these observers it appeared inevitable that Japan's increased prestige in the Far East which the fortunes of war had brought would lead sooner or later to a clash with the United States. If Japan was to realize

fully the economic advantages which she cherished in China
it was difficult to see how this could be accomplished without
violating the principle of the open door which the United
States had proclaimed.

It was for the purpose, among other things, of checking
the growing feeling of suspicion and animosity between this
country and Japan that President Harding summoned the
Washington conference in 1921. While the stated object of
the conference was to reach an international agreement on
the limitation of naval armaments it was clearly recognized
that no such agreement was possible unless some of the
causes of international friction which make navies necessary
were cleared away. It was with this thought in mind that the
President coupled the questions of the Far East and the
Pacific with that of armament limitation in his call for the
Conference. Invitations to the Conference were sent to
Great Britain, France, Italy, and Japan, while China, Belgium, Holland, and Portugal were requested to send delegates to participate in the discussion concerning Pacific and
Far Eastern questions.

The work of the Conference in relation to naval armaments will be considered in a later chapter.[6] At this point we
shall note what was done at the Conference to clear the international atmosphere in the Far East. Great Britain and Japan
had been in a defensive alliance since 1902. With the growing
estrangement between the United States and Japan in the
years following the Great War many persons in Great
Britain, and more particularly in the British Dominions, expressed concern about Great Britain's obligations to Japan
in case of a war between that country and the United States.
There was a strong feeling in both Canada and Australia in
favor of Great Britain's abrogating the Japanese treaty.
However, to do so, without offering some alternative might
be taken as an affront by Japan. A solution was finally

6 See p. 559.

reached at the Washington Conference whereby a Four-Power treaty was substituted for the Anglo-Japanese treaty.

By the terms of this compact Great Britain, France, Japan, and the United States agreed "to respect their rights in relation to their insular possessions and insular dominions in the region of the Pacific Ocean." In case these rights should be threatened by the aggressive action of any other power the contracting parties agreed to "communicate with one another fully and frankly in order to arrive at an understanding as to the most efficient measures to be taken, jointly or separately, to meet the exigencies of the particular situation." Senator Lodge and Mr. Hughes had some difficulty in convincing the Senate that this compact did not bind the United States to guarantee and protect the imperial holdings of Great Britain, France and Japan in the Far East.

In dealing with the specific problems of China the conference succeeded, through private negotiations between the Chinese and Japanese representatives, in bringing about a solution of the Shantung question, by which Japan agreed to carry out its promise to restore the territorial sovereignty of China in this province. Agreements were also reached to restore to China a measure of the sovereign rights that had been impaired by the encroachments of foreign powers. China was to be allowed to increase somewhat tariff duties levied on foreign imports; a commission was to be appointed to study the administration of justice in China with a view to abolishing extraterritorial rights of foreigners; and the powers agreed to arrange to abandon their postal agencies in China and to take steps to provide a unified railway system under Chinese control. Finally the contracting powers once more solemnly pledged themselves to respect the territorial integrity and independence of China and to recognize the principle of the "open door." The attempt made by the American representatives at the conference to persuade the other powers to surrender existing privileges in China met with no success. In short, past aggressions were condoned with the understanding that they would not be repeated.

In general the Washington Conference served a useful purpose in removing, in a measure, the feeling of suspicion between this country and Japan, which had assumed rather alarming proportions in the years following the war. Then, too, the abrogation of the British-Japanese alliance was welcomed both in this country and in the British dominions as removing a possible cause of trouble in the future between the two English-speaking nations. A further contribution to Japanese-American accord was made by Hughes, in April, 1923, when he succeeded in persuading the Japanese government to cancel the troublesome Lansing-Ishii agreement.

ANTI-JAPANESE LEGISLATION

In addition to the rival interests of the United States and Japan in the Far East there were other causes of friction between these countries arising from the domestic legislation of a number of our western states. Japanese immigration to the United States began to assume considerable proportions after 1900. According to the Federal census of that year there were 24,326 Japanese in this country, chiefly located in the states of the Pacific coast. By 1910 their numbers had increased to 72,157, and by 1920 to 111,010. As their numbers grew the antagonism formerly directed against the Chinese shifted to the Japanese. In fact, the opposition to the Japanese was not confined, as in the case of the Chinese, to the forces of organized labor. Unlike the Chinese the Japanese were not satisfied to remain permanently in menial positions. They were more energetic and ambitious than the Chinese, more eager to acquire land and to educate their children, and they entered more actively into competition with the whites in agriculture and in industry. As a result, many middle class white farmers and business men joined

the laboring classes in the agitation against the Japanese.
In 1906 the California representatives in Congress proposed to introduce a bill to exclude all Japanese immigration
to this country. When President Roosevelt heard of this
move, he vigorously opposed it. Obviously it was not politic
to deal as haughtily with the Japanese as we had done with
the Chinese. The Japanese were a sensitive people, proud of
their country's marvelous development, and their victorious
war with the great Russian Empire at this time greatly enhanced their national pride. Clearly the situation called for
tact on our part.

With a view to checking Congressional action in the mat-
ter, President Roosevelt entered into negotiations with the
Japanese government as a result of which a "Gentlemen's
Agreement" was reached by which Japan undertook to stop
further immigration of Japanese laborers to the United
States by refusing to grant such persons passports, provided
that the United States would not pass an exclusion law.
Although this agreement moderated the agitation on the
Pacific coast, it did not by any means solve the problem. In
October, 1906, the San Francisco School Board adopted a
regulation requiring all Japanese, Chinese, and Korean
students to be segregated in special oriental schools. The
Japanese resented this action as an affront to their national
dignity. While President Roosevelt denounced the move of
the California authorities as "a wicked absurdity," he could
not prevent it in view of the fact that under our Federal system of government the control of education rests with the
states. In 1909 several more anti-Japanese bills were introduced in the California legislature, but at the earnest request of President Roosevelt they were not pressed. Again,
in 1911, the attack was renewed and once more the national
administration intervened to check it. Finally, in 1913, the
California legislature declined to heed any longer the pleas
of the national administration and enacted a law that pro-

hibited aliens ineligible to citizenship from owning agricultural land in the state or leasing such land for a longer period than three years. A similar restriction was to be applied to corporations in which a majority of the stock was owned by aliens ineligible to citizenship. In an effort to evade these laws many Japanese having children born in this country and hence citizens, transferred title to their property to their children. To meet this situation a further restrictive law was passed, in 1920, which prohibited aliens ineligible to citizenship from acting as guardians for minor children holding property which such aliens could not hold, and further withdrew from such aliens the limited leasing right allowed by the act of 1913. Other western states adopted similar anti-Japanese legislation.

Not content with these restrictive measures, the anti-Japanese leaders determined to force the abrogation of the "Gentlemen's Agreement," although it was generally conceded that Japan had lived up loyally to its terms. The opportunity for such action came in connection with the general immigration bill of 1924. This bill proposed to admit to this country in any one year not more than 2 per cent. of the number of immigrants from any country who were residents of the United States according to the census of 1890. To apply this quota provision to the Japanese would have meant that not more than one hundred and forty-six Japanese could have entered the United States in any one year. But the representatives from the western states were not willing to have even this negligible number of Japanese admitted and they insisted that a provision should be incorporated in the bill excluding all aliens ineligible to citizenship. This was done and the bill passed Congress by a large majority. In signing the measure President Coolidge stated that if the exclusion provision alone had been presented to him he would have disapproved it without hesitation, but that he felt constrained to approve the act because of the urgent need of a comprehensive immigration law.

In Japan the reaction to the exclusion act was immediate and ominous. Anti-American meetings were held throughout the country; the Japanese press denounced the act as an insult to their national honor; a tragic but characteristic protest was made by an unknown Japanese who committed suicide in front of the American embassy in Tokio leaving the statement that his deed was prompted by the humiliation put upon his country by the United States. After the first outburst of indignation the excitement gradually calmed down, but there is no question that the incident tended to nullify much that the Washington Conference had accomplished in removing the causes of friction between Japan and the United States.

THE UNITED STATES AND EUROPE, 1896-1914

In preceding pages we have traced the emergence of the United States as a world power and the remarkable expansion of American interests and activities in North and South America as well as in the Pacific through the opening years of the twentieth century. When we turn to the European scene during these years we do not find a corresponding expansion of American influence. In the momentous events of these critical years in Europe—events that were hastening the great cataclysm of 1914—the United States played an insignificant part. While there were many in this country who argued, with considerable force, that the Spanish war and its aftermath had made the traditional American policy of isolation a mere fiction, there was still a strong feeling among the American people that the logic of these events did not call for any alteration of our policy in relation to Europe. And in general the national administrations during these years pursued a course that reflected the popular aversion to participation in European international complications.

A notable exception to this aloofness from European affairs was the attitude of President Roosevelt in connection with the Moroccan crisis of 1905-1906. In adjusting their rival colonial claims in north Africa Great Britain and France in 1904 reached an agreement by which France was to be given a free hand in Morocco in consideration for abandoning her claims in Egypt and the Egyptian Soudan. When news of this agreement reached Germany, its government entered a vigorous protest. It insisted that Great Britain and France had no right to dispose of the independent country of Morocco without consulting the other powers in Europe, and it demanded that the status of that country be referred to a European congress. To this suggestion France replied with an emphatic refusal, and it was clear that Great Britain was prepared to maintain her bargain with France. As a result a serious European crisis was precipitated, and the press in all leading countries freely predicted a great European war.

In this critical situation the German Kaiser turned to President Roosevelt and requested him to use his influence to persuade France to agree to a conference as the only means of avoiding a great catastrophe. Although the interests of the United States in Morocco were slight the President felt justified in exerting his influence to preserve European peace. He not only persuaded France to agree to a conference, which met at Algeciras, in Spain, in January, 1906, but took an active part in preparing the program for the conference, and sent two American delegates to attend the meetings. Only one or two of Roosevelt's closest advisers knew of the President's activities in the Moroccan dispute, and it was not until 1920 that a full record of the incident was published. This episode cannot be cited as evidence of a change in policy on the part of this country toward European questions. The enterprise was entirely personal on the part of the President and he took great care to preserve the utmost secrecy concerning it. Moreover, when the conclusions of the Algeciras Conference were placed before the Senate for its approval, that body stated that its action in ratifying the work of the conference was not to be construed as a departure from the traditional policy of this country in holding aloof from European complications.

Although the American people at this time showed a decided reluctance to becoming involved in the mazes of European diplomacy there was, nevertheless, a lively interest displayed throughout the country in plans for the peaceful settlement of international disputes. Numerous societies, liberally endowed by men of wealth, were organized for the purpose of furthering the cause of peace. Conferences were held and large quantities of literature were circulated in which various plans for the settlement of international controversies were set forth.

When the Czar of Russia invited the representatives of the leading countries of the world to meet at The Hague in the summer of 1899 to discuss plans for relieving the peoples of Europe from the crushing burden of military armaments, President McKinley accepted the invitation with enthusiasm. At this conference the American delegates took a leading part in formulating plans for the peaceful settlement of international controversies. Three methods of settling such difficulties were agreed upon. The first provided that a neutral country might offer its good offices to disputants to avoid a rupture or, in case war had broken out, to bring hostilities to an end. The second stipulated that either party to a dispute might propose the submission of the question in controversy to an international commission of inquiry. Finally provision was made for the creation of a permanent court of arbitration at The Hague to which international disputes, by agreement, might be submitted. On the vital question of limitation of armaments the conference was unable to reach any agreement. At the second Hague Conference in 1907 the United States was again represented and the American delegates brought forward the question of neutral rights on the high seas in time of war, but the most they were able to accomplish was to have the matter referred to a special naval conference which was ordered to meet in London the following year.

Further evidence of a widespread interest in the pacific adjustment of international controversies was given by the negotiation, in 1904, under the leadership of President Roosevelt, of treaties with France, Great Britain, Germany, Switzerland, and Portugal by which the high contracting parties agreed in advance to submit to the Hague Court all disputes except those which involved "the vital interests, the independence, or the honor" of the contracting parties. When the treaties reached the Senate, however, that body declined to ratify them in the form in which they had been submitted. Some of the Senators from the Southern states feared that under the terms of the treaties foreign holders of repudiated bonds of these states might present their claims to the Hague Court. Furthermore the Senate objected to the use of the word "agreement" in the treaties. The clause in question stated: "In each individual case the high contracting parties, before appealing to the Permanent Court of Arbitration, shall conclude a special agreement defining clearly the matter in dispute." The question arose whether such "agreement" could be made by the President without the consent of the Senate and, when it was learned that President Roosevelt and Secretary Hay so interpreted the clause in question, the Senate insisted upon substituting the word "treaty" for "agreement" which, of course, meant that ratification by the Senate would be necessary in each case before submission to the Hague Court. In the amended form the arbitration treaties were ratified by the Senate, but President Roosevelt refused to transmit them to the other nations because he believed that the treaties as amended would hinder rather than help arbitration. However, Mr. Root, when he succeeded Secretary Hay in 1908, revived the treaties in the form which the Senate had approved and completed the agreements with most of the leading European powers.

In 1911 President Taft negotiated treaties with Great Britain and France extending the principle of arbitration to all "justiciable" questions, but again the Senate amended the treaties in such a way that the President refused to continue the negotiations. When Bryan, who had long been an earnest supporter of the peace movement, became Secretary of State, in 1913, he took up with enthusiasm the task of furthering the movement for arbitration. It was his view that war could be frequently averted if there was some assurance of delay, , after a controversy had arisen between two nations, before hostilities were resorted to. To carry out this idea President Wilson, at the suggestion of Bryan, submitted to all nations having diplomatic representatives at Washington a proposal that agreements should be entered into with the United States by which "all questions of whatever character and nature in dispute between them" should be submitted for investigation and report to an international commission. Bryan suggested that a year be allowed in each case for the commission to make a report and that in the meantime the parties to the dispute should not resort to war or increase their military strength. The suggestion was received with favor by most of the foreign powers and during the year treaties embodying these proposals were negotiated with thirty-one nations and the Senate, with unwonted alacrity, ratified the agreements.

Within less than a year after these promising advances in international good will had been made, all Europe was swept into the greatest war in history. The dreams of the advocates of peace were rudely dispelled and the unselfish efforts of thousands of men and women in all of the civilized nations of the world had apparently been expended in vain.

498   THE UNITED STATES AS A WORLD POWER

BIBLIOGRAPHICAL NOTE

For the relations of the United States and Mexico consult
C. W. Hackett, *The Mexican Revolution and the United States*
(1926); J. F. Rippy, *The United States and Mexico* (1926);
C. Beals, *Mexico: An Interpretation* (1923).
On Pan-Americanism and the Pan-American Conferences see
G. H. Blakeslee, *The Recent Foreign Policy of the United States*
(1925); R. L. Buell, *International Relations* (1925); *Pan-Americanism and The Pan-American Conferences,* Foreign
Policy Association Information Service, Vol. III, No. 19; *The
New Pan-Americanism,* World Peace Foundation Pamphlets,
Vol. VI, No. 1; E. Root, *Latin America and the United States*
(1919).
For American relations in the Pacific see H. K. Norton,
China and the Powers (1927); J. W. Overlach, *Foreign
Financial Control in China* (1919); T. Dennett, *Roosevelt and
the Russo-Japanese War* (1925); W. W. Willoughby, *Foreign
Rights and Interests in China* (1920); T. Dennett, *Americans
in Eastern Asia* (1922). On the relations with Japan consult
S. L. Gulick, *The American-Japanese Problem* (1914); K. K.
Kawakami, *American-Japanese Foreign Relations* (1912); P. J.
Treat, *Japan and the United States* (1928); T. Iyenaga and
K. Sato, *Japan and the California Problem* (1921).
For American relations with Europe between 1900 and 1914
see J. H. Latané, *America as a World Power* (1907); J. B.
Bishop, *Theodore Roosevelt and His Times* (1920); G. H.
Blakeslee, *Recent Foreign Policy of the United States* (1925);
E. E. Robinson and V. J. West, *Foreign Policy of Woodrow
Wilson* (1917).

CHAPTER 21

THE UNITED STATES AND THE WORLD WAR

On June 28, 1914, the Austrian Archduke, Franz Ferdinand, and his wife were assassinated at the little town of Serajevo in Bosnia. The crime was committed by Serbian sympathizers and was an outgrowth of the bitter feeling that had developed between Austria and Serbia because of the annexation of Bosnia by Austria in 1908. The incident immediately aroused the diplomats in all of the leading European countries, for it was realized that any disturbance of the delicate balance of power in the Balkans carried a threat to the peace of Europe. For a month the world watched the maneuvers of the diplomats in the various European chancelleries in their vain efforts to avoid the catastrophe, or at least to escape responsibility if war should come. On July 28 the storm broke when Austria declared war on Serbia. Within a week, because of the intricate system of military alliances, Russia, Germany, France, and Great Britain, were swept into the maelstrom of war.

Among the mass of the people in the United States the first reaction to the European War was one of bewilderment. With the progress made in recent years toward the peaceful settlement of international disputes, many Americans had come to believe that such a calamity as had broken upon Europe was impossible. Not one person in a thousand in this country was familiar with the complex international situation that for years had threatened the peace of that continent. It is true that in informed government circles there were those who realized the gravity of the situation many months before the war started. In the spring of 1914 President Wilson had sent a personal representative, Colonel E. M. House, to Europe to make a study ot the situation and to see if some arrangement could be made to stave off the threatening war. But House found that he could do nothing to prevent the approaching conflagration, and when the conflict started he informed the President that he regarded it as the logical result of the age-old struggle for the balance of power in Europe and that he had little hope that the outcome would lead to any material improvement in the international situation. In these views President Wilson apparently concurred.

The confused state of the public mind in America, regarding the European struggle, coupled with President Wilson's conviction at the time that we were not concerned with the issues that brought on the war, made it perfectly natural for the President to follow our traditional policy and declare American neutrality. This he did in a proclamation issued on August 4, and he followed this a few days later by an appeal to the people of the country to be "neutral in fact as well as in name." Ex-President Roosevelt, who was as well informed as any person in the country concerning the historical background of the war, approved the President's action in declaring neutrality, although a short time afterwards he saw the situation in a different light and bitterly denounced Wilson for his refusal to support the cause of the Allies.

But neutrality "in fact as well as in name" was difficult to maintain. In the first place large numbers of American citizens had come from the nations at war, and it was only natural that their reactions toward the European struggle would be influenced by inherited loyalties. Thus, among Americans of German descent there was outspoken sympathy with the cause of the Teutonic Allies. Many Irish-Americans saw in the war an opportunity to weaken Great Britain and possibly gain Irish independence. Immigrant groups coming from the Allied countries were no less outspoken in their support of the countries from which they had come. To add to the confusion, both belligerent groups turned loose upon the American people a veritable deluge of propaganda in their efforts to influence American opinion. Official spokesmen from the Allied and Teutonic powers were sent to the United States with carefully prepared theses in which were set forth the supposed merits of their respective causes and more particularly the villainy of their opponents. Harrowing tales of German atrocities in Belgium, most of which were later proven to have been fictitious, were spread broadcast throughout this country and came to be widely believed. German apologists countered with the charge that thousands of innocent Germans were starving as a result of Great Britain's illegal blockade policy. In this war of propaganda the advantage lay with the British and French. Their work was better organized and more persistently pressed than was that of the Germans and as a result a great many Americans who had no inherited sympathies one way or the other came to accept the Allied version of the European catastrophe.

Quite apart from the activities of foreign propagandists public opinion in the United States was certain to be affected by the war in Europe because vital American interests, especially economic ones, felt the impact of the gigantic struggle across the Atlantic. The first reaction upon the economic life of the nation was unfavorable. Large amounts of American securities held in the belligerent countries were dumped upon the market and a serious panic was averted by the action of the Exchange authorities in closing the New York Stock Exchange. The shock, however, quickly passed, for it was realized that American business enterprises would be called upon by all of the belligerents to furnish vast quantities of supplies. A wave of war prosperity, therefore, soon struck the country.

The outbreak of hostilities in Europe placed the United States in a position similar to that which prevailed one hundred years before at the time of the Napoleonic wars. In both instances virtually the whole continent of Europe was involved in war and the United States was the chief neutral power capable of furnishing large quantities of supplies to the belligerents. Again, President Wilson was confronted with many of the same problems that had vexed Jefferson, concerning such questions as the right of neutrals to trade with belligerents and other neutrals, the enforcement of a blockade, and the definition of contraband goods. In point of fact all attempts to regulate sea law during the nineteenth century had been resisted by Great Britain, the mistress of the seas, because of her unwillingness to restrict her naval power in time of war. For example, when in 1908 the chief naval powers drafted the Declaration of London, defining contraband of war, that is, goods of military use liable to seizure by belligerents in time of war, Great Britain refused to ratify the agreement, and when the Great War came she exercised her right to determine the list of contraband, which she did by extending it to include virtually every commodity that could conceivably be of military value.

Within a few months after the war broke Great Britain established her complete control of the seas, except insofar as it was interrupted by German submarines and an occasional German commerce destroyer. In her effort to take full advantage of her sea power Great Britain adopted measures that gave rise to strong protests from neutrals, especially from the United States. Among these were the restrictions that she placed upon the shipment of contraband from one neutral country to another. On two sides Germany was bounded by neutral countries that touched the seas. To Holland and the Scandinavian countries contraband goods could be shipped from the United States and from other neutral countries and then be transshipped to Germany. In order to stop this trade Great Britain intercepted contraband shipments between neutral countries and seized the goods if she was satisfied that they were ultimately destined for the enemy. Against this action the United States' authorities entered a vigorous protest, insisting that England had no right to interfere with commerce between neutral countries simply because she suspected that some of the commodities might reach Germany. In reply Great Britain cited the principle of the "continuous voyage" and referred to the action of the United States during the Civil War. At that time the United States' naval authorities had seized goods in transit between Great Britain and Bermuda on the ground that they were ultimately destined for the Confederacy, and this action was upheld by the United States Supreme Court. The British authorities insisted that this precedent justified their seizure of goods en route between the United States and neutral European countries, if they were convinced that the goods' final destination was Germany.

It was not until six months after the outbreak of the war that Great Britain formally proclaimed a blockade of Germany and declared her intention to seize all goods of "presumed enemy destination, ownership, or origin." This raised the question of how such a blockade was to be maintained. Under the accepted rules of international law a blockade to be recognized must be effective, that is, a patrolling fleet of sufficient size must be maintained before the blockaded ports to prevent ships from entering or leaving such ports. But the appearance of the submarine made the maintenance of such a patrolling fleet before the German ports extremely hazardous. To meet this situation Great Britain adopted the policy of keeping a patrolling fleet in the English Channel and another from the northern part of Scotland to the coast of Norway, thus blockading the whole North Sea. The United States objected to this unusual form of blockade, characterizing it as "ineffective, illegal, and indefensible," and pointing out that it would result not only in blockading Germany but also the neutral Scandinavian countries.

Other causes of friction between the United States and Britain developed. Departing from the former practice of searching neutral vessels on the high seas, English naval authorities forced such vessels to enter British harbors to be searched, thus causing annoying delays. Again, the British officials insisted upon opening mail pouches coming from the United States to intercept contraband goods sent by parcel post. Finally the United States objected to the practice of British commanders in raising the American flag on their ships when approaching English ports in order to avoid attack by German submarines. Concerning this practice the British authorities insisted that it was warranted under international law and further cited the precedent of American vessels during the Civil War using the British flag as a ruse to avoid attack by Confederate cruisers.

For more than two years these questions in controversy between the United States and Great Britain gave rise to a voluminous correspondence, which at times threatened the peaceful relations between the two countries. In the end Great Britain made no substantial concessions to the demands of the United States, while on the other hand this country refused to concede the legality of the British actions, possibly with the intention of making a claim for damages when the war was over.[1]

---

[1] By an exchange of notes between the American Secretary of State and the British Ambassador at Washington on May 17, 1927, it was agreed that neither party would present any diplomatic claim or request international arbitration on behalf of any national alleging loss or damage through the war measures adopted by the other.

THE SUBMARINE CONTROVERSY

It was in the Great War that the submarine was first used on a large scale in naval warfare. Its use gave rise to new and perplexing questions. Being of frail construction, these vessels could.be easily sunk if seen by a war vessel or even if rammed by a merchant vessel. Their strength lay in their ability to attack unseen and to sink enemy vessels without warning. But the rules of naval warfare, evolved before the appearance of the submarine, provided that merchant vessels on the high seas could not be sunk without warning, and then only if provision was made for the safety of passengers and crew on board. Obviously the submarine could not operate under such conditions. Even if it risked the chance of being sunk by coming to the surface before attacking a merchant vessel the small size of the submarine would make it impossible to take on board the passengers and crew of the merchant vessel before sinking it.

Confronted by this situation, the German authorities determined to disregard the established rules of naval warfare and allow the submarines to sink merchant vessels without warning. They justified this action by citing Britain's violation of international law in enforcing the blockade of Germany and insisting that they were entitled to do likewise in order to allow the submarine to operate effectively. Accordingly, on February 18, 1915, Germany declared the waters around the British Isles a war zone, and served notice that she proposed to sink enemy merchant ships found in this zone without warning and further stated that neutral ships entering this proscribed area did so at their own risk.

This threat brought a prompt protest from the United States in which it was pointed out that very serious consequence would follow if Germany carried out the declared policy. To meet the critical situation the United States' authorities addressed an identical note to Great Britain and Germany proposing an agreement between the two powers respecting the conduct of naval warfare. The following suggestions were made: (1) that neither power would sow floating mines on the high seas or in territorial waters, and that anchored mines should be placed only within cannon range of harbors for defensive purposes, and that all mines should be marked with the stamp of the government planting them; (2) that both parties should agree not to use submarines except in accordance with established rules of war; (3) that the use of neutral flags for the purpose of disguise should be stopped. Britain was requested to allow foodstuffs to enter Germany consigned to agents, designated by the United States, who would guarantee that such imports went only to the civilian population in Germany. Neither of the belligerents showed a willingness to meet the suggestions made by the United States, and thus matters stood awaiting action by German submarines which would result in the loss of American property and lives. On March 28, 1915, news was received of the sinking of the British steamship *Falaba* causing the death of one American, and on May 1, the American tanker *Gulflight* was sunk and two of the crew drowned. Before definite action was taken by the American authorities in relation to these incidents, the civilized world was shocked by the news that the Cunard line steamship *Lusitania* had been sunk on May 7 by a German submarine off Old Head of Kinsale at the southeastern point of Ireland, resulting in the loss of over eleven hundred lives, of whom more than a hundred were Americans.[2]

The feeling of horror that this terrible event aroused in the United States was succeeded by a feeling of bitter resentment against Germany and a demand was voiced in many

[2] On the day that the *Lusitania* left New York a notice appeared in a number of leading American newspapers signed by the German Embassy warning Americans of the danger of traveling on British vessels passing through the war zone.

quarters for an immediate break with that country. President Wilson, however, determined to wait until he had full information of the circumstances before taking definite action. Germany promptly sent a note to the United States expressing regret at the loss of American lives in the sinking of the *Lusitania,* but insisting that the responsibility rested with the British authorities who, by their policy of starving the German civilian population, had forced Germany to adopt retaliatory measures.

After waiting a week to obtain all of the facts in the case, President Wilson, on May 13, 1915, sent a note to Germany in which he stated that the United States could not accept the German contention that illegal acts of her adversaries justified Germany in adopting retaliatory measures that infringed upon the rights of neutrals. Among these rights was that of persons to travel on merchant vessels on the high seas wherever their legitimate business might call them. In view of these long-established principles of international law the President called upon the German government to disavow the act of the submarine commander, to make reparations for the loss of American lives and property, and to take immediate steps to prevent the recurrence of such a deed. In conclusion he solemnly warned the German government that the government of the United States would not "omit any word or any act necessary to the performance of its sacred duty of maintaining the rights of the United States and its citizens and of safeguarding their free exercise and enjoyment."

Just before this communication was sent, Germany informed the United States that it had no intention of sinking American or other neutral vessels in the war zone and if any such should be destroyed by mistake the German government would "unreservedly recognize its responsibility therefor." Although this did not cover the question involved in the sinking of the *Lusitania,* namely, the right of neutrals to travel in safety on merchant vessels under a belligerent flag, it did constitute an important modification of the original war zone proclamation.

The first reply of the German government to the note sent by President Wilson stated that the American government had not taken into consideration all of the material facts of the case. It asserted that the *Lusitania* had guns mounted under deck and was therefore an auxiliary cruiser and not entitled to protection as a merchant vessel. It also contended that there were a number of Canadian troops on board and that in the cargo were large quantities of munitions. In view of these alleged facts it was stated that German commanders "were no longer in a position to observe the rules of capture otherwise usual." To this communication the American authorities returned a prompt reply in which it was stated that the charge that the *Lusitania* had guns mounted when she left New York was untrue. In regard to carrying contraband of war it was pointed out that this fact in no way affected the status of the ship as a merchant vessel. The American government insisted that it was "contending for nothing less high and sacred than the rights of humanity," and it "very earnestly and very solemnly" renewed the demands made in the former note.

It was at this time that Secretary of State Bryan resigned because of his inability to agree with President Wilson concerning the submarine controversy. It was his view that the German suggestion to submit the question of responsibility for the sinking of the *Lusitania* to arbitration should have been accepted and that in the interests of peace, Americans should be warned not to travel on belligerent merchant vessels.

For three months the correspondence between the two governments continued until, finally, on September 1, the German Ambassador at Washington notified the American authorities that he had been assured by his government that thereafter "liners will not be sunk without warning and without safety of the lives of non-combatants, provided that the liners do not try to escape or offer resistance." This statement indicated that the German government had accepted substantially the contentions made by the United States and President Wilson was warmly congratulated in the press of the country for having won a noteworthy diplomatic victory.

It was at this juncture, when the prospects of a peaceful solution of the submarine controversy seemed bright, that a new issue arose to complicate greatly the situation. International law sanctioned the placing of guns on merchant vessels for defensive purposes. This practice dated from the days of piracy and privateering and the guns were intended for use against these marauders of the high seas. But the appearance of the submarine placed the armed merchantmen in a new light. Against these frail craft the defensive armament of merchantmen could be used effectively. The German authorities contended that as piracy was no longer a menace and as privateering had been abolished by international law, the practice of arming merchant vessels was no longer warranted. The American government indicated that it was impressed with the reasonableness of this argument and that in view of the character of submarine warfare and the defensive weakness of these craft it was seriously considering instructing its officials to treat armed merchantmen as auxiliary cruisers.

To this suggestion the British government replied that it saw no reason for giving up a right sanctioned by international law and indicated its intention of continuing the practice of placing guns on merchant vessels. This unyielding attitude on the part of the British authorities created a very unfavorable impression in the United States. Resolutions were introduced into both houses of Congress calling upon the President to warn Americans not to travel on armed merchantmen. Had it not been for the opposition of the President there is little doubt that the resolutions would have been passed. Wilson took the view that action by Congress in this matter would interfere with his prerogatives in conducting negotiations with foreign countries and at his insistence the resolutions were tabled.

It was at this moment, when public sentiment in the United States seemed to be turning against the Entente Allies, that Germany saw fit to raise once more the submarine issue, thereby forfeiting a splendid opportunity to profit by the public feeling that had been aroused in this country against Great Britain. On March 24, 1916, word was received of the sinking of the channel steamer *Sussex,* resulting in the death or injury of eighty persons, among whom were several American citizens. The *Sussex* was not armed, and carried no troops, and was sunk without warning. This was such a flagrant violation of the assurance given in the previous September that President Wilson sent to the German government a communication that was clearly in the nature of an ultimatum. In it he stated that unless the German government "immediately declare and effect an abandonment of its present methods of submarine warfare against passenger and freight-carrying vessels, the government of the United States can have no other choice but to sever diplomatic relations with the German Empire altogether." This vigorous statement brought from the German government a prompt response in which it was stated that submarine commanders had received specific instructions that merchant vessels, both within and without the war zone, were to be destroyed only in accordance with the accepted principles of international law. Although this was a substantial agreement to the demands of the United States the German note went on to state that Germany would expect the United States to require Great Britain to observe the rules of international law and in case she did not do so "the German government would

then be facing a new situation, in which it must reserve
to itself the complete liberty of decision." In short this meant
that unless the United States succeeded in forcing Great
Britain to modify her blockade policy, Germany reserved
the right to resume submarine warfare without restrictions.
In reply to the German note the United States stated that it
would rely upon a "scrupulous execution" of the new policy
by Germany and at the same time insisted that it could not
agree that such action was to be made "contingent upon the
conduct of any other government."

Another issue that gave rise to an exchange of diplomatic
notes between the United States and Germany was that relating to the shipment of munitions by American firms to the
European belligerents. The Entente powers early in the war
placed orders in the United States for large quantities of such
supplies. On the other hand, Germany, because of British
control of the seas, was unable to obtain similar supplies.
In Germany the view came to be held that the United States
was not observing the true spirit of neutrality if it allowed
large quantities of munitions to be shipped to one belligerent
when the opposing side was not able to obtain any. On April
4, 1915, the German Ambassador at Washington brought
this matter to the attention of the American authorities and
suggested that a real spirit of neutrality called for an embargo
on the shipment of munitions to all belligerents. To this suggestion the state department replied that it was a clearly
recognized right of citizens of neutral countries to sell munitions as well as any other commodities to belligerents in time
of war and that this country would not be justified in changing an established principle of international law during a
war. Furthermore it was pointed out that if such trade was
prohibited it would compel every nation to maintain large
supplies of munitions in time of peace and thereby encourage
the spirit of militarism to which this nation was opposed.

During the nine months which followed the promise made

by Germany in the *Sussex* case there was a distinct lull in the
activities of German submarines and there were few, if any,
incidents in this period which appeared to violate the German
pledge. As the months passed the people of the United States
reached the conviction that President Wilson had won a
remarkable diplomatic victory. He had secured American
lives and property, and he had kept us out of war. It was
during these months that the presidential election of 1916
occurred and there is little doubt that President Wilson
profited materially in his campaign for reëlection by the
apparent success that he had made in handling the submarine controversy with Germany.

Two years of embittered disputes with both of the belligerent groups in Europe had brought a significant change in
the attitude of the American people toward the desperate conflict across the Atlantic. The position of a more or less disinterested observer, which was assumed in this country at the
beginning of the struggle, had given way under the pressure
of circumstances to the feeling that there was grave danger
of the United States becoming involved in the cataclysm.
Such a feeling gave an opportunity to the advocates of preparedness to press their views. Organizations such as the
National Security League and the American Defense Society
were formed which carried on a vigorous campaign for the
strengthening of the army and navy. Then, too, the views of
President Wilson had undergone a decided change. In his
message to Congress in 1914 he rejoiced that this country
was not ready, and never should be ready, to put into the field
"a nation of men trained in arms." Again, at the time of the
sinking of the *Lusitania,* although not said in reference to
that event he declared, "There is such a thing as a man being too proud to fight; there is such a thing as a nation
being so right that it does not need to convince others by
force that it is right." Such views gave great umbrage to the
advocates of preparedness and they accused the President of

being in sympathy with the pacifists. That such was not the case, Wilson clearly indicated early in 1916. He frankly confessed that he had "learned much in fourteen months" and that he had changed his opinion concerning the need for strengthening our military and naval forces. On a tour through the Middle West at this time he spoke in several important cities, pointing out the critical situation that confronted the country and emphasizing the necessity for immediate action to place our armed forces in a state of adequate preparedness.

Urged on by both official and unofficial advisers Congress responded by passing in June, 1916, the National Defense Act, which provided for the increase of the regular army to 186,000 men, to be still further increased in time of war; a federalized national guard of 424,800 men; civilian training camps and a reserve officers training corps at colleges and universities; and the construction of a government plant for the production of nitrates and munitions. This was followed by a naval appropriation bill that authorized the building of 10 dreadnoughts, 6 battle cruisers, 10 scout cruisers, 50 destroyers, 100 submarines, and other ships, at a total cost of over $502,000,000. In addition, provision was made for the organization of a Council of National Defense, consisting of six cabinet officers and an advisory commission of experts, "for the coördination of industries and resources for the national security and welfare." Finally to strengthen the merchant marine Congress provided for the appointment of a Shipping Board, which was authorized to spend $50,000,-000 to buy or build ships that were to be leased to private corporations or individuals or operated by the Board in case no satisfactory leases could be made.

Although these steps were taken by the administration to put the country in a position to meet the eventuality of war, there is no clear evidence that President Wilson had definitely reached the conclusion in 1916 that we would be drawn into the European conflict. It is true that his private secretary, Mr. Tumulty, later stated that the President had confided to him that he had been convinced from the very beginning of the war that this country would be sooner or later involved. On the other hand there is the testimony of Ambassador Page and Secretary Lane that they had been unable to convince the President of the righteousness of the cause of the Entente Allies, or of the moral responsibility of this country to come to their aid. It would seem that the President's mind in these critical days, despite some evident confusion of thought, was bent upon keeping this country out of the terrible catastrophe of war if possible.

The surest way to accomplish this purpose was to bring the war to an end before further untoward incidents forced the United States to abandon her neutral position. It was with some such thought in mind that President Wilson in 1916 actively took up the roll of peacemaker. In February of that year he sent Colonel House to Europe to interview the French and British authorities, to determine their willingness to join in a peace conference and suggesting that the terms of peace should include the restoration of Alsace and Lorraine to France, the acquisition of an outlet to the sea by Russia, and concessions to Germany outside of Europe. As an incentive to the Allies to accept these proposals the President stated that if Great Britain and France agreed and Germany declined he would use his influence to bring the United States into the war on the Allied side. This peace effort of the President came to nought, chiefly because Great Britain and France had agreed in the secret treaties of 1915 upon a different division of the spoils of war than that suggested by Wilson.

Undeterred by this rebuff, the President renewed his efforts to end the war in December, 1916. In an identical note which was sent to all of the belligerent powers he called attention to the fact that both sides had disclaimed any desire for aggression and that the objects that they had in mind were the same, as they were set forth in statements to their own people and to the world. Such being the case the President asked both sides for "such an avowal of their respective views as to the terms on which the war might be concluded and the arrangements that would be deemed satisfactory as a guaranty against its renewal" in order to discover if a comparison of views would lead to an understanding. He disclaimed the intention of offering mediation and declared that his purpose was to ascertain if possible, "how near the haven of peace may be for which all mankind longs with an intense and increasing longing." To these suggestions of Wilson's Germany returned a prompt reply, renewing the proposal for the calling of a general peace conference that she had made a few days before the President's note was sent, but declining to state in advance the terms upon which she would be willing to make peace. This suggestion was, of course, in no sense an answer to Wilson's communication. The Allied reply protested against the assumption made in the President's note that the purposes for which the two groups of belligerents were contending were the same. Concerning terms of peace the Allies stated that these could not be made known in detail "with all the equitable compensations and indemnities for damages suffered until the hour of negotiation." At the same time they indicated certain minimum conditions that would have to be met. These included the restoration of Belgium, Montenegro, and Serbia, with indemnities; the evacuation of France, Russia, and Roumania, with reparations; the liberation of Italians, Slavs, and Roumanians from foreign control; and the expulsion of Turkey from Europe.

These statements of the two belligerent groups were so far apart that it was obviously impossible for the President to take further steps looking to an immediate peace. Nevertheless, he did not abandon hope of accomplishing his purpose. In a remarkable speech delivered before the Senate on January 22, 1917, he stated that it was inconceivable that the United States should play no part in the great enterprise for establishing a durable peace. If such a peace could be established he asserted that the people of this country were prepared "to add their authority and their power to the authority and force of other nations to guarantee peace and justice throughout the world." A just and lasting peace would not come if there was formed at the close of this war a new balance of power. "There must be, not a balance of power, but a community of power; not organized rivalries, but an organized common peace." Turning from generalities to particulars he declared that it must be "a peace without victory," that is, it must be a negotiated peace, not a peace imposed by victors upon the vanquished. An imposed peace would leave bitterness and resentment and "only a peace between equals can last." Proceeding further, he maintained that a permanent peace must recognize equality of right among great and small nations; it must accept the principle that "governments derive all their just powers from the consent of the governed"; subject peoples should be freed; freedom of the seas should be guaranteed and "every great people" should have "direct outlet to the great highways of the sea"; and provision should be made for the limitation of armaments on land and sea.

Although President Wilson, in presenting these propositions, stated that he believed that he had said "what the people of the United States would wish me to say," nevertheless he realized that in suggesting that the United States would join with the rest of the world in guaranteeing a just peace he would be accused of proposing a radical change in the traditional American policy of isolation. Anticipating such a charge he insisted that his recommendation did not contemplate a breach either in our traditions or in our policy as a nation. It was rather a suggestion that the nations of the world should adopt the Monroe Doctrine as the doctrine for the whole world and that there were no "entangling alliances" when "all unite to act in the same sense and with the same purpose."

This notable address called forth sharp diversity of opinion in the country. Some persons were inclined to regard it as an "oration on the millennium," others, like Ex-President Roosevelt, denounced the President for uttering "the shameful untruth that each side is fighting for the same things, and to declare for neutrality between wrong and right." Senator Borah voiced the sentiment of those who saw in the league proposal a dangerous departure from our traditional policy of isolation from European affairs. On the other hand, there were many expressions of admiration for the fine idealism that the message displayed.

In the belligerent countries the proposals of the President met a varied reception. Many persons were willing to concede the disinterested purpose that actuated Wilson in formulating his suggestions and they also expressed approval of the ideals which he set forth. But among the Entente Allies there was much adverse criticism of the President's call for a "peace without victory." The official Allied thesis, that Germany was solely responsible for the war, was almost universally believed by the peoples of these countries and it seemed unjust to them that a country which had been the cause of so much suffering should be allowed to escape punishment. In Germany, where the people had been taught to believe that the Allied countries were bent upon the destruction of the Fatherland, there was similar criticism. In short the emotional strain that more than two years of war had brought in all of the belligerent nations made it difficult for the people of these countries to take a dispassionate view of the President's program. Nevertheless, if no new circumstances had arisen to change the course of events it is probable that sheer war weariness, coupled with the realization that neither side was apparently able to win a decisive victory, would have forced the belligerents to accept some such solution as Wilson had proposed. But events moved with startling rapidity to change the whole aspect of the situation, to bring to a close the trying period of American neutrality, and to end President Wilson's efforts as peacemaker.

On January 31, 1917, less than ten days after the President's Senate address, the German government served notice that on the following day it proposed to resume unrestricted submarine warfare in a zone around the enemy countries and that all vessels, neutral as well as belligerent, entering the war zone would be sunk without warning and without making provision for the safety of passengers and crew. As a concession to the United States the notice stated that one American ship a week would be allowed to go to England, provided that it sailed on a fixed day, over a specified course, and carried no contraband.

Germany justified this action on the ground that the condition that she had made at the time of the *Sussex* pledge, namely, that the United States would require Great Britain to modify her blockade policy, had not been met and therefore Germany had decided to resume her freedom of action. There were, however, other considerations that influenced the German authorities in adopting a policy which made it almost certain that the United States would be driven into the arms of her enemies. The British blockade had grown steadily more effective and threatened a slow strangulation of Germany. A war of attrition would at best result in a stalemate and at worst it threatened the defeat of Germany. The German military leaders therefore determined to risk the chance that the United States would enter the war on the side of the Entente, confident that by unrestricted submarine warfare they would be able to starve England into submission before American aid could become effective.

The German threat brought prompt action by the American authorities. President Wilson immediately broke off diplomatic relations with Germany and in an address before a joint session of the two houses of Congress on February 3, he recounted past negotiations with Germany and stated that her present action left no alternative to the United States but to sever relations. At the same time he stated that he was unwilling to believe that Germany would do what she threatened to do, but in case that his "inveterate confidence" should prove unfounded he would again come before Congress and ask for authority to adopt measures to protect American lives and property on the high seas.

Events soon demonstrated the reality of the German threat. During February a large number of merchant ships were sunk without warning, only two of which, however, were American. Nevertheless the menace of the submarine brought a virtual embargo on American shipping entering the war zone. Ship owners were unwilling to risk the loss of their property and insurance underwriters would not insure vessels passing through the proscribed area. If this condition continued Germany would accomplish her aim in preventing American supplies reaching her enemies. To meet this intolerable situation President Wilson appeared before Congress on February 26 and asked for authority to place defensive arms on American merchant ships, and "to employ any other instrumentalities and methods that may be necessary and adequate to protect our ships and our people in their legitimate and peaceful pursuits on the seas."

In Congress strong opposition appeared to granting the President the broad discretionary power which he asked but a bill passed the House appropriating $100,000,000 for purchasing arms to be placed on American merchant vessels. In the upper house a small group of Senators led by Senator La Follette, fearing that the passage of the measure would result in the United States becoming involved in the war, engaged in a filibuster and succeeded in preventing a vote on the bill before the adjournment of Congress on March 4. Aroused by this failure of Congress to meet the critical situation President Wilson appealed to the country, denouncing "the little group of willful men" in the Senate who had defeated the wishes of an overwhelming majority of Congress and of the people and he demanded that the Senate amend its rules so that such a situation would not recur. Popular approval of the President's position was so strong that the Senate in special session modified its rules so that in the future a two-thirds vote of the Senate could shut off debate and bring a measure to a vote.

While the debate on the Armed Ship bill was proceeding in Congress the state department published an intercepted dispatch that had been sent by Dr. Alfred Zimmerman, the German Minister of Foreign Affairs, to the German minister in Mexico in which he was instructed to inform the Mexican government that Germany proposed to resume unrestricted submarine warfare and that if this resulted in war with the United States he was to suggest to the Mexican authorities an alliance with Germany, promising financial aid and the restoration to Mexico of the "lost territory" of Texas, New Mexico, and Arizona. The minister was also instructed to suggest to the President of Mexico that he communicate with Japan proposing that she should desert the allies and join the Teutonic alliance. The publication of this note aroused bitter resentment against Germany in this country and did much to strengthen the President's hands.

Undeterred by the failure of Congress to act upon his suggestions, President Wilson obtained an opinion from his Attorney General that he had authority to place guards on American vessels without Congressional sanction and on March 12 he announced that he proposed to exercise this authority. There ensued three weeks of "armed neutrality," and it seemed inevitable that sooner or later a clash between American armed merchantmen and German submarines would bring the United States to the verge of war. When news was received on March 18 that three American vessels had been sunk and a number of American lives lost the die was cast. Three days later President Wilson summoned Congress to meet in special session on April 2, "to receive a communication concerning grave matters of national policy." On the evening of that day the President appeared before a joint session of the two Houses and read his historic war message.

With a gravity befitting the momentous occasion the President began by reviewing the long controversy with Germany over submarine warfare and with evident emotion, said: "With a profound sense of the solemn and even tragical character of the step I am taking and of the grave responsibility that it involves, but in unhesitating obedience to what I deem my constitutional duty, I advise that the Congress declare the recent course of the Imperial German government to be in fact nothing less than war against the government and people of the United States." But the President did not justify our entrance into the war solely on the ground of Germany's violation of American rights. He asserted that our purpose was "to vindicate the principles of peace and justice in the life of the world as against selfish and autocratic power, and to set up amongst the really free and self-governed peoples of the world such a concert of purpose and of action as will henceforth insure the observance of those principles." In short he held that the war had become, whatever may have been its causes, a great struggle between the forces of democracy and autocracy, and "the world must be made safe for democracy." [3] Continuing, he declared that,

[3] It would have been difficult for President Wilson to have made this claim if the Russian Revolution had not occurred eighteen days before he delivered his address; for it would have been a strange crusade for democracy with the most benighted autocracy in Europe as one of the Allies. With Russia a republic the central powers were left as the chief stronghold of autocracy.

"We are glad, now that we see the facts with no veil of false pretense about them, to fight thus for the ultimate peace of the world and for the liberation of its peoples—the German people included—for the rights of nations great and small and the privilege of men everywhere to choose their way of life and of obedience." Disclaiming any desire for conquest or for material compensation, he concluded his remarkable appeal in a flight of idealism: "We shall fight for the things which we have always carried nearest our hearts—for democracy, for the right of those who submit to authority to have a voice in their own governments, for the rights and liberties of small nations, for the universal dominion of right by such a concert of free peoples as shall bring peace and safety to all nations and make the world at last free. To such a task we can dedicate our lives and our fortunes, everything that we are and everything that we have, with the pride of those who know that the day has come when America is privileged to spend her blood and her might for the principles that gave her birth and happiness and the peace which she has treasured. God helping her she can do no other."

It is doubtful if a people had ever before been called upon to enter a great war for such unselfish reasons. The British Premier declared, "I do not use the language of flattery when I say that it is one of the most disinterested acts in history." President Poincaré of France rejoiced that the great American republic had proven faithful to its ideals and its traditions. In America there were doubtless those who were inclined to be cynical concerning the war for democracy, but there is little question that among the mass of the people President Wilson's effort to place America's war aims on a high plane did much to bring about the demonstration of loyalty and unselfish service throughout the trying days of the war.

When the President had concluded his address resolutions were introduced into both Houses declaring that a state of war existed between the Imperial German government and the United States. The resolution passed the Senate on April 4 by a vote of 82 to 6. The six negative votes were cast by Senators La Follette, Gronna, and Norris, Republicans, and Stone, Lane, and Vardaman, Democrats. In the House, after a debate which lasted from 10 A.M. on April 5 to 3 A.M. on April 6, the resolution passed by a vote of 373 to 50, nine not voting. The negative votes included 16 Democrats, 32 Republicans, 1 Socialist, and 1 Independent. The President issued the proclamation declaring a state of war with Germany on April 6.[4]

PREPARING THE WAR MACHINE

Having reached the momentous decision of war the President and Congress were confronted by a gigantic task in preparing the country for the part which it was to play in the great enterprise. "It is not an army that we must shape and train for war," said the President, "it is a nation." And the President faced this task with a determination and vigor which surprised those critics who had accused him of weakness during the period of American neutrality. Congress, with some grumbling, conferred upon the President almost dictatorial powers, and under his direction the whole economic life of the country was transformed. The price of wheat was fixed by the government and the consumption of various raw materials such as coal and gasoline was strictly regulated. To add to the food supply amateur farmers were encouraged to raise various crops in gardens and backyards.

[4] Diplomatic relations with Austria-Hungary were broken on April 8, and with Turkey on April 20. It became apparent that it would not be possible for the United States to fight Germany without opposing her most important ally. Therefore President Wilson in his message to Congress on December 4, 1917, called for a declaration of war against Austria. Congress responded December 7. The resolution passed the Senate 74 to 0, and the House 365 to 1. We did not declare war against the other Teutonic allies, Turkey and Bulgaria.

To conserve the wheat crop for the use of the army, the people were induced to use numerous unpalatable substitutes in making bread. Drastic measures were adopted to conserve the fuel supply for war purposes. In January, 1918, the Fuel Administrator ordered the closing of all manufacturing establishments east of the Mississippi River, except those engaged in the production of war materials, for a period of fifteen days and thereafter on Mondays for two months. Before the war ended the government had taken over the entire railroad system of the country as well as the telegraph, telephone, and cable lines. It has elsewhere been noted that during the war both capital and labor were subjected to strict governmental regulation and control. Strikes and lockouts were prohibited, the labor supply was apportioned among basic industries by governmental commissions, and wages, although not fixed by law, were virtually determined by public authorities. To all of these restrictions upon their normal freedom of action the people submitted with remarkably little resentment.

To carry out these multitudinous new functions, a large number of governmental agencies were organized. The Food Administration, the Fuel Administration, the War Finance Corporation, the Shipping Board, the Railroad Administration, the War Industries Board, and the War Labor Board were the most important in the vast array of governmental functionaries brought into being by the exigencies of war. Hundreds of men came to Washington, many of them giving up lucrative occupations, to offer their services to the government at a nominal salary of one dollar a year.

The success with which the nation raised and equipped an army of nearly four million men and transported a large proportion of them across three thousand miles of water was a cause for wonder and admiration both at home and abroad. That mistakes were made, due to the unprecedented size of the task and to the inexperience of those charged with its execution, was inevitable, but the accomplishment stands in striking contrast to similar efforts on a much smaller scale in previous wars. None of the scandals that humiliated the nation in the Spanish-American War or the class discrimination that marked the application of the drafts in the Civil War were repeated in our experience in the World War.

The act of June 3, 1916, which provided for an army of 175,000 officers and men, raised by volunteering, was soon seen to be wholly inadequate to meet the task before the country. The principle of voluntary military service was hallowed by tradition in the United States and when President Wilson, convinced of the necessity of making American military power available at the earliest possible moment, declared in favor of conscription, his suggestion met with determined opposition in Congress. But in the end his view prevailed.

By the law passed by Congress and signed by the President on May 18, 1917, the regular army was increased to 287,000 men to be raised by enlistment and the President was authorized to call into the service of the United States the entire National Guard and to raise a further force of 500,000 men by a selective draft, to be later increased to 1,000,000 men if such a number was deemed necessary. All male citizens between the ages of 21 and 31 were made subject to the draft. In addition the President was authorized, in his discretion, to raise a volunteer infantry force of not more than four divisions. This last provision was placed in the act at the suggestion of friends of Ex-President Roosevelt, who wished to have him sent immediately to France at the head of a volunteer force similar to that which he had led in the Spanish-American War. President Wilson, however, refused to accept this proposal, stating that he believed that it would interfere with the prompt organization of our military forces and would contribute nothing to the effective strength of the Allied forces in Europe. To satisfy the appeal made by the representatives of the Allied countries for the immediate despatch of American troops to France in order to arouse the drooping spirits of the Allies, President Wilson ordered a division of regulars under General John J. Pershing to proceed at once to France. The appearance of these American soldiers in Europe gave rise to remarkable demonstrations of popular enthusiasm in the Allied countries.

Enrollment under the selective draft resulted in the listing of over 9,500,000 men. The country was divided into 4,557 districts, and each man in a district was assigned a number ranging from 1 to 10,500. The drawing took place in Washington, where similar numbers were placed in a large bowl and the Secretary of War drew out the first number, 258. This meant that in each district the person holding that number was drafted. The process continued until 1,374,000 names were listed. The men drawn in this manner were ordered before medical examining boards and, if found physically fit, were assigned to the army.[5]

The training of this large force offered difficulties of no mean proportions, but they were met with a determination and effectiveness that confounded those who had maintained that a nation devoted to the arts of peace could not prepare for war. Officers' training camps were established to provide the large number of officers needed for the new army. With remarkable speed cantonments were built in various parts of the country to which the drafted men were sent. Various civilian organizations, including the Y.M.C.A., the Knights of Columbus, the Jewish Welfare League, and the Salvation Army, did splendid work at these cantonments in caring for the material and spiritual well being of the soldiers.

Criticism was made, some of it well meant and some for

[5] The law provided for liberal exemptions, including state and Federal officials, ministers of religion, members of churches that forbade the taking up of arms, artisans employed in munition works and in industries essential to the war, persons physically and mentally unfit for service, and men on whom other persons depended for support.

partisan reasons, that the war department had failed to perform its work satisfactorily. Senator Chamberlain, chairman of the Senate Committee on Military Affairs, went so far as to declare that the military establishment had virtually stopped functioning because of inefficiency in every department of government. Others denounced the administration because of the delay in building aircraft. Still others pointed to the alleged waste of money in building the army cantonments. To these criticisms Secretary of War Baker replied effectively by showing the remarkable progress that had been made despite the stupendous difficulties that had to be overcome. The war secretary had the energetic backing of the President. Efforts on the part of Congress to establish a congressional committee to supervise the conduct of the war were firmly resisted by President Wilson, who regarded such proposals as an invasion of the prerogatives of the executive.

When the United States entered the war the navy was in a much better condition of preparedness than the army, because of the fact that the navy had always been regarded as our first line of defense and had been kept in shape for immediate action. The naval defense act of 1916 had provided for a substantial increase in ships of various kinds and in the navy personnel. Rear Admiral Sims, who had been sent to England as an observer before we entered the war, was put in command of all of the naval forces of the United States in European waters. A fleet of American destroyers was despatched immediately to England, followed by battleships and cruisers, all of which coöperated effectively with the Allied naval forces in combating the German submarine menace. A notable service was performed by the American naval forces in protecting the transport of American troops to Europe. In all some two million troops were carried across three thousand miles of water with scarcely any loss of life, an achievement which reflects great credit on the navy.

ON THE FIGHTING LINE

It was not the expectation of the American authorities that any large number of American troops would be sent to France for some months after we entered the war. It was the original plan to give the preliminary training to the drafted troops in the camps in this country and to have about 1,000,000 men in France by the end of the year 1918. But in the summer and fall of 1917 the military fortunes of the Allies became desperate, necessitating a change in the plans of the American military authorities. In the first place, in October, 1917, the Italian forces in northern Italy suffered a disastrous defeat, which for a time threatened the complete collapse of the Italian front. Serious as this blow was to the Allies it was overshadowed by the course of events in Russia.

One month before the United States entered the war the Russian Revolution occurred. This event was hailed with joy in the Allied countries, for it was felt that an efficient and honest government would replace the corrupt régime of the Czar and the Russian military power would become a much more effective asset to the Allied cause. But this expectation was soon dispelled. Within eight months the control of the revolution passed from the hands of the moderate bourgeois element into the hands of the extreme Socialist forces led by Lenin and Trotsky. These latter, convinced that the war was being carried on in the interest of great capitalists, determined to end Russian participation in the struggle and before the close of 1917 Russia was no longer one of the Entente Allies. The Russian defection enabled Germany to transfer a large force of troops from the eastern front to the battlefields of France. This new menace caused consternation in Great Britain and France and frantic appeals were sent to the United States to hasten the despatch of American troops to Europe. The American authorities made every effort to respond to this call. By the close of the year 1917, 187,000 soldiers and 7,500 marines had embarked for France. Each month thereafter the number increased until it reached a maximum of over 2,000,000 by the time that the Armistice was signed. In anticipation of possible further demands Congress in August, 1918, changed the age limits of the draft to include all men between the ages of 18 and 45, which resulted in adding 13,000,000 registrants to the list. In addition Students' Army Training Corps were established in a large number of colleges to provide additional supplies of officers. All men of draft age were required to obtain registration cards and those not engaged in essential industries were made liable to assignment to such industries unless drafted into the army. Government officials inaugurated an intensive drive to round up slackers. Suspected persons were accosted on the streets, in automobiles, at places of amusement, or in their offices or homes, and unless able to show registration cards were sent to the training camps. There was some protest by those who regarded such action as a violation of the rights of American citizens, but in general the authorities were loyally supported.

To care for the tremendous American forces in France a veritable army of engineers and mechanics was engaged in construction work. Huge docks were built at French ports, new railroad lines were constructed and old lines rebuilt to meet the added strain; warehouses, supply depots, cantonments, recreation huts, sprang up as if by magic. Thousands of welfare workers accompanied the fighting forces to continue and expand the activities that they had started in the army camps at home.

The first contingent of the American forces to arrive in France comprised the First and Second Divisions of the regular army, followed shortly by the 26th, 41st, and 42d Divisions of the National Guard. It was contemplated that after these forces had finished a period of intensive training and had become familiar with the conditions of actual fighting they would be organized as an American army unit under the command of American officers and assigned to an American sector. But the critical position of the Allies made it impossible to realize this object for some months.

The German military authorities fully realized the significance of the gigantic preparations that were being made in the United States to place the full weight of its military and economic power at the disposal of the Allies and the Germans were determined to take full advantage of their increased military strength, which the Russian defection had given them, before the might of the United States could be thrown into the scales against them. With this end in view the Teutonic military leaders boldly proclaimed their intention of launching a gigantic offensive in the spring of 1918. General Ludendorff appeared before the German Reichstag and announced that he was prepared to guarantee a victorious ending of the war within six weeks, calmly remarking that this would necessitate the loss of another million men.

On March 21, 1918, the long-heralded German drive began with a terrific onslaught along a forty-mile front of the Allied line between Arras and La Fere. For more than a week the attack continued with unabated fury, and the British forces, which held this sector of the line, were driven back, at one point more than thirty-five miles. For a time it seemed as though the Germans would break through the Allied lines and Ludendorff would make good his boast. Only by the most heroic efforts were the Allies able to check the German advance when it had reached almost to the important railroad center at Amiens. Two important results followed this barely averted Allied disaster. For the first three years of the war the French, British, Italian, and other Allied armies had been under the command of their respective military leaders, coördinated only by means of a Supreme War Council. In the face of the crisis caused by the

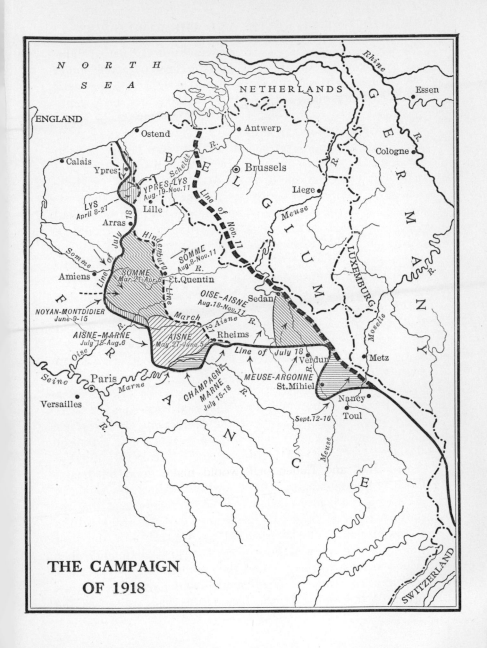

THE CAMPAIGN
OF 1918

German drive in 1918 the representatives of the Allies determined to provide a unified command for the Allied armies, and they selected General Foch as the supreme Allied commander. At the same time General Pershing, impressed by the serious situation which confronted the Allies, agreed to postpone the formation of a separate American army and offered to place all of the American forces at the disposal of General Foch. This generous offer was gladly accepted and the American forces were brigaded with the French and British until the crisis had passed.

Having failed in their effort to break the Allied line at Amiens, the Germans shifted their offensive further to the north and began a drive against the British near Ypres. Once more the Allies were forced back but were able to stop the Germans from breaking through to the Channel ports. Again the Germans shifted their point of attack, and in May and June carried on a terrific drive against the French along the Aisne River. A deep salient was driven into the French line reaching to the Marne River but once more the Allied line was stabilized and the Germans failed to break through. On July 15, the Germans launched their last offensive in an effort to enlarge the Marne salient, but this time they were stopped in their tracks by a combined French and American force. On July 18 Marshal Foch decided that the time had arrived for the Allies to assume the offensive. Accordingly the French and American contingent from Château-Thierry to Soissons began a drive against the western side of the Marne salient and within two weeks the Germans were forced to retire to their former position on the Aisne River.

By this time the American forces in France totaled more than a million men, and it was determined to carry out the original plan to have them organized as a separate army, and be assigned to a definite sector of the Allied front. At the request of General Pershing the first task given to the Americans was the capture of the Saint-Mihiel salient, which had been held by the Germans since the early months of the war. General Pershing had under his immediate command 500,000 troops, which included about 70,000 French troops and a large force of Allied tanks and airplanes. The attack began on September 12, and within three days the entire salient had been wiped out and more than 16,000 German prisoners taken, together with large quantities of war materials. The slight casualties on the Allied side were in part due to the fact that the Germans had realized the impossibility of holding their position and had begun to retire at the time that the American attack began.

This initial success of a distinctly American army encouraged Marshal Foch to assign General Pershing a much more difficult task, that of driving the Germans from the territory west of Verdun in the region of the Argonne forest. In some respects this region was the most formidable part of the whole German line. It was a rough country covered by thick forests and dense undergrowth, and during the three years that the Germans had held it they had planted hundreds of machine gun nests and erected many miles of barbed-wire entanglements. Both French and German military authorities had considered parts of this territory impregnable.

It would be beyond the scope of this book to describe in detail events of the seven weeks extending from September 26 to November 11, during which the Americans, numbering 1,200,000 men, drove the Germans step by step along a front of 23 miles until they had reached their final objective at Sedan and cut the important Carignan-Sedan railroad, the main artery of communication to the German front. Every foot of this advance was stubbornly contested, and the American losses were severe, numbering more than 100,000 men. Further operations were halted by the signing of the Armistice on November 11, 1918.

While these momentous military operations were going forward in France, significant maneuvers were made by the diplomats of the different belligerent countries to strengthen the morale of their respective peoples. Throughout the year 1917 there had been growing evidence of war weariness in all of the countries at war. The gigantic struggle had lasted three years with stupendous losses on both sides and the end seemed to be as far off as ever. Moreover, there were persistent rumors that the professions of the statesmen that the war was being fought without thought of aggression were not to be relied upon. These rumors received substantial verification when the Russian Bolsheviks obtained access to the Russian archives in November, 1917, and published the secret treaties that had been drawn up among the Entente Allies in 1915, providing for a division of the spoils in the event of an Allied victory. There is no doubt that the Teutonic Allies contemplated similar territorial aggressions at the expense of their enemies, as was shown by the treaty of Brest-Litovsk, which they forced upon Russia in 1918.

The publication of the secret treaties gave rise to much criticism in Allied liberal and radical circles. The Labor party in England came forward with a program that demanded a peace based upon justice. In France a defeatist movement attained serious proportions and in the summer of 1917 a threatened mutiny among the French troops at the front caused much concern to the military leaders. In Italy the disaster to the Italian forces at Caporetto was attributed to Communist agitation among the soldiers. The Bolshevik leaders in Russia set forth their program of a peace based upon the principles of self-determination with no annexations and no indemnities; a proposal which touched a responsive chord among the rank and file in the belligerent countries. And these doubts and questionings among the peoples in the Allied countries came just at the time that the Germans were preparing to launch their great offensive in the spring of 1918. Clearly the situation demanded a stiffening of the morale both of the soldiers at the front and of the civilians behind the lines.

Instinctively the statesmen of the Entente Allies turned to President Wilson to formulate the war aims of the United States and her associates in terms that would counteract the doubts and suspicions that had been aroused by the publication of the secret treaties. President Wilson essayed this task in a notable address to Congress on January 8, 1918, in which he outlined the war aims of the United States in the famous "fourteen points." Taking the long view and visualizing a permanent peace rather than confining himself to the particular issues of the war then in progress, he advocated open diplomacy, freedom of the seas, the removal of economic barriers to international trade, the reduction of armaments, and an impartial adjustment of colonial claims taking into consideration the interests of the populations involved. Turning to the specific problems that had been raised by the war he demanded the evacuation of all militarily occupied territory, the return of Alsace-Lorraine to France, the fixing of political frontiers in Italy and the Balkans in accordance with the principle of nationality, autonomous government for the peoples in Austria-Hungary, the resurrection of Poland, and the settlement of the vexing problem of Russia by giving her "an unhampered and unembarrassed opportunity for the independent determination of her own political development and national policy." In conclusion he called for the formation of an association of nations for the purpose of assuring world peace. Reiterating the statement that he had made many times since his war message, President Wilson asserted that there was nothing in his peace program which aimed at the humiliation or dismemberment of the German Empire and that his only purpose was to have her "accept a place of equality among the people of the world—the new world in which we now live—instead of a place of mastery." These pronouncements of President Wilson gave rise to a veritable diplomatic war. The spokesmen of the Teutonic powers, unwilling to concede a monopoly of virtue to their opponents, issued statements in which they expressed approval of many of the general principles stated by Wilson without being too specific as to details. Counterblasts from President Wilson in later speeches reaffirmed and elaborated the creed that he had formulated.

Throughout the United States and in the Allied countries President Wilson's idealistic program was hailed with joy and it went far to relieve the Entente statesmen of the embarrassment caused by the disclosure of the secret treaties. Although giving tacit approval to the various Wilsonian proposals, the Allied diplomats did so with important mental reservations, as was clearly shown when the serious business of peace making was undertaken.

Although the German political and military leaders belittled the efforts of President Wilson to drive a wedge between the German people and their autocratic rulers there is little doubt that the assertion that the German people could obtain a just peace if they would cease fighting for their imperialist masters contributed materially in undermining German morale. Then, too, Bolshevist propaganda, seeping into Germany through the eastern frontier, added to the difficulties of the German authorities. In short Allied and Russian propaganda behind the German lines in conjunction with the irresistible drive of the Allied armies broke the German power of resistance and brought the gigantic four years' struggle to an end.

As early as August 14, 1918, General Ludendorff admitted to his Imperial leader that the Germans were beaten. In one last desperate effort to save the situation the Kaiser made somewhat vague promises of giving to the German people a more effective control of their political affairs. As an earnest of this it was announced that thereafter the ministry in Germany would be responsible to the Reichstag. At the same time Prince Max of Baden, a liberal, replaced Count Von Hertling as Imperial Chancellor. In the meantime the military situation became daily more desperate for the Teutonic powers. On September 15 the Allied troops in the Balkans broke the Bulgarian line and two weeks later Bulgaria signed an armistice and withdrew from the war. The collapse of Bulgaria isolated Turkey, and the steady advance of the Allied forces in Asia Minor clearly foreshadowed the end of Turkish resistance. Still more ominous were the internal disturbances in Austria-Hungary, which paralyzed the military efforts of the Hapsburg monarchy.

The new German Chancellor fully realized that the hope of German military success had vanished, and on October 4 he sent to the American government the following communication: "The German Government requests the President of the United States to take in hand the restoration of peace, acquaint all of the belligerent states of this request, and invite them to send plenipotentiaries for the purpose of opening negotiations. It accepts the program set forth by the President in his message to Congress on January 8 [6] and in his later pronouncements, especially his speech of September 27, as a basis for the peace negotiations. With a view to avoiding further bloodshed, the German Government requests the immediate conclusion of an armistice on land, on water, and in the air."

Warned by the experience of Russia at Brest-Litovsk, President Wilson determined to ascertain the precise meaning of the German request before submitting it to the Entente powers. He asked the German authorities whether they accepted the Fourteen Points without question or simply wished to make them a basis of discussion at the peace conference. He further wanted to know whether the Chancellor was speaking for the German people or "merely for the constituted authorities of the Empire who have so far conducted

[6] The "Fourteen Points."

the war." He added that he would propose an armistice only on condition that the German armies would retire from French and Belgian soil. To these queries the German Chancellor replied that Germany was prepared to accept the Fourteen Points without qualification and would withdraw from the occupied territories in France and Belgium. He assured the President that he spoke in the name of the German people and not for the military and autocratic leaders. In a further exchange of communications President Wilson insisted upon the absolute necessity of being assured that the United States and the countries associated with her were dealing with veritable representatives of the German people and not their military masters. In addition he declared that any armistice to be accepted by the Allies must be of such a character as to make it impossible for Germany to resume hostilities.

Having obtained a satisfactory response to these demands President Wilson felt justified in submitting to the representatives of the Entente countries the correspondence that had passed between Germany and the United States. In reply the Entente diplomats agreed to enter into peace negotiations on the basis of the Fourteen Points and the subsequent statements of President Wilson with two qualifications. In the first place, they declared that the second of the Fourteen Points, dealing with the freedom of the seas, was open to various interpretations and that they must insist upon reserving complete freedom of action in considering this question at the peace conference. In the second place they asserted that the restoration of invaded territories was understood by them to mean that Germany should pay "for all damage done to the civilian population of the Allies and their property by the aggression of Germany by land, by sea, and from the air." In transmitting the Allied response to Germany President Wilson was silent regarding the first reservation made by the Allies and expressed approval of the second.

In the meantime the Supreme War Council of the Allies

538   THE UNITED STATES AND THE WORLD WAR

met at Paris to prepare the terms of the Armistice. Full advantage was taken of President Wilson's proposal that the terms should be made so drastic as to prevent Germany from renewing the war. Not only was she required to evacuate the occupied territories in the west but was also obliged to surrender to the Allies a large part of her military and naval equipment. As a further precaution the Allies insisted upon the military occupation of the German territory on the west bank of the Rhine pending the conclusion of the peace treaty. The terms of the Armistice were communicated to Germany and after a futile protest against their drastic nature the German representatives signed the Armistice on November 11, 1918.

News of the termination of hostilities brought forth wild demonstrations of joy in all of the belligerent countries. In the official proclamation to the American people announcing the conclusion of the Armistice President Wilson stated that "everything for which America fought has been accomplished. It will now be our fortunate duty to assist by example, by sober friendly counsel, and by material aid, in the establishment of just democracy throughout the world." It remained to be seen whether these hopeful views of the President were to be realized at the peace conference that gathered at Paris.

BIBLIOGRAPHICAL NOTE

Good single volume accounts of the relation of the United States to the World War are, C. Seymour, *Woodrow Wilson and the World War* (1921); J. S. Bassett, *Our War with Germany* (1919). On the relations of the United States with the belligerents during the period of American neutrality consult F. A. Ogg, *National Progress* (1918); J. B. Scott, ed., *President Wilson's Foreign Policy: Messages, Addresses and Papers* (1918); C. Seymour, *Intimate Papers of Colonel House* (4 Vols., 1926-1928); E. E. Robinson and V. J. West, *Foreign Policy of Woodrow Wilson* (1917); J. B. Scott, *A Survey of International Relations Between the United States and Ger-*

many, August 1, 1914—April 6, 1917 (1917). For a criticism of President Wilson's policy see T. Roosevelt, *Fear God and Take Your Own Part* (1916).

For a consideration of the mobilization of the economic resources of the country for war purposes and of the changes in governmental organization see B. Crowell and R. F. Wilson, *How America Went to War* (6 Vols., 1921); W. F. Willoughby, *Government Organization in War Time and After* (1919); C. R. Van Hise, *Conservation and Regulation in the United States During the World War* (1917); G. B. Clarkson, *Industrial America in the World War* (1923). See also several monographs published by the Carnegie Endowment for International Peace under the general title *Preliminary Economic Studies of the War* (1918-——).

For the operations of the American military forces in France consult J. J. Pershing, *Final Report to the Secretary of War* (1919); Colonel de Chambrun and Captain de Marenches, *The American Army in the European Conflict* (1919); R. J. Beamish and F. A. Marsh, *America's Part in the World War* (1919); L. P. Ayres, *The War with Germany: A Statistical Summary* (1919); F. Palmer, *America in France* (1919); S. Thomas, *The History of the A.E.F.* (1920). For naval operations see W. S. Sims and B. J. Hendrick, *The Victory at Sea* (1920).

CHAPTER 22

ISOLATION OR LEADERSHIP?

No past war had approached the gigantic struggle of the four years from 1914 to 1918 in the number of nations and warriors involved, the destruction of property and loss of life, the staggering financial burdens that were placed upon the nations involved, and the far-reaching political and social changes that came in its wake. There had been mobilized some sixty million men, of whom more than eight million had been killed in battle, not to mention many more million victims of disease due to war conditions. Billions of dollars of the nations' wealth had been destroyed and vast areas of agricultural land as well as thousands of towns and villages had been laid waste. Central and eastern Europe had been swept by revolution; the Romanoff, Hohenzollern, and Hapsburg monarchies had been overthrown. Out of the resulting political chaos came the cries of subjected national groups, such as the Poles, Czechs, Roumanians, Jugoslavs, and Finns, for political emancipation. To add to the confusion there appeared the menace of a proletarian revolution in Central Europe, led by the new masters of Russia.

Under the most favorable conditions the task of restoring peace and redrawing the map of the world was one calculated to test the qualities of the ablest statesmen and diplomats. And the conditions were far from favorable. Four years of terrible war and suffering, accompanied by vicious propaganda, had embittered the people of all of the warring nations and when the end came there arose loud cries for vengeance. All of the professed idealism of the war days vanished with the signing of the Armistice, and there ap-

540

peared in most of the belligerent nations an intense and selfish nationalism. The responsible statesmen of the victorious nations, even had they been so inclined, would probably have been unable to stem the tide of chauvinism that swept the people of their respective countries. Then, too, the commitments contained in the secret treaties that had been made by the Entente Allies could not be lightly disregarded. Great Britain, France, Italy, and Japan demanded the territorial rewards and other advantages that they had mutually pledged to one another. Of the nations associated in the victory only the United States came to the peace conference unembarrassed by treaty obligations and cherishing no desire for territorial or other material rewards.

It was amidst this welter of bitterness, national antagonisms, and selfish ambitions that the Peace Conference met at Paris to solve the momentous problems presented by the war and its outcome. And it was under these conditions that President Wilson, the prophet of a new world era, attempted to realize those ideals of peace and justice that he had so eloquently preached during the trying years of the war. Clearly it was a task to daunt the wisest statesman and Woodrow Wilson unhappily was handicapped by certain faults of temperament and personality which greatly enhanced the difficulties confronting him.

Throughout his political career President Wilson had aroused personal and political animosities without winning compensating loyalties. He lacked the instinct for coöperation with men of intellectual ability and political capacity. His inclination to play a lone hand gave rise to the belief that he was dictatorial, opinionated, and impatient with those who differed with him. He relied upon the soundness of the ideals which he pronounced without taking into consideration the difficulties to be overcome and the accommodations to be made in order to translate these ideals into realities. With apostolic fervor and something of the Scotch Covenanter's stubbornness he pursued his course unmindful of the human relationships that are so essential to success in the field of politics.

Just before the Armistice was signed the congressional elections of November, 1918, were held. Prior to the election the President had been induced to issue an appeal to the voters calling for the return of a Democratic Congress in order that he might have effective support in the critical days to come. This was not the first time that a President had made such an appeal. In 1898, McKinley urged the election of a Republican Congress stating that "this is no time for divided councils," and Roosevelt at the same time more emphatically called upon the voters to "remember that whether you will or not your votes this year will be viewed by the nations of Europe from one standpoint only. . . . A refusal to sustain the President will, in their eyes, be read as a refusal to sustain the war and to sustain the efforts of the peace commission."

But the Republican leaders resented Wilson's action as a reflection upon their patriotism. Ex-President Roosevelt, overlooking his own attitude at the time of the Spanish-American War, bitterly denounced the President. Republicans were quick to point out that their party members in Congress had loyally supported the President's policies, in a number of instances more earnestly than the members of his own party.

The election results brought great disappointment to the administration, for the Republicans succeeded in electing a majority in both houses of the incoming Congress. It would be incorrect to interpret the outcome of this election as a popular repudiation of President Wilson's war policies or of his program for world peace. In addition to the normal mid-term reaction against the party in power there were many factors connected with the domestic policies of the administration which contributed to the defeat of the Democrats.

It is going much too far to say as did Roosevelt that "our Allies and our enemies and Mr. Wilson himself should all understand that Mr. Wilson has no authority whatever to speak for the American people at this time. His leadership has just been emphatically repudiated by them. . . . Mr. Wilson and his Fourteen Points and his four supplementary points and his five complimentary points and all his utterances every which way have ceased to have any shadow of right to be accepted as expressive of the will of the American people." Nevertheless there is no doubt that the result of the election was a severe blow to the prestige of the President on the eve of his departure for the Peace Conference.

Despite his failure to obtain a vote of confidence from the American people President Wilson boldly proceeded with his peace program. He announced his intention to go to Paris in person as the head of the American delegation. This decision brought further criticism from his enemies. He was accused of wishing to satisfy his vanity and of deserting his constitutional duties as President at a critical juncture. But Wilson felt that only by his presence at the Peace Conference could he hope to have incorporated in the peace settlement the ideals that he had proclaimed.

In selecting his associates on the American delegation the President made a tactical blunder. It was probably necessary to take with him his Secretary of State, Robert Lansing. Then, too, the choice of Colonel House was eminently fitting, for he had become intimately acquainted with European statesmen in his capacity as spokesman for the President during the war and was moreover by temperament an able negotiator. But in selecting the other two members of the delegation Mr. Wilson had a fine opportunity to overcome, in a measure, Republican opposition to his program by choosing two influential and representative Republican statesmen. In this connection the names of Ex-President Taft and Elihu Root were prominently mentioned. Both favored the purpose that Wilson had nearest at heart, namely, the formation of a League of Nations, and both commanded great popular respect and wide influence among Republicans. It would have been difficult for a Republican Senate to have refused approval to a treaty signed by two such eminent leaders of their own party. Disregarding this opportunity to strengthen his position the President selected as the remaining members of the delegation General Tasker H. Bliss and Mr. Henry White. Both were men of unquestioned ability and Mr. White had had a wide experience in diplomacy, but neither of them aroused wide popular appeal nor commanded substantial influence in Republican ranks.

Accompanying the delegation was a group of more than a thousand aides and experts. Among these were some of the outstanding figures in the fields of economics, history, finance, law, geography, labor, and ethnology. Despite President Wilson's inclination to keep his own council we have the testimony of those who accompanied the delegation that he relied largely upon the advice of the American experts. "Tell me what is right," he said, "and I will fight for it. Give me a guaranteed position."

Upon his arrival in France President Wilson was greeted with wild demonstrations of popular acclaim. This outburst of enthusiasm was in part a personal tribute to the man who had formulated in memorable phrases the ideals of liberals in every country of the world, and in part it was a tribute to the American nation whose unselfish efforts had contributed so much to the winning of the war. Similar triumphs awaited the President upon his visits to the other Allied countries. But popular acclaim is an evanescent thing, and Wilson soon found that in translating his abstract principles into concrete proposals he ran counter to the national aspirations in Europe with the result that many who had hailed him with delight later showered him with bitter denunciation.

It was more than a month after the arrival of President

Wilson in France before the first session of the Peace Conference met. The delay was due in part to the great number of preliminary details that had to be settled and in part, if rumor is to be credited, to the desire of the diplomats of the Entente countries to allow the enthusiasm for Mr. Wilson to cool a bit before they came to grips with him concerning some of the provisions that they proposed to incorporate in the settlement and that did not square the principles enunciated by the American President.

President Wilson appears to have gone to the Peace Conference with certain definite objectives in view. Upon the detailed territorial and economic settlements that might be made he was not committed, except in so far as he was determined to make them square as nearly as possible with the Fourteen Points. But the one thing upon which his mind was firmly fixed was the creation of a League of Nations and the incorporation of its covenant as a definitive part of the treaty. As he said, "This is the central object of our meeting. Settlements may be temporary, but the actions of the nations in the interests of peace and justice must be permanent. We can set up permanent processes. We may not be able to set up permanent decisions." Over the objections of the French representatives Wilson succeeded in having the conference approve his proposal to undertake immediately the formation of the League and the President had himself appointed as chairman of the committee to draw up the Covenant. In less than a month this committee reported the first draft of the document, and on February 14 it was laid before the second plenary session of the Conference.

RECEPTION OF THE LEAGUE PROPOSAL IN THE UNITED STATES

Immediately after Wilson had accomplished his main objective at Paris he sailed for home taking with him a copy of the proposed League Covenant. He requested that the

Senate should defer consideration of the proposal until he had had an opportunity to explain it to them in person. But a number of leading Senators declined to be restrained, and expressed determined opposition to the League idea in general and to the specific Covenant that the President brought back from Paris. This Senatorial opposition was in part an expression of sincere objection to the principle or to the details of the League Covenant, and in part to personal and partisan opposition to Wilson. Senatorial dignity had been hurt as a result of the President's action in ignoring that body in the selection of the peace delegates and by his failure to take the Senate into his confidence in regard to the purposes and actions of the American delegation at Paris.[1]

Upon his arrival at Boston the President delivered an address in which he clearly indicated his intention of appealing directly to the people to support his program. "The people are in the saddle," he said, "and they are going to see to it that, if their present governments do not do their will, some other government shall." But Wilson lacked Roosevelt's ability to arouse popular enthusiasm and he failed to reply satisfactorily to some of the questions that had been raised in the minds of many persons concerning some of the articles of the Covenant. It must not be forgotten that, despite the influence of our war experience in broadening men's minds in regard to world affairs, there was still a deep-rooted provincialism among the mass of the American people. American isolation was still a tradition to be reckoned with, and much persuasive argument was needed to convert the people to a new world point of view.

At Washington the President met the Senate Committee on Foreign Relations and the House Committee on Foreign

[1] According to the statements of Henry White, the one Republican on the American delegation, he, White, kept Senator Lodge fully informed of the discussions at Paris and urged the Senator to let him have any suggestions that he might wish to make, but Lodge declined to offer any suggestions.

Affairs and attempted to convince them that there was nothing in the Covenant which violated the traditional policy of this country or endangered our interests. But his efforts met with little success. Before Congress adjourned thirty-nine Senators, more than enough to prevent ratification, declared their intention to vote against the treaty if it contained the proposed Covenant of the League. This action made Wilson more determined than ever to carry through his program. Upon the eve of his return to Paris, in a speech delivered at the Metropolitan Opera House in New York, the President said, "When the Treaty comes back, gentlemen on this side will find the Covenant not only in it, but so many threads of the Treaty tied to the Covenant that you cannot dissect the Covenant from the Treaty without destroying the whole vital structure." And he declared his purpose "to get the country so pledged in the view of the world to certain courses of action that the Senate will hesitate to bring about the appearance of dishonor which would follow its refusal to ratify." At the same time Wilson indicated his willingness to accept constructive suggestions for modifying the proposed Covenant from those who were in sympathy with the League idea. Accordingly he succeeded upon his return to Paris in having incorporated a number of changes suggested by Root, Hughes, and Ex-President Taft. Among these were provisions for a new article specifically recognizing the Monroe Doctrine; excluding domestic questions from the jurisdiction of the League; allowing members to withdraw from the League; requiring the Council to act by unanimous consent; and providing that no nation should be required to accept a mandate for colonies without its own consent. In regard to the much-discussed Article X, which provided that the members of the League "shall undertake to respect and preserve as against external aggression the territorial integrity and existing political independence of all States members of the League" the President insisted upon its retention without change, despite the fact that many persons professed to see in its provisions an obligation on the part of this country to send American soldiers to defend the sovereignty and independence of European and Asiatic states.

Upon his return to Paris to complete the work of the Peace Conference President Wilson was confronted with many formidable problems. He had scored his greatest success in securing from the Allied statesmen the approval of the League Covenant and its incorporation in the Treaty. But when the Conference took up the questions of territorial adjustments and financial compensations the President found it impossible to withstand the selfish national ambitions of the various Allied powers. France insisted upon the retention of the left bank of the Rhine as essential to her national security; Great Britain and the British dominions called for the division of the German colonies among the victors; Italy demanded not only the rewards promised in the Treaty of London but Fiume as well; Japan insisted upon obtaining Germany's former concessions in China; and both France and Great Britain called for huge indemnities to be paid by Germany. Obviously many of these demands could not be made to square with the peace of justice advocated by Wilson, and they were, moreover, in violation of the Fourteen Points, which had been accepted as a basis for the peace negotiations. Against some of the most extravagant claims of the European powers the President stood firm. He succeeded in preventing, at least for the time being, Italian annexation of Fiume; he resisted successfully France's efforts to annex the German territory along the Rhine; and he was able to prevent the formal distribution of the German colonies and Turkish provinces among the Allies by supporting the mandate system. On the other hand he reluctantly acceded to Japan's claim to Shantung, having received the promise of the Japanese ultimately to restore the territory to China, and he failed in his efforts to fix the reparations bill to be levied upon Germany at a reasonable sum. But Wilson believed that these flaws and others in the treaty could later be remedied through the instrumentality of the League.

On May 7, 1919, the completed treaty was laid before the German delegates and the following day President Wilson cabled from Paris a call for a special session of Congress. It was not, however, until the 28th of June that the treaty was signed in the Hall of Mirrors at Versailles. Immediately thereafter Wilson left for home to meet there the greatest crisis of his life. For more than a month before his arrival the Senate had been engaged in a heated discussion of the treaty, which had not as yet been officially laid before it. This discussion indicated that the Senators were divided into three fairly distinct groups. First was a group of "Irreconcilables," who were determined to defeat the treaty and the League at all costs. At the other extreme was a group, chiefly of Democratic Senators, who were prepared to support the President in his demand that the treaty be ratified without change. Between these two was a larger group of Republicans and Democrats who desired the ratification of the treaty provided certain interpretations and reservations were added, chiefly for the purpose of defining more clearly the obligations of the United States under the League Covenant.

Despite the fact that the Senate was controlled by the Republicans and that the chairman of the Committee on Foreign Relations, Senator Lodge, entertained a deep personal dislike for the President, it is probable that Wilson could have won in his contest with the Senate had he been willing to co-operate with the moderate Republican Senators. In the country there was no clear evidence of popular opposition to the League and the treaty. On the contrary, such representative and influential groups as the American Bankers' Association, the American Bar Association, and the American Federation of Labor adopted resolutions calling for the ratification of the treaty and the League. Had Wilson accepted the suggestions of the moderate group of Senators he could in all probability have secured the necessary two-thirds vote for ratification, but his inability or unwillingness to compromise convinced many Senators that he was bent upon having his own way, reckless of consequences.

In the Senate criticism was centered on the League Covenant. Senator Lodge led the attack despite the fact that in the past he had been a warm advocate of the League idea. As late as May 26, 1916, in an address before the meeting of the League to Enforce Peace, he had belittled the criticism that our participation in such an organization would involve a departure from our traditional policy. "I know," he said, "the difficulties which arise when we speak of anything which seems to involve an alliance. But I do not believe that when Washington warned us against entangling alliances he meant for one moment that we should not join with the other civilized nations of the world, if a method could be found to diminish war and encourage peace." Now, however, he professed to see in the proposed League a menace to American sovereignty. President Wilson appeared before the Committee on Foreign Relations and attempted to explain doubtful points and to defend the settlement made at Paris. He pointed out that most of the suggestions for changes in the wording of the Covenant made in this country had been adopted, and he insisted that the obligations contained in Article X were moral and not legal. He objected to amending the Covenant or the treaty because he felt that such action would necessitate doing over again much of the work that had been accomplished at Paris. At the same time he stated that he felt that there was no objection to setting forth American interpretations of certain provisions of the treaty if these did not constitute a condition of ratification. In the end the President failed to win a majority of the Committee to his point of view and the treaty was reported to the Senate accompanied by forty-five proposed amendments and four reservations.

From the Senate the President appealed directly to the people. In September he went on a speaking tour of the Middle and Far West. Enthusiastic crowds greeted him in the cities he visited but his efforts failed to arouse sufficient popular support to have any appreciable effect upon the Senate. While speaking at Pueblo, Colorado, on September 25th, he broke down and was forced to abandon his tour and return to Washington. A few days after his arrival at the Capital he suffered a paralytic stroke which incapacitated him during the following critical five months in which the treaty was being discussed before the Senate. His impaired health seemed to make the President more firm in his determination not to compromise with those who opposed his plans and he declined to listen to the advice of many friends of the treaty who were convinced that reasonable yielding on the part of the Executive would have saved the essential part of his program.

In the meantime the debate on the treaty continued in the Senate. All of the amendments reported by the Foreign Relations Committee were defeated. Senator Lodge then proposed a list of reservations in place of the amendments. Most of these reservations aimed to limit the obligations of the United States under the League Covenant. Most important was the reservation directed against Article X, which stated that the United States would assume no obligations to preserve the territorial integrity or political independence of any other country, or to interfere in the controversies between nations, unless in any particular case Congress should so provide. A majority of the Senators voted in favor of the Lodge reservations, but the resolution to ratify the treaty with the reservations attached failed to obtain the necessary two-thirds vote. A further motion made by Senator Under-

wood for unconditional ratification was likewise defeated.
Thus matters stood when Congress adjourned in November.
In his message to Congress at the opening of the regular
session in December, 1919, President Wilson made only an
incidental reference to the treaty in saying that the Republican leaders must bear the full responsibility for its fate and
for "the present condition of the world in consequence of
that fate." In January Senator Lodge called a bi-partisan
conference of Senators in an effort to reach a satisfactory
compromise, but to no avail. Finally on February 10, 1920,
Senator Lodge again reported the treaty back to the Senate
with the fifteen reservations adopted at the previous session
substantially unchanged. After five weeks of debate the final
vote was taken on a resolution of ratification with the reservations and understandings attached. The vote on this resolution lacked seven of the necessary two-thirds to ratify.
Twenty-eight Republicans and twenty-one Democrats supported it, and twelve Republican "irreconcilables" and twenty-
three administration Democrats voted for its defeat. The
Senate then voted to return the treaty to the President with
the information that the Senate had failed to consent to
ratification. This action was followed by the passage of a
resolution by both Houses declaring that the war with
Germany was at an end, but the President vetoed this resolution, characterizing it as "an ineffaceable stain upon the
gallantry and honor of the United States."

Such was the disheartening culmination to one of the
most inspiring periods of American history. We had entered
the World War stirred by an exalted spirit of unselfishness
that won for us an enviable position among the nations of
Europe; we closed our adventure amidst deplorable demonstrations of personal animosities and partisan feeling. Our
failure to ratify the treaty and to enter the League not only
shocked and disappointed the nations with which we had been
associated in the war but it was regarded by many persons

in this country as a deliberate repudiation of the principles for which so many American lives had been sacrificed in France. Agreement upon the responsibility for this deplorable outcome will probably never be reached. To the supporters of Mr. Wilson it appeared that the opposition in the Senate was based upon most unworthy motives; a desire to discredit a political opponent and a determination to humiliate the man whom many Senators personally disliked. It was a great misfortune that the debate on the treaty came on the eve of a presidential election, for there can be no doubt that much that was said and done in the course of the debate in Congress was influenced by considerations of the effects that Congressional action on the treaty might have upon the approaching presidential contest. On the other hand many believed that the action of the Senate in insisting upon reservations to the treaty was a wise precaution. If, as was stated by the advocates of the League, there would be no sacrifice of American sovereignty and no infringement upon the constitutional powers of Congress involved in our entrance into the League, there should be no objection to having this fact stated explicitly. Nor would the advocates of reservations concede the soundness of the President's contention that such reservations would necessitate redrafting the whole document drawn up at Paris. It was their conviction that Europe would welcome the United States into the League under whatever conditions she might see fit to lay down.[2] Failure to obtain ratification with reasonable reservations was attributed by those who favored conditional ratification to the stubborn determination of President Wilson to have his own way. Viewed in retrospect ten years after the controversy, it appears that the unfortunate outcome of this episode

[2] Viscount Grey, British Ambassador to the United States, in an open letter to the London *Times* stated that the success of the League depended upon the adherence of the United States, and although he considered the Senate reservations serious, American coöperation should not be refused because conditions were attached.

was in considerable measure due to the unwillingness of either side to concede honest motives to their opponents. A little greater capacity to reconcile his personal and political opponents on the part of Mr. Wilson and a little less insistence upon Senatorial dignity and prerogatives by Senators might have brought a happier result.

However, it is not just to place upon the shoulders of a stubborn President and a jealous Senate the full responsibility for the failure of this country to underwrite the treaty and the League. Had public opinion among the mass of the American people at this time been definitely formulated in regard to the future relations of the United States to the rest of the world it might have had a decisive influence upon the Executive and Congress. But public opinion was in a confused state when the war ended. Our war experience had been too brief to bring about a profound and lasting change in the mental attitude of the majority of the people. It is true that during the war there had been a striking display of unselfishness on the part of the average American citizen. In the crisis persons had endured inconvenience and had submitted to governmental control of their normal social and business activities with remarkably little grumbling. But these experiences had not served to undermine the deep-seated individualism of the great majority of the people. Then, too, many persons had applauded President Wilson's idealistic pronouncements and his vision of the new rôle which this country was destined to play in world affairs without realizing all of the implications involved in his proposals. True, there was a minority of intellectuals who were internationally minded and who realized that the fiction of American isolation no longer fitted the realities of American life, but the large majority was still provincially minded. Moreover, the return of peace brought in this country as it did in most of the nations of Europe an outburst of intense nationalism. Bewildered by the experiences of the war and disillusioned by the demonstration of crass selfishness at the Peace Conference, many people in the United States came to the conclusion that the only safe policy for this country to pursue was to resume its pre-war attitude of aloofness from the affairs of Europe.

It was under these most discouraging circumstances that the advocates of a new world order urged upon the American people the policy of unselfish coöperation with the rest of the world. That their efforts failed is not astonishing. Novel experiments, whether in domestic affairs or in the field of foreign relations, aroused no great popular enthusiasm in this country at the close of the war. In general there was a yearning for a return to "normalcy." And those who led the opposition to the League proposal were quite ready to take advantage of the doubts, fears, and suspicion that stirred the public mind at the time. Exaggerated and frequently absurd statements were made concerning the dire results that would follow if we entered the League. And these statements could be denied but could not be disproved, for the test of their validity lay in the future.

Such was the complex of fears, suspicions, national pride, personal resentments, and partisan antagonisms which contributed to this dramatic but uninspiring episode in American history.

THE "SOLEMN REFERENDUM" OF 1920

President Wilson firmly believed that the mass of the American people sympathized with his views concerning the League and the Treaty, and that they would rebuke those who had frustrated his purposes in the approaching presidential election. Without attempting to dictate the party platform or to indicate his preferences for the party nominee for the presidency he urged the Democratic Convention which met in San Francisco on June 28 to endorse his policies and to select a nominee who supported his views on the League of Nations. To this appeal the party responded by adopting a platform which unequivocally pledged the ratification of the Treaty of Versailles with only such reservations as should be found necessary to define clearly the limitations imposed by our Constitution. The party nominee, Ex-Governor Cox of Ohio, was known to be a strong advocate of America's entrance into the League. In one of his early speeches after his nomination he said: "We promise you this, that after March 4, 1921, with the least amount of conversation possible, we will enter the League of Nations of the world. . . . We advocate the immediate ratification of the Treaty without reservations which impair its essential integrity; but do not oppose any reservations making clearer or more specific the obligations of the United States to the League associates."

The Republicans were in a quandary. Such outstanding Republican leaders as Root, Taft, and Hughes had on numerous occasions endorsed the league idea and had advocated the United States joining such a world organization. On the other hand, there were the "Irreconcilables" headed by Senators Johnson, Borah, and McCormick, who were for the repudiation of the League root and branch. Then, too, it was not certain that the voters would approve a complete repudiation of the league idea. Obviously a straddle was in order, and a plank was adopted that could be accepted by those who favored the League without at the same time alienating the "bitter-enders." On the one hand the platform declared that the proposed Covenant "ignored the universal sentiments of America for generations past in favor of international law and arbitration." On the other hand it was stated that, "The Republican party stands for agreement among nations to preserve the peace of the world" and favors the formation of "an international association" in which the nations shall "exercise their influence and power for the prevention of war." It was maintained that all this could be accomplished "without compromise of national independence" and without involving this country "in a multitude of quarrels, the merits of which they are unable to judge." The nominee of the party, Senator Harding of Ohio, entertained no deep convictions one way or the other concerning the League.

In the course of the campaign the Republican nominee seemed quite unable or unwilling to take an unequivocal stand in regard to the League. At one time we find him stating his belief that the League Covenant could be amended or revised "so that we may still have a remnant of the world aspirations of 1918 builded into the world's highest conception of useful coöperation." On another occasion he said that he did not want to clarify our obligations under the Covenant. "I want to turn my back on them. It is not interpretation but rejection I am seeking." Veering again, he declared that he had no desire to fling aside the good in the Covenant but that he was merely proposing "an amended form of it which may reasonably undertake all that is now said the League intends to do."

Throughout the campaign Republicans who favored the League insisted that the election of Harding would hasten America's entry into the League. Just before the election a group of thirty-one influential Republicans, including Root, Hughes, Taft, and Hoover signed an appeal to the voters to support the Republican ticket, assuring them that Republican success would mean the entrance of the United States into the League under proper limitations.

In view of these facts it seems quite absurd to consider the election of 1920 as a "solemn referendum" on the League or to regard the seven million majority that Harding received as an expression of an overwhelming popular disapproval of the proposal that the United States should join a world organization for the preservation of peace. It is very doubtful if any considerable number of voters voted as they did in this election simply because of their belief or disbelief in the League. One publicist has shrewdly analyzed the results of the election as follows: "The Republican majority was composed of men and women who thought a Republican victory would kill the League, plus those who thought it was the most practical way to secure the League, plus those who thought it the surest way offered to obtain an amended League. All these voters were inextricably entangled with their own desire or the desire of the other voters to improve business, or put labor in its place, or to punish the Democrats for going to war, or to punish them for not having gone sooner, or to get rid of Mr. Burleson, or to improve the price of wheat, or to lower taxes, or to stop Mr. Daniels from outbuilding the world, or to help Mr. Harding do the same thing."

In office President Harding promptly abandoned any attempt to bring the United States into the League. In his inaugural address he said, "We seek no part in directing the destinies of the world. . . . We are ready to associate ourselves with the nations of the world, great and small, for conference and counsel, for the suggestion of plans of mediation, conciliation, and arbitration; but every commitment must be made in the exercise of our national sovereignty." Again in a special message to Congress on February 2, 1923, he said, "I have no unseemly comment to offer on the League. If it is serving the Old World helpfully, more power to it. But it is not for us. The Senate has so declared, the executive has so declared, the people have so declared. Nothing could be more decisively stamped with finality." Shortly after Harding assumed office Congress was summoned in special session and the Knox resolution, declaring the state of war with Germany at an end, which had been vetoed by President Wilson, was repassed and signed by Harding.

The Republican administration at first took the view

that the League without American participation would be short lived and the state department at first ostentatiously adopted the policy of ignoring its existence. Communications from the Secretary General were allowed to go unanswered; invitations to this government to coöperate in the early humanitarian work of the League were declined; American assistance in the organization of the Permanent Court of International Justice was discouraged; and private American citizens were dissuaded from accepting positions on League commissions. But contrary to such expectations the League did not disappear; in fact its membership steadily grew until it has come to include fifty-five nations of the world while the activities of the League machinery have increased in scope and effectiveness as it has gained experience. In view of this situation the attitude of aloofness on the part of the American government became both futile and childish. Accordingly, the Washington authorities adopted the policy of sending "unofficial observers" to sit with the League committees dealing with non-political matters. From this grudging recognition of the League's existence the American authorities gradually passed to official coöperation with many of the activities of the League. In 1927 official American representatives sat with League commissions dealing with humanitarian, technical, economic, and armament questions, although the Washington authorities continued to withhold any participation in League activities dealing with purely political matters.

THE WASHINGTON ARMAMENT CONFERENCE

Whatever might be the policy of the American authorities toward the League of Nations, there were disturbing conditions in the foreign relations of this country in the post-war period which called for something more than a policy of negation. Our cordial coöperation with Great Britain during our participation in the war had not served to obliterate remembrance of the humiliation that we had suffered in the interference with our trade through the activities of the British navy during the period of our neutrality. The Paris Conference had done nothing to define sea law in time of war. Wilson's demand for the freedom of the seas had been ignored, presumably at the behest of Great Britain. In future wars, as in the late war, neutral rights on the high seas would presumably be determined by belligerents, provided they had adequate naval power to enforce their views. It was this situation that led to the agitation, supported by influential groups in this country, for the building of an American navy which would be able to enforce respect for American rights in any future war. The General Board of the navy in its report of September, 1920, advocated the building of "a navy equal to the most powerful maintained by any other nation in the world." The naval building program of 1916, which had been postponed when we entered the war, was revived as soon as the war was over and, if carried to completion, it would result in this country having a number of capital ships equal to, if not greater, than those in the British navy, unless Great Britain should see fit to engage in a competitive building program.

It must be remembered that the two countries, Great Britain and Japan, most concerned with the naval policy of the United States, were in an alliance, and any ambitious naval building program on our part was calculated to strengthen the Anglo-Japanese alliance. Clearly here was a situation that might easily disturb the peaceful relations among these three countries unless something should be done to clear the atmosphere.

Whatever naval experts at Washington might say or recommend, popular opinion in the United States in 1920 was anything but jingoistic. Memories of the late war were still too fresh. Whether we joined the League or not there was a strong undercurrent of feeling in the country that we should do our part to remove the menace of future wars and to lighten the burden of military and naval armaments. This feeling found expression in Congress when in December, 1920, Senator Borah introduced a joint resolution urging the President to invite Great Britain and Japan to a conference for the purpose of promptly entering into an understanding or agreement by which the naval expenditures of the three powers should be reduced. Popular approval of this proposal came from all parts of the country with the result that the resolution passed the Senate unanimously and the House by a vote of 330 to 4.

Fortified by the expressions of popular sentiment President Harding not only carried out the suggestion contained in the Borah resolution but extended its scope by including the proposal that the conference should take up questions concerning the Pacific and the Far East in the hope of removing the danger of war in this region.[3]

The conference held its first session in Washington on November 12, 1921. After a welcoming speech by President Harding, Secretary Hughes, who had been chosen chairman of the conference, startled the delegates by immediately proposing not only a limitation upon future naval building but also a substantial scrapping of ships already built or in process of construction. In substance he proposed that the United States scrap ships amounting to some 845,000 tons, while Great Britain was asked to scrap about 583,000 tons, and Japan similarly was to scrap some 448,000 tons. As the United States was in an economic position to outbuild any of its competitors and as we were offering to scrap the largest tonnage it was difficult for the other powers to oppose the proposed cut, and the Hughes program was immediately accepted in principle. It was then proposed that the tonnage of

[3] See p. 488.

capital ships [4] of the five chief naval powers be fixed at the following amounts: Great Britain and the United States 525,000 tons each, Japan 315,000 tons, and France and Italy 175,000 tons. This provided the so-called ratio for capital ships of 5–5–3–1.67–1.67. The effort to extend the limitation to cruisers and submarines failed, as did also the attempt of Mr. Hughes to have the subject of land armaments included in the discussions of the conference.[5]

As a result of the discussions at Washington nine treaties were drafted and signed: (1) A five-power treaty between the United States, Great Britain, France, Italy, and Japan, limiting the tonnage and fixing the quota of capital ships; (2) a five-power treaty between the same countries restricting the use of submarines in war by the accepted rules of naval warfare, and also outlawing asphyxiating gases as a war weapon; (3) a four-power treaty between the United States, Great Britain, France and Japan, binding these states to respect the existing rights of the signatories in their insular possessions in the Pacific; (4) a four-power treaty between the same countries by which they agreed that in case of "aggressive action" by one or more other powers in the Pacific they would "discuss fully and frankly the most efficient measures to be taken" to assure their mutual interests; this agreement carrying with it the abrogation of the existing Anglo-Japanese treaty of alliance; (5) a nine-power treaty signed by all of the states represented at the conference guaranteeing the territorial integrity and independence of China and recognizing the principle of the "Open Door" in that country; (6) a similar treaty granting to China greater control of her customs tariff; (7) a treaty between Japan and China providing for the restoration of Kiaochow and the Shantung peninsula to China; (8) a treaty between Japan and the

---

[4] Capital ships included all ships over 10,000 tons displacement or having guns larger than 8 in. caliber.

[5] The work of the conference in connection with Far-Eastern questions is considered in Chapter 20.

United States confirming American cable rights in the island of Yap; and (9) a six-power treaty between the United States, Great Britain, Japan, France, Italy, and China allocating the former German cable lines in the Pacific.

In submitting the treaties to the Senate President Harding assured that body that there was nothing in any of them which committed the United States to "any kind of alliance, entanglement, or involvement." Some of the Senators who had bitterly opposed the Treaty of Versailles were not easily convinced of this optimistic point of view. In fact, to persons given to strict logical reasoning it appeared somewhat inconsistent to maintain that there was no departure from American traditions to have this country join with three of the great powers of the world to preserve peace in the Pacific and at the same time to argue that it would violate such traditions to have us join these same and other powers to assure peace in other parts of the world. However, Senator Lodge and most of his Republican associates professed no difficulty in reconciling these two points of view and all of the treaties were ratified with the face-saving reservation disclaiming any intention on the part of the United States of departing from the old tradition against entangling alliances and participation in the affairs of other nations.

Although the Washington Conference did not accomplish all that was claimed for it at the time by its more enthusiastic supporters it was not on the other hand a futile gesture, as some of its critics claimed. Though much remained to be done before any adequate limitation of armaments could be realized, at least the Conference had made a notable beginning in this direction.

CONTINUED EFFORTS AT DISARMAMENT

Perhaps the most significant result of the Washington Conference was not so much the specific agreements entered into by the nations involved as the fact that the Conference stimulated popular interest in the problem of disarmament and paved the way to further efforts in the same direction. Through the instrumentality of the League of Nations a conference was summoned at Rome in 1924 in an effort to secure "the extension to the rest of the world of the principles of the Washington Naval Conference." This attempt failed largely because it was a meeting of military and naval experts who had no authority to consider the political questions involved in the extremely complicated problem of armaments. Again in 1926 the Preparatory Commission for a General Disarmament Conference of the League of Nations gathered at Geneva. Invitations to attend the sessions were extended to Russia and the United States, the two most important countries not members of the League. Frankly abandoning the attitude of aloofness from League activities the Washington authorities accepted the invitation and appointed a strong American delegation. Once more the effort to reach a practical program of disarmament failed because of the inability of the conference to divorce technical questions from political considerations.

Undiscouraged by these failures, President Coolidge in February, 1927, announced his purpose to invite the five Powers that had signed the naval treaty in Washington— the United States, England, France, Italy, and Japan—to discuss the extension of the ratio system to the categories of warships not covered by the Washington Conference. France and Italy declined the invitation, chiefly because they were unwilling to separate the question of naval armaments from that of land armaments. Despite these refusals the representatives of the three remaining countries met at Geneva. Prolonged and somewhat heated discussions between the British and American delegates ended in a deadlock. Great Britain was willing to concede equality to the United States in cruiser strength, but agreement could not be reached upon the question of total tonnage to be allowed to each nation or upon the type of ships to be built. In announcing the failure of the Geneva Conference President Coolidge in his message to Congress in December, 1927, said, "We now know that no agreement can be reached which will be inconsistent with a considerable building program on our part." The navy program subsequently submitted to Congress by the Secretary of the Navy called for the construction of 74 vessels at an estimated cost of $740,000,000. An energetic campaign of opposition to this huge expenditure was launched by a number of peace societies, religious groups, and women's organizations, with the result that the naval construction program was cut to fifteen cruisers and one aircraft carrier.

SEA POWER AND SEA LAW

Directly involved in the question of naval strength is the question of sea law. For more than a century the United States, except during the Civil War, had consistently contended for the principle of the sanctity of private property on the high seas in time of war and for the right of neutrals to trade at will with belligerents and neutrals. Great Britain, in command of the seas, resolutely resisted all attempts to write these principles into international law. In time of war, therefore, neutral rights were at the mercy of any belligerent having adequate naval power to enforce its views. The experiences of neutrals in the Great War gave pointed evidence of this fact. In such a situation it seemed futile to expect any satisfactory agreement between the two chief naval powers, Great Britain and the United States, concerning the limitation of naval armaments until the existing chaotic condition of maritime law should be remedied.

It was this conviction that led Senator Borah, Chairman of the Foreign Relations Committee, to introduce a series of resolutions in the Senate on February 21, 1928, calling for the restatement and recodification of maritime law governing the conduct of belligerents and neutrals in war; such action to be taken prior to the meeting of the Conference on the Limitation of Armaments scheduled to meet in 1931.[6] No immediate response to this suggestion came from the British authorities, but there was not lacking evidence that among liberal circles in England the opinion prevailed that the American proposal should be accepted. Added weight was given to this view from a realization of the fact that if the two countries should engage in a program of competitive naval building the United States had it within its power, because of its tremendous financial resources, to wrest from England the control of the seas. The likelihood of an understanding being reached on this thorny question appeared to be materially increased as a result of the significant agreement, signed by the United States and the other leading nations of the world at Paris, August 27, 1928, providing for the renunciation of war as an instrument of national policy.

THE PEACE PACT OF PARIS

In the course of the prolonged discussion on the question of disarmament among the European nations after the Great War one fact was clearly demonstrated, namely, that no satisfactory progress could be made in the direction of disarmament until the closely associated problem of security was solved. The nations of the continent of Europe, with a keen realization of historic rivalries among European states, were unwilling to agree to any substantial disarmament until they were assured that such action would not expose them

---

[6] In the bill for the construction of fifteen cruisers before July 1, 1931, passed by Congress, February 5, 1929, there was a provision favoring the negotiation of a treaty restating sea-law and providing for the inviolability of private property on the high seas in time of war. In case of an international agreement being reached for the further limitation of naval armaments the President was authorized to suspend in whole or in part the building program provided by the bill.

to the danger of attack. The guarantee contained in the League of Nations Covenant appeared to the statesmen of some of these countries to be inadequate. Various efforts were made to satisfy the demand for additional guarantees, notably in the Draft Treaty of Mutual Assistance submitted by the Council of the League in 1923 and in the Geneva Protocol of 1924. For a variety of reasons which cannot here be discussed, both of these proposals failed of adoption. There followed the important Locarno Treaties of 1925 which went far to remove one important area of international friction along the frontier between France and Germany.

It became apparent, however, that any understanding looking toward world peace and disarmament which did not take into consideration the attitude of the United States and Russia would at best be only partially successful. Considerations of domestic politics made it inexpedient for the authorities at Washington, whatever might be their personal convictions, to sponsor any proposal emanating from the League of Nations. A fortunate circumstance gave an opportunity to the state department at Washington to assume the initiative in bringing about American coöperation in a significant international agreement without arousing the latent fears and suspicions concerning our relations to the League of Nations.

On June 20, 1927, M. Briand, the French Foreign Minister, submitted the draft of a pact of perpetual friendship between France and the United States which provided that the high contracting parties condemn "recourse to war and renounce it respectively as an instrument of their national policy towards each other." After a delay of six months Secretary of State Kellogg replied that it was the view of the American government that instead of a bilateral treaty between the United States and France all of the principal nations of the world should be invited to adhere to a declaration similar to that proposed by M. Briand. The French authorities agreed to this proposal, with the understanding that the contemplated treaty should not affect the obligations that France had assumed under the League Covenant and the Locarno Treaties for safeguarding the peace of Europe. Secretary Kellogg took the view that there was no conflict between the contemplated treaty for the renunciation of war and the obligations of the European powers under the League and the Locarno agreements and he therefore extended an invitation to the leading nations of the world to join in signing the proposed treaty. The representatives of fifteen states—Germany, the United States, Belgium, France, Great Britain, Canada, Australia, New Zealand, South Africa, the Irish Free State, India, Italy, Japan, Poland, and Czechoslovakia—met at Paris and, on August 27, 1928, signed the multilateral agreement.

The treaty consists of three brief but comprehensive articles. Article 1 states that the High Contracting Parties "condemn recourse to war for the solution of international controversies, and renounce it as an instrument of national policy in their relations with one another." Article 2 provides that the settlement of all disputes "of whatever nature or of whatever origin they may be, which may arise among them, shall never be sought except by pacific means." Article 3 stipulates that all other powers of the world that have not participated in signing the treaty be allowed to indicate their adherence to it.

Having in mind the fate of the Treaty of Versailles there was some doubt whether the Paris Pact would be approved by the United States Senate, at least without substantial reservations. However, the Senate restricted itself to an explanatory statement submitted by the Committee on Foreign Relations to the effect that it was to be understood that the ratification of the treaty did not curtail or impair the right of self-defense; that the maintenance of the Monroe Doctrine is included as part of our system of self-defense; and that the treaty did not obligate the United States to engage in any punitive or coercive measures against any nation violating it. With this understanding the treaty was ratified January 15, 1929, with only one dissenting vote.

There are many who maintain that the Paris Pact is nothing but an empty gesture. It does not outlaw war. It merely renounces war as an instrument of national policy without attempting to define these terms. It does not deprive nations of their inherent right to defend themselves against attack. But it does place upon nations resorting to war the burden of proof that they are not acting as aggressors. Most important of all, it brings the United States into coöperation with the other nations of the world for the preservation of peace. It imposes a moral if not a legal obligation upon the United States not to give aid or comfort to any nation that resorts to war in violation of its pledge given in the treaty. It gives an added guarantee to defenseless nations that they will not be made the victims of aggression, and thereby removes one more obstacle to general disarmament. Finally, it places the seal of world approval upon the peaceful instead of the warlike settlement of international disputes.

THE LONDON CONFERENCE ON DISARMAMENT

The signing of the Paris Peace Pact by fifty-six nations paved the way for further efforts to limit armaments. In October, 1929, the British Premier, J. Ramsay MacDonald, visited the United States to discuss with President Hoover "the mutual relations of the two countries in the light of the situation created by the signing of the peace pact." As a result of their conversations a joint statement was issued in which the heads of the two governments declared that they regarded war between the United States and the British Empire as "unthinkable." With obvious reference to the much mooted question of the freedom of the seas it was stated that in view of the signing of the Paris Pact "we approach these old historical problems from a new angle and in a new atmosphere" and, assuming that war between the two countries has been banished, "these problems have changed their meaning and character and their solution, in ways satisfactory to both countries, has become possible."

During Premier MacDonald's visit an official invitation was sent by the British government to the five chief naval powers that had participated in the Washington Conference to send delegates to a second conference to meet in London in January, 1930, to discuss the extension of limitation of naval armaments to the categories of ships that had not been covered by the Washington Conference, and also to consider the total prohibition of submarines.

THE UNITED STATES AND THE WORLD COURT

Efforts to establish machinery for the judicial settlement of international controversies have in the past received earnest support in this country. The American delegation to the first Hague Conference in 1899 was instructed by President McKinley to act upon "the long-continued and widespread interest among the people of the United States in the establishment of an international court." Largely due to American initiative the Conference provided for the organization of a Permanent Court of Arbitration. In fact this Permanent Court was neither permanent nor even a court. It was merely a panel containing the names of about a hundred and fifty men from which contending states might select arbiters for particular disputes. In 1907 the American delegates to the second Hague Conference were instructed to work for the establishment of a more formal court, but their efforts in this direction did not meet with success. It required the tragic experience of the World War to bring the nations of the world to a realization of the necessity of providing some such international judicial organization as had been proposed by the United States.

The Covenant of the League of Nations provided that the Council of the League should formulate plans for the establishment of a Permanent Court of International Justice. Acting under this mandate the Council invited a group of distinguished jurists to frame a plan for the new court. This body drafted a protocol which provided for the organization, competence and procedure of the proposed court. The court was to consist of fifteen members, eleven judges and four deputy judges, who were to be elected by the Council and Assembly of the League of Nations from a list of persons nominated by the Hague Court of Arbitration. The jurisdiction of the court extended to all international disputes submitted to it by states subscribing to the protocol. In addition the court might render "advisory opinions" on questions submitted to it by the Council or Assembly of the League. The protocol was approved by the Council and Assembly of the League in December, 1920. All nations of the world, whether members of the League or not, were entitled to subscribe to the jurisdiction of the Court by signing the protocol.

To a large number of persons in the United States it appeared appropriate that we should join the World Court, whatever might be our attitude toward the League of Nations, for the establishment of the Court was the realization of an ideal for which this country had long striven. Such was the view taken by Secretary of State Hughes in a letter to President Harding on February 17, 1923, in which he earnestly advocated our adhesion to the Court with the distinct understanding that such action should not involve any legal relation on the part of the United States to the League of Nations, and with the further provisos that this country should be permitted to participate in the election of judges and that the protocol should not be amended without the consent of the United States. President Harding transmitted Mr. Hughes' letter to the Senate with his endorsement, and with the recommendation that the Senate give its favorable advice and consent, but memories of the bitter controversy over the League were still too fresh to obtain the requisite senatorial support and the matter was allowed to rest. In three successive annual messages President Coolidge urged upon the Senate favorable action upon the Court proposal and the House of Representatives on March 3, 1925, by an overwhelming vote expressed its approval of American adhesion to the Court. Finally on January 27, 1926, the Senate adopted a resolution giving its consent to the proposal but attached a number of important conditions. In addition to the provisos suggested by Mr. Hughes the Senate stipulated: (1) that the United States may at any time withdraw its adherence to the protocol; (2) that the Court shall not render any advisory opinion except publicly after due notice and shall not, without the consent of the United States, entertain any request for an advisory opinion on any dispute or question in which the United States has or claims to have an interest; (3) that recourse to the Court in disputes involving the United States can be made only by treaty agreement; and (4) that our adhesion to the protocol shall not be construed to require the United States to depart from its traditional policy of not intruding upon or interfering with political questions of any foreign state or to imply a relinquishment by the United States of its traditional attitude toward purely American questions. Finally it was stated that the signature of the United States to the protocol should not be affixed until the powers which had signed the protocol had indicated their acceptance of the conditions made by the United States.

On invitation from the Secretary General of the League, the nations that had signed the Court protocol sent representatives to Geneva to consider the American conditions. Little difficulty was encountered in obtaining acceptance of all of the American reservations except the one referring to the right of the Court to render advisory opinions. It was felt by the representatives of several of the European states that such a restriction would hamper the work of the League of Nations. In an effort to reach a satisfactory agreement on this question it was proposed that the United States should be assured an equal right with League members in objecting to a request for an advisory opinion from the Court. This suggestion did not meet with the approval of the Washington authorities and as a result the attempt to bring the United States into the World Court was for the time being abandoned.[7]

Those who favored the entrance of the United States into the Court did not give up hope. In January, 1929, Mr. Elihu Root, then approaching his eighty-fourth birthday, accepted an invitation to join a committee of international jurists appointed to consider the revision of the statute of the Court as it was drawn up in 1920. To this Committee Mr. Root submitted a long explanatory formula which was aimed to meet the reservation made by the Senate concerning advisory opinions rendered by the Court. In brief this formula provided that the Court shall not, without the consent of the United States, render an advisory opinion touching any dispute to which the United States is a party. In regard to disputes in which the United States is not a party, but in which it claims an interest, if the United States declines to consent to the Court rendering an advisory opinion and the interested parties demand such an opinion, then the United States may exercise its right to withdraw its adhesion to the Court protocol "without any imputation of unfriendliness or unwillingness to coöperate generally for peace and

[7] In 1928 the Council and Assembly of the League of Nations chose Charles Evans Hughes to fill the vacancy in the World Court caused by the resignation of John Bassett Moore.

good-will." This formula was accepted by the Committee and subsequently ratified by the Council and Assembly of the League of Nations. It remained to be seen whether the United States Senate would accept this formula as satisfying its former reservation.

THE UNITED STATES AND GERMAN REPARATIONS

We have seen that President Wilson had failed at the Peace Conference to persuade the Allies to fix the total reparations to be demanded of Germany. He had also been induced, against his own judgment and against the advice of the American experts, to agree to the inclusion in the reparations bill of the total sum paid by the Allies to their subjects in the form of pensions and separation allowances. The Peace Conference adjourned leaving the problem of determining the total amount of German reparations to an Allied Reparations Commission. After nearly two years' study the Commission on April 27, 1921, submitted a report fixing Germany's obligation at the stupendous figure of 132,-000,000,000 gold marks. Economic experts were generally agreed that it would be utterly impossible to extort any such fanciful sum from Germany, even if it could be theoretically justified under the Armistice terms and the Peace Treaty. Regarding the Allied demands as both unjustified and impossible of fulfillment, Germany adopted a policy of passive resistance and declined to make such reasonable payments as her circumstances would have warranted. In retaliation France determined upon military occupation of the important German industrial region of the Ruhr valley. For two years from 1921 to 1923 the European situation grew steadily more menacing. The German mark collapsed, and Germany's currency became virtually worthless. Not only Germany but the whole of Central Europe appeared to be headed for economic and political chaos.

In the face of these momentous events in Europe the Washington authorities assumed, officially, an attitude of detachment. President Harding declined the proposal of Germany that he should arbitrate the dispute with her creditors. But official detachment of the American authorities could not obscure the fact that the chaotic conditions in Europe were reacting unfavorably upon business conditions in this country. The business depression in 1920 and 1921 was at least in part due to the disturbed economic conditions in Europe. Obviously the United States was in the most favorable position to relieve the intolerable situation in Europe and despite the professed aloofness of the Harding administration Secretary Hughes in a speech delivered at New Haven, December 29, 1922, suggested that a committee of economic and financial experts, with American participation, be appointed to make a study of German conditions for the purpose of determining her ability to pay reparations. France was at first disinclined to accept the proposal but she finally consented on condition that the authority of the committee should be strictly limited. The result was the appointment of the so-called Dawes Commission of which three members were Americans, General Charles G. Dawes, Owen D. Young, and Henry M. Robinson.

It is not possible here to describe the work performed by this body or even to outline the details of the report that it made. Suffice it to say that it proposed a plan for the stabilization of the German currency and indicated a schedule of annual payments to be made by Germany on account of reparations, which were graduated from 1,000,000,000 gold marks in the first year (1924-25) to 2,500,000,000 gold marks in the fifth year (1928-29). The whole plan was conditioned upon the restoration of the economic unity of Germany, that is, upon the withdrawal of France from the Ruhr. The Dawes plan did not solve the reparations problem, for it did not fix the total amount which Germany was to pay in reparations but it did serve to relieve an extremely critical situation in Europe.[8]

Although the American government assumed no obligation to underwrite the Dawes plan the fact remains that it would not have been adopted had it not been for the moral support given to it by this country and it would have been impossible of realization without the aid of American capital. As a further step to assure the coöperation of American financial interests in the working of the Dawes plan the Allied powers selected an American, Mr. S. Parker Gilbert, as Agent General of Reparations.

After five years of experience under the Dawes plan during which time Germany faithfully met the annual installments which she was required to pay, it was felt that the time had arrived to clear up the whole reparations problem and particularly to determine the total amount that Germany should be called upon to pay. With this in view an agreement was made between Germany and the five powers chiefly interested in reparations, France, Great Britain, Italy, Belgium, and Japan, on September 16, 1928, for the setting up of a commission to reconsider the problem of German reparations. Convinced that the success of the work of the commission depended upon the financial support of American banking interests the six powers concerned indicated to the government at Washington their desire to have American experts serve on the commission. Having received assurance from Secretary Kellogg that the government of the United States had no objection to Americans serving on the commission in an unofficial capacity, the six powers invited Mr. Owen D. Young and Mr. J. Pierpont Morgan to accept membership on the commission. This international commission, with Mr. Young as chairman, after prolonged discussions drew up a

[8] At a conference of the Finance Ministers of the Allied powers held at Paris, January, 1925, it was agreed that the United States should receive 2¼ per cent. of the annual payments made by Germany under the Dawes plan to satisfy American claims against Germany.

report which aimed to settle finally the problem of German reparations. The outstanding features of the report were: (1) the establishment of a fixed number of annuities to be paid by Germany extending over fifty-eight years; (2) the establishment of an international bank from the profits of which Germany's payments during the final twenty-two years should be made; (3) the continuance of deliveries in kind by Germany for ten years only; (4) provisions for commercializing a portion of the reparations obligations; and (5) the abolition of the Reparations Commission.

Although the United States authorities had consistently maintained that the payment of the debts owed to the United States by the various Allied countries should not be conditioned upon the amount that the Allies received from Germany, nevertheless the Young plan clearly recognized that there was an economic and financial connection between war debts and reparations. In the first place, the period over which the German reparations payments were to run was made to correspond with the period of the war debt payments. In the second place, the amounts of the German annuities and the condition of their payment are definitely related to the amounts which the Allied governments are required to pay to the United States under the war debt settlements. In fact the French Chamber of Deputies in ratifying the debt settlement agreement with the United States on July 21, 1929, passed a resolution which declared that the amounts paid to the United States should be covered by German reparations payments. If Germany should default, France would doubtless ask the United States for a revision of the debt agreement.

THE UNITED STATES AND INTER-ALLIED DEBTS

When the United States entered the World War the Allied governments had about exhausted their financial resources. President Wilson in his war message recommended the ex-

GERMAN REPARATION PAYMENTS

WHAT GERMANY PAYS

WHAT EACH CREDITOR OF GERMANY RECEIVES

DOMINIONS FRANCE OTHER COUNTRIES AMERICA ITALY BELGIUM BRITAIN

WHAT EUROPEAN COUNTRIES DO WITH IT

A. PAID TO BRITAIN
B. " " AMERICA
C. RETAINED BY COUNTRY CONCERNED

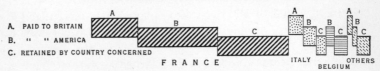

FRANCE ITALY BELGIUM OTHERS

WHAT BRITAIN PAYS AMERICA & WHERE SHE GETS IT FROM

FROM GERMANY FROM FRANCE FROM ITALY FROM OTHER COUNTRIES

WHAT AMERICA RECEIVES

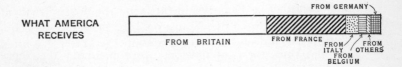

FROM BRITAIN FROM FRANCE FROM GERMANY FROM ITALY FROM BELGIUM FROM OTHERS

WHAT FINALLY HAPPENS TO GERMANY'S PAYMENTS

DOMINIONS ITALY OTHERS

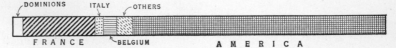

FRANCE BELGIUM AMERICA

tension to these governments of liberal credits so that our resources might be made effective as quickly as possible. Congress responded by authorizing loans totaling $10,000,-000,000. Most of these advances were made to enable the various European countries to pay for war supplies purchased largely in this country. Some of the loans were made after the Armistice was signed for relief purposes or as advances for the payment of surplus American war materials left in Europe at the close of the war. The amount of these government loans made to foreign countries are indicated in the following table:

Armenia	$ 11,959,917.49
Austria	24,055,708.92
Belgium	379,087,200.43
Cuba	10,000,000.00
Czechoslovakia	91,879,671.03
Esthonia	13,999,145.60
Finland	8,281,926.17
France	3,404,818,945.01
Great Britain	4,277,000,000.00
Greece	15,000,000.00
Hungary	1,685,835.61
Italy	1,648,034,050.90
Latvia	5,132,287.14
Liberia	26,000.00
Lithuania	4,981,628.03
Nicaragua	166,604.14
Poland	150,666,972.39
Rumania	37,922,675.42
Russia	192,601,297.37
Jugoslavia	54,758,486.55

At the time these obligations were incurred the representatives of the borrowing governments signed promissory notes for their indebtedness in much the same manner as would be done in an ordinary commercial transaction. With the close of the war the question of the funding and ultimate payment of this large indebtedness gave rise to a prolonged and somewhat acrimonious discussion between the United States and the debtor nations. Among the latter, and especially in France, there was a feeling expressed in both official and unofficial circles that all of the inter-allied debts should be canceled. It was argued that as the United States had entered the war late and had therefore not suffered as great losses in men and money as had her Allies she should regard the loans as contributions to the general cause of the Allies. This proposal did not meet with approval in this country, at least in official circles. It was pointed out that any such arrangement would mean placing upon the shoulders of the American taxpayers a large and unjustified burden. Convinced of the impossibility of bringing about complete cancellation of the inter-allied debts the suggestion was then made in Europe that the United States should agree to limit the amount which she would demand from the Allies to the amount which they in turn could exact from Germany in the shape of reparations. This proposal was firmly resisted by the American authorities, for it was realized that to accept any such arrangement would involve this country in the complicated reparation controversy. It was the view at Washington that the question of German reparations had no legal or moral relation to that of the inter-allied debts.

In 1922 Congress took official action to bring the debt issue to a head. An act was passed creating a World War Foreign Debt Commission, which body was authorized to enter into negotiations with the representatives of foreign countries for the purpose of funding their obligations to this country. In carrying out these powers the Commission formulated the principle of "capacity to pay" as the basis of negotiating the debt-funding agreements. Arrangements were ultimately made with all of the governments for funding their obligations. All of the agreements provided for the payment of the principal and interest of the debts in installments running over a period of sixty-two years. In applying the principle of "capacity to pay" the Commission provided for different rates of interest in the various debt settlements.

These rates varied from a maximum of 3.3 per cent. in the case of the British debt to a minimum of .4 per cent. in the Italian settlement. Assuming that all of these agreements will be carried out, there will be paid to the United States by the debtor states during the first ten years an average annual payment of $233,000,000, which will increase to a maximum annual payment of $414,000,000 during the last twelve years.

Viewed in the large the record of ten years of post-war foreign relations of the United States has not served to enhance the respect for America among the nations of the world. On the contrary there is much evidence to show that our country, a decade after our great adventure in the World War, is regarded abroad with a feeling compounded of fear, suspicion, and resentment. To the nations associated in the League it appeared that our attitude toward that body had been ungracious. Beginning with a determination to ignore the existence of the League we soon found that circumstances forced us into a grudging coöperation with it. To European statesmen it appeared that this country wished to enjoy the advantages which might come from a world organization without being willing to assume any responsibility or to forego any of its sovereign rights. Then, too, the inclination of some American publicists and statesmen to lecture Europe on its shortcomings and to read moral lessons to other peoples has been a source of much irritation. Such pronouncements have been regarded abroad as savoring too much of hypocrisy and condescension. Although this unfortunate European reaction toward the United States in recent years is understandable and perhaps inevitable, there is little doubt that it does not truly reflect the attitude of the great mass of intelligent Americans towards Europe. As the Honorable Elihu Root has well said: "We have allowed insensate prejudice, camouflaged futile phrases, to appear, but falsely appear, to represent the true heart of the American people with all its idealism, with its breadth of human sympathy, with its strong desire that our country should do its share for peace and happiness and noble life in all the world."

BIBLIOGRAPHICAL NOTE

A large number of works have appeared describing the work of the Paris Peace Conference. Among these the following may be noted: H. W. V. Temperley, ed., *A History of the Peace Conference of Paris* (6 Vols., 1920-24); R. S. Baker, *Woodrow Wilson and the World Settlement* (3 Vols., 1922); E. M. House and C. Seymour, *What Actually Happened at Paris* (1921); B. M. Baruch, *The Making of the Reparation and Economic Sections of the Treaty* (1920); R. Lansing, *The Peace Negotiations: A Personal Narrative* (1921); A. Tardieu, *The Truth About the Treaty* (1921), gives a French view. H. C. Lodge, *The Senate and the League of Nations* (1925), contains a defense of the attitude of the Senate toward the treaty and a strong criticism of the policy of Wilson. See also C. Seymour, *Intimate Papers of Colonel House* (4 Vols., 1926-28).

For the Washington Conference consult H. A. Gibbons, *Introduction to World Politics* (1926); R. L. Buell, *The Washington Conference* (1925). For the League of Nations and the World Court see J. S. Bassett, *The League of Nations* (1928); S. P. Duggan, ed., *The League of Nations* (1919); M. O. Hudson, *The Permanent Court of International Justice and the Question of American Participation* (1925). Consult also the pamphlets and handbooks published by the World Peace Foundation and the Carnegie Endowment for International Peace.

On the questions of German reparations and the inter-allied debts see C. P. Howland, *American Foreign Relations: 1928* (1928); C. Bergman, *History of Reparations* (1927); R. L. Buell, *International Relations* (1929).

For the controversy over the freedom of the seas consult J. M. Kenworthy and G. Young, *Freedom of the Seas* (1928). For a consideration of the Paris Pact see J. T. Shotwell, *War as an Instrument of National Policy and Its Renunciation in the Pact of Paris* (1929).

CHAPTER 23

SOCIAL AND CULTURAL CONDITIONS, 1900-1929

The progress of scientific inventions and the development of industry in the first quarter of the twentieth century have brought profound changes in the social life and cultural conditions of the American people. Indeed, it is impossible to foresee at the present time how far-reaching these changes are destined to be. Mention need only be made of the development of the telephone, the automobile, the radio, the motion picture, and innumerable electrical and mechanical devices in the industrial activities and in the home to make one appreciate how far the life of the average American of today is removed from that of only a generation ago.

The population of the continental United States increased in the first three decades of the twentieth century from about 92,000,000 to approximately 120,000,000. The rate of increase in these decades was less than it had been in the period before 1900, largely because of the falling off in immigration caused by the Great War and of the post-war restrictive immigration laws. The distribution of the increased population reflected the trend of economic development during these years. In the older agricultural states only a moderate increase was registered, and in some cases even a decline. Some of the newer agricultural states, as the Dakotas, showed substantial gains, but it was the states affected by the rapid industrial development of this period that claimed the largest percentage of growth. Industrial states like New York, Connecticut, Pennsylvania, and New Jersey showed an average increase of more than 20 per cent., while the very large growth of such states as Texas, Oklahoma, and California is accounted for, in considerable measure, by the development of the oil industry.

The shift of population from rural areas to urban centers noted in the earlier years continued unabated in the period after 1900. The urban population which stood at 40 per cent. of the total in 1900 reached 45.8 per cent. in 1910 and 51.4 per cent. in 1920. There was 144 cities of over 50,000 inhabitants in 1920, 68 with more than 100,000, nine having between 500,000 and 1,000,000, and three more than a million.

Conditions of life in the cities show important contrasts with those of the period before 1900. The numbers of persons of large wealth who resided, for a part of the year at least, in urban centers had increased substantially. The income tax returns for the years from 1914 to 1927 show that the number of persons reporting net incomes of between $50,000 and $100,000 increased from 5,161 to 22,573; those receiving between $500,000 and $1,000,000 rose from 114 to 557; while those enjoying an income of a million dollars or more advanced from 60 to 290. It has been estimated that there were in the United States in 1929 in the neighborhood of 50,000 millionaires.

Among those who possessed great fortunes there appeared a tendency to avoid the ostentatious display of wealth that had characterized the "Gilded Age" before 1900. The monkey dinners and other exotic pastimes of the earlier days were seldom if ever repeated in the homes of the wealthy. There seemed to be among those richly endowed with this world's goods a greater appreciation of the responsibilities of wealth, coupled with a greater sensitiveness to criticism coming from the middle and lower classes. While some of the older wealthy families continued to maintain their handsome homes along fashionable boulevards in New York and other cities, an increasing number of this class established city residences in the luxurious apartments and hotels built in the large cities after 1900.

Life among the urban middle class showed marked changes in these years. Although the members of this class had not drawn the great prizes from the increase of national wealth there is no doubt that the standard of living in this social stratum rose steadily. Even more than the rich, the middle class city families gave up their private dwellings and moved into apartments. In every city large areas were covered with blocks of apartment houses, somewhat less pretentious than those occupied by the wealthy, but still having conveniences unknown to middle class families of the previous generation. Other members of this class, unwilling to conform to the standardized apartment house life, left the cities and moved to suburban areas, where they were able to maintain some of the features of the family life of former years.

Conditions of life among the laboring masses of the cities were steadily improved in the early decades of the twentieth century. Although there remained slum areas in cities like New York, Boston and Chicago, in which living conditions were far from ideal, nevertheless the disgraceful rookeries with their unspeakable filth which housed the workers of earlier years were replaced by tenements having at least a minimum of comforts and conveniences. Municipal authorities, urged on by social workers and financially supported by philanthropists, undertook plans for building model housing accommodations for the poorer classes. Greater care, too, was given to health conditions. Urban centers were provided with adequate sewerage systems and the street cleaning departments kept the streets in at least a tolerable condition of cleanliness. These advances were reflected in the steadily declining death rate, which was reduced from 15.5 per one thousand at the beginning of the century to 11.8 in 1926. In these years cities were rarely visited by the scourges of disease that had marked the earlier decades.

Life in the rural sections of the country was profoundly affected by scientific advances in the first quarter of the twentieth century. The rapid extension of the telephone has given the farmer an easy method of communication with the outside world, the appearance of the automobile has provided him and his family with cheap and swift transportation to town and city, the moving picture and the radio have furnished him with the same quality of entertainment as that enjoyed by the city resident, and the large mail order houses and the parcels post have enabled him to obtain the same standard commodities to be found in the shops and markets of the cities. In short, rural life in these years tended more and more to conform to the modes and tastes set by the urban dwellers.

The change in the status of women noted in the latter part of the nineteenth century, continued at an accelerated pace in the years that followed. Women in steadily increasing numbers found their way into the various trades and professions. For those women who did not, either from choice or necessity, enter the business or professional world, there came a release from many household cares as a result of the introduction of a large number of labor-saving devices. Provided thus with additional leisure, many women found opportunity to extend their cultural interests, others engaged in charitable and civic betterment movements, while many others doubtless merely frittered away their leisure time in idle amusements.

It was in these decades, as we have seen, that the long campaign for the political enfranchisement of women was brought to a successful conclusion. Having obtained the ballot, women found their political influence materially increased. Politicians of all parties found it expedient to grant women representation in political conventions and on party committees. In the legislative halls of state and nation, as judges in the courts and in various other governmental positions women took their place beside men. The results that followed from this increased political activity on the part of women justified neither the dire predictions of those who had opposed women's suffrage nor the hopeful anticipations of its advocates. Apparently politics remained much as it had been before.

Having won the right to vote, some of the more radical women leaders demanded the complete equality of men and women before the law. To this end they proposed a constitutional amendment which would prohibit any legislative discrimination against women on account of their sex. This proposal was vigorously opposed by other women leaders, who pointed out that whatever gains might come from such action to some women by way of increased economic opportunities, such gains would be more than offset by the destruction of protective legislation for safeguarding the health of women.

The emergence of women into a man's world was reflected in changing feminine manners and dress. Women's habits were patterned after those of men as much as possible. Both "flappers" and grandmothers cut their hair in mannish fashion; and women smoked and drank in public as freely as men. Many persons who recalled the earlier days of feminine retirement deplored these new habits while others, less romantic, were inclined to regard them as the normal "self-expression" of women in the new era.

Coincident with the changed status of women went important modifications in family life. The substitution of apartments for private dwellings frequently made homes little more than places in which to sleep. Moralists also pointed to the ominous growth in divorce, and to the loosening of parental authority over children as evidences of the disintegration of the old family ties. Just how far these tendencies foreshadow fundamental changes in the position of the family in the society of the future is a matter of interesting speculation.

Educational development in the first quarter of the twentieth century showed the continuance of some of the same tendencies noted in the preceding decades, together with certain novelties. Public expenditures for elementary and secondary education mounted steadily, reaching the huge figure of more than two billion dollars in 1926. In this year more than twenty-seven million pupils were enrolled in the public, private and parochial schools of the country. In the cities school buildings, housing in some instances more than five thousand children, were built and equipped with all manner of educational devices. Every town of any size boasted at least one fine school, and even in rural districts in many sections of the country, the old one-room school houses were replaced by modern buildings.

Colleges and universities, too, experienced a remarkable expansion both in the numbers of students enrolled and in the variety of subjects offered. In 1926 there were more than 800,000 students in the universities, colleges, and professional schools of the country, an increase of more than 400 per cent. in twenty-five years. There was a widespread belief that a college education was an open sesame to economic success and social position. Pressure upon the colleges became so great that many institutions found it necessary to limit the number of students, either by raising entrance requirements or by fixing a definite limit upon their enrollment. In keeping with the industrial development of this period there came the growth of business education, in both secondary and higher fields. Colleges of commerce and business took their places beside liberal arts colleges and technical schools in many institutions of higher learning.

Changes of note in the content and methods of education marked these years. Some modification in the system of free electives in the colleges was made in the direction of making the college course less discursive and more purposeful. On the other hand a number of institutions introduced so-called honors courses in which capable students were allowed to concentrate their efforts in some field of major interest and were relieved from regular attendance at lectures. In keeping with the vogue for standardization and classification in the business world of the time was the application of educational tests and measurements in the field of education. The fervent advocates of these devices essayed to grade and classify all students and to assign to each his or her appropriate I.Q. (intelligence quotient), but educators were far from agreed as to the meaning and value of these tests.

Supplementing these traditional forms of educational activity came the extension courses offered by many colleges and universities for those who could not devote full time to college training. Appealing to the same clientele were correspondence courses, and the large number of popular lectures on a wide range of subjects. In short, the educational process reached out into every field of knowledge and activity and made its appeal to all classes and ages, from infancy to old age. If the American people remained unenlightened, it was not because of lack of opportunity.

Hand in hand with advancing enlightenment, and perhaps because of it, came a remarkable expansion and diversification in the field of literature. In this quarter of a century the publishing business in America grew at an amazing rate. In this deluge of printed matter there was, of course, much of fugitive value and much more that was worthless. On the other hand there was a considerable output of literature of a high order of merit.

It is difficult to classify the literary work of these years. It was a period alive with movements and tendencies. In the better grade of frankly popular writing a high level of artistic execution and technical strength was reached. Of the better known novelists mention should be made of Gertrude Atherton, Owen Wister, Robert W. Chambers, Meredith Nicholson, Booth Tarkington, Mary Johnston, Edith Wharton, Winston Churchill, and Stewart Edward White. If these writers offered no particular philosophy of life and did not propound any economic or social program, others like Upton Sinclair and Jack London surveyed the American scene and found therein material to bolster up their economic theories.

There appeared also a group of critically minded writers less bent upon any scheme of economic salvation than were Sinclair and London. Theodore Dreiser, in a spirit of rigorous scrutiny of contemporary conditions, perhaps with an emphasis upon the seamy side, presented powerful, if unpleasant, descriptions of American life. Sinclair Lewis set forth the crudities, intolerance and insularity of contemporary America. Willa Cather, although admired chiefly for the perfection of her style and her remarkable gift of characterization, expressed a distaste for much that was crass in the spirit of the day and a preference for what she considered the superior independence and vitality of earlier America. Sherwood Anderson and James Branch Cabell penetrated behind the mask of contemporary humanity and found there much that was sickly and repellent. If their work was characterized by cynicism and despair it at least had the merit of courage in seeking and facing the truth.

In the field of poetry also the first quarter of the twentieth century beheld a revolt against the traditional forms of poetical writing. It was then, for example, that Whitman came into his own and the recognition of the validity of his art made easier the reception of Edgar Lee Masters and Carl Sandburg, two notable leaders in the use of free verse. The same general upheaval, the same demand for spirit as opposed to convention, brought to the fore the Imagists, under the leadership of Amy Lowell; the return to rural simplicity in Robert Frost; and the varied gifts of Lindsay, Robinson, and Edna Millay. Two results mark the general movement of these years: the liberation from devitalized conventions, and the renaissance of fresh, vital imagery.

In the field of historical writing these years produced a number of noteworthy figures. James Harvey Robinson departed from beaten paths. In place of the staples of history— kings, courtiers, and wars—he turned to a consideration of the contributions to civilization made by the great minds of the past. In American history Frederick Jackson Turner and a group of scholars trained under his direction disclosed the influence of the West in the making of the nation. Charles A. Beard made a number of significant studies of the influence of economic forces in American history and then produced the most penetrating and comprehensive synthesis of American civilization yet published. Herbert L. Osgood, after an exhaustive study of the original sources, wrote the institutional history of the colonial period. A group of other historical scholars subjected to a fresh examination many of the traditional beliefs concerning various aspects of American history, particularly the Revolutionary period, and reached conclusions shocking to a large number of super-patriots. If some of these productions lacked the literary qualities of a Bancroft, a Parkman, or a Fiske, they had the merit of sound scholarship and scientific accuracy not always found in the writings of earlier historians.

In scientific advance the chief contributions of Americans in the first quarter of the twentieth century were, as in the preceding decades, mainly in the field of applied science. In electrical appliances, in radio transmission, in aëronautics, and in the automotive industry, were produced a bewildering number of inventions. The biologist and the chemist turned their scientific knowledge to the improvement of plants and animals, to the study of foods, and to the production of a variety of new commercial articles. In the realm of pure science, although the contributions of Americans in these years were relatively slight, nevertheless mention should be made of the work of A. A. Michelson and R. A. Millikan, in physics, and R. A. Richards, in chemistry, whose scientific investigations were acclaimed both in this country and abroad.

In American journalism some of the same tendencies noted in the decades before 1900 continued in the years that followed. The increased size of newspapers together with the steadily mounting costs of labor and materials made it increasingly difficult for any but the most prosperous journals to keep their heads above water. In many cities long-established newspapers were forced either to cease publication or to seek combination with other papers. Some communities that formerly boasted three or four morning and evening papers found themselves with but one. Although this trend was in keeping with the general tendency toward combination in the business world it had certain unfortunate results. Doubtless large advertisers welcomed a change which meant substantial reduction in the cost of advertising, but the reading public was thereby deprived of the variety of editorial opinion on public questions.

In 1918 there came an innovation in American journalism with the appearance of the "tabloid" newspaper. The way had been prepared for this new venture by the increased number of illustrated magazines, by the issuance of picture supplements with the old-established newspapers and by the wide appeal of the motion pictures. Through these agencies a large number of Americans became accustomed to receiving their knowledge of daily events from pictures rather than from the printed word. Inaugurated with the appearance of the *Illustrated Daily News* of New York, this new type of journalism quickly attracted imitators, and tabloid papers were soon published in many of the large cities. With remarkable ingenuity the directors of these enterprises obtained and published pictures of sensational events in the day's news. Lurid pictorial illustrations, some real photographs and others cleverly fabricated, of sordid crimes, formed a considerable part of the make-up of these papers. Despite the rapid growth of the tabloid press there was no appreciable diminution in the circulation of the older type of newspaper. Apparently the picture newspaper had touched a stratum of the population, much as had the yellow press of the previous generation, that had never before been reached by the newspapers.

The periodical press experienced remarkable growth in these years. Some of the more popular magazines such as the *Saturday Evening Post,* the *Ladies Home Journal,* and *Liberty,* counted their circulation by the million. Appealing to a smaller circle of readers of liberal inclinations was the *New Republic,* founded in 1914. Shortly afterwards the *Nation,* under the direction of Oswald Garrison Villard, took up the defense of unpopular ideas and individuals, to the discomfiture of many of its former readers. Of a somewhat different type of critical magazine was the *American Mercury.* Under the editorship of Henry L. Mencken this publication held up to scorn most of the time-honored conventions of the comfortable classes in America. Regarding the general run of Americans as "boobs," Mencken made his appeal to what he confidently called "the civilized minority."

Although American artists in this period produced an abundance of excellent work they did not give evidence of departing materially from the trend in European art circles. Many painted portraits and landscapes in accordance with established canons of art, while others brought from Europe recent innovations. Childe Hassam and Twachtman, despite the disapproval of the upholders of the classical tradition, won recognition with their vivid impressionist paintings. The devotees of other new artistic ideas such as Cubism, Futurism and Vorticism, placed upon canvas weird geometric designs and strange formless figures. Despite the scorn of the conservatives these radical experimenters firmly maintained that their work would usher in a new era in art.

In architecture American genius showed greater originality than in painting. The development of steel construction in building prepared the way for the erection of huge "skyscrapers" in all important cities in the country, rising, some of them to more than fifty stories. Although built for utilitarian purposes and frequently severely plain in design, not a few of these towering buildings presented a strikingly artistic appearance. Notable instances are the Woolworth Tower in New York and the Tribune Building in Chicago. As these tall buildings increased in numbers and in height, making streets appear like narrow canyons, municipal authorities required their builders to set back the upper stories in order to conserve light and air. As a result the newer skyscrapers present a striking appearance with their terraced fronts rising to dizzy heights.

Interest in music, noted in the earlier decades, continued unabated after 1900. In New York, Chicago and other large cities operatic performances were given, rivaling the best productions in Europe. Singers from all parts of the world came to America, attracted by the munificent rewards that were offered. Symphony orchestras of the first order, directed by the most eminent European and American conductors, presented the best of orchestral music to large and enthusiastic audiences. In fact there were those who maintained that the musical center of the world had shifted from Europe to America. Supplementing operatic and orchestral productions in spreading popular appreciation of music were the mechanical devices for the reproduction of musical compositions. Through the player-piano, the phonograph, and the radio, the masterpieces of music and the finest voices, together, it is true, with much that was cheap and tawdry, were carried into homes in the remotest parts of the country.

Two noteworthy trends in the development of music came

in the years under review. The first was the revival of interest in the folk music of the Negro and the Indian. The Negro spirituals, with their plaintive notes reminiscent of the days of slavery, found their way into the programs of musical organizations or were used along with the equally characteristic barbaric chants of the Indians as themes for new orchestral and operatic compositions. The other American contribution to the realm of music was "jazz." Despite the condemnation that came from musical authorities the syncopated rhythm quickly won popular acclaim and was used in innumerable song and dance compositions. From America the craze for jazz music spread to many foreign countries, ultimately receiving the stamp of respectability from some of the musicians who had greeted it with derision at its inception.

The statistics of religious organizations in America in 1926 showed that about 30,000,000 Protestants, 18,600,000 Roman Catholics and 4,000,000 Jews were members of organized religious bodies. These figures indicate that less than half the people of the United States maintain church membership and they give force to the laments heard in clerical circles that religious influence has not kept pace with the growth of other influences in American life. Various suggestions for remedying this situation have come especially from religious leaders in Protestant denominations. Some, like Harry Emerson Fosdick and John Haynes Holmes, have boldly asserted that the churches must rid themselves of creeds and dogmas that do not meet the needs of modern life or that run counter to advances in the scientific world. Others, less radical, have urged greater coöperation among Protestant churches with the aim of bringing about ultimately a combination of the various Protestant sects. Prominent in this work is the Federal Council of Churches of Christ in America. Still other groups have insisted that the churches must grapple with some of the vital social and industrial problems confronting the country if they are to hold the support of the mass of its people. Acting along these lines the Interchurch World Movement made an investigation of the strike in the steel industry in 1919 and rendered a report that strongly condemned many of the conditions disclosed.

On the other hand, there were many, both among clergy and laity, who insisted that the remedy for religious laxity was to be found not in modification of creeds or dogmas, nor in socialization of religious activities, but rather in a revival of the old-time faith and in the preaching of "Christ and Him crucified." Under the militant leadership of such preachers as John Roach Straton these Fundamentalists declared war upon the Modernist wing of the clergy and denounced all scientific knowledge and theories that reflected in any way upon the literal interpretation of the Bible. Assuming the offensive, the Fundamentalists brought pressure to bear upon the legislatures of several states and succeeded in having placed upon the statute books in these states laws prohibiting the teaching of the theory of evolution in state-supported educational institutions.

The amusements and pastimes of the American people in the first quarter of the twentieth century call for passing notice. Organized sports, especially professional baseball, increased greatly in popularity. In schools, colleges, and universities, athletic activities engaged a substantial part of the time of the students of both sexes. Intercollegiate contests in football and other sports attracted huge crowds and athletic heroes received greater acclaim on the campus than did those who made their mark in intellectual pursuits. The remarkable extension in the use of the automobile in these years offered new opportunities for pleasurable pastime to hundreds of thousands of persons. Within a few hours whole families could go from congested urban centers to the open country where they obtained at least a passing acquaintance with the beauties of nature. The automobile, too, was responsible for the rapid development of the country club. The popularity of these clubs is indicative of the steadily increasing wealth and leisure of the American business and professional classes.

In theatrical amusements the passing years brought important changes. In place of the crude melodrama of the earlier generation came more sophisticated plays nearly always involving a sex problem and not infrequently verging on the vulgar. For variety there were offered innumerable musical comedies, good, bad and indifferent, usually staged in sumptuous fashion with the women performers wearing as little as the law would allow. The period was not however entirely devoid of plays having dramatic qualities of a high order. The movement noted in the preceding decades connected with the work of Bronson Howard was carried on by Clyde Fitch, whose plays contain a social history of the United States between 1900 and 1910. He did not depart from the type of drama made popular in England by such men as Pinero and Jones, but he did reveal the comic pettiness of a society in a state of perpetual change and the ceaseless imitation of a civilization it did not understand. He created in drama a parallel to the international novel of Henry James, though unlike the latter he sought to attract the vast body of the American public rather than a select few. In *The Truth* he produced a genuine comedy of manners and in *The City* a more serious study of American problems. The transition to a drama of ideas seen in his last play is also found in the work of Augustus Thomas, whose *The Witching Hour* was a notable success, and in that of Willam Vaughn Moody, whose *The Great Divide* sets forth the source of the conflict between the western and eastern portions of the country. Most important of all, perhaps, is the work of the Little Theatre movement, out of which came Susan Glaspell, whose *The Verge* has been hailed by an English critic as comparable to the work of Chekhov, and Eugene O'Neill, who first

598 SOCIAL AND CULTURAL CONDITIONS, 1900-1929

made American drama of international importance. His searching analysis of elemental passions as disclosed by his *The Hairy Ape, Desire Under the Elms, Emperor Jones,* and *Strange Interlude* has placed him in the front rank of contemporary dramatists.

But this form of entertainment was for the few. The multitude found relaxation from daily cares chiefly in motion pictures. Nearly every village throughout the land boasted at least one moving picture theater while in the large cities were erected palatial buildings which surpassed in size and splendor the theaters devoted to legitimate dramatic and musical performances. At Hollywood, California, were gathered moving picture "stars" whose salaries made the compensation received by great actors and actresses of the past seem pitiable by comparison. By the end of the first quarter of the twentieth century the motion picture business had become one of the leading industries of the country. By the combination of the spoken voice with the motion picture this form of entertainment was given an added attraction. Although millions of dollars were expended in portraying elaborate spectacles and thrilling adventures, rarely did the moving picture make any serious appeal to the intelligence of the spectator. The producers of these pictures, primarily concerned with box office receipts, shrewdly figured that the average spectator desired to have his emotions rather than his intellect stirred when seeking entertainment.

Taking a broad view of American life at the close of the first quarter of the twentieth century the question may well be asked whether the machine age, which had poured forth such an abundance of commodities for the comfort and amusement of the American people, has made them any happier or has advanced America as a civilized community. A keen observer of social and industrial conditions, Stuart Chase, has attempted to assess and to strike a balance between the losses and gains of the present age. Among the manifest benefits that mechanical and scientific progress has brought to mankind he enumerates the following: increase in the life span because of medical and mechanical controls; higher living standards for a larger fraction of the population than has ever before been attained; shrinkage of space brought about by mechanical devices such as railroads, steamships, automobiles, telephones, cables, radios, and airplanes, thereby increasing the social and economic unity of the world; material decrease in the hours of labor; decline in superstition furthered by scientific explanations of mysterious occurrences; increase in self-confidence promoted by the handling of machines such as the automobile; breaking down of class distinctions founded on land ownership and patents of nobility; expansion of the limits of human knowledge through scientific researches; decrease in human cruelty and a growth of social sympathy as evidenced by the formation of great philanthropic foundations and the outpouring of money for the relief of human distress. On the other hand he lists the following evils of modern life: the menace to civilization from mechanized warfare; the danger to the social equilibrium in the interlocked industrial structure when a crisis occurs such as a strike in a key industry or the failure of a strategic material; the exhaustion of natural resources; the monotony and wearisomeness of mechanical work; the divorce of work, play, and art due to the performance of specialized tasks; the vogue for mechanical amusements, which has led to watching and listening rather than active participation in recreation; the displacement of workmen by machines, which has aggravated the problem of unemployment; the speeding up of industrial activities, which has placed an added strain upon the workers, with the result that they are being scrapped at an earlier age; the overvaluation of industry at the expense of agriculture; the growth of congested centers of population; the increase in noise, dust, and smoke to the detriment of health. Other effects noted having both good and evil results are: An increase and redistribution of population; the decline in community self-sufficiency bringing greater efficiency along with greater dependence on other communities; the economic independence of women together with the breaking up of the old family life; the standardization of commodities, cheapening the cost of production but frequently sacrificing quality and artistic craftsmanship; an increased economic dependence of the worker upon the machine.

It is no easy task to strike a balance in this formidable catalogue of good and evil consequences of the machine age. There are, however, hopeful signs that earnest efforts are being made to grapple with some of the most serious evils noted—war, overspecialization, failure of natural resources and unemployment. "If these menaces," says Chase, "can be held in check, it may well be that we shall find no limit to the greatness of the civilization before us. The penalty of power is the creation of sufficient intelligence to direct it. Most of us are still too busy in our own little backyards to realize the awful magnitude of that challenge."

BIBLIOGRAPHICAL NOTE

An excellent survey of American social and cultural development since 1900 can be found in C. and M. Beard, *Rise of American Civilization,* Vol. II, Chap. 30 (1927). See also S. Chase, *Men and Machines* (1929); J. T. Adams, *Our Business Civilization: Some Aspects of American Culture* (1929). For a consideration of the growth of urban population in America consult J. V. Thompson, *Urbanization: Its Effects on Government and Society* (1927); J. F. Steiner, *The American Community in Action* (1928). For rural life see L. Mac Garr, *The Rural Community* (1928); N. L. R. Sims, *Elements of Rural Sociology* (1928). On the problem of the family consult E. R. Groves and W. F. Ogburn, *American Marriage and Family Relationships* (1929); E. R. Groves, *Social Problems of the Family* (1927).

For a discussion of recent tendencies in education, in addition to the references noted in Chapter 10 consult I. L. Kandal, *Twenty-five Years of American Education* (1924); E. W. Knight, *Education in the United States* (1929).

For literature and the drama consult the references in Chapter 10. On art, architecture, and music the references in Chapter 10 are useful. See also H. O. Osgood, *So This Is Jazz* (1926); L. Mumford, *Sticks and Stones* (1924). For a discussion of the trend in historical writing see H. E. Barnes, *The New History and the Social Studies* (1925).

On amusements see J. P. Sizer, *The Commercialization of Leisure* (1917); M. M. Davis, *The Exploitation of Pleasure* (1911); J. P. Kennedy, ed., *The Story of the Films* (1927); W. M. Seabury, *The Public and the Motion Picture Industry* (1926).

CHAPTER 24

FACING THE FUTURE

In the foregoing chapters has been traced the remarkable development of the American nation over a period of sixty-five years. Within these years we have seen the population of the country grow from about 30,000,000 to approximately 120,000,000. In addition to the development of the resources of over three million square miles of territory, extending from the Atlantic to the Pacific and from the Gulf to the Great Lakes, we have seen the extension of American authority over distant lands totaling over 700,000 square miles in area. The national wealth in this period increased from a little more than sixteen billions of dollars to about four hundred billions. From this bounteous store a few acquired fortunes counted in millions of dollars while at the same time the large majority were enabled to enjoy a degree of comfort never before approached in any age or country. Accompanying this material prosperity went the expenditure of large sums of money for cultural purposes and for social and philanthropic enterprises. Finally we have seen in these years the emergence of the United States as a world power of the first magnitude. This story represents an accomplishment of which Americans can justly be proud. At the same time we should not overlook certain serious problems and national weaknesses which confront us as we face the future.

First may be noted various problems of social adjustment. The people of this country, as we have seen, have come from the four quarters of the globe. According to the census of 1920, 55 per cent. of the white population of the country were natives of native parentage while 45 per cent. were either foreign born or had parents one or both of whom were foreign born. For many years Americans held the comfortable belief that the assimilation of this large foreign element presented no serious difficulties. It was assumed that the immigrant having foresworn allegiance to the country of his birth would quickly and easily adopt the traditions and customs of his adopted home. In many cases this was true, if not among the immigrants themselves, at least among their children. Nevertheless the experience of the Great War showed how deep-rooted were the spiritual attachments to their native countries of many Americans who had come from across the seas.

To add to the concern among native Americans caused by these evidences of divided allegiance came the writings of Lothrop Stoddard and Madison Grant in an effort to prove that the "superior" Nordic civilization of the United States was menaced by the "inferior" civilization of the immigrant groups from southern and eastern Europe. They pointed to the low birth rate among the middle and upper class Americans, made up largely of Anglo-Saxon stock. It was shown that 60 per cent. of women with college degrees do not marry and of those who do 36 per cent. have no children. On the other hand the birth rate among the recently arrived immigrant groups is relatively high. The conclusion was reached that unless something were done to remedy these conditions the Anglo-Saxon element would at no distant date become a negligible factor in the American population.

To meet this supposed danger Americans of the old persuasion adopted two lines of action. First, as has been noted, they brought about the enactment of restrictive immigration laws to stop the flow of immigration to this country. The second move was the insistence upon a program of 100 per cent. Americanism which meant the acceptance by all Americans of certain traditional beliefs and customs. The revival of the Ku Klux Klan, with its anti-Catholic, anti-Jewish and anti-Negro propaganda, represented an extreme form of this agitation. To those who supported these views the ideal of American civilization was not an amalgam of the cultures of the peoples of Europe but rather a civilization based upon Protestant, Anglo-Saxon traditions.

It was in the nature of things that those elements in the population coming from so-called inferior races or holding religious and social views out of harmony with those of the 100 per centers should resist the effort forcibly to "Americanize" them. This racial and religious cleavage in the body politic constitutes a national weakness that should not be minimized. It may be that the restrictive immigration laws, if retained, will sufficiently reduce the "undesirable" immigrant element to quiet the fears of the nativist group, but in any event the adjustment of the different cultural elements among the American people constitutes a problem that calls for sympathetic understanding rather than for dogmatic theorizing.

A special problem of social adjustment is that involving the relations of the negroes to the white population. Until recently this question was confined largely to the Southern states. There, as we have seen, in the years following the Reconstruction period the negroes were reduced to political impotence, were subjected to social discrimination, and were kept in economic dependence upon the whites. For many years there appeared to be little disposition on the part of the southern whites to modify their attitude toward the negro. In fact, it was generally held that the racial question had been definitely "solved" by placing the negro in a permanent position of inferiority to the whites. But in recent years, especially in the decade since the Great War, the negro question has undergone significant changes in many of its aspects. During the war more than a half million negroes migrated from the southern states to northern industrial centers. As a result the negro problem became national rather than sectional in scope. Northern communities to which came large numbers of negroes showed no greater willingness to receive them on a basis of social and economic equality than had the whites of the South. Race riots occurred in Washington, Chicago, Omaha, East St. Louis, and Tulsa. As the negroes moved into residential sections of northern cities the whites moved out. The Harlem section in New York City and a large area stretching from the stockyards to Lake Michigan in Chicago became almost entirely colored in population. While northern communities were thus coming to grips for the first time with the race question, the South, fearful of losing more of its cheap labor supply, hastened to modify some of the more acute restrictions and abuses of which the negroes complained. At the same time prominent white citizens of the South, both men and women, frankly proposed a sympathetic study of the relations of the two races. The Atlanta Plan of Interracial Coöperation was started to discuss the sources of unrest among the negroes, to forestall violence and to influence public opinion. Interracial committees, consisting of prominent members of both races, were formed in a large number of southern communities.

In recent years the attitude of the negroes themselves has undergone an important change. During the World War thousands of negroes were drafted into the army. In Europe they were received on a basis of social equality with the whites and many of them returned to America determined to resist the discrimination to which they had been formerly subjected. Moreover the negroes who had moved North exercised there the right to vote and they demanded and received political recognition from party organizations. Self-consciousness and race pride among the negroes was further stimulated by the artistic accomplishments of negroes like Roland Hayes, Harry F. Burleigh, and Paul Robeson, and by the wide popularity of negro folk creations—the spirituals,

African art, jazz, and the Blues. In short, intelligent negroes of the present generation refuse to accept any longer the stigma of inferiority.

It would be optimistic to maintain that any final solution of the negro problem in this country has been found. But there are hopeful signs of a more reasonable and tolerant attitude on the part of intelligent members of both races. In addition to the activities of the interracial committees in the South noted above mention should be made of the Negro-Caucasian Club at the University of Michigan, the Interracial Discussion Groups at the University of Chicago and the International House at Columbia University, where youthful members of both races mingle freely. At the University of North Carolina negro lecturers have been listened to by the student body with respect. Such activities as these may pave the way for a solution of one of the most delicate problems of social adjustment confronting the country at the present time.

Somewhat related to racial intolerance is the manifestation of intolerance toward unpopular ideas and individuals that has been prevalent in recent years. Since the Great War many states have passed laws that have been so administered as to prevent any advocacy of basic changes in the political and economic institutions of the country, and these laws have been upheld by the highest courts of the land. The privileges guaranteed by the Bill of Rights, if they have not been scrapped, have certainly been materially curtailed. Public meetings, especially those under radical auspices, have been repressed by government officials. Persons have been blacklisted by patriotic societies for advocating the outlawry of war. All this seems strange in the land of Jefferson and Lincoln and it is disheartening to those who still cherish the principles proclaimed in the Declaration of Independence. It may be that this repression of civil liberties represents merely a passing hysteria induced by the Great War and its aftermath but if it registers a permanent change in the attitude of the government and in the thought of the American people then it is a more serious matter. Freedom of discussion in a democratic state is an important safety-valve. It makes possible social change without recourse to force and violence. The use of coercion to prevent certain types of discussion inevitably leads to the advocacy of violence by those who are dissatisfied with things as they are.

If we turn to the field of government and politics the query arises whether political conditions in this country are better or worse than they were in the past. There are those who bemoan our political decadence and ruefully contrast those who sit in our legislative halls today with bygone statesmen and orators. To these complaints it may be remarked that there is always a tendency to idealize the great figures of the past. We are likely to remember their fine qualities but fail to recall their frailties. Every American school child has read Webster's great orations but few have heard of his moral shortcomings or of his inability to make nice distinctions between his obligation to the public and his own private financial interests. When we deplore the evidences of political corruption in recent years let us not forget that former generations of Americans were confronted by similar evidences of human frailty.

Whether our political morals are better or worse than those of our fathers the fact remains that there are certain aspects of American political life at the present time that leave much to be desired. A large number of citizens do not take the trouble to avail themselves of the privilege and duty of voting to say nothing of taking an intelligent interest in public affairs. This may be due to apathy induced by the feeling that the machinery of government has become so large and impersonal that the political activity of the individual voter is largely futile, or it may be due to a feeling that things will go on much the same whether one votes or not, or, finally, to our preoccupation with money-making, but in any event it is not a healthy political condition. Then there is our naïve belief in the potency of law-making to cure all manner of social and political ills. Thousands of laws, many of which are hastily drafted and rushed through with slight consideration, are placed each year upon the statute books of the states and of the nation. More serious is the widespread disrespect for law. The statistics of crime in the United States are truly appalling. Various explanations have been put forward to account for this reign of lawlessness. Some have attributed it to the tendency of individuals and private groups to take the administration of justice into their own hands, a heritage of frontier days when courts of justice were not available. Others have pointed to the technicalities of our criminal law, which enable offenders with the aid of clever lawyers to escape punishment for their crimes. Whatever may be the explanation, these conditions are surely a national disgrace. In fact they have become so disquieting that President Hoover, in 1929, deemed it necessary to appoint a commission of eminent lawyers and jurists to make a thorough study of our system of law enforcement and to recommend remedies for existing weaknesses.

The organization of political parties and prevailing party practices offer material for interesting speculation as we face the future. It has previously been noted that neither of the two major parties in the United States is homogeneous in membership. In the Democratic party we find the conservative, dry, nativist, and rural South together with the somewhat progressive, wet, immigrant and urban groups of the North. In Republican ranks are found such widely divergent views as those held by Senator Borah, Senator La Follette, and Ex-President Coolidge. Leaders in both the major parties, confronted by the necessity of satisfying the widely divergent interests of their followers, found it expedient, as we have seen, to adopt party platforms that are evasive, ambiguous or meaningless on controversial questions. In fact, neither the Republican nor the Democratic party is a national party in the European sense of that term. Only once in four years do American parties function as national organizations in the election of a President of the United States. In the intervening years they operate as state bodies and their policies are determined largely by the local interests of the individual states. But it is not only the nature of the American Federal system that accounts for the heterogeneous character of political parties. In America, until recent years, there had not appeared that tendency toward fixed social and economic groups which is found in most European countries. In the absence of such settled groups, political parties did not represent, except in the case of the Socialist party, a cleavage along class lines. But the trend of economic development in the United States since the opening of the twentieth century has modified to a considerable degree the former fluidity of social classes. We have not as yet reached the condition of stratification of social and economic groups found in European countries, but the pertinent question has been raised whether the two major political parties can much longer hold within their ranks the increasingly divergent elements that now make up their memberships. Keen political observers foresee the likelihood of a realignment of parties, one distinctly conservative and the other progressive or radical, or, perhaps, one representing the urban and industrial interests and the other the rural and agricultural.

It is a difficult task to attempt to forecast the future economic development of the United States. The remarkable material growth of the United States in the first quarter of the twentieth century, the resourcefulness of business leaders, the genius for invention among the American people, the still ample natural resources of the country, the deep-rooted confidence in the continued prosperity of the country, are all factors which make any prediction as to the future likely to be falsified by events. Still it is worth while to direct our attention to certain shortcomings in the trend of our economic development in recent years which may become problems of serious moment in future years.

The outstanding feature of recent industrial development in the United States is the mass production of standardized commodities. That this has led to increased output at less cost—a distinct economic gain—we have already seen. But it has not been an unmixed blessing. By encouraging the use of standardized goods it has emphasized that drab uniformity in the tastes and method of life of the American people which has impressed both foreign and native observers. "Nine-tenths of the American towns," says Sinclair Lewis, "are so alike that it is the completest boredom to wander from one to another. Always, west of Pittsburgh, and often east of it, there is the same lumber yard, the same railroad station, the same Ford garage, the same creamery, the same box-like houses and two-story shops. The new, more conscious houses are alike in their very attempts at diversity; the same bungalows, the same square houses of stucco or tapestry brick. The shops show the same standardized, nationally advertised wares; the newspapers of sections three thousand miles apart have the same 'syndicated features'; the boy in Arkansas wears just such a flamboyant ready-made suit as is found on just such a boy in Delaware, both of them iterate the same slang phrases from the same sporting pages, and if one of them is in college and the other is a barber, no one may surmise which is which."

But mass production of standardized commodities has not only stimulated in national habits a monotonous sameness that is esthetically unpleasant; it has given rise to other problems of more practical significance. It is not possible as yet to pass final judgment on the effect upon the workers of mass production and the speeding up of industrial processes through the widespread use of machinery. It is a question whether the monotony of machine labor and the nervous strain of high speed production is offset by the increased leisure time that laborers have acquired in recent years through the reduction in the number of working hours. Again, mass production is not adaptable to a large number of industries in which machinery cannot be used on an extensive scale and which demand individual initiative, artistic ability and a high degree of skill on the part of the worker. In the production of finer grades of textiles, scientific instruments, optical lenses, and other delicately made articles America lags behind Europe despite the artificial stimulus of an extremely high protective tariff. In agriculture, too, the possibilities of standardization and the technique of mass production appear to be distinctly limited. The question may be raised whether the emphasis which has been placed in recent years upon mass production and standardization is not leading to a one-sided economic development.

The outstanding facts in the economic life of the United States are that the bulk of the commodities produced in the country is consumed within its geographic limits, and that domestic products constitute a large percentage of the total national consumption. Less than 10 per cent. of the total national production is exported to foreign countries and likewise less than 10 per cent. of domestic consumption is represented by imported commodities. In short, we have, up to the present time, lived largely unto ourselves, producing what we consumed and consuming what we produced. It is this situation that has enabled America to maintain her exceptional standard of living. But is this condition likely to continue indefinitely? This depends upon two factors: first, that our natural resources enable us to remain independent of imported raw materials and, second, that domestic consumption keeps pace with the steadily mounting national production. Concerning the first of these factors it is to be noted that we have exploited certain of our important natural resources, notably timber and petroleum with such reckless waste that there have been authoritative warnings that the exhaustion of these commodities can be predicted at no distant future date. As to the ability of domestic consumption to continue to absorb the bulk of domestic commodities, this will depend upon a growth in population and upon the ability of the average consumer to maintain his present standard of living. But the increase in population is likely to be affected by the policy of restricted immigration unless there is a material increase in the national birth rate, while the maintenance of the present standard of living depends upon the continuance of high wages and general prosperity. In short, it seems doubtful whether the conditions which have made the United States largely economically self-sufficient in the past will continue in the future. When and if American production greatly exceeds the ability of domestic consumption then will arise the necessity of paying greater attention to the development of foreign markets. Moreover, as our natural resources are depleted we shall have to depend more and more upon imported raw materials. American economic life will then be affected much more than it is at present by the economic conditions in the rest of the world. American products will have to meet the competition of goods made in countries having a much lower scale of wages. It may be that American ingenuity will be able to cope with this situation without reducing the standard of living of the American worker to the general world level, but it is a problem to which much thought has been given by those who are looking forward to the time when American economic life will be international instead of predominantly national.

If the huge business organizations and mass production, the two characteristic features of American industrial life today, have increased efficiency in both production and distribution, they have, on the other hand, raised important social and economic problems. By the elimination of duplication and by the extensive use of machinery they have reduced materially the amount of human labor employed in industrial processes and have thereby increased the danger of unemployment, particularly among those who have passed middle age. Moreover they have made it increasingly difficult for an individual with limited capital to establish an independent business or to continue one already established. If the present tendency toward business integration continues in the future, it is not difficult to foresee the time when the large majority of the American people will depend for a livelihood upon a limited number of great business organizations. Even granting that these enterprises will be conducted with the highest degree of intelligence and with a sympathetic regard for the interests of those in their employ still it is doubtful whether it is a desirable social condition which decreases the opportunities for young men and young women to establish themselves in independent economic positions. Does our modern industrial organization offer compensating advantages for the loss of that self-reliance and individual initiative which were such marked characteristics of former generations of Americans?

Nor should the fact be overlooked that the tremendous power possessed by the large business enterprises may not always be used in the interests of the public. The recent attempts of certain public utility corporations to gain control of a chain of newspapers, presumably for the purpose of influencing public opinion, and their similar efforts to spread propaganda through educational institutions are instances of the possibilities of misuse of unrestrained economic power. Without wishing to be unduly alarming or pessimistic, it is important to direct attention to these shortcomings in the economic life of the nation today as we are attempting to forecast the future.

American extravagance and wastefulness are national

traits that have been widely commented upon by foreign observers, and have brought warnings from thoughtful leaders in this country. Attention has already been directed to the senseless waste of our natural resources. Then there are the hundreds of millions of dollars spent annually for luxuries, not only by those who can well afford them but also by a large part of the middle and working classes. To quote Stuart Chase once more: "Today one feels naked without silk stockings, lipstick, a manicure set, a permanent wave, Arrow collars, Fisher ·bodies, a radio, a copy of *The Story of Philosophy,* a cocktail shaker, a gasoline cigarette lighter, and a membership in the Elks. We have bathrooms loaded down with toothpowders, dental floss, shaving creams, bath salts, patent sprinklers, old safety razor blades, germ destroyers, and lotions guaranteed to increase our popularity at dances." Eighty per cent. of all of the automobiles in the world are to be found in operation in the United States. One person out of every five in this country owns or operates a motor car. More than $350,000,000 are spent annually for confectionery, nearly $50,000,000 for chewing gum, and more than $800,000,000 for cigars and cigarettes. Of course such huge expenditures for luxuries are a reflection of our present national prosperity, but if less prosperous times come there will have to be some painful readjustments made in our national habits of waste and extravagance.

In our survey of the problems confronting the United States as we face the future there is, finally, the question of the relation of this country to the rest of the world. In previous chapters we have considered the traditional policy of isolation that this country has assumed toward the outside world, and especially the violent controversy that arose over the proposal to modify this policy at the close of the World War. It is idle to claim that the outcome of the bitter partisan conflict of 1920 was a final judgment upon the future of American foreign policies. In fact, within less than a decade after our war experience the attitude of national aloofness was materially modified. Starting with an ostentatious ignoring of the existence of the League of Nations, we passed to a furtive and indirect coöperation with it and finally to open participation in its activities. The important, if unofficial, part played by Americans in the efforts to solve the reparations problem by means of the Dawes and Young Plans, our association with the rest of the civilized world in renouncing war, our efforts to bring about international agreements for the limitation of armaments, are all indications of how far we have gone in the direction of international coöperation.

After all, personal and partisan animosities, narrow and selfish provincialism, and even the most cherished traditions, cannot ignore stubborn economic facts. The Great War clearly demonstrated how intimately the economic interests of this country were bound to the economic interests of the rest of the world. And these ties have been greatly strengthened by the course of American economic development since the war. The large-scale investment of American capital in European industries in these years has given to America, or at least American banking interests, a substantial reason for desiring peace and prosperity to be maintained in Europe. And these same interests have played in the past an important part in shaping American foreign policies, and presumably will continue to do so in the future.

Another factor likely to aid in dispelling the fiction of American isolation is the increasing knowledge of foreign affairs among the American people. In the newspapers and periodical press there is today a much greater and more dependable body of news about foreign nations than there was before 1914. Societies and clubs all over the country are engaging at the present time in serious discussions of the problems of foreign relations. We are beginning to get a realistic understanding of the causes of international strife. The glamour and romance of war are far less appealing today than they were formerly. Present-day military heroes do not arouse the enthusiastic popular acclaim that greeted their predecessors of former generations. Among thoughtful persons, especially of the younger generation, there has come a realization of the sordidness, the inhumanity, and the economic waste of war.

There are, then, indications that the American people are beginning to realize that this country cannot play a lone hand in the closely integrated world of today. We have not joined the League of Nations but we have at least lost the senseless fear of that body which prevailed when it was organized. Many of those who vigorously denounced the League a decade ago are now willing to concede that it has done useful work in settling a number of important international disputes and in promoting a better understanding among the nations of the world.

Concerning our relations with the nations of Latin America, the fine work of Ambassador Morrow in Mexico, the conclusion of our unfortunate adventure in Nicaragua, the disappearance in the press of the United States of much of the irritating and self-righteous material relating to Latin American affairs, are all hopeful indications that we are beginning to take a sympathetic attitude toward the problems and aspirations of our neighbors to the south. It remains for us in the future to make our actions square with our repeated pronouncements of disinterested friendship for the other nations on the American continents.

To recount some of our national short-comings and to point out some of the problems that will confront coming generations of Americans is not to indicate despair of our future. America has still the strength and enthusiasm of youth. Its people have a deep-rooted belief in the possibilities of unlimited national progress and an abiding faith in the ability of democracy to solve its most perplexing problems. Endowed with wealth, courage and resourcefulness, and with high faith in her destiny, it is in a spirit of confidence rather than of fear that America faces the future.

BIBLIOGRAPHICAL NOTE

A keen analysis of present political, economic and social conditions in America, with an attempt to foresee their future trend can be found in the work of a foreign observer, A. Siegfried, *America Comes of Age* (1927). For a consideration of the supposed threat to Anglo-Saxon civilization in the United States see M. Grant, *The Passing of a Great Race* (4th ed., 1923); F. L. Stoddard, *The Revolt Against Civilization* (1922); by the same author, *Reforging America, the Story of Our Nationhood* (1927). Numerous studies of the negro problem have been published of which the following are useful: B. G. Brawley, *The Negro in Literature and Art in the United States* (1918); by the same author, *A Social History of the American Negro* (1921); J. Dowd, *The Negro in American Life* (1926); E. B. Reuter, *The American Race Problem* (1927).

On the suppression of civil liberties see Z. Chafee, *Freedom of Speech* (1920); by the same author, *The Inquiring Mind* (1928); T. J. Norton, *Losing Liberty Judicially* (1928); A. G. Hays, *Let Freedom Ring* (1928).

On the political trend consult Siegfried noted above and C. A. Beard, *The American Party Battle* (1928). For the effects of recent economic development upon social conditions in America consult S. Chase, *Men and Machines* (1929). For the American habits of extravagance and wastefulness see S. Chase, *The Tragedy of Waste* (1925). On the subject of crime see C. S. Darrow, *Crime: Its Cause and Treatment* (1922); J. L. Gillin, *Criminology and Penology* (1928).

On the position of the United States in world affairs consult A. Bullard, *American Diplomacy in the Modern World* (1928); H. A. Gibbons, *America's Place in the World* (1924); C. P. Howland, *Survey of American Foreign Relations 1928 and 1929* (2 Vols., 1928-1929).

INDEX

Abbey, Edwin A., 204
Adams, Charles Francis, quoted, 49; 53, 54
Adams, Charles Francis, Jr., 104
Adamson Law, 395; upheld by Supreme Court, 404-405
Addams, Jane, 212
Advisory Commission, 396
Aëroplane, development of, 381
Agassiz, Louis, 209
Agrarian revolution, 79 ff.
Agriculture, introduction of machinery in, 80; increase in tenant farming, 80; specialized farming in West, 80-81; urban and agricultural wealth, 81; decline in prices of products of, 82, 85
Agricultural Wheel, 85
Agricultural Conference, 345, 384
Agricultural Credits Act, 345-346
Agricultural discontent, 82 ff., 382 ff.
Aguinaldo, leader of insurrection in the Philippines, 257
Alabama, restored to the Union, 24
Alabama Claims, 39-41
Alaska, purchased from Russia, 41-42; Bering Sea controversy, 216; boundary dispute with Great Britain, 218
Aldrich, Nelson M., Senator, 434
Aldrich-Vreeland Act, 423
Alger, Russell A., Secretary of War, 244
Alien Contract Labor Law, 125, 129
Allen, James Lane, 201
Allison, W. B., Senator, 169
Altgeld, J. P., and the Pullman strike, 123, 180
Alverstone, Lord Chief Justice, 218
American Academy, 204
American Defense Society, 512
American Federation of Labor,

116, 117; and eight-hour day, 121, 124, 126; opposition of to formation of labor party, 126, 127; growth of, 388, 394; in the World War, 395; decline in membership of, 400; and five-day week, 402
American League of Nations, proposal for, 474
American Reform party, 126
American Sugar Refining Company, prosecuted, 284-285
American Telegraph and Telephone Company, capitalization of, 376; stock ownership in, 378
American Tobacco Company, prosecuted, 284; dissolution of, 369
Ames, Oakes, 55
Anderson, Sherwood, 590
Angell, James B., 199
Anthony, Susan B., 196, 299
Anti-Imperialist League, 251
Anti-Monopoly party, 107, 126, 142 n.
Anti-Saloon League, 336
Amalgamated Copper Company, organization of, 362
Arizona, territorial government in, 88; woman's suffrage in, 300
Arkansas, reconstruction in, 8, 12; restored to the Union, 24; overthrow of carpetbag rule in, 33
Arthur, Chester A., 135; nominated for Vice-President, 138; elected, 139; succeeds to Presidency, 140; and the Stalwarts, 141
Atchison, Topeka and Santa Fé Company, 69
Atherton, Gertrude, 590
Atlantic and Pacific Company, 69
Atlantic and Pacific Tea Company, 379
Automobile industry, growth of, 380

619

630 INDEX

Ossawatamie, speech of Roosevelt at, 311

Page, Thomas Nelson, 201
Page, Walter H., 314
Pago-Pago, 227
Palmer, A. Mitchell, suggested for Democratic nomination for President (1920), 340
Palmer, John M., 185
Panama, activities of French Canal Company at, 225-226, 448; sale of interests in to United States, 449; revolution in, 450-451; establishment of republic of, 451
Panama Canal, early project for building, 225; purchase of French interests in, 449; construction of, 451; question of tolls on, 452-453
Panic of 1873, 55, 94, 99
Pan-American Congresses, 223-224, 471-479, 477 n.
Pan-American Union, 472, 474-475, 477
Parker, Alton B., nominated for President, 282-284, 319
Parker, John M., nominated for Vice-President, 332
"Parson Brownlow," 33
Patrons of Husbandry, 82
Payne-Aldrich Tariff, 308, 434-435
Pearl Harbor, 228
Peace Pact of Paris, 566-569
Peirce, Benjamin, 209
Pendleton Bill, 140
Pennell, Joseph, 205
Pennsylvania, oil found in, 95, 96
Pennsylvania Railroad, stock ownership in, 378
People's Party, convention in St. Louis, 85; in Cincinnati, 86; in Omaha, 86; platform of 1892, 86-87; attitude of conservatives to, 87; in election of 1892, 88, 151-152, 185-186
Peirpoint, Governor, 12
Pendleton, George H., 25
Pershing, J. J., General, in Mexico, 468; in France, 531, 532
Philippine Government Act, 260

Philippines, in Spanish-American War, 241-242; question of acquisition of, 247; ceded to United States, 247; conditions in, 249; revolt in, 257-258; establishment of government in, 259-260; disposal of church lands in, 261; question of independence of, 261-264 and n.; economic and cultural conditions, 264
Pinchot, Gifford, and conservation movement, 290-291; and the Ballinger controversy, 309, 311
Platt, Orville, Senator, 248; and relations with Roosevelt, 270-271
Platt, Thomas C., resigns from Senate, 139; quoted, 141, 294
Platt Amendment, 253-254
Plumb, Glenn E., 399
Plumb Plan, 399-400
Population, urban, 195; rural, 195; growth of, 196; after 1900, 583; shift from rural to urban centers, 584
Populist movement, 84 ff.
Porter, Noah, 210
Porto Rico, 245; ceded to the United States, 246, 249; conditions in, 255; government of, 255-256, 256 n.; economic relations of with the United States, 256-257, 266
Preparedness, agitation for, 512; attitude of President Wilson toward, 512-513; the Selective Draft Act, 525-526
Presidential Preference Primaries, 298
Presidential Succession Act, 146
Pribilov Islands, 216
Progressive Labor Party, 126
Progressive movement, 294 ff., 314 ff.; in election of 1924, 351-352; revival of insurgency, 358-359
Progressive party, formation of, 321; national convention of (1912), 321; platform of, 322; in the election of 1916, 332
Prohibition, early movement for, 336; effect of Great War on, 336; constitutional amendment

South, influence of planters, 3; demoralization of, 5; problems of reconstruction in, 5 ff.; economic changes in, 35 ff.; social changes in, 37; opposes withdrawal of greenbacks, 45, 136
South Carolina, restored to Union, 24; overthrow of carpetbag rule in, 33; and election of 1876, 61, 62
South Dakota, admitted to Union, 88
South Improvement Company, 98
Southern Farmers' Alliance, 85
Southern life, 195
Southern Pacific Company, 69-70
Spain, relations with United States concerning Cuba, 235 ff.; war with United States, 239 ff.; armistice with United States, 246
Spencer, Herbert, 209-210
Spooner Amendment, 260
Stalwarts, 135 n., 137, 139, 141
Standard Oil Company, 97-98; and rebates, 100; prosecution of, 284; of New Jersey, 362; dissolution of by Supreme Court, 369; stockownership in, 378
Stanton, Edwin M. and Johnson, 22, 23
Stanton, Elizabeth Cady, 196, 299
Star Route Frauds, 139
Stephens, Alexander H., 11, 13
Stephens, Uriah S., 114
Stephenson, Adlai E., nominated for Vice-President, 272
Stevens, J. S., minister to Hawaii, 229
Stevens, Thaddeus, 12, 13; theory of reconstruction, 13-14, 19
Stimson, Henry L., nominated for governor of New York, 311; in Nicaragua, 461
Stoddard, Lothrop, 603
Strasser, Adolph, 116
Straton, John Roach, 596
Strikes, 118-124, 345, 390-392, 394-395, 397-398
Suarez, M., 465
Submarine controversy, 505 ff., 518 ff.

Sumner, Charles, Senator, attitude toward Southern reconstruction, 13; relations with Grant, 40; and the Alabama Claims, 40
Supreme Court, and reconstruction, 20-21; and Greenbacks, 48-49; and the granger laws, 83-84; and income tax, 163-165; and Insular cases, 267-268; criticism of by Progressives, 358-359; and Sherman Anti-Trust Law, 368-370; and the United States Steel Corporation, 375; and Child Labor Law, 404; upholds Adamson Law, 404-405; and minimum wage law, 405; and labor legislation, 406 ff.
Sussex, 510

Taft, William H., on Philippine Commission, 259, 260; civil governor of Philippines, 260; nominated for President (1908), 304-305; election of, 306; character of, 307; and Payne-Aldrich Tariff Act, 308; and the Ballinger controversy, 309; and the insurgent Republicans, 311; and Canadian reciprocity, 313; and split with Roosevelt, 316; renominated for President (1912); defeated, 323; chairman National War Labor Conference Board, 396; attitude as Chief Justice to labor legislation, 408; vetoes literacy test when President, 416; and Monroe Doctrine, 473; and Chinese loan, 486; and arbitration treaties, 497; suggested as member of Paris Peace Conference, 543; attitude toward League of Nations, 556
Tammany Hall, 57
Tampico, arrest of American marines at, 466
Tariff, Morrill Act, 43; reduction in duties, 45; and the surplus. 156-158; of 1883, 158; President Cleveland and the, 158; Mills Bill, 159; McKinley Act, 160; Wilson Act, 161-162; Dingley Act, 162; Payne-Aldrich